RN

"A fascinating portrait . . .
the voice of the prose reflects its author more distinctly than does that of any other American political memoir I can think of . . . that voice continues to hypnotize throughout."

— Christopher Lehmann-Haupt,
New York Times

"Deeply impressive . . . splendidly readable . . . remarkably persuasive. There is a disarming frankness about this book that is very rare in the memoirs of a public man . . . there is a dimension of true drama and real tragedy which raises it to the realm of literature . . . My guess is that posterity will come to acclaim this work as a political classic."

—Peregrine Worsthorne, Associate Editor of
The London Sunday Telegraph, in a special book
review essay for *The American Spectator*

Also by Richard Nixon

Memoirs Volume I
Six Crises

Published By
WARNER BOOKS

THE MEMOIRS OF RICHARD NIXON

VOLUME 2

WARNER BOOKS

A Warner Communications Company

WARNER BOOKS EDITION

Some of the factual events in this book were treated
in greater detail in *Six Crises* (Doubleday & Company, Inc.
copyright © 1962 by Richard M. Nixon).

Book design: H. Roberts

Warner Books, Inc., 75 Rockefeller Plaza,
New York, N.Y. 10019

 A Warner Communications Company

Printed in the United States of America

First Printing: October, 1979

10 9 8 7 6 5 4 3 2 1

Library of Congress Cataloging in Publication Data

Nixon, Richard Milhous, 1913–
    RN, the Memoirs of Richard Nixon.

    Reprint of the ed. published by Grosset & Dunlap,
New York.
    Includes index.
    1. Nixon, Richard Milhous, 1913–   2. United
States—Politics and government—1945–   3. Presi-
dents—United States—Biography.   I. Title.
[E856.A35 1979]   973.924′092′4 [B]   79-9271
ISBN 0-446-93260-4 (v.2)

For
Pat, Tricia, and Julie

CONTENTS

The Presidency
1972

My attitude and outlook as this climactic year began were reflected in a note I dictated on January 9, 1972—my fifty-ninth birthday.

Diary

The 59th year, now complete, has been perhaps the most successful from the standpoint of accomplishment to date. The 60th offers immense opportunities and, of course, equally great dangers. The main thing is to maintain a cool and objective attitude throughout and if possible to stay above the battle and not be buffeted by ups and downs in the polls and by the inevitable political attacks.

On the third anniversary of my inauguration as President, I held a dinner for the Cabinet and the White House senior staff. In my after-dinner remarks I talked about the year ahead: "This is January 20, 1972, and tonight the fourth quarter begins. The football analogy tells us that the fourth quarter really determines the game," I began. "We are only here for about four quarters—maybe longer, but

3

you can only assume the fourth quarter. But in those four quarters, let us be sure that nothing was left undone that could have been done to make this a more decent country, in terms of our relations between ourselves and in terms of all the infinite problems we have."

PRESIDENTIAL POLITICS: 1972

On January 5, 1972, I sent a letter to the chairman of my New Hampshire campaign committee announcing my candidacy for re-election. Eleven Democrats and two other Republicans sought the presidential nomination in 1972. The other Republicans were antiwar California Congressman Paul McCloskey and right-wing Ohio Congressman John Ashbrook.

Some of the Democratic candidates—Edmund Muskie, George McGovern, Wilbur Mills, and Vance Hartke—were already campaigning in New Hampshire, each hoping to make a national impact by a decisive showing in this first primary contest on March 7. Others—including Hubert Humphrey, George Wallace, Henry Jackson, and John Lindsay—calculated that it was better not to risk an initial battering but to emerge as fresh faces in the second primary a week later in Florida.

Because the Republican National Committee would have to preserve an official neutrality until the convention and because after our 1970 experience I wanted to keep politics out of the White House, I decided to set up a separate campaign organization. It was called the Committee to Re-elect the President, a name we abbreviated with the initials CRP.

The front-runner on the Democratic side was Edmund Muskie. At the end of 1971 he was running even with me in the public opinion polls. Muskie's liabilities were an explosive temper and a reputation in political circles for indecisiveness. His principal problem was the ambition of his former running mate, Hubert Humphrey, whose entry into the race would draw away from him the support and votes of many traditional rank-and-file Democrats.

Of the other Democratic candidates, George Wallace was the one we had to take most seriously. If he ran again as a third-party candidate, he would undoubtedly draw a large number of conservative votes from me.

George McGovern, the extreme liberal dark horse, attracted only mild interest because his chances of getting the nomination seemed so remote. If by some miracle he could be nominated, I had no doubt that he would be the easiest Democrat to beat. The hardest would be the one who resolutely avowed his noncandidacy: Teddy Kennedy.

Noncandidacy would have been the best strategy for Kennedy in any event, but he probably had no choice in the aftermath of the party at Chappaquiddick, Massachusetts, in July 1969, when his car went off a bridge and a young woman in the car was drowned. Kennedy was given nation-wide television time to explain his version of the events. His speech was finely crafted, but many felt that his story was full of gaps and contradictions. I could not help thinking that if anyone other than a Kennedy had been involved and had given such a patently unacceptable explanation, the media and the public would not have permitted him to survive in public life.

Personally, however, I felt deeply sorry for Ted Kennedy. When I saw him at a meeting in the Cabinet Room a few days later, I was shocked by how pale and shaken he looked. I spoke to him in the Oval Office for a few minutes afterward and tried to reassure him that he must resolve to overcome this tragedy and go on with his life.

In politics it is possible to feel genuine personal concern for an opponent and still be coldly objective about his position as a competitor. Even as I felt real sympathy for Teddy Kennedy, I recognized, as he must have done, the far-reaching political implications of this personal tragedy. In the short term, I knew that Chappaquiddick would undermine Kennedy's role as a leader of the opposition to the administration's policies. In the longer term, it would be one of his greatest liabilities if he decided to run for President in 1972.

It was clear that the full story of what had happened that night on Chappaquiddick had not come out, and I suspected that the press would not try very hard to uncover it. Therefore I told Ehrlichman to have someone investigate the case for us and get the real facts out. "Don't let up on this for a minute," I said. "Just put yourself in *their* place if

5

something like this had happened to *us*." In fact, our private investigator was unable to turn up anything besides rumors.

After a grand jury heard the case, the presiding judge, James Boyle, issued a report stating that Kennedy could not have been telling the truth in his testimony. Kennedy immediately issued a statement saying that Judge Boyle's report was "not justified." Public opinion polls showed that most people did not think that Kennedy was telling the truth about Chappaquiddick; but they also showed that Massachusetts voters did not think he should have to resign from the Senate because of it. The following year they gave him an overwhelming vote of confidence by returning him to the Senate with 63 percent of the vote. Even with Chappaquiddick to overcome, Teddy Kennedy would still have been the most formidable Democratic nominee in 1972.

I thought that Muskie had a fair chance of beating me and that Humphrey, backed by labor, could come very close. Any Democrat would have the advantage of the sheer size of the Democratic party, which in 1972 outregistered the Republican party by millions of voters. It also seemed possible that they would have the added assistance of George Wallace running against me at the head of a third party.

Finally, it seemed increasingly likely that all of the candidates would be able to campaign against a war that I was not going to be able to win and that I would not yet be able to end.

George McGovern was the most extreme of the antiwar candidates. His solution to an immensely complex problem was appealingly easy to his supporters. "If I were President," he said, "it would take me twenty-four hours and the stroke of a pen to terminate all military operations in Southeast Asia." He said he would withdraw all troops within ninety days, whether or not our POWs were released. He said that President Thieu should plan to flee to whatever country would take him. Even if the POWs were not released, McGovern would not resume fighting because, as he put it during the campaign, "begging is better than bombing."

The difference between McGovern and the other Democrats on Vietnam was fundamental: for the others, the war was an issue; for McGovern, it was a cause.

Muskie beat McGovern in New Hampshire, 46 percent to 37 percent. Considering Muskie's commanding lead at the beginning of the campaign, the commentators described the 9 percent margin as a serious setback for him. Virtually overnight this media attention transformed McGovern from a fringe candidate to a serious contender.

In the second primary, in Florida, George Wallace aroused the voters with his call to "send a message to Washington." The message was: no busing. Wallace won the Florida primary with 41.5 percent of the votes. Hubert Humphrey was second. Senator Henry Jackson was third. Muskie, who had denounced Wallace as a racist, came in fourth with only 8.8 percent.

McGovern won the important Wisconsin primary on April 4 and also won in Massachusetts and Nebraska. To me his steady climb was as welcome to watch as it was almost unbelievable to behold. By the end of the spring, only Humphrey and Kennedy were left to stop him.

On our side, the primary results were no less gratifying because they were expected; despite the fact that I did no campaigning, I received overwhelming majorities in all the Republican primaries.

CHINA

At 7:30 on the evening of July 15, 1971, I spoke to the nation from a television studio in Burbank, California. I talked for only three and a half minutes, but my words produced one of the greatest diplomatic surprises of the century.

I began, "I have requested this television time tonight to announce a major development in our efforts to build a lasting peace in the world." Then I read an announcement that was being made at that very moment in Peking:

> Premier Chou En-lai and Dr. Henry Kissinger, President Nixon's Assistant for National Security Affairs, held talks in Peking from July 9 to 11, 1971. Knowing of President Nixon's expressed desire to visit the People's Republic of China, Premier Chou En-lai, on behalf of the Government of the People's Republic of China, has extended an invitation to President Nixon to visit China at an appropriate date before May

1972. President Nixon has accepted the invitation with pleasure.

The meeting between the leaders of China and the United States is to seek the normalization of relations between the two countries and also to exchange views on questions of concern to the two sides.

Behind this brief announcement lay more than two years of complex, subtle, and determined diplomatic signals and negotiations. Despite the almost miraculous secrecy we had been able to maintain, the China initiative was actually one of the most publicly prepared surprises in history.

The first time I raised the idea of the importance of relations between the United States and Communist China was in my article in *Foreign Affairs* in 1967. In my inaugural address I had referred indirectly to it when I said, "We seek an open world . . . a world in which no people, great or small, will live in angry isolation." Less than two weeks later, on February 1, I wrote a memorandum to Kissinger urging that we give every encouragement to the attitude that the administration was exploring possibilities of rapprochement with the Chinese. "This, of course, should be done privately and should under no circumstances get into the public prints from this direction," I added. During 1969 the Chinese ignored the few low-level signals of interest we sent them, and it was not until 1970 that we began a serious approach to opening a dialogue to see where, if anywhere, it might lead.

The first serious public step in the China initiative had been taken in February 1970 when I sent the first Foreign Policy Report to Congress. The section on China began:

The Chinese are a great and vital people who should not remain isolated from the international community. . . .

The principles underlying our relations with Communist China are similar to those governing our policies toward the U.S.S.R. United States policy is not likely soon to have much impact on China's behavior, let alone its ideological outlook. But it is certainly in our interest, and in the interest of peace and stability in Asia and the world, that we take what steps we can toward improved practical relations with Peking.

The leaders in Peking clearly understood the significance of the language in this report. Two days later, during a meeting in Warsaw with U.S. Ambassador Walter Stoessel, the Chinese ambassador dramatically suggested moving their hitherto sporadic and unproductive meetings to Peking. He also hinted that they would welcome a high-ranking American official as head of the delegation.

In March 1970 the State Department announced a relaxation of most of the official restrictions against travel to Communist China; in April we announced a further easing of trade controls.

Plans for moving the Warsaw talks to Peking received a setback in May when the Chinese canceled a scheduled meeting in protest of the Cambodian operation. For a few weeks it seemed as if the China initiative had collapsed. But the underlying logic of the initiative was based on clear-cut assessments of mutually advantageous interests, and I was not surprised when, after a few months, the Chinese signaled that they were willing to resume our diplomatic minuet. In July, they released American Roman Catholic Bishop James Edward Walsh, who had been arrested in 1958 and held as a prisoner for twelve years.

Early in October I gave an interview to *Time* magazine. I said that: "If there is anything I want to do before I die, it is to go to China. If I don't, I want my children to."

On October 25 President Yahya Khan of Pakistan came to see me, and I used the occasion to establish the "Yahya channel." We had discussed the idea in general terms when I saw him on my visit to Pakistan in July 1969. Now I told him that we had decided to try to normalize our relations with China, and I asked for his help as an intermediary.

"Of course we will do anything we can to help," Yahya said, "but you must know how difficult this will be. Old enemies do not easily become new friends. It will be slow, and you must be prepared for setbacks."

The next day President Ceauşescu of Romania arrived on a state visit. I had also discussed the need for a new Chinese-American relationship with him in Bucharest in 1969. My toast at the dinner in his honor was the first occasion on which an American President had intentionally referred to Communist China by its official name, the People's Republic of China; even my Foreign Policy Report had called it "Communist China." This was a significant diplomatic signal.

In my meeting with Ceaușescu the next day, I said that, even short of the ultimate ideal of re-establishing full diplomatic relations with China, there could be an exchange of high-level personal representatives. He agreed to pass this word along to Peking, and this was the beginning of the "Romanian channel."

A month later, on November 22, I dictated a memorandum for Kissinger:

> On a very confidential basis, I would like for you to have prepared in your staff—without any notice to people who might leak—a study of where we are to go with regard to the admission of Red China to the UN. It seems to me that the time is approaching sooner than we might think when we will not have the votes to block admission.
>
> The question we really need an answer to is how we can develop a position in which we can keep our commitments to Taiwan and yet will not be rolled by those who favor admission of Red China.
>
> There is no hurry on this study but within two or three months I would like to see what you come up with.

In fact, things were to move much faster than I had anticipated.

On December 9 Chou En-lai sent word through President Yahya that my representative would be welcome in Peking for a discussion of the question of Taiwan. Chou stressed that the message did not come from him alone but had been approved by Chairman Mao and by Lin Piao, still a powerful figure at that time. With characteristic subtlety, Chou concluded with a play on words. "We have had messages from the United States from different sources in the past," he said, "but this is the first time that the proposal has come from a Head, through a Head, to a Head." Through Pakistani Ambassador Agha Hilaly we replied that any meeting should not be limited to a discussion of Taiwan, and we proposed that Chinese and American representatives meet in Pakistan to discuss the possibility of a high-level meeting in Peking in the future.

On December 18, American writer Edgar Snow had an interview with his old friend Mao Tse-tung. Mao told him that the Foreign Ministry was considering the question of allowing Americans of all political colorations—left, right, and center—to visit China. Snow asked whether a rightist like Nixon, who represented the "monopoly capitalists," would be permitted to come. Mao replied that I would be welcomed, because as President I was, after all, the one with whom the problems between China and the United States would have to be solved. Mao said that he would be happy to talk to the President, whether he came as a tourist or as President. We learned of Mao's statement within a few days after he made it.

Early in 1971 the Romanian channel became active. Ambassador Corneliu Bogdan called on Kissinger with the news that after our conversation in October, Ceauşescu had sent his Vice Premier to Peking, and Chou En-lai had given him a message for me. It read:

> The communication from the U.S. President is not new. There is only one outstanding issue between us—the U.S. occupation of Taiwan. The P.R.C. has attempted to negotiate on this issue in good faith for fifteen years. If the U.S. has a desire to settle the issue and a proposal for its solution, the P.R.C. will be prepared to receive a U.S. special envoy in Peking. This message has been reviewed by Chairman Mao and by Lin Piao.

Chou En-lai had also commented that in view of the fact that I had visited Bucharest in 1969 and Belgrade in 1970, I would be welcome in Peking.

We were encouraged by this message. As Kissinger noted, the tone was reassuringly free of invective, and the absence of any references to Vietnam indicated that Peking would not consider the war an insurmountable obstacle to U.S.–Chinese rapprochement.

I did my best to make sure that the Lam Son operation at the beginning of 1971 did not cut off this budding relationship as the Cambodian operation had threatened to do the year before. In a press conference on February 17 I stressed that our intervention in Laos should not be interpreted as any threat to China. In Peking the *People's Daily*, the official government newspaper, vehemently rejected my statement: "By spreading the flames of war to the door of China, U.S. imperialism is on a course posing a grave menace to China. . . . Nixon has indeed fully laid bare his ferocious features, and reached the zenith in arrogance."

On February 25, 1971, five days after this tirade was published, I submitted to Congress my second Foreign Policy Report. This time a section dealing with the People's Republic of China canvassed the possibilities for an expanded relationship between our nations and reflected the eventuality of Peking's admission to the UN. It concluded:

> In the coming year, I will carefully examine what further steps we might take to create broader opportunities for contacts between the Chinese and American peoples, and how we might remove needless obstacles to the realization of these opportunities. We hope for, but will not be deterred by a lack of, reciprocity.
>
> We should, however, be totally realistic about the prospects. The People's Republic of China continues to convey to its own people and to the world its determination to cast us in the devil's role. Our modest efforts to prove otherwise have not reduced Peking's doctrinaire enmity toward us. . . . So long as Peking continues to be adamant for hostility, there is little we can do by ourselves to improve the relationship. What we can do, we will.

On March 15 the State Department announced the termination of all restrictions on the use of American passports for travel to mainland China. On April 6 a breakthrough occurred in a totally unexpected way: we received word from the American Embassy in Tokyo that an American table tennis team competing in the world championships in Japan had been invited to visit the P.R.C. in order to play several exhibition matches.

I was as surprised as I was pleased by this news. I had never expected that the China initiative would come to fruition in the form of a Ping-Pong team. We immediately approved the acceptance of the invitation, and the Chinese responded by granting visas to several Western newsmen to cover the team's tour.

On April 14 I announced the termination of the twenty-year-old embargo on trade between us. I also ordered a series of new steps taken for easing currency and shipping controls applying to the P.R.C. The same day Chou En-lai personally welcomed our table tennis players in Peking.

When I spoke to the convention of the American Society of Newspaper Editors in Washington, a few days later, I was asked about the meaning of the recent events involving the P.R.C. I replied that we were seeing an ordered policy process beginning to bear fruit. I said that I would have to disappoint the editors if they were looking for hot headline news, but the very nature of the new relationship made that impossible. I concluded with an observation that I am sure many of my listeners dismissed as simply a personal digression; in fact, it was a direct clue.

"The other day was Easter Sunday," I began. "Both of my daughters, Tricia and Julie, were there—and Tricia with Eddie Cox—I understand they are getting married this June—and Julie and David Eisenhower.

"And the conversation got around to travel and also, of course, with regard to honeymoon travel and the rest. They were asking me where would you like to go? Where do you think we ought to go?

"So, I sat back and thought a bit and said, 'Well, the place to go is to Asia.' I said, 'I hope that sometime in your life, sooner rather than later, you will be able to go to China to see the great cities, and the people, and all of that, there.'

"I hope they do. As a matter of fact, I hope sometime I do. I am not sure that it is going to happen while I am in office. I will not speculate with regard to either of the diplomatic points. It is premature to talk about recognition. It is premature also to talk about a change of our policy with regard to the United Nations."

At this point a bull in the form of Ted Agnew inadvertently careened into this diplomatic China shop. During a long postmidnight session with a group of reporters in his hotel room after he arrived for the Republican Governors Conference in Williamsburg, Virginia, Agnew told them that the favorable media coverage of the table tennis team's visit to Peking had helped the Communist Chinese government score a propaganda triumph. He noted that some reporters had sent back almost lyrical descriptions of the contented and productive lives led by the residents of Peking.

Agnew had expressed his reservations about our trade and visa overtures to the Chinese Communists at a recent NSC meeting, but I had never imagined that he would discuss his doubts with reporters. I told Haldeman to get word to Agnew to stay off this topic.

The tempo began to speed up considerably. On April 27 Ambassador Hilaly came to the White House with another message from Chou En-lai via President Yahya. After the ritual insistence that Taiwan was the principal and prerequisite problem, which had to be resolved before any relations could be restored, the message added that the Chinese were now interested in direct discussions as means of reaching that settlement, and therefore "the Chinese government reaffirms its willingness to receive publicly in Peking a special envoy of the President of the U.S. (for instance, Mr. Kissinger) or the U.S. Secretary of State or even the President of the U.S. himself for a direct meeting and discussion."

In some important respects this message raised as many problems as it solved. Taiwan was still mentioned as the central issue. Further, the Chinese spoke of publicly receiving an envoy in Peking. I felt that in order for the initiative to have any chance of succeeding, it would have to be kept totally secret until the final arrangements for the presidential visit had been agreed upon. With advance warning conservative opposition might mobilize in Congress and scuttle the entire effort.

Kissinger and I spent the next few days trying to decide who to send to Peking for these initial talks.

The best man, we agreed, would be David Bruce, but we ruled him out because he was our negotiator in Paris and the Chinese would undoubtedly resent our sending someone so closely identified with Vietnam. We also considered Cabot Lodge, but he was even more identified with Vietnam than was Bruce.

"Well, what about Bill then?" I asked. "If we send the Secretary of State, they'll sure as hell know we're serious."

14

Kissinger rolled his eyes upward. I knew that he would have opposed Rogers on personal grounds regardless, but in this case he had good policy reasons. The Secretary of State had too high a profile for these first talks. Besides, there was almost no way he could go to China secretly.

Finally I said, "Henry, I think you will have to do it."

He objected that, like Rogers, he had too much visibility.

I said, "I am confident that a man who can come and go undetected in Paris can get in and out of Peking before anyone finds out."

At my news conference on April 29 I gave another major clue to what was afoot. But once again even the most rigorous monitors and analysts of Nixon rhetoric failed to pick up the point I was making.

Since none of the reporters had asked me anything about the specific possibility of a visit to China, I asked it of myself. At the end of my reply to a general question about our China policy, I said, "I would finally suggest—I know this question may come up if I don't answer it now—I hope, and, as a matter of fact, I expect to visit mainland China sometime in some capacity—I don't know what capacity. But that indicates what I hope for the long term. And I hope to contribute to a policy in which we can have a new relationship with mainland China."

About the same time the issue of *Life* containing Edgar Snow's December interview with Mao appeared on the newsstands. Now it was public that Mao would welcome me to Peking.

Messages and signals had been going back and forth for more than two years. We had proceeded carefully and cautiously through the Yahya and Romanian channels. Now Kissinger and I agreed that we had reached a point at which we had to take the chance of making a major proposal, or risk slipping back into another long round of tentative probing. I decided that the time had come to take the big step and propose a presidential visit.

On May 10, therefore, Kissinger called in Ambassador Hilaly and gave him a message for Chou En-lai via President Yahya. It stated that because of the importance I attached to the normalizing of relations between the two countries, I was prepared to accept Chou's invitation to visit Peking. I proposed that Kissinger undertake a secret visit in advance of my trip in order to arrange an agenda and begin a preliminary exchange of views.

The die was cast. There was nothing left to do but wait for Chou's reply. If we had acted too soon, if we had not established a sufficiently strong foundation, or if we had overestimated the ability of Mao and Chou to deal with their internal opposition to such a visit, then all our long careful efforts would be wasted. I might even have to be prepared for serious international embarrassment if the Chinese decided to reject my proposal and then publicize it.

For almost two weeks we waited, wondering what kind of decision-making process was under way in Peking.

Then on May 31 we received a message from President Yahya Khan through Ambassador Hilaly. It read:

1. There is a very encouraging and positive response to the last message.
2. Please convey to Mr. Kissinger that the meeting will take place on Chinese soil for which travel arrangements will be made by us.
3. Level of meeting will be as proposed by you.
4. Full message will be transmitted by safe means.

Two nights later, we gave a state dinner for President Somoza of Nicaragua. After Pat and I had finished having coffee with our guests in the Blue Room, I went to the Lincoln Sitting Room to do some paperwork and reading. In less than five minutes Kissinger walked in. He must have run most of the way from the West Wing, because he was out of breath.

He handed me two sheets of typewritten paper. "This just arrived in the Pakistani Embassy pouch," he said. "Hilaly rushed it over, and he was so excited when he gave it to me that his hands were shaking."

Kissinger stood beaming as I read the message:

Premier Chou En-lai has seriously studied President Nixon's messages of April 29, May 17, and May 22, 1971, and has reported with much pleasure to Chairman Mao Tse-tung that President Nixon is prepared to accept his suggestion to visit

Peking for direct conversations with the leaders of the People's Republic of China. Chairman Mao Tse-tung has indicated that he welcomes President Nixon's visit and looks forward to that occasion when he may have direct conversations with His Excellency the President, in which each side would be free to raise the principal issue of concern to it. . . .

Premier Chou En-lai welcomes Dr. Kissinger to China as the U.S. representative who will come in advance for a preliminary secret meeting with high level Chinese officials to prepare and make necessary arrangements for President Nixon's visit to Peking.

"This is the most important communication that has come to an American President since the end of World War II," Kissinger said when I had finished reading.

For nearly an hour we talked about the China initiative—what it might mean to America and how delicately it must be handled lest we lose it. It was close to midnight before we noticed the time, and Kissinger rose to go.

"Henry, I know that, like me, you never have anything to drink after dinner, and it is very late," I said, "but I think this is one of those occasions when we should make an exception. Wait here just a minute."

I got up and walked down the corridor to the small family kitchen at the other end of the second floor. In one of the cabinets I found an unopened bottle of very old Courvoisier brandy that someone had given us for Christmas. I tucked it under my arm and took two large snifters from the glass cupboard. As we raised our glasses, I said, "Henry, we are drinking a toast not to ourselves personally or to our success, or to our administration's policies which have made this message and made tonight possible. Let us drink to generations to come who may have a better chance to live in peace because of what we have done."

As I write them now, my words sound rather formal, but the moment was one not just of high personal elation, but of a profound mutual understanding that this truly was a moment of historical significance.

On July 6 I flew to Kansas City to address a large group of Midwestern news media executives attending one of the periodic briefings on administration policies that we held in different parts of the country.

17

Kissinger was in the middle of a ten-day mission to the Far East and just days away from his secret trip to Peking. Before he got there I wanted to place on the record an outline of the reasons for approaching China.

I told the gathering that the potential of China, though obscured to most American observers by its isolation, was such that no sensible foreign policy could ignore or exclude it. "That is the reason why I felt that it was essential that this administration take the first steps toward ending the isolation of mainland China from the world community," I said. Despite the recent flurry of activity I said that I did not hold out any great hopes of rapid advances in our relations. "What we have done is simply opened the door—opened the door for travel, opened the door for trade," I said. "Now the question is whether there will be other doors opened on their part. . . . Mainland China, outside the world community, completely isolated, with its leaders not in communication with world leaders, would be a danger to the whole world that would be unacceptable, unacceptable to us and unacceptable to others as well. So consequently, this step must be taken now. Others must be taken, very precisely, very deliberately, as there is reciprocation on the other side."

My speech received relatively little attention in Kansas City. As we were to learn later, however, it received a great deal of attention in Peking.

We arranged that Kissinger would fly to Vietnam for consultations early in July and then stop in Pakistan on the way back. There he would develop a stomachache that would require him to stay in bed and not be seen by the press. Then, with President Yahya's cooperation, he would be taken to an airport where a Pakistani jet would fly him over the mountains into China. The stomachache was scheduled for July 9–11. Kissinger would then fly to San Clemente to report to me.

Kissinger's trip was given the codename Polo after Marco Polo, another Western traveler who made history by journeying to China. Everything went without a hitch. His indisposition in Islamabad received only minor attention from reporters covering him. They accepted the story that he would be confined to bed for at least a couple of days and began making arrangements for their own entertainment.

Because of the need for complete secrecy and the lack of any direct communications facilities between Peking and Washington, I knew that we would have no word from Kissinger while he was in China. Even after he had returned to Pakistan it would still be important to maintain secrecy, so before Kissinger left, we agreed on a single code-word—Eureka—which he would use if his mission were successful and the presidential trip had been arranged.

Although I was confident that the Chinese were as ready for my trip as we were, I did not underestimate the tremendous problems that Taiwan and Vietnam posed for both sides, and I tried to discipline myself not to expect anything lest I begin to expect too much.

On July 11 Al Haig, who knew our codeword, phoned me to say that a cable from Kissinger had arrived.

"What's the message?" I asked.

"Eureka," he replied.

Kissinger's description of his time in China was fascinating. The Chinese had agreed to virtually everything we proposed regarding the arrangements and schedule for my trip. The preliminary talks had covered the whole range of issues and problems that lay between our two countries. He found the Chinese tough, idealistic, fanatical, single-minded, remarkable, and uncomfortably aware of the philosophical contradictions involved in their arranging a visit by their capitalist archenemy. "These were men in some anguish," Kissinger said.

Most of all, Kissinger was impressed by Chou En-lai. The two men spent seventeen hours together in meetings and informal conversation, and Kissinger found that "he was equally at home in philosophic sweeps, historical analysis, tactical probing, light repartee. His command of facts, and in particular his knowledge of American events, was remarkable." At one point Chou asked about my Kansas City speech, and Kissinger had to admit that he had read only the press reports. The next morning at breakfast Kissinger found a copy of my speech, with Chou's underlinings and marginal notations in Chinese, lying on the table with a note requesting that he return it because it was Chou's only copy.

In a brilliant summing up of his long report after the trip, Kissinger wrote:

> We have laid the groundwork for you and Mao to turn a page in history. But we should have no illusions about the future. Profound differences and years of isolation yawn between us and the Chinese. They will be tough before and during the summit on the question of Taiwan and other major issues. And they will prove implacable foes if our relations turn sour. My assessment of these people is that they are deeply ideological, close to fanatic in the intensity of their beliefs. At the same time they display an inward security that allows them, within the framework of their principles, to be meticulous and reliable in dealing with others. . . .
>
> Our dealings, both with the Chinese and others, will require reliability, precision, finesse. If we can master this process, we will have made a revolution.

On July 15 I made the televised announcement that I would be going to Peking. Most of the initial reactions were overwhelmingly positive. Max Lerner wrote, "The politics of surprise leads through the Gates of Astonishment into the Kingdom of Hope."

Some commentators joined the more partisan Democrats in tempering their praise with speculation that my motives had been political. Most of the serious criticism, however, came, as I had expected, from the conservatives. Congressman John Schmitz of California charged me with "surrendering to international communism" by accepting the invitation. George Wallace did not actually condemn the trip, but he warned me against "begging, pleading, and groveling" before the Chinese Communists. He told reporters that he suspected the trip was actually a diversionary tactic to get people's minds off "inflation and the high cost of pork chops."

The reaction abroad to our China initiative was generally favorable, but there were some understandable reservations. Our friends in Taiwan were terribly distressed. However, they were reassured that we did not withdraw our recognition of their government and did not renounce our mutual defense commitment. The Japanese presented a particularly difficult problem. They resented the fact that they had not been informed in advance, but we had no other choice. We could not have informed them without informing others, thus risking a leak that might have aborted the entire initiative.

As soon as I returned to Washington from San Clemente, I held a briefing for the bipartisan leadership in the Cabinet Room. I stressed the need for secrecy, because the more we had to put things into words, the less freedom of movement we would have in our dealings with the Chinese. I understood how difficult it would be for many of them, but I had to ask that they trust me. To a man, they came through splendidly. John Stennis said, "The President has made a good move; now it's up to him to follow through, and I'm going to back him up."

Mike Mansfield said, that the China initiative was like the Manhattan Project: secrecy was absolutely essential to the success of each.

Kissinger returned to China on October 20 for Polo II. This time his six-day trip was publicly announced. Its purpose was to prepare the agenda for the meetings I would have with the Chinese leaders and to work out the basic language of the communiqué that would be issued at the end of my trip.

The draft communiqué that I had approved for submission to the Chinese had followed the standard diplomatic formula of using vague and conciliatory language to patch over the most heated and insoluble problems.

Kissinger was somewhat taken aback when Chou stated that our approach to the communiqué was unacceptable. He said that unless it expressed our fundamental differences, the wording would have an "untruthful appearance." He dismissed our proposed draft as the sort of banal document the Soviets would sign without meaning it and without planning to observe it.

The Chinese then handed Kissinger a counterdraft that took his breath away. If ours had smoothed over differences, theirs underscored them. With great self-control, Kissinger read it and calmly said, "We cannot have an American President sign a document which says that revolution has

21

become the irresistible trend of history, or that 'the people's revolutionary struggles are just'!"

The Chinese seemed disconcerted, but Kissinger continued. We could not allow any references to racial discrimination; we opposed it as much as did the Chinese, but mention in this communiqué would be interpreted as criticism of American domestic problems. Similarly, their proposed references to China as "the reliable rear area" of North Vietnam, and to Chinese support for the Indochinese peoples' "fighting to the end for the attainment of their goal" were unacceptable phrasing while Americans were fighting or being held prisoner in Indochina.

After this initial session, Kissinger found that the Chinese were willing to compromise on a communiqué that would state the underlying goals of the summit while retaining each side's basic position expressed in noninflammatory language.

Kissinger summed up these long and sometimes difficult sessions by saying that the Chinese were willing to pursue their objectives by banking on the thrust of history rather than on the specific wording of a communiqué. "They will continue to be tough," he wrote, "but they essentially accept our arguments that we can often do more than we say, that the process must be gradual, and that some issues must be left to evolutionary pressures. This involves great risks for them, at home and abroad, given their past public demands and dissidents in their own camp."

Kissinger reported that toward the end of the talks Chou had specifically pointed out that they could be in real trouble if my administration was not in power. "He shares what he described as your wish that you preside over the 200th anniversary of America's birth."

While Kissinger was in China on Polo II, the United Nations General Assembly moved to vote on the question of admitting the People's Republic of China as a member nation. I instructed Kissinger to stay away an extra day so that he would not have just arrived home when this controversial vote was taken.

As early as August we had publicly withdrawn our

opposition to consideration of this question and indicated our support of the concept of the "two Chinas," Chiang Kai-shek's Republic of China on Taiwan and the Communist People's Republic of China, each to have membership in the world organization.

It had not been easy for me to take a position that would be so disappointing to our old friend and loyal ally, Chiang. I had learned as early as the spring, however, that the traditional vote bloc opposed to Peking's admission had irreparably broken up, and several of our erstwhile supporters had decided to support Peking at the next vote. Personally, I have never believed in bowing to the inevitable just because it is inevitable. In this case, however, I felt that the national security interests of the United States lay in developing our relations with the P.R.C. Besides, regardless of what happened in the UN, I was determined to honor our treaty obligations by continuing our military and economic support for an independent Taiwan.

On October 25 the UN voted 76 to 35, with 17 abstentions, to expel Taiwan and to admit the P.R.C. as the sole government representing China. This went much further than we had expected: we had thought that our greatest problem would be in convincing Taiwan to stay after the P.R.C. had been admitted to equal status.

A few days before leaving for China, I invited the great French writer and philosopher André Malraux to the White House.

Malraux had known Mao Tse-tung and Chou En-lai in China during the 1930s and had kept up intermittent contact with them through the years. His description of the Chinese leaders in his *Anti-Memoirs* was among the most valuable and fascinating reading I had done in preparation for my trip.

Malraux was then seventy years old. Time had not dimmed the brilliance of his thought or the quickness of his wit. Even after his elegant French had been filtered through a State Department interpreter, his language was original and striking.

During the talk I had with him in the Oval Office, I

asked whether just a few years ago he would have thought that the Chinese leaders would agree to meet with an American President.

"This meeting was inevitable," he replied.

"Even with the Vietnam war?" I asked.

"Ah yes, even so. China's action over Vietnam is an imposture. There was a period when the friendship between China and Russia was cloudless, when they allowed Russian arms to pass over their territory on the way to Vietnam. But China has never helped anyone! Not Pakistan. Not Vietnam. China's foreign policy is a brilliant lie! The Chinese themselves do not believe in it; they believe only in China. Only China!

"For Mao, China is a continent—it is an Australia by itself. Only China is important. If China has to receive the Sultan of Zanzibar, then China will. Or the President of the United States. The Chinese don't care."

I asked Malraux for his impressions of Mao. "Five years ago," he said, "Mao had one fear: that the Americans or the Russians, with ten atom bombs, would destroy China's industrial centers and set China back fifty years at a time when Mao himself would be dead. He told me, 'When I have six atomic bombs, no one can bomb my cities.' " Malraux said that he had not understood what Mao meant by that. He continued, "Then Mao said, 'The Americans will never use an atom bomb against me.' I did not understand that either, but I am repeating it for you because often it is what one does not understand that is most important. I did not ask Mao any more questions about it, because one does not ask Mao questions."

Malraux rushed on with a torrent of words and ideas.

"You will be dealing with a colossus," he said, "but a colossus facing death. The last time I saw him he told me, 'We do not have a successor.' Do you know what Mao will think when he sees you for the first time?" he asked. "He will think, 'He is so much younger than I!' "

That evening at a dinner in his honor in the Residence, Malraux advised me on how to approach my conversation with Mao.

"Mr. President, you will meet a man who has had a fantastic destiny and who believes that he is acting out the last act of his lifetime. You may think he is talking to you, but he will in truth be addressing Death. . . . It's worth the trip!"

I asked him again what came after Mao. Malraux replied, "It is exactly as Mao said, he has no successor. What did he mean by it? He meant that in his view the great leaders—Churchill, Gandhi, de Gaulle—were created by the kind of traumatic historical events that will not occur in the world anymore. In that sense he feels that he has no successors. I once asked him if he did not think of himself as the heir of the last great Chinese emperors of the sixteenth century. Mao said, 'But of course I am their heir.' Mr. President, you operate within a rational framework, but Mao does not. There is something of the sorcerer in him. He is a man inhabited by a vision, possessed by it."

I remarked that this kind of mystique was present in many great men. People who knew Lincoln said that they always felt he was looking beyond the horizon—as if there were a space between the earth and the sky where his gaze was focused. On the day of his assassination he had told his Cabinet about a dream he had the night before: he had seemed to be in some "singular indescribable vessel" moving with great rapidity toward an indefinite shore. "We don't know where or what the shore is but we must avoid the shoals in trying to reach it," I said.

Malraux said, "You have spoken of avoiding the shoals to reach the shore. I feel that Mao has the same view. And even though both you and he are aware of the shoals, neither of you knows what lies on the shore beyond. Mao knows, however, that his harbor is Death."

Later, over coffee, Malraux told me, "You are about to attempt one of the most important things of our century. I think of the sixteenth-century explorers, who set out for a specific objective but often arrived at an entirely different discovery. What you are going to do, Mr. President, might well have a totally different outcome from whatever is anticipated."

At the end of the evening I escorted Malraux to his car. As we stood on the steps of the North Portico, he turned to me and said, "I am not de Gaulle, but I know what de Gaulle would say if he were here. He would say: 'All men who understand what you are embarking upon salute you!'"

On February 17, 1972, at 10:35 A.M. we left Andrews Air Force Base for Peking. As the plane gathered speed and then took to the air, I thought of Malraux's words. We were embarking upon a voyage of philosophical discovery as uncertain, and in some respects as perilous, as the voyages of geographical discovery of a much earlier time.

Diary
As Henry and Bob both pointed out on the plane, there was almost a religious feeling to the messages we received from all over the country, wishing us well. I told Henry that I thought it was really a question of the American people being hopelessly and almost naïvely for peace, even at any price. He felt that perhaps there was also some ingredient of excitement about the boldness of the move, and visiting a land that was unknown to so many Americans.

We stopped briefly in Shanghai to take aboard Chinese Foreign Ministry officials and a Chinese navigator; an hour and a half later we prepared to land in Peking. I looked out the window. It was winter, and the countryside was drab and gray. The small towns and villages looked like pictures I had seen of towns in the Middle Ages.

Our plane landed smoothly, and a few minutes later we came to a stop in front of the terminal. The door was opened, and Pat and I stepped out.

Chou En-lai stood at the foot of the ramp, hatless in the cold. Even a heavy overcoat did not hide the thinness of his frail body. When we were about halfway down the steps, he began to clap. I paused for a moment and then returned the gesture, according to the Chinese custom.

I knew that Chou had been deeply insulted by Foster Dulles's refusal to shake hands with him at the Geneva Conference in 1954. When I reached the bottom step, therefore, I made a point of extending my hand as I walked toward him. When our hands met, one era ended and another began.

After being introduced to all the Chinese officials, I stood on Chou's left while the band played the anthems. "The Star-Spangled Banner" had never sounded so stirring to me as on that windswept runway in the heart of Communist China.

The honor guard was one of the finest I have ever seen. They were big men, strong-looking, and immaculately turned out. As I walked down the long line, each man turned his head slowly as I passed, creating an almost hypnotic sense of movement in the massed ranks.

Chou and I rode into the city in a curtained car. As we left the airport, he said, "Your handshake came over the vastest ocean in the world—twenty-five years of no communication." When we came into Tienamen Square at the center of Peking, he pointed out some of the buildings; I noticed that the streets were empty.

Madame Chou was waiting for us when we arrived at the two large government guesthouses where our official party was to stay. We had tea in the sitting room, and then Chou said that he was sure everyone would like to rest before the state banquet.

About an hour later I was getting ready to take a shower when Kissinger burst in with the news that Chairman Mao wanted to meet me. Late that night I described the atmosphere of the meeting.

Diary

Coming in on the plane Rogers had expressed concern that we ought to have a meeting with Mao very soon, and that we couldn't be in a position of my seeing him in a way that put him above me, like walking up the stairs or him standing at the top of the stairs.

Our concerns in this respect were completely dissipated at about two o'clock when Henry came into the room breathlessly, and told me that Chou was downstairs and said that the Chairman wanted to see me now at his residence. I waited about five minutes while Henry went downstairs, and then we drove to the residence.

We were escorted into a room that was not elaborate, filled with books and papers. Several of the books were open to various pages on the coffee table next to where he was sitting. His girl secretary helped him to his feet. When I shook his hand, he said, "I can't talk very well." Chou later told me that he had been sick for about a month with what was described as bronchitis. This, however, was not known to the Chinese public.

Everybody, including Chou, showed him the deference that was due him. Two or three of the military and the civilian people were standing in the room, and about ten minutes through the conversation Chou waved them out. I noted, however, that they remained standing in the hall watching.

The transcript of the conversation may not have caught probably the most moving moment, when he reached out his hand, and I reached out mine, and he held it for about a minute.

It is obvious that he has a remarkable sense of humor. He kept bringing Henry into the conversation, and while it was supposed to be ten or fifteen minutes it extended to almost an hour. I saw Chou look at his watch two or three times and realized that I probably should break it up in order not to tax him too much.

It was interesting to note that later at the plenary session, Chou constantly referred back to the meeting with Mao and what Mao had said.

Several Chinese photographers had rushed in ahead of us in order to record our first meeting. We all sat in overstuffed armchairs set in a semicircle at the end of the long room. While the photographers continued to bustle around, we exchanged bantering small talk. Kissinger remarked that he had assigned Mao's writings to his classes at Harvard. Indulging in characteristic self-deprecation, Mao said, "These writings of mine aren't anything. There is nothing instructive in what I wrote." I said, "The Chairman's writings moved a nation and have changed the world." Mao, however, replied, "I haven't been able to change it. I've only been able to change a few places in the vicinity of Peking."

Although Mao spoke with some difficulty, it was clear that his mind was moving like lightning. "Our common old friend Generalissimo Chiang Kai-shek doesn't approve of this," he said, with a sweeping gesture that might have meant our meeting or that might have taken in all China. "He calls us Communist bandits. He recently made a speech. Have you seen it?"

"Chiang Kai-shek calls the Chairman a bandit," I replied. "What does the Chairman call Chiang Kai-shek?"

Mao chuckled when my question was translated, but it was Chou who answered. "Generally speaking, we call them 'Chiang Kai-shek's clique,'" he said. "In the newspapers sometimes we call him a bandit; he calls us bandits in turn. Anyway, we abuse each other."

"Actually," Mao said, "the history of our friendship with him is much longer than the history of your friendship with him."

Mao remarked on Kissinger's cleverness in keeping his first trip to Peking secret. "He doesn't look like a secret agent," I said. "He is the only man in captivity who could go to Paris twelve times and Peking once, and no one knew it—except possibly a couple of pretty girls."

"They didn't know it," Kissinger interjected, "I used it as a cover."

"In Paris?" Mao asked with mock disbelief.

"Anyone who uses pretty girls as a cover must be the greatest diplomat of all time," I said.

"So you often make use of your girls?" Mao asked.

"*His* girls, not mine," I replied. "It would get me into great trouble if I used girls as a cover."

"Especially during an election," Chou remarked as Mao joined in the laughter.

Referring to our presidential election, Mao said that in honesty he had to tell me that if the Democrats won the Chinese would deal with them.

"We understand," I said. "We will hope that we don't give you that problem."

"I voted for you during your last election," Mao said with a broad smile.

"When the Chairman says he voted for me," I replied, "he voted for the lesser of two evils."

"I like rightists," Mao responded, obviously enjoying himself. "People say that you are rightists—that the Republican Party is on the right—that Prime Minister Heath is also to the right."

"And General de Gaulle," I added.

29

Without dropping a beat, Mao said, "De Gaulle is a different question." Then he continued, "They also say the Christian Democratic Party of West Germany is to the right. I am comparatively happy when these people on the right come into power."

"I think the most important thing to note is that in America, at least at this time, those on the right can do what those on the left can only talk about," I said.

When the conversation moved to the history of our meeting, Mao remarked, "The former President of Pakistan introduced President Nixon to us. At that time, our ambassador in Pakistan refused to agree to our having any contact with you. He said that President Nixon was no better than President Johnson. But President Yahya said, 'The two men cannot be compared.' He said that one was like a gangster—he meant President Johnson. I don't know how he got that impression, although we on our side were not very happy with your former Presidents, beginning with Truman through Johnson. In between there were eight years of a Republican President. During that period probably you hadn't thought things out either."

"Mr. Chairman," I said, "I am aware of the fact that over a period of years my position with regard to the People's Republic was one that the Chairman and the Prime Minister totally disagreed with. What brings us together is a recognition of a new situation in the world and a recognition on our part that what is important is not a nation's internal political philosophy. What is important is its policy toward the rest of the world and toward us."

Although the meeting with Mao dealt mainly with what he called the "philosophy" of our new and potential relationship, I raised in general terms the major substantive questions we would be discussing. I said that we should examine our policies and determine how they should develop in order to deal with the entire world as well as the immediate problems of Korea, Vietnam, and Taiwan.

I went on, "We, for example, must ask ourselves—again in the confines of this room—why the Soviets have more forces on the border facing you than they do on the border facing Western Europe? We must ask ourselves, What is the future of Japan? Is it better—and here I know we have disagreements—from China's standpoint for Japan to be neutral and totally defenseless, or is it better for Japan to have some mutual defense relations with the United States? One thing is sure—we can leave no vacuums, because they can be filled. The Prime Minister, for example, has pointed out that the United States 'reaches out its hands' and that the Soviet Union 'reaches out its hands.' The question is, which danger does the People's Republic of China face? Is it the danger of American aggression—or of Soviet aggression? These are hard questions, but we have to discuss them."

Mao was animated and following every nuance of the conversation, but I could see that he was also becoming very tired. Chou had been discreetly glancing at his watch with increasing frequency, so I decided that I should try to bring the session to a close.

"I would like to say, as we finish, Mr. Chairman, that we know you and the Prime Minister have taken great risks in inviting us here. For us also it was a difficult decision. But having read some of your statements, I know that you are one who sees when an opportunity comes, and then knows that you must seize the hour and seize the day."

Mao's face beamed when the translator came to these words from his own poem.

I continued, "I would also like to say in a personal sense—and I also say this to you, Mr. Prime Minister—you do not know me. Since you do not know me, you shouldn't trust me. You will find I never say something I cannot do. And I always will do more than I can say. On this basis, I want to have frank talks with the Chairman and, of course, with the Prime Minister."

Mao pointed toward Kissinger and said, " 'Seize the hour and seize the day.' I think that, generally speaking, people like me sound like a lot of big cannons!" Chou laughed, and it was clear that we were in for another bit of self-deprecation. "For example, things like, 'The whole world should unite and defeat imperialism, revisionism, and all reactionaries, and establish socialism.' "

"Like me," I said. "And bandits."

Mao leaned forward and smiled. "But perhaps you as an individual may not be among those to be overthrown," he said. Motioning toward Kissinger, he continued, "They say that he is also among those not to be overthrown personally. If all of you are overthrown, we wouldn't have any more friends left."

"Mr. Chairman," I said, "your life is well known to all of us. You came from a very poor family to the top of the most populous nation in the world, a great nation.

"My background is not so well known. I also came from a very poor family, and to the top of a very great nation. History has brought us together. The question is whether we, with different philosophies, but both with feet on the ground, and having come from the people, can make a breakthrough that will serve not just China and America, but the whole world in the years ahead. And that is why we are here."

As we were leaving, Mao said, "Your book, *Six Crises,* is not a bad book."

Looking at Chou, I smiled and shook my head and said, "He reads too much."

Mao walked us to the door. His walk was a slow shuffle, and he said that he had not been feeling well.

"But you look very good," I replied.

"Appearances are deceiving," he said with a slight shrug.

The first plenary session with Chou at the Great Hall of the People was cut short because of the unscheduled meeting with Mao, and we talked only in general terms about the way our meetings would proceed. Chou preferred a format in which one side presented its views on a subject at one session and the other side responded at the next.

The most difficult and touchiest part of the trip would be the joint communiqué, and I reaffirmed our pragmatic approach to it. "The conventional way to handle a meeting at the summit like this, while the whole world is watching," I said, "is to have meetings for several days, which we will have, to have discussions and discover differences, which we will do, and then put out a weasel-worded communiqué covering up the problems."

"If we were to act like that we would be not only deceiving the people, but we would be deceiving ourselves," Chou replied.

"That is adequate when meetings are between states that do not affect the future of the world," I said, "but we would not be meeting our responsibility for meetings which the whole world is watching, and which will affect our friends in the Pacific and all over the world for years to come. As we begin these meetings we have no illusions that we will solve everything. But we can set in motion a process which will enable us to solve many of these problems in the future. The men in this room and the women in this room have fought a long hard struggle for a revolution which has succeeded. We know you believe deeply in your principles, and we believe deeply in our principles. We do not ask you to compromise your principles, just as you would not ask us to compromise ours."

Perhaps the mention of opposing principles triggered the thought, because Chou remarked, "As you said to Chairman Mao this afternoon, today we shook hands," he said. "But John Foster Dulles didn't want to do that."

"But you said you didn't want to shake hands with him," I countered.

"Not necessarily," Chou replied. "I would have."

"Well, *we* will shake hands," I said, and once again we shook hands across the table.

Chou seemed to warm to the subject, and he continued. "Dulles's assistant, Mr. Walter Bedell Smith, wanted to do differently, but he did not break the discipline of John Foster Dulles, so he had to hold a cup of coffee in his right hand. Since one doesn't shake hands with the left hand, he used it to shake my arm." Everyone laughed, including Chou. "But at that time, we couldn't blame you," he said, "because the international viewpoint was that the socialist countries were a monolithic bloc, and the Western countries were also a monolithic bloc. Now we understand that that is not the case."

"We have broken out of the old pattern," I agreed. "We look at each country in terms of its own conduct rather than lumping them all together and saying that because they have this kind of philosophy they are all in utter darkness. I would say in honesty to the Prime Minister that my views, because I was in the Eisenhower administration, were similar to those of Mr. Dulles at that time. But the world has changed since then, and the relationship between the People's Republic and the United States must change too. As the Prime Minister has said in a meeting with Dr. Kissinger, the helmsman must ride with the waves or he will be submerged with the tide."

By the time we met for the banquet at the Great Hall of the People an hour later, the Chinese group seemed to be much more at ease. Perhaps it was because Mao had now given his official blessing to the visit—or perhaps it was simply that we had already begun to get along well with each other.

In my toast I tried to give idealistic expression to the pragmatic underpinnings of the China initiative:

> We have at times in the past been enemies. We have great differences today. What brings us together is that we have common interests which transcend those differences. As we discuss our differences, neither of us will compromise our principles. But while we cannot close the gulf between us, we can try to bridge it so that we may be able to talk across it.
>
> So, let us, in these next five days, start a long march together, not in lockstep, but on different roads leading to the same goal, the goal of building a world structure of peace and justice. . . . The world watches. The world listens. The world waits to see what we will do. . . .
>
> There is no reason for us to be enemies. Neither of us seeks the territory of the other; neither of us seeks domination over the other; neither of us seeks to stretch out our hands and rule the world.
>
> Chairman Mao has written, 'So many deeds cry out to be done, and always urgently. The world rolls on. Time passes. Ten thousand years are too long. Seize the day, seize the hour.'
>
> This is the hour, this is the day for our two peoples to rise to the heights of greatness which can build a new and a better world.

After the toasts, the orchestra played "America the Beautiful," and I remarked that this was one of the songs I had chosen for my inauguration in 1969. Chou raised his glass and said, "Here's to your next inauguration!"

When we met at the Great Hall of the People the next afternoon I reminded Chou that despite what he might be reading in some American press reports of the trip, I had no sentimental illusions about what was going on: "Now we say, and most of our rather naïve American press buys this line, that the new relationship between China and America is due to the fact we have a basic friendship between our peoples. But the Prime Minister knows and I know that friendship—which I feel we do have on a personal basis—cannot be the basis on which an established relationship must rest; not friendship alone. I recall that a professor of law when I was a first-year student said that a contract was only as good as the will of the parties concerned to keep it."

Chou sat motionless, his face intent but impassive.

"I believe the interests of China as well as the interests of the United States urgently require that we maintain our military establishment at approximately its present levels," I said. "And, with certain exceptions which we can discuss later, I believe that we should maintain a military presence in Europe, in Japan, and also maintain our naval forces in the Pacific. I believe that the interests of China are just as great as those of the United States on that point."

As I had intended, this statement created a slight stir on the Chinese side of the table.

"Let me now make what I trust will not be taken as an invidious comparison," I continued. "By religion I am a Quaker, although not a very good one, and I believe in peace. All of my instincts are against a big military establishment and also against military adventures. As I indicated a moment ago, the Prime Minister is one of the world's leading spokesmen for his philosophy, and so he has to be opposed to powers such as the United States maintaining huge military establishments. But each of us has to put the survival of his nation first, and if the United States were to reduce its military strength, and if we were to withdraw from the areas of the world which I have mentioned, the dangers to the United States would be great—and the dangers to China would be even greater.

"I do not impute any motives to the present leaders of the Soviet Union," I said. "I have to respect what they say. But I must make policy on the basis of what they do. And in terms of the nuclear power balance, the Soviet Union has been moving ahead at a very alarming rate over the past four years. I have determined that the United States must not fall behind. If we did, our shield of protection for Europe, and for the nations of the Pacific with which we have treaties, would be worthless."

Applying this approach to the question of America's relationship with Japan, I said that the Chinese had framed their position on the subject in terms of their ideology and philosophy: they called for the withdrawal of American troops from Japan and the abrogation of our treaty of mutual defense, thus leaving Japan neutral and unarmed.

"I think that the Prime Minister, in terms of his philosophy, has taken exactly the correct position with respect to Japan," I said, "and I think that he has to continue to take it. But I want him to understand why I think strongly that *our* policy with respect to Japan is in the security interests of his country even though it is opposed to the philosophic doctrine which he espouses.

"The United States can get out of Japanese waters, but others will still fish there. If we were to leave Japan naked and defenseless, they would have to turn to others for help or build the capability to defend themselves. If we had no defense arrangement with Japan, we would have no influence where they were concerned.

"If the United States is gone from Asia, gone from Japan," I said, "our protests, no matter how loud, would be like firing an empty cannon. We would have no effect, because thousands of miles away is just too far to be heard.

"Now I realize that I have painted here a picture which makes me sound like an old cold warrior," I continued, and Chou laughed softly. "But it is the world as I see it, and when I analyze it, it is what brings us, China and America, together, not in terms of philosophy and not in terms of friendship—although I believe that is important—but because of national security I believe our interests are in common in the respects I have mentioned."

The Chinese regarded the Soviet Union with a mixture of utter contempt and healthy fear. Chou was completely aware of the symbolism and impact of my coming to Peking before going to Moscow, and he thoroughly enjoyed the fulminations of the Soviet press against my visit. "You have come here first," he said, "and Moscow is carrying on like anything! They are mobilizing a whole mass of their people, their followers, to curse us. But let them go on. We don't care."

Later on, when he had loosened up considerably, he told an amusing story that he said took place during a Sino-Soviet border flare-up in 1969. "We had a hot line between the Soviet Union and ourselves then," he said, "but it had already become cold because the Kremlin never used it. At the time of the Chen Pao border incident, however, Kosygin picked it up and called us. When our operator answered, he said, 'This is Premier Kosygin. I would like to speak to Chairman Mao.' The operator, completely on his own, said, 'You are a revisionist, and therefore I will not connect you.' So Kosygin said, 'Well, if you will not try to reach the Chairman, will you please connect me with Prime Minister Chou.' But the operator gave the same unauthorized reply and broke the connection."

About halfway through the meeting Chou took some small white pills. I guessed that they were for his high blood pressure. I was impressed by his mental acuity and his stamina; I noticed that some of the younger men on both sides became drowsy as the afternoon lengthened and the translators droned on and on, but despite his seventy-three years Chou remained alert and attentive throughout the four-hour session.

"The most pressing question now is Indochina, where the whole world is watching," he said. "The Democratic Party tried to put you on the spot by alleging that you came to China to settle Vietnam. Of course this is not possible. We are not in a position to settle it in talks."

I said that I fully understood the limitations of our talks and that I had no illusions about being able to settle the Indochina war in Peking. "This is simply an issue in which the only gainer in having the war continue is the Soviet Union," I said. "They want us tied down, because they want to get more and more influence in North Vietnam as a result. From all the intelligence we get, they may even be egging on the North Vietnamese to hold out and not settle."

Chou made clear that, in his opinion, the later we withdrew from Vietnam, the more difficult and unsatisfactory the withdrawal would be for us. He knew the tenacity of the North Vietnamese. "Ho Chi Minh was a very old friend of mine," he said. "I knew him in France in 1922." Chou pointed out that I had admitted that de Gaulle acted wisely in withdrawing from Algeria; despite the domestic political difficulties that a similar decision would cause me, he felt that it was nonetheless the right thing to do regarding Vietnam. He said, "Our position is that so long as you are continuing your Vietnamization, Laosization, and Cambodianization policy, and as long as they continue fighting, we can do nothing but to continue to support them."

When I summarized the American position, I said: "Let me cut away the eight points, the five points, and the thirteen points and all the other points and come right down to what our offer really is. If I were sitting across the table from whoever is the leader of North Vietnam and we could negotiate a cease-fire and the return of our prisoners, then all Americans would be withdrawn from Vietnam six months from that day. And let me also point out that when this was suggested to the North Vietnamese as far back as the middle of last year, they rejected it and insisted there had to be a settlement in which we had to impose a political settlement as well as to resolve the military side."

I said, "I realize that there are views to the contrary, but when a nation is in a position like we are in, where around the world there are nations that depend on us for their defense, if we did not behave honorably we would cease to be a nation worth having as a friend, and which the people of the world could depend upon as an ally."

While I was in these meetings with Chou, Pat carried out a full schedule that included visits to the Peking Zoo and the Summer Palace. When we met at the guesthouse that evening, she remarked that although the Chinese she had met were gracious and eager to cooperate, she felt that our reception was somehow restrained. She had been kept from meeting people, and the only contact she had had with anyone other than her official guides was on a visit to the kitchen of the Peking Hotel. We discussed the tremendous problems our visit presented to the Chinese leadership, not just in terms of their relations with the Soviet Union, North Vietnam, and the entire Communist world, but also in terms of their own internal politics. Two decades of virulent anti-American propaganda could not be undone overnight, and the Chinese masses would take time to assimilate the new line emanating from Peking.

That night we were taken to the Peking Opera by Chou and by Chiang Ching, Mao Tse-tung's wife. They had arranged a special performance of the theatrical extravaganza *The Red Detachment of Women,* which she had devised and staged.

From briefing material I was aware that Chiang Ching was an ideological fanatic who had strongly opposed my trip. She had led a checkered and contradictory life, from her younger days as an aspiring actress to her leadership of the radical forces in the Cultural Revolution of 1966. For many years she had been Mao's wife in name only, but there was no better name in China, and she had used it for all it was worth to build up her personal faction of supporters.

As we settled into our chairs, Chou mentioned that in 1965 Khrushchev had come to a performance of this show and had sat in the very place I was now sitting. He suddenly became flustered and corrected himself: "I mean Kosygin, not Khrushchev."

While we waited for the overture to begin, Chiang Ching told me about some American authors she had read. She had enjoyed *Gone with the Wind* and had seen the motion picture. She mentioned John Steinbeck, and she asked me why another of her favorite authors, Jack London, had committed suicide. I couldn't remember, but I told her that I thought it was alcoholism. She asked about Walter Lippmann and said that she had read some of his articles.

Chiang Ching had none of the easy humor or warmth of Mao, Chou, and the other men I met. I had observed the same characteristic in the young women who acted as interpreters and in several others we met during our week in China. The women of the movement, it struck me, were more humorless and more single-minded in their total dedication to the ideology than were the men. In fact, Chiang Ching was unpleasantly abrasive and aggressive. At one point that evening she turned to me and in a challenging voice asked, "Why did you not come to China before now?" Since the ballet was in progress at the time, I did not respond.

I had not been particularly looking forward to this ballet, but after a few minutes I was impressed by its dazzling technical and theatrical virtuosity. Chiang Ching had been undeniably successful in her attempt to create a consciously propagandistic theatre piece that would both entertain and inspire its audience. The result was a hybrid combining elements of opera, operetta, musical comedy, classical ballet, modern dance, and gymnastics.

The story deals with a young Chinese woman in prerevolutionary times who leads her townspeople in a revolt against an oppressive landlord. Emotionally and dramatically the production was superficial and artificial. In many respects, as I noted in my diary, it reminded me of the ballet *Spartacus* that we had seen in Leningrad in 1959—in which the ending was changed so that the slaves won.

After each evening's social event Kissinger would meet with the Vice Foreign Minister and go over each new draft of the official communiqué word by word. Sometimes Chou would join them; sometimes Kissinger would walk across the small bridge connecting the two guesthouses and report to me on the progress they were making or the problems they had run up against. As a result of these nocturnal negotiations, few of us got very much sleep, and Kissinger got hardly any.

Taiwan was the touchstone for both sides. We felt that we should not and could not abandon the Taiwanese; we were committed to Taiwan's right to exist as an independent nation. The Chinese were equally determined to use the communiqué to assert their unequivocal claim to the island. This was the kind of disagreement that our formula for drafting the communiqué was supposed to take into account: we could state our position and they could state theirs. In this case, domestic political considerations led Kissinger and me to try to convince the Chinese of the necessity of exercising moderation.

We knew that if the Chinese made a strongly belligerent claim to Taiwan in the communiqué, I would come under murderous crossfire from any or all the various pro-Taiwan, anti-Nixon, and anti-P.R.C. lobbies and interest groups at home. If these groups found common ground on the eve of the presidential elections, the entire China initiative might be turned into a partisan issue. Then, if I lost the election, whether because of this particular factor or not, my successor might not be able to continue developing the relationship between Washington and Peking. In the official plenary sessions with Chou, therefore, I spoke very frankly about the practical political problems a strongly worded communiqué on Taiwan would cause me.

We knew that no agreement concerning Taiwan could be reached at this time. While both sides could agree that Taiwan was a part of China —a position supported by both the Peking and Taiwan governments—we would have to oppose the use of military force by Peking to bring Taiwan under Communist rule.

Our lengthy discussions resulted as we expected; we could only agree to disagree and to reflect our differences in the communiqué. Thanks largely to Kissinger's negotiating skill and Chou's common sense, the Chinese finally agreed to sufficiently modified language.

One reason we found the Chinese appeared to be so agreeable to deal with was their total lack of conceit or arrogance. Unlike the Soviets, who ritually insisted that everything they had was the biggest and the best, the Chinese were almost obsessed with self-criticism and with seeking advice on how to improve themselves. Even Chiang Ching, when I told her how impressed I was with her ballet, said, "It is good to know that you find it acceptable, but tell me how you would go about improving it." As Chou continually referred to their need to understand and overcome their imperfections, I could not help thinking of Khrushchev's boastful bombast and how much healthier the Chinese approach was. Of course, I knew that it was only an approach, a conscious decision to view themselves in this way, and that in fact they were absolutely convinced of the ultimate superiority of their culture and philosophy, and that in time it would triumph over ours and everyone else's.

However, I found myself liking these austere and dedicated men. When Pat and I toured the Forbidden City, our host was the seventy-two-year-old Minister of Defense, Marshal Yeh Chien-ying.

Diary
He was a totally delightful man with great inner strength. He made the interesting comment that the

American music and the Chinese music seemed to fit in together, and that American and Chinese journalists hit it off well. I think he is totally correct in this respect, particularly where Americans have a little depth and subtlety and are not the abrasive, loud types that would grate upon the Chinese. One of the benefits of our relationship is that Americans today, as distinguished from the late nineteenth-century Americans, are very different from the Europeans, the British, French, Dutch, et al. We have no sense of arrogance—we honestly, almost naïvely, like people and want to get along with them. We lack often a sense of subtlety but that will come after we've had a few hundred more years of civilization. It is the subtlety of the Chinese which is most impressive to me. I had read about it and heard about it, and seen it in quotations. Chou En-lai, of course, adds to Chinese subtlety the far-ranging experience of a world diplomat.

On our third night in Peking, Pat and I were taken to a gymnastics and table tennis exhibition.

Diary
The gymnastic event was a colorful spectacle and, as was the case with the ballet the night before, had the feeling of enormous dedication and singleness of purpose in the whole production.

The way that they brought out their equipment, and the opening march with the red flag, was strikingly strong. The appearance of both the girls and men, as well as, of course, up to the superb Ping-Pong event left an impression that was not only lasting, but also foreboding.

Henry could not be more right in his warning that as the years went on, not only we but all the people of the world will have to make our very best effort if we are to match the enormous ability, drive, and discipline of the Chinese people.

When I went to bed that night I found that I could not get to sleep. At five o'clock I got up and took a hot bath. I climbed back into bed and lighted one of the Chinese-made

"Great Wall" cigars my hosts had thoughtfully provided, and sat puffing on the cigar and making notes about the events of the momentous week.

On Saturday, February 26, we flew with Chou in his plane to Hangchow, in eastern China. By this time he and I were talking quite freely to each other.

Diary

Chou En-lai and I had a very interesting conversation on the way to the airport in Peking. He spoke of Mao's poem which he wrote on returning to his hometown after thirty-two years. He returned to the point he has made quite often, that adversity is a great teacher. I related it to adversity generally, and pointed out that an election loss was really more painful than a physical wound in war. The latter wounds the body—the other wounds the spirit. On the other hand, the election loss helps to develop the strength and character which are essential for future battles. I said to Chou that I found that I had learned more from defeats than from victories, and that all I wanted was a life in which I had just one more victory than defeat.

I used also the example of de Gaulle in the wilderness for a period of years as a factor which helped to build his character. He came back with a thought that men who travel on a smooth road all their life do not develop strength.

Chou said that I had a poetic turn of mind like Mao, when I had in my last toast said that it was not possible to build a bridge across 16,000 miles and twenty-two years in one week. Much of the Mao poetry, of course, is simply a colorful and vivid example.

He referred again to his admiration for *Six Crises*, and I jokingly said that he shouldn't believe all the bad that the press said of me, and that I would follow the same practice with regard to him.

Hangchow is built around large lakes and gardens. In the days when the emperors used it as a summer resort, it was known as the most beautiful city in China. I knew that

Mao enjoyed taking vacations there and staying in an exquisite old palace that had been turned into a government guesthouse.

Even though we were in Hangchow in the cloudy off-season, it was easy to see why Mao was drawn to the city. Mountains rise mistily in the background, and the lakes are full of lotus flowers. The pagoda-like guesthouse, with its sloping green tile roofs, was set in the middle of a lake on an island called "Island of Three Towers Reflecting the Moon." It was rather musty, but it was immaculately clean, and Pat and I later agreed that our stay there was the most delightful interlude of the trip.

During the more than fifteen hours of formal talks I had with Chou we covered a wide range of issues and ideas. Since all our discussions during this trip were so frank, it was understandable that the Chinese were nervous about the possibility of leaks. I am sure that Chou had no trouble imagining the propaganda use the Kremlin would have for the transcripts of our talks. During a discussion of the internal opposition to some of my decisions during the Indo-Pakistan war, Chou referred to the Jack Anderson leak. "The records of three of your meetings were made public because all sorts of people were invited," he remarked with a sardonic smile. I felt a real concern beneath his bantering tone. In fact, in our first conversation on the way in to Peking from the airport, Chou had mentioned how important the Chinese considered confidentiality in our relationship, and Chairman Mao had made the same point very emphatically during our meeting.

To assuage Chou's fears, I outlined the strict procedures we planned to follow to keep our future contacts secret. "The Prime Minister may think we're being too careful," I said, "but as you know, we had the Pentagon Papers from the previous administration, and we've had the Anderson papers from this administration. Dr. Kissinger and I have determined that this will never happen in the new relationship that we have established with your government."

I said I was determined that when the fate of our two

countries—and possibly the fate of the world—was involved, we would be able to talk in confidence.

When we began to talk about the situation in the Middle East, Chou jokingly said, "Even Dr. Kissinger doesn't want to discuss this problem, because being Jewish he is afraid that they suspect him."

I said, "My concern in the Middle East—and, incidentally it is Dr. Kissinger's too, because while he is Jewish he is an American first—our concern is much bigger than Israel. We believe the Soviet Union is moving to reach its hands out in that area. It must be resisted. That is why we took a position in the Jordanian crisis, for example, warning the Soviets that if they move aggressively in that area, we will consider our own interests involved."

I emphasized that my visit had bipartisan support and that other visits by Democrats as well as Republicans would now be perfectly in order. "As I have indicated to the Prime Minister, it is important to have policy carried forward whoever sits in this chair next year," I said. "Under our system, I may be here next year, and I may not. I want to be sure that whether a Democrat or Republican occupies the presidency, this beginning we have made is carried forward. It is bigger than any one party or any one man. It involves the future for years to come."

As we became more at ease and more familiar with each other, our conversations occasionally became light, even humorous.

During one of our airport drives, Chou told me about a meeting between Chairman Mao and Emperor Haile Selassie a few months before my trip to China was announced. Mao had asked the old Emperor whether he thought that the "socialist devil," as he humorously called himself, should sit down and talk with the "capitalist devil." I said, "I expect that many of your colleagues must have thought the reason I didn't bring a hat with me was because I couldn't find one to fit over my horns."

A recurring theme in our conversations was age. As Malraux had said, the Chinese leaders were obsessed by the amount that remained to be done and by the little time that was left them in which to do it.

Chou came to the age factor two or three times. I said that I was enormously impressed by his vitality and that age really was a question of not how many years a person lived but how much he lived in those years. I seemed to sense that he felt that being involved in great affairs kept a person alive and young, but there was a haunting refrain throughout that he felt that the current leadership was near the end of the road with still very much to be done.

All the Chinese leaders we met seemed particularly struck by the youth of our entire party. In our first meeting Chou singled out Dwight Chapin, who was only thirty-one and looked even younger. "We have too many elderly people in our leadership. So on this point we should learn from you," he said. "I have found that you have many young men; Mr. Chapin is very young indeed, and Mr. Green is not very old either." Marshall Green, the Assistant Secretary of State for East Asia and Pacific Affairs, was fifty-six.

Despite the fact that I was almost a quarter of a century younger than Mao, I approached this trip as if it were the last chance I would have to do something about the Sino-American relationship. As I put it in a diary dictation shortly after returning home, "I am really probably older than they are—I have only ten months to live (politically)—or at most four years and ten months, and I must get results now. That is why now is the hour for me, even more than for them, despite the fact that they are older in conventional terms."

One afternoon as we were discussing the need for patience in the solution of problems, Chou said, "I can't wait ten years. You have ten years. Mr. President may be re-elected to a third term."

"That's against the Constitution," Kissinger interjected.

"After four years then you can run again, because your age permits you to do that. But in view of the age of the present leaders of China, it is not possible. They're too old," Chou said.

"Mr. Prime Minister," I replied, "former Presidents of

the United States are like British kings; they have great responsibility but no power. I mean one who is out of office."

"But your career is quite rare in history. You have been Vice President for two terms, then lost and then won an election again. It's quite rare in history."

Our joint statement, issued from Shanghai at the end of the trip, has become known as the Shanghai Communiqué.

Following the formula Kissinger had worked out during Polo II, the communiqué broke diplomatic ground by stating frankly the significant differences between the two sides on major issues rather than smoothing them over. Thus the text is surprisingly lively for a diplomatic document.

The first substantive section begins: "The U.S. side stated" and then details our positions on each of the major issues discussed. This is followed by a section that begins: "The Chinese side stated" and then covers the same ground in counterpoint.

Thus the U.S. side proclaimed its support for the eight-point peace plan proposed by us and the South Vietnamese in Paris on January 27; the Chinese side stated its support for the seven-point proposal put forward by the Vietcong in February.

We stated our intention to maintain close ties with and support for South Korea; the Chinese endorsed North Korea's plan for unification of the Korean peninsula, and called for the abolition of the UN presence in South Korea.

We affirmed that we placed the highest value on our friendly relations with Japan and said that we would continue to develop the existing close bonds; the Chinese side stated that it "firmly opposes the revival and outward expansion of Japanese militarism and firmly supports the Japanese people's desire to build an independent, democratic, peaceful and neutral Japan."

The Chinese stated their claim to be the sole legal government of China and their conviction that Taiwan is a province of China. They affirmed that the liberation of Taiwan was China's internal affair in which no country had a right to interfere, and demanded that all American forces and military installations be withdrawn from Taiwan. They concluded by stating that "the Chinese government firmly opposes any activities which aim at the creation of 'one China, one Taiwan,' 'one China, two governments,' 'two Chinas,' and 'independent Taiwan' or advocate that 'the status of Taiwan remains to be determined.' "

The wording of the American section on Taiwan avoided a clash by stating simply: "The United States acknowledges that all Chinese on either side of the Taiwan Strait maintain there is but one China and that Taiwan is a part of China. The United States government does not challenge that position. It reaffirms its interest in a peaceful settlement of the Taiwan question by the Chinese themselves." We stated our ultimate objective of withdrawing American troops from Taiwan but did not put any final date on it, and we agreed in the meantime to reduce our forces and installations on Taiwan progressively "as the tension in the area diminishes."

Perhaps the most vitally important section of the Shanghai Communiqué was the provision that neither nation "should seek hegemony in the Asia Pacific region and each is opposed to efforts by any other country or group of countries to establish such hegemony." By agreeing to this provision both the P.R.C. and the United States were imposing restraints on themselves. But far more important, particularly as far as the Chinese were concerned, was that the provision subtly but unmistakably made it clear that we both would oppose efforts by the U.S.S.R. or any other major power to dominate Asia.

As I look back on that week in China two impressions stand out most vividly. One is the awesome sight of the disciplined but wildly—almost fanatically—enthusiastic audience at the gymnastic exhibition in Peking, confirming my belief that we must cultivate China during the next few decades while it is still learning to develop its national strength and potential. Otherwise we will one day be confronted with the most formidable enemy that has ever existed in the history of the world.

My other most vivid memory of the trip is the unique personality of Chou En-lai. My meeting with Mao Tse-tung was too brief and too formal to have given me much more than a superficial personal impression. But many hours of formal talks and social conversation with Chou made me appreciate his brilliance and dynamism.

Unlike many world leaders and statesmen who are completely absorbed in one particular cause or issue, Chou En-lai was able to talk in broad terms about men and history. Even though his perspective was badly distorted by his rigid ideological frame of reference the extent of his knowledge was impressive.

After one of the banquets in Peking, I made notes of our conversation.

Diary
It was interesting to note the remarkable knowledge of history that Chou En-lai displays, and, also, how his historical perspective is shaped by his ideology. For example, he sees the French intervention in the Revolutionary War as being by volunteers [led by Lafayette] and not by the French government.

Chou also sees Lincoln [as one] who "after many defeats," as he put it, finally prevailed because he had the people on his side. While it is true that Lincoln is one of the few great figures in history, he was a total pragmatist. He did not fight the war for the purpose of freeing the slaves, although he was unalterably opposed to slavery; and when he freed the slaves, he did not free them as an end in itself—he did so as a purely tactical, military maneuver, freeing only the slaves in the South but not in the Northern border states.

I regret that Chou did not live long enough for me to meet him again when I visited China for the second time in February 1976. I feel that although our acquaintance was brief and necessarily somewhat restrained and even wary, we had formed bonds of mutual respect and personal esteem.

During our last long session together in the guesthouse in Peking, Chou said, "In your dining room upstairs we have a poem by Chairman Mao in his calligraphy about Lushan mountain. The last sentence reads, 'The beauty lies at the top of the mountain.' You have risked something to come to China. But there is another Chinese poem which reads, 'On perilous peaks dwells beauty in its infinite variety.'"

"We are at the top of the mountain now," I said.

"That's one poem," he continued. "Another one which I would have liked to have put up, but I couldn't find an appropriate place, is 'Ode to a Plum Blossom.' In that poem the Chairman meant that one who makes an initiative may not always be one who stretches out his or her hand. By the time the blossoms are full-blown, that is the time they are about to disappear." He took a small book from his pocket and read the poem.

"Spring disappears with rain and winds
          and comes with flying snow.
Ice hangs on a thousand feet of cliff
          yet at the tip of the topmost branch the plum blooms.
The plum is not a delicious girl showing off
          yet she heralds spring.
When mountain flowers are in wild bloom
          she giggles in all the color."

"Therefore," Chou continued, "we believe we are in accord with the idea you have expressed: you are the one who made the initiative. You may not be there to see its success, but of course we would welcome your return," he said.

Kissinger diplomatically pointed out that even if I won re-election, a return visit would not be very likely.

"I was only trying to illustrate the Chinese way of thinking," Chou said. "It does not matter anyhow."

Chou referred to the fact that I had changed the name of *Air Force One* to *The Spirit of '76* shortly before this trip. "Regardless of who is the next President," he said, "the spirit of seventy-six still exists and will prevail. From the standpoint of policies, I hope that our counterpart will be the same so that we can continue our efforts. We also hope not only that the President continues in office but that your National Security Adviser and your assistants continue in office. Various changes may be bound to come. For example, if I should suddenly die of a heart attack, you would also have to deal with a different counterpart. Therefore, we have tried to bring more people to meet you. I hope you won't complain that I am too lengthy in my words."

I assured him that, on the contrary, I was very interested in what he was saying.

"This belongs to the philosophic field, but also to the political point of view. For example," he said, pointing to the book of poems open in his lap, "this poem was written after a military victory over the enemy. In the whole poem there is not one word about the enemy; it was very difficult to write the poem."

"Of course, I believe it is very useful to think in philosophic terms," I said. "Too often we look at problems of the world from the point of view of tactics. We take the short view. If the one who wrote that poem took the short view, you would not be here today. It is essential to look at the world not just in terms of immediate diplomatic battles and decisions but the great forces that move the world. Maybe we have some disagreements, but we know there will be changes, and we know that there can be a better, and I trust safer, world for our two peoples regardless of differences if we can find common ground."

I described the real nature of my thinking behind the China initiative in notes I made at 2:30 A.M. on Friday, February 24, of points I planned to make in my meeting with Chou that afternoon. Perhaps if I could have publicized these notes the conservative critics of the China initiative would at least have felt reassured that I had not approached the Chinese naïvely.

The first was to emphasize the immense potential of the Chinese living overseas, and the need for the P.R.C. to use that potential and learn to live with it, rather than to blunt it by trying to drive them into the system.

The second was to emphasize that RN would turn like a cobra on the Russians, or for that matter on anyone else, if they break their word with him. My record in Vietnam helped in getting this point across.

The third was to emphasize, in a very personal and direct way, my intense belief in our system and my belief that in peaceful competition it would prevail. I think we have gotten that across. I believe that it is essential not to let the assumption exist at all on their part that their system will eventually prevail because of its superiority.

Related to this point is that we are not going to become weak—that our system is not coming apart at the seams—and that all of the public criticism, etc., of our system should not be taken as a sign of weakness.

In my toast at the banquet on our last night in China I said, "The joint communiqué which we have issued today summarizes the results of our talks. That communiqué will make headlines around the world tomorrow. But what we have said in that communiqué is not nearly as important as what we will do in the years ahead to build a bridge across 16,000 miles and twenty-two years of hostility which have divided us in the past."

I raised my glass and said, "We have been here a week. This was the week that changed the world."

ITT

The day after we returned from China, Jack Anderson began a series of newspaper columns in which he claimed to have unearthed a major administration scandal. His charges were based on a memorandum allegedly from Dita Beard, a lobbyist for International Telephone and Telegraph Corporation, to one of her ITT superiors. Anderson said that the memo implied that a government anti-trust settlement with ITT had been influenced by an ITT contribution toward the upcoming Republican convention and that John Mitchell and I had pushed for favorable treatment for ITT because of this contribution. Mrs. Beard supposedly managed this whole deal almost single-handedly.

In fact, the anti-trust settlement in question had been a favorable one for the government and not for ITT, which was required to divest itself of holdings representing $1 billion in sales. On the first trading day after this settlement ITT's stock fell 11 percent. Furthermore, the money that allegedly influenced the settlement was not a contribution to the Committee to Re-elect the President or to the Republican Party, but to the city of San Diego so that the city could bid to be the site of the 1972 Republican National Convention. It is standard practice for local businesses to help underwrite a city's convention bid, and the Sheraton division of ITT, which was in the process of opening a new hotel in San Diego, saw the contribution as a promotional investment: the nationwide publicity and prestige that would come with being the presidential staff headquarters during convention week would be worth the payment to San Diego.

My own role in the ITT anti-trust matter consisted of one angry phone call to Dick Kleindienst almost a year earlier at the time of three Justice Department anti-trust suits against ITT. Kleindienst, Mitchell's deputy, was in charge of the case due to the fact that Mitchell had excused himself because an ITT subsidiary had been a client of our former law firm.

As I saw it, the Justice Department suits were a clear violation of my anti-trust policy. I was convinced that American companies would be able to compete in the international market only if they were as big and strong as the government-sheltered monopolies in so many foreign countries, and therefore I had instructed that big businesses were to be broken up only when they violated the laws of fair competition and not simply because they were big. I had made this position clear at staff and Cabinet meetings—and now some subordinate officials in the Justice Department were pursuing a course that deliberately contradicted it. ITT officials felt they were being unfairly sued and descended upon Washington in an effort to get the suits dropped. They had seen members of Congress from both parties and also everyone they could reach in the administration who would give them a hearing. When one case came to trial at the end of 1970, the court agreed that the suit was groundless and ruled against the Justice Department.

Several weeks later I learned that the Justice Department was going to appeal this decision to a higher court. I called Kleindienst and ordered him not to do it. The original suit had been contrary to my specifically stated policy, and I was not going to countenance further defiance by any subordinate or by any department. Two days later, when my anger had cooled, I was approached by John Mitchell. He was sensitive to the tempers and the egos at the Justice Department. He urged me to retract my order to Kleindienst, advising that if I did not, there would be resignations within the department and that would mean noisy congressional hearings and a general political mess. He explained the policy conflict as the result of unintentional confusion. I agreed to refrain from interfering in the Anti-Trust Division's decision to appeal the case.

As it turned out—for reasons wholly unrelated to my call to Kleindienst or to any contributions toward the selection of the Republican convention site—the Justice officials prosecuting the case decided to settle it and not proceed with the appeal. Months later both Watergate Special Prosecutors, Archibald Cox and Leon Jaworski, investigated the ITT case and concluded that there had been no quid pro quo involved in the settlement. When the tapes of my conversations with Mitchell and Kleindienst were turned over, they proved that my motive in ordering that no appeal be filed was policy and not politics. But this vindication was more than a year away. In that pre-election spring of 1972, the Democrats played the ITT issue to the hilt. And by the way we reacted we played right into their hands.

Dick Kleindienst, who at the time of the Anderson columns had been nominated to succeed John Mitchell as Attorney General, immediately called for new Senate hearings at which he could defend his honor. This turned out to be a tactical disaster. The committee holding the hearings included Teddy Kennedy—a front-running noncandidate—and his friends Birch Bayh and John Tunney. They quickly turned the hearings into a forum in which to berate the administration. Larry O'Brien at the Democratic National Committee joined in and the networks gave prominence to the easy accusations while the sometimes complicated explanations got lost in the clamor. I thought that the committee's Democrats had traded in hearsay and indulged in melodramatics.

Diary

If I ever get time to write a book, at some time in the future, there is going to be a hard-hitting chapter on this point. Where a committee is investigating subversives, inevitably the press attacks the procedures which the committee is following. When a committee is investigating business or government officials, including even the President, the press is totally silent with regard to outlandish procedures that it would immediately condemn if the investigation were being aimed at subversives.

Of course, what is needed is a single standard. Fair procedures should be followed in both cases —something I have always insisted upon. It bugs the press that I have done so, because they know that their objection is not to *how* a committee investigation is conducted, but to *what* is being investigated.

They just don't like to admit they had a double standard.

A year later I was to find out how hypocritical Kennedy in particular had been. Testifying before Congress, former Chairman of the Securities and Exchange Commission William Casey reported that for all Kennedy's sanctimonious grandstanding during the ITT hearings, three months later he had phoned Casey to urge that an investment banking firm headed by one of his friends not be named as a defendant in a civil suit the SEC had filed against ITT. Casey ignored Kennedy's intervention.

Day after day the White House staff raced around trying to minimize the political damage and keep any embarrassing material from the committee's partisan clutches. There were rumors that the memo itself was a forgery, so Colson sent someone out to see Mrs. Beard and to encourage her to deny publicly its authenticity. I later learned the man's name: E. Howard Hunt. In fact, Mrs. Beard did subsequently testify that the memo Anderson had published was a forgery; her secretary filed an affidavit that she had not typed the Anderson version; the man to whom it was addressed testified that he had never received it.

The whole ITT episode left us, and particularly Mitchell and Kleindienst, worn out. We had lost a massive partisan public relations battle; ITT left a sour taste in the mouths of the public even though they did not know exactly what had been involved.

Since I had no other choice, I tried to be philosophical about this situation.

55

Colson gave me a report on the ITT case, and said that he had really tried to shake up the staff a bit in terms of their pessimism with regard to the attacks. I told him this is only the beginning of a much greater assault at a later point—for us to stand firm.

I think we have got to find tougher language to throw at some of our Democratic friends. Instead of doing the nation's business, they are spending all their time in smears.

Haldeman had pointed out that Joe Kraft in his column, and Connally later in the day, in recounting a conversation he had with [NBC news anchorman John] Chancellor, made the same point to the effect that the administration was reacting too much to the disclosures. It is likely that this is the case, but I think that at the beginning the problem was that we didn't know what really was involved, and the mistake was that we should have, as Haldeman suggested, simply laid the whole record on the table, and not have been concerned about it.

NORTH VIETNAM INVADES THE SOUTH

The optimistic days when I had envisioned ending the Vietnam war within a year were now long past. For more than a year the North Vietnamese had played a cynical game with the peace talks in Paris. Whenever Kissinger would make a substantial new proposal in one of the private sessions, they would either ignore or reject it. Then in the public sessions they would vehemently attack us for not showing any flexibility or interest in reaching an agreement. They would haggle about details, but on the bottom line they never wavered: they would not agree to a settlement unless we agreed to overthrow Thieu.

On August 16, 1971, we offered the complete withdrawal of American and allied forces within nine months after an agreement; on September 13 they rejected this proposal and continued to insist on the overthrow of Thieu as the sine qua non for reaching any agreement. In the meantime they used the public meetings in Paris to berate us for not wanting to negotiate seriously.

It was a very skillful propaganda maneuver, and it took in many American critics of the war. For example, in September 1971 McGovern visited Paris and spent six hours talking with Xuan Thuy. Afterward he told reporters that he had been assured that the North Vietnamese would return all our POWs as soon as we agreed to set a date for our withdrawal. *These were exactly the terms that we had offered on May 31, 1971, and they had rejected, on June 26, 1971.* When Kissinger confronted Xuan Thuy with this duplicity at their next meeting, Thuy coldly replied, "What Senator McGovern says is his problem."

More to make sure that we had overlooked no opportunity for a settlement than out of any belief that we would succeed in obtaining one, I decided to make another attempt at breaking the deadlock. Therefore in October we got Thieu's approval on a major new plan that provided for all U.S. and allied forces to be withdrawn from South Vietnam within six months of an agreement, for all POWs to be exchanged on both sides, and for a cease-fire throughout Indochina. Thieu also accepted an internationally supervised presidential election in South Vietnam within six months after an agreement was reached and went to the extraordinary length of agreeing that he and Vice President Ky would resign from office one month before the election so that all candidates would run on an equal footing.

Armed with this dramatic new plan, we proposed another secret session for November 1, 1971. The North Vietnamese countered by suggesting November 20, and we accepted. On November 17 they canceled, saying that Le Duc Tho was ill. We offered to meet as soon as he was recovered or to meet with any other qualified representative.

No further word came from Hanoi, but there were ominous reports of a big military buildup north of the DMZ as well as a continued stepping up of enemy activity in the South. When Saigon was shelled—in clear violation of the terms of the 1968 bombing halt agreement—I ordered that our bombing raids be resumed over North Vietnam. The domestic outcry was immediate and intense.

———————

On January 13, 1972, I approved the withdrawal of 70,000 more American troops from Vietnam over the next three months. Coming on the eve of a new session of Congress and just before the beginning of the presidential primaries, I felt that the number had to be significant in order to underscore the downward direction of my withdrawal policy. By May 1, less than four months away, there would be only 69,000 Americans remaining in Vietnam, and they too would be getting ready to leave. Even as I made this announcement, however, I was facing the unsettling prospect that a successful Communist invasion of South Vietnam might seriously jeopardize the safety of those decreasing numbers of Americans still there.

The leak to columnist Jack Anderson during the Indo-Pakistan war had added a disturbing new element to our situation. The Navy yeoman we suspected of being the source of the leak had had access to papers dealing with Kissinger's secret negotiations in Paris, and we had no way of knowing whether any information about them had been passed on to Anderson or others. If the American people learned about the secret negotiations through a newspaper leak, there would be political and diplomatic hell to pay. I was also concerned because one of Kissinger's aides who had resigned because of Cambodia was now working as Muskie's foreign policy adviser in his presidential campaign. Since this man had been privy to the secret negotiations in Paris, we could not be certain that he would not tell Muskie.

Therefore I decided to make a speech revealing publicly the peace plan that the North Vietnamese had not been interested in hearing from us privately and, at the same time, to reveal the existence of the secret channel. The time had come to show the sincerity of our approach and expose the cynical tactics of the Communists.

In the speech, which I made from the Oval Office on January 25, 1972, I said that Kissinger had been holding secret meetings with the North Vietnamese since August 1969. I explained that over the past thirty months Kissinger, Rogers, and I had carefully tailored our public statements to protect the secrecy of the meetings because we were determined to do nothing to jeopardize any chance they had for success. But there had been no success, and it was time to try another way.

Referring to the cynical game the North Vietnamese had played with McGovern regarding the POWs in September 1971, I said, "Nothing is served by silence when it misleads some Americans into accusing their own government of failing to do what it has already done. Nothing is served by silence when it enables the other side to imply possible solutions publicly that it has already flatly rejected privately."

I said that just as secret negotiations can sometimes break a public deadlock, I now felt that public disclosure might help to break a secret deadlock. I described the major points of our dramatic new proposal that Hanoi had not even deigned to receive.

I said that we were still interested in almost any potential peace agreement, but I repeated that the only kind of plan we would not consider was one that required us to accomplish the enemy's goals by overthrowing our South Vietnamese ally. I also warned, "If the enemy's answer to our peace offer is to step up their military attacks, I shall fully meet my responsibility as Commander in Chief of our armed forces to protect our remaining troops."

I concluded, "Honest and patriotic Americans have disagreed as to whether we should have become involved at all nine years ago; and there has been disagreement on the conduct of the war. The proposal I have made tonight is one on which we all can agree."

———————

While the path to the Chinese Summit had unfolded relatively smoothly, the way to the Soviet Summit was strewn with pitfalls. During the first few months of 1972, our intelligence indicated that vast quantities of Soviet arms were pouring into North Vietnam. "I think that what offends me most about the Soviets is their utter lack of subtlety," Kissinger said when we learned this. "They're just trying to blacken China's eyes because of your trip. They want to increase their influence in Hanoi, but they don't see the danger of giving new toys to the North Vietnamese fanatics."

On January 25, I wrote a letter to Brezhnev informing him of my speech that night and stating, "The Soviet Union should understand that the United States would have no choice but to react strongly to actions by the North Vietnamese which are designed to humiliate us. Such developments would be to no one's benefit and would serve to complicate the international situation." Dobrynin pretended to be surprised that we were thinking so negatively, and Brezhnev's reply a few days later was terse and testy.

On March 30 I was sitting in the Oval Office talking to Kissinger when one of his staff members sent a note in to him. He read it and said, "The North Vietnamese have attacked across the DMZ. This is probably the beginning of the offensive we have been expecting."

It was more than just an offensive. It was a full-scale invasion, and over the next few weeks the main force of the North Vietnamese Army—an estimated 120,000 troops —trampled across the internationally recognized neutral territory of the DMZ and pushed deep into South Vietnam.

Tragically, the Communist spring offensive also once again unleashed that barbaric strain of North Vietnamese brutality that so marked their conduct of the Vietnam war. I was shocked by the reports that came in. At both An Loc and Quangtri, as terrified civilians rushed to flee the scene of combat, North Vietnamese troops indiscriminately slaughtered thousands of them.

During the spring offensive, the Communists took over Binh Dinh province on the central coast of Vietnam, and intelligence reports came in telling of public executions by the Communists of hundreds of individuals suspected of having connections with the Saigon government. In one hamlet forty-seven local officials were reported to have been buried alive. A few months later we learned of still another barbaric mass murder near Quang Ngai province, where Communist forces gathered together more than a hundred civilians and selected forty of them for execution. They added a grisly twist by stringing land mines around the chosen victims and then, as their wives and children watched, detonated the mines, blowing the helpless captives to bits.

I viewed the North Vietnamese invasion as a sign of desperation. They clearly felt that Vietnamization was working. If it were not, they would have waited and let it fail. I felt that if we could mount a devastating attack on their home territory while pinning down their Army in the South, we would be in a very good position for the next round of negotiations. We decided to go all out in applying military pressure to North Vietnam and diplomatic pressure to its Soviet suppliers. I issued orders for the Pentagon planners to begin assembling a massive attack force of aircraft carriers, cruisers, and destroyers for sea bombardment and B-52s for aerial raids on North Vietnam. On April 4 the State Department publicly announced that Soviet arms were supporting the North Vietnamese invasion. At their next meeting, Kissinger confronted Dobrynin with the alternatives that either the Soviets had actually planned the invasion or their negligence had made it possible.

Despite this, Brezhnev gave a noticeably warm reception to Secretary of Agriculture Earl Butz when he arrived in Moscow to discuss trade agreements, and during this period we signed several joint agreements dealing with education and cultural exchanges. We also began talks aimed at settling the lend-lease debts the Soviets had owed since World War II. It seemed clear that Moscow was moving ahead on the summit regardless of the flare-up in the war.

Without making any specific promises, Dobrynin told Kissinger that the North Vietnamese would adopt a very responsive approach when the private talks resumed in Paris on April 24. He also repeated an earlier suggestion that Kissinger make a secret visit to Moscow so that Vietnam and other agenda items could be discussed with Brezhnev before the summit. I agreed with Kissinger that he should accept this invitation.

We were also completely agreed on our overall strategy and goals as he prepared for his trip to Moscow. However, his opinion on the tactics he should follow in his talks was somewhat different from mine. In my conversation with Kissinger and in the instructions I sent him in Moscow, I stressed that I wanted him to make Vietnam the first order of business and to refuse to discuss anything that the Soviets wanted—particularly the trade agreements for which they were so eager—until they specifically committed themselves to help end the war. Kissinger, however, continued to feel that flexibility must be the cornerstone of any successful negotiation, and he urged me to let him feel out the situation rather than risk everything by imposing any rigid preconditions.

We were in complete agreement on the importance of keeping up the military pressure on North Vietnam, including the bombing. Any sign of weakness on our part might encourage the Soviets to provide more arms in hopes of giving the North Vietnamese a military advantage. I also wanted the South Vietnamese to be confident that we still stood resolutely behind them. The morale of the South Vietnamese government and armed forces would be crucial to their ability to resist this attack.

I felt that the North Vietnamese invasion had moved the war into a final stage. Now one of two things must happen: if the South Vietnamese, with American air support, could repel the invasion or even halt it, then we would effectively have won the war and a negotiated settlement on favorable terms would result. If, however, the North Vietnamese armies were able to sweep down and join with the Vietcong in routing the South Vietnamese forces and taking Saigon, then the war would be lost and the remaining 69,000 American troops in serious danger.

Kissinger agreed, and, perhaps to cheer me up, said that even if the worst happened and we had to pull out in the face of an enemy victory, I would still be able to claim credit for having conducted an honorable winding down of the war by the dignified and secure withdrawal of 500,000 troops. Most people would give me credit for that, and everyone would be so glad the war was over that the domestic situation would not be impossible to handle.

I considered this prospect too bleak even to contemplate. "I don't give a damn about the domestic reaction if that happens," I said, "because if it does, sitting in this office wouldn't be worth it. The foreign policy of the United States will have been destroyed, and the Soviets will have established that they can accomplish what they are after by using the force of arms in third countries." Defeat, I said, was simply not an option.

I recorded my reflections on the situation that had now developed in Vietnam.

Diary

It is ironic that having come this far, our fate is really in the hands of the South Vietnamese.

If we fail it will be because the American way simply isn't as effective as the Communist way in supporting countries abroad. I have an uneasy feeling that this may be the case. We give them the most modern arms, we emphasize the material to the exclusion of the spiritual and the Spartan life, and it may be that we soften them up rather than harden them up for the battle.

On the other hand, the enemy emphasizes the Spartan life, not the material, emphasizes sacrifice and, of course, with the enormous Soviet technical help on missiles, guns, etc., they have a pretty good advantage.

I think perhaps I was too insistent and rough on Henry today, but I am so disgusted with the military's failing to come up with any idea, and failing to follow through that I simply had to take it out on somebody. Also, Henry, with all of his many virtues, does seem too often to be concerned about preparing the way for negotiations with the Soviets. However, when he faces the facts, he realizes that no negotiation in Moscow is possible unless we come out all right in Vietnam.

What really matters now is how it all comes out. Both Haldeman and Henry seem to have an idea —which I think is mistaken—that even if we fail in Vietnam we can still survive politically. I have no illusions whatever on that score, however. The U.S. will not have a credible foreign policy if we fail, and I will have to assume the responsibility for that development.

A subtle occasion to apply pressure on the Soviets arose when I attended a ceremony at the State Department for the signing of an international convention banning biological warfare. With Dobrynin seated among the ranks of diplomats listening to my remarks, I said that we must recognize that a great responsibility rests upon the great powers to follow the principle that they should not directly or indirectly encourage any other nation to use force or armed aggression against one of its neighbors. There was no doubt that I was talking about the Soviet Union and North Vietnam.

Just before I left the State Department Auditorium, I went over to shake hands with Dobrynin. I told him that Pat had greatly appreciated Mrs. Dobrynin's recent invitation to get together for a talk about our trip to Moscow. Later that afternoon Dobrynin called Kissinger and suggested that the ladies' meeting be arranged for the next day.

Pat had asked Kissinger to brief her on the situation. He told her, "You could say how much you're both looking forward to the trip, and that you hope nothing will poison it, such as the current developments in Vietnam."

The meeting was very successful. Pat showed great skill and subtlety. When she raised the point that we did not want anything like Vietnam to interfere with the summit, Mrs. Dobrynin had squeezed her hand and vigorously nodded in agreement.

During the next weeks we pursued a combined policy of applying military pressure on the North Vietnamese and diplomatic pressure on the Soviets. Even while the summit plans were going forward, I was determined not to indulge the Soviet fiction that they could not be held responsible for what North Vietnam did, despite the fact that the invasion had been made possible by the massive infusion of new Soviet weapons and ammunition.

In order to have the necessary military impact, I was convinced that the bombing, which had begun in the southern part of North Vietnam, would have to be brought to the enemy's heartland around the Hanoi-Haiphong area. The risks of aircraft loss and additional casualties and prisoners of war in these more heavily defended regions were very great, and Laird expressed grave concern about the congressional furor that would follow further escalation of the bombing while Rogers feared that it might endanger the Soviet Summit. Still, I felt that it had to be done, and I approved the plans for operation "Freedom Porch Bravo"—a weekend of heavy B-52 raids aimed at destroying the oil depots around Hanoi and Haiphong, which were being used to fuel the invasion.

The operation was a complete success, and on Sunday morning April 16 I told Haldeman, "Well, we really left them our calling card this weekend."

Meanwhile, on April 15 the situation took a very serious turn: the North Vietnamese canceled the Paris meeting scheduled for April 24. This was the meeting that the Soviets had hinted might be the decisive one for reaching a settlement. I told Kissinger that I did not think he should take his secret trip to Moscow until we found out what kind of game they were playing.

Kissinger complained to Dobrynin that we had trusted his assurances about this meeting, and warned that its cancellation created serious obstacles to his presummit trip. "The President questions what progress can be made in Moscow if the Soviet Union cannot assure even a meeting with the North Vietnamese on an agreed date," Kissinger told him.

That night I assessed some of the possible political ramifications of these events.

Diary

Henry obviously considered this a crisis of the first magnitude. I laid down the law hard to him that under these circumstances he could not go to Moscow. I told him that what the Russians wanted to do was to get him to Moscow to discuss the summit. What we wanted to do was to get him to Moscow to discuss Vietnam. I can see that this shook him because he desperately wants to get to Moscow one way or the other. He took it in good grace. Then I told him that we had to consider our option with regard to imposing a blockade.

He walked over with me to the EOB. We stayed down deep on the lawn because there were several groups of tourists, and I was in no mood to talk to anybody at this point.

Later on in the afternoon I had a pretty candid talk with Henry about what we had to look forward to in the future. I said that what we were really looking at was a cancellation of the summit and going hard right on Vietnam, even up to a blockade.

I said under these circumstances, I had an obligation to look for a successor.

I ran down the list, including Rockefeller, Burger, Reagan, and Connally—if we could get him to change his party. Somebody like Burger, or Connally, without the scars on him that I had and with my support, might make it against a fractured Democratic Party.

Henry threw up his hands and said that none of them would do, and that any of the Democrats would be out of the question. I said that if we could get Henry to stay on that we could get continuity in foreign policy. Henry then became very emotional about the point that I shouldn't be thinking this way or talking this way to anybody—which, of course, he would have realized I wouldn't. He made his pitch that the North Vietnamese should not be allowed to destroy two Presidents.

After the dinner for the OAS, the military aide came and said I had a call from Kissinger. I went up and took it, and he told me that Dobrynin was still desperate to have him come to Moscow. Vietnam would be the first subject on the agenda. There was some talk even of having the North Vietnamese Foreign Minister there.

After the dinner I told Henry that I had reconsidered the situation and felt that we had to have an open option on the summit. We had to play out the string completely on the negotiating front, and he should go to Moscow.

The next day our bombers accidentally hit four Soviet merchant ships at anchor in Haiphong Harbor. The Soviets immediately protested what they called our "gangster activities." One of Dobrynin's staff handed a note to one of Kissinger's staff warning that the Soviets would be taking "all appropriate steps" to protect their ships "wherever they would be." An oral protest was made and then a similar note was delivered to the American Ambassador in Moscow. Diplomatically it was interesting—and important—that these protests were kept relatively low-keyed.

I issued orders that we hold absolutely firm in our position. Soviet weapons had made the North Vietnamese offensive possible, and I was not going to let them get off the defensive on this point.

Before Kissinger left for Moscow, he sent me a memorandum describing the strategy he intended to use at the meetings. As I read it I felt the memo did not adequately reflect my instructions about insisting upon a Vietnam settlement as a prerequisite for discussions on any other subject. In our last meeting I had even told Kissinger that if the Soviets proved recalcitrant on this point, he should just pack up and come home.

In their first meeting, Brezhnev protested that the Soviet government did not have as much influence in Hanoi as we seemed to think. He said that the Soviets had refused to answer any new requests for military equipment from the North Vietnamese. When he claimed that they had not supplied all that much equipment in the first place, Kissinger reminded him of the massive tonnage they had sent. In the end Brezhnev refused to promise to put any pressure on Hanoi to achieve either a de-escalation or a final settlement. The most he would agree to do was to forward our latest proposal to Hanoi even though he expected it would receive a negative reaction there. This was a far cry from the Soviets' earlier assurances that the April 24 meeting in Paris, now canceled, would probably see the fruition of the negotiations.

Having reached this impasse, Kissinger proceeded to move on to further discussions of summit agenda items. He was able to arrange the entire agenda except for the most sensitive elements of SALT, which would require direct negotiation between Brezhnev and me. But I was disappointed as I read his daily cable reports, because I felt that we might have missed the last opportunity to see how far the Soviets were willing to go to get the summit. I also feared that they would interpret Kissinger's willingness to negotiate without first getting a firm Soviet commitment to restrain the North Vietnamese as a sign of weakness rather than a sign of pragmatism.

In the other areas of discussion, however, there was remarkable progress. Brezhnev produced a SALT proposal that was considerably more favorable than we had expected, and as Kissinger reported, "If the summit meeting takes place, you will be able to sign the most important arms control agreement ever concluded."

Given Kissinger's achievements on the summit issues, I felt that there was no point in gainsaying his performance after the fact. If he had followed my instructions and insisted on a Vietnam settlement as the first order of business, perhaps Brezhnev would have dug in, called his bluff, and told him to go home—and that might have meant the end of the summit, with everything that it could accomplish, while still producing no progress on Vietnam. That was a risk I had thought worth taking. In any event the summit was held, and undoubtedly it owed a large measure of its success to Kissinger's negotiations during this secret visit to Moscow.

Two days after Kissinger's return I decided to make a short televised speech announcing a troop withdrawal from Vietnam. I felt that a further reduction of our forces while the enemy's invasion was under way would dramatize our desire for peace. Therefore I announced that an additional 20,000 troops would be withdrawn from Vietnam over the next two months, bringing our total force there on July 1, 1972, to only 49,000 men.

I described the military situation in Vietnam in the plainest possible words: "What we are witnessing here—what is being brutally inflicted upon the people of South Vietnam—is a clear case of naked and unprovoked aggression across an international border. There is only one word for it—invasion." I said that the bombing of North Vietnam would continue until the military offensive had stopped. "I have flatly rejected the proposal that we stop the bombing of North Vietnam as a condition for returning to the negotiating table," I said. "They sold that package to the United States once before, in 1968, and we are not going to buy it again in 1972."

It was a tough speech, and afterward I wished that I had made it even tougher.

The North Vietnamese rescheduled the April 24 meeting for May 2. On April 30 Pat and I attended a barbecue party at John Connally's ranch in Texas. I made a few remarks and then answered questions. One guest wanted to know whether I had thought about bombing the dikes in North Vietnam. I replied that naturally I had thought about it, but that it would involve an enormous number of civilian casualties. I continued, "We are prepared to use our military and naval strength against military targets throughout North Vietnam, and we believe that the North Vietnamese are taking a very great risk if they continue their offensive in the South. I will just leave it there, and they can make their own choice."

I knew that the news of this reply would reach Hanoi before the May 2 meeting, and I thought that it might help to strengthen our hand.

That evening I dictated a memorandum for Kissinger outlining my instructions for dealing with the North Vietnamese:

> What you must have in mind is that if they get a delay as a result of their talk with you, we shall lose the best chance we will ever have to give them a very damaging blow where it hurts, not just now, but particularly for the future.
>
> Forget the domestic reaction. Now is the best time to hit them. Every day we delay reduces support for such strong action.
>
> Our desire to have the Soviet Summit, of course, enters into this, but you have prepared the way very well on that score, and, in any event, we cannot let the Soviet Summit be the primary consideration in making this decision. As I told you on the phone this morning, I intend to cancel the Summit unless the situation militarily and diplomatically substantially improves by May 15 at the latest or unless we get a firm commitment from the Russians to announce a joint agreement at the summit to use our influence to end the war.
>
> In effect we have crossed the Rubicon and now we must win—not just a temporary respite from this battle, but if possible, tip the balance in favor of the South Vietnamese for battles to come when we no longer will be able to help them with major air strikes.
>
> We know from experience, based on their record in 1968, that they will break every understanding. We know from their twelve secret talks with you that they talk in order to gain time. Another factor is that as we get closer to the Democratic Convention, the Democratic candidates and the supporters of

Hanoi in the Congress will increasingly give them an incentive to press on and not make a deal with us with the hope that they can make a deal with the Democrats after the election.

I will be talking with you about the statement you will make when you see them, but my present intuition is that you should be brutally frank from the beginning—particularly in tone. . . . In a nutshell you should tell them that they have violated all understandings, they stepped up the war, they have refused to negotiate seriously. As a result, the President has had enough and now you have only one message to give them—Settle or else!

MAY 1972

On May 1, the day Kissinger was to leave for Paris, I received a letter from Brezhnev that increased my fear that we had failed to impress upon the Soviet leadership my unshakable determination to stand up in Vietnam. Brezhnev bluntly asked me to refrain from further actions there because they hurt the chances of a successful summit.

Kissinger was completely absorbed in mapping out his strategy for his May 2 meeting with Le Duc Tho. I spent several hours trying to make sure that we agreed on the strategy he should follow at the meeting.

Late in the afternoon after an hour and a half session on SALT Kissinger came back into the Oval Office, where I was meeting with Haldeman. He had just received a message. "It's from Abrams," he said. "Quangtri has fallen to the Communists. The battle for Hué is beginning."

We were silent for a moment while he looked over the document. "Abrams says that Quangtri isn't that important except for the effect it will have on South Vietnamese morale, but the loss of Hué would be a very serious blow."

"What else does he say?" I asked.

Kissinger cleared his throat uncomfortably, and said, "He feels that he has to report that it is quite possible that the South Vietnamese have lost their will to fight, or to hang together, and that the whole thing may well be lost."

I could hardly believe what I heard. I took the cable and read it for myself.

"How can this have happened?" I asked.

"The South Vietnamese seem to go in cycles," Kissinger suggested. "They're very good for about a month and then they seem to fold up. This crisis has been building up for about a month, and now they're caving in on schedule."

"Whatever happens, this doesn't change my thinking about the negotiations," I said. "I don't want you to give the North Vietnamese a thing. They'll be riding high because of all this, so you'll have to bring them down to the ground by your manner. No nonsense. No niceness. No accommodations. And we'll just have to let our Soviet friends know that I'm willing to give up the summit if this is the price they have in mind to make us pay for it. Under no circumstances will I go to the summit if we're still in trouble in Vietnam."

And then I thought of the bleak possibility—it was conceivable that all South Vietnam would fall. We would be left with no alternative but to impose a naval blockade and demand back our POWs.

"And then we're defeated," I told Haldeman and Kissinger.

"Then we will just have to tighten our belts," Kissinger replied glumly.

———————

Shortly after I arrived in the office on the morning of May 2, 1972, Bob Haldeman came in with the news that J. Edgar Hoover had died in his sleep during the night.

I was deeply saddened by the news. I was also taken by surprise. Even though he was seventy-seven years old, Hoover had a vigor and drive that made him seem much younger. He had become the Director of the Bureau of Investigation in 1924. Over the next forty-eight years his strong patriotism and his political astuteness enabled him to be the loyal servant of seven Presidents. He had been a part of our national life for as long as I could remember; he was already a national hero when I first met him in 1947.

Information was one of the primary sources of Edgar Hoover's power. He usually knew something about everything that was going on, and that knowledge made him as valuable to his friends as it made him dangerous to his enemies. He reached a pinnacle of power and prestige during the Eisenhower years. When Kennedy became President, Hoover was already sixty-six years old, and many of

Kennedy's advisers urged him to replace Hoover. Robert Kennedy found some of his activist plans as Attorney General hampered by Hoover's influence in the Justice Department, and the result was a period of very strained relations.

I remember sitting with Hoover in his house during a visit to Washington in 1961, listening to him go on about "that sneaky little son of a bitch," who happened to be the President's brother and Hoover's boss. Never in all the years I knew him, however, did I hear him speak disrespectfully of John Kennedy or any other President he had served.

It was under Lyndon Johnson that Hoover became a presidential confidant. Lyndon Johnson's admiration for Hoover was almost unbounded. I remembered his telling me in 1968 that if it hadn't been for Edgar Hoover, he could not have been President. Johnson's fascination with information and gossip was as insatiable as Hoover's own. In many ways the relationship was probably not a healthy one because, as subsequent Senate investigations have shown, it was under Johnson that Hoover allowed the FBI to reach its peak of political involvement.

When I became President, I asked Hoover to stay on as Director, but I was aware that because of his advancing age and the internal problems his long tenure was causing within the Bureau, I would have to begin thinking about a replacement.

In 1971, John Ehrlichman and others on the staff felt strongly that in the interests of the FBI, the administration, and of Hoover himself, we should take the initiative and get him to resign voluntarily before we reached the point where he might be forced to resign under pressure. We heard the reports that the Bureau's morale was sagging and that the characteristics that had once been Hoover's source of strength—his discipline and his pride—were now seen as temperament and ego.

That year Robert Mardian, an Assistant Attorney General under Mitchell, was told about still other problems. He reported a message of concern from William Sullivan, who had been one of Hoover's closest aides in the FBI. Sullivan apparently felt that Hoover was trapped in outdated notions of the communist threat and was not moving with flexibility against the new violence-prone radicals. Sullivan also worried that Hoover was becoming personally erratic and had recently turned on Sullivan himself and planned to fire him.

Mardian reported that Hoover might try to use the seventeen wiretaps we placed on administration aides and reporters in 1969 as blackmail leverage in order to retain his position in the Bureau. I did not believe that he would ever do such a thing. There had long been rumors that Hoover kept his position because of threats and subtle blackmail of various Presidents, but I had always regarded them with skepticism. I was also convinced that however much he might be tempted to disclose political shenanigans, Hoover would never deliberately expose national security wiretaps, the disclosure of which might have an adverse effect on our efforts to end the war and on our other foreign policy initiatives. But the FBI was in a period of great upheaval, and even though the taps had been discontinued, I could not permit the reports of them to fall into the hands of someone who, like Ellsberg, would see the chance to publicize them and become a media hero.

Sullivan had the FBI's copies of the wiretap reports, so I told Mardian to get them from him so that all copies would be kept at the White House. Later Ehrlichman said he was going to keep them himself, and I approved. That was the last I heard of any supposed threat from Hoover. I never said anything to him about it.

In October 1971 Ehrlichman sent me a brilliantly argued memorandum written for him by G. Gordon Liddy, a member of the White House staff and a former FBI agent. The memorandum analyzed in detail the complex situation presented by Hoover's long tenure as Director and concluded with a strong recommendation that he should resign.

While Ehrlichman favored immediate action, John Mitchell had a more restrained view. He knew Hoover's weaknesses, but he felt that an attempt to replace him—especially if it involved a public confrontation—could be very difficult for me and could make the administration very unpopular. He pointed out that despite all' the criticism, Hoover still had very substantial support in the country and in Congress. To millions of Americans J. Edgar Hoover was still a folk hero.

I told both Ehrlichman and Mitchell that I thought most of the new wave of anti-Hoover criticism involved predictable charges from predictable sources. His most prominent public critics opposed him not because of his policies but because he was a symbol of beliefs and values that they opposed, particularly his crusade against domestic communism and subversion, his strong stand for tougher anticrime legislation, and his opposition to legal and judicial permissiveness. I would never desert a great man, and an old and loyal friend, just because he was coming under attack.

I did, however, have two other concerns: one pragmatic and one political. What bothered me most deeply was the fact that Hoover's increasingly erratic conduct was showing signs of impairing the morale of the FBI. I told Mitchell, "The real problem, as so often happens in cases like this, is that the man himself has become the issue. That great ego which for so many years was directed almost totally to serving the Bureau and the nation is now being put into the service of the man himself. I'm sure Edgar isn't even aware that it is happening. But we have to face the fact that he is thinking too much of himself and not enough about the cause he wants to serve."

My second concern was based on my own political realism: I could not be sure that I would be re-elected for a second term. I was aware of what could happen to the FBI in the hands of a politically motivated opposition party, and the last thing I wanted to do was give the Democrats a chance to appoint a new Director who would unquestioningly carry out their bidding against Republicans for the next four or eight years.

Mitchell finally suggested that the ideal compromise would be to persuade Hoover that he should voluntarily announce his decision to retire on his seventy-seventh birthday in 1972. Such an announcement would both undercut the mounting criticism and avoid charges that he had been forced out.

Since the Director of the FBI is under the administrative control of the Attorney General, Mitchell would ordinarily have been the one to raise the question of Hoover's voluntary resignation with him. But as Mitchell put it, "Mr. President, both you and I know that Edgar Hoover isn't about to listen to anyone other than the President of the United States when it comes to this question." I knew that he was right. Although it would be painful for both of us, I decided to invite Hoover to have breakfast with me at the White House and to raise the subject with him then.

At our breakfast Hoover was as alert, articulate, and decisive as I had ever seen him. It was obvious that he was trying to demonstrate that despite his age he was still physically, mentally, and emotionally equipped to carry on.

I told him that I knew he was sensitive about some of the recent attacks on him in Congress, and about a very negative conference on the FBI at Princeton University.

"You shouldn't let things like that get you down, Edgar," I said. "Lyndon told me that he couldn't have been President without your advice and assistance, and as you know, I have the same respect for you as well as a deep personal affection that goes back nearly twenty-five years." Having said this, I tried to point out as gently and subtly as I could that as an astute politician he must recognize that the attacks were going to mount in number and intensity in the years ahead. It would be a tragedy if he ended his career while under a sustained attack from his long-time critics instead of in the glow of national respect that he so rightly deserved.

He responded very directly. He said, "More than anything else, I want to see *you* re-elected in 1972. If you feel that my staying on as head of the Bureau hurts your chances for re-election, just let me know. As far as these present attacks are concerned, and the ones that are planned for the future, they don't make any difference to me. I think you know that the tougher the attacks get, the tougher I get."

It was obvious that he was not going to take the initiative in offering his resignation. I had been through this kind of situation in 1952 when I told Eisenhower that he should make the decision whether or not I was a liability to his campaign. Now Hoover was taking exactly the same position with me: he would submit his resignation only if I specifically requested it. I decided not to do so. My personal feelings played a part in my decision, but equally important was my conclusion that Hoover's resignation before the election would raise more political problems than it would solve.

It has now become fashionable to think of our years of concern over organized crime and subversive communism as a national neurosis. Because Hoover was at the forefront of the anticrime and anticommunist movements of the postwar period, he has been painted, since the revision, as the chief neurotic. But Hoover had done the job that the public demanded for forty-eight years.

During his long and controversial life he made many enemies. He received much criticism, some of it deserved. But he took a bad rap from the critics who charged him with being "anti" one group or another. He was strongly pro-American and only against any group or individual he concluded might be engaging in activities that threatened the security of his country.

Diary

He died at the right time; fortunately, he died in office. It would have killed him had he been forced out of office or had he resigned even voluntarily. I remember the last conversation I had with him about two weeks ago when I called him and mentioned the fine job the Bureau had done on the hijacking cases. He expressed his appreciation for that call and also expressed his total support for what we are doing in Vietnam. I am particularly glad that I did not force him out at the end of last year.

I tried Buchanan on the statement [on Hoover's death] and I think improved upon it in one respect when I said that while I had ordered the flags to be flown at half-mast the flag at the FBI would always fly high due to the courage of J. Edgar Hoover in resisting the vicious attacks on his organization.

―――――――――――

While we were trying to decide on Hoover's successor, I received Kissinger's report of his May 2 meeting with the North Vietnamese in Paris. The Communists had been icy and snide, and after putting up with three hours of insult and invective, Kissinger broke off the talks.

Diary

I found with no surprise that the North Vietnamese had given nothing whatever, and that it was the most unproductive of all of Henry's trips. This is the one weakness in his approach to some of these problems. He is so understandably obsessed with the idea that there *should* be a negotiated settlement and that we ought to be able to obtain it with everything that we have set in motion, that he cannot get himself to see clearly why there really isn't enough in it for the enemy to negotiate at this time. I had a long talk with Haig, in which we concluded that we had to have a two-day strike rather than the one-day-separated-by-another-day as Henry had recommended earlier in the week. We have very few cards to play at this point.

I have sent Henry a message indicating that I thought he should think seriously on the plane on the way back about our breaking off the summit before the Russians make that move.

Haig emphasized that even more important than how Vietnam comes out is for us to handle these matters in a way that I can survive in office. I am not sure that this will be possible and in any event I am totally committed to the idea that rather than going out like Johnson did, that I must make whatever hard choices have to be made, and take whatever risks need to be taken, to preserve the position of the U.S. in Vietnam.

Of course, the weak link in our whole chain is the question as to whether the South Vietnamese have the will to fight. Certainly Abrams has been very strongly shaken in this respect as we compare his memorandum of May 1, with his memorandum of just a week before. I wired Thieu today personally to keep his spirits up, because I think it is vitally important that we not be responsible for his losing his courage at this very difficult time when bad news is coming in from the war front. The real problem is that the enemy is willing to sacrifice in order to win, while the South Vietnamese simply aren't willing to pay that much of a price in order to avoid losing. And, as Haig points out, all the air power in the world and strikes on Hanoi-Haiphong aren't going to save South Vietnam if the South Vietnamese aren't able to hold on the ground.

When Kissinger returned from Paris that night he was still discouraged by Le Duc Tho's arrogant conduct. He felt that there was now almost no chance that the Soviet Summit could take place, and he agreed with my initial inclination that we should cancel it immediately in order to prevent the Soviets from doing so first.

We discussed the overriding questions: Would cancellation of the summit be the key to winning the war? Would it shock the Soviets into finally putting some pressure on the North Vietnamese? Would it free us to lift all restrictions and bomb them until they gave in? We agreed that it was unlikely to do any of these things.

Then, I said, I would have to consider the problems it would cause. It would dash a lot of domestic hopes for peace, and that would give the Democrats a real issue. It would unleash a worldwide propaganda offensive in which the Soviets could claim that they had crumbled our foreign policy. "It's hard to see how cancellation is a really rational choice when you look at it this way," I concluded.

The problem, as Kissinger saw it, was that we could not bomb and have the summit too. And now we would have to bomb because we had said we would unless we got some meaningful action in Paris. The Soviets knew this, and unless they thought we were going to back down on our threat, it was highly likely that they would cancel the summit themselves and blame the cancellation on our bombing. That would be the worst possible outcome: a domestic outcry over the bombing and cancellation of the summit as well.

The arguments on both sides seemed persuasive. It was hard to see how I could go to the summit and be clinking glasses with Brezhnev while Soviet tanks were rumbling through Hué or Quangtri. That would show callousness, or weakness, or both. For us to cancel the summit, however, would inevitably be criticized as an impulsive action that dashed the hopes for progress toward a more peaceful world.

I decided to take the risk of postponing a decision for at least a few days. In the meantime I was determined to keep up a strong front despite all the recent setbacks. I began by sending a blunt reply to Brezhnev's letter of May 1 in which he had warned me against taking any actions in Vietnam that might hurt the chance of a successful summit. I said that the North Vietnamese had tricked us and apparently hoped that their offensive would force concessions from us:

> But this, Mr. General Secretary, will not happen, and I must now decide on the next steps in the situation that has been created. In the light of recent events, there does not seem much promise in communicating to you additional substantive considerations; there is now no basis for believing that this will have a positive effect on the situation. As Mr. Le Duc Tho made clear, Hanoi is contemptuous of communications transmitted by a third party. The fact remains that Soviet military supplies provide the means for the D.R.V.'s [Democratic Republic of (North) Vietnam] actions and promised Soviet influence if it has been exercised at all has proved unavailing.

I told Haldeman that he and Kissinger should brief John Connally on the situation and get his opinion. Haldeman reported that Connally emphatically said, "Most important—the President must not lose the war! And he should not cancel the summit. He's got to show his guts and leadership on this one. Caution be damned—if they cancel, and I don't think they will, we'll ram it right down their throats."

I discussed the issue with Kissinger, Haldeman, Connally, and Haig: "As far as I'm concerned, the only real mistakes I've made were the times when I didn't follow my own instincts," I told them. "After the EC-121 was shot down I knew that we should have moved in and bombed North Korea. When we didn't, everybody figured we were pushovers, and we've been paying for that ever since. When we went into Cambodia, I knew that we should have bombed North Vietnam at the same time. If we'd done that then, the damned war would be over now. Now in this case, my instinct is that one thing is clear: whatever else happens we cannot lose this war. The summit isn't worth a damn if the price for it is losing in Vietnam. My instinct tells me that the country can take losing the summit, but it can't take losing the war."

I believed that it was essential that we take decisive action to cripple the North Vietnamese invasion by interdicting the supplies of fuel and military equipment the enemy needed for its push into South Vietnam. I consequently directed that plans be prepared immediately for mining Haiphong Harbor and for bombing prime military targets in Hanoi, particularly the railroad lines used for transporting military supplies.

I went to Camp David to prepare the speech announcing my decision. On Sunday night I recorded the events of that tense weekend.

Diary

Julie went up with me Friday at four o'clock, and Tricia and Eddie joined us around six o'clock. We saw a good comedy with Bob Hope that night.

I told Julie about the decision on Friday and Tricia on Saturday.

Julie seemed concerned about it in terms of whether it would work. She obviously has done a lot of reading about past failures on the military side in Vietnam. She also was aware of the fact that many had become so disillusioned with the war that we might not have enough public support for it. I mentioned the fact that if we did not do this the United States would cease to be a respected great power. She rejoined with the observation that there were many who felt that the United States shouldn't be a great power. This, of course, is the kind of poison that is fed into so many of the younger generation by their professors. She was sure, however, that David would totally agree with the decision, and she seemed sensitive to what the needs were.

Tricia's reaction was immediately positive because she felt we had to do something, and frankly didn't know what else we could do to avoid a continued deterioration in the battle areas.

Pat came up very late Friday night. I had just

come back from Birch where I had been working on the speech. I saw the light on in Pat's room, and when I went in, she got up and came over, and put her arms around me, and said, "Don't worry about anything."

Over the weekend I talked to John Mitchell and he said he thoroughly approved of the decision.

Henry seemed pleased by the fact that all but one of his staff were for the blockade, including his Vietnam expert, who is somewhat of a dove. All of his staff say that it will kill the summit. Mitchell disagrees with that as did Connally.

I discussed with Kissinger the necessity to prepare a contingency plan for summit cancellation. As of this morning, he had raised his 20 percent possibility of a noncancellation to 25 percent, although he still cannot see how the Russians can react otherwise. I constantly bring him back to the point that Connally had made when we reached the decision: we can lose the summit and a number of other battles but we cannot lose in Vietnam. Not only the election, but even more important, the country, requires that the United States not lose in Vietnam. Everything is to be concentrated toward the goal now of seeing that we do not lose now that we have crossed the Rubicon.

The drafts we went through on the speech will tell the story of how it developed. Perhaps the most important section was that on the Soviet Union, and Henry was very impressed with what I finally came up with on my own. It had to be done with great subtlety and I think we have stated the case as well as we possibly can to give them a way out if they want to find one.

This whole period has been terribly hard on the family. Tricia and Eddie have decided to stay up there at Camp David. I am so glad that both girls are making great use of it, because no one knows, as I told Rose, whether we will have it to use after this year, and I want them to have the most pleasant memories of these years.

On Monday morning I informed the NSC that I had decided to go ahead with the bombing and mining, and that

I would announce the decision in a televised speech that night.

Diary

Monday was a pretty tough day because the NSC meeting ran over three hours, with Laird opposing the decision and Rogers saying he would be for it if it worked. Connally and Agnew predictably took a very strong position for it. The record will speak for itself. Of course, in fairness to Laird and Rogers, both of their reputations are on the line, and I think they have very serious doubts about whether the action will succeed. The real test, of course, will be whether they support once the decision is made and on that I have no doubt.

The biggest question mark remained the Soviet reaction. On Monday morning I sent a four-page letter to Brezhnev explaining what I had decided to do and why. I reiterated my dedication to developing our new relationship into a foundation for world peace and said that I did not intend to let the situation forced upon us by the actions of the North Vietnamese divert us from the path upon which our two countries had embarked:

In conclusion, Mr. General Secretary, let me say to you that this is a moment for statesmanship. It is a moment when, by joint efforts, we can end the malignant effects on our relations and on the peace of the world which the conflict in Vietnam has so long produced. I am ready to join with you at once to bring about a peace that humiliates neither side and serves the interests of all the people involved. I know that together we have the capacity to do this.

The final copy of my speech was not ready until after five o'clock, and I marked it up for reading and then went to get a haircut at 5:30. I had my usual light prespeech dinner of a small bowl of wheat germ for energy around six, and then went over the text until half past seven.

I jogged in place for about ten minutes and took a long cold shower before going over to the West Wing for a meeting with the joint congressional leadership in the Roosevelt Room.

The room was comfortable and warm, with a fine fire burning in the fireplace. I looked around at the familiar faces, some tense, some wary, all alert: Carl Albert, Hugh Scott, Bill Fulbright, Mike Mansfield, John Stennis, George Aiken, Jerry Ford, Hale Boggs, and half a dozen others. Some would oppose me, others would only reluctantly support me while wishing that I had not made this decision. As I described the situation and the actions I had decided to take no one interrupted or asked any questions.

I acknowledged that this was very strong medicine. It had been a very difficult decision for me to make and I knew that it would be a very difficult decision for them to support.

"If you can give me your support, I would appreciate it," I said. "If you cannot, I will understand."

There was complete silence as I rose and left the room.

Kissinger had invited Dobrynin to come to the White House shortly before I was to deliver the speech. When he described what I was about to say, Dobrynin became terribly agitated. "Why are you turning against *us* when it is Hanoi that has challenged you?" he asked.

Kissinger remained cool. Dobrynin said that he did not see how matters could do anything except take a very bad turn.

I delivered the speech at 9 P.M. After describing the military situation and the deadlock in the negotiations, I said, "There is only one way to stop the killing. That is to keep the weapons of war out of the hands of the international outlaws of North Vietnam." I continued, "I have ordered the following measures which are being implemented as I am speaking to you. All entrances to North Vietnamese ports will be mined to prevent access to these ports and North Vietnamese naval operations from these ports. United States forces have been directed to take appropriate measures within the internal and claimed territorial waters of North Vietnam to interdict the delivery of any supplies. Rail and all other communications will be cut off to the maximum extent possible. Air and naval strikes against military targets in North Vietnam will continue."

I then presented a new peace proposal, which became the reference point for the terms of the final settlement the following January:

> First, all American prisoners of war must be returned.
>
> Second, there must be an internationally supervised cease-fire throughout Indochina.
>
> Once prisoners of war are released, once the internationally supervised cease-fire has begun, we will stop all acts of force throughout Indochina, and at that time we will proceed with a complete withdrawal of all American forces from Vietnam within four months.
>
> Now, these terms are generous terms. They are terms which would not require surrender and humiliation on the part of anybody.... They deserve immediate acceptance by North Vietnam.

I concluded with the carefully phrased message to the Soviet Union that I had personally drafted: "We expect you to help your allies, and you cannot expect us to do other than to continue to help our allies, but let us, and let all great powers, help our allies only for the purpose of their defense, not for the purpose of launching invasions against their neighbors.... Our two nations have made significant progress in our negotiations in recent months. We are near major agreements on nuclear arms limitation, on trade, on a host of other issues. Let us not slide back toward the dark shadows of a previous age. We do not ask you to sacrifice your principles, or your friends, but neither should you permit Hanoi's intransigence to blot out the prospects we together have so patiently prepared."

Criticism in Congress and the media was immediate and shrill. Teddy Kennedy said that the mining was a "futile military gesture taken in desperation. I think his decision is ominous, and I think it is folly." The St. Louis *Post-Dispatch* stated that the nation would not support me because "in this case, the cause of war isn't one of honor but of dishonor." The *Wall Street Journal* reported that informed diplomatic observers were now guessing that the summit would be postponed indefinitely. Most of the television reports were focused on this question, and the network commentators unanimously concluded that my speech had seriously jeopardized the summit. NBC's Moscow correspondent said that it would be hard for the Kremlin to swallow my decision, and that it would "practically kill prospects of a summit."

The reticence of the military planners continued to be a problem.

The bombing proposals sent to me by the Pentagon could at best be described as timid. As I wrote in a long memorandum to Kissinger, "I am concerned by the military's plan of allocating 200 sorties for North Vietnam for the dreary 'milk runs' which characterized the Johnson administration's bombing in the 1965–68 period."

Having gone through the agony of making the decision and having accepted the political risks it would involve, I was determined to have it carried out the way I intended. I continued the memo:

I cannot emphasize too strongly that I have determined that we should go for broke. What we have got to get across to the enemy is the impression that we are doing exactly that. Our words will help some. But our actions in the next few days will speak infinitely louder than our words.

I am totally unsatisfied at this time at the plans the military have suggested as far as air activities are concerned. . . .

Our greatest failure now would be to do too little too late. It is far more important to do too much at a time that we will have maximum public support for what we do.

What all of us must have in mind is that we must *punish* the enemy in ways that he will really hurt at this time. . . .

Now that I have made this very tough watershed decision I intend to stop at nothing to bring the enemy to his knees. I want you to get this spirit inculcated in all hands and particularly I want the military to get off its backside and give me some recommendations as to how we can accomplish that goal. . . .

I think we have had too much of a tendency to talk big and act little. This was certainly the weakness of the Johnson administration. To an extent it may have been our weakness where we have warned the enemy time and time again and then have acted in a rather mild way when the enemy has tested us. He has now gone over the brink *and so have we*. We have the power to destroy his war-making capacity. The only question is whether we have the *will* to use that power. What distinguishes me from Johnson is that I have the *will* in spades. If we now fail it will be because the bureaucrats and the bureaucracy and particularly those in the Defense Department, who will of course be vigorously assisted by their allies in State, will find ways to erode the strong, decisive action that I have indicated we are going to take. For once, I want the military and I want the NSC staff to come up with some ideas on their own which will recommend *action* which is very *strong, threatening* and *effective*.

The Soviet news agency TASS issued a stinging denunciation of the mining as "fraught with serious consequences for international peace and security" and an emergency meeting of the Politburo was held in the Kremlin on the morning after the speech. I was fully prepared for an official statement condemning my actions and canceling the summit.

The next day Dobrynin met with Kissinger in the Map Room. Ignoring the usual pleasantries, Dobrynin coldly announced that his government had instructed him to read an official note. To Kissinger's immense relief, it turned out to be a relatively mild and private protest about the blockade and about a Soviet seaman who had been killed when a bomb accidentally hit a Soviet ship in Haiphong Harbor. When they met again the next afternoon, Kissinger casually asked why the Soviets had made no mention of the summit.

"We have not been asked any questions about the summit," Dobrynin replied, "and therefore my government sees no need to make a new decision."

Kissinger said, "*Should* we have asked any questions about the summit?"

"No," Dobrynin replied, "you have handled a difficult situation uncommonly well."

During their meeting I had been visiting Manolo at the hospital where he was recuperating from surgery. The moment I returned Kissinger rushed into my office to tell me the news. "I think we have passed the crisis," he said exuberantly. "I think we are going to be able to have our mining and bombing and have our summit too."

The next day, Dobrynin called Kissinger saying he had a message from Moscow. It turned out to be about procedural details for the summit. He even brought up the question of the state gifts to be exchanged. The Soviets were planning to give me a hydrofoil for use at Key Biscayne, and he said that Brezhnev would not look unkindly on receiving a new car for his collection of luxury automobiles.

It now seemed certain that the summit had survived the speech. The media pundits and congressional critics who had been predicting disaster dropped the cancellation line and began to concentrate on allegations that our bombers were hitting civilian targets.

Early Monday morning, May 15, I was back at my desk ready for a heavy day of meetings and appointments. I was talking with Don Kendall late in the afternoon when Bob Haldeman came in and asked if he could see me for a moment in the private office. When the door was closed behind us, he said, "We just got word over the Secret Service wire that George Wallace was shot at a rally in Maryland."

I asked if he was alive. Haldeman said he was. He said that the gunman was white, but we didn't know anything more about him yet.

The shock of the Wallace shooting forced memories back to the horror of the assassinations of John Kennedy, Martin Luther King, and Robert Kennedy. However terrible and stunning this new blow, I was determined not to let the country be talked into a climate of fear.

An editorial in the New York *Times* the next morning suggested that because of the mood of violence in the country, candidates should stay away from outdoor rallies and campaign only on television or in closed halls where security could be assured. I told Haldeman that under no circumstances would I let my Secret Service detail be increased.

Around noon John Connally came to my office after

having announced his resignation and George Shultz's nomination as Secretary of Treasury. I told him and others in the room I was going for a walk.

"When?" Ron Ziegler asked.

"Right now," I said. "Come on."

I decided to walk with Connally back to the Treasury Building. When we emerged from the East Wing just across the street from the Treasury Building a small crowd gathered, and I stopped to talk with some young people with cameras and several foreign visitors. A rather distinguished-looking man said that he was a lawyer who had gone to the University of Virginia Law School. As I started to cross the street, he said, "Thank you for coming out today."

At the end of the week I went to see Wallace at the hospital.

Diary

I stopped in to see Wallace on my way to Washington Friday morning. I was again impressed about the attractiveness of Mrs. Wallace. She has great verve, and I can see must be an enormous asset to him in his campaigning.

He seemed very up for the meeting although I sensed that he did not hear or understand too well at times. He was very proud of the showing he had made in the primaries. I told him that I would send somebody out to brief him after the Russian trip, which pleased him. He said that he would like to consider going to Walter Reed at another time, and I told him it would be available at any time when he was in the Washington area—that it provided perfect security and was a particularly nice room.

He is, though a demagogue, somewhat sentimental in terms of his strong patriotism, like most Southerners, and it came through loud and clear in the meeting. He pointed out that he had taken on both Humphrey and Muskie on the ground that they had voted for all the actions that got the United States into the war in Southeast Asia and now were criticizing what I was doing to get us out. There was a floral flag by his bed, and as I left I told him to keep the flag flying high. He saluted and said, I certainly will to my

Commander in Chief. I saluted back and left the room.

SUMMIT I

On Saturday, May 20, *Air Force One* left Washington for Salzburg, Austria, en route to Moscow. After we were airborne, Kissinger came into my cabin and exuberantly said, "This has to be one of the great diplomatic coups of all times! Three weeks ago everyone predicted it would be called off, and today we're on our way."

At 4 P.M. on Monday, May 22, after staying overnight in Salzburg, we landed at Moscow's Vnukovo Airport.

A light rain had begun to fall just before we arrived. President Nikolai Podgorny officially greeted me; Kosygin and Gromyko were also there. Aside from a small crowd standing behind the fence and waving little paper flags, it was a very cool reception. As our motorcade raced along the broad and completely empty streets toward the Kremlin, I noticed that fairly sizable crowds were being kept behind police barriers a block away down the side streets.

Pat and I had been given an entire floor of rooms in one of the large wings of the Grand Palace inside the Kremlin. As we were looking around our ornately opulent quarters, Kissinger arrived with the news that Brezhnev was waiting to welcome me in his office.

Brezhnev's office was the same room in which I had first met Khrushchev, thirteen years before. Like Khrushchev, Brezhnev looked exactly like his photographs: the bushy eyebrows dominated his face, and his mouth was set in a fixed, rather wary smile. I was sure that neither of us, standing shoulder to shoulder in the kitchen at the American Exhibition thirteen years before, had imagined that we would one day be meeting at the summit as the leaders of our countries.

We shook hands and stood talking while tea was brought in for us. He gestured to a long table at one side of the room, and he and I sat down on opposite sides of it with the Soviet translator Viktor Sukhodrev at the end. There had been concern expressed that I should have a State Department translator present also. But I knew that Sukhodrev was a superb linguist who spoke English as well as he did Russian, and I felt that Brezhnev would speak more freely if only one other person was present.

Brezhnev's tone was cordial, but his words were blunt. He said that at the outset he had to tell me that it had not been easy for him to carry off this summit after our recent actions in Vietnam. Only the overriding importance of improving Soviet-American relations and reaching agreements on some of the serious issues between us had made it possible.

After he had made this almost obligatory statement, he warmed perceptibly as he began to talk about the necessity and advantages of developing a personal relationship between us. He said that the name of Franklin D. Roosevelt was warmly cherished in the memory of the Soviet people, who remembered him as the first President to extend diplomatic recognition to the Soviet Union in 1934 and as the leader of the alliance against Hitler during World War II.

I said that I had studied the history of the relationships between Stalin and Roosevelt and between Stalin and Churchill. I had found that during the war differences between subordinates were usually overcome by agreement at the top level. "That is the kind of relationship that I should like to establish with the General Secretary," I said.

"I would be only too happy, and I am perfectly ready on my side," he replied expansively.

"If we leave all the decisions to the bureaucrats, we will never achieve any progress," I said.

"They would simply bury us in paper!" He laughed heartily and slapped his palm on the table. It seemed to be a good beginning.

About a half hour later we met again for the state dinner in the beautiful fifteenth-century Granovit Hall in the heart of the oldest part of the Kremlin. The parquet floor had been polished to a high gloss, and the vaulted walls were covered with huge icon-like paintings in rich gold and brown tones. Sitting next to each other at the head table, Brezhnev and I looked directly across the room at a several-times life-size mural of Christ and the Apostles at the Last Supper. Brezhnev said, "That was the Politburo of those days." I responded, "That must mean that the General Secretary and the Pope have much in common." Brezhnev laughed and reached over and shook my hand.

As usual, the time change made it impossible for me to fall asleep that first night. I finally got up around 4:30 and pulled on slacks and a jacket and decided to go out for a walk around the Kremlin grounds. In Moscow's northern latitude it was already almost clear daylight. I could hear the boats on the river and the sounds of truck traffic from the streets outside the red brick walls. I paused for a minute to look up at the American flag flying atop our residence amid the gold onion-top domes and red stars of the Kremlin churches and towers.

In the first plenary session at 11 A.M. with Brezhnev, Kosygin, Podgorny, Gromyko, and Dobrynin, I decided to establish the straightforward tone I planned to adopt during the entire summit.

"I would like to say something that my Soviet friends may be too polite to say," I began. "I know that my reputation is one of being a very hard-line, cold-war-oriented, anticommunist."

Kosygin said dryly, "I had heard this sometime back."

"It is true that I have a strong belief in our system," I continued, "but at the same time I respect those who believe just as strongly in their own systems. There must be room in this world for two great nations with different systems to live together and work together. We cannot do this, however, by mushy sentimentality or by glossing over differences which exist."

All the heads nodded on the other side of the table, but I guessed that in fact they would have much preferred a continuation of the mushy sentimentality that had characterized so much of our approach to the Soviets in the past.

That afternoon Kissinger and I had a two-hour meeting on SALT with Brezhnev and Andrei Aleksandrov, his adviser on U.S.–Soviet affairs. Despite the impatience he affected with the details and numbers, Brezhnev was obviously very well briefed on the subject. He used a red pencil to sketch missiles on the notepad in front of him as we discussed the timing and techniques of control and limitation.

When I said we felt that specific provisions for verifying that each side was fulfilling its obligations would give necessary reassurance to both sides, he turned to me and in an injured tone of voice said, "If we are trying to trick one another, why do we need a piece of paper? We are playing clean on our side. The approach of 'catching each other out' is quite inadmissible."

We held another long meeting that evening to discuss the important and controversial question of how far the new Soviet ABM systems would be situated from Moscow. When we began our discussion, Brezhnev casually cut three hundred kilometers from the figure that had been agreed upon just a few hours earlier. "Regarding the ABM question," he said, "this now appears to be cleared up. Twelve hundred kilometers is OK with us."

"Fifteen hundred," I said.

"You mean we should put it in China?" he said with mock exasperation.

"Well, as the General Secretary will find out, I never nit-pick," I replied.

"Fifteen hundred kilometers is all right," he said without missing a beat. "You wanted us to move eastward and so now we agree. It would be easier for us to accept twelve hundred, but fifteen hundred is all right, too, and we won't speak of it anymore."

It is a technique of Communist negotiators to introduce some ideal but impractical change in an area where the details have already been agreed upon. When we were wrangling over specific provisions of the SALT proposal, which both sides had agreed would last for five years, Brezhnev suddenly asked, "Why not make it for ten years? Why only five?" Kissinger calmly pointed out that the Soviets themselves had originally wanted the agreement to last for only eighteen months.

"I would consider this interim agreement a great achievement for us and all the world," I said. "I want to reach a permanent agreement, but my time is limited—less than five years. After then, I am out—swimming in the Pacific. Maybe even before."

"Don't go out before that, Mr. President," Brezhnev said.

Surprise is another favorite technique of Communist negotiators. After the ceremony on Wednesday afternoon when we signed an agreement on cooperation in space exploration, Brezhnev and I walked out of the room together. He began talking about the dinner planned for us at one of the government dachas outside Moscow that evening. As we neared the end of the corridor, he took my arm and said, "Why don't we go to the country right now so you can see it in the daylight?" He propelled me into an elevator that took us down to the ground floor where one of his limousines was parked.

We climbed into the limousine and were on our way while the Secret Service and the others rushed around trying to find cars and drivers to follow us. The middle lane of all the main streets in Moscow is reserved solely for party officials, and we drove along at a very fast clip.

As soon as we arrived at the dacha, Brezhnev suggested that we go for a boat ride on the Moskva River. This was exactly what Khrushchev had done thirteen years before. But times had changed: he led us not to a motorboat but to a small hydrofoil bobbing gently in the water. The pilot was skilled, and we had a smooth ride. Brezhnev kept pointing to the speedometer, which showed us traveling at ninety kilometers an hour.

We discussed work habits, and he told me he did not use a Dictaphone. I recalled that Churchill had told me that he much preferred to dictate to a pretty young woman. Brezhnev and the others agreed, and Brezhnev jokingly added, "Besides, a secretary is particularly useful when you wake up at night and want to write down a note." They all laughed uproariously.

Everyone was in a good humor when we got back to the dacha, and Brezhnev suggested that we have a meeting before the dinner, which was scheduled for eight o'clock.

Kissinger and I sat with Winston Lord and John Negroponte of the NSC on one side of the table, facing Brezhnev, Kosygin, Podgorny, and Sukhodrev on the other side. For the next three hours the Soviet leaders pounded me bitterly and emotionally about Vietnam.

I momentarily thought of Dr. Jekyll and Mr. Hyde when Brezhnev, who had just been laughing and slapping me on the back, started shouting angrily that instead of honestly working to end the war, I was trying to use the

Chinese as a means of bringing pressure on the Soviets to intervene with the North Vietnamese. He said that they wondered whether on May 8 I had acted out of thoughtless irritation, because they had no doubt that if I really wanted peace I could get a settlement without any outside assistance. "It's surely doubtful that all of the American people are unanimously supporting the war in Vietnam," he continued. "Certainly I doubt that families of those who were killed or maimed or who remain crippled support the war."

When Brezhnev finally seemed to run out of steam, Kosygin took up the cudgel. He said, "Mr. President, I believe you overestimate the possibility in the present circumstances of resolving problems in Vietnam from a position of strength. There may come a critical moment for the North Vietnamese when they will not refuse to let in forces of other countries to act on their side."

This was going too far. For the first time I spoke. "That threat doesn't frighten us a bit," I said, "but go ahead and make it."

"Don't think you are right in thinking what we say is a threat and what you say is not a threat," Kosygin replied coldly. He said, "This is an *analysis* of what may happen, and that is much more serious than a threat."

Kosygin seemed to gather force as he concentrated his scorn on President Thieu, to whom he referred as "a mercenary President so-called." When I continued to show no reaction to this tirade Kosygin's composure began to break. "You still need to retain the so-called President in South Vietnam, someone *you* call the President, who had not been chosen by anyone?" he asked.

"Who chose the President of *North* Vietnam?" I asked him.

"The entire people," he replied.

"Go ahead," I said.

When Kosygin concluded, Podgorny came to bat. His tone was more cordial, but his words were just as tough. While Podgorny and Kosygin were taking their turns at trying to hammer me down, Brezhnev got up and paced the floor.

After about twenty minutes, Podgorny suddenly stopped and Brezhnev said a few more words. Then there was silence in the room. By this time it was almost eleven o'clock. I felt that before I could let this conversation end, I had to let them know exactly where I stood.

I pointed out that I had withdrawn over 500,000 men from Vietnam. I had shown the greatest restraint when the North Vietnamese began their massive buildup in March, because I did not want anything to affect the summit. But when the North Vietnamese actually invaded South Vietnam, I had no choice but to react strongly.

"The General Secretary remarked earlier that some people may have wondered whether the action I took last month was because of irritation," I said. "If that were the case, I would be a very dangerous man in the position I am in. But that is not the case. On the contrary, my decision was taken in cold objectivity. That is the way I always act, having in mind the consequences and the risks.

"Our people want peace. I want it too. But I want the Soviet leaders to know how seriously I view this threat of new North Vietnamese escalation. One of our great Civil War generals, General Sherman, said, 'War is hell.' No people knows this better than the Soviet people. And since this new offensive began, 30,000 South Vietnamese civilians, men, women, and children, have been killed by the North Vietnamese using Soviet equipment.

"I would not for one moment suggest that the leaders of the Soviet Union wanted that to happen. What I am simply suggesting is that our goal is the same as yours. We are not trying to impose a settlement or a government on anybody."

They listened intently to what I said, but none of them made an attempt to respond.

With that we went upstairs, where a lavish dinner was waiting for us. I made my usual joke about not giving Kissinger too many drinks because he had to go back and negotiate with Gromyko. They seemed vastly amused by this and they proceeded in a comic charade to pretend to ply him with vodka and Cognac. There was much laughing and joking and storytelling—as if the acrimonious session downstairs had never happened.

While we were eating, Kosygin remarked that it was a good omen for our future relations that after three hours of the kind of hard-hitting discussions we had just completed, we could still have a relaxed and personally friendly conversation over dinner. I responded that we must recognize our differences and discuss them honestly. He nodded his head vigorously and raised his glass in another toast.

It was after midnight by the time we got back to the Kremlin. Kissinger and Gromyko immediately began a meeting on the critical questions still standing in the way of a SALT agreement.

I was in my room getting a back treatment from Dr. Riland around 1:00 A.M. when Kissinger came in with the news that the Soviets were continuing to hold out for their position, which was unacceptable to us. It was possible that they were hoping that the domestic pressures on me to return home with a SALT agreement would force me to settle for their terms. I had anticipated this possibility before we left Washington, and I was ready to call their bluff.

Kissinger had further news, however, for which I was not prepared. He reported that the Pentagon was in almost open rebellion and the Joint Chiefs were backing away from the SALT position to which they had previously agreed. Kissinger did not have to remind me—although he did so in the most urgent terms—that if word of this split reached the press, or if the Pentagon refused to support a SALT agreement I brought back from the summit, the domestic political consequences would be devastating.

"The hell with the political consequences," I said. "We are going to make an agreement on *our* terms regardless of the political consequences if the Pentagon won't go along." I determined not to allow either the Pentagon on the right or the Soviets on the left to drive me away from the position I believed was in the best interests of the country.

"Just do the best you can," I said, "and remember that as far as I'm concerned, we don't have to settle this week."

Kissinger spent several more hours that night trying to hammer out an acceptable agreement. The meeting finally broke up in the early morning with the issue still dead-locked.

The next night we went to a gala performance of *Swan Lake* at the Bolshoi Theatre. I sat between Kosygin and Podgorny, with Pat on Kosygin's right. Protocol did not require Brezhnev to attend, and I welcomed the opportunity to see how his colleagues acted away from his forceful presence.

Between the second and third acts a woman in the audience stood up and, turning toward our box, yelled, "Viva Vietnam!" She was quickly removed. We later learned that she was the wife of an Italian journalist who worked for a pro-Communist newspaper. At the next intermission Kosygin remarked that if we left Vietnam our prestige would grow, rather than suffer the way French prestige did after the defeats at Dien Bien Phu and in Algeria. That was the only mention of substantive issues all evening, and Podgorny immediately moved on to say that his favorite part of the ballet was the dance of the four swans in the second act.

Kissinger resumed his meetings with Gromyko after the ballet. The next morning he reported that they had gone as far as they could with the actual negotiations. Their meeting had broken up without any agreement having been reached.

Later, Kissinger and I were meeting in my apartment when Dobrynin arrived with the news that the Politburo had held a special session and agreed to accept our final position.

Everyone's spirits were high at the dinner we gave at Spaso House, the ambassador's residence, that night. Brezhnev was at his most expansive. The pièce de résistance of the meal was a flaming Baked Alaska. When it was brought in, Brezhnev said, "Look! The Americans really are miracle workers! They have found a way to set ice cream on fire!"

Just after eleven that night in the Kremlin, Brezhnev and I signed the ABM treaty and the Interim Offensive Agreement, thereby establishing a temporary freeze on the numbers of ICBMs and submarine-launched missiles that each side could possess until a permanent agreement was negotiated. Pat had asked me if she could attend the historic ceremony. Since none of the other wives would be there, I suggested that she wait until the official party had entered and then slip in and stand behind one of the large columns. She did, and watched the signing.

The next day we flew to Leningrad. We visited the Piskaryev Cemetery, where many of the hundreds of thousands who died during the Nazi siege of the city are buried. We were running late, so the advance man recommended that I cut the scheduled stop at the small museum there. The young girl who was acting as our guide was obviously upset when she heard that I might not complete the itinerary. I said that of course I would visit the museum. I was deeply moved when she showed me the diary of Tanya, a twelve-year-old girl buried in the cemetery. She translated from the entries describing how one after another the members of Tanya's family died; the final sad entry read: "All are dead. Only Tanya is left." The girl's voice choked with emotion as she read these words. "Tanya died too," she said as she brushed tears from her eyes.

I was asked to sign the visitor's book before we left. I wrote: "To Tanya and all the heroes of Leningrad." As I walked away, I said, "I hope it will never be repeated in all the world."

We flew back to Moscow, and on the next day, Sunday, we went to services at Moscow's only Baptist church, the All-Union Council of Evangelical Christian Baptists. The unaffected singing of the congregation made me think of the early Christians. I was surprised to see such a large number of young people in the congregation. I was told later that many of the older men and women had either been frightened away or displaced by KGB agents.

I spent the rest of the day preparing my television broadcast to the people of the Soviet Union. As in 1959, I felt that this would be a very important opportunity for me to present the American viewpoint on international issues to the Russian people without any editing or control by the Soviet government.

In the speech I discussed the dangers of an unchecked arms race, and I underlined America's sincere desire for peace. At the end I described my experience the day before at the cemetery in Leningrad and said:

> As we work toward a more peaceful world, let us think of Tanya and of the other Tanyas and their brothers and sisters everywhere. Let us do all that we can to ensure that no other children will have to endure what Tanya did and that your

children and ours, all the children of the world, can live their full lives together in friendship and in peace.

Brezhnev told me after the broadcast that my conclusion had brought tears to his eyes.

The greatest surprise of the summit came during my next to last meeting with Brezhnev. I went to his office for what was supposed to be a half-hour courtesy call, and we ended up spending two hours talking about Vietnam. Unlike at our meeting at the dacha, however, he was calm and serious.

After some initial skirmishing, he said, "Would you like to have one of our highest Soviet officials go to the Democratic Republic of Vietnam in the interest of peace?"

I replied that such a visit might make a major contribution to ending the war, and I said that I would suspend bombing during the period the Soviet official was in Hanoi.

As I was leaving, we paused by the door, and I said, "You have my commitment that privately or publicly I will take no steps directed against the interests of the Soviet Union. But you should rely on what I say in the private channel, not on what anyone else tells you. There are not only certain forces in the world, but also representatives of the press, who are not interested in better relations between us."

The major achievement of Summit I was the agreement covering the limitation of strategic arms. The ABM treaty stopped what inevitably would have become a defensive arms race, with untold billions of dollars being spent on each side for more and more ABM coverage. The other major effect of the ABM treaty was to make permanent the concept of deterrence through "mutual terror": by giving up missile defenses, each side was leaving its population and territory hostage to a strategic missile attack. Each side therefore had an ultimate interest in preventing a war that could only be mutually destructive.

Together with the ABM treaty, the Interim Agreement on strategic missiles marked the first step toward arms control in the thermonuclear age. The Interim Agreement froze the levels of strategic missiles to those then actually

99

existing or under construction. Under this agreement, the United States gave up nothing, because we had no programs that were affected by the freeze. The Soviets, however, had a substantial missile deployment program under way. It is not possible to state how extensive that deployment might have been in the absence of the agreement. But had it continued, it would have put us increasingly at a disadvantage in numbers of missiles and would almost certainly have forced us into a costly building program just to maintain the then-current ratios. By maintaining those ratios the agreement would allow the two sides to begin negotiations for a permanent agreement on offensive weapons free from the pressures of an arms race.

In addition to these major achievements in the area of arms control, there were a number of other agreements signed at Summit I, including the establishment of a joint commercial commission to encourage more trade, and agreements on pollution control and on medicine and public health, especially research on cancer and heart disease. In addition to the establishment of a joint commission to expand cooperation in several areas of science and technology, there was an agreement on a joint orbital mission in space, which came to fruition in 1975 with the Apollo-Soyuz space docking.

Finally, we signed a document containing twelve "basic principles of mutual relations between the United States and the U.S.S.R.," which set forth a code of behavior both sides agreed to follow. This code dealt not only with bilateral relations and measures to reduce the risk of nuclear war but also with the reduction of tension and conflict, especially the kind that could involve the major powers, in their relations with other areas of the world.

These summit agreements began the establishment of a pattern of interrelationships and cooperation in a number of different areas. This was the first stage of détente: to involve Soviet interests in ways that would increase their stake in international stability and the status quo. There was no thought that such commercial, technical, and scientific relationships could by themselves prevent confrontations or wars, but at least they would have to be counted in a balance sheet of gains and losses whenever the Soviets were tempted to indulge in international adventurism.

Because of the pervasive bugging I did not dictate any diary entries while we were in the Soviet Union. The Soviets were curiously unsubtle in this regard. A member of my staff reported having casually told his secretary that he would like an apple, and ten minutes later a maid came in and put a bowl of apples on the table.

I did, however, keep extensive notes during the trip, and I made several long dictations from them the weekend after we returned.

Diary

I emphasized to Henry my evaluation of the Soviet leaders in which I said that Robert Conquest's comment to the effect that they were intellectually third-rate was simply off the mark. I said that we constantly misjudge the Russians because we judge them by their manners, etc., and we do not look beyond to see what kind of character and strength they really have.

Anybody who gets to the top in the Communist hierarchy and stays at the top has to have a great deal of political ability and a great deal of toughness. All three of the Soviet leaders have this in spades, and Brezhnev in particular. His Russian may not be as elegant, and his manners not as fine, as that of some of his sophisticated European and Asian colleagues, but like an American labor leader, he has what it takes, and we can make no greater mistake than to rate him either as a fool or simply an unintelligent brute. Chou En-lai had the combination of elegance and toughness, a very unusual one in the world today.

There is no question that the Russian leaders do not have as much of an inferiority complex as was the case in Khrushchev's period. They do not have to brag about everything in Russia being better than anything anywhere else in the world. But they still crave to be respected as equals, and on this point I think we made a good impression.

It was interesting to note that all the Soviet leaders like good clothes. Brezhnev was even somewhat of a fashion plate in his own way. He had an obviously very expensive gold cigarette holder and lighter.

I noted that all three of the Soviet leaders wore cuff links. I recalled how subtle the change had been from the days of Khrushchev, when he insisted on dressing more plainly than the rest of us.

Kosygin is really all business, a very cool customer with very little outward warmth. He is by Communist terms an aristocrat; while Podgorny is more like a Midwestern senator; and Brezhnev like a big Irish labor boss, or perhaps an analogy to Mayor Daley would be more in order with no affront intended to either.

They seemed to get along well and to have a good personal relationship with each other. I pointed out to Kissinger in a note when Kosygin, Brezhnev, and Podgorny were having one of their colloquies, that it sounded like the scrambler we had in our room which we turned on whenever we wanted to knock out the listening device.

Brezhnev was very warm and friendly. As we were riding in the car out to the dacha, he put his hand on my knee and said he hoped we had developed a good personal relationship.

[Austrian Chancellor Bruno Kreisky had] analyzed Brezhnev as being a "bear-hug" type of man who was likely to have physical contact with whoever came to see him. I couldn't help thinking that Brezhnev and Johnson would have been quite a pair if they had met at Glassboro, instead of Kosygin.

At one point, he said to me, "God be with you." At another point he referred to me as "the present President and the future President."

He told me how an older party man, when he had just begun party work, emphasized the importance of personal relationships in politics and government and party work. I rather wondered who it might have been because this sounded somewhat like Stalin.

There is no question about Brezhnev's overall strength. First, he is five years younger than the other two. Second, he has a strong, deep voice—a great deal of animal magnetism and drive which comes through whenever you meet him. Third, while he sometimes talks too much and is not too precise, he always comes through forcefully, and he has a very great shrewdness. He also has the ability to move off of a point in the event that he is not winning it.

His gestures were extremely expressive. He stands up and walks around, a device he often used during the course of our meetings. Henry recalled one instance in which Brezhnev said, 'Every time I stand up I make another concession.' He must, of course, have been affected by the fact that my own conduct was, by comparison, totally controlled. Some would say this was a mistake but, on the other hand, I am inclined to think it may have impressed him more than if I had been more outwardly emotional in responding to his various charges.

Brezhnev at one point said to me, "I am an emotional man, particularly about death in war." I told him that while my reputation was for being unemotional, I was just as emotional as he was about this issue.

He asked about Mao. I responded that despite poor health, he was sharp from an intellectual standpoint. Brezhnev responded that Mao is a philosopher, not practical, a God-like figure. He said the Chinese were terribly difficult to understand, and then went on to say, "We Europeans are totally different from them."

He said it was really shocking that in the Cultural Revolution they cut off people's heads in the public square. Of course, it's only been twenty years or so since the Communist leaders liquidated their opponents rather than letting them become non-persons, as had been the case with Khrushchev.

He made a great point of the fact that "some people" do not want this meeting to succeed—obviously referring to the Chinese.

An interesting sidelight: unlike the Chinese, who were totally obsessed with the smaller countries of Africa, Asia, and Latin America, the Soviet leaders hardly talked at all about any of the smaller countries except for North Vietnam and a brief mention of North Korea. It was also interesting to note that the

Soviet leaders did not raise the subject of Cuba at all, and they were very mild on North Korea.

I noted the great changes since 1959. There were far more cars in the streets, and the people were better dressed.

In a totalitarian state they have to put on a fetish of having some contact with people, but they really don't do much better than the Chinese in setting these things up in a way that appears to be spontaneous. I am constantly amazed by the total gulf that exists between the Communist ruling classes and the people. I always spoke to the waiters or nodded to them as we left the various dinners, but the Communist leaders acted as if they were non-persons. They treated them as a totally different class.

I pointed out on one of the occasions that our meeting was not a fortuitous affair. The situation in the world required that the meeting be held. The world expected much from the meeting, and we justified the world's hopes. The meeting was well prepared, and now we must go forward to do away with the hotbeds of war that exist in the world. What we must not do is to repeat history. Yalta led to an improvement of relations, but then to a sharp deterioration thereafter. Reading about Yalta gives one great pause because it was not what was agreed to at Yalta, but the failure of the Soviets to keep the agreement, which led to all the troubles after that time.

We are now faced with the major task of giving implementation to the documents we have signed.

JUNE 1972

The morning after our return from the Soviet Summit, I had a heavy schedule of meetings and a congressional briefing on the SALT treaty in an effort to line up support behind it. That afternoon I went with my family to Florida. I carried with me a briefcase full of the domestic reports and decision memoranda that had piled up while we were away.

John Connally came down on Monday. He was leaving the administration and was preparing for his return to Texas.

"Well, I saw Tommy Corcoran a couple of days ago," he said as he settled into a chair in my study, "and he told me Teddy Kennedy now says he wants the nomination. But I think it's too late. McGovern and his people have the bit in their mouths, and they're running with it."

I said that we should not underestimate Kennedy's residual appeal. Even McGovern's supporters, no matter how emotionally committed to their man, would rally around Kennedy. "I understand Hubert isn't going to make it," I said, and Connally nodded.

"Whatever you do," Connally said, "keep the door open for Democrats and independents. If McGovern is nominated, you will see an unprecedented defection."

"Don't worry," I said. "I learned something in 1960. The door will not only be open—I've been weaving a welcome mat."

On June 6 George McGovern won the California primary. The early polls had projected a 20-point landslide, but Hubert Humphrey narrowed the difference to only 5.4 percent; with one more week of campaigning, Humphrey might have won. But California settled it: McGovern would win the nomination.

The Democrats were about to nominate a man who had called for immediate unilateral withdrawal from South Vietnam without any assurances concerning the return of our POWs; who favored unconditional amnesty for draft dodgers; who proposed a reduction in the defense budget that would cut the Air Force in half, reduce the number of Navy warships, and slash the personnel assigned to NATO posts without requiring any reciprocal reductions from the Soviets; and who pledged to cut off aid to our NATO ally Greece while increasing overall foreign aid totals by some 400 percent, with most of the money earmarked for African countries.

McGovern's approach to welfare was for the federal government to give $1,000 to every man, woman, and child in America, funded largely by the tax-strapped middle-income group. HEW calculated that this program alone would cost some $50 billion a year.

His tax reform proposals, ostensibly aimed at closing

loopholes and redistributing the tax burden more fairly, were too much even for the New York *Times*, which described them as "drastic" with "often woolly estimates of potential gains and losses." Hubert Humphrey, during the California primary, had called them "confiscatory," and "a lot of bunk." By the end of the campaign, we estimated the domestic proposals put forth by McGovern would add $126 billion to the federal deficit.

McGovern told the Washington *Post* that busing was "essential" for integration. He called J. Edgar Hoover "a menace to justice." He said that when he was elected President, the demonstrators who had threatened chaos and spat obscenities at the police would be "having dinner at the White House."

All these extreme stands and statements were on the record, but as late as July only one panelist in ten on a *Time* magazine citizens' panel considered George McGovern a radical, while the rest were equally divided over whether he was really a liberal or a moderate conservative! This confusion existed largely because early in the campaign the media had played down the radical or inconsistent elements of McGovern's programs. Many reporters sympathized with McGovern's positions; many just liked his enthusiastic and engaging collection of amateur staff members and volunteer workers.

Fortunately, not all reporters abdicated their critical faculties or their obligation to be objective. "Reader beware," wrote Godfrey Sperling, columnist for the *Christian Science Monitor*, on June 8. "A love affair between a number of newsmen and George McGovern is bursting into full bloom and even though we are talking—by and large—about tough-minded, professional observers, this congenial relationship is bound to affect their copy." He continued:

> In fact, in this reporter's judgment, it already has. For months now Senator McGovern has been talking about a program that would pretty much revolutionize our society . . . Yet, at least until the last week or so Senator McGovern has pretty much been given a "free ride" from the press. . . . As of now, I would say that many of those newsmen who accompany McGovern along the campaign trail have already let

their bias show through—not so much by what they have written about McGovern but by what they have not written about him and his programs. Their omissions tell a great deal.

The biggest political danger McGovern could pose, as I saw it, would be if he decided to change his positions in order to pick up the support of moderate Democrats. I noted in a memo to Mitchell dictated on June 6, the day of the California primary:

> The McGovern strategy is becoming very clear now that he believes that he has the nomination wrapped up. His going to the Governors Conference for the purpose of "clarifying" his stand on amnesty, marijuana, abortion, and welfare is a case in point. I know there are those who will say that he can't get away with it any more than Goldwater was able to get away with it. . . . There are two very significant differences. McGovern is more clever and less principled than Goldwater and will say anything in order to win. And second, McGovern will have about 100 percent support from the media in his effort to clean himself up so that he can beat us in the final. This points up the necessity at this time to get *Democrats* and *independents*, not Republicans, to nail McGovern on the left side of the road which his record so clearly identifies him with.

By summer, when my campaign organization began moving into high gear, I almost immediately began hearing about problems connected with it. There were rumors about slack field organizations, about unnecessary discourtesies to local people, and, repeatedly, about the dislike local campaign workers were developing toward the size and slickness of the CRP's Washington headquarters. When I asked what was wrong, I was usually told, "Mitchell's too tired to focus on it," or "ITT nearly wore Mitchell out," or, more simply, "It's Martha."

Haldeman and I decided to send Fred Malek, then a member of the White House staff, over to the CRP to bring things under control. Malek was a tough young businessman whose specialty was organization and management. We decided to hold off for a few more weeks, however, primarily out of concern that Mitchell would view the move as an implicit criticism of his performance rather than as a recognition that he did not have the help he needed.

On June 12 we celebrated Tricia and Ed's first wedding anniversary with a trip on the *Sequoia*. Pat arranged for us to have the same hors d'oeuvres we had liked so much at the wedding reception. After the sail we watched a videotape of the wedding and reminisced about that day and about the year that had gone by so quickly.

President Luis Echeverría of Mexico arrived in Washington for a state visit on June 15. We had a long talk about water salinity problems and ended up with a lively but friendly discussion about the treatment of American private enterprise in Latin America. At the end, he said that he thought my re-election was vitally important to the world.

Later in the day the Saudi Arabian Defense Minister, Sultan ibn 'Abd-al-Aziz, came in to bring me greetings from his brother, King Faisal.

In the afternoon I met with Ehrlichman about what appeared at first glance to be a panicky position taken by Bill Ruckelshaus of the Environmental Protection Agency on banning the pesticide DDT. The long day ended with a state dinner in honor of President Echeverría.

Friday, June 16, began with a Cabinet meeting on the Republican platform proposals. Then I had an hour-long session with James Hodgson, Elliott Richardson, and members of my staff on welfare reform. My official schedule ended at 12:45 P.M. with a posthumous presentation ceremony of the Medal of Freedom for John Paul Vann, the courageous head of the Second Regional Assistance group in South Vietnam, who was killed in a helicopter crash.

In the afternoon, I left for a weekend in Florida. I was on my own; Pat was making appearances on the West Coast, and the girls were with their husbands. In my briefcase I had a Buchanan campaign memorandum, the briefing materials on welfare reform, and my well-thumbed copy of Irving Kristol's *On the Democratic Idea in America*. I also brought a copy of *Triumph and Tragedy*, the last volume of Churchill's World War II series, because after the recent Soviet Summit I wanted to reread his analysis of the Yalta conference.

THE WATERGATE BREAK-IN

I spent Friday afternoon and all day Saturday on Grand Cay, a small island in the Bahamas owned by my old friend Bob Abplanalp. The weather was spotty, but I went for a swim and took a walk around the island. The caretaker's wife gave me two brightly colored shirts she had made for me, and I talked with her twelve-year-old daughter, who showed me some of the turtles she had been raising.

On Saturday, June 17, I called the mainland only once, to check in with Haldeman. We talked for four minutes. I asked him to find out where I could reach John Connally, who was on a thirty-five-day trip around the world. I also told him to be sure that we had a plank in the Republican platform supporting federal aid to parochial schools. In the afternoon I went boating with Rebozo and Abplanalp.

On Sunday morning, June 18, Rebozo and I left for Key Biscayne. When I got to my house I could smell coffee brewing in the kitchen, and I went in to get a cup. There was a Miami *Herald* on the counter, and I glanced over the front page. The main headline was about the Vietnam withdrawals: *Ground Combat Role Nears End for U.S.*

There was a small story in the middle of the page on the left-hand side, under the headline: *Miamians Held in D.C. Try to Bug Demo Headquarters.*

I scanned the opening paragraphs. Five men, four of them from Miami, had been arrested in the Democratic National Committee headquarters at the Watergate, a fashionable hotel, office, and apartment complex in Washington. The story said that one of the five men had identified himself as a former employee of the CIA; three of the others were Cuban natives. They had all been wearing rubber surgical gloves. It sounded preposterous: Cubans in surgical gloves bugging the DNC! I dismissed it as some sort of prank. I looked at the feature story at the bottom of the page dealing with the campaign: *How McGovern Camp Figures to Win.* I left the paper on the counter and went to make some phone calls.

I reached Haldeman at the Key Biscayne Hotel, where he was staying with the rest of the traveling staff. We briefly discussed whether to have a signing ceremony for the higher education bill. Then we turned to some intriguing news about George Meany—news that had the potential of becoming one of the most important developments of the 1972 campaign. Meany had told George Shultz that if Humphrey failed to get the Democratic nomination, he would not support McGovern. Meany's—and that meant a large part of organized labor's—benevolent neutrality would breach the traditional Democratic coalition and be a tremendous boost to my campaign.

I called Tricia and Julie, who wished me a happy Father's Day, and I talked to Pat, who was in Los Angeles on a three-day series of appearances that had begun in Texas and was scheduled to end in South Dakota. I talked with Al Haig and then with Kissinger, who had stopped over in Hawaii en route to Peking. In the afternoon I called Chuck Colson to discuss the Meany development with him. Then I went for a long swim in the ocean.

Shortly after 6 P.M. I reached John Connally in Australia and received a glowing report on his trip. I called Colson again for a short talk about my concern that most of the media would be sympathetic to McGovern. Rebozo came over for dinner, and we watched a movie. Afterward I called Jack Nicklaus, who had just won the U.S. Open in Pebble Beach. I congratulated him on his victory and commiserated about the putts that had seemed to go in the hole and out.

I decided to make an early night of it. Before I went to bed, I sat in my study reading the last chapters of *Triumph and Tragedy.*

A steady sun and a light breeze made Monday a beautiful day. I did not bother to look at the morning paper but went straight to my study to make calls. The Watergate break-in was still the furthest thing from my mind as I talked with Julie, Tricia, Rose Woods, Al Haig, and Billy Graham. I also talked with Chuck Colson; the only note that I dictated in my diary about our conversation recounted our detailed analysis of a new set of poll figures covering everything from confidence in presidential leadership to the economy. I made two short calls to Haldeman concerning the day's schedule, and then he came over and we met for an hour. We discussed the possibility that George Wallace would become a third-party candidate, the increase in food prices, the appointment of a new Chief of

Protocol, and the schedule for the coming week. In the afternoon I went boating and took a long walk before dinner. At 7:48 P.M. I boarded *Air Force One* for the flight to Washington.

Late that night, back at the White House, I brought my diary up to date. Buried amid observations on the weekend's weather and reflections on the general benefits of relaxation was my first entry dealing with Watergate.

Diary

I almost decided to go back Sunday night, but a hurricane passed nearby, and the winds were so strong that we thought it would be a rather miserable ride although we probably could have gotten out without too much difficulty.

The following day the winds had passed on, and it was the best of all the days. In fact, the best of the six days, including the three immediately after returning from Moscow two weeks ago, and these three. The extra day, with good long swims in the morning and the afternoon, gave me, it seemed to me, a much bigger lift than I had realized was possible. I must make it a point to try to get three full days in the future, and, of course, always try to get the situation developed where I can have peace of mind and good weather if possible.

I am convinced that it is essential to get more exercise. I think one of the reasons that I feel tonight not only more rested but frankly more sharp and more eager to get work done is because I have had rest, and also have had the fresh air and the exercise. I am going to try a routine of bowling for a half hour at the end of each day before coming over to the Residence. This may have a good effect.

On the way back, I got the disturbing news from Bob Haldeman that the break-in of the Democratic National Committee involved someone who is on the payroll of the Committee to Re-elect the President. Mitchell had told Bob on the phone enigmatically not to get involved in it, and I told Bob that I simply hoped that none of our people were involved for two

111

reasons—one, because it was stupid in the way it was handled; and two, because I could see no reason whatever for trying to bug the national committee.

Bob pointed [out] one of Chotiner's operatives had said that a McGovern aide had told him that they had our committee rooms bugged. The problem here, of course, is to get somebody on the PR side who will get out some of the negatives on the other side like this, so that this story just doesn't appear to be a clumsy attempt on our part to get information illegally from the Democrats.

I also urged Bob to keep Colson and Ehrlichman from getting obsessed with the thing so that they were unable to spend their time on other jobs. Looking back, the fact that Colson got so deeply involved in the ITT was a mistake because it kept him from doing other things that in retrospect were more important to do. The best thing probably to have done with ITT was just to let it run its course without having our whole staff in constant uproar about it. I hope we can handle this one in that way.

Pat was in a very good mood tonight, and had felt that her visit to South Dakota was a success. She said the governor had expressed concern that I had always done so well in South Dakota, that he had to run this year as a Democrat and was worried about it. Of course, with McGovern on the ticket he may have a much better chance.

The CRP employee who had been arrested at the Watergate was James McCord. A former CIA security officer, McCord was employed by both the Committee to Re-elect the President and the Republican National Committee as a consultant on security for buildings, documents, and personnel. One of his responsibilities was to protect the Republicans from exactly the kind of thing he had been caught doing to the Democrats. Haldeman had also heard that the money found on the arrested men—over $1,000 in $100 bills—had apparently come from the CRP.

Because of McCord's connection to the CRP, his arrest had turned the Watergate break-in into a hot news story. Larry O'Brien in hyperbolic terms claimed that "the bugging incident . . . raised the ugliest questions about the integrity of the political process that I have encountered in a quarter century of political activity." John Mitchell, as chairman of the Committee to Re-elect, had issued a statement that the arrested men were not acting on behalf of or with the consent of the CRP, and that he himself was surprised and dismayed at the reports of McCord's involvement.

My reaction to the Watergate break-in was completely pragmatic. If it was also cynical, it was a cynicism born of experience. I had been in politics too long, and seen everything from dirty tricks to vote fraud. I could not muster much moral outrage over a political bugging.

Larry O'Brien might affect astonishment and horror, but he knew as well as I did that political bugging had been around nearly since the invention of the wiretap. As recently as 1970 a former member of Adlai Stevenson's campaign staff had publicly stated that he had tapped the Kennedy organization's phone lines at the 1960 Democratic convention. Lyndon Johnson felt that the Kennedys had had him tapped; Barry Goldwater said that his 1964 campaign had been bugged; and Edgar Hoover told me that in 1968 Johnson had ordered my campaign plane bugged. Nor was the practice confined to politicians. In 1969 an NBC producer was fined and given a suspended sentence for planting a concealed microphone at a closed meeting of the 1968 Democratic platform committee. Bugging experts told the Washington *Post* right after the Watergate break-in that the practice "has not been uncommon in elections past . . . it is particularly common for candidates of the same party to bug one another."

In fact, my confidence in the CRP was undermined more by the stupidity of the DNC bugging attempt than by its illegality. The whole thing made so little sense. *Why?* I wondered. Why then? Why in such a blundering way? And why, of all places, the Democratic National Committee? Anyone who knew anything about politics would know that a national committee headquarters was a useless place to go for inside information on a presidential campaign. The whole thing was so senseless and bungled that it almost looked like some kind of a setup. And yet the trail undeniably led back to the CRP. On Sunday morning the idea of Cubans in surgical gloves bugging the DNC had seemed totally ridiculous. By Monday night it had become a potential issue in the presidential campaign.

On Tuesday morning, June 20, my first day back in Washington, there was a new twist.

A front-page headline in the Washington *Post* proclaimed: *White House Consultant Tied to Bugging Figure.* The story, attributed to "federal sources close to the investigation," said that the name Howard Hunt had been found in the address books of two of the men caught inside the DNC headquarters. It stated that until March 29, 1972, Hunt, a former CIA agent, had worked at the White House as a consultant to Chuck Colson. The mention of Colson's name gave me a start. It was one thing if the CRP was involved, or even a former lower-level White House staff member like Hunt. But Colson was a member of my inner circle of aides and advisers, and if he was drawn in it was a whole new situation. I had always valued his hardball instincts. Now I wondered if he might have gone too far.

The Democrats were already mounting an attack. The DNC filed a $1 million suit against the CRP for invasion of privacy and violation of civil rights. This suit would enable their lawyers to call as witnesses and depose under oath almost the entire CRP and White House staff. In this way, while ostensibly probing the DNC bugging, they could ask questions about any and every aspect of our campaign. As *Time* put it, the true aim of the Democrats' suit was "to preoccupy Republicans in court during the fall, to keep the case in public view to subvert the seemingly unstoppable GOP campaign." Publicly the Democrats were full of righteous indignation at the Watergate break-in. Privately they were rejoicing at this unexpected election-year dividend.

Ken Clawson, our Deputy Director of Communications, received an insight into what we were going to be up against when he had lunch with Dick Harwood, an editor at the Washington *Post*. Before coming to the White House, Clawson had been a *Post* reporter, and after the lunch he visited with some of his former colleagues. He was told that Katharine Graham, the paper's publisher, was personally going to direct an army of reporters assigned to delve into the Watergate story. "We're in for a hell of a barrage," Clawson warned members of the staff.

At 2:20 Tuesday afternoon Colson came in to see me. We spent several minutes discussing the way the newspapers were stretching his connection with Hunt in order to draw him into the scandal and the question of who might be the source of the news leaks.

Colson said that Haldeman was "pulling it all together," and that, in Colson's own opinion, so far we had handled it the right way.

I thought that one problem we would have to deal with soon was what the arrested men were going to say. I thought we would be vulnerable to any charges or accusations—true or false—they might make. I said that I had been told they were all "pretty hard-line guys." I told Colson that, as I understood it, we were going to have "this funny guy" take credit for the whole thing. I meant McCord, but Colson evidently thought I meant his friend Howard Hunt.

Colson was quick to defend Hunt. He insisted that Hunt was just too smart and too sophisticated to have been involved in something as amateurish as the Watergate break-in. I agreed that if we didn't know better we would have thought that the whole thing had been deliberately botched up.

Colson said that after he heard about the break-in he figured it might have been something the Cubans had organized on their own. Everyone knew that the Cuban émigré community feared that McGovern would decide to resume diplomatic relations with Castro. Feelings ran sufficiently high that it was by no means impossible that anti-Castro Cubans would want to bug the Democrats to obtain information about such intentions.

I thought for a moment about the double standard that was sure to be adopted by McGovern and by the New York *Times* and the Washington *Post*: they had tacitly sanctioned Ellsberg's illegal release of top-secret government documents, but they were sure to register high moral dudgeon about something as comparatively minor as an unsuccessful break-in at a political party headquarters. I sardonically suggested that someone give a speech urging that the Watergate break-in crew be given a Pulitzer Prize like the one the

115

New York *Times* had been given for publishing the Pentagon Papers.

I told Colson that my understanding was that we were just going to leave the Watergate matter where it was, with the Cubans.

Colson came back to Hunt. He said the fact that Hunt's name was in the address books of the arrested men was the most logical thing in the world. The morning paper had pointed out that Hunt had been a CIA agent for more than twenty years, and that all the arrested men had CIA ties. But Colson told me that the connection was even stronger: Hunt had trained Cuban exiles for the Bay of Pigs operation. This information seemed to reinforce the whole Cuban connection.

Colson said that the biggest hazard Watergate represented for us was the risk of our becoming preoccupied with it simply because the media and the Democrats were sure to be. He said that the whole thing was "something which normally wouldn't amount to that much. They're just going to blow their cool out because they haven't got any other place they can lay a glove on us."

He then told me that the New York *Times* had a problem of its own. During my Soviet Summit trip the paper had run an ad calling for my impeachment because of my policy on the Vietnam war. A formal complaint had been filed against the paper, charging that it had failed to require the necessary identifications from the people who paid for the ad and therefore violated the campaign fund disclosure law. I was pessimistic about our ability to get any political mileage out of that. The *Times*, I knew, would just stonewall it.

Before Colson left my office, I tried to cheer him up. "Dumbest thing," I said. "Nothing loses an election. Nothing changes it that much. . . . You look at this damn thing now and it's gonna be forgotten after a while."

The main problem was that the Democrats would be able to keep the Watergate issue alive with their depositions. We were going to try to delay them until after the election, but there was no guarantee we could do so. Colson, however, was not at all worried about this. He said that he would love to have depositions taken from the White House staff, because "everybody's completely out of it. . . . This is once when you'd like for people to testify." He said it with complete conviction. I hoped that it was true.

I met with Bob Haldeman twice on Tuesday, June 20: from 11:26 A.M. until 12:45 P.M., and again from 4:35 until 5:25 in the afternoon. What was said during the morning meeting will never be known completely because the tape of that conversation is the one with the 18½-minute gap. Some of what we talked about during those 18½-minutes can be reconstructed from the notes Haldeman took. According to them, one of my first reactions to the Watergate break-in was to instruct that my EOB office be checked regularly to make sure that *I* was not being bugged by anyone. They also indicate a concern about the political ramifications of the Watergate incident and a desire to divert its impact by mounting our own counterattack.

The best indication of anything else that may have been said about the Watergate break-in in that morning conversation is our discussion of the same subject just a few hours later that afternoon. It has always been my habit to discuss problems a number of times, often in almost the same terms and usually with the same people. This is the way I try to elicit every possible piece of information and advice and examine every possible angle of a situation before making a decision. I am confident that our discussion about the break-in covered much the same points at 11:26 in the morning as it did just five hours later at 4:35 in the afternoon: that any of our own people, at any level, had embroiled us in such an embarrassing situation; and that the investigations and depositions, if they went too far in pursuing all the angles available, would hand the Democrats a major campaign issue.

In the afternoon meeting Haldeman said he thought that John Mitchell had not known about the break-in plan beforehand. I agreed. For one thing, Mitchell was just too smart to be involved in any such thing. I said that I thought Mitchell had been surprised by it. Haldeman observed that it was true, however, that the men who were caught were supposed to be a pretty competent bunch of people and had been doing other campaign-related things.

Haldeman told me what he had heard about the possible reasons for the break-in. Apparently the arrested men had gone in to repair some electronic equipment that had already been installed but was not working properly, and to take pictures of whatever they found inside. Later he mentioned they had expected to find some financial information about the Democrats.

In subsequent weeks and months I heard many other theories about the reason for the break-in and bugging of the DNC. One was that the men were trying to verify a tip that the Democrats were planning to disrupt our convention by printing counterfeit tickets for distribution to demonstrators; another was that they had been planning to photograph classified documents that were illegally held by the DNC. I heard so many different stories because I asked the same question so many times: *Why bug the DNC?*

In our conversation that afternoon Haldeman ran through some of the other information he had picked up during the day. Haldeman said that, as he understood it, McCord was going to say that he was working with the Cubans, who had been putting in the bug for their own political reasons. Haldeman told me that Howard Hunt had either disappeared or was in the process of doing so, but he would come back if wanted. Haldeman indicated that the appearance of Hunt's name in the address books would be explained on the basis of his ties to the Cubans; he told me, as Colson had, that Hunt had been involved in the Bay of Pigs operation while he was in the CIA; in fact Haldeman had learned that one of the Cubans had been Hunt's deputy for the operation. Haldeman said that our people were making an effort to keep the incident tied to the motive of Cuban nationalism. The problem, of course, was that now, through Hunt, ties to Colson and to the White House were being uncovered. The newspapers had reported that Hunt worked at the White House on projects involving international narcotics intelligence and the declassification of documents. Haldeman said that he was not sure exactly what else Hunt had done; he knew only that it had been based on his prior experience in intelligence. Later in the conversation, he mentioned that Hunt had been involved in the "Diem thing"—our effort to unearth the facts on President Kennedy's involvement in the coup against President Diem in 1963, a coup that resulted in Diem's death. I recalled that Colson had alluded to Hunt's intelligence background.

Haldeman said that as far as the intelligence activities for the CRP were concerned, all of us—including Colson—had known that some were going on. But despite the Hunt connection, Haldeman said that he did not think that Colson had known specifically that the Watergate bugging project was under way. I said I thought he had, but then I said that that was just second-guessing him. Later in the conversation Haldeman, however, reassured me even more strongly about Colson: he said that a check had been made and that he was sure Colson was not involved.

Haldeman reported that my offices in the White House and the EOB had been swept for bugs, and none had been found. Of course, he reminded me, there was our own taping system.

Haldeman said he felt like the whole thing was a nightmare; something like this just doesn't happen, he said. I agreed. Fortunately, he said, Mitchell had been several steps removed—or perhaps it was unfortunate, because if he hadn't been so far removed it probably would never have happened. There was always the problem of circumstantial evidence, however, and there was clearly still going to be an effort to try to tie Mitchell in. Haldeman said half jokingly that maybe it would be better if we just said that yes, we were spying on the Democrats and that we had hired McCord to do it because we were scared to death that a crazy man was going to become President and sell the country out to the Communists!

I asked Haldeman how Howard Hunt was involved in the Watergate incident. He said that on the night of the break-in Hunt had been waiting across the street from the Watergate in the motel room from which the bugs were going to be monitored. Haldeman was not sure, however, about Hunt's relationship to McCord or McCord's to the Cubans.

I was still confused about just how Hunt's name had come up, and Haldeman again ran through the story of the address books. He also told me that one of the Cubans had a check from Hunt for about $6.90, payable to Hunt's country club.

I said that in a sense the involvement of the Cubans, McCord, and Hunt made it appear that it was in fact some kind of Cuban operation. Whatever the case, I saw that a

Cuban explanation for the break-in would have two advantages for us: it would protect us from the political impact of the disclosure of the CRP's involvement, and it would undercut the Democrats by calling attention to the fact that the Cuban community in the United States feared McGovern's naïve policy toward Castro.

Haldeman mentioned in passing something about the wiretapping and concern about "Liddy's budget." He then returned to the problem of the Democrats' depositions, which, he said, were clearly the toughest thing for us. I expressed my continuing bafflement over the origins of the whole thing. "The Democratic committee isn't worth bugging," I said to Haldeman as our conversation on the subject drew to a close.

June 20 had been a full day. I had had an hour session with Ehrlichman on busing and other domestic issues; made several phone calls to members of Congress and the staff; and held a long meeting with Al Haig. As far as Watergate was concerned, as I walked back to the Residence that night I felt confident. My primary concern had been whether anyone at the White House was involved, and Haldeman and Colson had reassured me on that score. Haldeman had been equally reassuring that Mitchell had had nothing to do with it. With these reassurances, I was ready to go on the offensive.

That evening I called John Mitchell. We talked for about four minutes and I recorded what he told me in a brief diary note I made later that night: "He is terribly chagrined that the activities of anybody attached to his committee should have been handled in such a manner, and he said that he only regretted that he had not policed all the people more effectively . . . in his own organization."

On the phone Mitchell sounded so embarrassed by the whole thing that I was convinced more than ever that it had come as a complete surprise to him. He also sounded completely tired and worn out.

After talking with Mitchell, I called Haldeman. When both he and Colson had mentioned the Bay of Pigs that afternoon, they had stimulated my thinking, and I told him about my new idea for handling the public relations aspect of the Watergate incident. I suggested that if the Cuban explanation for the break-in actually caught on, I would call Rebozo and have him get the anti-McGovern Cubans in Miami to start a public bail fund for their arrested countrymen and make a big media issue out of it. If they used it to revive the Democrats' inept handling of the Bay of Pigs and to attack McGovern's foreign policy ideas, we might even make Watergate work in our favor.

I worked in the EOB office that night until nearly 11:30. I took some of the time to bring my diary up to date. After recounting the day's events, I closed with this note: "I felt better today than I have really for months—relaxed and yet able to do more work than even we usually do with far more enthusiasm."

Watergate was an annoying problem, but it was still just a minor one among many.

In our conversation on Wednesday morning, June 21, Haldeman told me that Gordon Liddy was "the guy who did this." I asked who Liddy was, and Haldeman said he was the counsel for the finance committee at CRP. When I said I thought McCord was the man responsible for the break-in, Haldeman said no, it was Liddy; we didn't know what McCord's position was, but everyone seemed to think he would hang tight.

Ehrlichman had come up with the idea of having Liddy confess; he would say he did it because he wanted to be a hero at the CRP. This would have several advantages: it would cut off the Democrats' civil suit and minimize their ability to go on fishing expeditions in the depositions connected with it; it would divert some of the press and political attacks by establishing guilt at a low level instead of letting it be imputed to a high one; and finally, since all the arrested men felt that Liddy had been in charge, once Liddy admitted guilt it wouldn't matter what else they thought because everything would tie back to Liddy. Then, Haldeman said, our people would make an appeal for compassion on the basis that Liddy was a poor misguided kid who read too many spy stories.

I said that after all this was not a hell of a lot of crime and in fact if someone asked me about Ziegler's statement that it was a "third-rate burglary," I was going to say no, it was only a "third-rate *attempt* at burglary." Haldeman said the lawyers all felt that if Liddy and the arrested men entered a guilty plea they would get only fines and suspended sentences since apparently they were all first offenders.

I said I was for Ehrlichman's plan. We had to assume the truth would come out sooner or later, so if Liddy was the man responsible, he should step up and shoulder the blame. My only reservation, I said, would be if this would involve John Mitchell—in that case I didn't think we could do it. A day earlier Haldeman seemed certain Mitchell was not involved. Now he was not so reassuring. He had already told me that Mitchell was concerned about how far the FBI's investigation was going and thought that someone should go directly to the FBI and get it turned off. Haldeman said, too, that Ehrlichman was afraid that Mitchell might be involved. When Haldeman had all but put the question directly to Mitchell when they had talked earlier that morning, he had received no answer; so he could not be sure whether Mitchell was involved or not. He indicated that Mitchell had seemed a little apprehensive about Ehrlichman's plan because of Liddy's instability and what might happen when Liddy was really put under pressure. In any case, he said, Ehrlichman had just developed the plan that morning, and everyone was going to think about it before anything was done.

I still believed that Mitchell was innocent; I was sure he would never have ordered anything like this. He was just too smart and, besides, he had always disdained campaign intelligence-gathering. But there were two nagging possibilities: I might be wrong and Mitchell might have had some involvement; and even if he had not actually been involved, if we weren't careful he might become so circumstantially entangled that neither he nor we would ever be able to explain the truth. Either way, I hoped that Liddy would not draw him in. I said that taking a rap was done quite often. Haldeman said that we could take care of Liddy and I agreed that we could help him; I was willing to help with money for someone who had thought he was helping me win the election.

I never personally confronted Mitchell with the direct question of whether he had been involved in or had known about the planning of the Watergate break-in. He was one of my closest friends, and he had issued a public denial. I would never challenge what he had said; I felt that if there were something he thought I should know, he would have told me. And I suppose there was something else, too, something I expressed rhetorically months later: "Suppose you call Mitchell . . . and Mitchell says, 'Yes, I did it,' " I said to Haldeman. "Then what do we say?"

We also talked about the White House side of the problem that morning. I said that I was concerned about what I thought was a bad rap the White House was getting because of the fact that Hunt had worked for Colson. I asked again about whether Haldeman thought Colson was involved, and Haldeman said that as nearly as anyone could be convinced of anything, he was convinced Colson was not.

Haldeman said that what he considered to be the real problem for the White House had nothing to do with the Watergate break-in itself, but concerned what he called "other involvements"—things that an investigative fishing expedition into the break-in could uncover and exploit politically. That was what made the Democrats' civil suit the biggest problem for the White House. Hunt had done a lot of unrelated things for Colson that could be uncovered in the kind of freewheeling legal depositions the Democrats clearly had in mind. I knew that Colson's major project in the last several months had been ITT; I asked Haldeman what he meant—the declassification of papers, or ITT? Haldeman identified Hunt as the man who had gone to Denver and talked to Dita Beard during the ITT investigation. He said there were apparently other "fringe bits and pieces" that would come out if Hunt was called. At one point he said that this was why it was important for us not to overdefend Colson and for Colson not to overreact: he was clean on the bugging, but vulnerable on his other connections with Hunt. Haldeman said that Hunt's political connection was the reason it was felt he should disappear. He also said that this was another reason for getting to the FBI: as of now there was nothing that put Hunt into the case except his name in the address books.

At the end of our discussion I came back to the frustrating situation concerning the break-in. I told Haldeman that it seemed that the Democrats had been doing this kind of thing to us for years and *they* never got caught. Haldeman agreed that the Democrats always seemed to get off easier. He said the press just never went after them the way they went after us. Later in the day, I said that every time the Democrats accused us of bugging we should charge that we were being bugged and maybe even plant a bug and find it ourselves!

When I saw Colson that afternoon, we talked about the morning's press coverage of the break-in, and about the McGovern campaign. Thinking ahead to my press conference scheduled for the next day, I came back to the break-in and observed that taking it at its worst we could at least knock down strongly the idea that the White House was involved. "We didn't know a goddamn thing about it," I said. The conversation ranged over several other topics and then came back to Watergate. I asked Colson what he thought about the plan to have Liddy take the rap and then just cut our losses. He said that he would be for anything that would cut our losses and get us out of it. But, he added, he was deliberately staying out of the whole thing so that he could make an honest affidavit that he knew nothing about it.

Colson again defended his friend Howard Hunt, calling him "a dedicated patriot." He just could not believe that Hunt had engineered the Watergate break-in.

On the morning of Thursday, June 22, I reviewed the briefing material for my press conference that afternoon. Ziegler and Buchanan had written me a memo warning that the reporters were pushing to escalate the break-in story and would try to force me to make a comment that would keep the story alive: *Nixon Concerned* or *Nixon Calls for Investigation* was the kind of headline they were after. It would be important for me to strike the right balance in what I said about the break-in; showing too little concern would cause as bad a news story as showing too much. There was not much more for me to say. Mitchell had already said that such activities could not be condoned and that he was surprised by them; and Ziegler had already issued a statement on Colson's behalf denying Colson's involvement.

When I saw Haldeman, I predicted that the main Watergate question at the press conference would be whether there was any White House involvement. I knew that the reporters would pounce on any modifiers or qualifiers in my answer, so I thought I should just state unequivocally that there was no involvement whatever. Haldeman said he thought that on the direct basis of White House involvement, we were absolutely clean.

He said that the day's Watergate news was all good. For one thing, the Democrats had made a legal mistake by filing a class action suit against the CRP. The Democratic judge who would have heard the case had been replaced by a Republican judge. When the lawyer for the Democrats, Edward Bennett Williams, had insistently demanded immediate depositions, the judge had said that he would meet with him after the weekend to make decisions about the timing.

Further good news was the fact that the FBI still had no case on Howard Hunt. We knew that he had been at the scene, but they did not. Haldeman said that the FBI had no warrant out for him and therefore did not care whether he had disappeared. The final good news was that the FBI could not trace the hundred-dollar bills that the break-in crew had been carrying the night they were arrested. This was good news, because the money was another route by which the break-in could be tied to the CRP. The FBI had got only as far as a Miami bank, and Haldeman said that they would evidently have to go through a South American country in order to trace it finally.

As of June 22, then, the situation provided at least some grounds for hope. The Cuban explanation for the break-in was still holding, and the issue was thoroughly confused. Haldeman said there would continue to be an effort to crank up the Cuban story. He observed that because of what we knew we tended to read too much into what we saw—things that others could not see.

I said that the main thing was what the networks would be doing if they thought they had something on the White House or the CRP. The Cubans were not much of a story, but the networks, I said, would "play it to beat hell" if they thought they had something on us.

Haldeman said that it was being arranged that some members of the Cuban community would start to say how scared they were of McGovern. They were also getting out the fact that two of the arrested men were registered Democrats. He said that there was even some thought of having Liddy leave the country. The FBI was not after him now, and he could come back if something on him surfaced—for instance, if some of the men in jail decided to talk. In the meantime, Haldeman said, McCord would stay in jail and keep an eye on the others. Later that afternoon I called Ron Ziegler into my office and asked him what he thought I should say about the bugging incident. Then I looked up over my glasses and asked, "Were you there?"

For a moment his round eyes in his boyish face grew wide. "At the bugging incident?" he asked, slightly choked.

"No, you were in Florida weren't you?" I said, and laughed out loud.

"Did you mean was I at the Watergate, Mr. President?" he repeated as he, too, started to laugh.

"Oh, I'll tell you," I said, adding that somebody should say the arrested men were just trying to win a Pulitzer Prize.

When I went into the press conference on the afternoon of June 22, there were two things about Watergate I was prepared to say: that no one in the White House had been involved in the break-in, and that I absolutely believed John Mitchell's statement denying that he had known anything about it. Of the seventeen questions asked that afternoon, only one involved the break-in, and my prediction about it turned out to be completely accurate:

Q: Mr. O'Brien has said that the people who bugged his headquarters had a direct link to the White House. Have you had any sort of investigation made to determine whether this is true?

A: Mr. Ziegler and also Mr. Mitchell, speaking for the campaign committee, have responded to questions on this in great detail. They have stated my position and have also stated the facts accurately.

This kind of activity, as Mr. Ziegler has indicated, has no place whatever in our electoral process or in our governmental process. And, as Mr. Ziegler has stated, the White House has had no involvement whatever in this particular incident.

As far as the matter now is concerned, it is under investigation, as it should be, by the proper legal authorities, by the District of Columbia police, and by the FBI. I will not comment on those matters, particularly since possible criminal charges are involved.

On Friday, June 23, 1972, I had breakfast with Jerry Ford and Hale Boggs, who were leaving on a trip to the People's Republic of China. After breakfast I went to the Oval Office and Alex Butterfield, one of Haldeman's assistants, brought in several routine papers and documents. Then Haldeman came in as he did every morning, unhurried, ready to begin the day.

We talked about the schedule for Kissinger's return from China that afternoon and about plans for a meeting with Rogers. Then we turned to what Haldeman referred to as the "Democratic break-in thing."

All the good news of the previous day had gone bad, and we were back in what Haldeman called "the problem area." The FBI, he said, was not under control because Acting Director Pat Gray did not know how to control it, and the investigation was leading into some productive areas. In particular, the FBI was apparently going to be able to trace the money after all. "And it goes in some directions we don't want it to go," Haldeman said. As I understood it, unless we could find some way to limit the investigation the trail would lead directly to the CRP, and our political containment would go by the boards.

Haldeman said that Mitchell and John Dean had come up with an idea on how to deal with this problem. Dean was a bright young man who had worked at the Justice Department until 1970, when he succeeded Ehrlichman as White House Counsel. In this capacity Dean had the responsibility for keeping track of and attending to any legal problems affecting the President or the White House.

As Haldeman explained it, General Vernon Walters, the Deputy Director of the CIA, was to call Pat Gray and tell him to "stay the hell out of this . . . business here. We don't want you to go any further on it." The FBI and the CIA had a longstanding agreement not to interfere in each other's secret operations. Haldeman said that this call would not be unusual. He said that Pat Gray wanted to limit the investigation but simply didn't have a basis on which to do so; this would give him his basis. Haldeman said that this would work well because the FBI agents on the case had already come to the conclusion that the CIA was involved in some way.

Haldeman explained that unless something was done, the money would be traced to the contributors who had given it and from there to the CRP. I asked what the contributors would say if they did not cooperate with the investigation—they would have to say that they had been approached by the Cubans. I asked if that was the idea. Haldeman said it was if they would go along; but that would mean relying on more and more people all the time, and the plan to call in Walters would prevent having to do that, and all it would take to set the plan in motion would be an instruction from the White House.

I asked how Haldeman planned to handle it and then observed that we had protected CIA Director Richard Helms from a lot of things. Helms had rarely approached me personally for any kind of assistance or intervention, but I remembered the visible concern on his face less than a year earlier over the possible publication of a book by two disaffected CIA agents. Helms had asked if I would back up legal action by the CIA, despite the fact that there would be cries of "suppression." I had told him that I would.

I mentioned Hunt; he had been involved in a lot of earlier CIA operations, including the Bay of Pigs. I postulated an approach by which we would say to Helms and Walters, "You open that scab and there's a hell of a lot of things." I told Haldeman to say that we felt it would be very detrimental to have the investigation go any further, alluding to the Cubans, to Hunt, and to "a lot of hanky-panky that we have nothing to do with ourselves."

I asked again what had become an almost ritual question: "Did Mitchell know about this thing to any much of a degree?"

"I think so," Haldeman answered. "I don't think he knew the details, but I think he knew."

I said I was sure that he could not have known how it was going to be handled—that had to have been Liddy. Haldeman speculated that the pressure on Liddy to get intelligence might have come from Mitchell.

"All right, fine, I understand it all," I said abruptly. "We won't second-guess Mitchell and the rest. Thank God it wasn't Colson."

Haldeman reassured me that the FBI, after interviewing Colson, had concluded that the White House had had no role in Watergate; they were convinced it was a CIA operation. I said that I was not sure of their analysis, but I was not going to get involved.

"You call them in. Good. Good deal," I said as we brought our discussion of the subject to a close. I told Haldeman to "play it tough," because that was the way the Democrats always played it "and that's the way we are going to play it."

We moved on and talked about the resignation of our Chief of Protocol, a congressional effort to attach a Social Security benefits increase to the bill extending the temporary national debt ceiling, the devaluation of the British pound, the media coverage of my press conference, and busing. Then I came back to the idea to call in Helms and Walters. Howard Hunt clearly provided the best justification for approaching Helms. Hunt's CIA background would give Helms and Walters a plausible reason for going to the FBI; and Hunt's involvement in the planning of the Bay of Pigs would give Helms added incentive.

I thought back again to the time I had instructed Ehrlichman to ask Helms for the CIA's files on the Bay of Pigs, and the Diem assassination. I remembered how he had been unwilling to give them up. Even after I had personally requested that he do so, the Bay of Pigs report he turned over to us was not complete. I saw that Howard Hunt would give us a chance to turn Helms's extreme sensitivity about the Bay of Pigs to good advantage. I was not sure whether the CIA actually had any bona fide reasons to intervene with the FBI. There was enough circumstantial evidence to suggest that they might. But, in any case, Howard Hunt would provide a good way of suggesting that they do so. If the CIA would deflect the FBI from Hunt, they would thereby protect us from the only White House vulnerability involving Watergate that I was worried about exposing—not the break-in, but the political activities Hunt had undertaken for Colson.

I was concerned that Haldeman handle the matter deftly. I did not want him to strong-arm Helms and Walters, nor did I want him to lie and say there was no involvement. I wanted him to set out the situation in such a way that Helms and Walters would take the initiative and go to the FBI on their own. I told Haldeman to say that I believed this thing would open up the whole Bay of Pigs matter—to say that the whole thing was a sort of comedy of errors and that they should call the FBI in and say that for the sake of the country they should go no further into this case.

After this half-hour meeting with Haldeman I held a ninety-minute session on the economy and then conducted several brief ceremonial meetings. When I had finished, I buzzed for Haldeman to come in again. I wanted him to understand that I was not interested in concealing Hunt's involvement in Watergate from Helms and Walters or even from the FBI; in fact, I said that he should level with Helms and Walters and tell them that we knew Hunt had been involved in Watergate. But then he should point out that the whole Cuban involvement in Watergate would make the CIA and Hunt look bad; and the whole thing might possibly reopen the Bay of Pigs controversy, and that would be bad for the CIA, for the country, and for American foreign policy. I also did not want Helms and Walters to get the idea that our concern was political—which, of course, it was. However, I also did not want Haldeman actually to misrepresent to them that our concern was *not* political. He should simply say that our concern was because of "the Hunt involvement."

When Haldeman came back from his meeting with Helms and Walters that afternoon, he said that he had not mentioned Hunt at the outset. He had simply raised the possibility that the FBI was exploring leads that would be harmful to the CIA and to the government. Helms had volunteered the information that he had in fact already received a call from Pat Gray expressing fear that the FBI investigation had run into a CIA operation. Helms said he had told Gray that there was nothing that the CIA knew of at that point, but Gray had asserted that that was what it looked like to him.

Haldeman said he had gone on to point out that the problem was that this matter would track back to the Bay of Pigs and to people who had no involvement in the Watergate matter except by contacts or connections. That was when he mentioned Hunt. At this point, Haldeman said that Helms got the picture and said he would be happy to be helpful but would like to know the reason. Haldeman said he made it clear to Helms that he was not going to get specifics but rather generalities. It had been left that Walters would go to see Gray and take care of the matter. It seemed that our intervention had worked easily. As far as I was concerned, this was the end of our worries about Watergate.

During the remaining few days in June when I discussed the Watergate break-in it was mainly to express my irritation that nothing seemed to be happening to settle the case and remove it from the public eye. Until that was done the media and the Democrats would continue to batter us with it. On June 26 I asked Haldeman if there was any way to get the people involved to plead guilty so that the White House could forget about the case and not have it hanging over us. I asked who was keeping track of the situation for us. He told me that it was being watched by John Dean, John Mitchell, and others.

Haldeman said that guilty pleas would have to await the indictments, and the indictments were being delayed because the FBI kept investigating and uncovering new things. But, he said, we could hope we had turned that off. Later in the day Haldeman said that one of the problems was that the CRP had used the men involved in the Watergate bugging on other standard intelligence and political projects as well. Otherwise, he said, we could cut them loose and sink them without a trace. Haldeman said that he did not know what the other projects were.

For all my concern about Mitchell's vulnerability and despite occasional doubts by me and others about the extent to which he might have been involved, I was still basically convinced of his innocence. I assumed that he had known about the campaign intelligence operations in general, but not about the bugging in particular.

On June 28 I said to Haldeman that, as I understood it, Mitchell had not known specifically about the bugging. Haldeman answered that, as he understood it, that was correct. The next day I said my hunch was that one of the lower-level people at the CRP had said to Mitchell that they were trying to get information. That was standard political practice by both sides. Mitchell would have assumed that

131

they were talking about planting an informant and said, "Don't tell me anything about it." Instead, they had gone and bugged the DNC.

On Friday morning, June 30, a newspaper story attributed to unidentified sources said that Howard Hunt's safe at the White House had been opened and among the contents turned over to the FBI were the architectural plans of the DNC offices, wiretapping equipment, and a gun. Ziegler immediately checked the story and found that there had been an unloaded gun. But there were no such plans, and the so-called wiretap equipment was a walkie-talkie. Haldeman said that some other things in the safe had been handled at a high, discreet level in the Bureau. I asked why Hunt had a safe at the White House if, as I had been told, he had not actually worked as a consultant for several months. Haldeman said that he had simply left these things behind. At one point Haldeman said that the whole thing was so ludicrous that Dean had not discounted the possibility that we were dealing with a double agent who purposely blew the operation. Otherwise it was just too hard to figure out.

I was surprised because this story indicated that the FBI was still going after Hunt. I had thought that they were going to keep away from him as a result of Haldeman's meeting with Helms and Walters. Haldeman said that apparently Pat Gray did not know how to follow through. The U.S. Attorney's office at the Justice Department was pushing hard, making it difficult for them to limit the investigation. I said that Walters should go see the Justice Department officials, too.

The story about Hunt's safe raised my concern that Colson might have had something to do with Hunt on the bugging project. But once again Haldeman said that Colson had told the FBI "the straight truth"—that he had worked with Hunt only on matters totally unrelated to the bugging.

Haldeman had informed me the day before that Liddy had been fired from the CRP after he refused to talk to the FBI investigators; Liddy had understood that this would happen and agreed to it. I asked again whether Haldeman thought Mitchell knew in advance of Liddy's bugging plans. Haldeman said he did not think Mitchell had known specifically but that Liddy had worked on general intelligence and counter-intelligence activity for Mitchell. I observed that such practices were standard in campaigns.

Then Haldeman told me that Gordon Liddy had once worked at the White House on narcotics problems for Bud Krogh on Ehrlichman's Domestic Council. Haldeman was not sure whether it was just Hunt or Liddy too who had worked on the Pentagon Papers investigations. I said that these were perfectly legitimate projects, and we went on to other things.

Later in the day Haldeman told me about the latest ideas for dealing with the Watergate matter. Liddy was going to write a "scenario" that would tie together all the loose ends: he would take responsibility for planning the entire Watergate operation and say that no one higher up had authorized it. As for the money used to finance his activities, he would explain that he had obtained it by cashing a check that he was supposed to have returned to the campaign contributor who wrote it. When I asked why Liddy had in fact been given this campaign check, Haldeman said that apparently Liddy was supposed to have converted it into cash in Mexico, exactly as he had done, but then had gone the further step of using it for his own covert operation. Haldeman said that they had not yet worked out how to handle the issue of Hunt's role.

I told Haldeman that I really believed that Mitchell was telling the truth—that he had not known. Haldeman agreed that he had probably ordered an information-gathering operation, not knowing that bugs were going to be planted.

I expressed my hope that some Cuban motive could be retained in our explanations of the origins of the break-in. I said that the story had to be true to some extent—why else would the Cubans have risked so much? Most of all, I urged Haldeman to move quickly on the whole matter. We should cut our losses and "get the damn thing done."

I was particularly concerned that Colson not get dragged in, which was almost bound to happen if the investigation continued as an endless fishing expedition. Haldeman, however, said that the problem went beyond Colson, because Hunt and Liddy were tied to Krogh, and all

133

of them were tied to Ehrlichman and his aide David Young.

I replied that if this connection was because of our Pentagon Papers investigations, there was nothing the matter with that. Haldeman said that it was the investigation itself—"the process," he called it—that was the problem. I asked what he meant. He said again that it was just "the process" that they had used. I did not pursue the question, but I repeated emphatically that in my view, it was perfectly all right.

My thoughts turned back to Liddy. Earlier I had asked Haldeman about his family, and Haldeman said that whatever needs they had, we would take care of them. Haldeman ventured that if Liddy were saddled with a very long sentence—which would clearly be unfair when measured against all precedents—we could wait a discreet interval and then parole or pardon him after the election. I agreed.

As the meeting was ending, I came back to the matter of Liddy's confession and urged that we get it over with. It would involve the CRP, and I didn't like it. But it wouldn't cripple us in the campaign; the Bobby Baker scandal had not hurt Johnson's margin. "You can't cover this," I said to Haldeman, adding that the best thing was just to get the guy in charge to go ahead and accept the blame. "It's just such a ridiculous goddamn thing," I said.

Shortly before I left Washington to spend the week of July 4 in California, Colson and I talked again about the exaggerated news coverage that was being given to the break-in. In sheer exasperation, I said it would help if someone broke into our headquarters and did a lot of damage—then we could launch a counterattack. Colson agreed and pointed out that several of our campaign files actually had been missing. I re-emphasized my desire to get the break-in off our backs because of the impression it would leave, if it lingered, that the White House had ordered bugging and snooping. I observed that Bobby Kennedy had actually *done* it; but we could not afford even the *impression* of having done it.

My extensive diary notes from June 21 to June 30 are predominantly about foreign policy, domestic issues, campaign planning, and personal and family observations. On

June 30, the night before I left for California, I dictated a brief reflection about where we stood on Watergate:

Diary
The major problem on the Watergate is simply to clean the thing up by having whoever was responsible admit what happened. Certainly I am satisfied that nobody in the White House had any knowledge or approved any such activity, and that Mitchell was not aware of it as well.

It was in these days at the end of June and the beginning of July 1972 that I took the first steps down the road that eventually led to the end of my presidency. I did nothing to discourage the various stories that were being considered to explain the break-in, and I approved efforts to encourage the CIA to intervene and limit the FBI investigation. Later my actions and inactions during this period would appear to many as part of a widespread and conscious cover-up. I did not see them as such. I was handling in a pragmatic way what I perceived as an annoying and strictly political problem. I was looking for a way to deal with Watergate that would minimize the damage to me, my friends, and my campaign, while giving the least advantage to my political opposition. I saw Watergate as politics pure and simple. We were going to play it tough. I never doubted that that was exactly how the other side would have played it.

I would have preferred to tell the story of these days as they really happened, with Watergate discussions of thirty and forty minutes interspersed among hours of conversations, deliberations, and decision-making on the whole range of interesting, boring, important, and insignificant matters that fill the days of a President. Instead perspective has been sacrificed to clarity, and several complex dimensions have been reduced to a single comprehensible one. Yet all the discussions about Watergate that took place during the week after the break-in totaled no more than a small fraction of the more than seventy-five hours I spent in the office and working at home. I have sometimes wondered whether, if we had only spent more time on the problem at the outset, we might have handled it less stupidly.

Martha Mitchell was vivacious and pretty in a flamboyant, self-amused way. She was flirtatious, determined to be outrageous, and bound to dominate any room she entered. When I first met her I thought that she might indeed be "the only fun that poor man has," as she later described herself. The man was her husband, who kept a watchful eye to protect her, smiled at her antics, and never seemed to let anything ruffle his calm exterior.

After the election, when Mitchell resisted my request that he come to Washington as Attorney General, I was sure that concern about Martha was behind his reticence. Finally I broached the matter directly with him. I said that I thought Washington might be just what Martha needed. The limelight and attention surrounding his position would give her confidence and do her good. He was skeptical, but in the end he agreed.

I was both right and wrong in my judgment. Martha blossomed like a sweep of azaleas in Washington. She was excellent news copy, and she cultivated a reputation for saying exactly what she thought by saying exactly what she thought. Before long she was a national celebrity. Her lively originality made her much sought after for television shows and party fund-raisers. At one point she had a phenomenally high 76 percent national recognition factor in the Gallup poll. Her constituency consisted of those who actually liked her opinions, those who liked the fact that she spoke out, and those who enjoyed the fact that she must be causing embarrassment to Mitchell and me. I knew she was not always in complete control of herself, and sometimes that worried me. But I kept such worries to myself because I did not ever want Mitchell to feel uncomfortable with me because of her.

Although Martha enjoyed great popularity and success in Washington, her troubles remained, and she was frustrated and tormented by emotional problems she could neither understand nor control. As early as March 1971 Bebe Rebozo had confidentially raised with me the fact that

Mitchell was having increasing difficulty with Martha. One day at Key Biscayne, I asked Rebozo why Mitchell put up with her. He said that he had once asked Mitchell the same question, and he had replied simply, "Because I love her."

In the past there had been long bouts of crying and hysterics. Now, with Watergate, there was talk of suicide.

John Mitchell had been exhausted and drained by the ITT attack. Now he was trying to run a presidential campaign amidst the worries and distractions of the Watergate publicity. In the two weeks after the break-in, Martha began a new series of phone calls to the press, saying that she had given her husband ultimatums to get out of politics and insisting that she was a "political prisoner." She drew added suspicion to Mitchell when she said, "I love my husband very much but I'm not going to stand for all those dirty things that go on."

"He can't cope with this," Haldeman told me. Billy Graham called Rose Woods to see if there was anything he could do to help. But we did nothing because we knew that Mitchell would have resented it. He would say that it was his problem, and he must deal with it himself. Only once in a low moment did he break down and confide to Haldeman, "You and the President don't realize how much time I have to spend keeping her on an even keel—or how much it's affected my ability to run the campaign."

I felt that some members of the press deliberately exploited Martha Mitchell during this period. Months later it would become clear to all that her wild claims that she had a manual containing procedures for the Watergate break-in and that she herself knew all the details were simply ploys to get attention. But even at the time it was obvious to those who came into contact with her that she had very serious emotional problems. Nonetheless, many reporters encouraged her to further excesses, primarily, I felt, because they thought that by doing so they were tightening the screws on Mitchell. By the end of June I was reluctantly beginning to think that Mitchell would have to leave the campaign.

I considered John Mitchell to be one of my few close personal friends. I believed that I owed my election as President in 1968 largely to his strength as a counselor and his skill as a manager. I had referred to him as one of the few indispensable men, and that was how I felt about him. The thought of losing his help was bad enough. The thought of his having to resign under pressure amid a barrage of controversy and negative publicity was very hard for me to accept. But the combination of having to fend off Watergate publicity and having to take care of Martha would inevitably distract him too much from important campaign tasks.

I had no illusions that Mitchell's departure would put an end to our Watergate problems. It would take much more than that. On June 26, when Haldeman and I were discussing this, he ventured that the only way to put an end to Watergate would be to hang the blame directly on Mitchell. "I won't do that to him. To hell with it," I said, "I'd rather lose the election."

Even as I had begun to think that Mitchell would have to resign, Mitchell was coming to the same conclusion himself. In personal terms, he saw that there was no other choice, and in typical Mitchell style, instead of bringing us a problem to solve, he came to us with a solution. On June 29 he met with Haldeman and told him that Martha's condition was very serious. She could not cope with the criticism he was getting on Watergate, and he was afraid she would harm herself. Later, when I asked Haldeman if Martha was aware of the real Watergate problem, he said no. Mitchell had commented, however, that Martha was smart, and she recognized that her public complaints would give him a reason to ease out of the front line of the controversy by resigning.

I had lunch with Mitchell in my EOB office on June 30. It was a painful session. He looked worn out and his hand shook so much that he had to put his soup spoon down after the first taste. Later in the afternoon I asked former Minnesota Congressman Clark MacGregor if he would take over the campaign, and he agreed. I felt that MacGregor would infuse new life and spirit into the CRP. He had a rare ability to charge people up, and he would do an effective job of reorganization. We also decided to follow up on our earlier plan to send Fred Malek over to shake things up. "We'll clean that son of a bitch up," I told Haldeman, "and we'll run this campaign."

We made the announcement of Mitchell's resignation and MacGregor's appointment on July 1.

Several weeks later on two different occasions I dictated about John Mitchell and the Watergate break-in.

Diary
Here I think we have had a slip-up due to the fact that Mitchell was so obsessed with the problems he had with Martha. Whether it was getting the organization at 1701 [Pennsylvania Avenue, the CRP headquarters] honed down, or whether it was watching over things like this we just didn't have the discipline we should have had and that we would have had had he been able to pay attention to business.

I am continually amazed whenever I am with John Mitchell about his vast knowledge of people over the country and also in all kinds of fields.

Mitchell has particular knowledge about all kinds of fishing, how the tides operate in various parts of the East Coast, as well as, of course, a wide knowledge of every kind of food and how it is prepared—in addition to having already the deserved reputation for knowing more about more political figures in both parties than perhaps any man in the United States.

Without Martha, I am sure that the Watergate thing would never have happened.

THE GRAY PHONE CALL

When I arrived in California on July 1 for an eighteen-day stay, I faced an unusually busy period. Al Haig and Sir Robert Thompson returned from Vietnam with a first-hand assessment of the situation there, and Kissinger and I were working on the strategy for his upcoming meeting with the North Vietnamese, the first since the May 8 bombing and mining. There was also a great deal of campaign planning to be done following Mitchell's departure. On July 6, I had a long meeting with MacGregor and Malek to discuss campaign organization and management. This day was to turn out to be memorable for a completely unexpected reason, and that night I recounted the events that would later assume such importance:

Diary

Today we got some of the disturbing news with regard to the developments in the Watergate case, almost by accident.

When I saw the account in the *Times* of the FBI's action on the hijacking case in which they killed two hijackers, and unfortunately a passenger as well, on Pacific Southwest Airlines, I called the new Director [Pat Gray] and told him to congratulate the men for me and also to give my congratulations to the Pan Am captain and the police sergeant or retired policeman who had been responsible for the spectacular killing of the hijacker in Vietnam at Saigon Airport.

When I had passed on the message, he proceeded to tell me that he was greatly concerned about the Watergate case and that Walters had come in to see him today indicating that the CIA had no interest in the matter and that pursuing the investigation would not be an embarrassment to the CIA.

He said that he and Walters both felt that some people either at the White House or at the committee were trying to cover up things which would be a mortal blow to me—rather than assisting in the investigation.

When Ehrlichman came in he was astounded to find out that I had had this conversation. He then told me that the problem was that the unraveling of the case would not be particularly embarrassing as far as this instant matter was concerned, but that it would involve the activities which were perfectly legitimate but which would be hard to explain in investigating the Ellsberg case, the Bay of Pigs, and the other matters where we had an imperative need to get the facts.

From my conversation with Haldeman on June 23, I had understood that Gray had *wanted* help from Walters in controlling an investigation that he agreed was getting out of hand. On June 30 Haldeman had told me that Gray wanted to limit the investigation but was under pressure from the U.S. Attorney's office. But now Gray was telling me, and in the most vivid language, that he was upset about what he saw as attempts on the part of the White House to frustrate the FBI's inquiry. I was suddenly confronted with the one thing that I had most wanted to avoid: White House involvement in Watergate. I told Gray emphatically to go ahead with his full investigation.

Diary
Certainly the best thing to do is to have the investigation pursued to its normal conclusion. In any event, we have to live with this one and hope to bring it to a conclusion without too much rubbing off on the presidency before the election. It is one of those cases where subordinates in a campaign, with the very best of motives, go off on some kick which inevitably embarrasses the top man. In this instance, however, how we handle it may make the difference as to how we come out.
In any event, as I emphasized to Ehrlichman and Haldeman, we must do nothing to indicate to Pat Gray or to the CIA that the White House is trying to suppress the investigation. On the other hand, we must cooperate with the investigation all the way along the line.

I told Ehrlichman to be sure that both Helms at the CIA and Gray at the FBI knew that I wanted a full investigation and that we were not attempting to suppress anything. I said we should also be sure to level with Clark MacGregor so he did not make statements he would have to retract later.
"Let's take the heat," I told Ehrlichman. "It won't be that bad."

The first mention I recall of Jeb Magruder's possible involvement in the Watergate break-in came while I was in California, when Ehrlichman told me that Magruder was going to be questioned in the investigation. Magruder had been brought into the White House by Haldeman in 1969 and was considered one of Haldeman's protégés, and it would be a personal blow to Haldeman if Magruder were drawn into the Watergate web. I dictated in my diary that night, "Haldeman is naturally very 'tender,' as Ehrlichman pointed out, with regard to Magruder. I feel just as deeply about it as he does." Magruder had left the White House staff in May 1971 to help set up the CRP, where he was assigned to handle the managerial details for Mitchell. Magruder had been Liddy's immediate superior and had been responsible for authorizing money for him.

Ehrlichman thought that Magruder might have to take the Fifth Amendment because even if the prosecutors could not establish any direct involvement in the planning and execution of the bugging, his relationship to Liddy was such that they might be able to draw him in as part of a conspiracy.

On Saturday afternoon, July 8, Ehrlichman and I went for a walk on the beach. It was a beautiful California day, and we could see the surfers bobbing on their boards in the water far down the coast. As we walked along the conversation turned to Magruder.

Diary

I told John Ehrlichman in a long walk on the beach that under the circumstances the question is whether Magruder is going to be better off in the event that he anticipates what will happen and voluntarily indicates what his role was and takes responsibility for the action, or whether he will face the fact that he will be questioned on such matters and then be forced at a later time to resign. I strongly urged the first course in his own interests.

Ehrlichman reflected on Gray's phone call and suggested that Gray and Walters might have failed to cooperate in limiting the FBI investigation because they felt that someone on the White House staff—perhaps Colson—was responsible for Watergate and was trying to put me on the spot in order to protect himself. Not knowing that in fact there was no White House involvement, Ehrlichman said, Gray and Walters probably thought that they were serving my interests by insisting on a wide-ranging investigation.

We discussed the subject of clemency. Watergate was a

political shenanigan, and Magruder, Hunt, Liddy, and th
five defendants were apparently first offenders. Three year
earlier the NBC television producer caught illegally buggin
the Democrats had been let off with a light fine and a
suspended sentence. The political climate that was being
built up around Watergate made it unlikely that there would
be such even-handed treatment for anyone involved in the
DNC bugging.

Ehrlichman and I agreed that there should be no com
mitments of any kind on clemency at this time.

In a later conversation with Ehrlichman I suggested
that if felonies were committed by demonstrators in this
campaign, as they had been in the past, and the participants
were booked and charged, I might grant a general political
pardon after the election that would encompass both the
Watergate bugging and the felonies committed by the opposition. This would not, however, include felonies that involved the use of violence, bombing, or physical injury. I did
not consider those to be in the same minor league with the
Watergate bugging.

There was certainly a precedent for pardons of political
offenses. When Harry Truman became President, dozens of
his fellow Democratic workers in the Kansas City Pender-
gast machine had been convicted of vote fraud in the 1936
elections. Truman began pardoning them before he had been
in office a month. By the end of his first year in the White
House, he had pardoned fifteen people and restored them to
full participation in future political activity.

My discussions with Ehrlichman were in no sense an
authorization or a promise of clemency or pardons. Any
decision would have to be made later. I summarized it at
one point in my diary: if there were equivalent offenses on
both sides, "that will provide the necessary basis we will
need for pardoning the individuals involved in this caper in
the event they are convicted."

Diary

    Everyone agrees that this incident was so clum-
sily handled that it probably doesn't deserve the criminal penalty that such incidents would ordinarily bring,
but in any event, with the political implications involved, we have to be prepared to deal with it firmly

before the election. After the election, of course, it will be very difficult to handle it in any other way than an evenhanded way, and I hope that such an opportunity presents itself.

THE DEMOCRATS' NOMINEE

The 1972 Democratic convention in Miami was a political shambles. After Humphrey's defeat in 1968, the party machinery had been taken over by radical reformers who sought to cleanse it of the "old politics" of the traditional organizations and power blocs by replacing them with the "new politics" of minority groups and radical activists. As a result the 1972 convention was unlike anything that had been seen before. Television audiences looked on hour after hour as representatives of the "new politics" used the convention to air and argue their currently fashionable frustrations: women, blacks, homosexuals, welfare mothers, migrant farm workers. Speakers were indulged and self-indulgent. There was no semblance of orderly procedure.

George McGovern had been one of the principal sponsors of the delegate reforms, and his nomination for President on July 12 was an indication of how well they had succeeded. He chose Senator Thomas Eagleton of Missouri as his running mate. Eagleton was young, attractive, Catholic, and a favorite with organized labor.

I invited John Connally to join me in San Clemente on the last night of the Democratic convention. After dinner we settled down in the living room to watch the acceptance speeches.

Hours passed as we waited for McGovern and Eagleton to appear. A new party charter was debated. Then thirty-nine other vice presidential candidates were nominated, including Mao Tse-tung and Martha Mitchell. The scene had the air of a college skit that had gotten carried away with itself and didn't know how to stop. Finally Connally gave up and went home. Pat and I continued to watch as first Teddy Kennedy took the microphone, then Hubert Humphrey, and then, at 2:48 A.M. in Miami—prime time on Guam, as some wit observed—McGovern himself at last appeared.

Diary

They panned to Humphrey on several occasions. He really looked like a very sad figure. I was glad that Henry called him today. He said that he wanted to be of assistance to us in foreign policy and seemed to be disappointed at what happened at the convention, not just from a personal standpoint, but generally.

I called Haldeman immediately after the acceptance speech and he said, "Well, they nominated the wrong man." Kennedy looked very good, although some thought he looked fat. He has a magnetic smile, a lot of style, and a brilliantly written speech.

As they had done on every other convention night in every other campaign, my family gave me their assessments of the opposition. Pat thought McGovern's best assets were a rather dignified bearing and an apparent sincerity. Julie had pneumonia and had not been able to stay up, but she thought Eagleton was too glib. Tricia said succinctly of McGovern, "He's a boring evangelist, and there's nothing more boring than an evangelist who's boring."

My thoughts returned to the look on Hubert Humphrey's face as he had watched McGovern's acceptance speech. Humphrey was an honorable and resourceful opponent. He did not fear showing his patriotism, his feelings, or his flaws. However close he might come to getting the nomination if he tried again in 1976, I knew that he would never make it. Time had now passed him by—just as it would have passed me by if I had lost to him in 1968.

The next day I sat in my study near the windows facing the ocean and wrote a letter to him.

I had very little by which to measure McGovern personally. I knew only what he said on the issues—but that was enough. I thought it was critically important to the future of the country that his radical ideas not prevail in November. I feared he would now ease off his radical positions—something, I observed, a far-right candidate would never do.

July 15, 1972

Dear Hubert,

As your party's convention comes to an end, I know how deep your disappointment must be.

You can take comfort in the fact that through the years you have earned the respect of your opponents as well as your supporters for being a gallant warrior.

As I am sure you will recall after Churchill defeat in 1945 his wife tried to console him by saying that maybe it was a "blessing in disguise"

Churchill answered - "If this is a blessing it is certainly very well disguised."

You must feel as he did. But like him -

146

you have many years of service ahead.

As friendly opponents in the political arena I hope we can both serve our parties in a way that will best serve the nation

Sincerely
Dick

Pat joins me in sending our best to Muriel & to you.

Diary

The extremists on the right of the Goldwater type would rather lose fighting for principle than to win by compromising principle. The extremists on the left, on the other hand, have usually shown that when the chips are down they will compromise principle in order to get power. This is why the communists usually beat the right-wingers, because the right-wingers are always fighting for principle, and the communists are willing to compromise principle until they get into power and then they, of course, crush out their opposition.

Putting it in a nutshell—the radicals of the left want power. They will compromise on issues in order to get power, recognizing that when they get power they can do what they want on the issues. They don't believe as deeply in principle as they pretend, and not nearly as deeply as do the radicals on the right.

In the first three days following his nomination George McGovern irretrievably lost the support of his own party.

Indications of his unreliability had appeared during the convention, when he had ignored or reneged on embarrassing or inconvenient commitments. For example, he had said that he would support a feminist challenge to the South Carolina delegation, but backed out when the challenge was made. Both before and after the nomination he asked Larry O'Brien to remain as Democratic National Chairman, and then backed down when his own staff raised objections. He introduced Pierre Salinger to a public meeting as his personal candidate for vice-chairman of the DNC, and then abandoned him when opposition arose. John Connally shook his head in disbelief. "Lack of character," he said. "It will do him in before the campaign is over." In March 1973 the new DNC Chairman, Robert Strauss, told Haldeman after the Gridiron Dinner, "You fellows just don't know McGovern—you think he's an evil man. He is just the stupidest man there ever was."

In San Clemente the reaction to McGovern's nomination and conduct was little short of exuberant. He had consciously abandoned conservative and moderate Democrats; and the ethnic groups, traditionally a Democratic blue chip, could find in him nothing of the hearty patriotism and pride that they had looked for in their party in the past. With these defections we had a chance not just to win the election but to create the New Majority we had only dreamed of in 1970. Only organized labor and George Wallace remained in doubt.

There were rumors that George Wallace was disgusted with the turn of events in Miami and was once again considering making a bid for the presidency as the nominee of a third party. Harry Dent, a former Republican State Chairman of South Carolina who served as a political aide on the White House staff, and several other White House political contacts were on the phone to Montgomery daily, keeping abreast of the situation there. Finally I asked

Connally to take over the "Wallace watch." "Go down there and see him, and let me know what he wants," I said.

On Tuesday, July 25, Connally saw Wallace and told him frankly what he himself believed: that Wallace would not help himself by becoming involved with a third party, and that the only way to get the Democratic Party back on its feet for the future was to "beat the hell" out of McGovern in November.

Connally called me the next day to report that Wallace would announce that he was definitely not going to run for President on a third-party ticket. "And all he really wants from you is to be sure that his message on the issues was heard. He said the Democrats hadn't listened to a word he and his constituents were saying." Connally later told Colson, "We might well say that this was the day the election was won."

I called Wallace and told him I knew it had been a terribly hard decision for him to make. "But you can't let yourself get discouraged by this," I said. "You have so many good years left." I told him that Connally was my closest political adviser, and if there was anything he wanted to discuss with regard to political matters, Connally would be available to him at any time. I also told him that Haig would give him foreign policy briefings, because I knew Wallace supported me on national defense issues.

Diary

I spoke to Haldeman and he was going to have *Sunrise at Campobello* taken to Wallace so he can see it.

I am also going to look into the possibility of a salt-water swimming pool for him, since I told him this would enable him to swim with his feet afloat and would greatly reduce the effort he would have to make swimming only with his arms.

On July 17 I received word that after a three-hour meeting, the executive board of the teamsters' union had voted 16 to 1 to endorse me for re-election. I invited their president, Frank Fitzsimmons, and his board to come to San Clemente.

Diary

This could have been one of the most important watershed meetings in American politics in this century.

I told them that when I had a tough decision to make sometimes members of the Cabinet, members of the administration, most of the media, and even most businessmen were reluctant to stand up and stand with me; but that I found that representatives of labor were really tough and strong in the crunch when the interests of the country were involved. This, of course, is the gospel truth, and they all knew that I meant it very sincerely when I said it.

I also pointed out that as far as they were concerned that most of them were registered Democrats—however, I did not consider that Democrats this year would be deserting their party, because the issues, particularly of national defense and foreign policy, transcended party lines, and that the Democratic candidate, who was undoubtedly sincere and against whom I had no personal animosity and hoped he had none against me, simply took a line which was out of tune and out of step with that of great numbers of his party.

I had walked out to the driveway with Fitzsimmons. I asked him what he thought George Meany's reaction would be to the teamsters' decision to endorse me. "Well," he said, "the old son of a bitch really has a problem now. I happen to know that 90 of the 130 members of the AFL-CIO board won't take McGovern. Hah," he chuckled, "after Meany hears what we did today, he'll be in such a stew he's gonna piss down his leg."

On July 19, my first full day back in Washington, I spent most of the morning going over domestic and legislative items. Then I asked Ehrlichman for an update on Watergate. He said that Dean was meeting with Mitchell that very morning to discuss it. He said that he did not think that the defense that had been worked up for Magruder was going to work. In Ehrlichman's judgment, Magruder would probably have to "take a slide."

I asked what that would mean. Ehrlichman said that Magruder would just have to take the lumps whatever they were; he would have to take the responsibility. Ehrlichman said he did not think a story could be contrived that indicated that Magruder had not known what was going on. But, he said, Dean was working on the problem that morning.

I asked if Magruder had in fact known. Ehrlichman's opinion was typically emphatic. Lord yes, he said, he was in it with both feet.

In that case, I said, there must not be any "contrived" story. I said I would like to see the thing worked out, but I knew that the two worst actions in this kind of situation were to lie and to cover up. If you covered up you would inevitably get caught, and if you lied you would be guilty of perjury. That was the story of the Hiss case and the 5 percenters under Truman. It was a tragic thing for Magruder, I said, and I hated to see it happen, but that was the way it was. I reiterated what I had said in San Clemente in early July: it would be easy to pardon Magruder later along with others in both parties who were charged with political offenses during the campaign.

That would do it, Ehrlichman agreed—as he put it, lay the foundation—but we would have a better feel for everything after Dean had talked with Mitchell. He told me that Hunt and Liddy were about to be drawn into the grand jury proceedings through the testimony of a lawyer Hunt had contacted on the night of the break-in and asked to represent the arrested men.

Still thinking about Magruder, I asked if he could invoke the Fifth Amendment. Ehrlichman did not think so and speculated that if he did he would still be convicted by someone else's testimony. He felt that Magruder should simply go in and say that it was a bad thing, but that he had got carried away and now he felt terrible about it.

Magruder's whole life would be ruined for this one mistake. I wondered if he could not accept only the ultimate responsibility by saying that he had simply given an instruction to get all the information possible but had not expected it to be carried out this way. I said I thought it would be unfortunate if he should say that he had actually ordered wiretapping. Ehrlichman agreed that it should be kept at the

Liddy level if possible, but repeated that he had too little information at that point to say anything more.

I said that the problem was a tough one, but the important thing was just to get it over and done with. Ehrlichman said he had told Dean that things must move as quickly as possible.

I asked whom Dean was working with on this, Ehrlichman or Haldeman. He said that both of them had been talking with Dean more or less together right along. I asked what Magruder was saying. Ehrlichman said that Magruder was saying that he had wanted to get a lot of information for a lot of different reasons, and that he had given Liddy the responsibility for getting it.

As Ehrlichman saw it, the problem was that once Magruder started talking, no one could tell what the scope of the examination might be and where it might end up.

I said that I supposed the main question was whether it would stop with Magruder or whether it would go on to Mitchell or Haldeman. Ehrlichman agreed and said that he and Haldeman had raised that question with Dean. Dean was unsure whether Magruder was tough and stable enough to be able to hold the line if pressed by interrogators.

I asked Ehrlichman if he thought Mitchell had known about the bugging. He replied that he assumed so but that he did not really know. I said I could not believe that Mitchell knew. Ehrlichman said that transcripts had been made of the tapped DNC calls, and he had a feeling— which, he acknowledged, might be unfair—that Mitchell might have seen them. I asked if Haldeman had seen them. Ehrlichman said no—in fact, he could not find anyone in the White House who ever saw them or who ever knew about the Watergate bugging operation. He said that Haldeman and Dean had had a meeting with Mitchell, Magruder, and some others on an earlier and different intelligence plan that had been proposed but had been disapproved. As a result of their decision in that earlier meeting Haldeman and Dean had a right to feel that nothing like the Watergate operation was going on. After this earlier plan had been disapproved, however, others in the CRP went ahead with the Watergate bugging operation without there ever having been another meeting involving White House people, Ehrlichman said.

Ehrlichman said it was still a tough question whether Magruder would assume responsibility and say that Mitchell had not known anything. He observed that sometimes tough questioning can lead a man into saying things he does not intend to say. I thought surely Magruder would be able to hold up when so much stood or fell on whether Mitchell became implicated. But Ehrlichman said that a good lawyer could keep at him until he broke him down. This was a particular danger in the Democrats' suit against the CRP: their lawyer was Edward Bennett Williams, who was well known for his dazzling courtroom technique.

I asked Ehrlichman what the best tactic would be on the criminal case. He said that if we had our way, it would be to let Liddy and Hunt go and to hold it there. But if Magruder was going to be involved through third-party testimony, he said, the next best tactic would be to rationalize a story that would not lead to his conviction.

I tried to estimate the public relations effect on the charges of a "cover-up" if the five men arrested at the Watergate and Hunt and Liddy were actually convicted. I said that even though Hunt had worked at the White House, I was not really bothered by the negative publicity that would ensue from his conviction. Ehrlichman observed that Liddy had also worked in the White House, and there would be some of that in the news stories as well.

Ehrlichman said that he was still hopeful that Dean and Mitchell would conclude that what Ehrlichman called the "Magruder scenario" would work. But, he said, there was no sense in starting it if it was going to be disproved; that would only be doubly damaging. I agreed. Then we would have both a cover-up and a conviction, which is what had happened to Truman in the Hiss case.

Ehrlichman said that Dean had been admonished not to contrive a story that might not succeed. He repeated his feeling that if any risk remained, Magruder might as well just go "whole hog."

I was still worried about Magruder when I saw Colson later that afternoon. I told him, as I had Ehrlichman, that we simply had to get the thing done and cut our losses. Since Howard Hunt was about to go before a grand jury, I asked Colson how he assessed the situation. He replied that in the first place he did not think that Hunt would feel he had done anything wrong. Hunt, he said, was such an ideologue and so committed to the country that, if he had a good lawyer and were properly coached, he would take the heat rather than talk. He said that the only place that he would worry about Hunt was that he might say that he had tried to "psychoanalyze" Ellsberg because the SOB was an enemy. I said I didn't see any way Ellsberg could be relevant to this case. "I wouldn't worry about that," I said.

We discussed Magruder's situation and my concern whether he would hold up under questioning. Colson said that if it weren't for the political notoriety the whole bugging episode would mean nothing more than a suspended sentence for those involved, as happened in cases of industrial espionage. We agreed that it would be a terrible thing for Magruder to go through and have on his record. I mentioned to Colson the idea I had discussed with Ehrlichman of granting a general pardon after the election covering both Democrats and Republicans who were guilty of political offenses.

When Haldeman came in that afternoon, he was pessimistic about Magruder's chances of not being indicted. He said that there would be testimony implicating Magruder and that the only thing to do now was to try to cut it off before it hit Mitchell. I asked if Magruder could do that. Haldeman said that Magruder said he would, but there was some question whether he could.

Haldeman reported that Ehrlichman felt that we should just get it over with quickly. Haldeman agreed that it was probably better to take whatever losses there were. I said it was just a damn shame about Magruder and repeated my feeling about the possibility of an eventual pardon. We talked about other things, but then I came back to Magruder and asked what we could do to help the "poor son of a gun." Haldeman said he would be assisted in getting legal help. I told Haldeman that I hoped Magruder would leave the campaign before he was indicted. It would be better for him, and for us.

Haldeman and I agreed that the main thing now was that Mitchell come out clean. Whatever the actual case, I told Haldeman, Magruder simply had to draw the line on anything that might involve Mitchell.

I asked Haldeman if Colson had been called before the grand jury. He said no, but he might be called for a deposition in the civil suit. He then told me that the grand jury was apparently talking about calling Ehrlichman. I was surprised and asked why. Haldeman said it had to do with Hunt's having worked for Bud Krogh. I again asked what could be the interest in Ehrlichman, and Haldeman said that Dean had tried to find out from the Justice Department but apparently they were not saying.

The next afternoon Haldeman told me that it looked as if Magruder was not going to be indicted for the Watergate break-in. Evidently there was a distinction that could be drawn about whether the decision was *knowledgeable*—and therefore indictable. Haldeman said that Magruder's line would be that he had not known of this specific action— "which apparently is true," Haldeman added. Magruder would say that he had authorized sums of money for Liddy without knowing the uses to which they would be put. He would admit to being guilty of stupidity but not of criminal conduct.

So Magruder was now at least technically safe. He had been part of the campaign's intelligence-gathering operation, but he had not been specifically aware of the Watergate break-in. At least that was what he was apparently saying. I was skeptical, as I think we all were, but I nonetheless thought that it was now up to the Justice Department to make its case against him if they could.

Haldeman said that Mitchell did not think we should make Magruder leave the CRP. There would be advance warning if he was going to be indicted; if he was, he could leave then. Haldeman observed that Ehrlichman and Mitchell represented two different approaches to handling the entire matter: Mitchell was of the "stonewall-it-to-hell-with-everybody" school, while Ehrlichman was of the "complete-panic-cut-everything-off-and-sink-it-immediately" school. Haldeman felt both were wrong.

In the late afternoon of July 25 Haldeman brought me a wire service bulletin from McGovern's post-convention vacation headquarters in South Dakota. McGovern and Eagleton had just held a press conference at which the vice presidential candidate disclosed that on three separate occasions between 1960 and 1966 he had admitted himself to hospitals for treatment of mental depression; on two of them his treatment had included electroshock therapy. He said that he still occasionally took tranquilizers.

After Eagleton's statement McGovern had said, "Tom Eagleton is fully qualified in mind, body, and spirit to be the Vice President of the United States and, if necessary, to take over the presidency on a moment's notice. I wouldn't have hesitated one minute if I had known everything that Senator Eagleton said here today." A reporter asked him if the decision to keep Eagleton on the ticket was irrevocable, and McGovern replied, "Absolutely."

My diary records the prediction I made that day to John Connally on how McGovern would handle the situation: "I suggested that McGovern would give him four or five days and then have his major newspapers call for him to resign and then have him replaced by the national committee."

I was therefore surprised the next day when McGovern made an even stronger statement, telling reporters that he was "1000 percent" behind Eagleton and that he had no intention of dropping him from the ticket. But when Haldeman came in with that afternoon's New York *Post* calling for Eagleton's resignation, I felt sure that despite McGovern's public statements, this was the beginning of the process I had predicted to Connally.

Diary

It is my view that if Eagleton is not dropped from the ticket this weekend that they have a very serious problem in letting the thing ride along. It will appear that they have a finger in the air, waiting for public opinion and the polls to tell them what to do. As I pointed out, this tells us a hell of a lot about McGovern.

The main test of a man is whether he has the character to make tough decisions and then to lead his associates to follow him on those decisions.

156

On July 27 Jack Anderson reported a shockingly false story: he charged that Eagleton had been arrested several times on charges of drunken and reckless driving. In short order the Washington *Post,* the Los Angeles *Times,* and the New York *Post* were calling for Eagleton to get off the ticket. McGovern repeated that he was 1000 percent behind his running mate, and Eagleton denied the charges and gamely defended himself. He insisted that he would stay on the ticket. His gutsy and unshakable belief in himself won sympathy, if not real political support.

On Sunday, July 30, Eagleton appeared on *Face the Nation.* Jack Anderson was one of the panel of questioners. He apologized for the drunk-driving charges but refused to retract them, claiming he was still checking them. I thought back to the fund crisis in 1952 and about how Anderson's mentor, Drew Pearson, had done a similar thing to me. I could empathize with Eagleton's frustration, and I admired his aplomb. He was as courageous as Anderson was contemptible.

At one point the program took a turn that bordered, I thought, on the incredible. One of the reporters remarked how much Eagleton was sweating. Eagleton pointed out that the lights were very hot. The reporter persisted and pointed out that others on the show were not sweating that much and then commented on Eagleton's nervous fidgeting with his hands. I dictated that night, "I perspire even though I may not be under any tension whatever!" I thought it was a predatory performance.

In the meantime McGovern had started to seed the ground for a reversal of his support for Eagleton.

Diary
The way the McGovern-Eagleton thing adds up now, it seems to me, is that McGovern probably will be forced to put him off the ticket because of the opposition of the McGovern media and the professionals in the party. In the event he is able to replace him with Kennedy, this will make it a whole new ball game. If he is unable to get Kennedy, it's difficult to see how he could improve the ticket.

The next night McGovern dropped Eagleton. I thought immediately of Eagleton's family. I knew that their agony must have been like that we suffered during the fund crisis—except that our suffering had been redeemed by a happy ending. I remembered that Eagleton had brought his young son to the Oval Office the year before, and I wrote a letter to the boy. A few weeks later I received his reply.

Personal

THE WHITE HOUSE

WASHINGTON   August 2, 1992-

Dear Terry-

When I saw the picture in Life a week ago I was reminded of our meeting at the White House when your father introduced you to me after I signed the Construction Safety Bill. I thought you might like to have a copy of the White House Photographer's picture of that meeting.

I realize these past few days have been very difficult ones for you and the members of your family. Speaking as one who understands + respects your father's decision to continue to fight for his party's nominees and against my administration's policies, I would like to pass on to you some strictly personal thoughts with regard to the ordeal your father has undergone.

Politics is a very hard game.

158

Winston Churchill once pointed out
that politics is even more difficult
than war. Because in politics you
die many times; in war you die
only once."

But in these words of Churchill
we can all take some comfort.
The political man can always
come back to fight again.

What matters is not that
your father fought a terribly difficult
battle and lost. What matters
is that in fighting the battle
he won the admiration of foes and
friends alike because of the
courage, poise and just
plain guts he showed against
overwhelming odds.

Few men in public life
in our whole history have
been through what he has
been through. I hope you
do not allow this incident
to discourage or depress you.

Years later you will look
back and say "I am proud of
the way my dad handled
himself in the greatest trial of his life".
            Sincerely Richard Nixon

PS I hope your arms are completely healed.

Friday, September 1, 1972

Honorable Richard Nixon
The White House
Washington D.C.

Dear Mr. President,

I just came home from summer
camp. That explains why I did not
answer your letter sooner.

I guess very few thirt-keen-
year-olds get hand-written letters from
the President. Although I am a
Democrat, I think you must be a
wonderful man to take the time
to write to some unimportant
person like me.

Do you know what my Dad
said when he read your letter?
He said, "It's going to make it
all the tougher to talk against
Nixon."

I think both Dad and
you are excellent politicians. Even
though you and Dad don't always
agree, I think the country is
lucky to have both of you.

My favorite subject in school
is history. I now feel I am
a part of history since you wrote
a letter to me.

Thank you, Mr. President very,
very much.

With appreciation,
Terry
Eagleton

The 1972 presidential election, with its landslide result, should have been the most gratifying and fulfilling of all my campaigns. Instead it was one of the most frustrating and, in many ways, the least satisfying of all.

During most of my first term I had assumed that my opponent in 1972 would be Kennedy, Muskie, or Humphrey. I thought that I could probably beat Muskie or Humphrey; a campaign against Teddy Kennedy would be much more difficult to predict because it would involve so many emotional elements. Any one of these men would have been a formidable opponent, and for three and a half years I fully expected to have to fight hard for re-election.

Even after McGovern emerged from the primaries as the front-runner, I still could not believe that he would actually be nominated. I thought, as did many political observers, that at the last minute the convention would turn to Kennedy. Only after McGovern was nominated did I accept the fact that I was virtually assured of re-election without having to wage much of a campaign.

Against Kennedy or Muskie or Humphrey I would have had to fight a close-in, one-on-one battle. Against McGovern, however, it was clear that the less I did, the better I would do. This was a totally unaccustomed situation for me, and it was not one in which I felt particularly comfortable or even knew instinctively what was best to do.

There were five basic components of my 1972 election strategy. First, I planned to spend the month and a half following the Republican convention in the White House doing my job. The choice between the candidates was so sharp and the issues spoke so clearly for themselves that there was no need for me to hammer them home.

Second, Senator Bob Dole of Kansas, the highly articulate Chairman of the Republican National Committee, and various members of the Cabinet and the administration would travel throughout the country as presidential "surrogates," talking about our general record and achievements as well as about their own specialized issues. Ideally, one surrogate would precede McGovern's appearance in each major city and another would follow him as soon as he left.

Third, I wanted to develop the most efficient and effective campaign committee organization humanly possible. We succeeded in this so well that Theodore H. White called the Committee to Re-elect the President "one of the most spectacularly efficient exercises in political technology of the entire postwar era."

Fourth, I planned to use the last weeks of the campaign to broadcast thirteen radio speeches covering my philosophy of government as well as my positions on the major campaign issues.

Finally, at the very end, I planned to emerge from the White House and campaign personally during the last two weeks before the election in states where the presidential vote might be close, or where my presence might pull in a Republican candidate in a tight local race. This was a dramatic reversal of roles for one who had been the party wheelhorse in so many other national campaigns. I knew there would be resentment on the part of some of the party workers and particularly by some Republican candidates who were hoping that my landslide could pull them in. But I thought then—and I still believe—that what we did was the only way to run the campaign of 1972 and the best way to pull in enough new blood from the Democrats to give the Republican Party the New Majority momentum that could give it a whole new lease on political life.

In view of my plans for highly limited personal campaigning, I decided that we should try to help Republican candidates with money. Nearly a million dollars went from our campaign funds into various Senate and House races. I posed for pictures and sent tape-recorded endorsements to every Republican candidate except the two running for the Senate in Mississippi and Arkansas. The Republicans in those races had no chance against Democratic incumbents James Eastland and John McClellan, who had stood with me in every international crisis in the first term and whose support I would need in the next four years.

After McGovern had been nominated I knew that the most difficult thing for us about the 1972 campaign would be the tendency to relax. Even if complacency did not cost us the election, it might cost us the renewed energy that comes with the completion of a campaign.

"We have to develop a sense of mission," I told Haldeman, "and not back into victory by default."

The most exciting aspect of the 1972 election for me was that McGovern's perverse treatment of the traditional Democratic power blocs that had been the basis of every Democratic presidential victory for the last forty years had made possible the creation of a New Republican Majority as an electoral force in American politics. I was confident that if we could only make a first inroad, we could follow through with these New Majority groups. I believed that I had a much greater affinity with most of them than had their erstwhile Democratic allies, and I made this point in two separate diary entries, one as a general observation and the other after a meeting with a group of labor union supporters in New York at the end of September.

Diary
    The American leader class has really had it in terms of their ability to lead. It's really sickening to have to receive them at the White House as I often do and to hear them whine and whimper and that's one of the reasons why I enjoy very much more receiving labor leaders and people from middle America who still have character and guts and a bit of patriotism.

    The meeting with the labor leaders was the best of all. They were friendly, all out, and I hope we can find a way to see that this alliance is not broken immediately after the election—and that they not revert to their usual partisan, Democratic position. Frankly, I have more in common with them from a personal standpoint than does McGovern or the intellectuals generally. They like labor as a mass. I like them individually. The same thing can be said of all other groups or classes, including young, black, Mexicans, etc.

I do not believe that any administration in history has gone into a re-election campaign with a more impressive record than ours in August 1972. There was no major area of American life in which we had not made progress or proposed dramatic new alternatives.

Inflation averaged 6.1 percent in 1969; after only one

year our New Economic Policy had cut it to 2.7 percent. The GNP had increased at an annual rate of only 3.4 percent in the first quarter of 1969; by the third quarter of 1972 it was rising at 6.3 percent, the fastest gain since 1965. All during the campaign the stock market was moving toward the 1000-point record that it achieved in November 1972.

The real earnings of Americans had not increased at all from 1965 to 1970; now they were moving up at an annual rate of 4 percent. Each year of the Nixon administration had set a new record in gross farm income. Average income per farm was 40 percent higher than the average from 1961 to 1968.

We had reduced federal income taxes by 66 percent for a family of four making $5,000, and by 20 percent for a family of four making $15,000. Overall federal taxes on individuals had decreased by $22 billion.

We had proposed the first major welfare reform since the program's inception. It was our proposal for a new national health insurance program—one that shared the cost between those who could afford to pay for health insurance, employers, and government—that survived the several socialized medicine schemes proposed by others. We had nearly doubled the funding for the fight against cancer and increased by ten times the funding for the attack against drug abuse. Seizures of narcotics and dangerous drugs had increased by 400 percent. The rise in crime had been 122 percent from 1960 to 1968; in 1971 it was only 6 percent; in the first half of 1972 it was only 1 percent.

We had proposed and won congressional approval for the nation's first formal research institute for learning and education. We passed a landmark mass transit bill which meant that funding which had been no more than $175 million per year rose to $400 million in 1971 and to $1 billion in 1973. We presented a revolutionary proposal for federal revenue-sharing with the states and hard-pressed cities. We also proposed a complete reorganization of the federal government. We offered the first comprehensive program for the environment in history, aimed at striking a balance between the dreams of the environmentalists and the realities of job-producing industry. Our Legacy of Parks program launched what would eventually become 642 parks in fifty states, parks designed not for elitists but the average citizen.

Our administration had completely changed America's spending priorities: in fiscal 1968, 45 percent of the budget was being spent for defense and 32 percent for "human resources," such as education, social services, health. By fiscal 1973 those figures had been reversed. We increased spending for the arts by almost 500 percent. We increased Social Security benefits by 51 percent.

Draft calls were 299,000 in 1968; they were 50,000 in 1972, and we were on our way to the elimination of the draft and the creation of an all-volunteer Army.

We had a superb record, but we had to make it known to the voters—or at least to remind them of our achievements. At the beginning of the summer I wrote a memorandum to John Ehrlichman asking him to move from his role of overseeing the conception of domestic policies to the role of overseeing their execution:

> You have handled the development of the programs with superb organizational ability and substantively have seen to it that they have come out along the lines of my own thinking. . . .
>
> As I look back over the past three years, our great failing, particularly in the domestic area, has been that once the President shoots the big gun, the infantry doesn't follow in adequately to clean up and to hold the territory. . . . As I see it now the gut issues are cost of living, busing, drug abuse, and possibly tax reform as it relates to the property tax. There are of course other subsidiary issues like the environment, revenue-sharing, etc. . . . And then of course there are always the issues where the opposition is on the attack. . . .
>
> The way that I look at most of our domestic programs is that we have done an excellent job of conceiving them and a poor job of selling them. . . . Great ideas that are conceived and not sold are like babies that are stillborn. We need some deliveries within the next few months even if they have to be Caesarean. I will approve any programs you have to bring about those deliveries, provided of course you recognize my total opposition to any abortions.

My relationship with George Meany during the first three and a half years of my first term as President could be described as tempestuous. I had known him for twenty-five years, from the days I served on the House Labor Committee. He was tough, smart, and combative. Philosophically, he was liberal on economic issues and conservative on social issues; politically, he was a partisan Democrat. But when it came to foreign policy and national defense, he was a patriot first and partisan second.

We knew that in June Meany had told George Shultz that he would not support McGovern if he won the nomination. After the Democratic convention he called Shultz again. He was outraged that McGovern had dumped Pierre Salinger—not because of any particular affection for Salinger, but because Salinger was McGovern's man, so McGovern should have stood by him. "He don't stick to his people," Meany said bitterly.

On July 19 a bulletin came over the wires announcing that, for the first time in its history, the AFL-CIO executive council had adjourned without voting any presidential endorsement. It was a moment to ponder and savor: for the first time in seventeen years the AFL-CIO was not going to endorse the Democratic candidate for President.

On July 28 I played golf with Meany, Bill Rogers, and George Shultz at Burning Tree, just outside Washington. As we went down the first fairway, Meany said brusquely, "Eagleton should have told McGovern, but now McGovern has handled it like a fool, vacillating from one side to the other."

It was about 6:30 when we got back to the clubhouse and sat on the porch to have a drink. Rogers and Shultz joined me in ordering cigars so that we could keep Meany company. We sat for almost an hour in the twilight, all of us smoking our cigars and three of us listening to Meany talk. He said that McGovern was going to lose by a virtual landslide. In the circumstances, he said, though labor disagreed with some of my policies, it was in labor's interest to remain neutral in the presidential race and concentrate on saving its favorite Senate and House members. Pouring money into McGovern's campaign would be tantamount to throwing it away.

As we left the porch and walked toward our cars, Meany cleared his throat and said to me gruffly, "I want you to know now that I am not going to vote for you, and I am not going to vote for McGovern. But you'll be doing all right with the Meany family." He said Mrs. Meany and two of his three daughters would vote for me. The other daughter, he said, "will just follow her old man and not vote for anybody."

Then, just as we were about to separate, he put his hand on my shoulder and said, "Just so you don't get a swelled head about my wife voting for you, I want to tell you why—she don't like McGovern."

During the first days of August McGovern sought a new vice presidential running mate. He tried Teddy Kennedy, Edmund Muskie, Abraham Ribicoff, Larry O'Brien, Hubert Humphrey, and Governor Reubin Askew of Florida—all without success.

I spent the weekend of August 4 at the vacation home of Tom McCabe, a good friend from the Eisenhower days, on Assateague Island off Maryland's Eastern Shore. Mitchell, Rebozo, and Abplanalp came with me. The television set at the house did not work so we listened to the radio to hear McGovern announce that Teddy Kennedy's brother-in-law Sargent Shriver would be his new running mate.

As early as June I had heard from visitors to the LBJ Ranch that Johnson was not going to support McGovern if he was nominated. After the Democratic convention I called Johnson and put the question to him directly.

"I don't want to embarrass you," I began, "but you know that John Connally is organizing Democrats who want to support me. A number of people have been contacted who are close to you, and they have indicated a desire to join the group, but only if it wouldn't embarrass you. I appreciate your position in your party, but I would like to ask if you would remain neutral with respect to supporters who want to join John's group."

"Let me just read you a letter, Mr. President," Johnson said, and I could hear a rustling of papers. "This is the standard reply I'm sending out to Democrats who write me about what they should do because they're so disenchanted with McGovern. It says that because of the honor I have been given by my party over forty years, I am going to support the Democratic ticket at all levels. However, I go on to say—and no one will fail to catch this—that I have always taken the position that what an individual does in a presidential campaign is a matter of conscience, and I'm not going to interfere with that decision. Now what do you think of that?"

"I can only say that I'm very grateful, Mr. President," I replied.

A few weeks later Johnson sent me some campaign advice through Billy Graham: "Ignore McGovern, and get out with the people. But stay above the campaign, like I did with Goldwater. Go to ball games and factories. And don't worry. The McGovern people are going to defeat themselves."

Billy said that when he had raised the question of the Watergate bugging business, Johnson had just laughed and said, "Hell, that's not going to hurt him a bit."

One of the first things I had to decide about the 1972 campaign was whether to change the ticket by choosing a new running mate. By the middle of 1971 Ted Agnew had become increasingly disenchanted with his role as Vice President. He felt, as does almost every Vice President to some degree, that the White House staff did not treat him with proper respect, and that I had not given him major substantive responsibilities. It was then that word came to us from Bryce Harlow that there was a very good chance that Agnew, on his own, would withdraw from the ticket early in 1972 to take advantage of attractive offers outside government.

During the first term Agnew had become an articulate and effective spokesman for conservative positions and issues. In this role he was wrongly underrated by the press as well as by his partisan critics. But as I began preparing for the 1972 election, I also had to look ahead to 1976. I believed that John Connally was the only man in either party who clearly had the potential to be a great President. He had the necessary political "fire in the belly," the energy to win, and the vision to lead. I even talked with Haldeman about the possibility of Agnew's resigning before the convention and my nominating Connally to replace him, although I knew that such a move was a remote possibility at best. The only serious option would be to replace Agnew with Connally as the nominee for Vice President at the convention.

Early in 1972 I discussed the vice presidency with Connally. His reactions ran from mixed to negative. I sensed that he did not think the second spot would be the best route to the White House for him. He said that none of us could calculate the depth of Republican opposition to him as a Johnny-come-lately.

I had a meeting with John Mitchell a few days later. I told him bluntly that I thought Connally should be President in 1976 and that I was weighing the possibility of giving him a head start, if he wanted it, by making him my running mate. Mitchell agreed that Connally was the man to run in 1976, but he argued strongly against making any changes in the ticket in 1972. Connally was still a Democrat, and Mitchell thought that putting him on the ticket might backfire with the conservative New Majority Republicans and Democrats, particularly in the South, among whom Agnew had become almost a folk hero. "Party workers have to believe that loyalty is rewarded, or there won't be any party workers," Mitchell warned.

He felt that Connally would be more helpful in the campaign as the Chairman of Democrats for Nixon than he would by becoming a Republican before the election. Moreover, Connally had told Mitchell that in no circumstances did he want to be Vice President.

In fact, Mitchell urged me to give Agnew a definite commitment. If we waited too long, he warned, Agnew might want to get a deal in exchange—possibly even a pledge to support him for the nomination in 1976. "Besides," Mitchell said, "I feel sorry for him. He's having some financial problems, and he needs to be able to plan his future."

On June 12 I asked Mitchell to tell Agnew that I had made the decision definitely to have him on the ticket again as my running mate. I said that we would not announce it until after the Democratic convention. This would generate interest by creating suspense; it might also lead the Democrats to soft-pedal their attacks on him at their convention just in case I decided to choose someone else.

At the beginning of August I tried to block off time to work exclusively on my acceptance speech, but there were inevitably distractions that made concentration difficult. I mentioned a particularly nettling one in my diary on August 16: "McGovern is striking out more wildly now, trying to say that I was indirectly responsible for the bugging of the Democratic headquarters." McGovern indeed was pulling out all the stops on Watergate. In one of his speeches at this time he had said that the break-in was "the kind of thing you expect under a person like Hitler." Other Democratic leaders were equally vehement in their denunciations, having seized upon Watergate as the best way to distract public attention from their own candidate.

The Democrats had mounted a particularly strident attack based on the fact that a large number of the contributors to my campaign preferred that their contributions remain anonymous. Many of them were Democrats of long standing and considerable prominence who thought it important to defeat McGovern but who would find it awkward to be named publicly. Anonymity for contributors was legal if the contribution was made before April 7, 1972, but the Democrats framed the issue and the media presented it as a case of secrecy versus openness in the political process and thus put us on the defensive in the battle for public opinion. By September the Washington *Post* would be printing leaks from anonymous sources on partisan congressional staffs. For example, there was one that charged Finance Chairman Maury Stans with being tied to $700,000 in illegal campaign funds that had been laundered through Mexico. Stans categorically denied the story. In the months ahead the CRP finance committee would be accused of monitoring the private bank accounts of potential contributors, of having laundered contributions in Luxembourg, and of having raised money from high-ranking Arabs and other illegal foreign sources. The charges were all false.

From the very beginning, I wanted to fight back. I saw no reason why McGovern and his supporters and contributors should be immune. If there was any campaign advantage to incumbency, it had to be access to government information on one's opponents. I remembered the IRS leaks of my tax returns to Drew Pearson in the 1952 campaign and the politically motivated tax audits done on me in

1963. The Democrats, while in office, had made little effort to camouflage their political pressure on the key government agencies. It seemed that even when they were out of power their supporters—particularly among the bureaucrats in the IRS—continued to do the job for them. I heard numerous reports—clearly too frequent to be coincidental—of close personal and political friends who had been subjected to constant and, in my view, vindictive, investigation by the IRS since the time I lost to Kennedy in 1960.

So far our own efforts to use this power had been halfhearted and ineffective. I dictated a diary note about this in the spring of 1972: "This has really been a shameful failure on our part, and it is hard for me to understand it, in view of the fact that I had so often pointed out that after what they did to us when we were out of office we at least owed it to ourselves in self-defense to initiate some investigations of them." Even now it frustrates me to think that our efforts to gain whatever political advantage we could from being in power were so tentative and feeble and amateurish in comparison to the Democrats'. I prodded my staff to change this; on August 3 I reflected on the situation we faced and the problem I saw behind it.

Diary

I emphasized to Haldeman and Ehrlichman the necessity of our getting information on some of our Democratic opponents that they constantly were getting out against us. It is ironic that when we were out of office they really used to crucify us—now that we are in office they still do, due to the fact that the bureaucrats at the lower level are all with them.

The problem we have here is that all of our people are gun-shy as a result of the Watergate incident and don't want to look into files that involve Democrats. Haldeman said after the election we really could then take the steps to get loyalists in various positions that were sensitive. Of course, we should have long ago. Certainly we have been above reproach in this respect and have not used the enormous powers of the office—the Internal Revenue files, the Justice

Department files—to go after some of the hanky-panky operations of our Democratic opponents.

I repeatedly urged Haldeman and Ehrlichman—though without apparent success—to have IRS checks made on McGovern's key staff and contributors. In one memo on the subject I said that anything that came up that might indicate "shady dealings" should be got out early. "Of course, if nothing turns up, drop the whole matter," I wrote. "But let's be sure that we've gone the extra mile and developed material before we drop the matter."

Larry O'Brien was one Democrat who was a grand master in the art of political gamesmanship. O'Brien had been tutored in the Kennedy political machine and further shaped by his years with Lyndon Johnson. He was a partisan in the most extreme and effective sense. After the Kent State tragedy, he virtually accused me of killing the four students. Whether the issue was Vietnam or Watergate, he could be counted on to hit hard, and not always above the belt.

An IRS investigation of Howard Hughes's financial empire had revealed that Hughes was paying O'Brien's Washington lobbying firm a large yearly retainer, reportedly almost $200,000. There were rumors about whether O'Brien had reported all the money and paid taxes on it. I was as doubtful as I was hopeful that we would nail him on this issue; as I noted in my diary, "I would be very surprised if he would have allowed himself to get in such a box." The IRS had planned to interview O'Brien at some point regarding the Hughes retainer; I ordered Haldeman and Ehrlichman to have the audit expedited and completed before the election.

Whatever the findings of the audit, I thought, it would be a pleasant—and newsworthy—irony that after all the years in which Howard Hughes had been portrayed as my financial angel, the Chairman of the Democratic National Committee was in fact the one profiting from a lucrative position on Hughes's payroll.

In the end the IRS cleared O'Brien after a routine audit, and my desire to check up on him and on McGovern's supporters was soon deflected by the heightening demands of the campaign schedule and the major new developments at the Vietnam peace talks.

On August 20, the day before the Republican National Convention opened, Pat and the girls went to Miami while I stayed at Camp David to put the finishing touches on my acceptance speech.

I watched television the next night to see the documentary about Pat that was shown on a huge screen in the convention hall. Jimmy Stewart had already given her an unforgettably eloquent introduction, and when the lights came up after the film, Pat suddenly appeared in person at the podium, standing with her arms out wide. It was a gesture uniquely hers, graceful and gracious. The program was running late, and, with infallible instinct, she spoke just a minute to say thank you. The cameras cut to Julie and Tricia, and I could see the loving pride in their smiles. I noted, "That was characteristic of the whole convention as far as the appearance of Pat, the girls, David and Ed are concerned. No First Family ever looked better than they did. No family looked more the all-American type than they did."

I flew to Miami on Tuesday afternoon, August 22. That night I made an unscheduled appearance at the open-air youth rally, and the reception I received overwhelmed me. Pam Powell, the daughter of Dick Powell and June Allyson, escorted me onto the stage. Hands above their heads, four fingers outstretched, the thousands of young people took up a chant that I was hearing for the first time: *"Four more years! Four more years!"* It was deafening. It was music. This was a new kind of Republican youth: they weren't square, but they weren't ashamed of being positive and proud.

The picture that is probably most remembered from the 1972 convention is of Sammy Davis, Jr., impulsively hugging me on the stage at the youth rally. When the crowd finally quieted down, I described my first meeting with him at a White House reception a few weeks earlier. We had both talked about our backgrounds and about how we both came from rather poor families. "I know Sammy is a member of the other party," I said. "I didn't know when I talked to him what he would be doing in this election campaign. But I do know this. I want to make this pledge to Sammy. I want to make it to everybody here, whether you happen to be black or white, or young or old, and all of those who are listening. I believe in the American dream. Sammy Davis believes in it. We believe in it because we have seen it come true in our own lives." For me—and, I think, for many others—the youth rally was the highlight of the convention. That night at the convention hall I was renominated for a second term by a vote of 1,347 to 1.

The next night outside the hall the frustrated demonstrators attempted to set fire to buses filled with delegates. They slashed tires, pelted delegates with rocks and eggs, and marched on the hall wearing their own gas masks and brandishing night sticks. My eyes burned from the lingering sting of tear gas as I entered the hall to accept my fifth and last nomination by a Republican convention.

Inside the hall neither the predictability of a well-organized program nor the absence of a hard-fought nomination battle could mute the enthusiasm of the crowd. The delegates had picked up the slogan I had heard at the youth rally. Over and over they shouted: *"Four more years! Four more years!"*

The day after the convention I addressed the American Legion in Chicago and then spoke at the dedication of Dwight D. Eisenhower High School in Utica, Michigan. Then we flew across the country to San Diego, where another big crowd was waiting, and then took the short helicopter flight up the coast to San Clemente. The enthusiasm of all these crowds was exciting and contagious and deeply satisfying. There was an emotional quality to their receptions and reactions that neither the staff nor I had been able to sense in Washington, where many of the columns and news stories attributed my support more to the widespread disappointment with McGovern than to any intrinsic quality in my own candidacy.

Diary
　　Certainly, no one could say that we didn't have the jumpers and the squealers in Michigan and San Diego and San Clemente, although it will, as usual, be difficult to get the press to write it. I am inclined to

think that our people are going to be far more the jumpers and squealers than the McGovern people unless he begins to catch on and begins to inspire and lift up, rather than simply talk in the dour, Calvinistic way which characterizes his approach up to this time.

The crowd in San Diego was really fantastic. It must have been about 15,000. My talk was not really up to what it should have been. By this time I was having some fatigue and I just wasn't able to put that much into it.

We then went on to San Clemente. It was a beautiful flight over the coast, and when we got here the staff, of course, had prepared me for a surprise. They had said that it was simply going to be the four mayors and a few friends from the area. It turned out to be one of the great crowds of the day. It was a very emotional crowd.

By the time we got back to the residence we were really bushed. Pat had dinner with me in the study—she had a second helping of chicken but I was not really in a condition to eat much and was glad that King came in to finish off my steak. Pat has been a really tremendous trouper in this past week.

I finished the day sitting out at the pool and smoking a cigar from Iran.

On Wednesday, August 30, Haldeman came in with a morose look. "Bad news," he said glumly, "I really mean it—it's really bad." Then he handed me the latest Gallup poll:

Nixon	64%
McGovern	30%
Undecided	6%

When I looked up he was smiling. So was I. It was the largest post-convention point spread in favor of a Republican candidate in Gallup's history.

My first presss conference of the campaign was scheduled for August 29. Watergate was obviously going to be one of the subjects raised. Ehrlichman assured me that there was still one thing of which we were certain: John Dean, the

Justice Department, and the FBI all confirmed that there had been no White House involvement.

In the press conference I was asked whether I thought that there should be a Special Prosecutor appointed for Watergate. I answered that a Special Prosecutor was hardly necessary, since the FBI, the Justice Department, the Senate Banking and Currency Committee, and the General Accounting Office were all conducting investigations. I said that I had ordered total cooperation by the White House. "In addition to that," I continued, "within our own staff, under my direction, Counsel to the President Mr. Dean has conducted a complete investigation of all leads which might involve any present members of the White House staff or anybody in the government. I can say categorically that his investigation indicates that no one in the White House staff, no one in this administration, presently employed, was involved in this very bizarre incident. . . . What really hurts in matters of this sort is not the fact that they occur, because overzealous people in campaigns do things that are wrong. What really hurts is if you try to cover it up."

At a Cabinet meeting on September 12, Attorney General Kleindienst reported that the indictments on the Watergate break-in and bugging would be handed down in three days and that no one at a high level in the CRP or anyone in the White House would be named. He had anticipated the predictable Democratic charges of a whitewash and had therefore totted up some impressive statistics. The FBI had made this the biggest investigation since the Kennedy assassination: 333 agents in fifty-one field offices had followed 1,897 leads through 1,551 interviews for a total of 14,098 man-hours.

The indictments handed down on September 15 named only Hunt, Liddy, and the five men arrested in the Democratic headquarters. My lengthy diary entry for that day indicates the relative unimportance I continued to attribute to Watergate at that time. In it I described a meeting with Nelson Rockefeller and a two-hour session on taxes with Connally, Burns, Shultz, Stein, and Ehrlichman; I reflected on several passages from Robert Blake's *Disraeli*, which I was currently rereading; I noted a conversation with Julie in which she was concerned about the way she had handled a reporter's question on Vietnam; I mentioned my concern because Pat was suffering from a prolonged earache but would not slow down her schedule; I commented on a recent radio speech by Connally; and I recounted a meeting in the Oval Office with singer Ray Charles. My only reference to Watergate was one short sentence near the end: "This was the day of the Watergate indictment, and we hope to be able to ride the issue through in a successful way from now on."

At Haldeman's suggestion, I saw John Dean later that day and thanked him for his work. I had known ever since the week after the break-in that Dean, as White House Counsel, was keeping track of all the different Watergate problems for us, including the FBI investigation, the grand jury, the Democratic civil suit, the libel suit Maury Stans had filed against Larry O'Brien and the CRP's countersuit against the DNC, and Texas Representative Wright Patman's attempt to hold pre-election hearings on the CRP's finances. Summing up his status report on these matters, Dean said, "Three months ago I would have had trouble predicting where we'd be today. I think that I can say that fifty-four days from now [Election Day] that not a thing will come crashing down to our—our surprise."

I said that the whole thing was a can of worms, and a lot of what had happened had been "awfully embarrassing." But I told Dean that the way he had handled it had been "very skillful, because you—putting your fingers in the dikes every time that leaks have sprung here and sprung there."

Dean covered the whole range of the different cases he was handling. The GAO report charging that the CRP had violated campaign finance rules had been referred to the Justice Department, Dean said, where there were reports of hundreds of other alleged violations—including charges against McGovern, Humphrey, and Jackson as well. The GAO was also planning to audit the use of funds by the White House staff. "I think we can be proud of the White House staff," Dean said, adding that the GAO would find nothing if they did investigate. Patman's unabashed partisan attempt to hold hearings on CRP finances was the next pre-election assault we faced. I told Dean that the whole thing was simply "public relations," and he agreed.

"We just take one at a time," Dean said.

"And you really can't just sit and worry yourself about it all the time, thinking 'the worst may happen' but it may not," I replied. "So you just try to button it up as well as you can and hope for the best...and remember that basically the damn thing is just one of those unfortunate things and, we're trying to cut our losses."

Then we turned to my long-time determination to restructure the bureaucracy in Washington—so that even if it were not favorable to us, at least it would no longer be serving the Democrats.

Two days later I recalled my impressions of this meeting.

Diary
I had a good talk with John Dean and was enormously impressed with him. I later told Haldeman, who said that he brought him into the White House, that he had the kind of steel and really mean instinct that we needed to clean house after the election in various departments and to put the IRS and the Justice Department on the kind of basis that it should be on. There simply has to be a line drawn at times with those who are against us; and then we have to take the action to deal with them effectively. Otherwise, they will be around to deal with us when their opportunity comes to them.

As the polls continued to indicate a Nixon landslide, McGovern and Shriver became desperate. They launched a strident campaign of personal attacks. McGovern said that my policy on Vietnam sought a "new level of barbarism" in order to save my own face. Three times he compared me to Hitler and the Republican Party to the Ku Klux Klan. He said that any working man who supported me "should have his head examined."

Shriver called me "Tricky Dicky," a "psychiatric case," "power-mad," the "greatest con artist" who spent most of the time "figuring out ways to keep America number one in the power to kill and destroy people abroad," and "the number-one bomber of all time." I told George Christian, President Johnson's former Press Secretary who was working with Connally in Democrats for Nixon, that Johnson should be pleased that Shriver had called *me* the number-one bomber. Christian laughed and said, "I don't believe so, Mr. President. LBJ never likes to be number two in anything."

While these increasingly shrill and acrimonious charges were being hurled against me I continued to stay on the job in the White House, aloof from the rising emotional tides of the campaign. Some diary notes I made after a weekend at Camp David in early September convey the striking contrast between the campaign as I experienced it and as McGovern and Shriver waged it.

Diary

Around noon, since it was such a beautiful day—clear blue—I went into the pool for a while. It was one of those days when I was able to lie on my back and look up at the leaves. I was reminded of the fact that in the spring the leaves turned over in the wind and the leaves in the spring and the fall were really so very much alike. One portrays the beginning of summer, the other the beginning of winter—one the beginning of life, the other the beginning of death.

I expect the situation to get rougher in the next week and throughout. It is very clear that McGovern had finally learned that what he has to do is simply to attack and he is doing so in a very vicious and irresponsible way. Our people, of course, as I pointed out to Colson, are reacting in their usual honest and stupid way, by defending rather than attacking.

McGovern's going to all the big cities at this time for street rallies is an indication of their desperation because eight weeks before the election is much too soon to hit the big cities.

My campaign was running like clockwork. Ted Agnew, Clark MacGregor, Bob Dole, and their teams were doing a magnificent job. They were not only effective spokesmen for the administration but kept McGovern on the defensive with sharp thrusts against his far-left views. In September I began adding some political appearances to my schedule, but it was still the most restrained campaign of my career; consequently, I remember it primarily as a series of episodes.

179

One of the most memorable was a campaign trip I made to Texas on September 22 that ended with an enthusiastic Democrats for Nixon barbecue at the Connally ranch.

Diary

I told Connally as we were sitting around about 11:30 or 12 it is vitally important that Teddy Kennedy not pick up the pieces after this election. It is important that people like John Connally pick them up because the country simply can't afford to have the likes of Kennedy and McGovern as even possible Presidents in the years ahead.

Pat pointed out a New York *Times* article on Mrs. McGovern said that the Nixons were from the fifties and the McGoverns from the seventies. I just hope the press continues to think this way because in the end they're going to take a hell of a beating.

I woke up twice in the night, once at 2, and once at 4—even though I was terribly tired when I went to bed. Finally at 7 o'clock I woke up again. When I got up, opened the blinds, looked out on beautiful green countryside, at the cows in the pasture, rang for breakfast, to my great pleasure instead of my wheat germ they insisted on sending in some of their country sausage, which was totally and perfectly delicious. I am going to have to mix up the breakfasts and lunches just a bit in order to get away from such a drab and uninteresting diet.

At the end of September George McGovern received the official editorial endorsement of the New York *Times*. The Washington *Post* withheld a formal endorsement but made clear its preference for McGovern. In my diary I noted my reaction when I heard about the *Times*'s endorsement: "I said that I learned the news with relief because I didn't want anybody on the staff to urge me to meet with their editorial board and thank God we had not done so. Nobody had had the temerity to suggest that I do so. And as I pointed out to Haldeman there should be a letter to the *Times* or a statement that the *Times* basically *should* endorse McGovern because he stood for everything they stood for—permissiveness, a bug-out from Vietnam, new isolationism, etc."

The *Post*'s decision came as no surprise either. On June 26 I had dictated this note on a report Kissinger gave me from columnist Stewart Alsop, who had been to dinner with the paper's publisher: "Henry told me of an interesting conversation he had had with Stewart Alsop. Stewart, apparently, is still critically ill and had been out to dinner with Kay Graham. He had been arguing emphatically with regard to the necessity to support RN because of what he had accomplished in foreign policy, and also the danger of having McGovern in the presidency. He said that Kay Graham finally blew up and said, " 'I hate him and I'm going to do everything I can to beat him.' "

On September 26 we held a dinner in New York for campaign contributors. One encounter during that evening particularly stayed in my mind.

Diary
 One thing that made a very great impression upon me was when a relatively young man—at least he seemed young to me; I would imagine he was forty, he could have been forty-five—said to me that he'd lost his son in Vietnam in 1970 and he was still for me and for my foreign policy.
 When I think of such men as this and the mothers of the boys as well as their wives, I realize how very important it is to see not only that we end the war, but that we end it in a way that will make their sacrifices not be in vain, which is what I told him as we were being hauled away.

The crowd that turned out to greet Pat and me in Atlanta on October 12 was estimated at between 500,000 and 700,000. To the dismay of the Secret Service, a man in the crowd outside the hotel grabbed me and shouted above the noise, "Thanks for making the South a part of America again." I later told Ehrlichman, "The South is teaching the Democratic Party a lesson about patriotism."

 During a long motorcade in Ohio I was warned that

there were some unfriendly demonstrators waiting for us a short way ahead. Since there had also been a bomb threat, the Secret Service wanted to close the top of my car and increase the speed during this particular part of the route.

Diary

One thing I did do was when the Secret Service wanted to speed up, I told them to slow down. I said we must not run from these people, so we slowed down to a snail's pace and I waved out the window, as did Pat on the other side, at all the nutheads in the nasty crowd.

When I saw some of the antiwar people and the rest, I'd simply hold up the "V" or the one thumb up; this really knocks them for a loop, because they think this is their sign. Some of them break out into a smile. Others, of course, just become more hateful. I think as the war recedes as an issue, some of these people are going to be lost souls. They basically are haters, they are frustrated, they are alienated—they don't know what to do with their lives.

I think perhaps the saddest group will be those who are the professors and particularly the younger professors and the associate professors on the college campuses and even in the high schools. They wanted to blame somebody else for their own failures to inspire the students.

I can think of those Ivy League presidents who came to see me after Kent State, and who were saying, please don't leave the problem to us—I mean, let the government do something. None of them would take any of the responsibility themselves.

Now the responsibility is theirs, although I imagine they will find another issue. The black power thing is gone—the environment has fizzled out—the war will be gone—the question is, what next? I suppose it will be big business or corruption or what have you, but it will be difficult to find one that emotionally will turn the kids on like the war issue.

It will be good that the college administrators and professors will have to look within themselves—look in the mirror—and realize that it is they who have the

182

responsibility—that they are at fault if the young people are not inspired. They can't blame it on government or anybody else.

Although my direct involvement in the campaign was limited, it was intense. By the end of the campaign I had made dozens of speeches and informal remarks.

Diary
I had a rather curious dream of speaking at some sort of a rally and going a bit too long and Rockefeller standing up in the middle and taking over the microphone on an applause line. Of course, this is always something that worries a person when he is making speeches, as to whether he is going too long. It is a subconscious reaction. It is interesting.

Since my strategy was to minimize my own campaigning, my family took over the burden of crisscrossing the country making appearances. All together, Pat, Julie, and Tricia covered seventy-seven cities in thirty-seven states in the nine weeks from the end of August to Election Day. David was in the Navy and had to stay on the sidelines, but Ed Cox plunged right in and went onto college campuses to face some of the toughest audiences of all. His easy manner and quick, organized mind enabled him to hold his own and make a strong impression everywhere he went.

In all their speeches and in all their press conferences, there was never a misspoken word. They were heckled, shoved, hissed, and subjected to obscene shouts from demonstrators, but they pressed on like professionals, with poise and grace. Even when Pat was being cursed by angry young men and women in Boston, she was serene and natural—which infuriated them even more; I am sure they had no idea how much they hurt her. Tricia passed on to us her strategy when confronted by a crowd of burly demonstrators: "Please," she would say quietly, "don't push the children."

Julie, who was steely enough to mean it when she said that she would give her life for South Vietnam's freedom, was soft enough to leave the dinner table in tears when she thought about how David, who loved politics so much, would miss the election because his ship would be in the Mediterranean.

Diary

Julie called me after the Gromyko dinner, very thoughtfully waiting until then, to ask me about whether she could go to see David since he could not return for the election. I, of course, approved it all the way.

To hell with the election if it interferes with a few days that they may have together at this time when it means so much to them.

I recall that in 1960, after the defeat, Julie was the one who at least as far as her open feelings were concerned really never gave up. I remember going in to her bedroom at the Forest Lane house just to kiss her good night, and she would say, "Daddy, can't we still win?" This was two weeks or so after the election.

In 1960 during the first debate she had been worried about whether Daddy had won or not. Tricia had very loyally stepped up and said, "Of course he did."

I remember in 1962 the reaction was somewhat different. Julie had said congratulations on taking on the press after the election, whereas Tricia seemed more reserved and more worried about it.

Looking back that ten years I certainly made it hard for the family with my own reactions and I shall never forget how when I told them we were going to New York, Tricia went in and tore up all her notebooks. They had really hated the school in California because of the number of Birchers that were always giving them hell.

I knew that the road had been hardest of all for Pat. For almost twenty years of public life she had been wife, mother, and full-time campaigner. She had done it all not because she loved the attention or reveled in the publicity—she didn't. She had done it because she believed in me. And she had done it magnificently. Now she was loved by millions, and no woman ever deserved it more. My deepest hope was that she felt that it had all been worth it.

As we anticipated, the summer of 1972 produced another series of propaganda maneuvers by Hanoi in an attempt to exploit American domestic opinion. This time they used the ploy of claiming—falsely—that American bombers were deliberately hitting the crucial system of dikes and dams in North Vietnam in order to kill large civilian populations in the resulting floods. Antiwar leaders accepted these claims uncritically. Teddy Kennedy charged that we had a "policy of deliberately bombing dikes." In one of my press conferences I tried to introduce at least an element of logic regarding this charge: if in fact we had decided on a policy of deliberately bombing the dikes and dams, we could have destroyed the entire system in a week. But despite all the propaganda claims, no major junctures were hit and there were no massive floods.

On July 27 former Attorney General Ramsey Clark, the man described by George McGovern as "perfect for head of the FBI if you could get him," left for Hanoi under the auspices of a Swedish group inquiring into "U.S. crimes in Indochina." He made a broadcast over Radio Hanoi stating that our bombing should be stopped immediately. On August 12 he told reporters that he had visited a POW camp and found the health of the American POWs "better than mine, and I am a healthy man." On Clark's return, Teddy Kennedy had him come to Capitol Hill to testify on the good treatment the POWs were receiving.

While Clark was in Hanoi, Shriver waded in, "revealing" that the Nixon administration, as he put it, "blew" a historic opportunity for peace in 1969 when I failed to follow up on progress that had been made in the Paris peace talks during the last months of the Johnson administration. Shriver also claimed that he had resigned as ambassador to France in protest of my war policy. Bill Rogers was furious when he heard about this. He publicly denounced Shriver's claims as "bunk" and political fantasy. Rogers's statement was particularly effective; it was characteristic of the forceful and articulate way he defended my foreign policy in public forums during the campaign. The next day the State Department released Shriver's letter of resignation as ambassador. It was hardly a protest. On the contrary, he wrote that he had "accomplished the objectives I went to Paris to achieve—the beginnings at least of peace in Vietnam and the reawakening of friendship between the U.S.A. and France."

Connally called me to say that President Johnson was "mad as hell" about Shriver's charge. Johnson had indicated that his already minimal support for McGovern would be even less because of this incident. Johnson called Haldeman to tell him that he had never informed Shriver of what was going on in the Paris negotiations. "I never trusted him, the SOB, not even then," Johnson said.

A few days after Ramsey Clark returned from Hanoi, a UPI report revealed that Pierre Salinger, on George McGovern's instructions, had directly approached the North Vietnamese delegation in Paris. His purpose was to see if the Communists would release some American POWs. The goal was laudable, but the contact had all the earmarks of a political ploy. Moreover, the Logan Act prohibits a private citizen from unauthorized contacts with foreign governments with the intent to influence disputes between our government and theirs. McGovern, therefore, had some serious questions to answer about the Salinger mission.

When confronted with this story, McGovern told reporters, "Pierre Salinger had no instructions whatsoever from me." Salinger evidently was stupefied by this statement, because McGovern had not only sent him on the mission but had made the arrangements through a prominent antiwar leader. McGovern had been caught in a serious and discreditable falsehood.

All McGovern's efforts to attack me on the war were to no avail. At the end of August we received word that public support of my conduct of the war had actually risen. A Harris poll found in early September that 55 percent supported continued heavy bombing of North Vietnam, 64 percent supported the mining of Haiphong Harbor, and 74 percent thought it was important that South Vietnam not fall into the hands of the Communists. McGovern and his followers were out of touch with the majority of the American people. But the North Vietnamese, who were avid observers of American public opinion, apparently got the message.

After three years of disappointing and unproductive stalemate the U.S.–North Vietnamese private channel suddenly became active in August 1972. For the first time the Communists actually seemed to be interested in reaching a settlement. Kissinger and I assumed that they had come to the conclusion that McGovern did not stand a chance of becoming President and had therefore decided to explore the possibility that they could get better terms from me before the election than after it. In addition they were undoubtedly concerned by our contacts with Moscow and Peking and with the success of Vietnamization; we knew also that the May 8 mining and bombing had taken a heavy military toll.

At a two-day session on September 26 and 27 the North Vietnamese presented a new ten-point program. Although it was more forthcoming than anything in the past, on the key political and military issues it was still unacceptable. The next meeting, scheduled for October 8, would clearly be the decisive one for determining whether the new momentum could carry through to a settlement before the November 7 election. I was not optimistic in this regard, but I decided to orchestrate as much pressure on the meeting as possible.

When Soviet Foreign Minister Andrei Gromyko arrived in Washington for the signing of the SALT agreement on October 3, I invited him to come to Camp David. When he repeated the familiar refrain that U.S.–Soviet relations could improve if the problem of Vietnam were removed, I told him that when Kissinger returned to Paris the next week, he would lay on the table the last offer we were going to make. If the North Vietnamese said no, then the negotiating track would be closed and we would have to turn to some other methods after the elections.

It seemed unlikely that, even if the North Vietnamese wanted to, we would be able to negotiate an acceptable agreement in just five weeks. Nonetheless I felt that we should prepare Thieu for the outside possibility that the Communists really were determined to conclude a settlement before our election. Haig flew to Saigon and assured Thieu that we would not rush headlong into an agreement. But he also described the difficult domestic situation we would face if the Communists made a reasonable offer and we refused to act upon it. Then they would be able to put the blame on Thieu for blocking peace.

Thieu was visibly shaken. He was suspicious of the motives behind the North Vietnamese proposals and unsettled by our willingness to accept them as even a basis for negotiations. He railed against Kissinger, who, he said, did not "deign" to consider Saigon's views in his negotiations. Haig tried to reassure him. Finally Thieu broke into tears.

I sympathized with Thieu's position. Almost the entire North Vietnamese Army—an estimated 120,000 troops that had poured across the DMZ during the spring invasion—were still in South Vietnam, and he was naturally skeptical of any plan that would lead to an American withdrawal without requiring a corresponding North Vietnamese withdrawal. I shared his view that the Communists' motives were entirely cynical. I knew, as he did, that they would observe the agreement only so long and so far as South Vietnam's strength and America's readiness to retaliate forced them to do so. But I felt that if we could negotiate an agreement on our terms, those conditions could be met. I sent Thieu a personal message: "I give you my firm assurance that there will be no settlement arrived at, the provisions of which have not been discussed personally with you well beforehand." Knowing his penchant for headstrong action, however, I reminded him of the dangers inherent in stirring up his domestic situation as well as our own.

On October 5 we received word of a recent conversation between Premier Pham Van Dong of North Vietnam and the French Delegate General in Hanoi. For the first time Dong had sounded optimistic regarding the likelihood of peace. He had admitted that his experts had paid too much attention to American antiwar leaders and added that I would probably have a freer hand after the election.

In my press conference that same day the questions focused on the prospects for a peace settlement before the election. I replied that in no circumstances would the election determine the character of our negotiations: "If we can make the right kind of a settlement before the election, we will make it. If we cannot, we are not going to make the wrong kind of a settlement before the election."

As the October 8 meeting approached, I felt that we

had done everything possible to encourage Hanoi toward a settlement: their troops were being pounded by our renewed bombing, and now presumably the Soviet leaders would be urging the North Vietnamese to take the best terms they could get and end the war before the election. In the meantime, the prospects of my re-election by a landslide were increasing every day.

Kissinger and Haig arrived in Paris on Sunday, October 8, for the crucial meeting with the North Vietnamese. That evening they sent a brief reporting cable: "Tell the President that there has been some definite progress at today's first session and that he can harbor some confidence the outcome will be positive."

On Monday Kissinger reported that the meetings were tense and volatile but that "we are at a crucial point." On Tuesday we received only a one-paragraph message that was more tantalizing than enlightening: "The negotiations during this round have been so complex and sensitive that we have been unable to report their content in detail due to the danger of compromise. We know exactly what we are doing, and just as we have not let you down in the past, we will not do so now."

That night George McGovern made a much-heralded nationally televised campaign speech on Vietnam. He said that on the day he was inaugurated President, he would stop all bombing and begin the immediate withdrawal of all American troops and military equipment from South Vietnam. He also committed himself to stop all military and economic aid to Saigon. He had no plan for ensuring the return of the POWs but said that he expected Hanoi to respond favorably to his policies. James Reston wrote that McGovern "went so far in meeting Hanoi's war aims that he may actually have lost more support by his TV speech than he gained." Joseph Kraft said of McGovern's speech that "apparently without knowing it, he is prepared to accept worse terms than the other side is offering."

On October 11 Kissinger reported only that both sides had decided to stay another day in the anticipation that they were sufficiently close to a major breakthrough. On that day we established a ten-mile bombing-free circle around Hanoi.

Kissinger and Haig arrived back at the White House on the evening of October 12 and came immediately to the EOB office to report to me.

Since the first days of the administration Kissinger and I had talked about the "Big Three" in foreign policy—China, the Soviet Union, and Vietnam—and our goals involving each of them. So far we had succeeded with two of them: we had achieved an opening to China and we had embarked upon a new relationship with the U.S.S.R. Only the third goal—a settlement of the war in Vietnam—had continued to elude us. As Kissinger began his report of the Paris negotiations, he was smiling the broadest smile I had ever seen. "Well, Mr. President," he said, "it looks like we've got three out of three!"

He described the negotiating sessions in great detail. After some rhetoric and bluster, Le Duc Tho had presented a new proposal that met almost all our major requirements: there would be a cease-fire, followed in sixty days by the withdrawal of American forces and the return of POWs on both sides. The North Vietnamese would not specifically agree to withdraw their troops from the South because they maintained the fiction that they had no troops in South Vietnam at all. This charade was particularly galling to Thieu. Now Kissinger had brought back terms that would achieve our and Thieu's objective while allowing the North Vietnamese to save face: no troop withdrawals would be required of them, but the provisions of the agreement regulating the replacement of forces and closing the border sanctuaries in Laos and Cambodia would effectively cut them off from their source of supplies and force them either to return to the North or gradually to wither away in the South. The Communists had finally dropped their demands for a coalition government and had agreed to the face-saving substitute of a National Council of Reconciliation and Concord to be composed of representatives of the government, the Vietcong, and neutral members. Unanimity would be required in its votes; thus Thieu would be protected from being outvoted by the Communists and their supporters. Equally significant, they dropped their demand that Thieu resign. These provisions alone amounted to a complete capitulation by the enemy: they were accepting a settlement on our terms.

There was also a provision embodying the principle of American economic aid to North Vietnam, which I considered to be potentially the most significant part of the entire agreement. The Communists tried to claim that this money would be reparations for the war they charged we had unleashed upon them; but however they tried to justify it, taking money from the United States represented a collapse of communist principle. More important, our aid would inevitably give us increasing leverage with Hanoi as the North Vietnamese people began to taste the fruits of peace for the first time in twenty-five years.

Several unresolved issues remained to be negotiated at a final session in Paris on October 17. Only two of them were major. The first involved the release of Vietnamese civilian prisoners. The North Vietnamese would be accused of betraying their Vietcong allies unless they tried to secure their release as part of the agreement. The second involved the provision for replacement of war matériel by both sides. The Communists wanted it done on the "principle of equality." Neither we nor the South Vietnamese could ever accept this, however, because it would immediately reduce the arms advantage that South Vietnam held over the Vietcong, which we saw as essential for maintaining the peace. Our position was that worn-out existing armaments should be replaced on a one-to-one basis.

Cautioning Le Duc Tho that I would have to review the agreement and approve it, Kissinger had agreed that after the final session in Paris on October 17, he would go to Saigon for three days in order to present the agreement to Thieu and to obtain his approval of it. Kissinger would then go to Hanoi on October 22, where he would initial the agreement with the North Vietnamese leaders. He would return to Washington, and a joint announcement would be made on October 26. The cease-fire would begin on October 30, when the agreement would be signed in Paris by the Foreign Minister of each party.

I asked that some steaks be brought over on trays from the White House mess, and I asked Manolo to bring a bottle of Château Lafite-Rothschild so that we could toast Kissinger's success. I noticed that Haig seemed rather subdued, but I assumed that he was just tired after the exertions of the last few days. Finally I asked him directly how he felt about these terms from Thieu's point of view. He replied that he honestly felt this was a good deal for Thieu. He was worried, however, about how Thieu himself would react to it.

Kissinger had promised to let the North Vietnamese know my reaction within forty-eight hours after his return to Washington. The next day, I instructed the Pentagon to reduce our bombing of North Vietnam to 200 sorties and ordered restrictions on B-52 raids. That night we sent a message to Paris: "The President accepts the basic draft for an 'agreement on ending the war and restoring peace in Vietnam' except for some technical issues to be discussed between Minister Xuan Thuy and Dr. Kissinger on October 17, and subject to the following substantive changes without which the U.S. side cannot accept the document." One of the changes I asked for was the deletion of a paragraph that tied various military obligations of the two South Vietnamese parties—the Saigon government and the Vietcong—to political sections of the agreement. We wanted political matters to be covered solely in the political chapter. Two other changes clarified ambiguities in the text.

The North Vietnamese replied with an official note saying that they felt we were demanding changes in points that had already been agreed upon. They said that only minor technical changes could now be considered and demanded that we not make changes like the ones I had listed. The election deadline was clearly a two-way street: just as we would use it to pressure them to accept our terms, they would try to use it to stampede us into a hasty and ill-considered settlement.

Therefore when I read this message I told Kissinger that in no circumstances should we consider any terms that we felt were less than acceptable.

Diary

I said that as far as the election was concerned, a settlement would not particularly help us, that there were risks insofar if Thieu blew it or the North Vietnamese blew it which could hurt us. But nothing that happened could be fatal—it could probably just narrow the gap. Under the circumstances, we had to do what was right. As I pointed out to him, if it was the right time to settle the war and if this was the right plan we should not delay it until after the election, when the pressures upon the enemy might be less than now.

My study of previous settlements indicates that there come pressure points when a settlement can be made, and if the opportunity is missed then the war will drag on for months, and even years, before it comes again. This probably is one of those pressure points. It is an opportunity we must play out to the hilt, because we would never forgive ourselves if we miss this opportunity and then had the election go by and found that the thing would drag on and on. In any event, we have it in the right posture now. We will do what is right without any regard for what effect it will have on the election, and that will probably turn out best for the election as well.

Kissinger raised the possibility of a bombing halt as a demonstration of good will on our part. I ordered another reduction of our daily attack sorties from 200 to 150, but there was no question that a total bombing halt would be a far more dramatic action. I told him, however, that I was absolutely opposed to one before the election. If everything worked out satisfactorily in Paris and Saigon and he was able to go on to Hanoi, then I would consider a bombing *pause* for the few days he was there. But there would be no bombing *halt* until the agreement was signed. I was not going to be taken in by the mere prospect of an agreement as Johnson had been in 1968. Just before Kissinger left for Paris, I gave him a letter I had written the night before. In it I told him to do what is right for an honorable peace, without regard to the election.

Kissinger's meeting with Xuan Thuy on October 17 was tense and pressured. On the prisoner issue, Kissinger rejected as unacceptable the Communist position that we free all Vietcong civilians held by Saigon; some of these prisoners were terrorist murderers. Kissinger told Xuan Thuy that the South Vietnamese would never accept this and there was no point in his writing down something that could not be implemented. The Communists also opposed our strict interpretation of the provisions for the replacement of war matériel and failed to give us satisfactory language regarding American POWs being held in Laos and Cambodia. It was obvious that there would have to be some slippage in the schedule for completion. They pushed for Kissinger to settle the remaining issues in Hanoi. Knowing my adamant views on this point, Kissinger replied that he could not go to Hanoi until we had a completed agreement. Although some of the points were left unresolved, Kissinger departed for Saigon. He had already cautioned the Communists that Thieu had to be consulted before we would sign any agreement. Kissinger had only been able to schedule three days in Saigon to go over the agreement, even though he knew Thieu would be skeptical about its terms and unhappy that it had been suddenly and unexpectedly concluded without his participation. There was no question that the North Vietnamese were trying to use the pressure of the election deadline to strain our relations with Thieu and to create domestic political problems for him by making it appear that the agreement was being imposed on him from Washington without allowing him time to prepare his public opinion for some of its superficially less than advantageous terms. But Kissinger had gambled that Thieu would overlook such problems and seize the tremendous advantages the agreement would give him if he approached it positively and treated it like the victory it was.

The next day I sent a note to the North Vietnamese informing them that, in my opinion, another meeting would be needed before Kissinger could go to Hanoi and before we could stop the bombing. I reiterated that the questions relating to civilian prisoners and replacement of matériel still had to be settled, as well as understandings relating to the withdrawal of North Vietnamese forces from Laos and Cambodia. I offered a new schedule that would extend the original one for three or four days to allow another meeting between Kissinger and Le Duc Tho. I added that as a sign of good will we would maintain the current restrictions on bombing sorties and B-52 raids while the negotiations were in progress, and I reaffirmed my intention to complete the agreement within the proposed new schedule.

The North Vietnamese were now clearly determined to

get a pre-election agreement. They sent a reply completely accepting our position on the questions of arms replacement and unconditional release of our POWs in North Vietnam. I sent a cable to Pham Van Dong saying that the agreement could now be considered complete. Only the matter of the unilateral declarations, which included the arrangements for a cease-fire and the return of American POWs in Laos and Cambodia, still had to be clarified, and I therefore suggested a further twenty-four-hour delay so that these questions could be considered and settled. I said that once these problems had been taken care of, we could be counted on to proceed with the schedule as amended, leading to the signing on October 31. On October 21 the North Vietnamese replied by accepting our position on the unilateral declarations.

When Kissinger arrived in Saigon on October 18, he carried with him a letter I had written to Thieu. In it I said, "I believe we have no reasonable alternative but to accept this agreement." I assured Thieu that I would view any breach of faith by the Communists with the utmost gravity.

Kissinger found Thieu polite but noncommittal. During one tense and emotional session with the entire South Vietnamese National Security Council and the ambassadors to the Paris talks, he was bombarded with skeptical questions. Reporting afterward, Kissinger said that the South Vietnamese leaders had exhibited a surprising awe of Communist cunning and a disquieting lack of confidence in themselves. It was clear that they were having great psychological difficulty with the prospect of cutting the American umbilical cord. As Kissinger saw the situation, we were up against a paradoxical situation in which North Vietnam, which had in effect lost the war, was acting as if it had won; while South Vietnam, which had effectively won the war, was acting as if it had lost.

There were undoubtedly psychological reasons for this attitude, but there were also practical personal, political, diplomatic, and military factors behind Thieu's conduct. Because of the way the U.S. media portrayed Thieu, many Americans thought of him as a petty tyrant who suppressed his political opponents. Political dissent was substantially curtailed in South Vietnam, but Thieu still had to deal with an elected National Assembly and face a formidable range of open domestic political opposition. It was by no means certain that he could survive in power unless he could convince his people that the peace agreement was one that would benefit South Vietnam. They had fought and sacrificed too much and they knew the enemy too well to be seduced by the Communists' professed sincerity or willingness to abide by the terms of any agreement. They were the ones who would have to remain in their country after the last Americans had left, and they were naturally reluctant to accept any agreement that might put them at a disadvantage. Since the provisions of any agreement were bound to be controversial, Thieu would have to make it clear that he was neither surrendering any of South Vietnam's vital interests nor accepting terms dictated to him by Washington. The problem was that this would take time, and time was the one thing we did not have if we were to keep to the agreed signing schedule.

Thieu would also be concerned about the military consequences of an immediate agreement. Many military analysts believed that the North Vietnamese were so insistent on keeping October 31 as the deadline for a cease-fire agreement because they had geared up to capture and control as much territory in South Vietnam as possible by that date. As early as the beginning of October a captured COSVN directive had revealed plans to draw South Vietnamese forces into the northern regions so that the provinces in the Mekong Delta and around Saigon would be vulnerable to a last-minute offensive; the document also set out plans for terrorist activities after the cease-fire. Haig was seriously concerned about this.

Diary

Haig believes the real problem is the fact that the North Vietnamese are moving very, very strongly around Saigon at this time to get as much territory as they can. Some of the intelligence indicates that they instructed their cadres the moment a cease-fire is announced to kill all of the opponents in the areas that they control.

This would be a murderous bloodbath, and it's something that we have to consider as we press Thieu to accept what is without question a reasonable political settlement but which must also be justified on security grounds.

On October 20 we began Operation Enhance Plus, a massive airlift of military equipment and supplies to South Vietnam. If the agreement was signed on schedule on October 31, we would have to adhere immediately to its provisions for limited matériel replacement. Therefore it was important to complete as much of the envisaged Vietnamization as possible before the cutoff deadline.

I wanted to make sure once again that Kissinger understood my feelings about not rushing to reach a settlement before the election and about not forcing a break with Thieu by pushing him too fast, so that night I sent him another cable:

> As you continue discussions with Thieu, I wish to re-emphasize again that nothing that is done should be influenced by the U.S. election deadline. I have concluded that a settlement which takes place before the election which is, at best, a washout, has a high risk of severely damaging the U.S. domestic scene, if the settlement were to open us up to the charge that we made a poorer settlement now than what we might have achieved had we waited until after the election . . . .
>
> As I outlined yesterday, we must have Thieu as a willing partner in making any agreement. It cannot be a shotgun marriage.

On October 21 Dobrynin delivered what he described as an urgent message from Brezhnev. The North Vietnamese had complained to him that we were reneging on our agreement and he wanted to let us know that the Soviet government expected us to adhere to the proposed schedule.

Also that day word reached Washington that Pham Van Dong had given an exclusive two-hour interview to Arnaud de Borchgrave of *Newsweek*. When asked whether Thieu could be part of a tripartite coalition government after the cease-fire, Dong had given the opposite impression of what the North Vietnamese had agreed to in Paris. He replied that the National Council of Reconciliation and Concord might actually be or become a coalition government.

This was bound to infuriate Thieu and make it even more difficult for him to accept the agreement.

The North Vietnamese were pursuing a cleverly calculated strategy. By agreeing to every point we raised they were building a perfect record in the event they decided to publicize the story of the negotiations. By positioning the agreement as a Communist victory—as Dong had done with de Borchgrave—they were not only saving face domestically and internationally but initiating a psychological battle against Thieu. And by such heavy-handed ploys as deliberately changing words in their translation of the text of the agreement into Vietnamese, they were trying to create friction and suspicion between Saigon and Washington. Thus, even as they were reeling from the effects of our bombing and mining and were troubled by our relationship with their allies in Moscow and Peking, the North Vietnamese were trying to achieve the stunning irony of accomplishing from a position of weakness what they had not been able to attain from a position of strength. They were trying to drive a wedge between us and Thieu; if they succeeded, they might yet use our public opinion to force us to withdraw and give them the chance they wanted to destroy Thieu's government and conquer South Vietnam. I was determined not to let them succeed.

I had Haig send Kissinger another cable on October 21, urging him to push Thieu as far as possible, short of actually making him break with us. I added that if there appeared to be no chance of obtaining Thieu's agreement, Kissinger should inform him that we would have to consider making a separate agreement with the enemy. At this point this was not something I considered doing or that I thought would be necessary, but I wanted to impress Thieu with the seriousness of my determination to complete a settlement as soon as the terms were right.

In Kissinger's judgment the problem was not so much that Thieu would reject the agreement outright and provoke us into breaking with him as that he would stall without giving any answer and thus force us past the signing deadline. He therefore proposed that, in the absence of any indication of Thieu's reaction to the agreement, or even in the event that he refused to go along with it, he should go on to Hanoi as scheduled. With urgent eloquence he pointed out that cancellation of "the final leg," as he called it, would cause many difficult problems, of which the most serious was his continuing conviction that once our election was over the Communists would feel far less pressure to settle and might decide to resume fighting:

> In recent weeks we have played a tough, ruthless game of using our election deadline as blackmail against the other side. In this process we have obtained concessions that nobody thought were possible last month, or for that matter last week. . . .
> Washington must understand that this is not a Sunday school picnic. We are dealing with fanatics who have been fighting for twenty-five years and have recently lost the cream of their manhood in the war. They have taken very painful decisions to make the major concessions they have. We cannot be sure how long they will be willing to settle on the terms that are now within our grasp. To wash out the final leg could cost us dearly.

I felt strongly, however, that the North Vietnamese would exploit Kissinger's presence in Hanoi as a propaganda victory and use it to turn American public opinion against Thieu, and I refused to consider the final leg as an option unless and until the settlement had been agreed to by all parties.

On the morning of October 21 Kissinger met with a South Vietnamese working group headed by the Foreign Minister, who opened the session with a prayer and then presented twenty-three proposed changes in the draft agreement. Kissinger immediately accepted sixteen of them as minor and probably manageable. The remaining seven, however, raised impossible demands, including the specified withdrawal of North Vietnamese troops from South Vietnam and the virtual elimination of the National Council of Reconciliation and Concord. He explained that the Communist forces, already weakened by battle and deprived of reinforcements, would eventually wither away; he also pointed out that with the unanimity required for any vote, the Council would end up being a protection rather than a handicap for Saigon. The meeting was cordial, and Kissinger felt that he had been able to present his arguments persuasively. But there was still no word from Thieu, and time was passing. In his cable after the meeting with the South Vietnamese working group Kissinger said:

> I have requested an appointment with Thieu this evening to determine his intentions. Clearly we cannot wait much longer to make our choice since we are rapidly becoming prisoner of events. In retrospect, it is now clear that I made a mistake in agreeing to a fixed date for the final leg. Doing so got us more concessions than any of us thought possible, but it is clearly making us pay at this end. That is water over the dam. I think when you read the records of our talks here you will find that we have been extremely patient with Thieu.

In the meantime the North Vietnamese accepted our formulation of the unilateral declarations regarding Laos and Cambodia. I immediately sent a letter to Kissinger for him to give to Thieu when they met. In it I said that I had now studied the entire agreement, including Hanoi's recent concessions, with the utmost care, and I urged him to accept it for the most practical and compelling reasons:

> Were you to find the agreement to be unacceptable at this point and the other side were to reveal the extraordinary limits to which it has gone in meeting demands put upon them, it is my judgment that your decision would have the most serious effects upon my ability to continue to provide support for you and for the government of South Vietnam.

As the presidential campaign moved through the summer and fall of 1972, the conventional political wisdom was that I might try to turn the war to my political advantage by producing a settlement right before the election. It was ironic that, primarily because of McGovern's extremism, but also because of his inept campaign, the political pressure turned out to be exactly the opposite. The opinion polls confirmed my own intuition that, in terms of voter support, my handling of the war was generally viewed as a positive issue for me and a negative one for McGovern, who was perceived as weak and favoring surrender. Therefore any settlement that was hastily completed in time for the election would look cynical and suspicious. The hawks would charge, however unfairly, that I had given away too much in order to meet a self-serving deadline, and the doves would claim, however erroneously, that I could have obtained the same terms in 1969.

As Kissinger pointed out, the risk in waiting until after the election was that the Communists might decide to keep fighting. I was prepared to step up the bombing after the election, but there was no way of knowing whether that would make them adopt a more reasonable position before the American public's patience ran out, before the bombing began to create serious problems with the Chinese and Soviets or before Congress just voted us out of the war.

Diary
> The problem, of course, is that we just don't know whether the enemy has a breaking point or, if it has, when it will come. We don't know, too, whether that situation may become too difficult for us from a political standpoint in the United States after the election, despite the fact that we may win a very significant mandate.
>
> I am inclined to think that the better bargaining time for us would be immediately after the election rather than before. Before the election the enemy can still figure there is an outside chance their man can win or at least that he could come closer and that we, therefore, would be under pressure to have a settlement.
>
> Immediately after the election we will have an enormous mandate, we hope, for bringing the war to a successful conclusion, and the enemy then either has to settle or face the consequences of what we could do to them.

My advisers differed about whether it would be easier to get a peace settlement before the election or after it. Kissinger felt strongly that the North Vietnamese would be under much more pressure to negotiate before the election because they would expect to get better terms from me while the war was still an issue in the campaign. He was concerned that once the election had passed, they might revert to their earlier intransigence and let the war drag on at a reduced level in the hope that American public opinion would eventually force us to withdraw.

Others, Haig among them, felt that the North Vietnamese would be more likely to make concessions after the election when I would be armed with a landslide mandate and when I would at any rate be less constrained than I had been during my first term. Personally, I leaned toward this opinion, but I was completely prepared to conclude an agreement before the election if the North Vietnamese would agree to the terms we required and if Thieu could be persuaded to come along. Thieu's apparent determination to postpone an agreement as long as possible presented us with a difficult problem. The knowledge that the North Vietnamese were playing out a cleverly calculated strategy aimed at separating us from Thieu and getting us over a barrel in terms of public opinion did not make that problem any easier to handle.

So far, in fact, it looked as if the North Vietnamese strategy had succeeded. If the negotiating record were made public, it would show that they had virtually capitulated and agreed to everything we required. If we now decided to delay signing the agreement because of Thieu's objections to it, or if we demanded changes in it because of him, then the North Vietnamese were likely to go public with their case and demand that we sign. Thus Thieu would be isolated as the sole obstacle to peace. American public opinion would be stirred up against him by the antiwar leaders and the media, and there would be tremendous pressure brought to bear to jettison him and sign the agreement on our own.

I did not feel that I could let this happen. Even in November, when Thieu's conduct became infuriating, I still felt that if we abandoned him South Vietnam would fall to the Communists within a matter of months, and our entire effort there would have been for naught. I was confident that Thieu would eventually join us in signing an agreement at some point before Congress returned in January and took matters out of our hands by voting to cut off all appropriations for the war and for aid to South Vietnam. So while I hoped that Thieu would accept the agreement before the November election, I was prepared to give him until the end of December to make whatever domestic preparations he felt were necessary before agreeing to sign. In the meantime,

I felt that the most important thing was to keep the negotiations going.

On Sunday, October 22, at 8 A.M. in Saigon, Kissinger was finally summoned to Thieu's office. If Thieu had decided to go along, there would still be time for Kissinger to go to Hanoi as we had agreed and for the agreement to be signed in Paris according to the schedule on October 31. Immediately after this meeting Kissinger sent a cable that was phoned to me at Camp David as I was getting ready for bed just after midnight: "We have just finished two-hour meeting with Thieu that was tense and highly emotional. However, I think we finally made a breakthrough and can keep to the original schedule with his support."

I felt an enormous sense of relief and satisfaction when I received this news. By the time I awoke the next morning, another cable had arrived from Kissinger:

> Thieu has just rejected the entire plan or any modification of it and refuses to discuss any further negotiations on the basis of it. He insists that any settlement must contain absolute guarantees of the DMZ, total withdrawal of North Vietnamese forces, and total self-determination of South Vietnam without any reference as to how this is to be exercised.
>
> I need not tell you the crisis with which this confronts us.

Later in the day Kissinger sent a cable explaining how Thieu had called him back in the late afternoon and completely reversed the position he had taken in the morning. "It is hard to exaggerate the toughness of Thieu's position," Kissinger stated. "His demands verge on insanity."

I immediately sent a message to Pham Van Dong through the North Vietnamese delegation in Paris, reminding Hanoi that we had always taken the position that we could not proceed unilaterally: "Unfortunately the difficulties in Saigon have proved somewhat more complex than originally anticipated. Some of them concern matters which the U.S. side is honor-bound to put before the D.R.V. [Democratic Republic of Vietnam] side." Citing the breach of confidence of the de Borchgrave interview as a major reason for the problems with Saigon, I informed them that I was calling Kissinger back to Washington for consultations, and asked that they take no public action until we could send a longer message within twenty-four hours. I reaffirmed our commitment to the substance and basic principles of the draft agreement and our commitment to achieving a negotiated settlement at the earliest opportunity.

Haig called Dobrynin in and explained that difficulties in Saigon required us to postpone the arrangements for signing a settlement. He said that it was important that the Soviets enjoin restraint on their partners, and that Hanoi not indulge in public polemics over the delay.

In the meantime we received a sternly worded reply from the North Vietnamese, stating that they could not accept the reasons I had given for requesting a delay and warning that unless we strictly carried out our commitments regarding the agreement and the schedule for signing it, we would bear the "consequences" for continuing the war.

On October 23 Kissinger and Thieu had a final meeting. Thieu repeated his three main objections to the agreement: its failure to establish the DMZ as a secure border; the potential of the National Council of Reconciliation and Concord to become a coalition government; and the continued presence of North Vietnamese forces in South Vietnam. Kissinger repeated his belief that, while Thieu's concerns were not unjustified, the terms of the agreement were, in fact, a major victory over the Communists. He nonetheless agreed to invite the North Vietnamese to Paris and present Thieu's demands to them there, but he stressed that it was unlikely we would be able to achieve all of them. "What is important is that all the sacrifices that have been made should not have been made in vain," Kissinger told Thieu. "If we continue our confrontation you will win victories, but we will both lose in the end. It is a fact that in the United States all the press, the media, and intellectuals have a vested interest in our defeat. If I have seemed impatient in the last days it is because I saw opportunity slipping away. This is why I leave with such a sense of tragedy."

The next day I sent another message to Premier Dong requesting one final meeting. I declared that the text developed at this meeting would be considered final, and as a token of good will I offered to suspend all bombing of North Vietnam north of the 20th parallel. This message crossed wires with a curt statement from the North Vietnamese insisting that the agreement was complete and no further meeting was necessary. They were ready to receive Kissinger in Hanoi as scheduled; if we delayed, the war would continue. They requested an answer by the next day.

Our answer, which we sent on October 25, was tempered but firm. We stated that we shared their regret that a brief delay in signing was necessary, but we pointed out that we could not sign a document that asserted the concurrence of one of the parties when that concurrence did not exist. We repeated our request for one more meeting between Kissinger and Le Duc Tho and repeated that the text they agreed upon would be considered final. We went even further than I had the day before and undertook that as soon as the text had been completed and while we were consulting with our allies, we would completely stop the bombing of North Vietnam. The message concluded:

> It is up to the D.R.V. to decide whether to sacrifice all that has been achieved by a policy of public vilification and private intransigence. For the D.R.V. to insist on demands beyond the power of the U.S. to fulfill will permit no other conclusion than that it seeks a pretext for prolonging the conflict.

At this point Thieu made a speech to the National Assembly in Saigon. Although he railed against the major provisions of the agreement, he did so in a way that did not rule out his coming along at some later time.

Diary

Thieu's speech was sort of a mixed bag. The most important thing that came out of it, however, was that of the two theories that Henry had laid out—either Thieu was crazy or that he was crazy like a fox—the second proved to be true.

What happens here is that really he is preparing himself for a cease-fire but also proving that he is participating in it in insisting that he is not going to have a coalition government, etc.

On the day of Thieu's speech I signed two veterans' benefits bills at a ceremony in the East Room.

Diary

As I spoke to the veterans I was again terribly moved when I saw the blind veterans and those in wheelchairs.

It makes me realize what a debt we owe to these people, and how important it is to have the kind of peace that will really contribute to no more wars, rather than one that is simply a hiatus between two wars.

How they can still be for us is difficult to understand, but there must be a lot of character in our people, that they will suffer so much and still stand up for what is right for the country.

On Thursday, October 26, what we had been fearing happened: the North Vietnamese went public with the peace agreement. They broadcast the general provisions of the agreement over Radio Hanoi, including the October 31 signing timetable. They revealed two of my cables to Pham Van Dong and insisted that we were dragging out the talks in order to cover up our "scheme of maintaining the Saigon puppet regime for the purpose of continued war of aggression."

Kissinger had already planned to hold a press conference on October 26 in order to reassure the North Vietnamese that we were serious about reaching an agreement as well as to distract attention from Thieu's obstructionism. Now his press conference took on an additional purpose and importance: we had to use it to undercut the North Vietnamese propaganda maneuver and to make sure that our version of the agreement was the one that had greater public impact.

In his opening remarks Kissinger said, "We believe that peace is at hand. We believe that an agreement is within sight, based on the May 8 proposals of the President and some adaptations of our January 25 proposal, which is just to all parties."

Public attention focused on this turn of phrase, "Peace is at hand." Another statement later in the briefing would also come back to haunt us. Kissinger said, "We believe incidentally, what remains to be done can be settled in one more negotiating session with the North Vietnamese negotiators, lasting, I would think, no more than three or four days, so we are not talking of a delay of a very long period of time." When Ziegler told me that the news lead from Kissinger's briefing was "Peace is at hand," I knew immediately that our bargaining position with the North Vietnamese would be seriously eroded and our problem of bringing Thieu and the South Vietnamese along would be made even more difficult. No less disturbing was the prospect of the premature hopes for an early settlement that would be raised at home, while the McGovern supporters would naturally claim that we were trying to manipulate the election. Kissinger himself soon realized that it was a mistake to have gone so far in order to convince the North Vietnamese of our bona fides by making a public commitment to a settlement.

On the positive side, there was no doubt that Kissinger's briefing had succeeded in completely undercutting the enemy's ploy and superseding their false interpretation of the proposed peace agreement.

Diary

The North Vietnamese thought they were going to surprise us by going public through the NLF with a somewhat distorted and garbled version of the peace plan. Consequently, Henry went public and indicated that "peace was at hand." This was really going considerably further than I would have gone, and I know Henry was worried about it. However, when I talked to him about what I should say when we went to [campaign in] Kentucky, he very much did not want me to back off from what he had said.

The North Vietnamese ignored Kissinger's briefing and delivered a message that they were still expecting him in Hanoi to initial the agreement. We sent them a note repeating that we understood their disappointment at our inability to meet the October 31 signing schedule and proposing a final meeting on November 1 with November 20 as the new target date for initialing the agreement.

We agreed not to request any further changes after the agreement had been reached at this final session, and we repeated the offer to suspend all bombing of North Vietnam as soon as the agreement had been completed and while we were consulting our allies about it. We said: "The U.S. side wishes to reaffirm its belief that with a cooperative attitude and good will on both sides, all remaining obstacles can be overcome. The major problem now is to focus on the future and to end recriminations about the past." In a reference to their having publicized the negotiations we added: "Public pressure tactics can only retard progress."

At the same time, we sent a note to Peking saying that it would be greatly appreciated if the Chinese would use their considerable influence in Hanoi to help bring about the peace that was now so near; and I wrote to Brezhnev asking him to use his influence to urge North Vietnam to work with us to complete the agreement on a realistic schedule.

I also sent a strong message to Thieu: "If the evident drift towards disagreement between the two of us continues, however, the essential base for U.S. support for you and your government will be destroyed."

Diary

We are now in a position where if he doesn't come along after the election we are going to have to put him through the wringer. I think then he will come along.

What really concerns him, Henry believes, and I am inclined to think he is right, is that he is terrified of the idea of the Americans being gone from South Vietnam. Abrams, on the other hand, who is certainly no opponent of Thieu's, feels strongly that the time has come for us to get out and that we simply have to cut the umbilical cord and have this baby walk by itself. If they can't do it now, with all we have fed it in the way of arms and ammunition and training, etc., they will never be able to do it.

The avalanche of speculation created by Kissinger's "peace is at hand" statement put us in a very delicate position. Although I did not want to dampen optimism needlessly, I could not allow the impression to remain that a settlement would be the guaranteed outcome of the next Paris meeting. Even if the North Vietnamese gave in to every requirement, there was no assurance that Thieu would go along. In fact, he had made a public speech condemning the proposed settlement as an "agreement to surrender." Therefore, on November 2, in a televised campaign speech, I stated: "We are not going to allow an election deadline or any other kind of deadline to force us into an agreement which would be only a temporary truce and not a lasting peace. We are going to sign the agreement when the agreement is right, not one day before. And when the agreement is right, we are going to sign, without one day's delay." McGovern responded with a charge that I had purposely misled the people about the prospects of peace.

On the same day that I made this speech I authorized some relaxation of the restriction on B-52 raids over North Vietnam that had been in effect since October 13. The plan now was to exert increasing pressure on Hanoi by beginning the bombing near the DMZ and then moving it slightly farther north each day. It seemed to work almost immediately: two days after it began the North Vietnamese agreed to meet with us in Paris on November 14. The election would be over by then; the American people would have chosen their President for the next four years and their decision would have a determining impact on the outcome of the war. Although the differences between McGovern and me were fundamental in almost every area, we were most diametrically opposite in the matter of the Vietnam war. He had pledged to end the war immediately by beginning a unilateral withdrawal without insisting on any arrangements for the return of our POWs. I had pledged to continue fighting until I was convinced that we had achieved a peace that was worthy of our sacrifices, that preserved the independence of South Vietnam, that had a chance of lasting after we had withdrawn our forces, and that assured the return of our POWs and an accounting of our MIAs.

THE CORRUPTION ISSUE

Ignored or rebuked by the majority of voters on the Vietnam war and nearly every other issue, McGovern and the Democrats began to focus on "corruption in government." It may have been completely coincidental that at the same time the Washington *Post* ran a series of news reports—attributed largely to anonymous "sources"—about alleged corruption in the Nixon campaign. As McGovern was quick to recognize, the *Post*'s articles had far more influence in Washington and on the rest of the national media than his or Shriver's campaign rhetoric, and he began to incorporate the charges made by the *Post* into his speeches. These stories reached their peak two weeks before the election, on October 25, and then ended as soon as the election was over. This too may have been coincidental, but that is not the way we saw it in the White House at that time.

For example, on October 3 the *Post* reported an allegation by "sources" that Bill Timmons had been named as one of the people who had received reports from the Watergate wiretaps. The allegation was false, and Timmons denied it. It was still false when the *Post* repeated it three days later, this time on the front page under a big headline.

On October 8 I commented in my diary on the effect this kind of story had.

Diary
Julie was worried about the story in the paper to the effect that Timmons, [Robert] Odle, and one other White House aide had had access to the reports on Watergate. She said that if any of them are really guilty that we really ought to get rid of them. I told her not to be concerned about it, that the reports were false. It does show how sensitive she, and probably others like her in the campaign, are about this issue.

She mentioned the fact that she had seen Sherman Adams. It is a tragedy really what happened to Adams and I must remember to have him to the White House for some occasion. After all of his service to Eisenhower, he should not have been forced to leave under a cloud for an offense that was, at best, a question of judgment and not one of illegality or morality. I tend to agree with Jerry Persons when he says that Adams is an impeccably honest man and left his job a relatively poor man.

On October 10 the *Post* had a new front-page allegation. Under the headline *FBI Finds Nixon Aides Sabotaged Democrats,* the story began: "FBI agents have established that the Watergate bugging incident stemmed from a massive campaign of political spying and sabotage conducted on behalf of President Nixon's re-election and directed by officials of the White House and the Committee for the Re-election of the President."

The story charged that a young man named Donald Segretti had recruited fifty operatives for an undercover campaign that involved "following members of Democratic candidates' families; forging letters and distributing them under candidates' letterheads; leaking false and manufactured items to the press; throwing campaign schedules into disarray; seizing confidential campaign files and investigating the lives of dozens of Democratic campaign workers."

Donald Segretti had been a college friend of my Appointments Secretary Dwight Chapin and of Gordon Strachan, an aide to Haldeman. Chapin and Strachan had hired Segretti to become what they called "a Republican Dick Tuck." Tuck was a Democrat whose name had become synonymous with ingenious gags aimed at Republican candidates; he was the master of what were then called "dirty tricks": planting embarrassing signs in campaign crowds, changing schedules in order to create confusion, and generally spreading disruption. Segretti, like Tuck, was supposed to use his imagination and his sense of humor to cause minor disarray among the opposition.

Chapin read the *Post*'s story with incredulity. He had not kept tabs on Segretti's activity, but the sinister implications of the *Post*'s account were nothing like what he had authorized. Segretti expressed outrage.

As I saw it then, by printing this story less than a month before the election, the *Post* was accusing Segretti of spying and sabotage for the same kind of thing that had been dubbed creative mischief when Tuck had done it. Furthermore, it was grossly untrue and unfair to link Segretti to the Watergate break-in.

A few days later reporters from the *Post* phoned the White House to warn that they were about to run a new story that would charge that Chapin and Hunt were

Segretti's contacts and directed his activities. This would tie Chapin by implication into the Watergate break-in stories. The reporters also said that they were going to charge that Chapin and Hunt had briefed Segretti on what the grand jury would ask about his activities. Both these charges were untrue, and Chapin issued a statement denying them.

The story that was actually published on the front page of the *Post* on October 15 had been subtly changed from the one the reporters had described to us over the phone. They did not, however, inform Chapin that any changes were going to be made or give him an opportunity to modify the wording of his denial accordingly. The story as run did not accuse Chapin of briefing Segretti on the grand jury, and weakened the alleged connection with Hunt. The story now began: "President Nixon's Appointments Secretary and an ex-White House aide indicted in the Watergate bugging case both served as 'contacts' in a spying and sabotage operation against the Democrats."

Of course the problem was that there was no way of separating facts from fiction in this kind of story three weeks before a presidential election. The most damaging parts were completely false; but it was true that Chapin had hired Segretti to cause disarray in the Democrats' campaigns. And there were other political hazards involved in trying to set the story straight. Haldeman had given Chapin approval to have Segretti paid by my lawyer and campaign aide, Herb Kalmbach. Thus there was the danger of focusing the story more strongly on the White House. Ziegler denied that Chapin directed any campaign of spying and sabotage, denounced the "hearsay, innuendo, and guilt by association," and then doggedly refused to comment on the specifics. The White House press corps was furious.

The diary note I dictated that night conveys the way I felt about these charges against Chapin stemming from his Segretti contacts.

Diary
> The big story on Chapin broke today and it was certainly guilt by association, hearsay, etc. McCarthyism at its very worst. In any event, as I told Haldeman, we could not be knocked off balance by

these stories because they were going to be stepped up in tempo this week.

Haldeman indicated that Chapin felt he was expendable. I said under no circumstances would we move in that direction because it was not fair since the press were simply using a double standard on all of this. It is rather ironical that they excused the Dick Tuck and other operations as being just good clean fun, but where we are doing it, it is grim and vicious espionage and sabotage of the worst type.

A few days later I added a further observation.

Diary
I passed on to Haldeman my midnight thought to the effect that the latest attack on Chapin et al. was the "last burp of the Eastern establishment."

As the news reports about Segretti and the Watergate affair continued, McGovern announced that he knew *he* was being sabotaged, and on October 19 he called my administration a "cutthroat crew . . . a corrupt regime." On October 24 he charged—falsely—that the Republicans wiretapped the phones of Democratic presidential candidates in the primaries and "had us followed and members of our families followed all the time." In the meantime Teddy Kennedy decided that this was the sort of thing he should investigate personally. He announced that his Senate Subcommittee on Administrative Practices would begin a probe of Segretti and questionable campaign tactics.

On the morning of October 25, the Washington *Post* ran a large front-page picture of Bob Haldeman under the headline: *Testimony Ties Top Nixon Aide to Secret Fund.* The story said that Haldeman was one of five men authorized to approve payments from a secret cash fund at the CRP. It claimed that the fund had been "uncovered during the FBI Watergate bugging investigation. It financed an apparently unprecedented spying and sabotage campaign." The story stated that Haldeman had been one of those who had approved expenditures of hundreds of thousands of dollars for these activities. The reporters said that Hugh Sloan, the CRP's treasurer, had given testimony to this effect before the grand jury and that Haldeman had been questioned about it by the FBI.

It was true that there was a cash fund at the CRP set aside for intelligence-gathering and other campaign projects that had to be handled discreetly. And Haldeman, acting in my name, theoretically could presumably approve money from any fund connected with my campaign. But he had not directed the payments from the CRP fund, nor had he been interviewed by the FBI. Nor had Hugh Sloan given the testimony described in the story.

Diary

We got the news with regard to the *Post* story on Haldeman. It obviously disturbs him but he is a strong man and took it very, very well. He says that the story was inaccurate insofar as the Hugh Sloan testimony was concerned, but in any event the *Post* is going to continue to nibble away. Haldeman spoke rather darkly of the fact that there was a clique in the White House that were out to get him. I trust he is not getting a persecution complex.

I called Haldeman after I got back to the Residence and tried to reassure him by saying that I was relaxed about it, that I knew we were going to have to take some heat in the next two weeks, but that we would sail through and not be knocked off balance.

It is interesting to note that Ben Bradlee of the *Post* says that this administration is committed to the destruction of the press. This of course is total nonsense and he knows it. I think what he fears is what's going to happen to the Washington *Post* news sources after the election—and we have every right, in fact every responsibility, to see to it that people who would give us a fair shake get a break over others who are going to give us the knife.

Considering that McGovern was supposed to be the peace candidate, his supporters resorted to surprisingly violent and destructive attacks against my campaign and even against my supporters. At one of my appearances in San

Francisco there occurred what one observer called a "state of siege": the hotel was ringed by helmeted police in riot gear while groups of demonstrators stopped traffic and threw rocks. This demonstration was promoted by leaflets distributed from the McGovern headquarters in nearby Berkeley. In Los Angeles, McGovern's Southern California campaign coordinator admitted to approving the use of telephone banks at their headquarters to promote a massive demonstration against me there; leaflets advertising this effort were handed out at approximately fifty McGovern headquarters. The Ervin Committee was later told that a McGovern spokesman had falsely represented to the press that this effort had not been authorized. In Morgantown, West Virginia, demonstrators tried to shout down a speech by Tricia. In Columbus, Ohio, guests attending a Republican fund raiser at which Ted Agnew spoke were spat upon and subjected to shouts and obscenities. In Washington, D.C., the Democrats for Nixon headquarters was stormed by nearly a hundred people who tore down posters, destroyed campaign material, damaged office equipment, and stole office supplies. When the violators departed, they left McGovern campaign leaflets behind.

Far more serious was the use of outright violence aimed at my campaign. CRP headquarters in Phoenix and Austin were completely destroyed by arsonists. Our headquarters in Dayton, Ohio, was broken into twice and equipment and records damaged; the second time, McGovern slogans were painted on the walls and windows. In Minnesota one of our headquarters buildings was broken into, and materials and literature were destroyed and motor oil dumped over boxes containing mailing literature. At the Alameda County headquarters in California, a bomb exploded, causing extensive damage.

It became routine to find scurrilous literature handed out in advance of appearances. One pamphlet passed out by McGovern campaign workers in Los Angeles neighborhoods with heavy Jewish populations included the line: "Nixon brings the ovens to the people rather than the people to the ovens."

After the campaign it was revealed that, for all its sanctimony, the McGovern high command was not above considering organized spying of its own. At the highest levels of their campaign it was proposed that a paid operative be planted aboard Ted Agnew's campaign airplane to spy on Agnew and report his activities to the McGovern camp. According to Senate Watergate Committee records, one of those responsible for this plan claimed that the same thing had been done successfully against my campaign in 1968.

There was also a break-in at the office of Dr. John Lungren, my personal physician in Long Beach, California. No money or drugs were taken, but my medical files were removed from a locked closet and left strewn about the floor of the office.

Diary
     Haldeman and Ehrlichman talked about it during the day. Colson was ecstatic and wanted to get it out right away. Ehrlichman, however, probably had the better judgment and said that it might lead to the conclusion either that we had set it up, or it really didn't amount to anything at all. The most important thing, as I told Haldeman, was to conduct an investigation—to report the situation so that there would be no indication of cover-up in the event that the people that broke in had something.

The demonstrators and arsonists detracted heavily from the spirit of this last campaign. More frustrating to me, however, was the double standard that permitted massive and frequently distorted coverage of Watergate while virtually ignoring the many serious violations of law and ethics committed against us. In light of what I saw being done against us in this campaign, the righteous moralizing about Segretti's activities rang hollow.

The last political rally of my career as a candidate took place at Ontario, California, a few miles and twenty-six years from where the first one had taken place in Pomona. We arrived at night, after a two-day final campaign swing through Illinois, Oklahoma, Rhode Island, North Carolina, and New Mexico. The night before we left Washington,

Tricia had come into the Lincoln Sitting Room and said, "I want this week to be a real last hurrah."

The overflow crowd at the Ontario airport seemed to sense the emotional and symbolic meaning of the moment for me. I told them how I had been all across the nation during the past few weeks. I said, "I want to tell you something about this country. . . . There was a time, and it was not too long ago, when if you traveled through the country, you would see it deeply divided—the West against the East, the North against the South, the cities against the farms, and so forth. But let me tell you, wherever you go across America, this nation is getting together."

I talked about our goals and then turned back to California and talked about how good the people of California had been to us, sharing our victories and standing by us in our defeats.

"This, of course, not only is the last rally of this campaign that I will speak to," I said in conclusion, "it is the last time I will speak to a rally as a candidate in my whole life, and I want to say to all of you here who worked on this, to all of you who took the time to come, thank you very much for making it probably the best rally that we have ever had."

On election eve, November 6, 1972, I dictated various recollections of my day in San Clemente.

Diary

Today I went down to the Red Beach, walked two miles, went in the water for about twenty minutes. The tide was out further than I have ever seen it—a real ebb tide. Whether this is a good sign or a bad sign only time will tell.

When I went further down the beach—I decided to first go just to the half-mile mark and then went on to the peace sign which someone had carved in the red sandstone cliff, which is about three-quarters of a mile. Interestingly enough, the peace sign had been worn down by the weather. It was very dim. It looked like a man with a frown on his face. This may be an indication that those who have held up this sign finally have had their comeuppance and they are really in for some heavy depression.

Rose joined Pat and me for dinner that evening. On the East Coast millions had already watched a brief election eve address that I had recorded on videotape earlier in the day. I said that I would not insult anyone's intelligence by rehashing the issues and making a last-minute plea for votes. I said that this election was probably the clearest choice between the candidates for President ever presented to the American people in the twentieth century.

My diary for election eve concluded on a rather subdued and analytical note.

Diary

> Well, this wraps it up for the first four years, because as I have often thought over this past year I really only had until November 7 to be President because if I lost the election on November 7— tomorrow—then the presidency would be in someone else's hands.

> We are not going to lose it, of course, lacking a miracle beyond which nothing has been seen up to this point. When I think of the ups and downs through the years, and particularly in this last year, I must say that someone must have been walking with us. The Peking trip, the Moscow trip, the May 8 decision, and then the way we have handled the campaign—must deserve some grudging respect from even our critics. The only sour note of the whole thing, of course, is Watergate and Segretti. This was really stupidity on the part of a number of people.

We flew back to Washington on Election Day. When we arrived at the White House at 6 P.M., we were greeted by a cheering staff. In my room I found an envelope propped up on my pillow. It contained a handwritten letter from Henry Kissinger:

Election Day 1972

Dear Mr. President—

It seems appropriate before the votes are counted to tell you what a privilege the last four years have been. I am confident of the outcome today. But it cannot affect the historic achievement—to take a divided nation, mired in war, losing its confidence, wracked by intellectuals without conviction, and give it a new purpose and overcome its hesitations—will loom ever larger in history books. It has been an inspiration to see your fortitude in adversity and your willingness to walk alone. For this—as well as for the unfailing human kindness and consideration—I shall always be grateful.

With warm and
respectful regards,
Henry

Our family had dinner together while waiting for the polls to close and for the first returns to come in. About an hour later the cap on one of my top front teeth snapped off. It had held firmly in place for twenty-five years, since the time it had been fitted in 1947.

I was to appear on television in a few hours, so we called my dentist, Dr. William Chase. He came to the White House, and after a half hour's work he was able to give me a hastily crafted temporary cap. I was in considerable discomfort, and I knew that if I smiled too broadly the cap might fall off.

I returned to the Lincoln Sitting Room and continued putting down notes for the remarks I would be making later. After a while I got up and put on a tape of *Victory at Sea*.

Ed and David brought me the first reports at 7:30. They were elated because it was already apparent that I was going to win by a landslide. Even if it was not really a surprise, the moment was still exciting for all of us.

Shortly after eight o'clock Haldeman began phoning over more detailed reports from the election-monitoring teams that had been set up in the West Wing offices. In state after state we were winning big. Texas, for example, was going to be ours by more than a million votes. But there was also bad news: we were not picking up enough congressional seats to provide the legislative support my own New Majority mandate would need. When all the results were in, Republicans gained 12 seats in the House, but lost two seats in the Senate. The new lineup of governors—31 Democrats to 19 Republicans—meant a loss of one state house for the

Republican Party. I was concerned about our failure to do better in Congress, but I was at least certain that no Republican candidate had lost for lack of money. On examination I found that in many cases our candidates had been defeated by younger liberals who had labor support and labor money. I thought that this would be our challenge as a party before the 1974 off-year elections: to revamp and renew ourselves so as to get candidates who could successfully appeal to voters and wage winning campaigns.

At about 11:40 P.M. George McGovern conceded and sent me a telegram:

> CONGRATULATIONS ON YOUR VICTORY. I HOPE THAT IN THE NEXT FOUR YEARS YOU WILL LEAD US TO A TIME OF PEACE ABROAD AND JUSTICE AT HOME. YOU HAVE MY FULL SUPPORT IN SUCH EFFORTS. WITH BEST WISHES TO YOU AND YOUR GRACIOUS WIFE PAT. SINCERELY, GEORGE MCGOVERN.

Ed thought the message was gracious, but Tricia and Julie thought it cold and arch. I thought it was merely carefully worded. I expressed my reaction in my diary: "It was a tough experience for him and I am not as hard-nosed about it as some might be because with all the mistakes he made, he feels that he has done the best he can and he is being put upon."

Thousands of calls and cables began pouring in to celebrate the great victory. One was from Johnson City:

> THE WAY IN WHICH YOUR FELLOW MEN EXPRESSED THEIR APPROVAL OF YOUR RECORD THESE LAST FOUR YEARS MUST BE A GREAT COMFORT TO YOU AND I KNOW IT WILL GIVE YOU THE STRENGTH SO NECESSARY IN THE TIMES AHEAD. YOU AND YOUR FAMILY HAVE ENDURED MUCH BUT I KNOW TODAY THAT IT IS WORTH IT ALL. LADY BIRD AND I WILL DO ANYTHING

WE CAN TO EASE YOUR BURDEN AND HELP YOU MAKE A GOOD PRESIDENT IN THE DAYS AHEAD. LYNDON B. JOHNSON.

The dimensions of the victory were gratifying. I received 47,169,841 votes, and McGovern received 29,172,767: 60.7 percent to 37.5 percent. This was the second largest percentage of the popular vote in our history of two-party politics, and the greatest ever given a Republican candidate. Only Lyndon Johnson, running against Goldwater in the unique circumstances of 1964, had received fractionally more: 61.1 percent. I received the largest number of popular votes ever cast for a presidential candidate and the second largest number of electoral votes. No presidential candidate had ever won so many states.

The support was both wide and deep—it was truly a New Majority landslide of the kind I had called for in my acceptance speech in August. I won a majority of every key population group identified by Gallup except the blacks and the Democrats. Four of these groups—manual workers, Catholics, members of labor union families, and people with only grade school educations—had never before been in the Republican camp in all the years since Gallup had begun keeping these records.

A few days later I described in my diary a curious feeling, perhaps a foreboding, that muted my enjoyment of this triumphal moment.

Diary

It makes one feel very humble at a time like this.

I had determined before this election evening to make it as memorable a one as possible for everybody concerned. The tooth episode probably interfered to a considerable extent. Certainly by the time that I had to prepare for the office telecast I was not as upbeat as I should have been.

The rest of the family seemed to think that they got enough of a thrill out of it. I think the very fact that the victory was so overwhelming made up for any failure on my part to react more enthusiastically than I did.

I am at a loss to explain the melancholy that settled over me on that victorious night. Perhaps it was caused by the painful tooth. To some extent the marring effects of Watergate may have played a part, to some extent our failure to win Congress, and to a greater extent the fact that we had not yet been able to end the war in Vietnam. Or perhaps it was because this would be my last campaign. Whatever the reasons, I allowed myself only a few minutes to reflect on the past. I was confident that a new era was about to begin, and I was eager to begin it.

THE END OF THE WAR

My first priority after the election was to end the war. Now that the pressure was removed, I hoped that both parties would enter the negotiations with the idea that after some hard bargaining each would accept an agreement embodying less than their most extreme position. I knew that it was not going to be easy. None of the objective factors had changed, but now that there was no election deadline, it remained to be seen what the Communists' negotiating tactics would be. Both Saigon and Hanoi were already playing a frustrating game with us. Thieu, while urging that we put forward his demands—some of which were bound to be unacceptable to the North Vietnamese— was still pretending that he was prepared to go it alone. And Le Duc Tho was pretending that the Communists were completely sincere in their desire to conclude an agreement on its merits and then to observe its terms. From our intelligence sources we knew that Thieu was secretly telling his military leaders to be ready for a cease-fire before Christmas; and we knew that the North Vietnamese were still planning to capture as much territory as possible just before the cease-fire in order to be able to turn it to their advantage.

The next meeting with the North Vietnamese was scheduled for mid-November. If anything was to come from it, Thieu's cooperation was now essential. I decided that Haig, whom Thieu trusted and liked, would once again be the best emissary. He left for Saigon on November 9, carrying another letter I had written to Thieu. In it I dealt point by point with the objections Thieu had raised to the terms of the October agreement and clarified the positions that we would present to the North Vietnamese at the next Paris meeting. "We will use our maximum efforts to effect these changes in the agreement," I wrote. "I wish to leave you under no illusion, however, that we can or will go beyond these changes in seeking to improve an agreement that we already consider to be excellent."

I also urged Haig to remind Thieu that although I had won the White House by a landslide, he must remember that the Senate was now even more dovish than it had been before the election. There was no question that if we did not have a settlement completed before Congress returned in January, and if it appeared that Thieu was the obstacle to achieving one, the Senate would cut off the funds that South Vietnam needed to survive. The situation was as simple, and as certain, as that.

Thieu handed Haig a reply that repeated his objections, particularly regarding the presence of North Vietnamese troops in South Vietnam. I responded by reiterating that we would not be able to obtain all the adjustments he had requested. I pointed out that far more important than what was *said* in any agreement was what we would *do* in the event the enemy renewed its aggression. "You have my absolute assurance that if Hanoi fails to abide by the terms of this agreement it is my intention to take swift and severe retaliatory action," I wrote.

Haig left Saigon convinced that Thieu would come along in the end. There was no doubt in his mind that Thieu knew that total intransigence would be fatal. In the meantime, however, he had been careful not to push Thieu too far. He reported on November 12:

> We are now dealing with a razor's edge situation. Thieu has firmly laid his prestige on the line with his entire government and I believe if we take a totally unreasonable stance with him, we may force him to commit political suicide. I am not sure that this would serve our best interests and therefore recommend the scarier approach of trying to work this problem with Thieu right up to the wire.

Haig correctly pointed out that if we broke with Thieu and then found that the North Vietnamese were still intransigent, we would have burned both our bridges. He concluded, "The price of keeping Thieu aboard is of course risky but I do not believe unacceptable at this juncture."

I agreed with Haig's assessment, and in my diary I noted, "Of course, we may come to the hard place where we have to simply tell Thieu it's this or else, but this does not need to come at this moment." I told both Kissinger and Haig that I felt December 8 was the final date by which we must have signed an agreement in order to make sure that everything was completely settled by the time Congress reconvened. If Thieu could not be convinced to come along by then, I could be reluctantly prepared to reach a separate agreement.

Whether we could meet the December 8 deadline would depend upon the outcome of the November 20 meeting in Paris.

Diary
Assuming that we get any kind of movement from the North Vietnamese on the agreement this week, and assuming we get what we consider to be a good agreement—well, as a matter of fact, we consider the present one to be good, but this will make it better—then we have to put it to Thieu hard: he either accepts the agreement and goes along with it, or we will have to go our separate ways.

As I told Henry when he began to rumble around to the effect that we have a very good record in this instance, I said, Henry, we're not concerned about being right on the record. What we are concerned about is to save South Vietnam and that's why we had to temporize with Thieu as much as we did, because our interest is in getting South Vietnam to survive and Thieu at present seems to be the only leader who could lead them in that direction.

It would, of course, be a disappointment in the event that Thieu does not go along, but under those circumstances we shall simply have to make our own deal, get our prisoners, have our withdrawal, try to save Cambodia and Laos, and then say that Vietnamization has been completed and Thieu then can do what he likes.

On November 20 Kissinger met with Le Duc Tho for more than five hours. Tho opened by reading a lengthy speech complaining that we had reneged on the October agreement. While its tone was no different from the standard rhetoric we had come to expect, the charges that we had unilaterally prevented an agreement were unacceptable. Kissinger immediately cited chapter and verse from earlier sessions in which he had informed the Communists that the South Vietnamese would have to be consulted before any agreement could be signed. Kissinger finished his opening remarks by reiterating our desire to negotiate seriously to end the war and our intention to maintain the essence of the agreement that had been achieved in October.

He then presented the proposed changes. By the time the ones requested by the South Vietnamese had been applied to the text of the agreement and added to the changes and clarifications we wanted, there were more than sixty of them. Le Duc Tho seemed somewhat taken aback by their number. Most of the changes were relatively minor and uncontroversial. But a few were substantive, the most significant of them involving Thieu's insistence on a pull-back of some of the North Vietnamese forces out of South Vietnam. There was also a proposal that the DMZ be respected by each party; the presence of North Vietnamese troops in the South would be a violation of this provision. Le Duc Tho simply took note of the list and indicated that he might have some changes of his own to propose. Kissinger had made no distinction between the changes we wanted and those we were presenting on behalf of the South Vietnamese. His approach, however, made it clear that we were prepared to negotiate on all of them. At the close of the meeting he was asked whether this was actually our final proposal. Kissinger replied, "I would put it this way. It is our final proposal, but it is not an ultimatum." Kissinger suggested that the technical experts meet that night to study the proposed changes. As the session adjourned on a friendly note, it seemed possible that the Communists would treat the proposals as a basis for negotiation and that an agreement might be reached during this round. That morning I dictated in my diary, "The next two days will tell the tale as to whether we get an agreement."

At the meeting the next day, however, the North Vietnamese countered our proposed changes and hardened their position on the remaining unresolved issues; in some areas they even pulled back to their position *before* October 8. It seemed that Kissinger's fears had been realized and that the North Vietnamese, relieved of the pressure of our election deadline, were prepared to stall the negotiations in an attempt to exploit our differences with Thieu. When Kissinger reported that there had been another tense and totally unproductive meeting on November 22, I sent him a message, which I said he could use if and when he saw fit—or not at all—in an effort to get the negotiations moving. The message was in the form of a directive stating that unless the other side showed the same willingness to be reasonable that we were showing, he should discontinue the talks and we would have to resume military activity until they were ready to negotiate. It continued:

> They must be disabused of the idea they seem to have that we have no other choice but to settle on their terms. You should inform them directly without equivocation that we do have another choice and if they were surprised that the President would take the strong action he did prior to the Moscow Summit and prior to the election, they will find now, with the election behind us, he will take whatever action he considers necessary to protect the United States' interest.

After the next session in Paris on November 23 Kissinger reported that although he had made limited progress in specific areas, we were still far apart on some of the provisions that Thieu considered most important. Therefore we had to face the fact that barring a sudden change by the North Vietnamese, we were not going to have an acceptable deal. He felt that as long as Saigon held out for so many substantial alterations, not only would no agreement be reached but the North Vietnamese would continue to retract concessions they had already granted.

Kissinger considered that we now had two options open to us. Option One would be to break off the talks at the next meeting and dramatically step up our bombing while we reviewed our negotiating strategy in order to decide what kind of agreement we would be prepared to accept with and without the South Vietnamese. This was the option Kissinger favored. Option Two would be to decide upon fall-back positions on each of Thieu's major objections and present them as our final offer. If the North Vietnamese agreed to them, we could still claim to have improved on the October terms. This proposal, as Kissinger put it, "would be substantially better optically, and marginally better substantively, than the agreement we concluded in October. It gives Thieu the minimum that he has asked for if he wanted to be reasonable, which he shows absolutely no inclination of being at this time."

The corollary of Option Two would be a complete break with Thieu if he refused to accept the agreement it produced. I knew that this would be a serious step to take, but I strongly opposed breaking off the talks and resuming the bombing unless it was absolutely necessary to compel the enemy to negotiate. I was also becoming irritated by some of Thieu's tactics, and I felt that we could no longer be in the position of forestalling an agreement solely to buy him time. Therefore, if Kissinger could reach a satisfactory agreement, I wanted him to do so. Then Thieu could make his own decision about joining us or going it alone.

In my message replying to Kissinger's cable I made it clear that I did not consider that Option One was open to us any longer:

> In my view the October 8 agreement was one which certainly would have been in our interest. You should try to improve it to take account of Saigon's conditions as much as possible. But most important we must recognize the fundamental reality that we have no choice but to reach agreement along the lines of the October 8 principles.

Almost immediately I became concerned that, in my attempt to encourage Kissinger to pursue Option Two, I might have overstated my reluctance to resume the bombing if there was no other choice left to us to make the enemy negotiate seriously. I felt it was essential that he not be denied this bargaining chip, and consequently I sent him a cable the next morning, November 24, saying that if the Communists remained intransigent, he could suspend the talks for a week so that both sides could consult with their principals. I said that I would be prepared to authorize a massive bombing strike on North Vietnam in that interval:

> I recognize that this is a high-risk option, but it is one I am prepared to take if the only alternative is an agreement which is worse than that of the October 8, and which does not clear up any of the ambiguities which we and Saigon are concerned about in the October 8 draft.
>
> Our aim will continue to be to end the war with honor. And if because of the pursuit of our strategy and the accident of the timing of the election we are now in a public relations corner, we must take our lumps and see it through.
>
> In giving this direction, we all must realize that there is no way whatever that we can mobilize public opinion behind us as in the case of November 3, Cambodia, and May 8. But at least with the election behind us, we owe it to the sacrifice that has been made to date by so many to do what is right even though the cost in our public support will be massive.

When Kissinger informed Le Duc Tho that I was prepared to take actions as strong as the ones of May 8, the North Vietnamese immediately became more conciliatory. This seemed to confirm our suspicions that their intransigence was in fact a negotiating tactic. They did not want the talks to end any more than we did and were therefore prepared once again to engage in serious negotiations.

The problem, as Kissinger presented it in his reporting cable that afternoon, was that while we had now considerably improved the agreement over the October 8 terms, there was no possibility that we could come near anything that would satisfy all of Thieu's requirements. We knew from cable intercepts that Thieu was in a deliberate stalling pattern; this meant that no improvements in the agreement would have any effect on him until he decided that he had sufficiently prepared his people to accept it. So despite our intensive efforts and the improvements we had been able to make in the agreement, a major break with Thieu seemed inevitable if we were going to complete the agreement right away. Kissinger therefore once again recommended a

228

week's recess during which we could force a reckoning with Thieu and then, on the basis of his decision, formulate our own final position.

I still believed, however, that it was important to keep the negotiating channels open and working. I considered Thieu's position to be ill-advised, and I felt more strongly than ever that if we could get a good agreement, we should do so and let Thieu make his choice accordingly. I immediately replied to Kissinger that I thought it preferable for him to stay in Paris and continue talking as long as there was even a remote chance of reaching an agreement. I said that I would even "take risks in that direction."

The North Vietnamese were still stonewalling the negotiations, however, so after another inconclusive session on November 25, Kissinger and Le Duc Tho agreed on the desirability of recessing the talks for several days.

I met with Kissinger as soon as he returned from Paris.

Diary

He arrived back around 10:30 and we spent an hour on it at that time. I had to back him off the position that we really had a viable option to break off the talks with the North and resume the bombing for a period of time. It simply isn't going to work. While we must play the card out with the North Vietnamese as if it would work that way, we must have no illusions that we now have no option except to settle.

We sent a message to the North Vietnamese that we would return to the talks with the idea of making one last effort. In order to demonstrate our good faith and desire to reach a settlement, I ordered a reduction of the bombing of North Vietnam.

On November 29 Kissinger ushered Nguyen Phu Duc, President Thieu's personal representative at the Paris talks, into the Oval Office. We thought that if I made a brutally tough presentation to Duc, that would succeed in bringing home to Thieu the precariousness of his position and the danger of being left on his own. I said that it was not a question of lacking sympathy for Saigon's predicament; but we had to face the reality of the situation. If we did not end the war by concluding a settlement at the next Paris session, then when Congress returned in January it would end the war by cutting off the appropriations. I had already informed Thieu that I had canvassed the staunchest congressional supporters of my Vietnam policy regarding the October terms, and they had unanimously avowed that if Thieu alone were standing in the way of accepting such terms, they would personally lead the fight against him when Congress reconvened.

On November 30 I met with Kissinger, Haig, Laird, and the Joint Chiefs of Staff to discuss our military plans in the event that the talks were broken off or that the agreement reached was subsequently violated by the Communists. In the former case there were contingency plans for three-day and six-day bombing strikes against North Vietnam. In the latter case I was adamant that our response be swift and strong. "If Hanoi violates an agreement, our response must be all out," I said. "We must maintain enough force in the area to do the job, and it can't be a weak response. Above all, B-52s are to be targeted on Hanoi. We must have our own unilateral capability to prevent violations."

Kissinger's next meeting with the North Vietnamese was scheduled for Monday, December 4. If no settlement emerged from this meeting, it would be very difficult to predict how or when the war would end. Kissinger would need all his formidable skills not only to convince the North Vietnamese that we would stay in and continue fighting unless they agreed to a settlement, but to convince the South Vietnamese that we would stop fighting and get out unless they agreed to one. Kissinger himself was optimistic that it would take only a few days to conclude an agreement; in fact, he said, there was a 70–30 chance that he could have the whole thing "wrapped up" by Tuesday night. He blamed his "peace is at hand" statement for having caused many of our present troubles, and he talked about resigning if he was unable to conclude an agreement. I told him that he should not even be thinking in such terms.

On Sunday night I noted: "We enter a very tough week and a very crucial one, but some way I think it's got to come out because the great forces of history—what is really right—are moving us in those directions. Only insanity and irrationality of some leaders may move us in other directions."

All our hopes were dashed on Monday. Le Duc Tho not only categorically rejected every change we had requested, but also withdrew some that had already been agreed upon during the last round and introduced several new and unacceptable demands of his own. Now, even if we decided to conclude an agreement without Thieu, the terms were no longer acceptable to us. Kissinger cabled: "We are at a point where a break-off of the talks looks almost certain." In a long report analyzing the meeting he stated:

It is not impossible that Tho is playing chicken and is waiting for us to cave tomorrow. But I do not think so. There is almost no doubt that Hanoi is prepared now to break off the negotiations and go another military round. Their own needs for a settlement are now outweighed by the attractive vision they see of our having to choose between a complete split with Saigon or an unmanageable domestic situation. . . .

The central issue is that Hanoi has apparently decided to mount a frontal challenge to us such as we faced last May. If so, they are gambling on our unwillingness to do what is necessary; they are playing for a clear-cut victory through our split with Saigon or our domestic collapse rather than run the risk of a negotiated settlement.

This is the basic question; the rest is tactics. If they were willing to settle now, I could come up with acceptable formulas and would not need to bother you. Assuming they are going the other route, we are faced with the same kind of hard decisions as last spring.

Kissinger felt that Le Duc Tho's conduct once again left us with only two options: either we must agree to go back and accept the terms of the October agreement without any changes, or we must run the risk that the talks would break off. He pointed out that the first option was unacceptable. It would be tantamount to overthrowing Thieu; as Kissinger put it, "He could not survive such a demonstration of his and our impotence." It would leave us with no way of explaining our actions since October, and it would provide Hanoi with an enormous propaganda victory. Most important, agreeing to return to the October terms would deprive us of any credibility in policing the agreement, because the Communists would know that if we were willing to swallow this backdown, we would also lack the capability to react to any violations. Kissinger concluded that while the October agreement had been a good one, intervening events had made it impossible to accept now.

Kissinger continued: "Therefore I believe we must be prepared to break off the negotiations. The question is how we do it." He felt that we now had two tactical choices in this regard. The first was to propose settling on the basis of where we had stood in the previous week's round; that would at least enable us to keep the changes and improvements Le Duc Tho had agreed to. The problem with this option was that neither Hanoi nor Saigon was likely to accept it.

The second tactical choice, and the one Kissinger recommended, was to insist on retaining those changes to which the North Vietnamese had already agreed while boiling down our remaining requirements to only the most basic ones involving the clear delineation of the non-governmental nature and functions of the National Council of Reconciliation and Concord and the necessity of having in the agreement some formulation of the principle that North Vietnamese troops did not have the right to remain indefinitely in the South. The Communists were unlikely to accept these requirements, but if for some reason they did, we could use the improvements they represented over the October terms as a lever to bring Thieu along. None of these points was sufficiently critical that the North Vietnamese, if they had genuinely wanted an agreement, could not have accepted them.

If the Communists refused and the talks broke off, we would have no choice but to step up our bombing as a means of making them agree to a redefined negotiating position. Kissinger recommended that I go on television to enlist the support of the American people for the stern measures that would be required. "I believe that you can make a stirring and convincing case to rally them as you have so often in the past with your direct appeals," he wrote.

I disagreed with Kissinger in this regard. Instead of a frantic and probably foredoomed attempt on my part to rally American public opinion behind a major escalation of the war, I preferred an unannounced stepping up of the bombing. This would be coupled with a press conference by Kissinger to explain where we stood in terms of the new attempts at reaching a settlement, and why the negotiations had broken down. In my opinion, however, this was still only the option of last resort. .

Diary

What Henry does not understand is what I tried to get across to him yesterday before he left, and that is that rallying the people as we did November 3 on Cambodia, and then May 8 has now reached the point of no return.

Expectations were raised so high prior to the election and since the election that to go before the American people on television and say that we have been tricked again by the Communists, that we were misled by them, and that now we have to order resumption of the war with no end in sight and no hope, is simply going to be a loser.

In his cable Kissinger raised the idea of his resigning. "I have no illusions about what a break-off in the talks will do to us domestically," he wrote. "If this happens, I will talk to you upon my return about my own responsibility and role."

Diary

I told Col. [Richard] Kennedy [of the NSC staff] that Henry simply has to get out of his head this idea of resigning and all that sort of thing. This is not personal. This is just one of those things where we are in a box and we have to do the very best we can to do what is right and work our way out of it. It will be tough but in the end we are going to win.

On Tuesday morning, December 5, I received a cable from Kissinger. In the event the negotiations broke off, he saw no alternative to stepping up the bombing drastically, and seizing the public relations initiative by using a presidential speech to rally the American people. He suggested in another cable that he insist upon Thieu's demand for the withdrawal of all North Vietnamese troops from South Vietnam as a way of causing Tho to break off the talks. Then he would return to Washington, and I would deliver the television address, in which I would set forward clear and achievable objectives that would essentially add up to a complete American withdrawal in exchange for the return of our POWs. We would then continue bombing until the North Vietnamese agreed to return all our prisoners; he estimated that this would take between six and eight months. "These are issues that the American people can understand. . . . And I am confident that you can rally them once again," he concluded.

I remained unconvinced of the wisdom and the feasibility of this course of action. It was my firm conviction that we must not be responsible—or be portrayed as being responsible—for the breakdown of the talks.

Diary

We must cast this if we possibly can in the light that the North Vietnamese rather than we were responsible for the breakdown in negotiations; and then we should talk in as low-key a manner as possible, and act as strongly as possible without making a big to-do about the fact that we were stepping up the bombing, etc., and in effect resuming the war with no end in sight after raising the expectations of the people primarily as a result of Henry's now-famous "peace is at hand" statement.

As far as the people are concerned, they assume that we have been bombing all along which, of course, is a fact, although the level of bombing has been lower than the high level immediately after May 8. Time will tell us tomorrow as to whether or not we have a way out, but I must say that four weeks after the election the situation is certainly not a very happy prospect.

There was clearly a difference of opinion between Kissinger and me regarding the best strategy to pursue. Once again he felt that we had reached a point where the only thing we could do was break off the talks and step up the bombing to make the North Vietnamese agree to a settlement. And once again I believed it was important to keep the talks going for as long as there was even a remote chance that they might yield a settlement.

Lest there be any misunderstanding about the way I wanted to proceed at what was likely to be the most critical and delicate stage of the entire negotiations, I gave Haldeman detailed instructions for a message to be sent to Kissinger outlining the course he should follow in his next meeting with Le Duc Tho:

> We should avoid any appearance of a dramatic break-off by our side. Instead we should treat the situation as a case where the talks have reached an impasse at this time and each side is returning home for consultation. If there is any such dramatic break-off, it should come from their side, not ours. In any event, our side should not appear to be taking the initiative in ending the talks. We should ask for a recess for the purpose of further consultation.
>
> Then when you return to U.S. you should conduct a low-key, non-dramatic briefing to explain the current situation very briefly and to indicate our continuing plan to maintain military operations until a satisfactory settlement is reached. You would indicate that we are ready to resume negotiations at any time when it will be productive to do so.
>
> I have talked to a very few of the hard-liners here in total confidence, and it is their strongly unanimous view that it would be totally wrong for the President to go on TV and explain the details of why the talks have failed.

Kissinger sent his reply through Haldeman. "We had better face the facts of life," he said. "If there is no agreement in the next forty-eight hours, we may be able to pretend that the talks are in recess long enough to permit me to give a briefing after my return. But soon after there will be no way to keep either of the Vietnamese parties from making the stalemate evident. Furthermore, if we resume all-out bombing this will be even more true. Thus in the event of a stalemate we have only two choices: to yield, or to rally American support for one more effort which I do not believe the North Vietnamese can withstand. If we are to attempt to rally the American people only the President can adequately do that eventually."

On Wednesday, December 6, Kissinger and Le Duc Tho met for six hours. The North Vietnamese position remained essentially unchanged. After the meeting Kissinger sent a cable stating that we had reached a crossroads and must decide what we wanted to do. Again, he refined the choices to two options. Option One involved making one last attempt at reaching a settlement: we would scale down our requirements to the absolute minimum and then present them as our rock-bottom position. There was no reason to think that the North Vietnamese would respond to this approach, and there was a risk involved even if they did, because Thieu was almost certain to reject it and break with us. As Kissinger pointed out, "You must therefore realize that if you authorize me to proceed along the above lines and we succeed, you will face a major confrontation with the G.V.N. Unless you are prepared to undertake such a confrontation you should not instruct me to follow this course."

Option Two involved provoking a break-off of the talks by making some unacceptable demand and resuming massive bombing until the North Vietnamese agreed to return our POWs in exchange for our military withdrawal from Vietnam. Kissinger still felt that if we could keep up the bombing for six months—through the summer of 1973—the North Vietnamese would be forced to accept this straight prisoners-for-withdrawal trade as the basis of a settlement. It was to be presumed that Congress would not cut off funds if it could be shown that the North Vietnamese were not willing to return our POWs. Kissinger said: "If we are willing to pay the domestic and international price, rally the American people, and stay on our course, this option has fewer risks than the other one, given the G.V.N. attitude."

After giving Kissinger's cable the most serious consideration, I responded with a long message containing my step-by-step instructions for the next morning's session:

> After reading all your messages, I am again enormously impressed by the skillful and dedicated way that you're handling a terribly difficult situation.

Before a decision of this importance is made, it is imperative that I talk with you personally. To accomplish this goal, I suggest that you start tomorrow's session by saying that the President has read all of your messages and a full transcript of the conversations to date. He is, frankly, shocked by the total intransigence of the North Vietnamese and particularly by the fact that they have backed off of the commitments they made in October. Then, I want you to go down a list of specific questions on all of the proposals that are contained in your minimum position contained in your last message, adding to it the specific question about whether they will agree to any language covering the withdrawal of North Vietnamese forces from South Vietnam. I assume that their answers to virtually all of these questions will be negative, but the purpose is to make the record clear once and for all. I then want you to ask them what is their final offer. You will then tell them that you will report the answers they have given to the President directly and then you will contact them as to the time and the conditions for further meetings.

If the negotiations are to be broken off, it must be absolutely clear that they were responsible for breaking off the negotiations rather than me.

I also am firmly convinced that we should not paint ourselves into a corner by saying things like "This is our last offer" or "This is our final meeting." Leave a crack of the door open for further discussion.

I realize that you think that if I go on television that I can rally the American people to support an indefinite continuation of the war simply for the purpose of getting our prisoners back. I would agree that this is a possibility at this time. But, that can wear very thin within a matter of weeks, particularly as the propaganda organs—not only from North Vietnam but in this country—begin to hammer away at the fact that we had a much better deal in hand, and then because of Saigon's intransigence, we were unable to complete it.

However your meeting comes out today, if it does not end in a settlement, and of course I know and agree with you that there is a very remote possibility that you will make a breakthrough on the settlement side, we will embark on a very heavy bombing in the North. But we are going to do it without a dramatic television announcement of it. The thing to do here is to take the heat from the Washington establishment, who know the difference, for stepping up the bombing which will occur for a few days, and simply act strongly without escalating publicity about our actions by what we say about them.

On December 6 we gave Dobrynin an urgent message that we would be presenting our rock-bottom position at the next meeting and that failure to make progress would result in termination of the talks. He seemed to be very disturbed, and reiterated that the Soviets had been working continuously on North Vietnam to get them to accept an agreement. A few days later I stepped up the pressure by calling him and telling him that it was definitely in Moscow's interest that the negotiations wind up now because both Moscow and Washington had bigger fish to fry and it was in our mutual interest to eliminate this irritant in order to enable our mutual relations to continue to improve. We also informed the Chinese ambassador in Paris that the situation had become critical, and that before taking "grave steps" we wanted to bring the issues before Chou En-lai, because such action would obviously affect our ability to develop Sino-American relations in the ways that both our governments wanted.

When Kissinger and Le Duc Tho met on December 7, very little was accomplished. There was some progress the next day, however, and by the morning of December 9 there remained only one major unresolved issue, the DMZ. In fact, the North Vietnamese had already agreed to it during the November negotiations. But now Le Duc Tho was insisting on a new and vague clause about both sides "assessing regulations" for movement across the DMZ, which had the effect of calling its integrity into question. I sent a cable to the North Vietnamese, saying that I felt the inclusion of their new clause would make rapid conclusion of the agreement difficult and suggesting that the language they had agreed to at the November 23 session be restored.

On December 9, with only this one remaining item to negotiate, I allowed myself to begin feeling optimistic about the possibility of having an agreement before Christmas. It would be painful if Thieu refused to go along, but there was no question that we had done everything possible to help him and that now we had to look to our own interests and conclude an agreement if the terms were acceptable. I thought back over the roller-coaster events of the past week, which had begun with Kissinger's recommending breaking off the talks and bombing, and which seemed to be ending with a settlement in sight.

Diary

In essence, as Haldeman and I add things up we think what happened here is that Henry went back to Paris firmly convinced that he would quickly, within a matter of two days, reach agreement with the North Vietnamese. As a matter of fact, he told me that the meetings would only last two days—Monday and Tuesday.

The North Vietnamese surprised him by slapping him in the face with a wet fish.

The North wants to humiliate the South and us as well if possible. The South wants to drive the North out of South Vietnam and get us to stick with them until this goal is accomplished. As far as we are concerned, we must bring the war to an end on an honorable basis as quickly as possible.

Expectations have been built so high now that our failing to bring the war to an end would have a terribly depressing effect on this country, and no television speech is ever going to rally the people, despite Henry's feelings based on past performances that this could be the case. As I have pointed out in previous memos, and as I see it now very clearly, the country can be rallied when it's on its back and when you ask it to get up and fight. On the other hand, when the country is already very optimistic, to go in and tell them that things are in a hell of a shape doesn't rally them—it simply rallies our opponents and depresses our friends.

For better or for worse, we are on a course now where we have no choice but to make the very best settlement that we can and then to do the best that we can to see that it is enforced.

On December 10 the North Vietnamese replied to my cable, saying that they considered their position on the DMZ to be very reasonable. It seemed clear that they had made a decision to stall the negotiations.

That afternoon I decided to stir things up and remove any doubts about our resolution. I telephoned Dobrynin and told him that I personally did not favor any of the compromise language that Kissinger was suggesting regarding the DMZ. I said that Hanoi should abide by the language it had already agreed to, and I told him bluntly that it was definitely in Moscow's interest to aid the negotiations and get them over with since we both had bigger fish to fry. As it stood, I said, Hanoi's preoccupation with changing the DMZ arrangement could risk concluding an agreement that had now been largely achieved. Dobrynin asked for some time to communicate with Moscow.

At the meeting on Monday, December 11, the North Vietnamese were totally inflexible on the DMZ issue. Kissinger's report characterized their conduct as composed of equal parts of insolence, guile, and stalling.

They were somewhat more forthcoming the next day, but there was still no real progress. That night Kissinger reported that he had come to the conclusion that Hanoi had decided to play for time: Le Duc Tho was purposely trying to prevent either a settlement of the war or a break-off of the talks. It was possible that they simply planned to exploit the increasingly obvious split between us and Saigon, and I could not help thinking it was ironic that the North Vietnamese intransigence at the negotiating table may have been at least in part a result of our unsuccessful attempts to pressure Thieu into accepting an agreement. There was no doubt that the Communists had infiltrated the Saigon government, and that Hanoi was therefore aware of our warnings of congressional fund cutoffs in January. I noted in a diary entry a week later on December 18: "We are right on a tightrope here and I fear that as a result of the infiltration of the South Vietnamese that the North Vietnamese figure that they have us where the hair is short and are going to continue to squeeze us. That is why we had to take our strong action."

Of course it was also possible that the leaders in Hanoi were divided and were still making up their minds about whether to conclude the agreement. In any case, the result was the same: stalemate. Kissinger described the situation in his cable:

Their consistent pattern is to give us just enough each day to keep us going but nothing decisive which could conclude an agreement. . . .

On the other hand, they wish to ensure that we have no solid pretext for taking tough actions. They keep matters low key to prevent a resumption of bombing.

They could have settled in three hours anytime these past few days if they wanted to, but they have deliberately avoided this. For every one of their semi-concessions they introduce a counterdemand. . . .

The North Vietnamese strategy seems to me to be as follows: they have reduced the issues to a point where settlement can be reached with one exchange of telegrams. I do not think they will send this telegram, however, in the absence of strong pressures.

At the next meeting, on December 13, Le Duc Tho made it clear that he had no intention of reaching an agreement. He was scheduled to return to Hanoi for consultations the next day, so Kissinger suggested that the talks be recessed and no more meetings be held until after Christmas. That night I noted, "As I had somewhat anticipated, this day, December 13, is really one of the toughest days we have had during the administration."

Kissinger and I completely agreed on the cynicism and perfidy of the North Vietnamese. He even thought that Le Duc Tho's occasional fainting spells during the talks had been contrivances aimed at gaining a negotiating advantage by eliciting sympathy for him. Gritting his teeth and clenching his fists, Kissinger said, "They're just a bunch of shits. Tawdry, filthy shits. They make the Russians look good, compared to the way the Russians make the Chinese look good when it comes to negotiating in a responsible and decent way!"

I had reluctantly decided that we had now reached the point where only the strongest action would have any effect in convincing Hanoi that negotiating a fair settlement with us was a better option for them than continuing the war. Kissinger and I agreed that this meant stepping up the bombing. The only question was how much bombing would be needed to force Hanoi to settle. Kissinger recommended reseeding the mines of Haiphong Harbor, resuming full-scale bombing south of the 20th parallel, and intensifying bombing in southern Laos. My intuition was that something far more extensive was required. When I checked and found that the area south of the 20th parallel was largely rice paddies and jungle, I told Kissinger, "We'll take the same heat for big blows as for little blows. If we renew the bombing, it will have to be something new, and that means we will have to make the big decision to hit Hanoi and Haiphong with B-52s. Anything less will only make the enemy contemptuous."

Kissinger pointed out that Hanoi and Haiphong were heavily defended with Soviet surface-to-air (SAM) missiles. If we attacked them, we would have to be prepared for new losses and casualties and POWs. "I know," I said, "but if we're convinced that this is the right thing to do, then we will have to do it right."

On December 14 I issued an order, to become effective three days hence, for the reseeding of the mines in Haiphong Harbor, for resumed aerial reconnaissance, and for B-52 strikes against military targets in the Hanoi-Haiphong complex. The bombing plan included sixteen major transportation, power, and Radio Hanoi transmitter targets in Hanoi, as well as six communications command and control targets in the outlying area. There were thirteen targets in the Haiphong area, including shipyards and docks. When the first plans came in for the bombing, I was appalled to find that the planes had to be borrowed from different commands, involving complicated logistics and large amounts of red tape. The day after the bombing began, I think I shook Admiral Moorer when I called him and said, "I don't want any more of this crap about the fact that we couldn't hit this target or that one. This is your chance to use military power effectively to win this war, and if you don't, I'll consider you responsible." I stressed that we must hit and hit hard or there was no point in doing it at all. If the enemy detected any reticence in our actions, they would discount the whole exercise.

The order to renew bombing the week before Christmas was the most difficult decision I made during the entire war; at the same time, however, it was also one of the most clear-cut and necessary ones.

Henry talked rather emotionally about the fact that this was a very courageous decision, but I pointed out to him that there was no other choice—that we were going to be here for four years and that even though we made a good, cheap peace now, to have it break within a matter of a year or two would leave us with nothing to be proud of and beyond that would leave us with terrible choices—much worse choices—later than we would have at the present time. We are going to face up to the music at this time with the hope that this will gain their attention and keep them from reacting to us later.

We decided that Kissinger would conduct a public briefing on the state of the negotiations. It was vitally important that we lay responsibility for the current impasse where it belonged—squarely on the North Vietnamese. I met with him several times to review what he would say; I also dictated two long memoranda covering the points I considered it important for him to make. I felt that we had to get across that the North Vietnamese had agreed to a settlement, then reneged on a number of points, and now were refusing to negotiate seriously. I also said that Kissinger should criticize Thieu for insisting on total victory when what we wanted was a just peace that both sides would be able to keep and live with.

In the early morning hours of Sunday, December 17, our planes reseeded the mines in Haiphong Harbor. Within twenty-four hours 129 B-52s took part in bombing raids over North Vietnam.

Diary
The tough decision has now been made and is under way with regard to the bombing around Haiphong. I have just learned about one B-52 shot down. Henry said they expected as many as three. Of course, there are two more waves to go, but they expect on the second and third waves the amount of SAM opposition to be down or at least suppressed. At least, we can

only pray that that will be the case and hope that it is the case.

Two more B-52s were shot down during the day.

Diary
I suppose all the decisions are hard—the May 8 one in retrospect may have been the most difficult one, although Cambodia was just as difficult in its way, and November 3 was difficult. But this one was heartrending due to the fact that everything was moving along in the right direction. And, also, because there is such great uncertainty as to what reaction there will be as a result of what we have done.

In any event, the decision is made and we cannot turn back. Henry has been up and down, understandably. For example, this morning he seems to be down more than up. I have called Moorer to be sure to stiffen his back with regard to the need to follow through on these attacks. I suppose that we may be pressing him too hard, but I fear that the Air Force and the Navy may in carrying out orders have been too cautious at times in the past, and that our political objectives have not been achieved because of too much caution on the military side. We simply have to take losses if we are going to accomplish our objectives.

I remember Churchill's admonition in his book on World War I, that one can have a policy of audacity or one can follow a policy of caution, but it is disastrous to try to follow a policy of audacity and caution at the same time. It must be one or the other. We have now gone down the audacious line and we must continue until we get some sort of a break.

Many people could not understand why I did not "go public" with the reasons for the December bombing. As I have already indicated, I did not feel that the American people were ready to be rallied at this time as they had been on November 3 and on May 8. But more important, I was convinced that any public statements on my part would have been directly counterproductive to the possibility of resumed negotiations. If I had announced that we were resuming bombing for the purpose of forcing the North Vietnamese to negotiate, their national pride and their ideological fanaticism would never have allowed them to accept the international loss of face involved in caving to such an ultimatum. So I did it with the minimum amount of rhetoric and publicity, and it succeeded exactly as I had intended. Our brief but massive use of force got the message through to Hanoi while still allowing them to back off their intransigent position without having to acknowledge that they were doing so because of military pressure from us.

On the morning of December 18, in a message to the North Vietnamese in Paris, we said that after having carefully reviewed the record of the recent negotiations, we had decided that they were deliberately and frivolously delaying the talks. We proposed returning to the text of the agreement as it had stood after the November 23 session, with the addition of one or two subsequently negotiated changes. On this basis we would be prepared to meet again at any time after December 26 to conclude an agreement.

I decided that we would also make every possible effort to convince Thieu that in the event the North Vietnamese agreed to resume negotiations, it was imperative that he join us in offering reasonable terms Hanoi would be willing to accept. We considered Agnew, Laird, and Connally for this unenviable job, but finally I said, "Haig is still the man to carry the message to Garcia."

Haig arrived in Saigon on December 19, carrying the strongest letter I had yet written to Thieu. In it I stated: "General Haig's mission now represents my final effort to point out to you the necessity for joint action and to convey my irrevocable intention to proceed, preferably with your cooperation, but, if necessary, alone. . . . I have asked General Haig to obtain your answer to this absolutely final offer on my part for us to work together in seeking a settlement along the lines I have approved or to go our separate ways." Haig told Thieu that I had dictated the letter personally and that no one else in our government had seen it. After Thieu had read the letter through twice, he looked up and said that it was obvious that he was not being asked to sign an agreement for peace but rather an agreement for continued

American support. Haig replied that as a soldier and as someone completely familiar with Communist treachery, he agreed with Thieu's assessment.

Thieu seemed almost desperate. He argued that the cease-fire would not last more than three months: then, when the last American had gone, the Communists would resume their guerrilla warfare. But this time they would fight with knives and bayonets, being careful not to do anything sufficient to justify American retaliation. In this way my guarantees to enforce the agreement would never be put to the test, and the Communists would have a free hand against him and his government.

After this meeting Thieu leaked word to reporters that we had tried to force him to accept an ultimatum and that he had refused. I was shocked when I learned this, and I felt we would now be justified in breaking with him and making a separate peace with Hanoi. But I was still reluctant to allow our annoyance with him to lead us to do anything that might bring about Communist domination of South Vietnam.

December 20 was the third day of heavy air strikes over North Vietnam. Ninety B-52s flew three waves of attacks against eleven targets. Six planes were lost. On December 21 there were thirty B-52 sorties flown against three new targets. Two planes were lost.

My major concern during the first week of bombing was not the sharp wave of domestic and international criticism, which I had expected, but the high losses of B-52s. I noted on December 23, "I raised holy hell about the fact that they kept going over the same targets at the same time. I was, therefore, not surprised, although deeply disappointed, when we lost five planes on the second or third day. Finally, we got the military to change their minds." The Pentagon began scheduling the strikes at different times and on different routes, thus denying the enemy the knowledge of when and where the strikes would take place and thereby reducing their ability to shoot down our planes.

On December 22 we sent a message to the North Vietnamese requesting a meeting for January 3. If they accepted, we offered to stop the bombing north of the 20th parallel on December 31 and suspend it for the duration of the meeting.

The media reaction to the December bombing was predictable. The Washington *Post* editorialized that it caused millions of Americans "to cringe in shame and to wonder at their President's very sanity." Joseph Kraft called it an action "of senseless terror which stains the good name of America." James Reston called it "war by tantrum," and Anthony Lewis charged that I was acting "like a maddened tyrant." In Congress there were similarly critical outbursts from members of both parties. Republican Senator William Saxbe of Ohio said that "President Nixon . . . appears to have left his senses on this issue." And Mike Mansfield said that it was a "stone-age tactic."

Diary

On the negative side, the columnists and the media broke down about the way they had during the election and on all the Vietnam decisions previously.

The record of the liberal left media on Vietnam is perhaps one of the most disgraceful in the whole history of communications in this country. I am not referring to the honest pacifists who have been against the war from the beginning, but to those in the media who simply cannot bear the thought of this administration under my leadership bringing off the peace on an honorable basis which they have so long predicted would be impossible.

The election was a terrible blow to them and this is their first opportunity to recover from the election and to strike back.

It was especially gratifying to receive calls of support from Nelson Rockefeller and Ronald Reagan. Senator James Buckley also stood behind me, as did Howard Baker, Bob Taft, and Chuck Percy. One of my strongest supporters was John Connally, who called daily to report some new and positive sampling of public opinion.

As the criticism outside mounted, the pressure inside the White House became intense. I could feel the tension in the people I passed and greeted as I walked back and forth to the EOB. I knew how sincerely troubled many of them were because of the bombing; I understood how difficult the bombing made it for many of them to face their friends and even their families during what should have been a happy holiday season.

Pat and I spent Christmas at Key Biscayne. It was the first Christmas we had been alone without the girls. Tricia and Ed were in Europe traveling, and Julie was also there to be with David. Pat and I naturally urged them to go, but I think we were both depressed to find how empty the house seemed without them. Casting a dark shadow over everything was the knowledge that if the bombing did not succeed in forcing the North Vietnamese back to the negotiating table, there was no way of knowing how—or whether—the Vietnam war would end. I made several diary entries during this holiday period.

Diary

This is December 24, 1972—Key Biscayne—4 A.M.

The main thought that occurred to me at this early hour of the morning the day before Christmas, in addition to the overriding concern with regard to bringing the war to an end, is that I must get away from the thought of considering the office at any time a burden. I actually do not consider it a burden, an agony, etc., as did Eisenhower and also to a certain extent Johnson. As a matter of fact, I think the term glorious burden is the best description.

On this day before Christmas it is God's great gift to me to have the opportunity to exert leadership, not only for America but on the world scene, because of the size of the mandate and also the strength of the country.

In a sense, of course, this is not true because immediately after World War II our power was greater because of the monopoly of the bomb and the weakness of Europe and Japan as well as the weakness of China and Russia. But then, there were other world leaders on the scene. Today, except for Chiang Kai-shek most of the World War II greats are gone. This, on the one hand, imposes an enormous responsibility but, of course, at the same time the greatest opportunity an individual could have.

From this day forward I am going to look upon it that way and rise to the challenge with as much excitement, energy, enthusiasm, and, wherever possible, real joy that I can muster.

God's help will be required as will the help of loyal people on the staff and the family.

A new group of Nixon loyalists, of course, is an urgent necessity, but this really begins a new period and this tape concludes with that thought—a period of always reminding myself of the glorious burden of the presidency.

At 6 P.M. Saigon time on December 24 a twenty-four-hour Christmas truce I had approved began in Vietnam. No planes flew. No bombs were dropped. For a day we were at peace.

On Christmas Day I made phone calls to many of our long-time friends and supporters across the country.

Diary
All in all, the Christmas calls didn't produce anything important or different, except not too much talk about the bombing. My guess is that they were all concerned about the media handling of it. Reagan mentioned that and said CBS under World War II circumstances would have been perhaps charged with treason.

Martha Mitchell sounded very up when I called her, which is encouraging because John Mitchell has gone through hell with her and I am glad that she is finally recovering. Perhaps the two weeks or so down here will make a great difference in getting all of them back on the track in a way that John can continue to be effective politically because he is one of the wisest men, one of the strongest men, we have on our whole team.

Henry called to wish us a Merry Christmas but obviously needed a little cheering up, which I was totally able to do because I am confident we are doing the right thing.

It is inevitable that not only the President but the First Lady become more and more lonely individuals in a sense who have to depend on fewer and fewer people who can give them a lift when they need it, even though ironically there are millions more who know them and who would help if they could just be given the chance to do so. It is a question not of too many friends but really too few—one of the inevitable consequences of this position.

As this Christmas Day ends I am thankful for Manolo and Fina, for the wonderful Filipinos and the staff, for Bebe, for Julie and Tricia, Pat, for all of those who basically are our family at a time that the girls are so far away.

Harry Truman died on the day after Christmas. According to his wishes, he lay in state at the Truman Library in Independence, Missouri. On December 27 Pat and I flew there to pay our respects to him and to call on Mrs. Truman.

There was considerable pressure from some of the staff to continue the Christmas truce for a few more days. But I disagreed completely. In fact, I personally ordered one of the biggest bombing raids for December 26: 116 B-52 sorties were flown against targets in the Hanoi-Haiphong area.

That afternoon the North Vietnamese sent the first signal that they had had enough. We received a message from them condemning what they called "extermination bombing," but they did not require that the bombing be stopped as a precondition to their agreeing to another meeting, which they proposed for January 8 in Paris. We replied that we would like the technical talks to begin on January 2 if the Kissinger meeting was to be delayed until January 8. We offered to stop the bombing above the 20th parallel once the arrangements for the meeting had been completed and had been publicly announced. On December 28 the North Vietnamese gave in and confirmed the January 2 and January 8 dates.

At 7 P.M. Washington time on December 29 bombing above the 20th parallel was suspended. The next morning we announced that the Paris negotiations would be resumed and that Kissinger would meet with Le Duc Tho on January 8.

Diary

The real question is whether the announcement today will be interpreted in the public mind as having been the result of a policy that worked. Of course, it will not be so interpreted by our opponents in the media and the Congress.

I have gone over this with Chuck Colson and he in turn with John Scali [Special Consultant to the President]. They both recognize that much of the media will try to say, "Why was the bombing necessary?" or might even try to say we were forced back to the table because of the world outcry and all that sort of thing.

Henry always looks at it in terms of the merits, and on the merits we know that what this is is a very stunning capitulation by the enemy to our terms.

Most of the TV reporters and the next morning's newspapers put the emphasis on the bombing halt rather than the resumption of talks, and most of them indicated that it was not clear whether the return to negotiations was the result of the bombing, or whether the bombing halt was the result of the enemy's agreement to return to negotiations. It was frustrating not to be able to set them straight. As I said to Colson, "We'll just have to trust to the good judgment of the people to see it. Certainly the press isn't going to make the point for us."

Pat and I spent New Year's Eve at Camp David. I watched the Redskins beat the Cowboys on television, 26 to 3. Just before midnight I looked back over the day and then ahead to the coming year.

Diary

I let all the staff off today and had Manolo cook

some eggs and bacon [for dinner]. I had about half a martini and then some white wine, bacon and eggs.

As the year 1972 ends I have much to be grateful for—China, Russia, May 8, the election victory, and, of course, while the end of the year was somewhat marred by the need to bomb Hanoi-Haiphong, that decision, I think, can make the next four years much more successful than they otherwise might have been.

1973 will be a better year.

On January 2 I called Lyndon Johnson at his ranch in Texas. We shared a few reminiscences of Harry Truman, and he said that he did not know whether he would be able to attend the memorial service in Washington because he had experienced severe heart pains after attending the recent Texas-Alabama football game and his doctor had told him not to travel.

The conversation turned to Vietnam, and Johnson said, "I know what torture you're going through over the war, and I want you to know that I'm praying for you every day."

I told him, "I know that you tried to do the right thing when you were here, and that is what I am trying to do as well."

We continued to play the Soviet and Chinese strategies for whatever they might turn out to be worth. Kissinger went to see Dobrynin and told him that the things the Soviets wanted—a Mideast settlement, a European security conference, nuclear weapons agreements—would have to stay on the back burner until Vietnam was settled. And I wrote a letter to Chou En-lai, saying that the Vietnam war impeded the kind of further progress that would benefit both our countries.

On January 2, 1973, the day before Congress officially reconvened, the House Democratic Caucus voted 154 to 75 to cut off all funds for Indochina military operations as soon as arrangements were made for the safe withdrawal of U.S. troops and the return of our POWs. Two days later Teddy Kennedy proposed a similar resolution to the Senate Democratic Caucus, where it passed 36 to 12. The atmosphere of the congressional leadership breakfast at the White House the next morning was tense. At the end I made a short speech about my reasons for the bombing and why I was sure it was the only way to get a settlement. I concluded, "Gentlemen, I will take the responsibility if these negotiations fail. If they succeed, then we will all succeed."

I was not surprised at the conduct of the Democratic liberals. Ever since the election I had virtually written off any hope of receiving support or cooperation from them. I could see that they were going to try to use the Vietnam issue to pull themselves together after the McGovern debacle. Their strategy seemed obvious: if we got an agreement, they would say that it was because they had pressured me to stop the bombing and return to the negotiating table; if we failed to get an agreement, they would insist on the military withdrawal that most of them had favored all along.

On January 6, before he left for Paris, Kissinger and I met at Camp David to discuss the negotiating strategy he should follow. During the last round of negotiations in December he had described the two options from which we had to choose. Under Option One we would agree to an immediate settlement on the best terms we could negotiate. Under Option Two we would break with Thieu and continue the bombing until the North Vietnamese agreed to return our POWs in exchange for our complete withdrawal.

I was determined that this round of negotiations would produce an agreement, and I strongly conveyed my sentiments to Kissinger.

Diary
Adding it all up I put it to Henry quite directly that even if we could go back to the October 8 agreement that we should take it, having in mind the fact that there will be a lot of details that will have been ironed out so that we can claim some improvement over that agreement. I told him that a poor settlement on Option One was better for us than Option Two at its best would be.

He has finally come around to that point of view, although he believes that both from the standpoint of

South Vietnam and perhaps our own standpoint in the long term, we might be better off with Option Two. I think he overlooks the fact that as far as our situation here is concerned, the war-weariness has reached the point that Option Two is just too much for us to carry on.

The war continues to take too much of our attention from other international issues, such as the Mideast, and it also has a detrimental effect on our international relations, not only with the Soviet and the Chinese but even with our allies.

As I told him goodbye at the door of Birch Lodge, I said, "Well, one way or another, this is it!" That night I tried to list all the pluses and minuses to see if I could find some clue to the way things would turn out.

Diary

The first day may tell us a great deal. Certainly as of the end of last week there was a good chance that the enemy was coming back to negotiate a settlement. The international support they have had and the support from the Democrats in Congress may cool them off and convince them that they can hang on longer.

Henry, of course, is going to continue to play the hard line, indicating that I might resort to resumption of the bombing in the Hanoi area, even though I have told him that as far as our internal planning is concerned we cannot consider this to be a viable option.

He feels that another card we have is the threat to withdraw the agreement altogether. He believes that Hanoi wants an agreement now for the reason that this gives them some standing in the South, whereas an American bug-out ironically would still leave them with the necessity of winning militarily in the South.

Some minor straws in the wind are that the technical talks have made some progress this week on the four easier issues, with the four tougher ones left for next week. Also, the fact that the North Vietnamese have launched offensives in the South may indicate that they are trying to grab territory and villages, etc., prior to the time that a cease-fire takes place.

Another plus item is that the South Vietnamese seem to be coming more into line. Our intelligence indicates that Thieu is telling visitors that it is not a peace agreement that he is going to get, but a commitment from the United States to continue to protect South Vietnam in the event such an agreement is broken. This, of course, is exactly the line I gave him in my letter which Haig delivered to him.

In the midst of the tense days of the December bombing and the furore it provoked, new Watergate problems began to surface. On December 8 Howard Hunt's wife was killed in a plane crash; since then Hunt had apparently been disconsolate and on the verge of a breakdown. Now that Hunt was about to face a jail term, Colson began to worry about him.

On the White House staff there were the first signs of finger-pointing, tentative and without evidence. I could sense that people were getting unsettled and worried. I dictated in my diary on January 3.

Diary
One disturbing note was Haldeman's comment to the effect that Colson may have been aware of the Watergate business. I am not sure actually that he was. Haldeman's point was that Colson was insisting on getting information with regard to attempts of the Democrats to disrupt our convention, etc. Of course, Colson may have been insisting on such information but he may not have been aware of what means were being used to obtain this information. I simply can't believe, based on my conversations with Colson, that he would have been so stupid as to think we could get such information through attempting to bug the other side.

I made another note about this problem three days later, on Saturday, January 6.

Diary
    Colson told me on Friday that he had tried to do everything he could to keep Hunt in line from turning state's evidence. After what happened to Hunt's wife, etc., I think we have a very good case for showing some clemency.
    It was Colson's view apparently that either Haldeman or Ehrlichman or both might have been more deeply involved than has been indicated. Of course, it is all hearsay. Colson's point is that Magruder is a name-dropper and that Magruder may have mentioned the names of Haldeman and Ehrlichman in telling the Watergate people to get information. Apparently, according to Colson, too, some of the meetings took place in Mitchell's office at the Justice Department. This would seem hard for me to believe but then again during the campaign people are not as rational or responsible as they normally would be. This, I know, must be a great burden for Haldeman and Ehrlichman during this past tough week and I could see that something was eating them without knowing what.

    I was concerned about these speculations, but I saw them at least in part as manifestations of the routine staff animosities that had long existed between Colson and Mitchell and Colson and Ehrlichman.
    It now seems clear that I knew Colson was sending messages of reassurance to Hunt through his lawyer— messages that Hunt took to be signals of eventual clemency. I did not believe that any commitments had been made. I cannot even rule out the possibility that I knew similar reassurance was being given the other defendants. I certainly do not remember it, but where Watergate is concerned I have learned not to be categorical. In any event, I was relieved when, in early January, Hunt and the others pleaded guilty. I thought this would spare us the difficulties of a noisy public trial and all the distraction that would produce at such a critical time.

256

On Monday, January 8, Kissinger met with Le Duc Tho for four and a half hours. Nothing was accomplished, but in Kissinger's report to me that night he pointed out that it would probably not be realistic to expect the Communists to give in or give up on the first day back after the bombing. I was naturally disappointed, but there was nothing to do but wait and hope. That night I recorded some reflections on the eve of my sixtieth birthday.

Diary

All in all, as the day is finished I look back over the past ten years and realize how life can seem to be at an end as it appeared to be on January 9, 1963, and then has turned completely around by January 9, 1973. It all has to do with spirit, as I emphasized to Colson, who is only forty-one years of age. He was obviously depressed tonight, probably because of the Hunt matter, etc., but I think I lifted him a bit by what we said.

We will get a report from Kissinger today which should tell us one way or another whether there is going to be any breakthrough in the talks.

I noted in the paper this morning that they made a great point out of the fact that the protocol was icy when Henry arrived. This does not bother me because so far when they have had a warm reaction to Henry's arrival, they make no progress. Perhaps having it exactly the opposite may bring a different result.

About noon on January 9 Haldeman came into the Oval Office with a cable from Kissinger.

"What happened?" I asked.

"I think you should read this for yourself, Mr. President," he said solemnly.

I took the paper, put on my glasses, and began to read: "We celebrated the President's birthday today by making a major breakthrough in the negotiations. In sum, we settled all the outstanding questions in the text of the agreement."

Kissinger warned against undue optimism: "The Vietnamese have broken our heart several times before, and we just cannot assume success until everything is pinned down, but the mood and the businesslike approach was as close to

October as we have seen since October." He concluded, "What has brought us to this point is the President's firmness and the North Vietnamese belief that he will not be affected by either congressional or public pressures. Le Duc Tho has repeatedly made these points to me. So it is essential that we keep our fierce posture during the coming days. The slightest hint of eagerness could prove suicidal."

I immediately dictated my reply:

> I greatly appreciated your birthday greetings and your report. I totally agree with the need to maintain absolutely "eyes only" secrecy on developments until we have everything completely nailed down. . . .
>
> You should continue a tough posture and, above all, not let the other side filibuster. If the other side stays on this track and doesn't go downhill tomorrow, what you have done today is the best birthday present I have had in sixty years.

The momentum continued through the next session, and Kissinger reported that at the current rate of progress the agreement should be concluded within three or four days.

On January 11 Kissinger cabled, "We finished the complete text of the agreement, including the provisions for signature." It was nine days short of four years since I had entered the White House and inherited the task of ending the Vietnam war.

When the announcement was made that Kissinger was going to fly directly to Key Biscayne from Paris in order to report to me on the progress of his meetings with the North Vietnamese, there was widespread speculation that an agreement had been concluded. In a brief statement at the airport before leaving Paris, Kissinger flashed one of his enigmatic, owlish smiles and said the talks had been "useful."

He arrived in Key Biscayne several hours later, and we talked until after 2 A.M. He described all the tension and drama of the intricate negotiations. Even though he was tired from the talks and the long flight, he still displayed his characteristic thoroughness and enthusiasm. In the early hours of the following morning I recorded some notes about the conclusion of our meeting.

Diary

After we met, I walked out to the car with him and I told him that the country was indebted to him for what he had done. It is not really a comfortable feeling for me to praise people so openly. I prefer to do it a little bit more discreetly. I recall this was one of Eisenhower's characteristics as well. On the other hand, Henry expects it, and it was good that I did so. He, in turn, responded that without my having the, as he put it, courage to make the difficult decision of December 18, we would not be where we are today.

On January 15 at ten o'clock in the morning all bombing and mining of North Vietnam were stopped for an indefinite period, and we made a public announcement of our actions. The bombing had done its job; it had been successful, and now it could be ended. It was good news for all of us.

Diary

I had Henry call Pat and give her a rundown on affairs shortly after the announcement. Henry said that the four years he had known Mrs. Nixon he had never heard her sound so elated—that she was enormously pleased.

Julie just wanted to call. She was bubbly and upbeat and she and her mother, who was apparently in the room with her, were very proud of what had happened. I began to answer by indicating that the stopping of the bombing I suppose was pretty popular and all that sort of thing. She says, no, that isn't what she meant. She and her mother were proud of the fact that I had gone ahead and done what was right.

I had heard that Mike Mansfield was telling people how restrained and responsible the Senate had been during the past week of negotiations, and I noted in my diary, "It is interesting to note that Mansfield had reacted as he had. Of course, they cut Henry's legs off before he ever went."

There was also a discordant note to record that same day.

Diary

It is ironic that the day the news came out stopping the bombing of North Vietnam, the Watergate Four plead guilty. When I saw the headlines in the *Times*—spies plead guilty in Watergate—I realized what the press would have done if they had not had another story that would override it.

There is a new wrinkle to this which is rather curious. Colson told me that the problem in Hunt's case and with the case generally was that a confession might lead to Haldeman and even Ehrlichman. On the other hand, Haldeman told me that what the *Time* magazine and New York *Times*'s exposés were going to say was that the line ran from Liddy to Colson to Mitchell. Only an ultimatum served on the *Times* that if they used this they would be subject to a libel suit with malice being proved kept them from using that particular item.

I frankly am at a loss to know how it happened and it is probably just as well, but my guess is that Colson was not as aware of it as Haldeman et al. thought he was.

Whether Haldeman was aware of it, I simply don't know, although I think he would be intelligent enough to have stayed a mile away from such stupid activity.

Obviously the judge is going to throw the book at them and this will present quite a problem when it comes to a pardon. It is interesting to note that funds for providing income for them are coming from a Cuban committee here in Florida and it is also interesting to note that just this week Teddy Kennedy comes out with an article indicating that we should renew relations with Castro. Certainly these men would not have taken such enormous risks unless they felt deeply that the McGovernites et al. and the Democrats generally represented a threat to institutions and ideas they deeply believed in.

We had reached agreement on terms with the North Vietnamese but we still had to persuade Thieu to join us in signing the agreement. Thieu had made good use of the time since October and was in a considerably stronger position vis-à-vis the Communists than he had been then. I had always believed that his common sense and patriotism—if not his instinct for survival—would make him come along when we reached the absolute deadline for concluding an agreement before Congress intervened and took the conduct of the war out of my hands. Now we were at that point, and my estimation of Thieu would be put to the test. Soon after Kissinger had returned to Washington on January 14, Haig left for Saigon.

On the morning of January 16 he met with Thieu and handed him a letter from me. In it I said that I had irrevocably decided to initial the agreement on January 23 and sign it on January 27. "I will do so," I wrote, "if necessary, alone." I continued:

In that case I shall have to explain publicly that your government obstructs peace. The result will be an inevitable and immediate termination of U.S. economic and military assistance which cannot be forestalled by a change of personnel in your government. I hope, however, that after all our two countries have shared and suffered together in conflict, we will stay together to preserve peace and reap its benefits.

To this end I want to repeat to you the assurances that I have already conveyed. At the time of signing the agreement I will make emphatically clear that the United States recognizes your government as the only legal government of South Vietnam; that we do not recognize the right of any foreign troops to be present on South Vietnamese territory; and that we will react strongly in the event the agreement is violated. Finally, I want to emphasize my continued commitment to the freedom and progress of the Republic of Vietnam. It is my firm intention to continue full economic and military aid.

With this letter and this guarantee I did not feel that I could do any more. Up to this point I had not felt that I could do any less. The decision now lay with Thieu.

Diary

Thieu's choice is simply whether he wants to commit suicide or go along with a settlement that could save his country as well as himself. The question, as he put it to his National Security Council, was whether he should be a hero now by turning down the settlement, or a statesman that would save his country later. This is exactly the case. I just told Henry, however, that I doubted if he would be a hero if he turned down the settlement, because the South Vietnamese are losing upward of 250 to 300 killed in action every week, and I imagine they are pretty tired of the war too and would like to have a cease-fire.

It appeared that, true to form to the end, Thieu was going to play it right down to the wire.

In their second meeting on January 17 Haig and Thieu had a brief and emotional encounter during which Thieu gave him a sealed letter addressed to me. Haig returned to the embassy and read the letter. It was, as Haig described it, brittle and uncompromising. I immediately sent a letter in return challenging Thieu's points one by one and confronting him with an inescapable conclusion: "We have only one decision before us: whether or not to continue in peacetime the close partnership that has served us so well in war."

On January 18 it was jointly announced in Washington and Hanoi that the Paris negotiations would resume on January 23 "for the purpose of completing the text of an agreement." Peace fever broke out everywhere, and reporters flatly stated, with an assurance they could not know was justified, that a settlement was in the bag.

As we anxiously awaited further word from Saigon, Bunker cabled that he had not been able to get an appointment with Thieu because he was engaged in all-day religious ceremonies connected with his daughter's marriage. Bunker and Haig both felt that Thieu was stalling simply in order to be able to say that he had done all he could. They felt he saw my inauguration on January 20 as his last deadline.

In the meantime Haig had traveled to Bangkok and Seoul. The Thai leaders and President Park had no confidence that the North Vietnamese intended to abide by the agreement. But they understood the political realities of the American scene, and they agreed to support the settlement publicly and privately to urge Thieu to sign it.

After one last stab at resistance and another series of letters between us, Thieu finally decided to accept the agreement. Looking across his desk at Bunker, he said, "I have done my best. I have done all that I can do for my country." Even though his conduct had been almost unbearably frustrating, I had to admire his spirit.

Now we had to wait while the final arrangements were made and until the North Vietnamese locked themselves into signing the agreement by announcing it publicly in Hanoi.

On January 20 I was sworn in for my second term as the thirty-seventh President of the United States. I had hoped that my second inauguration would take place in peacetime. But the inevitable delays, added to the dangers of becoming committed publicly to any specific date, pushed the peace agreement into the post-inaugural period. Instead of being able to describe in my inaugural address the blessings of a peace achieved, I could only describe a peace that was near achievement and talk about the ways we could try to make it more than just an interlude between wars.

I am sure that many who heard my words on that cold January afternoon thought I was engaging in conventional inaugural rhetoric when I said, "We have the chance today to do more than ever before in our history to make life better in America—to ensure better education, better health, better housing, better transportation, a cleaner environment—to restore respect for law, to make our communities more livable—and to ensure the God-given right of every American to full and equal opportunity." But I fully believed that, backed by my November mandate and based on my determination to proceed despite the opposition or the political cost, we could actually succeed during my second term in bringing America closer than ever before in history to the attainment of these goals.

This would be my last inaugural address, and I had decided to use it in order to impart a sense of the inspirational tone that I wanted to give to my second term.

I concluded, "We shall answer to God, to history, and

to our conscience for the way in which we use these years. As I stand in this place, so hallowed by history, I think of others who have stood here before me. I think of the dreams they had for America and I think of how each recognized that he needed help far beyond himself in order to make those dreams come true. Today I ask your prayers that in the years ahead I may have God's help in making decisions that are right for America, and I pray for your help so that together we may be worthy of our challenge. . . . Let us go forward from here confident in hope, strong in our faith in one another, sustained by our faith in God who created us, and striving always to serve His purpose."

That night, before leaving for the inaugural balls, I went to the Lincoln Sitting Room and recorded some memories and impressions, beginning with inaugural concerts at the Kennedy Center the night before.

Diary

When Mike Curb stepped up at the end of the performance and said that the President had done more to bring peace in the world than anybody else, I thought we would get a few boos. Interestingly enough, he got a pretty good cheer for it, which allayed one of the fears I had as we went to these inaugurals, having read earlier that eleven of Eugene Ormandy's orchestra members requested the right not to come, and he had put his foot down and told them to come. When Steve Bull informed him that I would not be coming down to the platform because it simply couldn't be worked out from a logistic standpoint, Ormandy said that he would have liked to have me come to the stage and stand there beside him "just to show those left-wing sons of bitches." What a man he is.

Inaugural morning, after getting up, I ran 500 steps in place. It left me a little breathless, but I thought it was a good idea to be in as good shape as I could for the ceremonies to take place later in the day.

Before going downstairs, I stepped into the Lincoln Bedroom in the spot where the Emancipation Proclamation was and where I understood Lincoln's desk was located and bowed my head for a moment, and prayed that I might be able to give the country some lift, some inspiration, and some leadership in the rather brief inaugural that I had prepared.

The ride down to the Capitol gave us some indication of what we could expect later in the way of demonstrators. Little clusters of them had gotten into strategic places along the route. Pat and the others didn't hear them, but they were yelling "f-u-c-k," etc., and were a pretty vicious lot.

The inauguration went on schedule—perhaps the best of any that I have seen. The public address system was superb, no hecklers could be heard, although way in the background I think there were a few who let out a few obscenities as I began to speak and then subsided or probably somebody subsided them.

Mrs. Agnew kissed Agnew—Pat did not kiss me. I am rather glad she didn't. I sometimes think these displays of affection are very much in place, as was the case election night. Other times, I don't think they quite fit and on this occasion I didn't really think it quite fit.

[At the inaugural luncheon in the Capitol] I could feel somewhat of a chill. I was thinking how much worse it would have been if we hadn't had the recent developments this week with regard to the possible settlement in Paris. It came not far ahead of the sheriff, and not far enough, I am sure, to avoid some jolt in the polls.

I don't give one damn what the polls say insofar as affecting my decisions. I only care about them because they may affect my ability to lead, since politicians do pay attention to them.

I stood up all of the way through the inaugural parade. Pat got up about a third of the way down and when the demonstrators began to throw eggs and debris, the Secret Service asked her to sit down, and she refused. She was absolutely right. There was one incident where a demonstrator broke out and started to charge the car. The Secret Service agents were on top of him like lightning and brought him down with a tackle.

My feeling is that this may well be the last of the inaugural balls. I just can't imagine that people pay all that money to stand in that huge mob. One girl from Massachusetts was practically hysterical crying, "I love and respect you so much!" Even though we were leaving, I danced with her for a few minutes. Pat, who notices those things a little more than I do, said that the girl was dressed in a rather plain gown, one that perhaps she had made herself, and it had probably cost her a great deal to come. In any event, the dancing was the great hit of the evening. People who came in afterward said the girls and even some of the boys were crying because we had mixed with them so much.

It is obvious that we have to get across more of what Rossiter has called "affability." The staff just hasn't been able to get it across and so I am going to have to do all of these things publicly which demonstrates that. On the other hand, you can't overplay it.

Time passed slowly waiting for January 23 and the announcement of the Vietnam settlement. In the early evening of January 22, while our waiting had yet to be rewarded, Lyndon Johnson died.

Diary
With his death there will be, I trust, the same reappraisal of his place in history as was the case of Truman on his death, although, of course, it will not be nearly as fulsome because not enough years have passed and because there are too many current hatreds which divide the country.

The sadness in Johnson's case is that he did not live to see his position in history really established by reason of our winning a peace with honor in Vietnam. On the other hand, his family will see it and that is, of course, extremely important, and he will know it I am sure.

I also had an interesting reaction as I was thinking about the reason LBJ went down in the polls and so forth in early 1968. What happened was that he did isolate himself—he quit fighting for his policies in public—he did not generate the public support for them. As a matter of fact, he seemed to be running away from them. It was when my November 3 speech came along that we really ginned up some public support for winning a peace with honor. LBJ gave away this ground, and that was why he really failed in the end and was driven out of public office.

I think that Lyndon Johnson died of a broken heart, physically and emotionally. He was an enormously able and proud man. He desperately wanted, and expected, to be a great President. He drove himself to outdo his predecessor.

After I won the election in 1968, and through the remaining years of Johnson's life, I saw what some have described as the "better side" of his character. He was courteous, generally soft-spoken, and thoughtful in every way. He was not the pushing, prodding politician or the consummate partisan of his earlier career.

Above all Johnson wanted to be loved—to earn not only the approval but also the affection of every American. Much of his overblown rhetoric and many of his domestic policies were rooted in this compulsive quest for approbation. Johnson should have allowed himself to be guided by his moderately conservative instincts, which would have led him to avoid huge spending programs at a time when America was deeply involved in a costly war. Seeking both guns and butter is a policy that works only in the very short term. I think that Johnson belatedly came to understand this, because through the four years of my first term I cannot recall an instance when he urged me to go forward with any of his Great Society programs.

Johnson's slogan in the 1964 campaign was "All the way with LBJ." But he found that where the liberals in the media and the left wing of his own party were concerned, it was either all the way with them or none of the way. They applauded his liberal domestic programs, and they praised the Great Society. But the consensus he worked so hard to develop disintegrated when he would not follow their demands for a U.S. bug-out in Vietnam, and they turned on him with a bitterness and ferocity that depressed him and hurt him deeply. He had catered and almost pandered to them, but he could no longer win them.

The hatefulness of the attacks on Johnson's Vietnam policy was symbolized by that awful, mindless chant shouted by antiwar demonstrators: "Hey, hey, LBJ, how many kids did you kill today?" First it frustrated him, then it disillusioned him, and finally it destroyed him. Like Herbert Hoover, he had the misfortune of being President at the wrong time. He might have been a great peacetime President, but the combination of war abroad and at home proved too much for him.

I kept in frequent touch with Johnson while I was President, either directly or through mutual friends. When he returned to Texas he was busy with the preparation of his memoirs—a project from which he derived no enjoyment—and the plans for his presidential library—a project from which he drew much satisfaction. He had his wife and family, including his grandchildren, and his beloved Texas land. But he still longed for the popular approval and affection that continued to elude him. He was uniquely able to understand some of the things I was experiencing, particularly with Congress and the media over Vietnam, and we became quite close. Although I was glad that he did not support McGovern, I thought it was sad that his party treated him so badly. I made a diary note at the beginning of October 1972 that captured something of my feelings and something of our relationship.

Diary

LBJ had told Bobby Baker that he felt he only had a couple of months to live. He ought to have an operation but he was afraid that the operation for removing some of his lower intestines—he has suffered from diverticulosis for years—might be fatal as far as his heart was concerned. He apparently finally got a haircut after getting some criticism about the length of his hair. He is terribly sensitive to how people criticize him on a personal basis. He said, according to Bobby Baker, that President Nixon was probably the best President in history. Whether this is a real view held by him or not is irrelevant. He is in one of those rather emotional states which often come over him. He must be terribly depressed because he is such a proud man and is now being left alone by his party. He doesn't want McGovern under any circumstances but, of course, feels that he can't leave his party. As he puts it, he has been sucking at the tit of the Democratic Party for years and can't let go now, even though the milk may have turned a bit sour because of what the poor cow is eating.

A few weeks earlier I had made a note of a message from Johnson that Rogers Morton passed on to me.

Diary
Morton had talked to Johnson by phone. He said that Johnson seemed to be in one of those moods when he was concerned about going into the hospital again for a rather serious operation, and was looking down toward the end of the road. He said that he closed his conversation in a very sentimental vein, and said, "Tell the President I love him." This, of course, is typical of Johnson who has his violent ups and downs, but is a man strongly motivated by the heart rather than the head.

A week after Johnson's funeral I learned the answer to a question that had bothered me ever since his death.

Diary
I had an interesting little historical note. I asked Kissinger about whether LBJ really knew that we had an agreement. In addition to the call I had made on the 2nd, Haldeman called him on the 15th and told him that we had stopped the bombing. Johnson had answered, "Well, I know what that means." Haldeman said there had been a breakthrough in the talks. And Kissinger had sent him some papers with regard to the peace settlement the same day. So actually before he died he did know what had happened.

———————————

At 10 P.M. on January 23, I made a brief statement announcing that a settlement had been reached in Paris and that a Vietnam cease-fire would begin on January 27.

After I finished the broadcast in the Oval Office, I went back to the Residence. As I entered the Solarium, Pat came over and put her arms around me. Julie and Tricia and Ed were also there, and we sat talking about how my announcement had made it official that America was finally at peace for the first time in twelve years. I went to the Lincoln Sitting Room and had a light dinner there by myself. I played several records and sat watching the fire. I had specifically asked that all telephone calls be shut off. Just before I went to bed, I wrote a short note:

Dear Lady Bird,

I only wish Lyndon could have lived to hear my announcement of the Vietnam peace settlement tonight.

I know what abuse he took—particularly from members of his own party—in standing firm for peace with honor.

Now that we have such a settlement, we shall do everything we can to make it last so that he and other brave men who sacrificed their lives for this cause will not have died in vain.

On January 25 I met with Kissinger.

Diary

I had a good talk with Kissinger, sitting over by the fireplace in the Oval Room. I told him what a superb job he had done.

He told me about his daughter, who had been approached in Cambridge to sign a resolution against the bombing. He said that to try to involve a thirteen-year-old was a terribly vicious thing.

He seems at the moment convinced that he should talk to our friends and not try to pander to our enemies. I told him that I didn't want us to have any hatred or anything of that sort toward our enemies.

On the other hand, we had to recognize—and that's one of the things that our terribly difficult decision in December meant—we had to recognize that our enemies had now been exposed for what they really are. They are disturbed, distressed, and really discouraged because we succeeded, and now we have to start to play to those who are willing to give us somewhat of a break in writing the history of these times.

At midnight on January 27 the cease-fire went into effect and the killing stopped—at least for a time. I had always expected that I would feel an immense sense of relief and satisfaction when the war was finally ended. But I also felt a surprising sense of sadness, apprehension, and impatience. Sadness, because Lyndon Johnson had not lived a few extra days to share the moment with me and receive the tribute I would have paid him. Apprehension, because I had no illusions about the fragile nature of the agreement or about the Communists' true motives in signing it. And impatience, because I was acutely aware of all the things we had postponed or put off because of the war.

On January 28 I convened a special Cabinet meeting. Commenting on Johnson's death, I remarked that this was the first time in years that we did not have a living former President, and I talked a little about the ages of various Presidents when they died. "TR was sixty-one," I said, and FDR was only sixty-two or -three. Coolidge was sixty-one. In fact it looks like the sixties are the dangerous age! I don't have any fears for myself in that regard. Whatever happens will happen. The important thing is that each of us has to approach each day as if it might be our last day here. That's why each of us has to make every day count and do something with it."

Then I passed around the table leather binders that I had asked Haldeman to have made. Inside each was a large desk calendar covering the four years from January 20, 1973, to January 20, 1977. Next to each of the dates was printed the number of days left in my administration.

I had written a special message for the front of each calendar.

Every moment of history is a fleeting time, precious and unique. The Presidential term which begins today consists of 1461 days--no more and no less. Each can be a day of strengthening and renewal for America; each can add depth and dimension to the American experience.

The 1461 days which lie ahead are but a short interval in the flowing stream of history. Let us live them to the hilt, working every day to achieve these goals.

If we strive together, if we make the most of the challenge and the opportunity that these days offer us, they can stand out as great days for America and great moments in the history of mankind.

Richard Nixon

Washington, D.C.
January 20, 1973

The Presidency
1973-1974

1973

In an interview just before the 1972 election I said that over the next four years my administration would become known as having advocated the most significant reforms of any administration since that of Franklin Roosevelt in 1932. But the reforms I had in mind would be very different from those of the New Deal. I told my interviewer, Garnett Horner of the Washington *Star*, "Roosevelt's reforms led to bigger and bigger power in Washington. It was perhaps needed then. . . . The reforms that we are instituting are ones which will . . . diffuse the power throughout the country and which will make government leaner but in a sense will make it stronger. After all, fat government is weak, weak in handling the problems." In a brief talk to the White House staff on the day after the election I put it more simply: "There are no sacred cows," I said. "We will tear up the pea patch."

At the beginning of my second term, Congress, the bureaucracy, and the media were still working in concert to maintain the ideas and ideology of the traditional Eastern liberal establishment that had come down to 1973 through the New Deal, the New Frontier, and the Great Society. Now I planned to give expression to the more conservative values and beliefs of the New Majority throughout the country and use my power to put some teeth into my New American Revolution. As I noted in my diary, "This is going to be quite a shock to the establishment, but it is the only way, and probably the last time, that we can get government under control before it gets so big that it submerges the individual completely and destroys the dynamism which makes the American system what it is."

During my first term, all my attempts at reorganizing or reforming the federal government along more efficient and effective lines had been resisted by the combined and determined inertia of Congress and the bureaucracy. This was partly for partisan reasons: Democratic institutions naturally resist a Republican President. But it was also because the plans and programs I submitted threatened the entrenched powers and prerogatives that they had built up over many decades through several administrations. For various reasons I had had to acquiesce in this situation and accept the fact that no major reorganization reform or voluntary fiscal restraint would come from Congress during my first term. Now, however, armed with my landslide mandate and knowing that I had only four years in which to make my mark, I planned to force Congress and the federal bureaucracy to defend their obstructionism and their irresponsible spending in the open arena of public opinion.

In my first press conference of the second term, on January 31, 1973, I minced no words. I said, "The problem we have here is basically that the Congress wants responsibility. . . . But if you are going to have responsibility, you have to be responsible, and this Congress . . . has not been responsible on money. The difficulty, of course, and I have been a member of Congress, is that Congress represents special interests."

During the first term I had also had to contend with the increasing hostility of the media. Agnew had told some home truths about their power and their bias, but I had had to observe the official fiction that the President and the media do not have a fundamentally adversary relationship. Now in the second term, however, I planned to let them know that I would no longer uncomplainingly accept their barbs or allow their unaccountable power to go unchallenged.

I took off the gloves in the January 31 press conference when I announced the peace settlement in Vietnam. I said that we had done the best we could against great obstacles and had finally achieved a peace with honor. "I know it gags some of you to write that phrase," I said, "but it is true, and most Americans realize it is true."

By the time a new President was elected in the bicentennial year of 1976, I hoped to have given America the beginning of a new leadership class whose values and aspirations were more truly reflective of the rest of the country. This was not a uniquely conservative perspective. Pat Moynihan had written gloomily in 1969, "Since about 1840 the cultural elite in America have pretty generally rejected the values and activities of the larger society."

My fears about the American leadership classes had been confirmed and deepened by what I had seen and experienced during my first four years as President. In politics, academics, and the arts, and even in the business community and the churches, there was a successful and fashionable negativism which, in my judgment, reflected an underlying loss of will, an estrangement from traditional American outlooks and attitudes. The Vietnam war had completed the alienation for this group by undermining the traditional concept of patriotism.

I had watched this malaise continue to grow and spread during my first term. I saw it in the way the media made heroes out of student rebels while either ignoring those who held to traditional values or presenting them as uninformed or unenlightened. In 1970 Pat Moynihan had added another observant note: "Someone should be pointing out that when an upper-middle-class Ivy Leaguer says something particularly outrageous, official America is supposed to respond that 'he is trying to tell us something.' But when a young construction worker says something in response, we are to conclude that he is a dangerous neo-fascist who must be silenced."

I also saw it in the more subtle attitudes that permeated the liberal-dominated cultural milieu. The fact that they seemed to be less significant did not, in my opinion, make them any less disturbing. During the campaign, for example, I had been annoyed by something I saw in a film we watched one night at Camp David.

Diary

We saw an interesting movie last night called *The Man*, and what really struck me about it was the way that they had an American flag in the lapel of the Secretary of State—who was, of course, depicted as a very bad character. Haldeman told me that he had seen the picture *The Candidate* and that in that case too they put an American flag on the Republican candidate. I told Haldeman that I was going to wear the flag, come hell or high water, from now on, and he said that MacGregor was now letting people know that since the President wore a flag many of them might want to do so also to show their support of the President and their support of the country. Of course, this must be carefully done so that there is no indication of throwing doubts on the patriotism of people who are on the other side. It's really curious how people have come to run down the country the way they do.

This was not a politically motivated prejudice on my part. I felt that we were at a historical turning point. My reading of history taught me that when all the leadership institutions of a nation become paralyzed by self-doubt and second thoughts, that nation cannot long survive unless those institutions are either reformed, replaced, or circumvented. In my second term I was prepared to adopt whichever of these three methods— or whichever combination of them—was necessary.

I thought that America needed a new sense and spirit of positive pride, and now that the Vietnam war was over I felt that I could be instrumental in creating it. I felt that the Silent Majority of Americans, with its roots mainly in the Midwest, the West, and the South, had simply never been encouraged to give the Eastern liberal elite a run for its money for control of the nation's key institutions.

It may seem ironic in view of the scandal that was

278

about to overtake me and my administration and bring my presidency to an untimely end, but in the first weeks and months of 1973 I was planning to provide America with a positive and, I hoped, inspirational example of leadership that would be both a background and an impetus for a new rebirth of optimism and decisiveness and national pride.

I had three main areas of reform in mind for my second term. I wanted to reform the budget and terminate wasteful and ineffective programs, and I planned a massive reorganization and reduction of the federal bureaucracy and White House staff. As columnist Nicholas von Hoffman later wrote, "What Richard Nixon contemplated doing was actually running the government, something no President in seven decades had attempted." Finally, I intended to revitalize the Republican Party along New Majority lines. I had no illusions about the reaction such reforms would provoke from the bureaucracy and Congress or the kind of coverage they would receive from the media. But I was ready, willing, and, I felt, able to do battle for them because I believed in them and because I thought they were the right thing for America.

I summarized all my hopes and plans in some notes I made on January 11 on my large desk blotter in my study at Key Biscayne. This was to have been the blueprint for my second term as President.

Before the election I had asked Caspar Weinberger, Director of the Office of Management and Budget, and John Ehrlichman to make a review of the federal grant programs. They found that of the more than a thousand programs they studied, at least 115 were riddled with waste. For example, the federal farm subsidy program was making 42 percent of its payments to the richest 7 percent of the farmers. Another federal program was still promoting student enrollment in teaching programs, even though we now had a national surplus of 70,000 teachers that was causing serious unemployment problems. Despite a surplus of hospital beds, we were still subsidizing hospital construction. All told, the budget cutbacks I proposed in the first federal budget of my second term, which I sent to Congress on January 29, would have saved $6.5 billion in 1973 and $16.3 billion in 1974. It

1-11-93

Goals for 2d term:

Substantive:

Peace — SALT
China — Exchange
Mideast — Settlement
Europe — Community, Trade —
Latin America —

Defense + Intelligence —
Cut duplication
Improve Hardware,
Restore respect

Full Monetary + Trade

Domestic:
Crime — Drugs —
Education —
Health —
Land Use —
Race —
Labor — Management —
Price + wages —
Growth — GNP ?

3 Reform goals
3 Foreign goals —
3 Domestic goals

Spending T —
Environment ? —

Cut size of govt — make efficient
Reorganize —

Political
Strengthen Party.
Better Candidates for '74
New Majority —
New Establishment.
Press —
Intellectual
Business —
Social,
Arts —

An campaign for '74 ?

Personal
Restore Respect for Office —
New idealism, respect for flag — country
Compassion — understanding —

was a bold suggestion to cut programs that were receiving millions of dollars a year and represented thousands of jobs and government contracts, but I was prepared to take that heat. "Cynics," wrote Eileen Shanahan in the New York *Times*, "who never believe that anyone is committed to anything, have had a hard time grasping the seriousness that Mr. Nixon accords these goals."

We finally moved to reorganize, reduce, or abolish the remaining behemoths of the Great Society that had done little to aid the poor, and which were now primarily serving the interests of the federal bureaucrats who administered them. Of the $2.5 billion it took to run the Office of Economic Opportunity, 85 percent was filtered out in salaries and overhead before it ever reached the poor. It disserved the poor to keep funding programs that didn't work, but I was prepared for the inevitable accusations from the poverty lobby and the liberals in Congress and the media that we were callous and heartless in proposing these cuts—and I did not have to wait long. "President Nixon's new budget takes the breath away," Joseph Kraft wrote in words of intended criticism that came as music to my ears. "It moves to impose on our whole society his belief in the work ethic."

A year earlier, on January 24, 1972, I had sent Congress a request for placing a ceiling on federal spending. Since Congress had never established a method for staying within an overall budget as it voted on individual appropriations, congressmen and senators had never before been forced to accept responsibility for the fact that passage of some worthwhile project might have the ultimate effect of forcing the government into deficit spending. The legislators had thus been enjoying the best of both worlds: they could vote for whatever spending measures their consciences, their constituents, or their party leaderships urged upon them, while not having to accept the blame for the inflation and tax increases that result from federal deficit spending. Needless to say, there was not much congressional enthusiasm for blowing this comfortable cover, but they did establish a committee to recommend new procedures for budgetary control.

I came back again in January 1973 with a challenge to Congress not only to hold spending to $250 billion that year but to agree to establishing projected spending limits through 1975. Many congressmen had sincere and serious questions concerning who would establish the spending priorities and what criteria would be used. But others were simply frightened by the prospect that budgetary restraints might inhibit their ability to campaign for re-election on a platform of how much federal money they had obtained for their districts. I had made a choice on which programs deserved priority. It was up to Congress to do the same. A reporter wrote in the New York *Times*, "The new budget proposed so sweeping a challenge both to programs and to Congress that it provoked not just surprise but shock, awe and anger. . . . Congress showed signs that it would rally to the defense one by one of the sacred cows the President had so badly defiled."

While my budget with its proposed spending ceiling was sending shock waves through Congress, my plan for government reorganization was sending seismic tremors through the federal bureaucracy. Congress had smothered my attempt in 1971 to streamline the government, so I had asked Ehrlichman and Roy Ash, the incoming Budget Director, to set up task forces and consult with constitutional lawyers to determine how much reorganizing I could legally do on my own. They advised that I could in fact create by executive authority a system closely resembling the one I had requested in the 1971 reform proposal.

We decided to organize six of the eleven Cabinet departments and some of the hundreds of federal agencies under four general management groups: Human Resources, Natural Resources, Community Development, and Economic Affairs. George Shultz would head Economic Affairs and one of the current Cabinet secretaries would be named Counsellor to the President for each of the remaining three areas. These men would then be directly responsible to me for all the programs under their supervision. For example, in 1972 it took seventy-one different signatures to buy one piece of construction equipment for certain federally funded urban renewal projects; five agencies and fifty-six signatures could be required in order to hire one person. Nine federal departments and twenty agencies all had responsibilities for educational programs. Local water and sewer projects alone involved seven different agencies. Under my reorganization plan, the Counsellor in charge would be responsible for eliminating duplication and inefficiency.

I also announced my renewed determination to break the hammerlock the federal government had on the nation's taxes and return some of the revenue to local levels. From 1960 to 1970 the number of categorical programs—programs that gave local and state governments federal money for projects which were then controlled and monitored by federal officials—had multiplied from 44 to more than 500. In 1969 a poll found that a majority said big government was a bigger threat to the country than either big business or big labor. I did not consider this an unreasonable fear.

In 1969, 1970, and 1971 I had introduced proposals embodying the principle of revenue-sharing, by which money would be returned from the federal government to state and local governments to spend according to their own needs and priorities. General Revenue-Sharing was passed by Congress in 1972; it provided for a simple return of money without program or project restrictions. During its first year of operation, over $5 billion was designated for return to state and local governments. There were also several Special Revenue-Sharing programs, which would return money with only the provision that it be spent for programs within broadly defined areas: urban development, law enforcement, education, job training, transportation, and rural development. Special Revenue-Sharing would have replaced 125 categorical grant programs that were bound up in red tape, but so far Congress had not passed any of its component parts. I reintroduced four of them in 1973.

On a practical level, revenue-sharing was a way of revitalizing local government and local responsibility. On a philosophical level, it was the first change in the direction of federal growth in forty years—no less than the New American Revolution we called it.

On a political level, revenue-sharing exacerbated the hostilities in Washington, where it threatened sections of the bureaucracy with obsolescence, and where no one was eager to relinquish any amount of power or control.

I moved immediately after the election to pare down radically the size of the executive branch. When I took office in 1969, the executive office of the President numbered more than 4,700 employees. We announced that by the end of 1973 we intended to cut that figure by 60 percent. I regretted that during the first term we had done a very poor job in the most basic business of every new administration of either party: we had failed to fill all the key posts in the departments and agencies with people who were loyal to the President and his programs. Without this kind of leadership in the appointive positions, there is no way for a President to make any major impact on the bureaucracy. That this was especially true of a Republican President was confirmed a few years later by a study reported in the *American Political Science Review*. Researchers Joel Aberbach and Bert Rockman found that in 1970 only 17 percent of the top career bureaucrats in the executive branch were Republican; 47 percent were Democrats and 36 percent were independents, who "more frequently resemble Democrats than Republicans." The authors of this study confirmed that the frustration we felt with the bureaucracy was based on solid reasons: "Our findings document a career bureaucracy with very little Republican representation but even more pointedly portray a social service bureaucracy dominated by administrators ideologically hostile to many of the directions pursued by the Nixon administration in the realm of social policy." A different study, by Bernard Mennis, concentrated on the foreign service bureaucracy and found that only 5 percent of foreign service officers considered themselves Republicans.

I was determined that we would not fail in this area again, and on the morning after my re-election I called for the resignation of every non-career employee in the executive branch. Most of the resignations would not be accepted: my action was meant to be symbolic of a completely new beginning. In the weeks before the election, while rereading Blake's *Disraeli,* I had been struck by Disraeli's description of Gladstone and his cabinet as "exhausted volcanoes." I announced that my second term would not suffer the same malady; I was determined that we would not settle into the lethargy that had characterized Eisenhower's second term after an overwhelming re-election victory in 1956. I also wanted the Cabinet members, especially the new ones, to feel that they had complete freedom to choose their staffs for the second term. In some cases I planned to transfer White House staff members into the Cabinet departments to see to it that our policies would be followed.

As much as it was within my power, I was determined during the second term to break the Eastern stranglehold on the executive branch and the federal government. I urged that we reach out into the West and Midwest for fresh talent. I told Haldeman and Ehrlichman that I wanted an administration infused with the spirit of the 1972 New Majority. I gave them four explicit criteria for selection: loyalty, breadth, creativity—and moxie. I wanted to appoint labor leaders, women, and members of ethnic groups, such as Poles, Italians, and Mexican Americans, that had not been adequately represented in the government in the past.

The call for resignations included the entire White House staff and all Cabinet members. I see this now as a mistake. I did not take into account the chilling effect this action would have on the morale of people who had worked so hard during the election and who were naturally expecting a chance to savor the tremendous victory instead of suddenly having to worry about keeping their jobs. The situation was compounded by my own isolation at Camp David, where I spent eighteen days in the four weeks after the election, holding more than forty meetings with old and new appointees and making plans for the second term.

It was one thing for the Democrats to hold all four aces in Washington—the Congress, the bureaucracy, the majority of the media, and the formidable group of lawyers and power-brokers who operate behind the scenes in the city. It was another thing to give them the fifth ace of a timid opposition party.

As I began the new term I had a sense of urgency about the need to revitalize the Republican Party lest the New Majority slip away from us. We even deliberated for several days about starting a new party. There was no question that the party had ability—it had some of the most able and principled men and women in public life. It seemed to me that what we most lacked was the ability to *think* like a majority party, to take risks, to exhibit the kind of confidence the Democrats had because of their sheer numbers. During the campaign I made a note about this after I had addressed the Democrats for Nixon rally at John Connally's ranch.

Diary

We simply need more people on our side who have the love of politics that many of our Democratic friends seem to have in such great abundance. As I have told Connally, the Republicans are more inhibited, more restrained, more proper. The Democrats let it all out and love to shout and laugh and have fun. The Republicans have fun but they don't want people to see it. The Democrats, even when they are not having fun, like to appear to be having fun.

We made plans to revamp the party's organizational structure. I talked with Bob Dole, George Bush, Clark MacGregor, Barry Goldwater, and Jerry Ford about ways we could get the best candidates in every nationwide race in 1974 and 1976. I felt there was a sense of excitement growing about our opportunities and prospects; if we worked hard and were lucky, by 1974 we might have laid the foundations for the first Republican Congress in twenty years.

———————

It was clear that Congress was determined to do battle. Connally reported to me that the mood on Capitol Hill was "the most vicious thing I have ever seen. They are mean and testy." No sooner had the Vietnam peace agreement been announced than the complaints began over the reorganization plans, the proposed budget cuts, the December bombing, and what was soon labeled as the attitude and style of the "Imperial Presidency." In the past there had been similar instances of attempts by Congress to reassert its power and re-establish its prerogatives after the ending of a war. With this precedent in mind I prepared myself for a long and hard fight to get my programs passed and working.

Congressional frustration was exacerbated by the Gallup poll in January, which showed me with an approval rating at 68 percent. Respect for Congress, as measured at the end of 1971, had fallen to an all-time low of 26 percent.

Walter Lippmann said that he did not believe that Congress had the wisdom to decide what programs should be proposed or how the country should be led.

I was a man of the Congress and I was proud of the fact. But by 1973 I had concluded that Congress had become cumbersome, undisciplined, isolationist, fiscally irresponsible, overly vulnerable to pressures from organized minorities, and too dominated by the media.

I knew that part of my disenchantment was the simple result of seeing things from the perspective of the White House end of Pennsylvania Avenue rather than from Capitol Hill. Nevertheless, I thought that dramatic changes had taken place in Congress in the twenty-six years since I first came to Washington.

In 1947 it was still possible for a congressman to run his office, do his homework, keep in touch with his constituents, and have his eye on his political fortunes. But the federal government had become so big and the business of government so extensive that even the most conscientious congressman had to delegate a large part of his responsibilities to the personal and committee staffs that had correspondingly swelled in size and influence.

Then radio and television had demonstrated their power to make a politician a national figure overnight, putting a premium on color and controversiality rather then steady industriousness. This situation had a fundamental impact not only on the relationship between Congress and the White House but on the traditional relationships within Congress itself. More and more members refused to accept party discipline and, in effect, went into business for themselves.

Vietnam had precipitated perhaps the most serious and significant change of all: the passing of the tradition of bipartisan support for a President's foreign policy. The long years of war and the national confusion over Vietnam had eroded this concept and further divided Congress against the President, and the two houses against themselves.

In early 1973 it seemed to me that Congress was looking everywhere except to itself for solutions to its problems of inefficiency and ineffectiveness. I thought it was absurd for members of Congress to complain that the executive branch had stolen their power from them. On the contrary, modern Presidents had merely moved into the vacuum created when Congress failed to discipline itself sufficiently to play a strong policy-making role.

The "Imperial President" was a straw man created by defensive congressmen and by disillusioned liberals who in the days of FDR and John Kennedy had idolized the ideal of a strong presidency. Now that they had a strong President who was a Republican—and Richard Nixon at that—they were having second thoughts and prescribing re-establishment of congressional power as the tonic that was needed to revitalize the Republic.

Congress was naturally anxious to find a scapegoat for its problems. The Democratic leadership decided that the best way both to assert their party's majority power and to recover Congress's former prestige would be to take a piece out of the executive branch's hide. After I proposed my budget ceiling and my government reorganization programs, Washington columnists Evans and Novak consulted their inside sources and reported that a "venomous" congressional counterattack was being planned. Hubert Humphrey announced that a "constitutional crisis" was fast approaching.

The first battle lines were drawn in the ostensibly peripheral areas of procedural prerogatives. In early January the Senate Democratic Caucus voted 35 to 1 to narrow the President's traditional authority to invoke executive privilege. The same day a bipartisan bloc of fifty-eight senators introduced legislation that would for the first time in our history limit the President's war powers. On February 5 the Senate voted to require confirmation of the Budget Director, a position that had been filled by presidential appointment without confirmation for the fifty-two years since it had been created.

The major public battles in the executive-legislative conflict were also being fought on the issue of the impoundment of funds. Presidents since Thomas Jefferson had considered it their prerogative, and indeed their responsibility, to withhold the expenditure of congressionally appropriated funds for projects that were not yet ready to begin or if inflation was especially severe and putting more money into the economy would make it worse. This is known as im-poundment. In fact, as of January 29, 1973, I had 3.5 percent of the total budget impounded; Kennedy im-pounded 7.8 percent in 1961, 6.1 percent in 1962, and 3 percent in 1963; Johnson impounded 3.5 percent in 1964 but increased steadily to a high of 6.7 percent in 1967. The Democratic Congress had not challenged my Democratic predecessors for their heavier use of the practice, so I saw the 1973 impoundment battle as a clear-cut partisan attack on me.

Despite my plea for fiscal restraint and my requests for a budget spending ceiling, by March Congress had already prepared fifteen major spending bills that alone would have exceeded the 1974 budget by $9 billion. As a Washington *Post* article on March 28 pointed out, despite "pious state-ments" about the need for economy, I continued to get re-sistance on spending cuts. Nor was it a strictly partisan phenomenon. For example, very few Senate Republicans regularly stood with me on opposing the major budget-busting spending bills. I told Hugh Scott that I was going to give up on the Senate unless we got some solidarity in our ranks.

In the midst of this developing confrontation between Congress and the presidency, the Senate Democratic Caucus called for a full-scale investigation of 1972 campaign prac-tices. What they meant, of course, was an investigation of *Republican* campaign practices and of Watergate in particu-lar. Mike Mansfield chose Senator Sam Ervin of North Carolina to head the probe.

Some of my staff and advisers felt that Ervin was a lucky choice for us. They thought that the media would be hard pressed to make much of a hero out of someone whose voting record many liberals viewed as downright segrega-tionist. But I knew that Ervin, for all his affected distraction and homely manner, was a sharp, resourceful, and intensely partisan political animal. As I noted in my diary, I saw Mansfield's move as a purposeful ploy in the congressional campaign to put the presidency on the defensive: "An indi-cation of the fact that we are going to have a very hard four years is Mansfield's announcement that he wants Ervin's committee to investigate Watergate. Mansfield is going to be deeply and bitterly partisan without question. The Democrats actually are starting four years early for their run for the White House."

WATERGATE RECURS

At the time of my re-election I had known that for almost five months we had done everything we could to minimize the impact of the Watergate break-in. John Dean, who had ended up with the day-to-day responsibility in this area, had parried the problems of the Democrats' civil suit depositions, the Patman hearings, the GAO investigations, and the various exposés by the press. He had followed the grand jury and the progress of the FBI investigations in order to keep us from being surprised by anything that emerged from them; he had counseled people who were called to testify; and he had urged officials of the Justice Department to be sensitive to the political ramifications of the case and not to veer off into unrelated areas. I thought that he had acted like a smart political lawyer handling a volatile political case.

As certain as I was that we had done everything we could to contain the scandal, I was equally as confident that we had not tried to cover it up. For one thing, there was no question that the FBI's investigation had been extensive. Mitchell and Colson had both been questioned; even Magruder, about whom we all had suspicions, had testified before the grand jury three times and, however narrowly, had pulled through. Despite the tremendous political sensitivity of the whole case, I had not put personal pressure on the Justice Department, as I was sure other administrations would have done. After all this, there was no evidence that anyone in the White House had been involved in the Watergate break-in.

I could sense that a cloud of suspicion still hung over the White House, but I attributed that to all the election-eve publicity about Segretti and to McGovern's charges of corruption. I felt sure that it was just a public relations problem that only needed a public relations solution.

I decided after the election that both Chuck Colson and Dwight Chapin should leave the White House. Colson was a lightning rod for criticism for political reasons quite apart from Watergate and Ehrlichman in particular urged that he leave as soon as possible. I thought that his departure would help reduce our political vulnerability and give us a fresh start. Colson was naturally concerned that if he left the White House it would look as if he were guilty of something, and our solution was to announce that he would be leaving but to postpone his actual departure until March. I analyzed the decision on November 13, and again on November 18.

Diary

There are risks involved as we know because of the attacks to which Colson will be exposed. However, I do not want to leave the impression that he is leaving under fire because it is an unfair rap for him and also would be an inaccurate way to interpret my actions for getting in a new team as we start the new administration.

Colson is probably right on the issue—I think he is actually clean on Watergate and Segretti—but in the minds of most people he has become the issue. It is a very sad commentary that an individual can be bruised and battered and maligned and libeled and then becomes expendable. But in politics I fear that is the case.

Of course John Ehrlichman would go further than most. We would have lost half the staff by this time had he had his way because of course he is a stickler for getting rid of anybody who has even the appearance of wrongdoing. I would never take this approach because of the human equation.

I believe that where it is the appearance of evil, that an individual should be given a chance to clean the record, to defend himself. The consequences of backing off of people when they come under attack could simply encourage the piranha fish to go to work with a vengeance and leave nothing but the skeleton.

Dwight Chapin's case was even more painful for me. He had been with me since the beginning of my bid for the presidency in 1967. He was young and bright, and he had his whole career ahead of him. But his association with Segretti had made it impossible for him to stay in the White

House. My feelings were complicated even more by the knowledge that it was I who had insisted to Haldeman and others on the staff that in this campaign we were finally in a position to have someone doing to the opposition what they had done to us. They knew that this time I wanted the leading Democrats annoyed, harassed, and embarrassed—as I had been in the past. Segretti just turned out to have been the wrong choice for that role.

When John Dean had made his initial report concerning Segretti in early November, he had described Segretti's activities as standard political mischief, and I had observed in my diary that "I was glad to note from talking with Haldeman today, after his talk with Dean, that the Segretti group were not involved in anything other than the Dick Tuck kind of games even though they were perhaps better organized than some of the Dick Tuck operations, although if anything less effective."

But in mid-November, after we had Dean interview Segretti so that we would know exactly what he had done and what Chapin's vulnerability might be, we had learned then that all his activities had not been so innocent as we had originally thought.

Segretti had hired a plane to fly over Miami during the Democratic convention trailing a sign that read: "PEACE POT PROMISCUITY VOTE McGOVERN." Pretending to be one of the organizers, he ordered 200 pizzas and flowers and entertainment for a big Muskie dinner in Washington. On April Fool's Day he printed flyers inviting people to an open house with free lunch and drinks at Humphrey's headquarters in Milwaukee. He paid people to carry "Kennedy for President" signs outside Muskie meetings. All of this was in the realm of standard political fare. But he crossed the boundaries of pranks when he sent out phony letters on stationery from different Democratic campaign offices claiming that two of the Democratic candidates had records of sexual impropriety and that another had a history of mental instability.

I felt that an element of double standard was at work in the media's treatment of Chapin and Segretti. I remembered, for example, that little was written about the vicious anti-Catholic mailers that were sent to heavily Catholic precincts in Wisconsin during the 1960 primary between

Humphrey and Kennedy. The letters, postmarked from Minnesota, were designed to look as if they came from Humphrey supporters. A magazine investigation later traced the letters to a friend of Bobby Kennedy's.

I felt too that the *Post*'s stories about Segretti were exaggerated and unfair. As it turned out, the reporters who uncovered the story had not been above dirty tricks of their own in using private sources to obtain access to Segretti's telephone bills and confidential credit information. As John Dean would say to me a few months later, "The intent when Segretti was hired was nothing evil, nothing vicious, nothing bad, nothing. Not espionage, not sabotage. It was prank-sterism that got out of hand." Even so, Chapin was irreparably damaged. I believed that it was in his own interest that he leave rather than endure the press assault that was sure to come if he remained in the White House. He was able to get a good job in private industry, but the experience was still sad and painful. As I indicated in my diary, "Chapin took it like a man, and is going to be well placed and will do a superb job. On the Segretti thing, the decision to let it all hang out is, of course, right. I think also the decision to have Chapin leave is the right thing to do. As I have pointed out to Haldeman, time is a great healer."

In mid-November I was still looking for some kind of positive action that would put us out in front and leave Watergate, at last, behind us. On November 22 I read Haldeman and Ehrlichman a letter from one of our supporters who had written to the White House urging me to clean things up. "This theory that it's just going to go away won't work," I said. "It looks like I'm trying to hide something." At the same time a number of conservative columnists had begun to criticize us because of our failure to dispel the residue of suspicion. "Our friends," I dictated one night, "are even harder on us than the other side: conservatives are held up to a higher standard."

I said that we should get out some kind of public statement highlighting the findings of the FBI and grand jury investigations: that there was no White House involvement in Watergate, and no involvement by high-ups at the CRP. I was also ready to go with a detailed accounting of the Segretti episode, regardless of the embarrassment that would cause us.

Not everyone agreed with such a course of action. I heard that Dean in particular thought we should just leave well enough alone. The news stories had died down, so there was no immediate need to respond to new charges. There was, in fact, the danger that anything we did would only create new publicity that would focus new pressure on Magruder or even Mitchell. Finally, there was the legal argument that the Watergate trial was about to begin and anything said by the White House would prejudice the jury about the evidence.

These were all good arguments, but I still wasn't satisfied with inaction. On December 8 I suggested to Haldeman that Dean talk to the press. On December 10 and again on December 11 I pushed for a public statement of some kind that we could issue. But nothing happened. Haldeman and Ehrlichman and I were all working long hours on reorganization, a far more gratifying and, in our view at the time, more important task than the knotty Watergate problem. And then, in the weeks before Christmas, my own time was almost completely absorbed by the unfolding events concerning Vietnam.

While our main attention was focused elsewhere, the Watergate situation became considerably more complicated. In the last weeks of December and the beginning of January, the ground began to shift, however subtly. The Watergate trial was about to begin and the pressure was mounting on the defendants. The vibrations were felt in the White House, particularly in the case of Howard Hunt, whose despair following the death of his wife had been communicated to Colson.

Colson cared deeply about Hunt personally; they had been friends for many years. It is also true that implicit in Hunt's growing despair was a threat to start talking, although I was never sure exactly about what.

In this period, just as had been the case in the days immediately following the Watergate break-in, we began to act on unspoken assumptions, presumptions, and unverified fears. Each person began expressing concern that the others were vulnerable: Haldeman and Ehrlichman said that they thought Colson might be more involved than he was acknowledging; Colson said the same about both of them. This was the period when Colson went to see Hunt's lawyer to reassure Hunt. We were on the verge of a Vietnam settlement, engaged in a wrestling match with Congress over the budget, and about to face some highly publicized Watergate hearings. No one wanted to take any chances.

On January 8, I made a diary note about a conversation with Colson.

Diary
Colson made the interesting point that those that engaged in this activity did so with the thought that in the event they were apprehended that we would move on whoever was the prosecutor and see that nothing happened. Of course, this is very hard for me to believe that they could have had such ideas but I suppose they were thinking back to the Johnson era when he used all the powers of his office to protect himself and others at the time of the Bobby Baker investigation.

By February I was still concerned about the widespread impression of a cover-up that had set in, yet there was little we could do. Whatever our suspicions, we did not actually know who was responsible, and I was not going to force someone to change his testimony just to solve a public relations problem for me. Still, as I said to Colson, "The President's losses got to be cut on the cover-up deal," because "we're not covering up a damn thing." Colson emphatically agreed.

A diary note I dictated on February 14 summed up the situation as I saw it during those first weeks of the new year.

Diary
The real concern here on Colson's part seems to be the possibility that Hunt may blow. He seems to have the obsession that he killed his wife by sending her to Chicago with the money or whatever it was that she was doing at that particular time. He doesn't want to take the $250,000 insurance because of the fact that he takes the blame for killing his wife. Under these cir-

cumstances I can see how if the judge calls him in, threatens him with thirty-five years in jail, that he is very likely to be tempted to take immunity and talk about everything he knows.

I really don't know what he knows. Ehrlichman and Haldeman claim they don't know, and of course the same is true of Colson. I think all of them may know a little more than they indicate but how much I simply can't say. The real problem in the whole thing I think is Mitchell and of course the second man there [Magruder].

I don't know what the situation is, but in any event we are going to have to take our lumps and get the thing over as quickly as we can. I say as quickly as we can although the strategy may be to delay as long as we can and let it drag on and on. I am inclined to think that perhaps the latter is the better thing although it seems to draw blood little by little all the way along.

After Edgar Hoover's death in May 1972 I had named Pat Gray, then an Assistant Attorney General, as Acting Director of the FBI. Gray had earned a reputation in Washington as one of the most efficient, sound, and genial administrators in the city. As Acting Director during the summer and fall of 1972 Gray had overseen the Bureau's Watergate investigation. He was proud of the extent and intensity of that investigation, and he was eager to defend it in any forum.

I decided to nominate Gray to be the FBI's permanent Director, and I met with him on February 14 to discuss the post. I assured him that I was not worried about anything that might come out at his nomination hearings involving Watergate: "I'm not concerned about the substance, about the facts coming out," I said. My only concern was the condition he would be in after the partisan battering he could expect to receive in the hearings.

He responded that he was ready. "I'm not ashamed for it to hang out because I think the administration has done a hell of a fine job in going after this thing," he said. He told me that at the end of the first week he had called in the agents working on the investigation and "just gave them unshirted hell and told them to go and go with all the vim and vigor possible." He said that the week after the break-in even Larry O'Brien had said that he was very happy with the job the FBI was doing.

Gray was sure that he could convince even non-believers that the FBI had proceeded without showing favor in the Watergate investigation. He certainly believed it himself.

Diary

At least getting Gray before the committee he can tell a pretty good story. It is a true story of a thorough investigation and this of course knocks down the cover-up. As I emphasized to Ehrlichman and Haldeman and Colson, but I am not sure that they all buy it, it is the cover-up, not the deed, that is really bad here. Of course, the deed may prove to be pretty bad if it involves Mitchell and to a lesser extent if it involves Magruder.

Suddenly it was the end of February and the Ervin hearings were breathing down our necks, and we had still not decided the critical issue of whether we would invoke executive privilege and refuse to let any White House aides testify. Haldeman's, Ehrlichman's, and Dean's efforts to come up with a strategy always seemed to get sidetracked by other things. At the same time, the Republicans in Congress were beginning to grow anxious; some were even insisting publicly that I do something about Watergate. I reflected in my diary: "It is hard to understand how those we have supported so strongly have to make asses of themselves by taking up the cry of the opposition on a matter of this sort when they know very well that there could not possibly be any involvement at the White House level." Ehrlichman and I decided that instead of working through him and Haldeman, I would work directly with John Dean. I thought that perhaps this way I could break the roadblock. For months I had deliberately left the Watergate strategy and planning to others. But not only had the problem not been solved or contained; now it was starting to snowball. I decided to give it my personal attention.

When I met with Dean on February 27, it was the first time I had talked with him since he had reported to me on September 15, the day the Watergate indictments were handed down.

Diary

The talk with John Dean was very worthwhile. He is an enormously capable man. Dean went through quite an amazing recitation as to how Johnson had used the FBI. Apparently he had the FBI do bugging or at least intelligence work on even the New Jersey Democratic convention [in 1964].

I made another note after I had met with him again the next day, February 28.

Diary

I had another very good talk with John Dean. I am very impressed by him. He has shown enormous strength, great intelligence, and great subtlety. He went back and read not only *Six Crises* but particularly the speech I made in the Congress and it made the very points that I am trying to get across here—that the Truman administration had put up a stone wall when we tried to conduct an investigation. They wouldn't allow the FBI or the Justice Department or any agency of government to cooperate with us and they were supported totally by the press at that time.

I am glad that I am talking to Dean now rather than going through Haldeman or Ehrlichman. I think I have made a mistake in going through others, when there is a man with the capability of Dean I can talk to directly.

As Dean and I walked to the door at the end of that conversation, we speculated on all the people the Ervin Committee would hope to get up before them in hearings—they would like nothing better than to interrogate Haldeman, Colson or Ehrlichman.

"Or possibly Dean," Dean added.

I was quick to reassure him, "In your case I think they realize you are the lawyer and they know you didn't have a goddamned thing to do with...the campaign," I said emphatically.

"That's right," Dean stated.

"That's what I think," I said.

Dean and I continued to meet during the first weeks of March. We discussed Ervin Committee strategy and the statement that we issued on March 12, asserting our right to claim executive privilege on all present and former White House aides. We talked about Pat Gray's confirmation hearings. We also discussed the information he was gathering on Democratic political abuses. And on March 13 we went over the questions he thought I was likely to be asked about Watergate in my press conference in two days.

This press conference on March 15 was bound to be an even more heated one than usual. With equal measures of naïveté and stubbornness, Gray had allowed his hearings before the Senate Judiciary Committee to become a disaster. He turned over raw FBI files to the committee for public release, thereby managing to outrage everyone from the American Civil Liberties Union to his subordinates in the FBI. In each successive appearance he had brought John Dean's name further and further into the controversy; at one point he even implied that Dean might have illegally shown FBI reports to Donald Segretti. Dean had the White House press office deny that he had mishandled FBI reports, but the Democratic members of the Judiciary Committee saw that they were on to a live issue and they began to insist that Dean had to testify before Gray could be confirmed.

I was fully prepared to defend Dean, and in our meeting on March 13 we agreed that if I were asked about the demands that he appear as a witness that I would say that he would respond to questions under oath in a letter. I said I would finesse other Watergate questions by reasserting our intention to cooperate with the Ervin Committee's investigation. Dean added that I could say we had cooperated with the FBI in the past and would cooperate with a proper investigation by the Senate committee.

"We will make statements," I said.

"And, indeed, we have nothing to hide," Dean affirmed.

"We have furnished information; we have nothing to hide," I repeated.

Then Dean and I began a review of the facts, first from the standpoint of my press conference and then from the standpoint of our potential vulnerabilities before the Ervin Committee. I thought that I knew them all. On Watergate I thought that our principal worries were Magruder and Mitchell, although I was sure the Ervin Committee would try to draw in Haldeman as well. I was still prepared to assert unequivocally and to defend unreservedly that there was no White House involvement in the Watergate break-in.

Dean cautioned me that there would be new revelations during the Senate Watergate hearings, but he added that he did not think that it would "get out of hand." I thought I knew what he meant: the Democrats on the committee, spurred on by the media, were going to try to increase the drama by drawing in a "higher-up."

"Let's face it," I said. "I think they are really after Haldeman."

"Haldeman and Mitchell," Dean agreed.

I said that Haldeman's problem was Chapin. Haldeman had given Chapin and Gordon Strachan, another Haldeman aide, the approval to start the Segretti operation, and the press was continually trying to link Segretti to Watergate. But Dean reassured me that Chapin had not known anything about Watergate.

"Did Strachan?" I asked, almost perfunctorily.

"Yes," Dean answered.

I was startled. "He knew?"

"Yes."

"About the Watergate?"

"Yes," he repeated.

I was stunned. Until two months ago, Gordon Strachan had worked in the White House. If he had known about the break-in, that would be bad enough in itself, but I immediately saw the even deeper problem it would pose. It was well known that Haldeman's staff acted as an extension of Haldeman; it would not seem likely that Strachan would have known about anything as important as the Watergate break-in plan without having informed Haldeman of it.

"Well, then, Bob knew," I said. "He probably told Bob then." But in the same breath I added, "He may not have."

Dean was reassuring on this point. He said that Strachan was "judicious" in what he relayed to Haldeman. He described Strachan as "tough as nails." He told me that Strachan had been questioned on two separate occasions and had said, "I don't know anything about what you are talking about." Dean seemed to be implying that Strachan had lied.

"I suppose we can't call that justice, can we?" I remarked. "The point is, how do you justify that?"

"He didn't have to be asked," Dean said. "It just is something that he found is the way he wanted to handle the situation."

Strachan had been such a peripheral and minor figure in all our thinking about Watergate during the past few months that it was difficult to believe that he was suddenly a major problem.

"But he knew? He knew about Watergate? Strachan did?" I asked again.

"Uh huh," Dean answered.

"I'll be damned. Well, that's the problem in Bob's case, isn't it? It's not Chapin, then, but Strachan, 'cause Strachan worked for him."

I still had difficulty accepting the fact that, according to Dean, Strachan had known about the Watergate bugging. If this was true, then nine months of denials of White House involvement were undermined. Later in the meeting Dean seemed to modify the problem presented by Strachan. He said that we could still truthfully say that there had been no White House involvement in that no one had known about the DNC break-in. Strachan had evidently known about the existence of the bug after the fact, but he had not been part of any criminal conspiracy. It was a lawyer's distinction, but by that technicality at least, the White House was still not "involved." In any case, my first instinct was not to accuse or even criticize, but to consolidate.

Running down the list of other potential vulnerabilities, Dean gave me his conclusions about each of them. He said that Magruder had known even more than Strachan; that Colson had not known specifically about Watergate; and that Mitchell had known about the overall intelligence-gathering but not about the actual details of the break-in. Dean observed that his own name had come up—he had been dragged in as the man who sent Liddy to the CRP. It was true, he said, but he had done so only because they had asked for a lawyer, and he had been told that Liddy was a good one. He had passed on that information to Magruder and Liddy had been hired.

We were on the eve of a partisan Senate inquisition, suddenly facing serious new and undefined vulnerabilities. "Well, what about the hang-out thing? . . . Is it too late to, frankly, go the hang-out road?" I asked and then answered my own question, "Yes, it is."

"I think it is," Dean replied.

"I know Ehrlichman always felt that it should be hang-out," I said.

Dean said that he thought he had convinced Ehrlichman that he would not really want to "hang-out" either. "There is a certain domino situation here," Dean said. "There are going to be a lot of problems if everything starts falling. So there are dangers, Mr. President. I'd be less than candid if I didn't tell you . . . there are. There's a reason for us not—not everyone going up and testifying."

I raised again the possibility of issuing some kind of White House statement. But Dean argued that regardless of the truth of our assertion that there had been no White House involvement in the Watergate break-in, the partisan Democrats and the media would never believe any statement we issued. He also warned that people would not believe or understand the true story of the Segretti case. "They would have to paint it into something more sinister," he said, "something more involved, a part of a general plan."

At my press conference on March 15 the first question was on Watergate and on John Dean's role in the investigation.

I defended Dean and said that it was unprecedented and unthinkable that the Counsel to the President would accept a summons to appear before a congressional committee. Dean was covered not only by executive privilege but also by the time-honored confidentiality of the lawyer-client relationship. I said that I was prepared to allow him to furnish information; this in itself was more cooperation than was required by the Constitution or by precedent. I reminded the reporters that other administrations had been less cooperative than we; I reminded them that I was cooperating in a way that Truman had refused to during the Hiss case.

The questioning kept returning to Watergate with a relentlessness, almost a passion, that I had seen before only in the most emotional days of the Vietnam war. It was during this conference that for the first time I began to realize the dimensions of the problem we were facing with the media and with Congress regarding Watergate: *Vietnam had found its successor.*

I also knew immediately—even while I was answering the questions in the way that Dean and I had discussed and agreed upon—that our current approach to Watergate was not going to work. We were already on the defensive. We were already behind. We already looked as if we had something to hide.

With the doggedness of one who suddenly finds himself surrounded by a raging storm, I clung to my one landmark—even though it was now apparently anchored upon a technicality: that no one in the White House had been involved in the Watergate break-in. I had been told that Strachan had known about the bugging after the fact—but he had not been part of the decision to do it. Even if that was all we could say, I felt that we should at least be finding persuasive new ways in which to say it. Then we could start defending ourselves from there.

After my press conference I decided to press more firmly than ever for a written statement from Dean that would repeat what he had been saying to us all these months: that there was no evidence against Colson, Chapin, or Haldeman on Watergate.

When I saw Dean again on March 16, I suggested that he go to Camp David and concentrate exclusively on preparing this statement. I was pushing Dean for a statement again the next day, when he told me that he, Dean himself, had been present at meetings in John Mitchell's office at the Justice Department at which Gordon Liddy's intelligence-gathering plans had been discussed. Dean hastened to add that he had said that such things should not be talked about in front of the Attorney General. He said that he had reported to Haldeman and had told him that if something like that was going on, the White House had to stay "ten miles away from it—because it just is not right and we can't have any part of it." He said that Haldeman had agreed with him. "That was where I thought it was turned off," he said.

"But you didn't hear any discussion of bugging, did you?" I asked. "Or did you?"

"Yeah, I did," he answered. "That's what distressed me quite a bit." He explained that Liddy had said at the meeting that they ought to do some bugging. Mitchell had not agreed to it but had simply sat puffing on his pipe, saying nothing. I could visualize the scene and Mitchell's inscrutability—the manner he always adopted when having to tolerate amateurs.

I told Dean that he would not have to mention the talk about bugging when he described this meeting in the statement he was going to prepare. I rationalized that, after all, he had tried to stop it, and Mitchell had not approved it. Dean said that it would be an embarrassment that the White House knew about the existence of an intelligence operation, even though we thought it was to be a legal one. I was not bothered by that and said that if we had to justify it we could, on the basis of all the violence and demonstrations against us. At least, unlike previous administrations, we hadn't used the FBI.

Later I came back to the problem of our vulnerabilities. I said that, as I understood it, in Dean's view they were Mitchell, Colson, Haldeman indirectly and possibly directly; and, on the second level, Chapin. Dean said that he would add his own name. I asked why. He said it was because he had been "all over this thing like a blanket." I said I knew that, but his activities had taken place after the bugging and I did not see the problem. I said that, unlike the others, he had no criminal liability. "That's right," Dean agreed.

When we came back to Strachan, Dean appeared to be altering what he had told me four days earlier when he said that Strachan had not known about the break-in. He said that Liddy had told him that he was not really sure how much Strachan knew.

Dean told me that Liddy had named Magruder as the man who had pressured him to go ahead with the break-in. I asked who had pressured Magruder, and Dean theorized that Strachan had probably urged in general terms that people get moving on gathering intelligence. Once again I asked what kind of intelligence they were after. But now, nine months after the break-in, even Dean still had no answer to why, of all places, they had gone into the DNC. "That absolutely mystifies me," he said.

Things seemed to grow more complicated every day. There was a rumor that Magruder was saying in private that Colson and Haldeman had known about the break-in. I did not believe the accusation, but I thought that, as Dean observed, if Magruder ever saw himself sinking he would reach out to grab anyone he could get hold of. Now there were all these other circumstantial associations and involvements. I told Dean I could see no alternative to trying to "cut her off at the pass" by saying simply that Liddy and his bunch had done the break-in as a part of their job. Then we would put everything out on Segretti. "It isn't nearly as bad as people think it was," I said.

Then Dean said that there was one other potential difficulty: Ehrlichman had a problem with both Hunt and Liddy. "They worked for him?" I ventured, thinking that some kind of circumstantial mud might be slung because of that. Dean then told me that Hunt and Liddy, laden with CIA equipment, had broken into the office of Daniel Ellsberg's psychiatrist.

"What in the world—" I said.

Dean told me that they had done it in an effort to get Ellsberg's psychiatric records in connection with the Pentagon Papers. But he didn't know why. "This is the first I ever heard of this," I responded.

Dean added that it was possible that Ehrlichman had not known beforehand that this break-in was going to take place. As I noted in my diary, "I had my talk with Dean. He mentioned the vulnerability that would be involved with Ehrlichman apparently with something that had to do with an investigation in the Ellsberg case which seemed to me to be somewhat ridiculous. Apparently they were trying to get some information on him from Ellsberg's doctor about his psychiatric conditions."

The ground had shifted once again. Just four days earlier Dean told me that Strachan had had knowledge of the Watergate bug. And now this.

Still, I was convinced that nothing to do with Ellsberg would ever come up during the Ervin hearings, and that meant that we had more important problems than Ellsberg now.

The old pattern of delay and inactivity continued to plague our handling of Watergate. At one point Dean proposed sending a letter to the Gray hearings saying that he had recommended Liddy to the Re-election Committee solely as a legal counsel and that the White House had fully cooperated with the FBI. I urged that he sign it under oath, and the idea lapsed and died.

I needed desperately to get my mind on other things. We were faced with the possibility of having to resume bombing in Laos as retaliation for the failure of the North Vietnamese to abide by the cease-fire provision of the Paris peace agreement. The domestic economy was disturbingly volatile, and George Shultz was about to concede that the relaxation of controls in Phase III of the economic policy had been premature.

I was also thinking about the need to set new foreign policy goals for the second term. Now that the Vietnam war had ended, we could turn our attention to the other area of the world where war was always imminent and where the danger of a great-power nuclear confrontation was far greater than in Southeast Asia. On February 3 I had made the first of several similar notes.

Diary

I hit Henry hard on the Mideast thing. He now wants to push it past the Israeli elections in October, but I told him unless we did it this year we wouldn't get it done at all in the four-year term.

The Egyptian [Hafez Ismail, adviser to President Sadat] is coming over. What he works out I don't know, but I feel that some way we have got to get the Israelis moved off of their intransigent position. Needless to say, we can't move to the all-out Egyptian or Arab position either, but there is some place in between there where we can move. The interim settlement is, of course, the only thing we can talk about—that's the only thing the Israelis will ever go for—and the Egyptians are just simply going to have to take a settlement of that sort—or the Arabs are —with the assurance that we will do the best we can to get a total settlement later.

I spoke to Henry about the need to get going on the Mideast. I am pressing him hard here because I don't want him to get off the hook with regard to the need to make a settlement this year because we won't be able to make it next year and, of course, not thereafter with '76 coming up. He brought that up himself so apparently the message is getting through. What he's afraid is that Rogers, et al. will get ahold of the issue and will try to make a big public play on it and that it will break down. This is the point that I had made to Heath—that we couldn't go to the summit here and fail and, of course, the British understand this totally.

On the other hand, Henry has constantly put off moving on it each time, suggesting that the political problems were too difficult. This is a matter which I, of course, will have to judge. He agreed that the problem with the Israelis in Israel was not nearly as difficult as the Jewish community here, but I am determined to bite this bullet and do it now because we just can't let the thing ride and have a hundred million Arabs hating us and providing a fishing ground not only for radicals but, of course, for the Soviets. I think actually the radicals are our greater danger because the Soviets will have their people be somewhat responsible whereas the radicals are likely to act in totally unmanageable ways.

As I told Bob, I thought that Henry was having a letdown now because he realized that he had participated in the three great events perhaps of the postwar era—the Soviet, the China, the Vietnam—and that everything else would pale by significance. The Mideast he just doesn't want to bite, I am sure because of the enormous pressures he's going to get from the Jewish groups in this country.

Henry needs to have another great goal. Haig feels strongly that it should be Europe. Henry I noticed had picked up this theme in my last talk with him. I kept hammering, however, with Haig the necessity of doing something about the Mideast.

I also needed some personal time to work on my own schedule. So far I had been keeping up a frenetic pace. In the two months since the second term had begun, I made ten major speeches, held three press conferences, submitted the 1974 budget with the proposed spending ceiling, and sent up new legislative proposals on the environment, health, education, manpower training, law enforcement, and transportation. Golda Meir, King Hussein of Jordan, and British Prime Minister Edward Heath had visited Washington. So far there had been little opportunity to make the public appearances that would be necessary to build support for my policies, and I needed to begin getting out into the country. In fact, I had planned to make a national tour after the end of the war to express my gratitude to the people for their steadfastness during that long ordeal. I was also thinking about making a trip to Latin America after Easter.

Haldeman shared my frustration that the White House was doing and saying nothing on Watergate. He was especially eager to go public on Segretti, tell exactly what had happened, and clear up the mystery. When we met on Tuesday evening, March 20, he complained that others kept insisting that anything he might say on Segretti would hurt people involved "on the Watergate side."

"I still think I'm being had in a sense . . . being tarred in order to protect some other people," Haldeman said; he added that Chapin, who was also ready to go public with a full explanation on Segretti, was being "far worse tarred in order to protect other people." I said the problem was that the people who seemed to have Watergate vulnerabilities were our friends. Haldeman agreed. He observed that whereas Segretti might represent bad judgment, Watergate was a serious problem, and Dean kept insisting that the whole situation was linked: to break loose and tell everything on Segretti might jeopardize others.

But this brought us back full circle to an unacceptable

conclusion, because to follow Dean's advice and to accept his cautious admonitions, was to stay stuck right where we were: making no public statements, fighting with Congress over executive privilege, and giving the impression of a White House cover-up—the worst possible situation for us to be in.

"It isn't really worse—it isn't worse than John Mitchell going to jail for either perjury or complicity," Haldeman countered. I had to agree. I said that I had also considered that. I had questioned, too, whether Magruder would have done such a thing on his own.

Haldeman pointed out that whatever our own conjectures about Mitchell's involvement might be, Dean seemed to think it was possible that Mitchell had not approved the break-in. And Magruder had claimed under oath that he himself had not, which was possible if you accepted the premise that Liddy was acting under a broad authority. But there was always the question of whether Liddy would take the heat or start throwing off onto others. In any event, Dean's approach continued to be containment at Liddy. If no new factors—such as White House statements—were introduced, Dean seemed to think that there was a chance Mitchell would not be drawn in, Haldeman said.

So it was now March 20 and we were back exactly where we had been four days after the break-in nine months earlier: no one was sure about Mitchell or—on a firsthand basis—even about Magruder, but the circumstantial involvements and vulnerabilities surrounding Watergate were so great that even false allegations made by a Liddy or a Magruder could be fatal.

At the end of the meeting Haldeman and I again discussed the idea of putting out a public statement of a general kind. When I mentioned Dean's argument that it would open too many doors, Haldeman said we should just make the statement and see. The doors were evidently going to open anyway, he said. That was exactly how I felt. If the facts were going to come out, I said, "I would rather have us get them out to the extent we can in a forthcoming way." We agreed that the statement should not purport to be complete lest something come up later and undermine it. Rather it should indicate a willingness to answer further questions as they arose.

Before our meeting ended, almost as an afterthought, Haldeman brought up one other problem that Dean had raised with him. He explained that $350,000 in cash had been transferred out of campaign funds in 1972 and brought to the White House to help pay for such political projects as private polling. The money had not been used, and after the election it had been transferred back to CRP. I asked what the problem was with that and he said that it would establish the existence of a "secret fund" which the papers would exploit. "Not that it worries me, not that it's ever worried me," he said. But he added, "Maybe there's more to it than . . . I've found."

I phoned Dean shortly after Haldeman left my office. He seemed slightly agitated. He told me that he would like to meet with me to review the "broadest implications of this whole thing." He said, "You know, maybe about thirty minutes of just my recitation to you of facts so that you operate from the same facts that everybody else has. . . . We have never really done that. It has been sort of bits and pieces."

I said that we should meet at ten o'clock the next morning, March 21. Then I turned to my continuing request that he draw up some kind of general statement that we could release from the White House. I suggested that he might give an oral report to the Cabinet, just to reassure them of what he had told me: that no one in the White House was involved in the break-in. As usual when the idea of a statement arose, Dean's reaction was cool. He repeated his suggestion that before issuing any kind of a statement he should meet personally with me. "No, I want to know. I want to know where all the bodies are first," I replied. Thinking of my discussion with Haldeman about the need to avoid any statement that purported to be definitive, I said that I was thinking about a "complete statement but make it very incomplete"—by that I meant no chapter and verse, just general conclusions such as "Haldeman is not involved in this, that and the other thing; Mr. Colson did not do this. . . . Taking the most glaring things. If there are any further questions, please let me know."

Diary

It was a rather hard day here because we began to get more and more involved in what was really at the bottom of the Watergate-Segretti business, and we seemed always to come up with answers that were basically dead ends as far as getting facts were concerned.

I don't mean to leave it that way actually. It isn't getting at the facts but it's really getting out our side of the story.

I got Dean late in the day, about seven o'clock. He apparently, according to Ehrlichman, had been a little bit discouraged today, although I have been spending a lot of time with him and apparently it bucked him up considerably. He had been trying to keep all of these loose ends from coming apart and he said he would like to have a half hour with me at some point where he could just lay it all out so that I would know everything that he knew and would know all the hazards of whatever might be involved in having members of the White House staff either testify and make statements or what have you. I set it for tomorrow at ten o'clock in the morning.

All in all, though, from what Dean said tonight, he and Moore have come down on the side of not putting out any statement at this point, simply stonewalling the thing.

The point that I raised with both Haldeman and Ehrlichman was that if these questions are going to come out anyway, perhaps it is best just to let them come out on our own initiative rather than having them forced out.

I had also learned that the district court judge was about to hand down sentences on Hunt, Liddy, McCord, and the other men arrested at the Watergate.

Diary

One of the major concerns is what will happen when the judge moves on Friday. He is apparently going to be extremely tough, which does not surprise me.

They think that McCord in this instance might crack because he doesn't want to go to jail and that he might say to the judge after a few days that he is willing to tell all. The question is how much he knows. Certainly he knows a hell of a lot about Mitchell. Mitchell is the one I am most concerned about.

All in all, recalling the fact that a few years ago this would have been inauguration day—March 20—we have many problems that are residues of the campaign. Haldeman said ironically that it was just one of those breaks where if it hadn't been for a night watchman who saw the tape on the door or something like that the Watergate thing would never have come out and none of the other things would have been involved. But that's one of the costs of trying to run a campaign and of having some well-intentioned but rather stupid or at least people with very poor judgment working for you.

Mitchell just didn't keep his hand on the tiller at a time when he was having all the problems with Martha although I do not blame him for it. I know why it happened. No one could have a better friend or supporter than Mitchell and no man who is stronger in the crunch, but at the present time we are really caught here without really knowing how to handle it.

THE MARCH 21 CONVERSATION

It was just after ten o'clock on Wednesday morning, March 21, when John Dean came into the Oval Office.

After some desultory remarks about the Gray hearings, he said he had thought that we should talk because in our earlier conversations about Watergate he had had the impression that I did not know everything he knew. And that, he said, made it difficult for me to make judgments that only I could make.

"In other words, I've got to know why you feel that . . . we shouldn't unravel something," I said.

"I think . . . there's no doubt about the seriousness of the problem . . . we've got," he began. "We have a cancer—within—close to the presidency, that's growing. It's growing daily. It's compounding—it grows geometrically now, because it compounds itself. That'll be clear as I explain, you know, some of the details of why it is, and it basically is because, one, we're being blackmailed; two, people are going to start perjuring themselves very quickly that have not had to perjure themselves to protect other people and the like. And that is just—and there is no assurance—"

"That it won't bust," I supplied.

"That it won't bust," he repeated.

He began reciting details. Some of them I had heard before. Some were variations of things I had heard before. And some were new.

Haldeman, he began, had asked him to set up a "perfectly legitimate" intelligence operation at the CRP. Dean had asked one of his aides to draw up a plan for "normal infiltration . . . buying information from secretaries and all that sort of thing." Dean said that Ehrlichman, Mitchell, and others reached a consensus that the aide he had selected was not the right person to handle the matter; they wanted a lawyer. It was at that point, he said, that he recommended Liddy to handle the intelligence functions. This was the first time Dean told me this: earlier he had said only that he had recommended Liddy to the CRP to act as a legal counsel.

Dean repeated the story of his own indignation when Liddy had presented his incredibly outlandish intelligence plan to Mitchell in the Attorney General's office, and of how he had told Liddy and Magruder, "You just can't talk this way in this office and . . . you should re-examine your whole thinking." He repeated his account of Haldeman's subsequent agreement that Dean and the White House should stay away from such activities. "I thought, at that point, the thing was turned off," he said.

That, as I understood it, was the extent of his firsthand knowledge. He then turned to details he had learned only after the break-in, while he was trying to put together what had happened; these were his extrapolations and conjectures.

It appeared that after the meeting in Mitchell's office, Hunt and Liddy had appealed to Colson for help in getting the authorization for their plans. Colson had thereupon called Magruder, urging him to "fish or cut bait" on Hunt and Liddy. I asked if Colson had known just what Hunt and Liddy's plan was. Dean said he assumed that Colson had had "a damn good idea what they were talking about."

Colson! My earliest fears returned. Up to now I had been told by everyone, including Dean, that Colson was not involved. "Colson then, do you think, was the person who pushed?" I asked. Dean said he thought Colson had *helped* to push. He also thought that Haldeman had pushed through Strachan, but Haldeman's push for some intelligence-gathering had been based on the innocent assumption that nothing illegal was being planned. "I think that Bob was assuming that they had something proper over there," Dean affirmed.

Dean conjectured that Magruder had reported the Colson and Strachan "pushes" to Mitchell, and in the face of all this pressure Mitchell had puffed on his pipe and said, "Go ahead," without really reflecting on what it was all about. That was Dean's theory of how the DNC bugging got under way. I was finding it hard to keep my bearings: just twenty-four hours earlier Haldeman had implied that Dean thought Mitchell had *not* approved the break-in.

Dean said that after the bug was installed, Strachan had received some of the information from it and passed the report on to Haldeman. Haldeman might not have known where the information came from, Dean said, but Strachan did.

Magruder, Dean said, was "totally knowledgeable" and had perjured himself. Dean said that Magruder had set up a "scenario" that he ran by Dean, asking, "How about this?" Dean said that he had responded, " 'Well, I don't know . . . if this is what you're going to hang on, fine.' " Dean said that, despite Magruder's testimony, Magruder had specifically instructed Liddy to go back into the DNC. Dean said, however, that he honestly believed that no one in the White House had known that; but he added, in apparent contradiction, that he thought Strachan had known.

Turning to the post-break-in activities, Dean said that he himself was "under pretty clear instructions not to really investigate this," that he had acted "on a theory of containment." "Sure," I said, remembering Haldeman's comment the night before, that Dean hoped to contain the blame for the break-in at Liddy and not let it be pushed higher to Mitchell.

Dean said that he had followed the FBI and the grand jury's investigations at all times. He said that soon after the arrests at the Watergate the defendants had warned, "We've got to have attorneys' fees . . . if you are asking us to take this through the election." Dean said that arrangements were made for the payments at meetings where he and Mitchell were both present. "Kalmbach was brought in. Kalmbach raised some cash," he added.

I asked if this had been put under the cover of a Cuban committee. Dean said yes, and that Hunt's lawyer had also been used. I added that "I would certainly keep that cover for whatever it's worth. Keep the committee."

Then Dean delivered his punch line: "Bob is involved in that; John is involved in that; I'm involved in that; Mitchell is involved in that. And that's an obstruction of justice."

I didn't understand. I thought Dean had to be overdramatizing.

"How was Bob involved?" I asked.

Dean said that Haldeman had let him use a $350,000 cash fund, which had been held at the White House, to make payments to the defendants. Dean said that he, Haldeman, and Ehrlichman had decided that there was "no price too high to pay to let this thing blow up in front of the election." This was a new twist. The night before, Haldeman had said that the money had been returned unused to the CRP and that the only problem it presented was that the media would call it a "secret fund." "I think you should handle that one pretty fast," I said. Dean agreed.

Dean said that McCord had talked to someone in the White House about commutation of his sentence. "And as you know, Colson has talked to, indirectly to, Hunt about commutation," he said. "All these things are bad . . . in that they are problems, they are promises, they are commitments. They are the very sort of thing that the Senate is going to be looking most for."

Now Dean arrived at the heart of what had precipitated his current state of concern. Five days earlier a lawyer for the CRP had received a message from Howard Hunt and had passed it directly to Dean: Hunt was demanding

$122,000 for attorneys' fees and personal expenses. Dean said that when he had received this message, he told the CRP lawyer, "I'm not involved in the money. I don't know a thing about it, can't help you."

Hunt's message had been accompanied by a threat: " 'I will bring John Ehrlichman down to his knees and put him in jail. I have done enough seamy things for he and Krogh that they'll never survive it.' " Hunt's deadline, according to Dean, was "close of business yesterday."

"What's that, on Ellsberg?" I asked. Dean replied, "Ellsberg, and apparently some other things. I don't know the full extent of it."

"I don't know about anything else," I said, thinking back to January and Colson's speculation that Hunt could draw in Haldeman or Ehrlichman and their simultaneous speculation about what Hunt would do to Colson. Dean said that he didn't either, and then he told me about all the other people who knew about the Ellsberg break-in, among them the Cubans who had been arrested at the Watergate and their lawyers.

Hunt's threat was just the most urgent and dramatic example of the larger problem of the continuing blackmail possibilities for all the defendants. If we continued to pay it, that would compound the obstruction of justice. Beyond that, there was the question of how to raise the money, and even how to deliver it, without involving the White House. I asked how much money he would need. Dean estimated that payments for all the defendants would require a million dollars over the next two years.

I said that it would not be easy, but that I knew where we could get the money. In fact, I had no specific way in mind, but I assumed that, if it were sufficiently urgent, we could raise it from some of the people who had been large contributors in the past.

Dean went back to his account of the "growing cancer" on the presidency. He said that Bud Krogh was forced to perjure himself on the Ellsberg matter. This news about Krogh came as another blow to me. He was one of my favorites among the younger staff members; I knew he was a principled man. But apparently he had testified that he did not know the Cubans, when, in fact, he did—not from Watergate, of course, but from Ellsberg.

"Perjury is an awful hard rap to prove," I said without much conviction.

We returned to the threat from Hunt. Out of all the new details and confusion one thing was clear: Howard Hunt was a time bomb, and his deadline was yesterday. In two days he would be sentenced, and he would be sure to make good on his threat.

"Just looking at the immediate problem, don't you have to handle Hunt's financial situation damn soon?" I asked. "You've got to keep the cap on the bottle that much in order to have any options—either that or let it all blow right now."

"That's right," Dean said. I told him to go ahead with his discourse on the facts. After he had finished, he returned to what he called the growing situation. The problem would be if the Watergate case started breaking and there was a criminal case against Haldeman, Mitchell, Ehrlichman, and himself. He said he thought that he, Haldeman, Ehrlichman, and Mitchell should talk about the whole thing and about how to carve it away from the presidency.

"You're not involved in it," he said to me.

"That is true," I replied.

"I know, sir, it is. Well, I can just tell from our conversations that these are things that you have no knowledge of."

We had arrived at the real question and the real problem: what were the alternatives? I posed the hypothesis that when he met with Haldeman, Ehrlichman, and Mitchell, they might conclude that there was nothing that could be done to keep the whole matter from breaking open. I asked Dean what would be done then: "Are you going to put out a complete disclosure? Isn't that the best plan? That'd be my view on it," I said.

Dean hedged. He introduced the alternative of calling another grand jury with immunity for some witnesses. I thought he had Magruder in mind, but it became clear he was thinking of himself. He told me he thought he faced the possibility of a jail term.

"Oh, hell no," I said, "I can't see how you can." By his own account, he had denounced Liddy's bugging plan; he was not involved in the handling of the money; and he had not offered clemency or given any perjurious testimony. But he was obviously worried, so I asked him to explain to me again his own problems on obstruction of justice. I told him that I couldn't see how a legal case could be made against him. He explained that he had been a "conduit for information" about the blackmail.

As he had talked I had been worrying about the blackmail and the risks of not paying it. I told him, "Let me put it frankly: I wonder if that doesn't have to be continued," and I started to work my way through that maze. At least if we had the million dollars and a way of delivering it, that would hold off everything for a while. Or would it? There was the problem of Hunt and his expectation of clemency: money would not satisfy him if he had been led to expect his freedom. Dean said that the others would be after clemency, too, and added, "I am not sure that you will ever be able to deliver on the clemency. It may be just too hot."

"You can't do it till after the '74 elections, that's for sure," I said. "But even then your point is that even then you couldn't do it."

"That's right," he replied. "It may further involve you in a way you shouldn't be involved in this."

"No, it's wrong; that's for sure," I said.

That was no answer; we were back at the starting point.

Dean was clearly depressed. He said almost apologetically that there had been some bad—as well as some necessary—judgments made before the election, but now it had become a burden in the second term that would not go away. I tried to reassure him; this was no time for recriminations. "We're all in on it," I said, and I told him again that I thought he was overplaying the possibility that he himself might have criminal liability.

Dean said that he did not have a solution to all these problems, but he thought we should think about cutting losses rather than compounding the matter with further payments. I agreed with him—with the exception of Hunt. We were already out of time on him, and if he started hurling charges at the White House there was no way of knowing what damage he could do to my closest aides—Colson, Ehrlichman, Haldeman, Mitchell—and therefore to me.

"But at the moment, don't you agree that you'd better

get the Hunt thing?" I asked. "I mean, that's worth it, at the moment."

"That's worth buying time on, right," Dean replied.

We then agreed that Dean would meet right away with Mitchell, Ehrlichman, and Haldeman. "We've never had a real down-and-out with everybody that has the most to lose," he said.

I buzzed for Haldeman to join us. In our conversation Dean had told me that he and Haldeman had talked that morning about the same things he and I were discussing, and at the time I assumed that Haldeman understood all the problems Dean had described to me. But when Haldeman joined us, he seemed to be learning for the first time about Hunt's blackmail demand; about Colson's phone call to Magruder, which may have triggered approval of the Watergate plan; and about Colson's apparently flat promise of a Christmas pardon for Hunt.

When Haldeman was seated I told him that we were at the point of decision. As I saw it, in terms of our overall strategy, we had two options. If we decided that the potential criminal liabilities for everyone were too great, we could yield nothing, fight back, and refuse to testify before the Ervin Committee. "Hunker down," Dean had called it earlier; "cover it up, is what we're really talking about." This was undeniably attractive—if it would work. "I don't want any criminal liability," I told Haldeman. "That's the thing that I am concerned about for members of the White House staff, and I would trust for members of the committee."

At the same time, this option only locked us into a vicious circle, which I described for Haldeman: the only way to stall off disclosures from the defendants would be to pay blackmail; it was possible to do that; but even if we decided that such a desperate measure was justifiable and worth the risk for now, we still had the problem of having to deal with eventual demands for clemency—and clemency was something we simply could not offer; so we ended up back where we began.

On the other hand, if we decided, as I said to them, that "in the end we are going to be bled to death and it's all

319

going to come out anyway, and then you get the worst of both worlds. . . . And we're going to look like we covered up. So that we can't do"—then we had to go with the second option: to get ourselves in the best possible position, whether by offering to go before the grand jury or the Ervin Committee, or by putting out a public statement, and then to let it all blow, take our chances, and just try to survive.

Haldeman was unequivocal about the course we should take. "I don't see how there's any way you can have the White House or anybody presently in the White House involved in trying to gin out this money," he said. I asked Dean if our consensus then was not to say to the defendants, "I'm sorry, it is all off," and let them talk. "That's the way to do it, isn't it? . . . If you want to do it clean?" I asked. Dean did not seem sure; but Haldeman was and said, "See, then when you do it, it's a way you can live with." He stated the problem with blackmail: paying the initial sum was one thing; "but what do you need tomorrow and next year and five years from now?" He pointed out that he had told Dean this during previous months when Dean had said there was a money problem.

As for the payments up to this time, I said that our cover story was going to be that the Cuban committee had taken care of the defendants through the election.

"Well, yeah. We can put that together," Dean said. "That isn't of course quite the way it happened, but—"

"I know, but it's the way it's going to have to happen," I said.

I again asked Dean if his recommendation was to go "the clean way," just letting it all go now.

This time he did not hedge. His answer was no. He again urged the desirability of having our people go before a grand jury, where, unlike the Senate Watergate Committee, there would be rules of evidence.

"You can say you forgot, too, can't you?" Haldeman asked.

A lawyer always advises his client that it is better to say he doesn't recall and err on the side of forgetfulness than hazard a guess or try to reconstruct a memory. Yet this would not help much in committee hearings where taking the Fifth Amendment, or claiming inability to recall, would mean automatic conviction in the eyes of the public. Dean reminded Haldeman that a grand jury also has its hazards—it was a high-risk perjury situation. The Hiss case demonstrated the dangers of a perjury charge. "That's right," I said, "just be damned sure you say I don't remember; I can't recall, I can't give any honest answer to that that I can recall."

I favored the grand jury idea. Ehrlichman had recommended as a solution that we request the Watergate grand jury be reconvened to hear testimony from the White House staff. That would provide an orderly way for us to present the facts. "It should be done through a grand jury, not up there in the klieg lights of the committee," I said at a later point.

I came back one last time to the problem of Hunt. We agreed that no more payments should be made to all the defendants, but Hunt was still the time bomb. I told Haldeman that the reason the Hunt problem worried me was that "it had nothing to do with the campaign . . . it has to do with the Ellsberg thing." Even the grand jury approach would be too late if, in two days' time when the sentencing of the defendants took place, Hunt lashed out. It was Hunt who threatened to leave us with no options, not even the option to do in any orderly way what was responsible and right.

I turned to Dean. "That's why for your immediate thing you've got no choice with Hunt but the 120 or whatever it is. Right? Would you agree that that's a buy-time thing, you better damn well get that done, but fast?"

"I think he ought to be given some signal, anyway to—" Dean said.

"Well, for Christ's sakes get it in a way that. . . . Who's going to talk to him?" I interjected.

Dean reiterated that the problem was having no way to get the money, and we talked about the problems with delivering it. Once again we discussed the idea of recalling the grand jury. Then I came back to Hunt.

"Try to look around the track. We have no choice on Hunt but to try to keep him—" I began.

"Right now we have no choice," Dean said.

"But my point is, do you ever have any choice on Hunt? That's the point," I said. We had arrived once again back at the beginning, the inescapable circle now complete.

Even the extreme measure of paying blackmail was not a solution; it would only buy us a little time.

Then Dean came up with an alternative, another way of buying time for ourselves: we might get Judge Sirica to postpone his sentencing for two weeks. That would take the pressure off as far as Hunt was concerned and give us the time we needed to get everyone before the grand jury. I liked this idea immediately and told Dean to go ahead with it.

"I think it is good, frankly, to consider these various options," I said as the meeting closed, "and then once you . . . decide on the plan—John—and you had the right plan . . . before the election. And you handled it just right. You contained it. Now after the election we've got to have another plan because we can't have, for four years, we can't have this thing—you're going to be eaten away. We can't do it."

Haldeman agreed. We had to turn off any further involvement at the lowest possible cost but at whatever cost it took; because as he pointed out, it was now beginning to get near me.

"Well, the erosion is inevitably going to come here apart from anything, you know, people saying that the Watergate isn't a major concern. It isn't," I said, "but it will be. It's bound to be."

"We cannot let you be tarnished by that situation," Dean said earnestly. I was grateful for his concern—and fully in agreement with it.

"I say that the White House can't do it. Right?" I said, and the meeting ended.

Only two decisions had emerged: Haldeman was to have Mitchell come down from New York immediately for a talk with Dean and Ehrlichman; and Dean was to try to get the sentencing postponed.

I went directly from this meeting to greet the young Russian Olympic gymnast Olga Korbut and some of her teammates, who were visiting the United States. After that there was a session on our efforts to hold down federal spending. But all the time Howard Hunt and his threats and demands for money were weighing on my mind.

As soon as these meetings were over I called in Rose Woods and asked her if we had any unused campaign funds.

322

She told me that we did—she would have to see how much. It turned out to be $100,000, and when Haldeman came in a little later I mentioned it to him. Once again he flatly rejected the idea of our involvement in paying more money. "You should stay out of this," he said.

Later that afternoon Haldeman, Ehrlichman, and Dean came over to the EOB office for a long talk about Watergate. Looking back on it now, I can see that we were all operating from different bases of knowledge and with different perceptions of our own personal vulnerabilities. Haldeman seemed primarily concerned about the danger that Magruder might falsely accuse him of having known about the break-in beforehand, rather than about his knowledge of the payments to the defendants, which Dean had indicated was the real danger. In fact, as late as the following morning Haldeman would still seem unaware of the severity of Dean's conclusion: I mentioned the fact that Dean was concerned about his own knowledge of payments to defendants, and Haldeman mused that he and Ehrlichman had worked on that with Dean. "Perhaps he thinks I'm tied into that, too," Haldeman commented.

On the afternoon of March 21 Ehrlichman seemed even less briefed than Haldeman on the details of the situation: he indicated that he still thought that Gordon Strachan's problem involved his failure to report disbursements of campaign funds. Ehrlichman appeared unaware that Strachan may have had knowledge of the bugging. These differing perceptions, and the chasms they created in our overall understanding, are apparent now. At the time, however, the problem only seemed very complicated, and our strategy sessions were just frustrating and inefficient minuets around the problem.

That night I dictated a long diary note about a day that was later to be seen as a disastrous turning point in my presidency. In it I noted:

Diary
    As far as the day was concerned it was relatively uneventful except for the talk with Dean. Dean really in effect let it all hang out when he said there was a cancerous growth around the President that simply was going to continue to grow and that we had prob-

ably to cut it out rather than let it grow and destroy us later. He obviously is very depressed and doesn't really see anything—other course of action open, but to move to let the facts out.

As I examined him it seems that he feels even he would be guilty of some criminal liability, due to the fact that he participated in the actions which resulted in taking care of the defendants while they were under trial. As he pointed out, what is causing him concern is that every one of the various participants is now getting his own counsel and that this is going to cause considerable problems, because it will be each man for himself, and one will not be afraid to rat on the other.

The next day, March 22, Haldeman and I again reviewed the increasingly volatile situation regarding Watergate. When our conversation turned to Liddy and the widespread rumors that he and the other defendants were going to be slapped with thirty-five-year sentences, I said that I thought it had been only right to raise money for them. "I don't mean to be blackmailed by Hunt, that goes too far," I told Haldeman, "but we're taking care of these that are in jail . . . we're sorry for them. We do it out of compassion." Haldeman agreed, saying that was why it seemed to him that there was no need for Dean to be concerned about an obstruction of justice. After all, the defendants had pleaded guilty, Haldeman said: "When a guy goes and pleads guilty, are you obstructing justice?"

I said I couldn't understand Dean's concern about his own involvement in an obstruction of justice—after all, by his own account he hadn't delivered the money to the defendants. I said that I thought that was why Hunt's direct demand to him for money had set him off in such a way. "You understand, that that would have constituted goddamn blackmail if Dean had gotten the money," I said. But since Dean had not done it, I could not see that he had any problem.

In retrospect it is clear that on March 21 John Dean was trying to alert me to the fact that what I had assumed for nine months was the major Watergate problem—the question of who had authorized the break-in—had been overtaken by the new and far more serious problem of the cover-up. I left the meeting only troubled by the new dimensions of what he had described rather than galvanized into action by the urgency and peril of our situation. Dean did not tell me the extent of his own active and conscious role in the cover-up, and so I treated much of what he said as conjecture and deduction, instead of as a firsthand report on an explosive situation that was already out of hand. I responded accordingly, by openly running through every available option. Even Dean's insistence that the authorization of payments to the defendants was an obstruction of justice seemed to me more a reflection of his personal depression than a statement of a considered legal conclusion. Only three weeks later, when I finally saw the whole cover-up mosaic in perspective and realized the position the payments to the defendants played in it, would I understand what Dean had really been trying to tell me.

I left the March 21 meeting more disturbed than shocked; more anxious than alarmed. The practical effect of my failure to grasp the full import of what I had been told was that I doggedly persisted in the same course I was on before the conversation: I continued to concentrate on the question of who was vulnerable because of prior knowledge of the break-in, and to look for some way to change our public relations posture so that the White House did not look so defensive where Watergate was concerned.

On the afternoon of March 22, in a meeting in the EOB with Haldeman, Ehrlichman, Dean, and me, John Mitchell urged that we waive executive privilege and allow all White House aides to testify before an executive session of the Ervin Committee. He said it was the only way to move the White House into a new public posture. When someone jokingly called this decision a "modified limited hang-out," I said, "Well, it's only the question of the thing hanging out publicly or privately."

"If we're in the posture of everything short of giving them a public session," Dean himself said at one point, "you're not hiding anything."

We also decided that it was time to get some kind of report or statement from Dean. "I think it's certainly something that should be done," he concurred.

Everyone agreed a statement or report was needed, but everyone seemed to have a different idea about what it was needed for. I wanted it as proof of the truth of my public statements that there was no one in the White House involved in Watergate. I wanted a document that would show that I had said it because I had been told it and believed it. I did not want it to include all of Dean's theories and conjectures—just answers to the broad charges. There was also talk of Dean's report as a document that could be given to the Ervin Committee to define the degree of the involvement of different individuals and therefore help limit the number of witnesses subpoenaed. And there was talk about publicizing the document in order to preempt some of Ervin's thunder by setting out some of the new facts about Watergate in a way that would make them old news before the hearings began. Ultimately, though, the use of the document would have to be defined by what was in it. "The proof is in the pudding," Dean said at one point. Whatever it was, I thought we had to have it. "If it opens up doors, it opens up doors," I said.

When the meeting ended I was relieved. The day before, I had posed two alternative courses: to yield nothing and fight back, or to try to position ourselves so the story would come out as much as possible on our own terms. Now, as of March 22, we had made the first move on the second course.

We had always thought that one important reason for avoiding public statements on Watergate or for volunteering any testimony would be to avoid putting increased pressure on John Mitchell. Therefore I worried about his reaction to this new strategy. I saw him alone after the others had gone. I did not want him to think that I was pushing him out on his own.

I said that I did not think Sherman Adams should have been sacked, even though he had made a mistake. That had been a cruel decision, and I was not going to react cruelly in this case. I was not going to turn against my friends. Then I thought of the beating everyone was going to take before the Ervin Committee. "I don't give a shit what happens," I said to Mitchell. As far as I was concerned they could "plead the Fifth Amendment, cover up or anything else, if it'll save it—save it for them. That's the whole point. On the other hand . . . I would prefer, as I said to you, that you do it the other way. And I would particularly prefer to do it that other way if it's going to come out that way anyway. . . . The story they get out by leaks, charges and so forth, and innuendos, will be a hell of a lot worse than the story they're going to get out by just letting it out there."

I knew that Mitchell would understand that this was my oblique way of confronting the need to make a painful shift in our Watergate strategy, a strategy that so far had been a dismal and damaging failure. Now we had to take a chance and go the other way. It was a relief to know that Mitchell had already come to this conclusion.

The next morning, March 23, Judge John Sirica called an open court session for the purpose of announcing the Watergate sentences. Shortly before the session began, he was handed a letter from James McCord. In it McCord said that political pressure had been exerted to keep him silent; that perjury had been committed at the trial; and that offers of clemency had been made in return for silence. Sirica read the letter in open court.

I had gone to Florida for the weekend, and I was in my study in Key Biscayne when a call came from Ehrlichman. I dictated a diary note soon after: "I have just received a telephone call from John Ehrlichman with regard to McCord's bombshell on the Watergate thing. I suppose this is something that had to be expected at some point and in my view it is just as well to get it over with now. Let's find out where the bodies are buried and what he has to say."

Sirica freed McCord on bond. He gave a provisional sentence of thirty-five years in jail to Hunt and forty years to each of the other four. Liddy, who had already been cited for contempt because of his refusal to talk, was given a final sentence: six years and eight months to twenty years in jail and a $40,000 fine. These sentences were an outrage. Murderers had received more lenient sentences in the District of Columbia. Sirica admitted severity and justified it as a tactic aimed at getting the defendants to talk. Later Gordon Liddy would wryly remark that he and Sirica were men of like minds because they both believed that the end justifies the means.

I rather gather that it may go more the Mitchell-Magruder route than the White House route. Whatever the case may be we are now forced to some sort of a position on Watergate. The main thing we have to get off our backs, of course, is the whole problem of political pressure.

As I told Ehrlichman, since the thing is going to come out, let's prick the boil early and get it over with. I asked him whether or not he didn't think we ought to have the President take the lead in calling for a grand jury and offer that everybody in the White House should be called upon to testify.

He said he would talk to Mitchell about that and also talk to Dean about it, but he is off to California for some church affair and will not be back until Sunday, so I will get ahold of Haldeman and Ziegler but I am going to have to make up my mind on this too. I am going to give Dean a call and get his judgment on it. Perhaps Kleindienst as well.

Of course, right at the moment, I guess we're all a bit depressed. I have to be with the Watergate thing going, and not knowing what's going to come out of it. But I think the most important thing now is to get the White House cleaned and cleaned fast on this matter. Now that the judge has moved, I think the more I lean to the idea that we should be calling for a grand jury.

The CPI figures came out—the worst in twenty years—the market continues to go down. So it's just one of the those bad Marches which seem to be congenital as far as our administration is concerned. March is usually a very bad month and then April is a month for action. We shall see.

I told Haldeman to get in touch with Colson and find out exactly what he had said to Hunt about clemency, including whether or not he had mentioned my name. Colson said that when he had met with William Bittman, Hunt's lawyer, Bittman had made references to the fact that Hunt hoped to be out of prison before the end of the year. In response Colson had told Bittman that he was Hunt's friend and would try to do what he could. He said that he had not been specific and had not mentioned me. Colson conceded that what Bittman inferred from his comments might be different from what was actually said.

Haldeman asked Colson about Dean's new disclosure that it had been Colson's call to Magruder urging action on Hunt's and Liddy's intelligence-gathering plans that may have precipitated the Watergate break-in. Haldeman reported that Colson had seemed startled by this question. He said he had not realized that the fact of the call was generally known. He swore that he had not known what it was that Hunt and Liddy were actually proposing.

Haldeman contacted Mitchell about my plan to request another grand jury to look into Watergate. He was against it. He said that at this point it would just give credibility to everything McCord had said and damage the rights of others. Dean agreed with Mitchell and said that we should not overreact. But at this point overreaction on our part was hardly the problem. McCord's letter was explosive news, and I kept pushing for something I could say or do that would enable us to get control of the rush of events: if not another grand jury, then perhaps I should appoint a Special Prosecutor of some kind. But there was always resistance from someone. On March 25 I made a note about the preceding day.

Diary

Yesterday continued our soul-searching with regard to the Watergate matter. I had a long talk with Haldeman, and he told me about Dean's plan of possibly going up to the grand jury, asking for immunity, and then telling all. I am not sure that this is in our interests because we would be giving in on our strongest case where executive privilege is concerned. I mentioned to Haldeman that everybody named by the grand jury, or particularly named in the letter on Thursday by McCord, would have to volunteer to go immediately before the grand jury and present everything that he knew.

Haldeman finally came down, and not reluctantly as a matter of fact, on my side that what we had to do was to have appearances before the grand jury.

Colson is the one that is dragging his feet the

most here and I can understand why, but he is the one perhaps who is the most clever in terms of being able to handle himself before the grand jury.

My concern is that the Cubans may have talked freely to McCord about their hopes and promises for immunity and that this is going to look like an administration cover-up in massive proportions or an obstruction of justice.

Colson swears that anything he said to Bittman he had made a thorough memorandum on later, and that he had limited it to Hunt only on the basis of old friendship. He said that he would intercede for him and he had reason to think that his intercession would be listened to. This, of course, is itself bad enough, and Colson overstated it somewhat.

I talked to Haldeman about the difficulty of any kind of clemency. He agreed nothing could happen before the 1974 elections and whether it could happen then or right at the end remains to be seen. Hunt might be an exceptional case because of his long-time service, the fact that he was not involved as the others were, the fact, too, that he has this very serious personal problem with his wife dead and his children having no one really to care for them.

I talked to Haldeman about the necessity of getting this whole thing cleaned up. I said that we simply wouldn't be able to govern, we couldn't do the job we could do for the country if we allowed it to go on. I said that each man had to go up there and I said when a man was charged he probably had to take a leave of absence. I was thinking then of Magruder.

I said the problem is that, if we go that far, what happens if someone in the White House is charged? Haldeman immediately reacted and said, "Well, that's exactly of course what they want. To drive somebody in the top command out of office and indicate that the whole White House is shot through with corruption." And he's right. We have to find a way to cut this thing off at the pass before it reaches that point, because there's no question in my mind that neither Haldeman or Ehrlichman are guilty.

The Colson matter is something else again. What happens there troubles me a great deal and only time will tell whether he can dig himself out of what appears to be a pretty complex and difficult situation.

I made a note on the 24th, yesterday, that it was exactly sixty days after the Vietnam speech, March 23, our high point in the polls, that the whole Watergate thing came apart, or at least blew up into its rather massive proportions. I recall, too, Theodore Roosevelt coming back after his fantastically successful trip abroad and being received virtually with a ticker tape parade in New York City, and then a few months later being turned down by his own party for leadership and not even being made a delegate to the convention.

It was also on Friday, March 23, that James McCord had a private interview with Samuel Dash, the chief counsel of the Ervin Committee. On March 25 Dash held a press conference and proclaimed McCord's account "full and honest." Even some of the reporters present were perplexed at such a blatantly prejudicial move; some of them speculated that Dash deliberately intended to heighten pressure on them to find leaks. As they soon found out, the search for leaks was not to be that difficult. As would become typical of the Committee's "fairness," the substance of McCord's secret session with Dash immediately leaked.

It turned out that one of McCord's particular targets was John Dean. On the night of March 25 we learned that the next morning's Los Angeles *Times* was going to report that McCord had "told Senate investigators" that Magruder and Dean had had prior knowledge of the Watergate break-in. Dean told Ziegler that the story was libelous and that his attorney was going to inform the paper to that effect. The story appeared regardless, under the headline: *McCord Says Dean, Magruder Knew in Advance of Bugging.* Haldeman called Dean again and received another flat denial. At first I thought about simply announcing that Dean would volunteer to go before the grand jury, but I decided to wait. When Ziegler came to see me before his regular morning press briefing, I told him to express confidence in Dean but to avoid statements on Magruder.

This story in the Los Angeles *Times* marked a major new stage in my perception of the seriousness of the Watergate issue.

Diary

We have tended to sort of live in the idea that while the Watergate wasn't all that big an issue in the country, that it was primarily a Washington–New York story, but now it is far more than that and with the media giving it an enormous assist, it will become worse, particularly as the defendants, if they do, begin to crack and put out various episodes of recollections which may or may not be true but which leave a terrible stigma of possible guilt on the part of the White House staff. Rogers told us that Roger Mudd had positively gloated while reporting the McCord letter.

The other side of the coin is that most of our friends in the press, including Dick Wilson, Bill White, Roscoe Drummond, Vermont Royster, are now pointing out that what was a caper in June now appears to be like a massive cover-up and one that could leave a serious mark on the President and the administration for the balance of the four years unless we take action frontally to clear the thing up.

I think this is correct.

The day has been a hard one, but all in all the day must be a terribly hard one for others. I think of the men who are in prison, I think of course of Haldeman and Ehrlichman, naturally, Mitchell who must be concerned. Needless to say, Magruder who knows he must have committed perjury before the court and Dean who is really the one who deserves the most consideration because he was acting always as a counsel, giving his best advice and always avoiding anything which would smack of illegal or improper activities.

Haldeman had talked with Dean during the day. Dean had said, "The more I look at it, the more I am convinced that if we try to fight it we're going to lose eventually, and the longer we take to lose, the worse we are going to look."

Dean told Haldeman that we should revive the idea of going before a grand jury to talk about everything, without invoking executive privilege. I still wasn't sure this was the right course. Dean also told Haldeman that earlier Mitchell had suggested someone be sent to "take McCord's pulse." Dean said that out of this somehow there seemed to be a view floating around that a one-year clemency commitment had been made. Dean also indicated concern because he himself had called Liddy at one point and reassured him not to worry. My diary continued:

Diary

There's also the question as to how much promises were made on the clemency side. Of course Dean puts it on the basis that they were blackmailing us, but on the other hand, as I told Haldeman, that while there might not be any legal basis for prosecution for people paying blackmail, on the other hand, in terms of the President keeping such people on his staff, there just wouldn't be any way to do so. I didn't put it quite so bluntly as that to him, but that is my considered judgment.

According to Haldeman, Dean's concern in testifying before the grand jury was that he told Haldeman he really didn't know how to answer insofar as Mitchell's involvement was concerned because he did not have what he considered to be totally substantiated evidence with regard to Mitchell's role.

Dean also told Haldeman that he didn't have any knowledge beyond a certain point on Magruder because Magruder had not confided in him. He told Haldeman that the only involvement he had with Magruder was that before Magruder went to the grand jury he came to see Dean and asked Dean to question him on the basis that Dean thought the grand jury would raise so that we could get a dry run, and that he, Dean, did that. He said that Magruder had acquitted himself well on the answers, but he said, "I have not gone on an off-the-record type thing in any way with Jeb to get the truth out of him, so I don't know what the truth is from Jeb."

Dean has also raised with Haldeman the point

that he did not know the full extent of Gordon Strachan's knowledge.

Haldeman said he asked Dean if Strachan had perjured himself, and Dean said, "No, he hasn't." I pointed out to Haldeman that if Dean went before the grand jury that the grand jury would then call Haldeman, Mitchell, Colson, Ehrlichman, and possibly others that would come out in Dean's questioning and that under those circumstances they would have to go before the grand jury too. Haldeman said again that Colson is very reluctant to expose himself to a grand jury. Dean told Haldeman that he purposely had not questioned Colson on activities other than Watergate which Colson seemed to be worried about because Dean really didn't want to know about those things. I told Haldeman that I didn't know of anything that Colson had done that was illegal unless he had the Cubans doing some damn thing in some other area. Haldeman answered, "He may have." I said, "Do you think he did?" Haldeman answered, "I don't know—I really don't know."

It was in this period that Dean called from Camp David and told Haldeman's assistant, Larry Higby, that while Dean's report might not be a good defense as far as the rest of the White House staff were concerned, it was a very good defense of John Dean.

Everything was growing more and more fluid on Watergate. I still sought some actions that would put the White House out in front of the controversy—some symbols to demonstrate that *we*, and not just the Ervin Committee, were on the side of right.

For a while I considered an idea Dean had suggested of appointing a special presidential commission somewhat like the Warren Commission that had investigated President Kennedy's assassination. Dean had said that he liked the idea because it would stretch things out beyond the 1974 elections. I could then consider granting clemency. But Bill Rogers, whom I had asked to give us advice about Watergate, was strongly opposed to the idea of such a commission. He warned that its members would all try to make names for themselves, and in the end it would be the main thing remembered about the Nixon administration. I finally came around to this view, and I told Haldeman and Ehrlichman, "The idea that a commission might get through the 1974 election. . . . I think the damn thing is going to come out anyway, and I just think you better cut the losses now and just better get it over with much sooner and, frankly, sharper."

I suggested another possibility: I would go to Judge Sirica and tell him to do whatever he thought was best—either call a new grand jury or appoint a Special Prosecutor. Rogers liked this idea. But Colson was against having a Special Prosecutor in any circumstances; he said bluntly that he thought nearly everybody in the White House except himself was involved in the post-June 17 activities, and therefore we should not deliberately increase our vulnerability. Dean also opposed the Sirica idea. He reminded Haldeman of the solution that he had proposed earlier whereby we would obtain immunity for him—that is, for Dean—and then send him to the grand jury. That way, he said, he would head off the possibility that Magruder would unfairly implicate everyone else.

On March 27 Dean phoned Haldeman. He said that he and Paul O'Brien, one of the attorneys retained by the CRP to deal with its Watergate litigation, had concluded that Mitchell had in fact approved the Watergate bugging plan. Dean believed that Mitchell was now using the White House to protect himself; he said Mitchell and Magruder were mixing "apples and oranges" for their own protection. Magruder, for example, was apparently saying that the whole intelligence plan had first been cooked up by Dean on Haldeman's instructions. Magruder even alleged that Strachan had once called him and told him that "the President wanted it done."

From a combination of hypersensitivity and a desire not to know the truth in case it turned out to be unpleasant, I had spent the last ten months putting off a confrontation with John Mitchell. Now it seemed impossible to avoid. I talked with Haldeman and Ehrlichman about having Mitchell come in to give us his personal account of what had actually happened regarding the bugging plan and the break-in.

Before we were able even to reach any decision on this, we had to deal with another problem that had recently emerged. Dean was now saying that if he went before the grand jury, he would contradict Magruder's—and possibly Mitchell's—earlier testimony. For one thing, there had in fact been *two* meetings in Mitchell's office at which the Liddy plan was discussed. Magruder had testified that there had been only one and that it had dealt with the new campaign spending laws. Dean was not sure how Mitchell had testified on this point. Dean and Magruder had both indicated that Mitchell was putting pressure on them to hold to the original version that there had been only one innocuous meeting. Haldeman said that he was going to advise Magruder to go to the court and say, "I lied," and correct the record. I asked if Magruder could not still stick to his original story, but Ehrlichman said that he could not because there were too many crosscurrents. I agreed and wondered if we could help him get immunity.

On March 28 Haldeman arranged for Mitchell, Magruder, and Dean to meet and see if they could settle the conflict over the number and subject of their meetings with Liddy.

First, Mitchell came in alone to see Haldeman. He said that his first mistake had been not turning the thing off when Liddy first proposed it. But, he said, he just had not paid much attention to it at the time.

Magruder told Haldeman that Liddy had been ordered to prepare a plan for campaign intelligence-gathering before he ever got to the CRP; he was not sure who had ordered it. Magruder was sure, however, that it had been John Dean's idea to lie about the number of meetings with Liddy. Although Magruder's version had to be regarded skeptically, we got a glimpse of how far Dean had gone to keep the Watergate situation under control. Magruder reported that Dean had not only suggested that Magruder say that there had only been one meeting but had urged Magruder to destroy his desk diary, in which there was a note of the two meetings. Magruder also said that it was Dean who had suggested that he lie about the purpose of the meetings and say that they were on the new campaign laws. In fact, Magruder said that he had testified the way he had only to protect Dean. He pointed out that he would not have hurt his own case by admitting that the meetings were on intelligence; but such an admission would have hurt Dean, by drawing him into the intelligence-planning network.

So Jeb Magruder had perjured himself to protect John Dean—and now Dean was going to do Magruder in by exposing him as a perjurer.

Haldeman said that Magruder had been pathetic and had asked about the possibility of clemency. Haldeman had tried to reassure him but made it clear he could make no commitments.

After these meetings with Mitchell and Magruder, Haldeman met with Dean, who said that he could not do what Mitchell and Magruder wanted him to do—to corroborate their accounts of no prior knowledge. He said the only way to avoid this problem would be for him not to testify at all. When Haldeman told me this, I debated whether we should use executive privilege to keep Dean from having to testify.

Dean told Haldeman that he had decided that we all needed the advice of a criminal lawyer. He said that he was going to get one himself whom we could all use to advise us.

The Ervin Committee continued to leak prejudicial stories, and big headlines now proclaimed that McCord had linked Mitchell to prior approval of the plan. At the same time a publicity-seeking Republican member of the committee, Lowell Weicker of Connecticut, began attacking Haldeman, accusing him of having been "fully aware" of the political espionage schemes. The senior Republican on the committee, Howard Baker of Tennessee, privately expressed dismay over Weicker's "histrionics," but there was nothing he or we could do as Weicker found in abundance the publicity he sought.

Conservative Republican Senators James Buckley, John Tower, and Norris Cotton publicly called on me to allow White House aides and former aides to testify before the Ervin Committee. George Bush, Chairman of the Republican National Committee, privately pleaded for some action that would get us off the defensive.

On the afternoon of March 29 I made the decision to waive executive privilege for Watergate testimony and send Dean to the grand jury. Ehrlichman wrote out a page of notes for the announcement, and we asked Ziegler to call a special press briefing.

Ziegler, however, raised practical objections: most of the reporters had already left the White House for the day, and we were only a few hours away from the major television speech I was to make that night. I agreed to Ziegler's suggestion that we wait until the next day to make the announcement. I have sometimes wondered what would have happened if the announcement had been made immediately, as I had intended. Since Dean himself had recently favored this idea, it had not occurred to me that he would have changed his mind in the matter of a few days. But when we talked with him about it, he strenuously objected and said that his lawyers now told him that he should not offer to go to the grand jury.

So we had to cancel this announcement and scrap this plan, and another day went by and nothing was done.

In my speech that night I announced a temporary price freeze on meat and warned Hanoi about its breaches of the Indochina cease-fire. I also heralded the homecoming of the last group of POWs. "For the first time in twelve years," I said, "no American military forces are in Vietnam." In Washington, however, attention was already focused on Watergate. Scarcely anyone in the media seemed to care about Vietnam anymore—not now that the Vietnam news was good and the Watergate news was bad.

At the end of the month there was a new volley of leaked Watergate stories. The Associated Press, in a story picked up by the networks, quoted sources who said McCord indicated Haldeman had to have known about the break-in scheme. In the New York *Times* "reliable sources" said that McCord had linked Haldeman only by hearsay but had flatly said that Colson knew. Other sources told the Washington *Post* that McCord had not implicated Haldeman at all.

In my diary I noted, "I marvel on the strength of Haldeman. He is a really remarkable man and I only hope to God that we can find a way to keep him immunized from all this, although it's going to be terribly difficult to do so with all the effort being made to get him."

Before we left for San Clemente on March 30, Ziegler announced that members of the White House staff would cooperate fully if they were called before the grand jury. He also revealed that negotiations were under way with the Ervin Committee for a relaxation of our stand on executive privilege.

I asked Ehrlichman to take over Dean's responsibility for handling the Watergate problem. Dean was under too much attack and was obviously going to be coming under still more. In order to establish a lawyer-client privilege, Ehrlichman drew up a letter for me to sign, officially charging him with these responsibilities.

The night after our arrival in California I presented the Medal of Freedom to film director John Ford at a dinner in his honor in Los Angeles. He was seventy-eight years old and terminally ill, but he insisted on being helped to the microphone to acknowledge the award. He told the large audience of celebrities that he had cried when he watched the POWs returning home. "Then," he said, "I reached for my rosary and said a few decades of the beads, and I uttered a short fervent prayer, not an original prayer, but one spoken in millions of American homes today. It is a simple prayer, simply 'God bless Richard Nixon.'"

On April 2 President Thieu arrived in San Clemente for a state visit. He was concerned about the blatant lack of good faith demonstrated by the Communists in their violations of the Paris peace accords. I fully shared his concern, and I reassured him that we would not tolerate any actions that actually threatened South Vietnam. He was grateful for my reassurances, but I knew that he must be concerned about the effect the domestic drain of Watergate would have on my ability to act forcefully abroad.

Ehrlichman moved decisively into his new role as the White House's Watergate man. He devised a negotiating strategy for dealing with the Ervin Committee and began a general fact-gathering inquiry.

On April 5 the CRP's lawyer, Paul O'Brien, came to San Clemente to give his assessment of the case. Ehrlichman found that O'Brien had still another version of the current facts and situation. According to O'Brien's information, Magruder was now saying that Colson had phoned him not once but twice to urge action on the Hunt-Liddy plan. And while only the week before Dean had told us that O'Brien felt that Mitchell had approved the plan, now O'Brien told Ehrlichman that Mitchell had not known of the break-in in advance, but that there was no question that Magruder had.

On April 5, the same day O'Brien met with Ehrlichman, we turned back to the problem of Pat Gray's confirmation hearings as FBI Director. The Senate Judiciary Committee had been holding the nomination hostage until Dean appeared to testify before them. The chances of getting Gray confirmed were slim, and even if we managed to get enough votes, he was now so damaged that I did not think he could be an effective Director. I therefore asked Haldeman to call him and ask that he request to have his nomination withdrawn. Gray called me back immediately and in a manly way did as I had asked.

Later that afternoon Ehrlichman met briefly with Judge Matthew Byrne, the man Attorney General Kleindienst and Henry Petersen had been enthusiastically recommending for weeks as a prospective FBI Director. Byrne was a Democrat and a respected member of the bench. The only drawback was that once Gray's nomination was withdrawn, it would be important to propose someone else right away. If we decided to name Judge Byrne, we would have to wait until he finished presiding over Daniel Ellsberg's trial for unauthorized possession of classified documents.

Diary

The call to Pat Gray was a difficult one. He has been really a great fellow. He said that he was always loyal to the President, and that the people on his staff he had already told were crushed. I said that nobody could feel worse about it than I do.

I met Judge Byrne, briefly, walked out the office door and talked to him for a moment. I was impressed by his real steel-like handshake. He has good tough, cold eyes and is the right age, forty-two years. Unfortunately his case isn't over for a month.

I had a call from Connally. As I expected, Connally was greatly disturbed about Watergate and thought that somebody had to walk the plank. Connally had raised the point with George Bush that there are too many people around the President and that they isolate the President from what is really going on. Of course what we have to realize here is that some of these people overlook the fact that we have some major successes and that we must be doing something right.

I received a rather astonishing message through Harlow from Agnew to the effect that he would speak up on Watergate, but only at a price and that was that he would have to see the President. I told Ehrlichman to pass the message to Harlow that I didn't want under any circumstances to ask Agnew to do something that he was not convinced he ought to do on his own, that under the circumstances he should just chart his own course and of course I would chart my own course. I only hope that Bryce delivered this message in the rather meaningful way that I tried to convey it.

I told Haldeman it was so fortunate that neither he nor I had been told about the Watergate thing before it broke. I am not sure what we would have said, although I think we would have turned it off because of its utter stupidity.

Kissinger came in. Told me that he thought I should stick by Haldeman. I said, "Suppose there is appearance of guilt?" He said, "Even if he is guilty in part they are after him because they know he is the strong man in the administration. He is the most selfless, able person you've got, and you have got to have him."

We have had in four months more problems than most second term Presidents have in four years. In December we had the charge of isolation and the bombing. In January, after it seemed that the war was going to be over, the charge of heartlessness, congressional relations, impoundment, and so forth in the budget. In February, they began to go on the economy, and in March it's Watergate. So every month there's something and each of them has an eroding effect.

One very perceptive point was made that Watergate would not hurt us in the event the other things held up reasonably well. But if, for example, the economy also goes to pot then Watergate accentuates other failures. That is why it is so important to get back to do the domestic things well and the economic things and so forth not just for the purpose of diverting attention, but so the people will not be thinking that the administration is coming apart at the seams, which is exactly what happened in the Truman years. It wasn't just the 5 percenters, it was the fact that added to the 5 percenters, they thought the Truman administration was just no damn good. We must not allow that thing to set in with us.

In early April Dean had advised us that his lawyers were going to meet with the U.S. Attorneys to feel them out on what would be involved if Dean went to the grand jury. Then on April 7 he told Haldeman, with whom he had been in frequent contact during the time we were in California, that he was going to have an off-the-record meeting with the U.S. Attorneys the next day. He said there was no interest in post-break-in activities. In anticipation of being called before the grand jury, he asked to meet with Haldeman and Ehrlichman as soon as they got back to Washington. On April 8, the morning of our return to Washington, I made a note about the unfortunate way the whole situation seemed to be developing, but which still expressed optimism about our ability to survive it.

Colson has been calling to say he has evidence that Mitchell may be trying to set up Haldeman as a scapegoat. I am not going to allow any of this division business to hurt any of our people. Everyone is going into business for himself for understandable reasons, but we're not going to let it go to the point that one destroys another.

In retrospect as I look back over the past months since the Congress came back into session, I think I've tended to become too depressed, and actually obsessed would be a better word, with the problems of the moment. We have three problems now, the question of prices, the question of Watergate, and the question of the increased disturbances in Vietnam. But compared with the massive problem we had with regard to the war and what we have gone through over the past four years, these problems do not appear all that difficult. They are solvable and they will pass. With the war we simply didn't know whether we were going to be able to see it through.

Haldeman and Ehrlichman met with Dean as soon as we returned to Washington. He told them that he was going to appear before the grand jury.

When I heard this I said that Mitchell would have to decide whether he was going to tell Dean to lie about the meetings with Liddy. I said of Dean, "John is not going to lie." Ehrlichman said that the smartest thing Dean could do would be to go down to the prosecutors and appear to be cooperative.

"Right," I replied.

Ehrlichman said that Dean's strong feeling was that this was the time when "you just have to let it flow." I agreed with this totally.

On April 10 Ted Agnew asked Haldeman if he could come over to his office; he wanted help on a problem. He told Haldeman that someone who had once worked for him in Baltimore was being questioned in a probe of kickbacks and campaign contributions. Agnew assured Haldeman that he himself was innocent of any wrongdoing, but the man apparently had records of efforts to solicit campaign contributions from those who had benefited from his administration, and Agnew thought that there was a potential for embarrassment. He wondered if someone from the White House would see Maryland Senator J. Glenn Beall, Jr., the brother of the Baltimore prosecutor, and alert him that we didn't want Agnew's name to come up in an unnecessary or embarrassing way.

Haldeman gave me a report on the meeting. I was very concerned at the prospect of Agnew's being dragged through the mud unfairly, but in view of all the other problems and our strained relations with Capitol Hill, I did not see how we could do anything to help him. In fact, the climate was such that anything we did to try to help might boomerang and be made to appear that we were trying to cover up for him.

On April 13 Dean told Haldeman and Ehrlichman that the White House was still not a target in the grand jury's Watergate investigation, even though the prosecutors were beginning to develop material on the post-June period.

Magruder, however, seemed to sense that his days were numbered. Earlier he had sent word to Haldeman that if he went to the prosecutors his testimony would bring down John Mitchell. This could mean only one thing: Magruder was going to claim that Mitchell had authorized the bugging. He had asked for Haldeman's advice, and Haldeman had responded that he should do what his lawyers told him to do—in other words, that he should come forward.

When Ehrlichman met with Colson and David Shapiro, Colson's lawyer, Colson said that after Howard Hunt testified before the grand jury on the following Monday, both Mitchell and Magruder would be indicted.

It seemed as if our return to Washington had somehow been a catalyst, and charges and countercharges were now flying in every direction. I did my best to gather everyone in and control the finger-pointing, but a panic was setting in that was beyond anyone's control. Colson said that Magruder was putting out the story that Haldeman, Mitchell, Colson, Dean, and I had all known about the Watergate break-in plans. Magruder, however, called one of Haldeman's aides and said that his testimony would hurt Mitchell, Strachan, and Dean, but not Haldeman.

Haldeman reported that Colson was claiming that Ehrlichman and Dean had told him to promise clemency to Hunt in January, but that he was smarter than that and had not done so. Ehrlichman had a different version. By his account he had instructed Colson not to tell Hunt anything about a pardon and not to raise the matter with me.

Things were obviously about to happen very quickly. We could no longer avoid facing the unpleasant fact that the whole thing was completely out of hand, and that something had to be done to get the White House out in front. Now it was not just a question of knowledge of the Watergate break-in or a subsequent cover-up, but the possibility of having to respond to accusations that I had not acted promptly on the knowledge obtained during the past few weeks. Regarding this last point, Ehrlichman observed that the information Dean had been giving us over the past weeks and months had not been direct. Dean had only presented different theories of what might have happened and who might have known about it, based on secondhand knowledge—so we had had no clear-cut legal responsibility to act on it. But Magruder's phone call to Haldeman's aide the day before, when he had said explicitly that he would bring down John Mitchell, was firsthand "action knowledge," and we could no longer afford to stand idly by.

About three weeks had now passed since John Dean had first told me that there was a cancer close to the presidency. Since then Watergate had been an almost constant preoccupation. I had tried to grapple with the facts only to find that they were not like the pieces of a puzzle that could be assembled into one true picture. They were more like the parts of a kaleidoscope: at one moment, arranged one way, they seemed to form a perfect design, complete in every detail. But the simple shift of one conjecture could unlock them all and they would move into a completely different pattern.

For example, on March 13 Dean told me that Gordon Strachan knew about the bugging and implied that Strachan had committed perjury. On March 17 he indicated it was possible Strachan had known about the break-in. On March

20, however, Haldeman said Strachan had not known about the break-in and had not lied—rather, "forgot" and had not been well questioned. On March 21 Dean said he thought Strachan knew about the break-in. On March 26 Dean told Haldeman that he did not know the full extent of Strachan's knowledge but that Strachan had not perjured himself. On April 14 Strachan would deny to Ehrlichman any advance knowledge of the break-in. At the end of April, however, I was told that Magruder had passed a lie detector test concerning Strachan's advance knowledge, and Strachan had taken the same test and failed. Years later Strachan told me that in fact he had passed that test. Strachan was never charged with knowledge of the Watergate wiretap.

There was also kaleidoscopic confusion surrounding the question of Colson's involvement. From the very beginning Haldeman and Ehrlichman had told me that Colson was not involved in any way. Then on March 13 Dean said that Colson did not know the specifics of Watergate but, like others, "knew something was going on over there." On March 21 Dean told me that a call from Colson may have triggered the bugging plan and that he "assumed" Colson had had "a damn good idea" what he was urging. On March 23 Colson completely denied any such knowledge. Five days later, however, both Magruder and Mitchell were speculating that Colson *had* known. An April 8 news report revealed Colson took a lie detector test on the question of prior knowledge and passed it. He was never charged with prior knowledge of the break-in.

A similarly confused and crucial question involved Haldeman. Both Dean and Magruder said that Haldeman and Strachan had received copies of the Watergate bugging reports and that Haldeman may have known what the information in them represented and where it had come from. Haldeman told me that while he may in fact have received these reports, he had not known anything about their source. As it later turned out, he and Strachan had *not* received any of them and had, when these charges were made against them, assumed that innocent intelligence reports they had received might have been the Watergate bugging transcripts.

The most basic and the most sensitive question of all involved John Mitchell's role. For ten months everyone had speculated about whether Mitchell knew in advance. On March 21 Dean told me that he did not know the answer. But on March 27 he told Haldeman that both he and Paul O'Brien had decided that Mitchell *had* approved the break-in. On April 5, however, O'Brien told Ehrlichman he had concluded that Mitchell *had not* approved it. On April 14 Mitchell would tell Ehrlichman he had not. No such charge has ever been brought against him.

We kept thinking that if we could only establish all the facts, then we could construct a way out of the situation that would minimize if not foreclose any possible criminal liability for the people involved. But we never felt confident of the facts, and every alternative course of action, from wholesale appearances before the grand jury to Special Prosecutors to presidential commissions, met with objections from one or the other of my aides and friends who suddenly found himself in a vulnerable position.

As a result, in the three weeks after March 21, when Dean had officially put me on notice about the implications of the cover-up, we did nothing more than stew and worry about the shifting facts and continue to look for any way to prevent damage. By April 14, when everything began to fall apart, all that was left to me was to try to get myself into a position to be able to claim that I had cracked the case, trying to garner some credit for leadership that I had failed to exert.

I decided that the step needed to show some action would be to ask John Mitchell to come down to Washington. That would also alert him to the fact that we were in a position where we had to act. Rather than simply turn over the information to the prosecutors, I wanted Mitchell to have the chance to go in on his own.

Ehrlichman said that he would tell Mitchell that "the President strongly feels that the only way this thing can end up being even a little net plus for the administration . . . is for you to . . . make a statement that basically says, 'I am both morally and legally responsible.'" Ehrlichman said that if both Mitchell and Magruder stonewalled, we would have no choice but to tell them that I was in possession of a body of knowledge that forced me to act.

For the first time I was in the position of having to face and force a confrontation about Watergate with John Mitchell.

Haldeman still did not believe Mitchell was guilty. "I don't think Mitchell did order the Watergate bugging, and I don't think he was specifically aware of the Watergate bugging at the time it was instituted. I honestly don't," he insisted. I agreed that the evidence was not enough to convince me that Mitchell was guilty. But it was almost certainly going to be enough to ensure that he would have to go before a grand jury. Haldeman suggested that perhaps if Mitchell went in and took the blame, the investigators and the press might not care about the cover-up anymore. I said pessimistically that they shouldn't, but they would.

"The Mitchell thing is goddamn painful," I said, and I told Ehrlichman to tell Mitchell that this was the toughest decision I had ever made—tougher than Cambodia, May 8, and December 18 put together. I said he should tell Mitchell that I simply could not bring myself to talk to him personally about it. I said to Ehrlichman, "Frankly, what I'm doing, John, is putting you in the same position as President Eisenhower put me in with Adams. But John Mitchell, let me say, will never go to prison. I agree with that assumption. I think what will happen is that he will put on the goddamnedest defense."

When we turned to the subject of John Dean, who was about to be called before the grand jury, Ehrlichman argued against making Dean leave. He felt that Dean's role in the post-June activities had not been at such a serious level that his departure was necessary. He also thought that Dean would get better and more respectful treatment from the grand jury if he still worked at the White House. Furthermore, as we all recognized, putting Dean outside the White House walls might make him turn against us.

"Dean only tried to do what he could to pick up the goddamn pieces, and everybody else around here knew it had to be done," I said.

"What Dean did was all proper," Haldeman added, "in terms of the higher good."

I picked up a theme that had first been introduced by Ehrlichman: if Dean was guilty, he was no more so than was half the staff—"and, frankly, than I have been since a week ago, two weeks ago," I added.

As far as Magruder was concerned, I asked Ehrlichman to talk to him and tell him that he was wrong if he thought that by keeping silent he was serving my interests. I told Ehrlichman to put in the personal "grace notes" that could help to ease the pain of the situation. I suggested that he tell Magruder of my affection for him and for his family. In fact, I had been thinking the night before about Magruder's young children in school, and about his wife. "It breaks your heart," I said. I thought back to Haldeman's comment two weeks before on how pathetic Magruder had been with his plea for clemency. I told Ehrlichman to tell Magruder that this was a painful message for me. "I'd just put that in so that he knows that I have personal affection," I said. "That's the way the so-called clemency's got to be handled."

Ehrlichman met with Mitchell at 1:40 P.M. on April 14. After their meeting he reported to me that Mitchell was an innocent man in heart and mind, but that he had not missed an opportunity to lob "mudballs" at the White House. He had refused to admit any responsibility for the break-in.

Mitchell confirmed Magruder's story that it was Dean who had talked Magruder into lying to the grand jury about the number and content of the meetings with Liddy. I was shocked, first by the report that Mitchell had been present at such meetings, and second by this apparent confirmation that Dean had talked Magruder into lying.

"What does Dean say about it?" I asked.

"Dean says it was Mitchell and Magruder," Ehrlichman replied. With a wry smile he added, "It must have been the quietest meeting in history, because everybody's version is that the other two guys talked."

Ehrlichman also had a disturbing report of his most recent talk with Dean, who was now saying that "everyone in the place" was going to be indicted. Dean had pointedly hinted to Ehrlichman that the prosecutors were after bigger targets than John Dean—they were aiming at targets like John Ehrlichman.

The problem was apparently the money—the fact that

Dean had asked Haldeman and Ehrlichman for money for the Watergate defendants. Dean's "hypothesis," as Ehrlichman called it, was that Haldeman's and Ehrlichman's approval of the use of Kalmbach to obtain funds had been as damaging as action. I said that I still could not believe that the prosecutors could charge Haldeman and Ehrlichman with conspiracy simply because they had been asked whether it was all right to raise the money in the first place. "Technically, I'm sure they could. Practically, it just seems awfully remote," Haldeman said, "but maybe that's wishful thinking."

In the early evening of April 14 I dictated a long diary entry about the day.

Diary

I have just had bacon and eggs and waiting to go over to the White House Correspondents' Dinner. It's rather ironic that the winners of the awards are from the Washington *Post*. While their stories for the most part were libelous, on the other hand it is significant that yesterday and today for the first time the Watergate case really broke apart and I learned the facts on it.

In meeting on Friday, I mentioned to Ehrlichman for the first time the idea of Haldeman and Dean taking a leave of absence. He came back and said it wouldn't work with Haldeman and I don't think he thinks it would work with Dean, because as it turns out Dean has ways that he could implicate both Haldeman and Ehrlichman, not in a way that they couldn't defend, but in a way that might be embarrassing. In any event, there is a solid reason for Dean not having a leave of absence because it would be in effect admitting his guilt before the ax fell on him.

Interestingly enough, Haldeman said that when Magruder came in to see him and say, "Goodbye, I'm going to jail," he said he was like a man with a terrible load lifted off him, a totally different man. He has resigned himself to what is going to happen and is going to live with his fate.

It seems that Colson is going to be a major target, according to Magruder, of the U.S. Attorney. If Dean cracks, Colson will have had it apparently. Colson is probably telling the literal truth when he says that he did not know that the Watergate was going to be bugged. On the other hand he seems to be deeply implicated in urging action on the Liddy project and so forth, and to get the material on O'Brien, whatever he meant by that I don't know, but Mitchell also had talked about getting material on O'Brien.

It is also quite clear that Dean was more of an actor in this whole thing than he led us to believe—or it may be that Magruder is shading it a bit this way too. Dean tells the story a very different way, particularly with regard to the question as to whether or not he advised Magruder how to testify. In this respect, Mitchell knocks Dean, because he indicates that Dean told Magruder how to testify in the meeting that Mitchell sat in with them. Dean seems to have been quite active in that.

I have a note here saying, "the loose cannon has finally gone off," that's probably what could be said because that's what Magruder did when he went in and talked to the U.S. Attorney. I am glad that he did so, however; it is time to get the whole damn thing out and cleaned up.

It's really a terrible thing what is happening to all these men. They all did it with the best of intentions, with great devotion and dedication, but they just went one step too far and then compounded the whole thing through this program of trying to cover it up. It's too bad we were unable to do something about it. I suppose during the election campaign there was a feeling we couldn't do anything for fear of risking the election. Yet that was a mistake, as it turned out, because we were just postponing the day that we would have to face up to it. Immediately after the election, of course, would have been the time to move on it frontally, and yet we did not move then for reasons that I probably will understand later. I just wasn't watching it that closely then and nobody was really minding the store. We were leaving too much to Dean, Mitchell, et al.

At the end of our conversation today, Haldeman brought up the subject himself of resignation. He said quite bluntly he didn't want to do it and didn't feel he should but that he might have to come to that. I didn't commit on it because I think we might have to consider it sometime, although my present inclination, as I indicated to Ehrlichman yesterday and to Kissinger this morning, is that we really had to draw the wagons up around Haldeman and protect him due to the fact, first, that he was really innocent, despite some tangential relationships with the whole affair, and also since it would be such a massive admission of guilt upon the part of the administration that it would really be hard to indicate that we had any character at all in the future.

It will be difficult enough to have Mitchell and most of the campaign people implicated, with Dean possibly a candidate, but to have Haldeman go I think would be the extra blow.

Here what we have to do of course is to enlist some of the Republicans to stand with us. And yet the very thing I predicted is beginning to happen when you see people like John Anderson, Johnny Rhodes, George Aiken, Mathias, of course, as would be expected, and Saxbe popping off, this is the kind of thing that could escalate and get into a general situation as happened in the case of Sherman Adams when Bridges stirred it all up.

Agnew denied the story to the effect that he was appalled by the way Watergate was being handled by the President. Agnew was apparently concerned about some grand jury investigation in Maryland which could involve one of his people and some very damaging memoranda apparently of conversation with Agnew with regard to contributors prior to the time they got state contracts. Of course this is a common practice in states. I said facetiously to Haldeman when he told me about it, "Thank God I was never elected governor of California."

Kleindienst seems to be a strange actor here. Ehrlichman called him at my direction and he had just finished playing golf. He seemed to be amazed the way the ball was bouncing, but still came out for a Special

Prosecutor, which Mitchell is totally opposed to and which I think would be a great mistake. Particularly now that the U.S. Attorney is moving so effectively in the case to substitute a Special Prosecutor, it would be a slap in the face for him and also a vote of lack of confidence in our system of justice.

An ironical note was the [Harold] Lipset revelation this morning, where he had been engaged in bugging in 1966, received only a misdemeanor after being charged with a felony, and got a suspended sentence. And yet he was chief investigator for the Ervin Committee. The double standard is really shocking here with the *Post* trying to put the very best face on it all and Dash saying that you have to have somebody as an investigator who has had some experience in doing some things that were wrong.

I told Haldeman today that Rogers must not leave. It's going to be a hell of a blow to Henry but it's the only thing to do, we cannot have anybody leave if we can possibly avoid it while we are under heat on this thing.

The only bright thing that happened over these past three days, one of the few bright things, was that the Gallup poll advance which is going to come out Monday indicated 60-33 [approval–disapproval]. This is probably the last time we will see one that high for some time unless we get a couple of breaks toward the end of the next year. But on the other hand, it does show that as of this time the Watergate has not seriously affected the public—only 5 percent apparently were affected, although Gallup is taking another poll which will probably indicate that more were affected as a result of the stories that have broken in the past few days.

I had a good meeting with Haig and Henry with regard to Vietnam. Everything seems to pile up here with Vietnam now a problem and the economic stuff.

I am going to get at that tomorrow if I can possibly get loose from some of this stuff to do so, and I will do so.

I had just made a note to suggest possibly that

Ehrlichman talk to Ervin about the disclosures of the day. It's sort of a way-out one, but we might take a crack at that.

In any event, that's all for this day.

This was to be my last full diary dictation until June 1974. Events became so cheerless that I no longer had the time or the desire to dictate daily reflections.

As my diary for January indicates, I knew by then that money was going to the defendants through a Cuban committee, at a time we were hoping Hunt and the others would plead guilty and avoid the publicity of a trial. I do not believe I was ever asked to approve Kalmbach's involvement in raising funds prior to that time, nor that I was aware of the transfer of the $350,000 from the White House to the Re-election Committee and then, at least in part, to the defendants. In early April Ehrlichman told me that O'Brien, the CRP lawyer, had said that in legal terms motive would be the key to guilt or innocence in the authorization of these payments: if the purpose had been to provide attorneys' fees and family support, then they were legal; if the purpose had been to buy silence from the defendants, that would be an obstruction of justice.

Diary
The purpose of course was to see that the defendants would get adequate counsel and that their families would be taken care of during the period when they were in jail, which I suppose would be a perfectly legitimate thing to do. But I suppose it could be said that they were being paid to shut up and not talk. Now whether or not this is a crime—not for the purpose of getting them to shut up about evidence they had about other people, but even about themselves, particularly in view of the fact that they were guilty—remains to be seen.

By mid-April it had become clear that these payments were going to be the biggest problem of all. When Haldeman and Ehrlichman began trying to reconstruct their motives they began to see how the shadow of the Watergate cover-up had fallen across everything and made it impossible to present earlier actions or decisions in their true earlier light. Were the payments intended to silence the defendants about the guilty involvements of others? Or were they simply intended—as I think they were—to pay attorneys' fees and provide family support lest the defendants grow bitter and begin hurling charges. They were a guard against human nature and a hedge against the political problem, not an effort to suppress information based on firsthand knowledge of guilt.

When it came to questions of motive the real answer lay in each man's mind and each man's conscience. I didn't know that answer, nor did I know what each participant was claiming. I did know, however, that the best chance to survive intact would be if everyone who had been involved in the whole unfortunate episode stayed together and maintained the position that the payments had not been intended to buy silence. Since the payments were open to different interpretations, it would take only one person's admission that they were hush money to taint everyone else's actions—including unthinking and innocent actions. That was what Dean would do if he said that the money had been raised for the protection of the guilty and that all the participants in the money-raising had known it. "I wish we could keep Dean away from that," I said, and I told Haldeman and Ehrlichman that ·I thought everyone involved should get together and stick to the line that they did not raise the money to obstruct justice. When we discussed it again a few days later, I said, "I don't mean a lie, but a line."

After I returned from speaking at the Correspondents' Dinner, I called first Haldeman and then Ehrlichman. I reiterated to both my concern that the participants in the money-raising have the same explanation of the motive for it. I also said that I wanted Colson alerted to what was happening so that if he were called before the grand jury he would not walk into a perjury charge. I also told both men that I had come to the view that the best way of handling the Ervin Committee was just to go ahead and send everyone up for public testimony. Haldeman had come to the same view himself and even thought we should agree to televised public sessions.

I told them both what I had been thinking that evening as I prepared my remarks for the Correspondents' Dinner. However melodramatic it might seem, it was true that what the American President did over the next four years would probably determine whether there was a chance for some kind of uneasy peace in the world for the next twenty-five years. It was in foreign affairs that presidential leadership could really make a difference. "Whatever legacy we have, hell, it isn't going to be in getting a cesspool for Winnetka," I told Ehrlichman, "it is going to be there." Then I added, "And I just feel that I have to be in a position to be clean—forthcoming."

I told Ehrlichman of my special concern for Haldeman—Haldeman was clearly the most vulnerable. "You have had a hell of a week—two weeks. And of course poor Bob is going through the tortures of the damned," I said, adding, "He is a guy that has just given his life, hours and hours and hours, you know, totally selfless and honest and decent." I said some people would argue that anyone against whom charges had been made should be fired. "I mean you can't do that," I said to Ehrlichman. "Or am I wrong? . . . Is that our system?"

"That isn't a system," Ehrlichman answered, "that is a machine."

"Whatever we say about Harry Truman," I said, "while it hurt him, a lot of people admired the old bastard for standing by people who were guilty as hell, and, damn it, I am that kind of person. I am not one who is going to say, look, while this guy is under attack, I drop him."

On Sunday afternoon, April 15, after the White House worship service, Dick Kleindienst came to my EOB office and told me that Haldeman and Ehrlichman were being drawn into the criminal case on Watergate. He did not think the information he had to date was sufficient to bring an indictment; but he felt that, circumstantially at least, very serious questions were being raised. He said that the main accuser was John Dean. Dean had in effect acknowledged his own role in obstructing justice and was now drawing others in. I asked him if there was enough evidence to ask Haldeman to take a leave of absence from the staff. He said that there was not now, but that there might be any day. He said that he thought I should consider whether Haldeman and Ehrlichman should take leaves of absence now, in anticipation of what might come.

Kleindienst was highly emotional and his voice choked periodically. He had been up nearly the whole night, and his eyes were red with fatigue and tears. He described the charges: Dean had alleged that shortly after the break-in Ehrlichman had told him to "deep-six" materials from Hunt's safe and to get Hunt out of the country; Haldeman was accused of knowing that the $350,000 he sent back to the CRP was used to pay the defendants; and there was a question whether Haldeman had actually seen budget proposals from Magruder that outlined the bugging plans.

These charges, based on Dean's accusations, did not seem to me to be sufficient evidence to indict either of them. And if I were to let them go now, I argued, it would label them as guilty before they had a chance to establish their innocence. I told Kleindienst that I wanted more details concerning the evidence and a concrete recommendation about what I should do.

He returned later that afternoon with Henry Petersen. I liked Petersen immediately. He was a Democrat who had served in the Justice Department for twenty-five years, first in the FBI and then in the Criminal Division. His allegiance was to the law and not to any administration. Kleindienst had found Petersen cleaning his boat and brought him straight to the White House, dressed in a smudged T-shirt, tennis shoes, and jeans.

Petersen told me that he thought Haldeman and Ehrlichman should resign. He acknowledged that the evidence against them was not solid. But he added, "The question isn't whether or not there is a criminal case that can be made against them that will stand up in court, Mr. President. What you have to realize is that these two men have not served you well. They already have, and in the future will, cause you embarrassment, and embarrassment to the presidency."

I defended them. Haldeman had denied any prior knowledge of the bugging and break-in; and both men claimed innocence of motive on the payments to the defendants. In effect, I was being asked to sentence them on charges that the prosecutors were not able to prove. I was being asked to prejudice their cases, perhaps irreparably, in the public eye, in order to avoid embarrassment.

"I can't fire men simply because of the appearance of guilt. I have to have proof of their guilt," I said.

Petersen straightened and said, "What you have just said, Mr. President, speaks very well of you as a man. It does not speak well of you as a President."

I urged him to talk to Haldeman and Ehrlichman and get their side of the story, but he said that first he wanted to build his case against them. I asked him if he would come back the next day and bring me the charges in writing.

It was after five o'clock. Bebe Rebozo had come up from Florida that morning, and he was waiting for me outside my office when I emerged. We decided to go for a sail on the *Sequoia*. It was a warm spring evening, and as we sat out on the deck I gave him an outline of the Justice Department's case against Haldeman and Ehrlichman.

I asked him how much money I had in my account in his bank. I said that whatever happened, they had served me loyally and selflessly and I wanted to help with their legal expenses. Rebozo absolutely rejected the idea that I use my own savings. He said that he and Bob Abplanalp could raise two or three hundred thousand dollars. He added that he would have to give it to Haldeman and Ehrlichman in cash and privately, because he wouldn't be able to do the same thing for the others who also needed and deserved help.

As the *Sequoia* prepared to dock, I dreaded having to go back to the White House and face the bleak choices I knew were waiting there.

I forced a cheerful voice as I greeted Haldeman and Ehrlichman when they entered the EOB office at 7:50 that evening.

While Rebozo and I had been on the *Sequoia*, they had been meeting with Bill Rogers. Rogers, they said, felt that no one should be suspended from the staff before formal charges had been brought against him. If an individual was indicted, Rogers thought he should then go on leave of absence. Rogers said that Dean, who had already confessed to the prosecutor his own criminal involvement, should submit his resignation now to become effective at some future date; in the meantime, he thought, Dean should take a leave of absence.

I gave Haldeman and Ehrlichman a report on my meetings with Kleindienst and Petersen and told them that Petersen had indicated that Dean was going to be offered the "good offices" of the U.S. Attorney in return for his cooperation. They were stunned, as I had been, that both Kleindienst and Petersen felt that they should leave the White House.

John Dean sent me a message that said that he hoped I would understand that the motivation for his action was loyalty, and that he was ready to meet with me at any time. I first checked with Petersen and then arranged to meet with Dean.

At 9:15 that night Dean entered the EOB office. I sat in my easy chair, and he sat in a straight-backed chair facing me. It was nearly three weeks since we had last talked.

His voice, as before, was uninflected. He said, "You ought to know that I briefed Bob and John every inch of the way on this." He said that regardless of what their motives may have been, Haldeman and Ehrlichman were involved in an obstruction of justice. "Obstruction of justice is as broad as the imagination of man," he commented dryly. He said that all of them were involved in a "conspiracy by circumstance." I was struck by the fact that whenever Dean talked about Ehrlichman, his voice would take on a vindictive edge.

As we went over some of the charges, Dean seemed almost cocky about his own position. It seemed clear from his comments that he was confident that his lawyers were going to succeed in plea-bargaining with the prosecutors, and I took this to mean that he expected to get immunity.

At one point I said that I could now see that I should not have discussed the question of clemency for Hunt with Colson. He made no response. When the meeting was over, we shook hands and said good night.

I met with Haldeman and Ehrlichman again at 10:15 P.M. I told them about Dean's verdict of "conspiracy by circumstance" and ran through some of the other things he had told me. They both still felt that I should follow Rogers's advice and get Dean's resignation in hand so that when it became known that he was plea-bargaining, it would not appear that I had condoned his crimes, but Petersen was insistent that I not fire Dean or even force him to leave the White House lest such a move adversely affect his decision to cooperate with the prosecutors.

I told Ehrlichman that Petersen had asked me about the fact that non-Watergate materials from Hunt's safe had been turned over to Pat Gray right after the break-in. Dean was claiming that Gray had been given these materials, but Petersen said that Gray had denied even receiving them. Ehrlichman had been present when Dean had turned them over to Gray; they had been given to him instead of to the FBI agents in charge of the investigation in order to reduce the risk of leaks. He could not understand why Gray would have denied receiving them. Ehrlichman picked up the phone and asked the operator to call Gray at home. Haldeman and I listened as he asked Gray about the documents from Hunt's safe. We watched the blood drain from his face as he listened to Gray's reply. After he replaced the receiver he turned to us, his lower lip thrust forward bitterly. "Well, there goes my license to practice law," he said. Pat Gray had destroyed Howard Hunt's files.

When I met again with Dean on Monday morning, April 16, I gave him two draft letters: one tendered his resignation, the other requested a leave of absence. In accordance with Rogers's recommendation, I told him that I wanted him to sign both letters, although neither would be released until his departure from the staff.

The night before, Dean had been self-assured and even cocky. Now he was tense. He challenged every mention of himself with a question about Haldeman and Ehrlichman. I told him they were willing to take leaves if I asked them. He said he would take the draft letters I gave him and do drafts of his own. Dean looked at me at one point late in the conversation and said, "I think there is a mythical belief . . . that [Bob and John] don't have a problem, I'm really not sure you're convinced they do. But I'm telling you, they do."

We talked again about the meeting in which he had

The historic handshake with Premier Chou En-lai in Peking on February 21, 1972.

The meeting in Chairman Mao Tse-tung's house in Peking.

One of RN's most vivid memories of the 1972 China trip
was this audience—made up of both men and women—
at the gymnastic exhibition they visited in Peking.

WHITE HOUSE PHOTO

At the Great Wall of China in 1972.

Shaking hands with Leonid Brezhnev after signing the SALT agreement in the Kremlin, May 26, 1972.

Campaigning for re-election in October 1972, in Atlanta, Georgia.

With Prime Minister Golda Meir of Israel following a White House dinner on March 1, 1973.

At the POW dinner, May 24, 1973, Irving Berlin leads the singing of "God Bless America." Sammy Davis, Jr., joins in. The flag made in captivity by a POW is displayed in the background.

Summit II: with Brezhnev on the South Portico of the White House after his arrival ceremony in June 1973.

Summit II: with Brezhnev in RN's second-floor study at La Casa Pacifica in San Clemente in June 1973.

With Pat and Bebe Rebozo in San Clemente, August 20, 1973.

The tense press conference of October 26, 1973, following the controversial firing of Archibald Cox as Watergate Special Prosecutor and after the military alert during the Yom Kippur War.

With President Anwar Sadat of Egypt in Alexandria during the Middle East trip in June 1974.

Summit III: sailing on the Black Sea in the Crimea in June 1974. Brezhnev (right) and translator Viktor Sukhodrev point out Yalta.

WHITE HOUSE PHOTO

With Tricia in the Rose Garden, August 7, 1974.

RN with Julie after informing the family of his decision to resign, August 7, 1974.

Meeting with Vice President Ford on August 8, 1974,
RN's last full day as President.

RN's farewell to the Cabinet and White House staff in the East Room on the morning of August 9, 1974.

told me of the "cancer on the presidency." He said it had taken place on the Wednesday before the sentencing of the Watergate defendants; that would have been March 21.

I asked him about what had happened after that meeting. He said that when Mitchell came down to Washington, Ehrlichman had asked if the Hunt matter had been "straightened out," and Mitchell had replied that he thought the problem was solved. Haldeman and Ehrlichman would have a different version of what had happened on March 22: they said that Mitchell had asked *Dean* if the problem had been handled, and then rhetorically answered himself by saying that he guessed it had been taken care of. I said that I was ready to assume some culpability for knowledge of the demands at that point, but he said that he did not think I had to.

I made a point of telling Dean that I thought all national security matters such as the 1969 wiretaps were privileged. He assured me that he agreed, and that he had no intention of raising them.

Dean reminded me that once he had said that he was incapable of lying. "I want you to tell the truth," I said emphatically. "That's the thing that . . . I have told everybody around here, said, 'Goddamn it, tell the truth.' 'Cause all they do, John, is compound it." I added, "That son of a bitch Hiss would be free today if he hadn't lied about his espionage."

Petersen came to see me again that afternoon, April 16. I told him that I had asked Dean for his resignation—not to announce it, but just to have it in hand. Petersen said he had no problem with that. I asked if he still felt that Haldeman and Ehrlichman should leave. "Mindful of the need for confidence in your office—yes," he said. "That has nothing to do with guilt or innocence." I wondered how he could expect me to live with myself if I deserted my friends simply for the sake of appearances. He gave me his written note of the allegations against them. In summary, the charges were:

Ehrlichman—the "deep-six" instruction and informing Liddy through Dean that Hunt should leave the country.

Haldeman—Magruder said that budget information on the Liddy plan had been given to Strachan, opening the possibility that it had gone to Haldeman. Dean had told Haldeman of the Liddy proposals after they were made and apparently no one had issued any instructions that the program be discontinued. Magruder said he had summaries of the bugging transcripts delivered to Strachan—again raising a possibility that they had been shown to Haldeman.

All our decisions and all our discussions in those days were taking place against a rising flood tide of pressure from the media and Congress. Watergate had acquired dominant status on the television news. Almost daily, every major newspaper had a story based on a leak about some aspect of the case.

I felt that some kind of statement had to be made from the White House, and on April 17 I walked into the press room and announced that we had reached an agreement with Senator Ervin by which all members of my staff would appear voluntarily to testify under oath when requested to do so by his committee. They would answer all relevant questions, unless executive privilege was warranted. Then I added:

> On March 21, as a result of serious charges which came to my attention, some of which were publicly reported. I began intensive new inquiries into this whole matter. . . .There have been major developments in the case concerning which it would be improper to be more specific now, except to say that real progress has been made in finding the truth.
>
> If any person in the executive branch or in the government is indicted by the grand jury, my policy will be to immediately suspend him. If he is convicted he will, of course, be automatically discharged.

At Ehrlichman's request I also expressed my personal opposition to the granting of immunity in this case:

> I have expressed to the appropriate authorities my view that no individual holding, in the past or at the present, a position of major importance in the administration should be given immunity from prosecution. The judicial process is moving ahead as it should. . . . I condemn any attempts to cover-up in this case, no matter who is involved.

I had formulated the language of this "no immunity" passage with Petersen. I indicated to him only that my concern was to avoid the appearance that would be created if high White House staff members, after acknowledging participation in crimes, were to get off without any penalty. But that was only part of the reason. Another part was Ehrlichman's and Colson's argument that if immunity were dangled before Dean it would be an incentive for him to lie about others, secure in the knowledge that he was protected from the consequences of his own testimony; the final part was my calculation that without immunity Dean might be less likely to turn against me in hope that I would grant him an eventual pardon.

Dean obviously understood what I had done. Len Garment sent word to me that the immunity passage of my statement had Dean "charging around the White House like a wild animal."

Two days later the Washington *Post* reported that Jeb Magruder was telling everything to the prosecutors and that his story would bring down John Dean. The story said that he had accused Mitchell and Dean of helping plan the break-in. This report, coupled with my April 17 statement, triggered Dean. He called Ziegler and said threateningly that he was going to have to "start calling in some friendly reporters." That afternoon he issued a statement: "Some may hope or think that I will become a scapegoat in the Watergate case. Anyone who believes this does not know me, know the true facts, nor understand our system of justice."

I told Ziegler to respond by saying that we were not after scapegoats, but the truth.

It was already clear that there was not one truth about Watergate. There was the factual truth, which involved the literal description of what had occurred. But the factual truth could probably never be completely reconstructed, because each of us had become involved in different ways and no one's knowledge at any given time exactly duplicated anyone else's.

There was the legal truth, which, as we now understood, would involve judgments about motive. There was the moral truth, which would involve opinions about whether what had been done represented an indictment of the ethics of the White House. And there was the political truth, which would be the sum of the impact that all the other truths would have on the American people and on their opinion of me and of my administration.

I can see that long before I was willing to admit it to myself consciously, I knew instinctively that Haldeman and Ehrlichman were going to have to leave the White House. Even while I believed that they had a good chance of being vindicated on the charges of criminal conduct, I knew that the circumstantial facts were so damning that they would not be able to survive the political test. I recognized that if they stayed, they would damage the White House and damage me.

I told myself that I had not been involved in the things that gave them potential criminal vulnerability. I was sure that I had heard nothing about the break-in in advance; I had seen none of the reports based on the phone bug; I had known nothing about Ehrlichman's alleged instruction to Dean to "deep-six" the material from Hunt's safe; and I was sure that no one had asked me about bringing in Kalmbach to raise funds, or about using the $350,000 cash fund for the payments to the defendants.

But there were things that I had known. I had talked with Colson about clemency; I too had suspected Magruder was not telling the truth, but I had done nothing about my suspicions; I had been aware that support funds were going to the defendants; and on March 21 I had even contemplated paying blackmail. The difference was that Haldeman and Ehrlichman had become trapped by their circumstantial involvement; so far, I had not.

I was faced with having to fire my friends for things that I myself was a part of, things that I could not accept as morally or legally wrong, no matter how much that opened me to charges of cynicism and amorality. There had been no thievery or venality. We had all simply wandered into a situation unthinkingly, trying to protect ourselves from what we saw as a political problem. Now, suddenly, it was like a Rorschach ink blot: others, looking at our actions, pointed out a pattern that we ourselves had not seen.

I was selfish enough about my own survival to want them to leave; but I was not so ruthless as to be able to confront easily the idea of hurting people I cared about so deeply. I worried about the impact on them if they were forced to leave; and I worried about the impact on me if they didn't. So the next two weeks were governed by contradictory impulses: I tried to persuade them to go—while I insisted that I could not offer up my friends as sacrifices. I said that we had to do the right thing no matter how painful it was—while I cast about for any possible way to avert the damage, even if it took us to the edge of the law.

This put me in an increasingly difficult situation with respect to John Dean. Since Haldeman's and Ehrlichman's defense lay in discrediting Dean, as long as I kept him on the staff I would appear to be lending credence to his charges against them. I felt that I could not ignore Henry Petersen's private request not to fire Dean, but I knew the detrimental impact that would have on the public perception of Haldeman's and Ehrlichman's guilt.

There was also a personal consideration I could not ignore. I had already alienated Dean by going along with the idea of preventing his obtaining immunity. Now I knew that if I seemed to turn on him, he would almost certainly turn on me. I wanted to handle John Dean very gingerly.

I also had to recognize and admit a confusion and ambivalence about Dean's role. He had been given the brief to contain the Watergate damage. If no one had known at the time all the lengths to which he was having to go to do so, was that his fault or ours? There was a legal difference, but how much of a real difference could we claim between the fact that he had coached Magruder's grand jury testimony while knowing firsthand that Magruder was lying, and the fact that we had wanted him to help Magruder get through the grand jury while only *suspecting* Magruder was lying—but doing nothing to confirm or dispel our suspicions?

It had come down in the end to a question of Dean's judgment: we had wanted Dean to do what had to be done to keep the matter under control—but with the unspoken assumption that he would stop short of getting us in trouble. Dean, however, had simply done what he thought had to be done while failing to project all the consequences.

It was too late to wonder whether someone else in that role—someone without Dean's vulnerabilities from having been present at the Liddy meetings—would have recognized earlier the trap being set for himself and us. By the spring of 1973 it mattered little anymore whether Dean had in fact acted from a genuine belief that what he was doing was necessary to protect the White House, or primarily because he had wanted to protect himself, or whether, under the great pressures he faced, he was even able to make the distinction.

Whatever Dean's motives before or after, I also believed that he was earnestly concerned about the presidency when he came to see me on March 21. Ulterior concern had partly been responsible for bringing him there—the press attention that resulted from Pat Gray's confirmation hearings; my pressure on him to prepare a written statement on Watergate and to answer the charges against him by a letter signed under oath, an idea born of my ignorance about what such action would do to him; and Hunt's direct demand for $122,000. When he walked into my office, however, I believe that he had genuinely hoped to save the presidency from an encroaching cancer. I am sure he hoped that I would react strongly and take charge of the situation. Instead I contemplated buying time with one more payment to Hunt and calmly analyzed the political problems involved in granting clemency to the defendants after the 1974 election.

As early as April 15 I had broached the idea that Haldeman and Ehrlichman possibly take leaves of absence by suggesting that they might find themselves being worn down by press leaks and press charges. On April 17 I did so again. They both disagreed. Ehrlichman said that Dean was the one who should leave. He asked if I felt that Dean's charges were valid. I assured him that I did not, and that I saw that Dean's involvement was on a much more serious level than his own. "Then that's the way it ought to be put," Ehrlichman said. "He brought in a lot of silly garbage about me which doesn't add up to a nickel's worth of a lawsuit."

Ehrlichman said that, furthermore, there were indications that during the original Watergate investigation, Henry Petersen had passed grand jury information to Dean, who was then acting as White House Counsel. That night I called Petersen and told him not to give me any information from the grand jury unless he specifically thought I should have it.

Despite their initially tough front, it was not easy for

Haldeman and Ehrlichman to sustain their optimism. That night they reported to me that while their lawyers did not think that the evidence against them was legally sufficient, they had advised them that there was a real chance that it would be a difficult case when so many fine points of motive and intention were involved. The law on obstruction of justice was very loose and broad. As Ehrlichman summed it up, it was possible for them to "beat the rap, but we're damaged goods."

I wanted to be reassuring, but I could think of nothing encouraging to say that any of us would believe. "I think we've just about had it," Ehrlichman continued, "I think the odds are against it."

The two of them joked mordantly about Ehrlichman's making a living handling traffic cases. I made an offer to help pay their legal fees. They thanked me but declined the offer.

After we had discussed the charges at great length, Ehrlichman said, "I'm just not willing to believe the process will result in an indictment . . . I just can't accept that."

"You've gotta have faith that the system works," Haldeman agreed.

I said that we would celebrate their acquittal together. "We'll have the goddamnedest party at Camp David," I promised. But it was just bravado. Deep inside I knew that none of us was confident of the outcome.

At Haldeman's and Ehrlichman's request I met with their lawyers. They told me that they did not think the cases against their clients were indictable, but they realistically admitted that the prosecutors were zealots and therefore anything could happen. They urged me not to force Haldeman and Ehrlichman to leave, because to do so would be taken as an admission of their guilt. They requested instead that I make a public statement of faith and support for both of them. They said that Henry Petersen was a man I should not trust, and they urged me to stay away from his advice. Later, when Haldeman reminded me of this, I could only say, "He's all I've got, Bob."

It was 7:40 on the night of April 19 that we received word of the first press leaks that Dean and his lawyers had designed as a way of bolstering his case for immunity. Each leak would go a little further: "upping the ante," I called it. In what soon became a grim pattern, we would receive a call, usually from the Washington *Post* or the New York *Times,* just a few minutes before the first-edition deadlines, asking for immediate comment on a complicated Watergate story. If we could not meet the deadlines, the stories would be printed without our response.

On this first night the Washington *Post* called to alert us that they were planning to publish a report that an associate of Dean's said he was "not going to go down in flames," and that he would implicate people "above and below himself." They said that Dean would charge Haldeman with having engineered the cover-up in order to hide the involvement of presidential aides in the DNC bugging, and that the so-called "Dean report" attesting to "no White House involvement" in Watergate had been more or less made up out of whole cloth.

The next morning the *Post* ran the story on the front page.

That same day, April 20, the New York *Times* reported without attribution John Mitchell's first alleged public acknowledgment that he had ever heard of the buggings in advance. According to the *Times,* Mitchell had told "friends" that he had heard of the bugging plot but rejected it and did not know who had ordered that it go ahead.

Throughout this whole period I had tried to keep up a fully active schedule. On Wednesday, April 18, for example, I spent nearly two hours in a congressional leadership meeting on energy policy and then proceeded into another meeting with congressmen on Soviet emigration policy. Prime Minister Giulio Andreotti of Italy was in Washington for a state visit and Rainer Barzel, the chairman of West Germany's Christian Democratic Union, came in for an informal talk. I met with John Volpe, our ambassador to Italy, and then attended a two-hour session on the economy. On April 19 I met with American Jewish leaders on the issue of the emigration of Soviet Jews. On April 20 I held a Cabinet meeting for two hours on energy and the economy and then flew to Florida for the Easter weekend.

Originally, Haldeman and Ehrlichman had planned to

come with me to Key Biscayne so that there would be no interruption of their normal duties. But as the weekend neared I felt that I needed time to think, and they felt the same way. They decided, therefore, to go to Camp David instead.

On the evening of April 20 Ron Ziegler came to my house. "Bob will accept the fact that they should leave if the inevitable happens," I told him as we watched the sun setting into Biscayne Bay, "but he won't accept that it is inevitable."

"I know the kind of thing we're going to be up against," Ziegler answered. "I saw Mitchell on television tonight. They were juxtaposing the public statements he made earlier with what he is saying now, trying to humiliate him. You can't have your Chief of Staff and your major domestic adviser going through that kind of thing every day." Ziegler said that in three days alone he had been asked over 300 questions on Watergate in his daily briefings. I asked him to call Haldeman and tell him this, as his own personal feeling about the situation. Before I had left for Florida for the weekend, Haldeman had urged that I not get just one-sided "panicky" advice about what I should do. He had asked me to check with Pat Buchanan and find out how he felt. I had done so, and I wanted Ziegler to read to Haldeman what Buchanan had written to me:

> Anyone who is not guilty should not be put overboard . . . however, presidential aides who cannot maintain their viability should step forward voluntarily . . . if done sooner it will be a selfless act . . . if it is dragged out, the result will be that they were forced . . .
>
> Howard K. Smith questioned on television: Will Nixon be the Eisenhower who cleans his house himself, or the Harding who covered up for his people? This in ruthless candor is the question.
>
> If Haldeman leaves without Ehrlichman, it is still a cover-up: they can't be separated. If there is any chance Ehrlichman's name is going to come up in the grand jury, he should go.
>
> There is a *Titanic* mentality around the White House staff these days. We've got to put out the life rafts and hope to pull the presidency through.

Later I phoned Ziegler to find out what had been said when he had delivered his message. He told me that Haldeman had been "thoughtful."

The next morning, April 21, the Miami *Herald* quoted "associates" of Mitchell who claimed that Magruder had gone over Mitchell's head to the White House to obtain approval of the bugging plan. The Washington *Post* said that Dean had documentary evidence to support his charges about the bugging and the cover-up. And the New York *Times* reported that Dean had supervised payoffs of more than $175,000 to defendants, a charge Dean denied.

On Easter morning there were four different Watergate stories on the front page of the Washington *Post.* According to the major one, the grand jury was investigating whether Haldeman had a fund of $350,000 from which he ordered payments to defendants to keep quiet. The story was attributed to a "high-placed source in the executive branch." Sources said that Dean had tried to stop the payments but was ordered to go ahead with them by higher-ups. A source also said that Dean was prepared to implicate Ehrlichman in Watergate.

The Washington *Star* said that Haldeman and Ehrlichman both were targets. The *Star* also quoted "sources" as saying that Mitchell had personally approved the bugging plans, although "sources" close to Mitchell were quoted as saying that Mitchell believed it was the White House that had done so. Colson, in an alleged attempt to take care of himself, was reported to have given the prosecutors documentary evidence establishing a cover-up.

Although not a single charge of any kind had been made against me directly, a Gallup poll reported that over 40 percent of the people thought I had known about the Watergate bugging in advance. In the same poll 53 percent thought that the bugging was nothing more than "just politics—the kind of thing both parties engage in."

It had been my habit for years to place phone calls to my staff on Easter Sunday. This troubled Easter morning I started with Chuck Colson. He heatedly denied "distorted stories" about him in the newspapers. He said that he wanted to tell me again that the phone call he had made to Magruder that was now being alleged to have precipitated the whole Watergate episode had been innocent. I said that I believed him completely. We wished each other well on Easter.

Next I called Dean. "On Easter morning, I want you to know someone is thinking of you," I began. "I want to wish you well—we'll make it through. You said that this is a cancer that must be cut out, I want you to know I am following that advice."

Dean said that he was grateful for the call. His appreciation seemed real. He said that at some point he would like to discuss with me how he should plead. He said he didn't know if he should take the Fifth Amendment. I told him that he should feel free to come see me.

At one point Dean said rather coolly, "I know how that line got in the statement, the one about no immunity." We talked about Gray's destruction of documents and the sequence of events surrounding Hunt's demand—the events that had led to our meeting of March 21.

I told him I still considered it proper for us to meet about his plea because he had not yet been dismissed from the White House. "You're still my counsel," I said.

At 9:45 I called Haldeman. "I don't want this Easter to go by without reminding you how much tougher it was last Easter," I said. He agreed that this was true.

I called Ehrlichman next. He wished me a good Easter, but he warned, "Don't move too fast and start picking up Carl Rowan's and Joe Kraft's lines that this entire government is corrupt because of all of this. Stay steady."

I went in to gather the family for the Easter church service. There is a kind of unspoken consensus that works in our family. During some crises they will be with me hourly, advising me on every change in mood they perceive and canvassing all the possible options. In this case, however, they had decided that my problem was that I had too many pressures coming in from every direction, and they tried to make it easier for me by talking about other things. Julie had sent me a note when we arrived in Florida. It said simply, "We love you. We stand with you."

When we had finally got the Vietnam peace agreement on January 23, I had told the family that one welcome personal benefit would be that we would no longer be harassed by sign-carrying hecklers as we had been during our first four years. The war was over, but now signs had reappeared. Now they were Watergate signs. Eventually they became even uglier and more personal than the antiwar signs had ever been.

When Pat and I left the church that morning, several people in the crowd held up signs. One of them read: "Is the President honest?" A woman rushed over in front of it, holding up a crudely done sign of her own: "Yes, the President is honest."

Later in the day Ziegler told me that Dean had called him to say how much he had appreciated my call. Ziegler had asked him about the newspaper reports that "sources close to Dean" were saying that his "Dean Report" to which I had alluded in my press conference of August 29, had never actually been written. "If I had a chance to discuss that statement with the President before he made it, it certainly would have been phrased differently," Dean told Ziegler. He added, "I wish someone had told me I was conducting an investigation, Ron—I just reported daily to John and Bob."

This exchange angered and depressed Ziegler. His office had kept the detailed notes from phone calls between Dean and Jerry Warren, the Deputy Press Secretary, when Warren had called Dean almost daily to ask him for guidance on responses to Watergate questions in the briefings. "No one in the White House involved" had been a staple of Dean's response. He had also talked frequently about his "investigation," which, he said, had begun on the day after the break-in. Dean had also given very clear instructions about how Ziegler should defend him when he was under attack: he should say that Dean had had no contact with Liddy on intelligence-gathering matters; that he had not shown FBI materials to anyone; and that he had not delayed turning over items from Hunt's safe to the FBI. Now Dean was completely undercutting Ziegler, who wondered if he would be able to go before the press and brief again.

On Monday morning, April 23, I had a three-hour session with Ziegler, Pat Buchanan, and Chappie Rose. I had asked Rose, a fine lawyer and personal friend from the Eisenhower days, to fly down to Florida to give me some outside counsel.

As Buchanan summarized the options, there were four: we could do nothing, but the evidence was too strong for that; we could fire everyone, but the evidence was too weak for that; we could ask them to take leaves, but that would just postpone the injury. "The answer is their resignation," he said. But Chappie Rose was less certain. He thought that it might be prejudicial to their rights to force them to resign. Ziegler played an effective devil's advocate against both views.

At the heart of the problem, as I had increasingly come to see it, was the White House itself. Haldeman and Ehrlichman had lost the confidence of the staff; no work was being done; everyone was tired, drained, and distracted.

For hours we debated the question, and the longer we went over the charges, the more inevitable the outcome seemed. At one point Rose sadly quoted Gladstone: "The first essential for a Prime Minister is to be a good butcher."

"Ten years from now," I said, as much for myself as the others, "this will be a few paragraphs. In fifty years it will be a footnote. But in the meantime I have got to run the office of President, and I can't when they are under constant attack. The country can't feel that the President is burdened and obsessed. The Mideast is boiling, and the international economic situation is in a crisis. There are too many things that need attention."

As the session drew to an emotional end, we all agreed that Haldeman and Ehrlichman had to resign.

I asked Buchanan if he would call Haldeman and tell him that I had come to this conclusion. I said that he should let them know that I was not forcing it. I still wanted it to be their decision. But this was my opinion. The next step would be theirs.

Buchanan said that he thought Ziegler should do it. The personal ties were closer there, and maybe that would make it less painful. Ziegler stared out the window. Haldeman had been responsible for bringing him on my staff; now he was being asked to pass on the word that Haldeman must resign. He said nothing.

"There are no good choices," I said for all of us.

After making the call, Ziegler told me that Haldeman had been predictably stoic and fair. He had said that while he disagreed with the decision, he would accept it.

Within a few hours, Haldeman called Ziegler back. Evidently he had talked to his lawyers, and also to Ehrlichman, who had resisted strongly and had persuaded Haldeman to change his mind. Ehrlichman maintained that he was in a different situation and that even if Haldeman resigned, he should not. Ehrlichman thought the charges against him were much weaker and that therefore he was detachable. And there was no question that he wanted to be detached.

Haldeman argued to Ziegler that I was overreacting. "In all the other important decisions the President has operated from strength," he said, "and just because this is painful doesn't mean it is strong." He urged that I see his lawyers again. "This would be the first real victory of the establishment against Nixon," he insisted. "This is what the media wants, and sooner or later they will see it as phony. It won't help."

Even though I knew that the decision would have to be mine, I sought the advice of several men I particularly trusted and respected. I asked Ziegler to call Bill Rogers, who said that it appeared to him that Haldeman could not survive in his job and that that should be the determining consideration. He felt that Ehrlichman was a closer case. John Connally's view was that if the allegations against them were untrue, then they should not have to go; but if they could not refute the allegations in a way that would demonstrate their untruth there was no alternative. "Someone has to walk the plank," he said, repeating what he had told me when the whole thing first broke open in March.

Bryce Harlow said, "If Haldeman, Dean, and Ehrlichman have undertaken actions which will not float in the public domain, they must leave quickly—they are like a big barnacle on the ship of state, and there is too much at stake to hang on for personal reasons." Leaves of absence would be wrong, he said, because they would only postpone the inevitable and in the end would be less fair to the men themselves. Kissinger, too, had come to the view that something had to be done to break what he called the "miasma of uncertainty" that had come to surround the working of the entire administration.

On Tuesday night, heading back to Washington from

Key Biscayne, I thought about Haldeman's argument that this decision should be made with the same toughness and disregard for the popular and easy course that had characterized the decisions on Cambodia, May 8, and December 18. But there was a difference. In those other decisions involving policy I always knew that if I were given a chance to present the whole case to the people they would be behind me. In those instances I had been acting on strong and recognizable principles. With Watergate there was no way to gain public support even on the principle of loyalty to one's staff or friends because the circumstantial case against them was too strong to be ignored or easily explained away.

Eisenhower had not saved me in the fund crisis; I was saved because I had been able to save myself. I did not believe Haldeman and Ehrlichman were guilty of criminal motives; but I did not know if they could ever prove their innocence. I told Ziegler, "What I am saying is that this, too, will *not* pass."

When Haldeman and Ehrlichman came in later that morning, they told me that they were not getting the same recommendations from Rogers and Connally as I seemed to think that Rogers and Connally were giving. I knew, however, that they were mistaking kindness for ambivalence. "Everyone," I said, "agrees we must do something."

Ehrlichman seemed uneasy and restless during this conversation, and suddenly he said that he had been thinking and had decided that there ought to be a candid assessment of the threat in all this to the President. "Now let me . . . just spin something out for you," he said, "probably a far out point." He said that if Dean were "totally out of control," it was "entirely conceivable" that I might be faced with a resolution of impeachment on the ground that I had committed a crime and no other legal process was available except impeachment. He knew in general of my conversation with Dean on March 21 about the break-in and the cover-up. He said that as far as he knew, what Dean had fell far short of any commission of a crime by me.

"I think really the only way that I know to make a judgment on this," Ehrlichman said, "is for you to listen to your tapes and see what actually was said then, or maybe for Bob to do it." He suggested that before I took "any precipitous steps" I'd better know what my "hole card" was.

I knew that what he was saying, both explicitly and implicitly, was true. Explicitly, he was saying that I should recognize how exposed I would be if he and Haldeman were forced to leave, and that before forcing them to, I should assess the worst possible consequences of that exposure. Implicitly, I believe, he was saying that if I decided I were equally as involved as they, I should consult my own conscience before forcing them to leave.

In the last two weeks of April I began seriously facing the possibility that I would be Dean's next target and that I had personally supplied him with the ammunition during our March 21 conversation. I became preoccupied with it and began bringing it up repeatedly. After reading the transcripts of these discussions, it is clear that I gave a number of different versions of it. In talks with Ehrlichman, Dick Moore, and Henry Petersen, I tried to make it sound more ambiguous than it really was, or even to pass it off as having been facetious.

When I was honest with myself, however, I had to admit that I had genuinely contemplated paying blackmail to Hunt—not because of Watergate, but because of his threat against Ehrlichman on the break-in at Ellsberg's psychiatrist's office and against the administration in general. I had also talked with Dean about the possibility of continuing payments to the other defendants. Furthermore, in that conversation Dean had made me aware of payments to defendants that he said constituted an obstruction of justice.

I told Haldeman and Ehrlichman at one point that we could not risk having Dean turn on me with this conversation, even if it meant having to give him immunity. Haldeman countered that I could not let Dean have the permanent handle of blackmail over me, either. I decided that Haldeman should listen to our tape so that we would know exactly what had actually been said and decided on that fateful afternoon.

Before long a disturbing thought occurred to me; I couldn't get it out of my mind: what if Dean had carried a tape recorder at our March 21 meeting, a small tape recorder, concealed in his jacket but capable of catching every word. He would be able to use parts of the conversation in a very damaging way.

In the afternoon of April 25 Kleindienst called me with an urgent request for a meeting. He had a new problem: he felt that the Justice Department would have to turn over material on the break-in at Ellsberg's psychiatrist's office to the court that was hearing the government's case against Ellsberg for having taken the Pentagon Papers. That had been the ruling within the department; besides, if they did not make their possession of the material known, Dean would undoubtedly hold it over their heads.

On April 18, a week earlier, at Ehrlichman's urging, I had talked on the phone with Henry Petersen about the break-in. I had told him to stay out of it. "Your charge is Watergate. This is national security," I had said. Dean had told me that Krogh had felt that he was acting on a national security mandate, and there was no question in my mind that the Ellsberg investigation as a whole was part of a national security crisis of the highest order.

When Petersen asked me if any evidence had been obtained during the break-in, anything that would have to be turned over to the court hearing Ellsberg's trial, I said no. "It was a dry hole," I told him.

Now Kleindienst was saying that the Justice Department felt that the material had to be revealed. Without hesitation I said that he should go ahead. As I did so, I thought how everything was about to become even bleaker for John Ehrlichman.

At 4:40 P.M. on April 25, Haldeman came back in to report on his first couple of hours of listening to the tape of my March 21 conversation with Dean. He said that it was interesting to learn that Dean had given me a different version of events from the one he had been telling Haldeman.

Haldeman confirmed that I had said to Dean, "We could get the money." But, he said, "You were drawing Dean out."

Haldeman was familiar with my habit of getting other people's ideas by indirection, by purposely not stating my own opinion until the end of a conversation lest it inhibit others, or alternatively, by stating an extreme position or proposition to see how others reacted. He also knew that in conversations I tend to think a problem through out loud, even considering totally unacceptable alternatives in the process of ruling them out—a lawyer's typical mental exercise. In this case all these factors were partial—but only partial—explanations for some of the things I had said.

I had only one other defense in the matter of the March 21 tape: no action had been taken as a result of that conversation. I had not finally ordered any payments be made to defendants, and I had ruled out clemency.

I thought about Haldeman's report during the afternoon and called him at home twice that night. I said that I had always wondered about the taping equipment, "but I'm damn glad we have it, aren't you?"

"Yes, sir," he answered, adding that even the one section he had been through that day was "very helpful."

I said that despite the passages I would have preferred not to have said, there were also some good things on the tape that helped balance it out.

By April 26 the prosecutors' talks with Dean had broken down. Dean immediately began sending threatening new signals to the White House. He talked with Len Garment and told him that Watergate was just the tip of the iceberg. He said that there were things that had been done in 1970 that he could expose. And he kept saying that he had documentary evidence of the cover-up.

That same day the New York *Daily News* had the story that Pat Gray had burned evidence from Hunt's safe. The source who leaked the story placed the blame squarely on Dean and Ehrlichman, saying that they had ordered Gray to do it. When I learned about the story, I called Kleindienst and told him that I thought Gray should resign. First, however, I wanted Henry Petersen's view of the situation.

Petersen said that Gray was going to accuse Ehrlichman and Dean of instructing him to destroy the papers, vowing that he had done it only because he had confidence in them. I was outraged. I knew from the genuine panic I had watched spread across Ehrlichman's face when he talked to Gray on the phone that he had never ordered such a thing. I said that Petersen must tell Gray that he could not solve this problem with another lie. I asked that he and

Kleindienst meet and give me a recommendation about what I should do in this situation.

Ehrlichman wanted the White House to put out a statement saying that the story was not true. When I called Ziegler in and told him this, he said that he thought Ehrlichman should put the statement out in his own name. He was right: eventually these would all be testimonial areas, and we could not be in the position of vouching for one side over the other.

"You must take a leave," I told Haldeman and Ehrlichman. I said that they should prepare letters requesting leaves of absence by Saturday. I said that Haldeman and Ehrlichman should go first, so that it would be clear that they were not being forced to go as Dean would be.

At 7:28 that night the *Post* called with another story: "sources" said that Haldeman and Ehrlichman had been told by Dean on March 20 that "the jig is up" and that they should be prepared to go to jail. The story was not true, but there was no way to fight Dean's guerrilla tactics. The stories revealing that Gray had destroyed documents also indicated that among these materials was a forged cable implicating President Kennedy in the Diem assassination. This had evidently come from Dean, who apparently had seen the material before giving it to Gray.

By the next morning, April 27, two new stories had surfaced about Ehrlichman on subjects unrelated to Watergate. The items were scurrilously false, and Ehrlichman tried valiantly to combat their effect on public opinion.

I flew to Mississippi that morning for a ceremony dedicating a naval training center being named in honor of John Stennis. I invited Stennis to come with me on *Air Force One.* On the way down, as we sat alone in my cabin, this old friend said that he wanted to give me some advice. "The time is now," he said. "We say down in our country that the rain falls on the just and the unjust. Time is running out."

When Stennis introduced me to the enthusiastic crowd at the dedication, he addressed me directly: "You do not panic when the going gets tough. I believe you have what it takes to tough it through. We admire that."

Pat Gray called while we were in Mississippi to say that he had decided to resign. William Ruckelshaus, head of the

Environmental Protection Agency, agreed to take over Gray's post temporarily.

I asked Ehrlichman to make up a list for me of all the national-security-related activities that he thought Dean might be able to expose. On the plane on the way back to Washington he went over three of them with me: Ellsberg, the 1969 wiretaps, and the yeoman episode during the Indo-Pakistan war. Ehrlichman was not sure what else there might be, because Dean's access to the files had been almost unlimited.

Ziegler came into my cabin to report that the Washington *Post* had a new story from "reliable sources" to the effect that "someone" had talked to the prosecutors and had implicated me directly in the cover-up. When we got to Washington, the New York *Times* had called with information that Dean was implicating me. Later the Los Angeles *Times* would call to get a comment on the same report.

I called Henry Petersen and asked him to come over. It was an emotional session. I demanded to know if the stories were true: had Dean implicated me? Petersen went out to check with his office, and a few minutes later he came back and said that the stories were not true. He said that earlier in the week Dean's lawyer had said, "We'll bring the President in—not on this case but in other areas." At the time the prosecutors had thought that this was just bombast and posturing as a part of the effort to gain immunity for Dean. And indeed, they had not yet produced any evidence implicating me. I called Ziegler in and told him that the story had to be killed immediately.

Before Petersen left, he said that he would like to recommend that I move on Dean now. He thought that the added pressure from me would be better for the government's position against him. And he urged once more that Haldeman and Ehrlichman also leave.

When Haldeman came in later, he told me that his lawyers felt that he and Ehrlichman were being taken advantage of because they were loyal and Dean was not. "They think Petersen and Dean are playing you."

I said that our plan should be that he and Ehrlichman would take leaves of absence beginning Sunday, or even Saturday. On Monday I would inform Dean that he was being fired. I asked that Ray Price begin preparing a speech for me, leaving open whether I would be announcing leaves of absence or actual resignations.

HALDEMAN AND EHRLICHMAN RESIGN

On Friday night, April 27, I flew to Camp David. On Saturday morning an early fog settled over the valley. I had breakfast on the porch and then went to the small library to work. About ten o'clock I walked into the living room looking for Manolo and a cup of coffee. I was startled to see the fire blazing and Tricia sitting on the couch in front of it.

She said that she had been awake all night talking with Julie and David about Watergate and the decisions that had to be made. They had talked with Pat for a long time early in the morning, and they wanted me to know that they all agreed that there was no choice but to have Haldeman and Ehrlichman resign. The attacks on them had destroyed their ability to serve in their high positions. "I want you to know that I would never allow any personal feeling about either of them to interfere with my judgment," she said. "You know I never felt that the way they handled people served you well—but I promise you that I made my decision carefully and objectively."

Tears brimmed in her eyes; but, unlike Julie, Tricia would seldom allow them to overflow. "I am speaking for Julie, David, and Mama as well," she said. "That is our opinion. But we also want you to know that we have complete confidence in you. If you decide not to take our advice, we will understand. Whatever you do, just remember we will support you, and we love you very much."

I asked her if she would like to stay with me through the day, but she said she knew it would be better if she went back. I hugged her, and she was gone.

Bill Rogers arrived at 11:30 and argued strongly that leaves of absence were no longer a viable answer—resignation was now the only choice. I valued his opinion because I had learned over the years that he had excellent political as well as legal judgment and that as a loyal friend he would tell me what I needed to hear and not just what I might want to hear. I told him I had come to the same conclusion. Otherwise we were just setting ourselves up for an even messier and more painful separation later on.

I asked him if he would convey this to Haldeman and Ehrlichman for me. He said that he did not think his relationship with them was good enough to do that—nor even objective enough, as mine had been with Adams. There had been some bitterness between them after the election during the reorganization, and he was concerned that they might feel that he was bringing personal feelings to the task.

That evening Ehrlichman called me. He was cordial but bluntly direct. He told me that he thought I should recognize the reality of my own responsibility. He said that all the illegal acts ultimately derived from me, whether directly or indirectly. He implied that I was the inspiration behind them and mentioned such things as the forged Diem cable. He also implied, I thought, that I should resign.

I was sitting in the living room after his call when Ziegler came in. He had just learned that the next morning's Washington *Post* had a story from "reliable sources" that Dean had evidence to prove that he was under the direction of Haldeman and Ehrlichman when he engaged in a cover-up and that he also had knowledge of "illegal activities" going back to 1969.

I asked Ziegler if he would call Colson for me and find out what had happened on the Diem cable. He came back a few minutes later and said that Colson had sworn that he himself had not known about the forgery. "The President," Colson had added, "knew zero."

Early on Sunday morning I called Haldeman and asked if he would come up to Camp David. He said that he would, and so would Ehrlichman—but that they would like to have separate meetings with me. I knew then that he realized what I was going to say. I knew that he realized we had reached the end.

Haldeman arrived in the early afternoon. We walked to the windows and haltingly attempted small talk. The fog and clouds had lifted by then, revealing the layers of green spring trees covering the mountainside.

Then I said that I believed resignation was the right course for him. I said this was the hardest decision I had ever made. I meant it. He knew that I rarely spoke about religion, and I thought he looked somewhat surprised when

I told him that from my first day as President on January 20, 1969, I followed my mother's custom of getting down on my knees every night and praying silently for those in my administration who were going through difficult times, but most of all for guidance that I would do what was right the next day in meeting my responsibilities. I told him that when I went to bed last night I had hoped, and almost prayed, that I wouldn't wake up this morning.

I said that I knew this wasn't fair, but I saw no other way. I told him I felt enormous guilt. I knew that the responsibility, and much of the blame for what had happened, rested with me. I had put Mitchell in his position, and Colson's activities were in many cases prompted by my prodding.

Even at this moment Haldeman's effort was to reassure me. He was proud and secure. He said that he accepted this decision even though he did not agree with it, and that I must always feel I could call on him. "What you have to remember," he said, "is that nothing that has happened in the Watergate mess has changed your mandate in the non-Watergate areas. That is what matters. That is what you do best." He said that he would go to another cabin and write his letter of resignation.

After he left I walked out onto the porch and was standing there looking down into the valley when Ehrlichman arrived. I shook hands with him and said, "I know what a terribly difficult day this is for you. I am sure you realize what a difficult day it is for me." When I told him about my feelings the night before, he put his arm around my shoulders and said, "Don't talk that way. Don't *think* that way."

Back in the sitting room I told him that I wanted to be as helpful in any way that I could, including assistance with the great financial burden I knew he would now be carrying, not only because of the need to support his family but because of the mounting attorneys' fees.

His mouth tightened and he said quickly, "There is only one thing I would like for you to do. I would like for you to explain this to my children."

With controlled bitterness he said that the decision I had made was wrong and that I would live to regret it. "I have no choice but to accept it, and I will," he said. "But I still feel I have done nothing that was without your implied or direct approval."

"You have always been the conscience of the administration," I said. "You were always for the cleanest way through things."

"If I was the conscience, then I haven't been very effective," he said.

Later that afternoon I had Kleindienst come up to see me. We both knew that his situation at the Justice Department had become intolerable. His close association with Mitchell now made it impossible for him to stay on. He had been the publicist of what he sincerely believed to have been the "greatest investigation since the Kennedy assassination," and it had blown up in his face. We agreed that he should resign and be replaced by Elliot Richardson, who was then Secretary of Defense. I deeply regret now that Kleindienst's departure was timed to coincide with the others; it falsely conveyed the impression that he was somehow involved in Watergate.

After Kleindienst left I stood for a few minutes waiting for Haldeman and Ehrlichman to return with their letters, looking out the picture window and watching the day darken into evening. Ziegler was standing silently near the couch behind me.

"It's all over, Ron, do you know that?"

"No, sir," he said. He thought that I was referring only to the terrible events of the past few days and hours.

"Well, it is. It's all over," I repeated.

When Haldeman and Ehrlichman returned, they showed their letters to me and to Bill Rogers, who had now joined us. Ehrlichman asked me to use the specific sentence, "John Dean has been fired," in my television speech. I knew how he felt. Ehrlichman had been loyal and would defend me and our administration. Dean was disloyal and would look out only for himself. By allowing Dean to "resign" I would be forcing Haldeman and Ehrlichman to share the same public disrepute as their accuser.

We walked out to their car. They said bolstering things like, "Get up for your speech tomorrow night."

"I wish I were as strong as you," I said. "God bless you both." The car drove away.

They had been my closest aides. They were my friends. I tried to make it up to them the next night by saying in my speech what I deeply believed: "Today, in one of the most difficult decisions of my presidency, I accepted the resignations of two of my closest associates in the White House—Bob Haldeman, John Ehrlichman—two of the finest public servants it has been my privilege to know."

They deserved the best possible chance to save themselves, and in asking them to leave I had ensured that they would never be able to prove that their motives had been innocent. I had done what I felt was necessary, but not what I believed was right. I had always prided myself on the fact that I stood by people who were down. Now I had sacrificed, for myself, two people to whom I owed so much.

I stayed at Camp David to work with Ray Price on the final draft of the speech I was to deliver the next night, Monday, April 30. As I handed him the draft, I said, "Ray, you are the most honest, cool, objective man I know. If you feel that I should resign, I am ready to do so. You won't have to tell me. You should just put it in the next draft."

He said that I should not resign, that I had a duty to complete the job I had been elected to do. He said he knew how heartbreaking my decision on Haldeman and Ehrlichman had been, but he tried to ease it for me by saying that I had done what I had to do.

I felt as if I had cut off one arm and then the other. The amputation may have been necessary for even a chance at survival, but what I had had to do left me so anguished and saddened that from that day on the presidency lost all joy for me.

My speech on April 30, 1973, was the first time I formally addressed the American people specifically on Watergate. All that most people understood of the complex situation that had precipitated the speech was that my two closest aides were being accused of participation in the Watergate cover-up, while one of my best friends, my former Attorney General, was being accused of having ordered the break-in and bugging.

No matter how much we protested to the contrary, as soon as Haldeman and Ehrlichman resigned, people assumed it was because they were, at least to some extent, guilty of the charges against them. The spotlight automatically turned next to me: people were waiting for a yes or no answer to the question of whether I was also involved in Watergate. That was what they looked for from my April 30 speech. I made the decision of how I would answer this question less on the basis of logical calculation than on political instinct. I made it without stopping to realize that this speech would be a major turning point and that my answer, once given, would have to see me through whatever lay ahead.

I believe that a totally honest answer would have been neither a simple yes or no.

If I had given the true answer, I would have had to say that without fully realizing the implications of my actions I had become deeply entangled in the complicated mesh of decisions, inactions, misunderstandings, and conflicting motivations that comprised the Watergate cover-up; I would have had to admit that I still did not know the whole story and therefore did not know the full extent of my involvement in it; and I would have had to give the damaging specifics of what I did know while leaving open the possibility that much more might come out later.

I sensed that the inept way we had handled Watergate so far had put us so much on the defensive that there would have been no tolerance for such a complicated explanation from me at this late date. And the instincts of twenty-five years in politics told me that I was up against no ordinary opposition. In this second term I had thrown down a gauntlet to Congress, the bureaucracy, the media, and the Washington establishment and challenged them to engage in epic battle. We had already skirmished over the limitations of prerogative and power represented in confirmation of appointments, the impoundment of funds, and the battle of the budget. Now, suddenly, Watergate had exposed a cavernous weakness in my ranks, and I felt that if in this speech I admitted any vulnerabilities, my opponents would savage me with them. I feared that any admissions I made would be used to keep the Watergate issue—and the issue of my behavior in office—festering during the rest of my term, thereby making it impossible for me to exert presidential leadership.

Given this situation and given this choice—given my belief that these were the stakes—I decided to answer no to the question whether I was also involved in Watergate.

I hoped that, after the agony of the past weeks, a firm statement of my innocence, accompanied by the symbolic cleansing of the administration with the departure of Haldeman, Ehrlichman, and Dean and followed by an active rebuilding with new people along open lines, would convince people that the various Watergate probes could and should be brought to a quick conclusion. I was counting on the polls, which showed that the majority of people, even some of the 40 percent who already thought I knew of the break-in in advance, still agreed with me that the whole thing was "just politics." I knew I was good at being President, at the really important things, and I was counting on people to become impatient with Watergate and exert pressure on Congress and the media to move on to something else and to get back to the things that mattered. I actually hoped that this speech would at last and once and for all put Watergate behind me as a nagging national issue. I could not have made a more disastrous miscalculation.

In the April 30 speech I gave the impression that I had known nothing at all about the cover-up until my March 21 meeting with Dean. I indicated that once I had learned about it I had acted with dispatch and dispassion to end it. In fact, I had known some of the details of the cover-up before March 21, and when I did become aware of their implications, instead of exerting presidential leadership aimed at uncovering the cover-up, I embarked upon an increasingly desperate search for ways to limit the damage to my friends, to my administration, and to myself.

I talked in terms of responsibility and the fact that "the man at the top must bear the responsibility. . . . I accept it." But that was only an abstraction and people saw through it. Finally, I clung to excuses. The fact that they happened to be excuses that I really believed made little difference. In a sense Watergate *had* grown out of the end-justifies-the-means mentality of the causes of the 1960s. It was also true that if we often made the mistake of acting like an administration under siege, it was because we *were* an administration under siege. And I believed it was true that if I had not been preoccupied with Vietnam and other policy issues, I might have probed until I sensed the full dimensions of the cover-up and perhaps precipitated action sooner—if not on ethical grounds, at least because I would have recognized that we were marching headlong into a trap with no exits.

But these were still only excuses. They were not an accounting of my role. They were not explanations of how a President of the United States could so incompetently allow himself to get in such a situation. That was what people really wanted to know, and that was what my April 30 speech and all the other public statements I made about Watergate while I was President failed to tell them.

———————————

It was as if a convulsion had seized Washington. Restraints that had governed professional and political conduct for decades were suddenly abandoned. The FBI and the Justice Department hemorrhaged with leaks of confidential testimony, grand jury materials, and prosecutorial speculation. And on Capitol Hill it seemed as if anything could be leaked and anything would be indulged, under the guise of righteous indignation over Watergate.

In reporting the story the members of the Washington press corps were fired by personal passion. They felt that they had embarrassed themselves by uncritically reporting the months of White House denials, and so they frantically sought to reassert their independence by demonstrating their skepticism of all official explanations. In their determination to prove they were not the tools of the White House they went to the other extreme and became the shills for faceless and nameless leakers.

In December 1971 the Washington *Post* had proudly announced a new policy: it would always insist on public accountability for public business—government officials would not be allowed to talk on a "source" basis. In the spring of 1973, however, the *Post* guaranteed anonymity to anyone who proffered an exciting and exclusive Watergate leak or story. Other papers followed this lead, reacting to the combination of commercial pressure and professional competitiveness. They called it "investigative journalism," but it was not that at all. There is nothing "investigative" about publicizing leaks from sources in the FBI, the Justice Department, or congressional committees who have easy access to confidential material. This was rumor journalism, some true, some false, some a mixture of truth and fiction, all prejudicial. That it was a dangerous form of journalism should have been understood by the *Post*, whose editor, Ben Bradlee, has since observed: "We don't print the truth. We print what we know, what people tell us. So we print lies."

A symbiotic relationship developed between the leakers on the Ervin Committee and its staff and the leakers in the prosecutor's office on the one hand, and their media publicists on the other. The reporters gathered daily outside the committee rooms or buttonholed bureaucrats in hallways to try to get a Watergate headline. The subject had already prompted a new ferocity in reporting: grand jurors were hounded by newsmen, itself a potential offense; in some cases other political dirt was ferreted out and traded for Watergate information. The emphasis was on having a story—any story—before someone else got it. The competition for Watergate stories debauched ordinary journalistic standards. No longer did reporters feel required to substantiate the truth of a charge before printing it. They shifted this traditional professional responsibility by saying that the person accused had the obligation to prove that the report was *not* true—and to do so before a stated deadline in order to get them to drop the story.

Many of the reporters argued that because there had been a cover-up of Watergate, the system of justice could no longer be trusted to work on its own. Before very long this argument became the self-justifying rationale for a vigilante squad of anonymous "sources" and competing reporters who, in effect, took the law into their own hands. Louis Nizer said during this period: "I fear McCarthyism in reverse. People are being perhaps destroyed by headlines where there are as yet no proven facts before a jury in a trial. ... It's one thing to dig up information and even to give it to a prosecutor to pursue, and it is another to become so drunk with the triumph as to begin taking rumor and putting it as a headline. ... This is the time to be cautious. You see, it is easy to agree with a violation of civil rights when the fellow who is getting it is a man that we are tickled to death is getting it."

But neither the pleas of conscience-stricken colleagues nor the criticism of dismayed outsiders could stop the stampede.

The New York *Times* carried at least one Watergate story on its front page every day but one during each of the months of May, June, and July 1973. A later study showed that an average of 52 percent of the front pages of the major American newspapers was occupied by Watergate stories on days when the Ervin Committee was in session; the average was 35 percent on days when the committee did not meet. The network news shows were devoting a third to half of their time to Watergate.

In many cases the sheer quantity of Watergate stories derived from the nature of the subject itself: each new disclosure seemed to ignite another, like a string of firecrackers. In other cases, however, the quantity of Watergate stories derived from the process of reporting: the competition for stories created a self-perpetuating momentum, and a day without a Watergate headline became a day you had been scooped. Often the same stories were repeated from day to day with only minor changes, and sometimes without any changes at all, and then rehashed again on the weekends in Watergate "updates" or "analyses."

In some cases the press created the monsters it denounced. For example, it was the Washington press corps that created the idea of the Plumbers as a repressive White House "police force." Many people are still astounded to learn that the Plumbers unit consisted of only four men who worked together for just a little over two months in 1971.

In early April 1973 allegations that Senators Muskie, Percy, Proxmire, and Javits had been under surveillance by the White House were being widely reported. *Newsweek* printed reports that the offices of Senators Mansfield and Fulbright had been bugged. Both stories were untrue. On May 3 the Washington *Post* claimed that the Nixon administration had tapped the telephones of at least two newspaper reporters as part of the Pentagon Papers investigation and that the taps were supervised by Hunt and Liddy. Hunt and Liddy were said to have overseen a "so-called 'vigilante squad' " of wiretappers, and, according to the *Post*'s story, it was decided at a campaign strategy meeting that some members of this squad would be used to wiretap the telephones of Democratic presidential candidates. This story was not true. On May 17 the *Post* claimed that a "vast GOP undercover operation" had originated in 1969, and asserted that both the Watergate and Ellsberg break-ins were part of an "elaborate, continuous campaign of illegal and quasilegal undercover operations conducted by the Nixon administration since 1969." The authority cited for this staggering accusation was "highly placed sources in the executive branch." In the story we were accused, among other things, of having had copies of Senator Eagleton's health records before they were leaked (which was not true); of having used paid provocateurs to encourage violence at antiwar demonstrations early in the first term and during the 1972 campaign (also untrue); and of having undertaken undercover political activities conducted by FBI "suicide squads" against people we regarded as opponents of the administration (also untrue). The reporters said that there were more instances of political burglaries and bugging than had yet been revealed (untrue). They said that groups of radicals, reporters, White House aides, and Democrats all got the same treatment of bugging, spying, infiltration, and burglary (untrue).

In early June the *Post* reported the accusation of "one Senate source" who claimed to have evidence of several other White House burglaries and to know who had participated in them and who had directed them. The charge was untrue; the alleged evidence was never produced. *Newsweek* said that the administration had a secret police force that undertook unauthorized wiretaps and burglaries against radicals (untrue). NBC's legal correspondent Carl Stern reported charges that "massive" wiretapping had been done on McGovern's phones by the Justice Department, ostensibly to monitor incoming radical calls, but in fact to provide information to the CRP (untrue). The Baltimore *Sun* said that testimony before the Ervin Committee would reveal a national network of wiretaps used to supply political information on the Democrats to the CRP (untrue). The Washington *Post* reported that taps had been placed on the phones of Ellsberg and of New York *Times* reporters Neil

Sheehan and Tad Szulc, and reports from them fed to the Plumbers (untrue). The New York *Times* reported that we had placed a bug on the phone of friends of Mary Jo Kopechne, who died in Teddy Kennedy's car at Chappaquiddick. None of these stories was true.

There was also a flagrant double standard. In 1973, thirteen years after the alleged event, John Kennedy's doctor claimed that his offices had been broken into during the 1960 campaign and described it as a break-in in a style similar to the burglary of the offices of Ellsberg's doctor. All three networks carried the story. John Lungren, my personal physician, thereupon told of the break-in at his office during the 1972 campaign and even offered reporters copies of the police photographs that had been made at the time. Only one network, CBS, bothered to carry this story.

When Bob Haldeman and John Ehrlichman left the White House, we knew their ability to make a defense before grand juries and in the courtrooms would depend on their ability to demonstrate that their motives had never been criminal or corrupt. Judgments about motives inevitably depend upon delicate and often intangible impressions of personal credibility. After the treatment they received from Congress and the media in the first few days of May, they had no hope of ever receiving a fair hearing.

On the first night after they had left the White House, John Chancellor of NBC proclaimed them "by far" the most unpopular of the 2½ million federal employees, and he quoted congressional "sources" who said that there was "dancing in the halls" over their downfall. ABC said that the reaction on Capitol Hill "couldn't have been happier" because they were both "thoroughly disliked." Hugh Sidey had already reviled them in his *Time* column.

By the end of April the news was full of leaks of John Dean's accusations against them and charges of "cover-up" by nameless congressional sources. But these were not their only malicious accusers. On April 25 a headline in the New York *Times* charged: *Data from Taps Reportedly Sent to White House.* The accusation came from anonymous "federal investigators" who said they had determined that officials of the White House were regularly apprised of the information obtained through the Watergate tap. They mentioned Haldeman as a possible recipient. The accusation was untrue.

On May 27 the *Times* said there was evidence that Haldeman was directly linked to the Ellsberg break-in. This was also untrue. On June 17 the Washington *Post* ran a large front-page story asserting that Gordon Strachan was going to say that Haldeman had been sent the plans for the bugging operation. The next day the New York *Times* ran the same charge. Strachan never made such a claim. Ehrlichman was similarly savaged. For example, on June 13 the Washington *Post* reported that "Watergate prosecutors" had a memo that had been sent to Ehrlichman that "described in detail" plans to burglarize the office of Ellsberg's psychiatrist. The story directly contradicted Ehrlichman's insistence that he had had no prior knowledge of the plans. There was no such memo.

Daniel Schorr of CBS described the situation succinctly when in the fall of 1973 he commented:

> This past year, a new kind of journalism developed, and I found myself doing on a daily routine some things I would never have done before. There was a vacuum in investigation, and the press began to try men in the most effective court in the country. The men involved in the Watergate were convicted by the media, perhaps in a more meaningful way than any jail sentence they will eventually get.

As the months went by and the leaks continued, some voices were raised in concern and protest. Democratic Senator William Proxmire likened the press coverage to McCarthyism. Elliot Richardson urged that reporters develop a code of fairness relating to the use of leaked information. And Special Prosecutor Archibald Cox accused the press of considering itself a fourth branch of government and said that he had misgivings about its role in Watergate. ABC's Harry Reasoner denounced *Time* and *Newsweek*: in a broadcast commentary about the way those news magazines had treated Watergate, he said that "Week after week their lead stories on the subject [of Watergate] have been more in the style of pejorative pamphleteering than objective journalism, and since they are highly visible and normally highly respected organs of our craft, they embarrass and discredit us all."

At the time of the Agnew investigation in September 1973 James Reston wrote:

> It is easy to understand why the Agnews and the Ehrlichmans resent all this, for they are condemned even before they can state their own cases, and obviously they have a justifiable grievance. The newspapers have not resolved or even grappled with the problem effectively. They know that they ought to try to do something to protect the grand jury process, but they have not. . . . The press is ducking this problem, but it cannot do so much longer. It cannot insist on policing the power of the government without policing itself.

The media's performance during this period was irresponsible. Yet to this day exhibiting the same arrogance they are quick to denounce in other institutions, most reporters prefer self-congratulation to self-examination where Watergate is concerned.

On May 2 Bob Haldeman came to see me. Just two days earlier he had been entrusted with some of the most important responsibilities in government. Now he slipped in privately to avoid causing me any embarrassment.

He said he had been thinking about the decision I had made not to replace him but to function as my own Chief of Staff. He wanted to urge that I change my mind. In fact, I had already reached a similar conclusion. Details drain away energy even in good times; now, with Watergate, there was no way that I could handle everything myself.

We had the same man in mind to succeed him: Al Haig. Haig had left Kissinger's staff in January to become Vice Chief of Staff of the Army. He was steady, intelligent, and tough, and what he might have lacked in political experience and organizational finesse he made up for in sheer force of personality. He also had the enormous stamina that the job required. He knew how to drive people, and he knew how to inspire them. Equally important to me, he understood Kissinger.

I asked Haldeman if he would make the initial approach. Haig said he would accept; he asked only that I think further about the public reaction to having a military man as the White House Chief of Staff. After talking with me about this, Haldeman called Haig back and said that he was still the man I wanted.

When I met with Haig at noon the next day I told him that I knew what a great sacrifice I was asking him to make. With his abilities he would certainly have been in a position to become Chief of Staff of the Army and possibly Chairman of the Joint Chiefs of Staff.

I explained that I did not want him to become involved in the handling of Watergate. I wanted him to stick exclusively to running the White House staff and organizing the information I needed for making policy decisions. Still, I knew that taking this job would mean far more for him than just forfeiting military advancement and perquisites. We were in for a long and bloody struggle, and for Haig it would be like volunteering to return to combat with no guarantee of the outcome and with no medals at the end.

A day earlier John Connally had courageously announced that he was switching his affiliation and allegiance to the Republican Party; it was, he said, his ideological home. On May 7 he agreed to come back on the White House staff as an adviser without pay. We decided that rather than define his duties specifically, we would tailor them to his abilities as he went along.

Over the next weeks we began to regain momentum rebuilding the administration as I appointed William Colby Director of the CIA and moved James Schlesinger from the CIA to the Pentagon as Secretary of Defense. I also appointed a strong new head of the FBI, Clarence Kelley, the Chief of the Kansas City Police. Mel Laird and Bryce Harlow agreed to return to the White House as Counsellors to the President, and Haig brought in Fred Buzhardt, the General Counsel of the Defense Department, to assist Len Garment in handling Watergate.

Much of the Watergate criticism had centered on the White House press office. Connally, Laird, and Haig all believed that Ron Ziegler should leave. They had nothing against him personally, but they felt he was a symbol of the old Haldeman order, and that his credibility with the press corps was irreparably damaged. I knew that this was true, but I thought it was unfair to Ziegler. So did Kissinger, who said that we would always regret it if we hurt innocent people in an effort to palliate the press.

Haig looked for someone who might restore the credibility of the press office. Not surprisingly, there were few volunteers for the bloodletting that now accompanied the daily briefings in the White House press room. Ziegler's deputy, Jerry Warren, began to take over the podium much of the time, and Ziegler became more of an adviser to me. Despite his youth and occasional brashness, Ziegler was tough-minded and could analyze problems with honesty and incisiveness.

We had taken some hard blows, but slowly we were gathering strength and beginning to climb back on our feet again. Many friends and supporters at home and abroad offered their reflections and their assistance.

I received a note from Harold Macmillan:

> Although I now live remote from current affairs, thinking more of the past than of the present, I feel impelled, in view of our long friendship, to send you a message of sympathy and good will.
>
> I trust that these clouds may soon roll away, and that you may be able to take up with enthusiasm the task of promoting the Peace and Prosperity of the world, to which you have already made such a notable contribution.

Our ambassador to Italy, John Volpe, wrote to me after an audience with Pope Paul VI at the Vatican:

> His Holiness said that history will record that you have done more than anyone else to capture world respect as an effective peacemaker during the last four years . . . He told me that he simply cannot understand how Americans writing in the American press can so brutally tear down their own country and its institutions. He is confident, however, that you will be able to pass through this difficult period and continue your fine work for world peace. The Holy Father said he will offer his prayers and a mass for your intentions.

I received a message from former Japanese Prime Minister Sato:

> With profound personal sympathy, today I heard you speak to the American people on the television. You are right when you said, "America is the hope of the world." As an old personal friend of yours, I have firm and quiet confidence in you that you, as the great leader of this hope, will succeed in re-establishing the greater authority and integrity of your own office. Would you please accept my own prayer.

And one afternoon a note arrived from my old friend Clare Boothe Luce:

> From "The Ballad of Sir Andrew Barton": "Sir Andrew Barton said, 'I am hurt, but I am not slain! I'll lay me doun and bleed awhile, and I'll rise and fight again!' "

Through the months of May, June, and July I held meetings with eleven different foreign leaders, presided over fourteen congressional meetings covering major legislation, conducted four Cabinet meetings, chaired thirteen major sessions on the economy and energy, delivered four major public speeches, and prepared for the upcoming summit meeting with Brezhnev.

During this period we also devised a new plan for election reform, moved to increase food production, and, in mid-June, reimposed a limited price freeze in order to steady the economy while we considered our post-Phase III moves. We set up a new Office of Energy Policy, and with Agnew standing by to cast the tie-breaking vote we pushed the vitally important Alaska pipeline bill through the Senate. We continued our efforts at budget reform and government reorganization; by June we had actually accomplished what our critics had said was impossible: we had kept federal spending for 1973 under $250 billion. And although the cost in terms of political abrasion was extremely high, every one of my vetoes of budget-busting legislation was sustained.

Despite this visible and productive activity, we were haunted by the specter of "paralysis." The threat was invoked constantly as the media monitored our pulse and judged that Watergate had sapped my ability to lead. For

397

me, it was a no-win situation. If I had no officially announced schedule for a particular day, it was reported that I was secluded, brooding, paralyzed; if I had an active schedule, it was reported that I was contriving activity in order not to appear paralyzed.

If I talked about Watergate, I was described as struggling to free myself from the morass. If I did not talk about Watergate, I was accused of being out of touch with reality. If I tried to summon the nation to consider economic or foreign policy problems, I was accused of trying to distract attention from Watergate. Watergate had become the center of the media's universe, and during the remaining year of my presidency the media tried to force everything else to revolve around it.

THE POWs RETURN

The fighting in Vietnam took place far from Washington, but scarcely a day passed when the sacrifice and suffering of those who served there were not brought home to me in a very personal and agonizing way. In the letters sent to the next of kin of the men who had been killed in action, I could never find words adequate to express the grief I shared with them. The posthumous presentations of Medals of Honor, at which the families accepted the decoration, were always emotionally wrenching experiences for me. From time to time I made telephone calls to the wives or mothers of men who had been killed in action. It tore me up inside to do it.

During the Christmas season of 1969 Pat and I met with twenty-six wives and mothers of POWs and MIAs. The women spoke respectfully but passionately of the urgent need to get their loved ones released as soon as possible. Tears filled Pat's eyes, and mine as well, as we listened to them tell of the effect of the years of waiting on them and their children, and the terrible uncertainty of not knowing whether their men were alive or dead. From that time on, each POW was an individual to me, and obtaining their release became a burning cause. My long-time friend and chief military aide General Don Hughes did a superb job of handling White House liaison with the families of our POWs and MIAs.

The most dramatic, and heartbreaking, attempt at their release came in November 1970. Late in the summer Mel Laird and the Pentagon presented me with a proposal that we make a daring swoop-and-seize rescue raid on a POW camp inside North Vietnam. They decided to make the raid on the large POW installation at Sontay, the same town outside Hanoi that Pat and I had visited in 1953, when it had served as a refugee camp. Complete secrecy and clockwork precision might allow us to surprise and overpower the camp's guards and remove as many as ninety Americans before a counterattack could be mounted. When I received the plan, I immediately approved it. Early in the month I had received reports that as many as twenty-eight American POWs had recently died because of torture and ill-treatment. I said that I wanted the POWs to have Thanksgiving dinner at the White House.

After two and half months of rigorous training and rehearsal, the raid took place on November 20. By midafternoon in Washington, we knew that it had failed. The raiding party had found the cells empty; the prisoners had been moved. Apparently all the intelligence reports used for planning the operation had been several weeks old. Even if I had known when the operation was being planned that the reports were out of date, I believe I would still have given my approval.

Although the raid did not achieve its purpose, it was a significant psychological success. From intelligence sources we learned that it caused serious concern among the North Vietnamese military and political leaders, because it revealed their vulnerability to a kind of attack they had not experienced before. Later, when the POWs were home, I learned that the raid had also had a positive effect on their treatment as well as on their morale. Shortly after the raid the North Vietnamese moved most of the men from scattered camps throughout the country to a single prison in Hanoi, which became known as the Hanoi Hilton. The men were then able to organize themselves, and obtained more consistent—if not substantially better—treatment from their captors.

Our POWs had been courageous in action; they were even more courageous in captivity. That was one of the reasons that as the war ended, I continued to oppose amnesty for draft dodgers and deserters. I said in one press conference, "I can think of no greater insult to the memories of those who have fought and died, to the memories of those who have served, and also to our POWs, to say to them that we are now going to provide amnesty for those who deserted the country or refused to serve."

The first of the 591 POWs were released in Hanoi on February 12 and flown directly from Hanoi to Clark Air Force Base in the Philippines. I wanted the flag to be flying proud and high on the day the first prisoners returned to American soil. I called Lady Bird Johnson and asked her if we might cut short the official thirty-day period of national mourning during which all flags were flying at half-staff for President Johnson. She said she would like to think about it and call me back in a few minutes. When she called to give her approval, she said she was sure that this was what Lyndon would have wanted.

The scene at Clark Air Force Base was tremendously moving as one by one the men came down the ramp, walking or hobbling on crutches, saluting the flag. Some made eloquent statements. Some fell to their knees to kiss the ground. I had been concerned that they might have been so scarred by what they had been through that they would be bitter and disillusioned, or broken and unable to adjust to the conditions they would find at home. But these were no ordinary men. These were true heroes.

The first man off the first plane, Navy Captain Jeremiah P. Denton, stepped before the microphones and said, "We are honored to have had the opportunity to serve our country under difficult circumstances. We are profoundly grateful to our Commander in Chief, and to our nation for this day. God bless America."

As a token of the joy I felt at the return of the men, I personally bought more than 600 orchid corsages and had one sent to each of the wives or mothers. I was delighted when I heard that some of them had worn the flowers to greet their husbands and sons as they arrived home.

Over the next few days the returning men talked to reporters. Air Force Colonel James Kasler said, "We went to Vietnam to do a job that had to be done. And we were willing to stay until that job was complete. We wanted to come home, but we wanted to come home with honor. President Nixon has brought us home with honor. God bless those Americans who supported our President during this long ordeal."

And Air Force Captain David Gray, Jr., spoke with warm simplicity. "A loving God made me an American, and to America I return. A loving President preserved my honor, and with honor I return. A loving wife waited with strong heart, and to her I return. Thank you, Heavenly Father. Thank you, President Nixon. Thank you, Lynda. Thank you, America."

On the morning of February 12, I received a call from Air Force Colonel Robinson Risner, the senior officer of the first POW group to return home. For seven and a half years he had been held captive in North Vietnam; for much of that time he had been kept in solitary confinement.

When I picked up the phone, he said, "This is Colonel Risner, sir, reporting for duty."

We talked for just a few minutes, and I told him that I looked forward to seeing him and all the other men at the White House. At the end of our brief conversation he said that talking to me had been the greatest moment of his life.

Diary

Risner's comment to the effect that this was the greatest moment in his life, of course, had a very sobering effect as far as I was concerned. It made me feel extremely humble, to hear this man who had suffered so long and had taken such great risks as far as his life was concerned, to speak in this way. He spoke at the very last by saying that he and the men with him would be supporting me as long as they lived.

On March 6 Captain Jerry Singleton and Major Robert Jeffrey, both Air Force officers, came to meet me at the White House.

Diary

At ten o'clock I met the first POWs I have seen. It was a very moving experience to see their wives and the two of them—gaunt, lean, quiet, confident, with enormous faith in the country, in God, and in themselves.

Apparently they had been exposed to enemy propaganda throughout and had never given in to it. For example, they were shown still photos of the big crowds demonstrating against the President. They, of course, heard tapes of messages from Ramsey Clark, Jane Fonda, and the other peacenik groups, but they had nothing but contempt for them.

I only hope that these men do not have a terrible letdown now that they are back. I don't think they will. I think after what they have been through they have become stronger as a result of being put through the fire of adversity. They are like fine steel rather than soft iron.

It was not long before the returning men had confirmed the widespread use of torture in the prison camps. Some were tortured for refusing to pose in propaganda photos with touring antiwar groups. Miss Fonda said that the POWs were "liars" for making such claims; one POW had his arm and leg broken because he refused to meet with Miss Fonda. It was during her trip to North Vietnam in 1972 that she broadcast appeals over Radio Hanoi asking American pilots to quit flying bombing runs over North Vietnam. I met with other POWs whenever I could arrange time in my schedule. Among them was the ranking officer of the group, Air Force Brigadier General John P. Flynn, who had been a POW for five and a half years. When I escorted him to the door after our talk, I told him how deeply sad I was that he had been away from his home and family for so many years and had had to endure such terrible conditions.

He said, "Mr. President, don't give that a second thought; how else could John Peter Flynn be standing here in the office of the President of the United States?" He smartly snapped to attention, saluted, and left the room before I could respond. It was fortunate that he did. I was so choked up with emotion that I don't believe I could have thought of anything to say worthy of the moment.

On March 12 I had long meetings with Colonel Risner and Captain Denton.

Diary

I asked Risner about how he was able to take what he had been through. I had not realized that he had been four years in solitary confinement. At this point he said, "It isn't easy for me to say this." His voice broke, and he said, "It was faith in God and faith in my country."

He obviously was a man who had been through the tortures of the damned. He explained in detail some of the torture he had gone through but did not make a big thing out of it.

He told me how he had gotten to the point that he was ready to break because his nerves had been shattered. He didn't know what was happening to him. He had a hot flash on the back of his neck—he felt that he was coming apart but he would exercise and then finally fall asleep for a few hours.

I asked about the effect of the bombing. They pointed out that as far as the other fighter planes were concerned, their captors would get out and make as if they were shooting at them and all that sort of thing. But when the B-52s came, they came out of the blue despite the bad weather and all the rest, with shattering effect.

He said that they all cheered and hollered and hugged each other when the bombing was going on. He said their captors thought they were all crazy. Apparently some of the plaster fell down off of the walls as a result of the reverberations—one of their captors came in and said, "Aren't you aware of the fact that they are trying to kill you or kill the civilians?" They answered that this was in no way what was involved, and that they knew the bombing was aimed at only military targets.

Denton spoke movingly about his deep concern about the country. He is a deeply religious man. He, whenever I mentioned his suffering and the rest, came back to what I had been through. He was most generous in his respect—said that he could see the same suffering in my eyes that he could see in the eyes of his fellow POWs. I told him that after knowing what they had been through, what I had been through was nothing. But he realized, as he said, that I had been pretty much alone in the decisions that I had made.

He pointed out that the North Vietnamese said that the trouble with Nixon is that he flip-flops. Of course, this was a compliment, not a condemnation. He said that the North Vietnamese knew that Nixon was a very tough fellow, and he was convinced that the recognition of that fact was what eventually brought them around to a settlement.

He made an interesting analogy on the point that the North Vietnamese really thought that the President was off his rocker—was totally irrational. He said that it was absolutely essential for them to think that. He said, as a matter of fact, that that is what saved the POWs because the North Vietnamese thought that they were so irrational that they could not break them and they could not take risks with them.

In fact, Risner or Denton said (I think it was Denton) that he would be willing to stay eight, twelve, or sixteen years if necessary to see that the United States came out of Vietnam in the right way. They did not want to come back with their heads down.

He said that the settlement that Harriman would agree to in '68 would have been a shameful thing and that they could not possibly have felt proud if it had ended on that basis.

Denton kept coming back to the fact that he didn't know what was going to happen to the country after I left the office. He feels very strongly we must use this precious time—he said three years or so—for the purpose of seeing that America's foreign policy role is played as well as it possibly can be.

I said that the history of civilization showed that the leader class rather than the common people were those that first disintegrated. That here in our country the problem was not the common people who stood by us—they were the silent majority.

It is now ten minutes until one on the 13th of March. As I sleep in this comfortable room with the blackout curtains, the air conditioning, a very comfortable bed, I think of how really easy we have it—I think of what they went through—and I realize how we could probably do far more than we do—take more physical punishment actually than we do—live certainly a much more austere life than we do.

On March 3 we had one of our evenings at the White House, at which Sammy Davis, Jr., performed. Afterward he suggested that we organize a gala entertainment honoring the POWs. I discussed this with Pat, and she said that we should go all out and also give a formal dinner in honor of the men and their families.

There were monumental problems involved. In the past the largest number ever served dinner at one time at the White House had been the 231 senior citizens we invited for Thanksgiving in 1969. Now we were considering having more than 1,300 people. Some of the staff members urged that we move the affair into one of the local hotel ballrooms that were properly equipped to deal with such a large number of people, but Pat and I felt that the whole point of the evening was to honor these men at the White House.

Since there was no way that we could possibly accommodate, much less seat, more than a few hundred people inside, Pat arranged for the construction on the South Lawn of a canopy that was itself larger than the whole White House. Then she found and rented enough china and crystal that were sufficiently elegant for an occasion of this importance. Hundreds of bottles of champagne were chilled in ice-filled aluminum canoes, and crates of strawberries for the dessert mousse were run through the blenders at the Pentagon kitchens because the White House simply could not handle such large quantities. Pat was busy for weeks making the preparations and supervising the arrangements for everything from individual place cards to the flower centerpieces on each of the 126 tables.

We wanted to arrange excellent entertainment for after dinner, and Pat and her staff worked with Sammy Davis and Bob Hope and our long-time California friend, television producer Paul Keyes. Her only condition was that she did not want a "girlie" show; she felt that would be inappropriate for the men and their families. The result was a beautifully produced, tasteful, and deeply moving program that everyone who saw it will always remember.

On May 24, the day the POW dinner was held, the flag flying over the White House was the same one that had flown at Clark Air Force Base on February 12 when the first group of POWs returned from Hanoi.

In the afternoon Pat and the girls attended a tea for the wives. Tricia recorded the scene in her diary:

> Mama, Julie, and I attended a reception honoring the wives of the POWs prior to the dinner at the White House.
>
> The press attended the reception too, and while we were scattered through the reception room surrounded by the wives, the reporters surrounded us. Instead of asking us questions about the occasion or even showing a humane concern about the POW families, the press immediately and gleefully bombarded us with Watergate questions.
>
> Finally the POW wives could support this attack no longer and they, unasked, began telling the reporters how fine Richard Nixon was. They said things like, "He is the greatest President our country has *ever* had" and "If it were not for him our husbands would still be prisoners."

While the women were having tea, I addressed the men in the State Department Auditorium. My speech was interrupted many times by applause, but I was surprised at the reaction to one particular sentence. Only two weeks earlier Daniel Ellsberg's trial had been dismissed, and he had gone free. When I said, "And let me say, I think it is time in this country to quit making national heroes out of those who steal secrets and publish them in the newspapers," the men leaped to their feet and shouted their agreement.

It had rained all day and much of the evening, and the South Lawn was soggy when the first guests began arriving for the dinner. Many of the women's long dresses got splattered with mud, but nothing could dampen the high spirits of that night. Pat had decided to open the entire White House, so the men and their families wandered through all the rooms, examining the decorations and taking photographs.

Before the dinner an invocation was offered by Navy Captain Charles Gillespie, the POW who had acted as their chaplain in Hanoi. Then the POW chorus of thirty-five men sang a hymn that one of them had written in prison.

Everyone stood at attention as a fanfare announced an all-service honor guard for the presentation of the colors. In place of the full-size American flag, there came a tiny flag held aloft on a short staff. It was the flag that had been secretly made by Air Force Lieutenant Colonel John Dramesi in a North Vietnamese prison, fashioned from a white handkerchief, patches of red underwear, gold trim from a blanket, blue cloth from an old jacket, and string from a Red Cross package. As the honor guard entered, all eyes turned toward the tiny patchwork flag, and beginning with the front tables, a cheer grew and grew until it filled the canvas tent.

During most of the dinner Pat and I walked around from table to table, posing for photographs and signing autographs. When I came to the table at which John Stennis was seated, he turned to the men and said, "You fellows wouldn't be here if it weren't for the guts of this man."

When the dinner was over, I rose to begin the toasts. "The most difficult decision that I have made since being President was on December 18 of last year," I said, and before I could continue there was a thunderous burst of cheering and applause. "And there were many occasions in that ten-day period after the decision was made when I wondered whether anyone in this country really supported it. But I can tell you this: after having met each one of our honored guests this evening, after having talked to them, I think that all of us would like to join in a round of applause for the brave men that took those B-52s in and did the job, because as all of you know, if they hadn't done it, you wouldn't be here tonight."

I said that I wanted to propose a toast not just to Pat as First Lady but to all the brave wives and mothers of the prisoners. Tricia noted in her diary, "When all the men rose to toast their wives and families, all the sacrifice, poignance, sadness, past and future, was caught in that moment."

General Flynn responded to the toast: "I would like to state . . . that we do not consider ourselves a unique group of men. Rather we are a random selection of fate. . . . Mr. President, concerning your decision on December 18, I would like to assure you, sir, that we knew you were in a very lonely position. The decision was contested, but I would like to also report to you that when we heard heavy bombs impacting in Hanoi, we started to go and pack our bags, because we knew we were going home, and we were going home with honor."

The men presented me with a plaque inscribed to "Our leader—our comrade, Richard the Lion-Hearted."

Bob Hope opened the entertainment. All the stars of the show had entertained the men in South Vietnam, many of them as part of Hope's annual Christmas shows. John Wayne got the biggest hand when he said to the POWs, "I'll ride into the sunset with you anytime." Just before he left the stage, he looked down at me sitting in the front row of tables and said, "I want to thank you, Mr. President, not for any one thing, just for everything."

There were famous pop and country singers, comedians and motion picture personalities on the program, and the place of honor at the end was for Sammy Davis, Jr. He sang and danced and, with tears in his eyes, had special praise for the women whose prayers had "brought you cats home."

Then I introduced Irving Berlin. His age and failing health had made it impossible for him to participate in any other part of the evening, but as he began the first notes of his most famous song, his voice came out loud and strong. Many now wept openly as we repeated the stirring and simple verse over and over until, at the end, some of the men almost seemed to be shouting so that the words could be heard all the way to Hanoi: "God bless America, my home sweet home."

The show did not end until after midnight and the dancing went on until after two o'clock, but Pat and I went upstairs around 12:30. I kissed her goodnight and then went to the Lincoln Sitting Room. As I sat before the fire, listening to the sounds of the music and laughter coming up from downstairs, I felt that this was one of the greatest nights in my life. There were no words then, and there are really none now, that could describe the joy and satisfaction that I felt at the thought that I had played a role in bringing these men back home, and that they, who were so completely courageous and admirable, genuinely seemed to consider the decisions I had made about the war to have been courageous and admirable ones.

I reached in my pocket and pulled out a small piece of paper that the wife of one of the POWs had handed to me. It was a short handwritten note on Statler-Hilton stationery:

Dear Mr. President:

When I was living in solitary confinement and conditions were especially bad, men would often send notes of encouragement to others who were under great pressure. The notes were hidden in the bath areas and were a great comfort to the recipient. The standard message was "Don't let the bastards get you down."

Don't let the bastards get you down, Mr. President.

Joy and Bob Jeffrey

The contrast between the splendid lift of this night and the dreary daily drain of Watergate suddenly struck me with an almost physical force. When Tricia and Julie came upstairs from the party a little later, I invited them to join me in the Lincoln Sitting Room. Tricia made a diary note of that meeting:

We went down expecting that he wanted to talk over the splendid event and what had led up to it and made it possible.

When we saw his face, we realized that his spirit was troubled. It was obvious that his low spirit was more than the natural letdown that frequently follows the conclusion of a speech or an event where much energy has been expended. He began to talk quietly, without undue passion, about the press's rather negative reception of all the POW ceremonies in Washington. He correctly stated the reason for this apathy: in giving a good play to the ceremonies they feared they would build him up.

He called Paul Keyes and thanked him for arranging the entertainment. They joked for a few minutes, but it was almost painful for us to see how sad Daddy's face looked despite the laughter in his voice.

After he hung up we were all silent for a moment and then, very simply, he said to Julie and me, "Do you think I should resign?"

It was not what he said but the way he said it that

produced an internal earthquake in us. Instead of saying it with levity, he said it with a seriousness that produced a wave of exclamations such as "Don't you dare!" and "Don't even think of it!" from us.

He really wanted us to give him reasons for not resigning. This was not difficult for us to do: we said he should stay in office because he had done nothing wrong. There was no reason to resign. The country would not thrive as well with anyone else in office. He smiled at us and tried to say something to cheer us up, but it was almost more than I could bear to stay there and see his sadness on what should have been a night of jubilant triumph for him as it was for everyone else.

And so the evening concluded—an evening representing a great historical and personal achievement for Daddy, marred by a great personal tragedy. I could not help but think how man lives in the hope of perfection, but lives in the reality of imperfection in himself and in those around him.

THE MAY 22 STATEMENT

John Dean's news-making accusations against Haldeman and Ehrlichman failed to gain him immunity from prosecution.

He later claimed that he had been very careful not to try his case in the press, and he testified before the Ervin Committee that he had not done so. But the New York *Times* reported flatly that Dean's attorney was behind the leaking.

On May 4 Dean had informed Judge Sirica that he had a safe-deposit box full of classified documents taken from the White House, which he planned to use to buttress his Watergate case. We had no idea what the documents might be. The only clues were the press reports noting that one of these documents was forty-three pages long and carried one of the highest security classifications in the government. Fred Buzhardt took the security classification and the number of pages mentioned in the press leaks and started searching until he found what he was sure was the document: the June 1970 Interagency Intelligence Report—the Huston Plan.

In April Dean had promised me categorically that he would not reveal anything involving national security matters, but now he seemed to be willing to breach that promise if it would help him gain immunity from prosecution.

Justice Department officials who had seen the document said that it involved a national security matter and did not relate to Watergate. But Senator Ervin pounced on the chance to make news. He told reporters that it was an "operation to spy on the American people in general," and he cited it as evidence of the administration's "Gestapo mentality."

Even so, I was almost relieved that this was Dean's bombshell document, because I was certain that we could completely defend and explain it in a way that people would understand.

A few days later General Vernon Walters, Deputy Director of the CIA, notified us that several of his "memcons"—memoranda of conversations—dating from June 1972 were about to be subpoenaed by the Senate Armed Services Committee, which was investigating the question of CIA involvement in the Watergate break-in and its aftermath. One of Walters's memcons covered the conversation held among Helms, Haldeman, Ehrlichman, and himself on June 23, 1972. Other Walters memcons covered subsequent conversations with John Dean and with Pat Gray. The subject of all the memcons was Watergate. Walters brought the memcons to the White House to get a ruling on whether they were covered by executive privilege. The minute we saw them we knew we had a problem.

Walters's memcon of the June 23 meeting with Haldeman and Ehrlichman noted that Haldeman had commented on the embarrassment being caused by Watergate and then said that it was my desire that Walters go to see Pat Gray and suggest that he not push the inquiry further, particularly into the Mexican money that appeared to have financed the break-in.

One of the things that made the memcons so troublesome was the fact that Walters was one of my old friends; he would not have contrived them to hurt me. In addition, his photographic memory was renowned, and he was universally respected as a scrupulous and honest man.

Buzhardt, however, noticed that the June 23 memcon had not actually been written on June 23, but five days later, on June 28. During those five days John Dean had ap-

411

proached Walters and asked if the CIA could help put up the bail for the Watergate defendants to get them out of jail and pay their salaries if they were convicted. He had also asked obliquely if the CIA might assume some of the responsibility for the break-in. Walters had reacted to Dean's overtures with dismay and alarm; he had refused, insisting that he would do nothing unless he received a direct order from me. In fact, Dean had undertaken this approach to Walters without my knowledge, and he dropped his request.

Buzhardt postulated that on June 28, when Walters wrote the memcon of the June 23 meeting, he had unconsciously reconstructed the conversation from the perspective of what he felt Dean was trying to do, rather than from what Haldeman and Ehrlichman had actually said.

It had been almost a year since that conversation; so much had happened in the meantime. But I was certain that the motive could not have been as transparently political as it looked. What could we have been thinking? It must have been concern over the perennial competition between the FBI and CIA. I saw Haldeman on May 10 and 11 and again on May 18. He was positive beyond a doubt that that had been our motive. He told me again, as he had when we met on April 25, that I had told Dean on March 21 that we could raise a million dollars but it would be wrong and it would not work.

Back in April I had talked to Haldeman and Ehrlichman about the difficulty of recalling events that were many months past. "How do you remember back that far? . . . You remember the things you want to remember." Now we ourselves rationalized the implications of Walters's memcons; we confusedly reconstructed events around our recollection of our motive—we remembered what we wanted to remember.

I was relieved by Haldeman's certainty. I asked whether he could recall even the slightest hint of political concern in calling in the CIA. He said he was positive that there had been no political concern whatever.

By mid-May we were inundated with new charges. In addition to all the Watergate allegations and accusations, the 1969–70 wiretaps were now public; so was the Plumbers unit, and we knew that Dean had a copy of the Interagency

Intelligence Report. No distinction was being made between legitimate national security concerns and exclusively Watergate problems. In the April 30 speech I had dealt in a very general way with the broad concepts of responsibility and blame. Now I could see that we were going to have to provide a detailed response to the many specific Watergate allegations.

In a statement issued from the White House on May 22 I described the 1969 wiretaps and the events that had created the need for them. I also described the 1970 Interagency Intelligence Report and the establishment of the Plumbers. Then I turned to Watergate. I denied prior knowledge of the break-in, and I made a blanket denial of any awareness of or participation in the cover-up. I said that we had called in the CIA to make sure that no secret CIA operations were uncovered by the Watergate investigation and that the investigation did not lead to any inquiry into the Special Investigations Unit. I stated, "It was certainly not my intent, nor my wish, that the investigation of the Watergate break-in or of related acts be impeded in any way." I said flatly that it was not until "my own investigation" that I had known of any fund-raising for the men convicted of the break-in at the DNC. And I said that I had not authorized any offer of executive clemency for any of these defendants. Thus I set more traps that would be sprung by the tapes months later.

The May 22 statement came as a shock to the American public. It was the first time that a President of the United States had publicly admitted that there had been such things as government-approved break-ins. At that time the activities that were later revealed by the 1975 Senate study of intelligence activity were not yet widely known outside some political and journalistic circles in Washington. Thus there was no cushion of preparation, no context of public awareness and acceptance, for my contention that what I had approved in the Huston Plan and the wiretaps was not only objectively justifiable but based on the precedent of presidential decisions and practices as far back as FDR. In 1973 *Newsweek* said that the Huston Plan was "the most wide-ranging secret police operation ever authorized."

Later William V. Shannon wrote in the New York *Times*, "There was nothing really new or unprecedented in the methods proposed in the 1970 plan."

There were even denials that any precedents existed. For example, the Washington *Post* reported that Kennedy and Johnson had generally felt that wiretapping was too damaging to employ. After a press conference in which I responded to questions about the history of government-authorized break-ins, Johnson's Attorneys General Nicholas Katzenbach and Ramsey Clark said that they did not know about such things. And Sam Ervin used the nationally televised forum of the Watergate hearings to pontificate erroneously that J. Edgar Hoover would not have authorized any break-ins. Thus were the conventional pieties kept intact and my explanation of my actions undermined.

In the face of the sanctimony that greeted my May 22 statement, I decided that I wanted all the wiretaps of previous administrations revealed. It was Robert Kennedy who had authorized the first wiretaps on Martin Luther King. Ultimately King was subjected to five different phone taps and fifteen microphone bugs in his hotel rooms. The Kennedys had tapped newsmen. They had tapped a number of people instrumental in the passage of a sugar import bill they considered important. I wanted to get out the particulars of Lyndon Johnson's political use of the FBI. He had had thirty FBI employees at the 1964 Democratic convention monitoring events and overseeing wiretaps on Martin Luther King. The Mississippi Freedom Democratic Party—a group that threatened to pose a political problem for him—was tapped, and the reports were relayed directly to the White House. His Press Secretary asked for name checks on Goldwater supporters. His Attorney General had authorized a tap on an author who had written a book about Marilyn Monroe and Bobby Kennedy. Hoover's aide, William Sullivan, wrote, "To my memory the two administrations which used the FBI most for political purposes were Mr. Roosevelt's and Mr. Johnson's. Complete and willing cooperation was given to both." I wanted everything out on the Democrats. My staff resisted me, and for several weeks we debated back and forth about it. I felt like a fighter with one hand tied behind his back: most of my advisers argued that if I revealed the activities of previous administrations, it would look as if I were trying to divert attention from myself by smearing others. If I did not, however, I was afraid that I would remain portrayed as a willful deviant from past practice and be condemned for my legal and legitimate uses of the same tactics my predecessors had used not only more extensively but for blatantly political purposes. In the end, I was persuaded against it, and we did nothing.

If the public reaction to the May 22 statement was negative, the reaction in the White House briefing room was almost violent. Len Garment helped Ziegler with the briefing, and the reporters interrupted them constantly, shouting and jeering.

By the summer the White House and my campaign organization were under investigation by the FBI, the Ervin Committee and four other congressional committees, the General Accounting Office, one House committee, grand juries in Los Angeles, New York, Florida, and Texas, and the Miami District Attorney's office. More than a dozen civil suits had been filed. Now we also had a Special Prosecutor, Archibald Cox, whose sole responsibility was the investigation of Watergate.

The Ervin Committee had a staff of 92; the Special Prosecutor's office had a staff of 80. We had fewer than 10 people: Fred Buzhardt and Len Garment, who bore the full-time burden; Charles Alan Wright, a distinguished constitutional scholar from the University of Texas Law School who helped on a part-time basis; and young lawyers to assist them. Compared with the forces ranged against us, we were like a high school team heading into the Super Bowl.

At the end of May it was clear that Dean's effort to gain immunity from the federal prosecutors had failed. All that was left for him was to push harder for Senate immunity in the hopes that his testimony before the Ervin Committee would renew pressure in his favor that might make the Justice Department reconsider its decision.

On Sunday morning, June 3, there were front-page headlines in the New York *Times* and the Washington *Post*: *Dean Said to Tell of 40 Meetings with Nixon in 1973* and *Dean Alleges Nixon Knew of Cover-up Plan*. I quickly scanned the *Post*'s story. It began: "Former presidential counsel John W. Dean III has told Senate investigators and federal prosecutors that he discussed aspects of the Watergate cover-up with President Nixon or in Mr. Nixon's presence on at least thirty-five occasions between January and April of this year, according to reliable sources." The story in the *Times* similarly reported that Dean had said that I had met with him alone and in small groups more than forty times between January and April, and that in these meetings I had shown "great interest" in making sure things were "taken care of."

I read on in the *Post* and felt a sudden sense of dread as I came to another part of the story. "One of the strongest charges," according to the *Post*, was Dean's assertion that in March 1973, shortly before the Watergate burglars had been sentenced, I had met with him and asked him how much the defendants would have to be paid to ensure their continued silence. Dean was said to have told me that the additional cost would be about $1 million, and I was said to have replied that there would be no problem in paying that much money. Dean claimed that after January I had begun calling him personally to "find out the status of the cover-up," and on March 21 he had told me that "to save the presidency" it would be necessary for Haldeman, Ehrlichman, and Dean himself to disclose fully their involvement in the Watergate affair. He charged that after that meeting I had met with Haldeman and Ehrlichman and then told Dean that I would not tolerate any division in the White House ranks and warned him that he would stand alone if he went to the prosecutors.

I felt discouraged, drained, and pressured. I asked Haig whether I shouldn't resign. His answer was a robust no, and he urged me to steel myself to taking whatever time and effort would be required to listen to the tapes of the Dean meetings and to construct an unassailable defense based on them. I agreed to see what we could do in this regard, and Haig said that he would make the necessary arrangements.

A check of my daily logs showed that I had met with Dean twenty-one times and made or received thirteen phone calls from him between February 27 and April 1973. Except for the March 21 conversation I had little or no recollection of any of the rest of them. As I sat looking at this list, an uneasy feeling came over me as I wondered what we might have talked about in all those conversations.

Monday, June 4, was the first time I listened to a tape. Steve Bull brought a tape machine to my EOB office and cued the first one for me. I put on the earphones and pressed the "play" button. The reel began unwinding. Sounds drifted in and out; voices overrode each other. Gradually, as my ears became accustomed, I could pick up more and more. I listened to conversation after conversation with Dean in February and March, all before March 21. At the end of the day I was both exhausted and relieved.

I knew that there would be problems, but I was sure that they could all be explained. I had said that I first learned about the cover-up on March 21, and the tapes showed that in the conversations prior to March 21, Dean and I had talked about Watergate, the Ervin Committee, executive privilege, and political retaliation against the Democrats strictly as political problems. Dean had told me that no one in the White House was involved in the Watergate break-in.

He had reassured me that from the White House point of view, Watergate and Segretti were not nearly so bad as they had been made to appear in the press. He had agreed with me that he himself had had nothing to do with campaign activities. And he had certainly not disclosed his own role in the cover-up to me before our meeting on March 21.

I called in Haig and Ziegler to tell them the good news: I felt the tapes proved Dean was lying. For just a moment after I had read all the newspaper stories, I was worried that maybe Dean and I *had* talked about a cover-up. But now that I had reviewed the tapes, I told Ziegler I felt enormously relieved. "Really, the goddamn record is not bad, is it?" I remarked almost cheerily.

The day that John Dean was scheduled to begin his testimony before the Watergate Committee, June 18, was also the day that Leonid Brezhnev was to arrive in Washington to begin the second U.S.–Soviet Summit. At the last minute Ervin—"with some degree of reluctance," as he himself said—postponed Dean's appearance for a week, until after the summit.

SUMMIT II

By early spring of 1973, the Soviets appeared to be moving full speed in pursuit of détente. Brezhnev, according to press and intelligence reports, had conducted a quiet purge of the Politburo, apparently in order to remove anti-détente recalcitrants. In February he wrote me a letter outlining his expectations for the summit, saying that he looked forward to the signing of a treaty on the nonuse of nuclear weapons; to useful discussions of the Middle East; to the completion of a further SALT agreement; to the signing of trade and economic agreements and agreements to cooperate in the areas of science, technology, health, and peaceful uses of nuclear energy; to discussion of relations between the two Germanys; and to talks concerning European security and mutual and balanced force reductions in Europe. Considerable progress had already been made in building on the agreements for cooperation in economic and other non-military areas we had reached in Moscow in 1972. The prospects for a successful summit appeared good.

But problems were beginning to develop at home, even apart from Watergate. In the year between the first and second Soviet Summits, a fusion of forces from opposite ends of the political spectrum had resulted in a curious coalition. Kissinger later described it as a rare convergence, like an eclipse of the sun. On the one side the liberals and the American Zionists had decided that now was the time to challenge the Soviet Union's highly restrictive emigration policies, particularly with respect to Soviet Jews. On the other side were the conservatives, who had traditionally opposed détente because it challenged their ideological opposition to contacts with Communist countries. My request in April 1973 for congressional authority to grant most-favored-nation trade status to the Soviet Union became the rallying point for both groups: the liberals wanted MFN legislation to be conditioned on eased emigration policies; the conservatives wanted MFN defeated on the principle that détente was bad by definition.

I have never had any illusions about the brutally repressive nature of Soviet society. But I knew that the more public pressure we placed on the Soviet leaders, the more intransigent they would become. I also knew that it was utterly unrealistic to think that a fundamental change in the Soviet system could be brought about because we refused to extend MFN status.

I felt that we could accomplish a great deal more on the Jewish emigration issue when we were talking with the Soviets than when we were not. As I said to one group of American Jewish leaders, "The walls of the Kremlin are very thick. If you are inside, there is a chance that they will listen to you; if you are outside you are not even going to be heard." That was the approach we adopted. Although we did not publicly challenge the Soviet contention that these questions involved Soviet internal affairs, both Kissinger and I raised them privately with Brezhnev, Gromyko, and Dobrynin. This approach brought results. In March 1973 Dobrynin informed Kissinger that the high exit tax, which the Soviets described as the repayment of state educational expenses by those who wanted to move abroad, had been removed and only a nominal fee was now being required of émigrés from the Soviet Union to Israel. He said that a similar approach would be maintained in the future. Brezhnev sent me a personal note claiming that 95.5 percent of the requests for emigration visas to Israel during 1972 had been granted. Whether or not this claim was exaggerated, the statistics are proof of undeniable success: from 1968 to 1971 only 15,000 Soviet Jews were allowed to emigrate. In 1972 alone, however, the number jumped to 31,400. In 1973, the last full year of my presidency, nearly 35,000 were permitted to leave; this figure is still the record high.

On December 11, 1973, the House of Representatives passed a trade bill that in effect prohibited MFN for the Soviet Union because of its restrictive emigration policies. I met with Dobrynin on December 26 and expressed my profound contempt for the alliance that had combined to defeat MFN, but I said that we must not let temporary setbacks, no matter how discouraging, interfere with or poison the relations between the two superpowers that still held the future of the world in their hands. In the end, the congressional action unfortunately but predictably had an effect that was exactly the opposite of what was intended: the number of Jews allowed to emigrate declined from 35,000 in 1973 to 13,200 in 1975.

Brezhnev's plane landed at Andrews Air Force Base on the afternoon of June 16. Because we had decided not to begin the summit officially until Monday, I had gone to Florida for the weekend. I called him from Key Biscayne shortly after he arrived at Camp David, where he would spend two days resting and adjusting to the time difference between Washington and Moscow. I had never heard him sound so friendly and completely uninhibited as he did on the phone that afternoon. I said that I wanted to welcome him to the United States. Even before Dobrynin, who was on an extension line to act as our interpreter, could begin the translations, Brezhnev said "thank you" three or four times in English.

I told him to get as much rest as he could because I knew from experience that it would take some time to recover from jet lag. He said that he appreciated my thoughtfulness in providing a place as private and comfortable as Camp David, and that he regretted that his wife had not been able to take the trip with him. I said that Pat and I would look forward to having her come with him during the Fourth Soviet Summit, which would take place in America in two years. At least as far as atmosphere was concerned, Summit II was off to the best possible start.

The Soviets were fully aware of Watergate, but they made little effort to conceal the fact that they could not completely understand it. Dobrynin told Kissinger that he was utterly dismayed by the way Americans were acting over the whole affair. He called it a "mess" and said that no other country would permit itself the luxury of tearing itself to pieces in public.

Dean's testimony before the Ervin Committee had been postponed until after Brezhnev's departure, but the drumbeat of Watergate leaks and accusations from him and his nameless associates, and from various anonymous Ervin Committee sources, continued. On the morning Brezhnev arrived, the Washington *Post* published a front-page report revealing that "sources" said I was going to abandon Ehrlichman and Haldeman in a last-ditch effort to save myself. The story was absolute fiction, but perhaps more than many others, it contributed to the impression that the Nixon White House was a viciously cynical place where I would turn on my closest aides to save myself. Our denial of this front-page fabrication was relegated to page five of the next day's edition. Archibald Cox also chose the day of Brezhnev's arrival to hold a press conference, at which, in reply to reporters' questions, he stated that he was studying whether or not he could indict me before an impeachment had taken place. Having said this, he hastened to add that, of course, such a study was only academic.

Just before eleven o'clock on Monday morning Brezhnev's car came up the curving driveway to the South Portico of the White House. In my welcoming speech I said, "The hopes of the world rest with us at this time in the meetings that we will have." His response was warm: "I and my comrades, who have come with me, are prepared to work hard to ensure that the talks we will have with you . . . justify the hopes of our peoples and serve the interests of a peaceful future for all mankind."

After the brief speeches we walked out onto the rain-soaked lawn to review the honor guard. As we came to the end of the front line of troops and were about to walk by the rear ranks, Brezhnev could no longer suppress his animation and joviality. He waved enthusiastically at the spectators, who were applauding and waving American and Soviet flags, and then strode over to them just like an American politician working the crowd at a county fair. He shook hands with several people and grinned broadly as they reached out to him until I reminded him that we had to complete the ceremony. As we walked back to the South Portico, he threw his arm around my shoulders and said, "See, we're already making progress!"

Our first meeting in the Oval Office was private, except for Viktor Sukhodrev, who, as in 1972, acted as translator. Brezhnev began by assuring me that he spoke for the entire Politburo. I replied that, despite domestic differences, I spoke for the majority of Americans. He nodded his head vigorously.

We reviewed our general schedule and agenda for the next few days. As we talked he became more animated. Several times he grabbed my arm and squeezed it to emphasize the point he was making. I couldn't help thinking that the last time such tactile diplomacy had been used in that room was when Lyndon Johnson wanted to make a point.

Brezhnev became very serious when explaining his views about the relationship between our two countries. He said, "We know that as far as power and influence are concerned, the only two nations in the world that really matter are the Soviet Union and the United States. Anything that we decide between us, other nations in the world will have to follow our lead, even though they may disagree with it." It was clear, although he did not mention China, that he wanted this summit to demonstrate that the U.S.–Soviet relationship was more important than the U.S–Chinese relationship, and that if we have to choose between the two our ties to the Soviet Union would prevail.

I replied that, while I recognized the reality of our pre-eminence as the two nuclear superpowers, we both had allies. "They are all proud people," I said, "and we must never act in such a way that appears to ignore their interests."

At 12:30 our private session ended, and the other participants for both sides came in. Brezhnev quoted the Russian proverb that he would invoke several times during the visit. "We say," he remarked to me, " 'Life is always the best teacher.' Life has led us to the conclusion that we must build a new relationship between our countries." Then he turned to the others in the room and announced that he had already invited me to return to Russia in 1974 and that I had accepted the invitation.

I thought back to 1959, when I had sat in this same office for the first meeting between Eisenhower and Khrushchev. Khrushchev had known that he was speaking from a position of weakness and had felt that it was therefore necessary to take a very aggressive and boastful line. Since then the power balance had evened out, particularly as the gap in the decisive area of nuclear development and capability had been closed. Brezhnev could afford to speak more quietly. In 1973 the United States overall still held the stronger hand, but Brezhnev could laugh and clown and vary his stern moods with warmth, based on the confidence that comes from holding very good cards.

That night there was a state dinner in his honor at the White House. As Brezhnev and I greeted the guests in a receiving line in the Blue Room, he was clearly impressed and somewhat surprised by the broad cross section of political, business, and labor leaders, many of whom opposed each other politically but who had gathered socially under the President's roof to meet the Soviet leader. I was reminded again of how isolated the Russians still are by history and geography, as well as by their communist ideology. Several times Brezhnev asked me, "Do they all support the new Soviet-American initiatives?" In my toast I said, "Not only in this room but across this country, regardless of whatever the organization may be, the overwhelming number of Americans support the objective of Soviet-American friendship."

The first talks with Brezhnev held few surprises. He expressed his disappointment that we had not been able to grant MFN status, but he understood that the fault lay beyond my control in Congress. The Soviets were not yet ready to have limitations imposed on their own multiple-warhead missile development, so he remained adamant against expanding the SALT agreements at this summit. He did, however, reluctantly acquiesce in my insistence that we set the end of 1974 instead of 1975 as the deadline for reaching a permanent SALT accord.

At public functions Brezhnev's demeanor remained ebullient. He obviously enjoyed the attention he was receiving, and, like a skilled actor or a born politician, he knew how to hold center stage. At one signing ceremony, he toasted the event so vigorously that he spilled champagne on his suit and hid his face behind a handkerchief in an exaggerated display of embarrassment. At another signing ceremony he initiated an elaborate pantomime of pretending to race me to see who could finish signing the various copies first.

On Tuesday night we went for a sail aboard the *Sequoia* and then boarded helicopters and flew to Camp David to continue our discussions there. I presented him with a windbreaker bearing the Seal of the President with "Camp David" beneath it on one side and "Leonid I. Brezhnev" on the other. He was delighted and wore it most of the time we were there, including during our photo session with the press. I also presented him with an official gift commemorating his American visit: a dark blue Lincoln Continental donated by the manufacturer. It had black velour upholstery and "Special Good Wishes—Greetings" engraved on the dashboard. Brezhnev, a collector of luxury cars, did not attempt to conceal his delight. He insisted upon trying it out immediately. He got behind the wheel and enthusiastically motioned me into the passenger's seat. The head of my Secret Service detail went pale as I climbed in and we took off down one of the narrow roads that run around the perimeter of Camp David. Brezhnev was used to unobstructed driving in the center lane in Moscow, and I could only imagine what would happen if a Secret Service or Navy jeep had suddenly turned a corner onto that one-lane road.

At one point there is a very steep slope with a sign at the top reading, "Slow, dangerous curve." Even driving a golf cart down it, I had to use the brakes in order to avoid going off the road at the sharp turn at the bottom. Brezhnev was driving more than fifty miles an hour as we approached the slope. I reached over and said, "Slow down, slow down," but he paid no attention. When we reached the bottom, there was a squeal of rubber as he slammed on the brakes and made the turn. After our drive he said to me, "This is a very fine automobile. It holds the road very well."

"You are an excellent driver," I replied. "I would never have been able to make that turn at the speed at which we were traveling."

Diplomacy is not always an easy art.

Our meetings at Camp David included long sessions on SALT, European security, and the mutual and balanced force reduction talks concerning the comparative military strengths of the NATO and Warsaw Pact countries.

The most difficult and significant subject we negotiated at Summit II related to the proposed Agreement for the Prevention of Nuclear War. In our contacts before the summit, Brezhnev had strongly urged that we agree to a treaty on the nonuse of nuclear weapons. But Kissinger and I recognized that the practical effect of such a treaty would be to prevent, or at least to inhibit, us from using nuclear weapons in defense of our allies or of our own vital interests. In fact, we felt that a major reason for Brezhnev's interest in a nonuse treaty might be his suspicion that we were about to conclude a military agreement with Peking. The Soviets felt that a renunciation of the use of nuclear weapons would greatly undercut our usefulness to the Chinese in the event of a Sino-Soviet war. The Soviet fears were unfounded as far as our relations with Peking were concerned. But a treaty of the kind they wanted would have wreaked havoc among our NATO allies in Europe and with countries like Israel and Japan that depended on our nuclear protection against the threat of Soviet attack.

In May Kissinger had worked out a formula that went part way in meeting the Soviet proposals without undercutting our allies and other nations that would look to us for assistance if they were subjected to a Soviet attack. Rather than a treaty renouncing nuclear weapons in the event of war, Kissinger proposed that we should both renounce the use of force not only between us but between each of us and third countries, and agree to consult with each other when the danger of the use of nuclear weapons seemed imminent. I knew that Brezhnev would not be completely satisfied with this formula because it did not preclude the further development of our relations with Peking. But it was better than nothing for his purposes, and he agreed to accept it. We signed the agreement on Friday, June 22, in a formal ceremony in the East Room of the White House.

Later that afternoon we flew to California. As we passed over the Grand Canyon en route, *Air Force One* made a low sweep so that Brezhnev could see the spectacular play of light and shadow on the canyon walls. "I've seen many pictures of this in newsreels and in cowboy movies," Brezhnev said.

"Yes," I replied, "John Wayne."

Suddenly he jumped back from the window, hunched his shoulders, put his hands to his hips, and drew imaginary six-shooters from imaginary holsters.

On the short helicopter ride from El Toro to San Clemente, I had Brezhnev sit by the window so that he could get a good view of the freeway network and the suburban landscape beneath us. I could sense that he was impressed, particularly by the number of cars on the roads and by the large number of private houses. I told him that some of the beachfront houses were owned by wealthy people, but most of the others belonged to people who worked in factories and offices and were typical of what he would see if he had the time to travel over other parts of the country.

It was a beautiful summer evening in San Clemente, so I took Brezhnev for a ride in my golf cart. We had suggested that he stay at the commandant's large house at nearby Camp Pendleton Marine Base, but he insisted on staying with us. I think that he wanted to do so in order to emphasize our personal relationship. Although our house in San Clemente is very beautiful, it is very small by the standards of Soviet leaders, who are used to the dachas and villas of Czarist nobles, and it is not at all equipped to accommodate state visitors. The only extra bedrooms were Julie's and Tricia's. Because Tricia had recently redecorated hers, we put Brezhnev there. The room is only about ten by fifteen feet, and Tricia had chosen wallpaper with a large floral design in soft lavender and blue. It was amusing to picture a bear of a man like Brezhnev ensconced amid such feminine decor.

During our talks in Washington and at Camp David, Brezhnev had been very restrained on the subject of China. In a meeting in my San Clemente office on Saturday afternoon, however, he spoke about China for several minutes with only thinly veiled concern. He was apparently still worried that we were contemplating some secret military arrangement, possibly a mutual defense treaty, with the Chinese.

I assured him that, while we would continue our policy of communication with China, we would never make any arrangement with either China or Japan that was inconsistent with the spirit of the Agreement for the Prevention of Nuclear War that we had just signed in Washington. I knew that this was not what he had been getting at, but I could not be in the position of agreeing to establish a reporting relationship with him on our dealings with the Chinese.

I told him that I really did not believe that his concern about the Chinese was justified. He asked me why, and I said that it was not a judgment based on any of the conversations I had had with the Chinese leaders but on the realities of military power. I expressed my opinion that it would be at least twenty years before the Chinese would acquire a sufficient nuclear capability to risk an aggressive action against the Soviet Union or any other major nuclear power.

Brezhnev said that he disagreed with me on this question.

"How long do you think it will be until China becomes a major nuclear country?" I asked him.

He held up his two hands with fingers outspread, and at first it struck me he was making some kind of gesture of surrender, but then he stiffened his fingers and said, "Ten, in ten years, they will have weapons equal to what we have now. We will be further advanced by then, but we must bring home to them that this cannot go on. In 1963, during our Party Congress, I remember how Mao said: 'Let 400 million Chinese die; 300 million will be left.' Such is the psychology of this man." Brezhnev gave the impression that he did not think that the Chinese policies would change, even after Mao's death; he was certain that the entire Chinese leadership was instinctively aggressive.

I turned the conversation to Cambodia, a subject I had already raised several times during our meetings. I pointed out that the renewed North Vietnamese activity there was a major threat to world peace. "If that continues," I said, "the reaction of many people in this country will be that Soviet arms made it possible." Brezhnev became highly agitated and strongly denied that any new Soviet military equipment had been sent to Indochina. He said that the Soviet Union was 100 percent for a speedy termination of the war in Cambodia and Laos, and he promised to speak in strong terms to the North Vietnamese. As far as the appearance of new weapons in the area was concerned, Brezhnev said he thought the Chinese might be responsible, not only for the weapons themselves, but for spreading stories that they were being sent by the Soviets.

At the end of the meeting Brezhnev urged as diplomatically as his obviously strong feelings allowed that we not

427

enter into any military agreements with China. He said that he had refrained from raising the question in 1972, but now he was worried about the future. He asserted that the Soviets had no intention of attacking China. But if China had a military agreement with the United States, he said, "that would confuse the issue."

We adjourned from the ideological rigors of the Sino-Soviet split to a poolside cocktail party. The guest list read like a Hollywood *Who's Who*, and we had a receiving line so that Brezhnev would have a chance to meet everyone. While a strolling mariachi band filled the twilight with gay music, Brezhnev greeted each guest warmly and in several cases showed a familiarity with old movies that indicated either that he had been very well briefed or that he had been spending time in the private screening rooms in the Kremlin.

In my remarks I noted that there were many cowboy and movie stars among the guests, but I reassured Brezhnev that they had checked their pistols and holsters at the door. In response he made a very gracious speech: "I am here in the home of President and Mrs. Nixon, and I feel happy."

After the reception we had a small dinner for him. Our dining room seats only ten people, and we made the dinner deliberately informal so that he could feel at home. In my toast I remarked that he had told me how he usually ate very lightly at the big state dinners, and went home afterward to have a late dinner with his wife, an excellent cook. I said that I considered this private dinner in our home to be even more meaningful than the formal and official dinners we were both so accustomed to attending. I pointed out that he was the first foreign visitor who had ever stayed in our house with us, that he was sleeping in Tricia's room, and that Dobrynin and Gromyko were sharing the small guest cottage that David and Julie stayed in when they visited us together.

"As you can see, Mr. Chairman," I said, "this is not a large house, but it is our home. On such an occasion our thoughts turn away from the affairs of state to our families and loved ones wherever they may be. I want our children to grow up in a world of peace, just as I am sure you want your children and grandchildren to grow up in a world of peace. What the meetings that you and I have had last year and this year have done is contribute to that goal. I only hope that Russians and Americans in future generations may meet as we are meeting in our homes as friends because of our personal affection for each other, and not just as officials meeting because of the necessity of settling differences that may exist between our two countries. Therefore I propose this toast of course to your health, and that of our other guests, but even more to Mrs. Brezhnev, to your children and our children and all the children of the world who, we trust, will have a happier and more peaceful future because of what we have done."

As my toast was translated, Brezhnev's eyes filled with tears. He impulsively got out of his chair and walked toward me. I rose and walked toward him. He threw his arms around me with a real bear hug and then proposed an eloquent toast to Pat and our children and all the children in the world.

After dinner he asked the other guests to excuse us for a moment. Then he took Pat and me aside and said, "We have already exchanged official gifts, but I have brought something with me which is for you and Mrs. Nixon alone." He gave Pat a scarf that had been handwoven by artisans in his home village. "It is a modest gift," he said, "but every stitch in this piece of fabric represents the affection and friendship which all the people of the Soviet Union have for the people of the United States and which Mrs. Brezhnev and I have for you and President Nixon." Tears again came to his eyes as he spoke.

After this rather emotional dinner, Brezhnev said that he was tired because of the three-hour time change from Washington, and he planned to go to bed early. I walked with him to the door of Tricia's room and we said good night there. I decided to have an early night myself, and I was reading in bed in my pajamas around 10:30 when there was a knock at my door. It was a Secret Service agent with a message from Kissinger: the Russians wanted to talk.

I asked Manolo to light a fire in my upstairs study, and I had just finished dressing when Kissinger came in.

"What is this all about?" I asked.

"He says he wants to talk," he replied.

"Is he restless or is this a ploy of some kind?" I asked.

"Who ever knows with them?" Kissinger answered with a shrug.

We went to the study, where Brezhnev, Dobrynin, and Gromyko soon joined us.

"I could not sleep, Mr. President," Brezhnev said with a broad smile.

"It will give us a good opportunity to talk without any distractions," I replied as I settled into my easy chair.

For the next three hours we had a session that in emotional intensity almost rivaled the one on Vietnam at the dacha during Summit I. This time the subject was the Middle East, with Brezhnev trying to browbeat me into imposing on Israel a settlement based on Arab terms. He kept hammering at what he described as the need for the two of us to agree, even if only privately, on a set of "principles" to govern a Middle East settlement. As examples of such principles, he cited the withdrawal of Israeli troops from all the occupied territories, the recognition of national boundaries, the free passage of ships through the Suez Canal, and international guarantees of the settlement.

I pointed out that there was no way that I could agree to any such "principles" without prejudicing Israel's rights. I insisted that the important thing was to get talks started between the Arabs and the Israelis, and I argued that if we laid down controversial principles beforehand, both parties would refuse to talk—in which case the principles would have defeated their purpose.

Brezhnev was blunt and adamant. He said that without at least an informal agreement on such principles he would be leaving this summit empty-handed. He even hinted that without such an agreement on principles he could not guarantee that war would not resume.

At one point he made a show of looking at his watch and furrowing his brow. "Perhaps I am tiring you out," he said. "But we must reach an understanding."

As firmly as he kept demanding that we agree on such principles—in effect, that we jointly impose a settlement that would heavily favor the Arabs—I refused, reiterating that the important thing was to get talks started between the parties themselves.

This testy midnight session was a reminder of the unchanging and unrelenting Communist motivations beneath the diplomatic veneer of détente. Brezhnev was aware of the slow but steady progress we had been making in reopening the lines of communication between Washington and the Arab capitals; and he was also aware that if America was able to contribute toward a peaceful settlement of Arab-Israeli differences, we would be striking a serious blow to the Soviet presence and prestige in the Middle East. From his point of view, therefore, his use of shock tactics at the ostensibly impromptu meeting in my study in San Clemente was a calculated risk. Brezhnev could not seriously have expected me to rise to the meager bait he held out in return for what would amount to our abandoning Israel. Whether he already had a commitment to the Arabs to support an attack against Israel is not clear, but I am confident that the firmness I showed that night reinforced the seriousness of the message I conveyed to the Soviets when I ordered a military alert four months later during the Yom Kippur War.

In the joint communiqué Brezhnev and I signed the next morning there was no effort to use diplomatic language to conceal that we had not been able to reach any common ground for our differing views on this difficult subject. The short section on the Middle East stated, "Each of the parties set forth its position on this problem."

Brezhnev and I made our parting remarks in front of microphones in the flower garden next to the house. He said that he would see me next time in Moscow. At the end he said "goodbye" in English.

After Brezhnev left, I tried to put Summit II in perspective. It was too soon after the 1972 SALT agreements for another major breakthrough in that area, but I did make it clear at every opportunity that 1974 would be the year of decision, when we would have to make progress in ironing out our differences, particularly on offensive weapons. I knew that the Soviets were moving much faster than we were in this area. Unless we got some agreement soon, we might face a situation in which we would be weaker than the

Soviets in the eyes of our allies, our friends, and the neutral countries. Therefore, in addition to pinning Brezhnev down to a new agreement by the end of 1974, I specified that we would be talking about reductions and not just limitations of nuclear weapons.

There were several important agreements signed at Summit II covering specific areas: transportation, agriculture, oceanic studies, taxation, commercial aviation, the peaceful uses of atomic energy, and trade. These continued the process that we had begun in 1972 of building an interlocking web of relationships to increase the Soviets' stake in stability and cooperation.

This summit also gave me an opportunity to get to know Brezhnev better and to try to take his measure as a leader and as a man. I had spent forty-two hours with him in 1972, and now thirty-five hours with him in 1973. However superficial this kind of personal contact may be, it can still provide important insights.

I found Brezhnev more interesting and impressive than I had during our first meeting. Away from the constraints of the Kremlin he was able to indulge the more human and political sides of his personality. At one of the signing ceremonies, when his antics made him the center of attention, I jokingly said, "He's the best politician in this room!" He seemed to accept my statement as the highest possible praise.

His conduct and humor were almost impish at many of his public appearances. Whenever possible, I acted as his straight man on these occasions, but it was sometimes difficult for me to balance politeness against dignity.

Brezhnev showed the typically Russian combination of great discipline at times with total lack of it at others. An amusing symbol of this inconsistency was his fancy new cigarette case with a built-in timer that automatically rationed out one cigarette per hour. This was the way he was going to cut down on his chain-smoking. As each hour began, he would ceremoniously remove the allotted cigarette and close the box. Then, a few minutes later, he would reach into his jacket and take another cigarette from the ordinary pack that he also carried. Thus he was able to continue his habit of chain-smoking until the timer went off and he could take another virtuous cigarette from the box.

432

At Summit I, I could not help making mental comparisons between Brezhnev and Khrushchev. During Summit II, however, I had a chance to observe and analyze the differences between them in more depth and detail. They were alike in the sense that they were both tough, hard, and realistic leaders. Both interlarded their conversation with anecdotes. Khrushchev was often quite vulgar; Brezhnev, however, was just earthy. Whereas Khrushchev had been crass and blustering, Brezhnev was expansive and more courteous. Both had a good sense of humor, but Khrushchev more often seemed to be using his at the expense of others around him. Khrushchev seemed to be quicker in his mental reflexes. In discussions, Brezhnev was hard-hitting, incisive, and always very deliberate, whereas Khrushchev had tended to be more explosive and more impulsive. Both men had tempers, and both were emotional. I was struck by the simple look of pride on Brezhnev's face as he told me that he was about to become a great-grandfather, and that we now had still another generation for which to guarantee peace.

Despite the shortness of Brezhnev's visit, I felt that he had seen a diversity of American life for which no briefing books and studies could possibly have prepared him. I know that he returned home with a far better understanding of America and Americans than he had before he came.

On June 25, the day Brezhnev left Washington, the House of Representatives agreed to a Senate bill immediately cutting off funds for U.S. bombing actions in Cambodia. The effect of this bill was to deny me the means to enforce the Vietnam peace agreement. We were faced with having to abandon our support of the Cambodians who were trying to hold back the Communist Khmer Rouge, who were being supplied and supported by the North Vietnamese in violation of the peace agreement. The Cambodians were completely and justifiably bewildered; they could not understand why we were suddenly deserting them—especially when the military tide seemed to be turning in their favor.

Congress, however, was not prepared to hear any arguments and was determined to go forward despite the consequences. This congressional insensitivity had been dramatically symbolized a few weeks earlier as Kissinger was preparing to leave for a meeting with Le Duc Tho over violations of the cease-fire agreement. We had pleaded with Congress not to send Kissinger to Paris with no negotiating leverage, but Mike Mansfield's response was typical: he offered his "sympathies" but nothing more. In short order, two separate Senate committees voted to cut off funds for combat activities.

The cutoff bill passed on June 25. I vetoed it, and in my veto statement I said, "After more than ten arduous years of suffering and sacrifice . . . it would be nothing short of tragic if this great accomplishment, bought with the blood of so many Asians and Americans, were to be undone now by congressional action." The House of Representatives sustained my veto the same day, June 27, but it seemed clear that another cutoff bill would be proposed and that I could not win these battles forever. Therefore, we agreed to a compromise that set August 15, 1973, as the date for the termination of U.S. bombing in Cambodia and required congressional approval for the funding of U.S. military action in any part of Indochina. At least this gave us more time, but the invitation to aggression represented in any cutoff date remained unchanged.

I was determined that the historical record would mark Congress's responsibility for this reckless act, and on August 3, shortly before the scheduled mandatory cutoff, I wrote to House Speaker Carl Albert and Senate Majority Leader Mike Mansfield:

> This abandonment of a friend will have a profound impact in other countries, such as Thailand, which have relied on the constancy and determination of the United States, and I want the Congress to be fully aware of the consequences of its action. . . . In particular, I want the brave and beleaguered Cambodian people to know that the end to the bombing in Cambodia does not signal an abdication of America's determination to work for a lasting peace in Indochina. . . .
>
> I can only hope that the North Vietnamese will not draw the erroneous conclusion from this congressional action that they are free to launch a military offensive in other areas in Indochina. North Vietnam would be making a very dangerous error if it mistook the cessation of bombing in Cambodia for

an invitation to fresh aggression or further violations of the Paris agreements. The American people would respond to such aggression with appropriate action.

I knew that since Congress had removed the possibility of military action I had only words with which to threaten. The Communists knew it too. During this period Kissinger held one of his regular luncheon meetings with Dobrynin. When Kissinger raised the question of the Communist violations of the cease-fire in Cambodia, the Soviet ambassador scornfully asked what we had expected, now that we had no negotiating leverage because of the bombing cutoff imposed by Congress. Kissinger tried to be as menacing as he could, even though he knew that Dobrynin was right.

"There should be no illusion that we will forget who put us in this uncomfortable position," he said.

"In that case," Dobrynin replied, "you should go after Senator Fulbright, not us."

For more than two years after the peace agreement the South Vietnamese had held their own against the Communists. This proved the will and mettle of the South Vietnamese people and their desire to live in freedom. It also proved that Vietnamization had succeeded. When Congress reneged on our obligations under the agreements, the Communists predictably rushed in to fill the gap. The congressional bombing cutoff, coupled with the limitation placed on the President by the War Powers Resolution in November 1973, set off a string of events that led to the Communist takeover in Cambodia and, on April 30, 1975, the North Vietnamese conquest of South Vietnam.

Congress denied first to me, and then to President Ford, the means to enforce the Paris agreement at a time when the North Vietnamese were openly violating it. Even more devastating and inexcusable, in 1974 Congress began cutting back on military aid for South Vietnam at a time when the Soviets were increasing their aid to North Vietnam. As a result, when the North Vietnamese launched their all-out invasion of the South in the spring of 1975, they had an advantage in arms, and the threat of American action to enforce the agreement removed. A year after the collapse of South Vietnam, the field commander in charge of Hanoi's final offensive cited the cutback in American aid as a major factor in North Vietnam's victory. He remarked that Thieu "was then forced to fight a poor man's war," with his firepower reduced by 60 percent and his mobility reduced by half because of lack of aircraft, vehicles, and fuel.

The war and the peace in Indochina that America had won at such cost over twelve years of sacrifice and fighting were lost within a matter of months once Congress refused to fulfill our obligations. And it is Congress that must bear the responsibility for the tragic results. Hundreds of thousands of anti-Communist South Vietnamese and Cambodians have been murdered or starved to death by their conquerors, and the bloodbath continues.

Congress's tragic and irresponsible action, which fatally undermined the peace we had won in Indochina, was buried amid the media's preoccupation with John Dean's testimony before the Ervin Committee. On Monday, June 25, when Dean took the stand, all over the country—even in the compound in San Clemente—the hypnotic monotone of his voice drew people to their television sets. The three television networks gave these sessions all-day gavel-to-gavel coverage.

JOHN DEAN TESTIFIES

Dean testified for five days. It took him one full day to read his 245-page opening statement, which contained most of his charges against me. The cornerstone of his testimony was his accusation that for at least six months, since my meeting with him on September 15, 1972, I had been an active complicitor in the Watergate cover-up. *Dean Tells Panel President Discussed Cover-up in September, March, April* was the Washington *Post* headline after his first day of testimony; *Dean Tells Inquiry That Nixon Took Part in Watergate Cover-up for Eight Months* was the headline in the New York *Times*.

I did not watch the hearings, but the reports I read filled me with frustration and anger. Dean, I felt, was re-creating history in the image of his own defense.

Dean testified that on September 15, 1972, he had expressly discussed the Watergate cover-up with me. He stated that he had specifically told me that he could make no assurance the whole thing would not "unravel" someday, and that he had expressed his concern that "the cover-up" could not be "maintained indefinitely." He said that he had told me that all he had done was "assist in keeping it out of the White House" and that I had expressed appreciation for the difficult job he had performed. Dean said that he, thinking of Magruder's perjury, had told me that others had done more difficult things than he.

As the tape of that conversation shows, Dean had not said anything about others having done more "difficult things" or about his "keeping it out of the White House." Nor had he said anything about things starting to "unravel." On the tape, in fact, he said exactly the opposite: "Three months ago," he said, "I would have had trouble predicting where we'd be today. I think that I can say that fifty-four days from now that not a thing will come crashing down to our surprise."

There were ambiguous statements on the tape, to be sure. For example, I had talked about "putting your fingers in the dikes every time that leaks have sprung." But I was thinking of the fact that he was monitoring so many congressional, civil, and criminal investigations that had potential political impact. It was clear from the tape that however much Dean was concentrating on the criminal vulnerabilities, I was concentrating solely on the potential for political embarrassment.

Dean testified that in our meeting on February 28, 1973, he had described for me his own legal problems concerning "obstruction of justice." He said that he had given me a "general picture" of his "conduit activities" and left me clearly aware of his role in the "cover-up." Here too the tape shows that exactly the opposite occurred. In that meeting I had said to Dean that he, at least, had no vulnerability to the Watergate committee: "I think they realize you are the lawyer and they know you didn't have a goddamn thing to do with the campaign," I said.

"That's right," Dean had replied.

The tape shows that I said that the important thing about the whole Watergate mess was my own isolation from it. "That, fortunately, is totally true," I said.

"I know that, sir," he had affirmed.

Now, four months later, he was testifying that this conversation was one of the reasons he was convinced of my involvement in the cover-up.

Dean testified that on March 13 he had told me about the money being paid to the Watergate defendants. If that were true, it would have undercut my public assertion that I had first learned about the cover-up on March 21. But Dean was wrong, and it seemed to me that he must have deliberately changed the correct date, because as recently as our conversation of April 16, 1973, he had remembered that our "cancer on the presidency" discussion had taken place "on the Wednesday before they were sentenced"—and that was March 21.

In his testimony concerning the meeting of March 17 Dean made another omission that seemed too significant to be accidental. This was the meeting in which he had told me about the break-in at Ellsberg's psychiatrist's office. As the tape shows, I had reacted with utter shock. But Dean apparently wanted to leave an impression that knowledge of the Ellsberg break-in was a motive for my role in the Watergate cover-up. He testified that the meeting consisted of a "rambling conversation" with only brief reference to Pat Gray's confirmation hearings and the general problems confronting the White House. That same day I observed that, unlike others, he had not participated in the break-in and had no criminal liability. "That's right," Dean agreed.

Dean testified that on March 21, 1973, he had finally told me everything. He said flatly under questioning: "On March 21 I certainly told the President everything I knew at that point in time." As the tape proves, however, he did not tell me the extent of his active involvement in suborning perjury, in promising clemency, or in revealing confidential FBI information to the lawyers for the CRP. He did not tell me, nor did he tell the Watergate Committee, that he had also destroyed evidence from Howard Hunt's safe. He minimized his role in the fund-raising and said his primary problem was the fact that he had been a "conduit of information" on paying blackmail to defendants. Because of all these things I thought he was being inadvertently, unfairly, and tangentially drawn in; as late as March 26 I had dictated in my diary that Dean had always acted as counsel, giving his best advice and "avoiding anything that would smack of illegal or improper activities."

Dean implied that since the first days after the break-in everyone in the White House shared the understanding that there was White House "involvement" in the Watergate bugging, even if there was no direct participation in ordering the June 17 break-in. But in March I was stunned by his assertion that Gordon Strachan knew about the existence of the bug, and the information that a Colson phone call may have triggered it—and this was nine months after the break-in.

In his testimony Dean said that I had "never at any time" asked him to write a report concerning Watergate. In fact, I had pointedly suggested on March 22 that he go to Camp David, away from the phone, and prepare a written report.

Dean now implied that from the beginning he had had actual knowledge of Magruder's involvement and perjury and that everyone else did too. Yet on a tape from March 22 Haldeman says of Magruder: "On the other hand, we don't, we can't, prove he perjured himself, that's Dean's opinion." On March 26 Dean was still saying that he did not have any firsthand "off-the-record" knowledge of whether Magruder was involved in the break-in and therefore he could not be sure whether Magruder had committed perjury.

In the spring both Haldeman and I had repeatedly urged Dean to put out the full story regarding Segretti, and he had consistently resisted; now he charged that the White House effort to "cover-up" the Segretti episode was "consistent with other parts of the general White House cover-up" which followed Watergate. Similarly, he now insisted that our efforts to thwart a partisan pre-election move to hold congressional hearings on Watergate were in part an effort to avoid "unraveling the cover-up"; at the time, however, I had analyzed the problem of the hearings this way: "That's what this is, public relations." "That's all it is," John Dean had agreed.

Dean claimed that during March and April Haldeman

and Ehrlichman had tried to protect themselves at his expense and that he had only been concerned that the truth be told. Ironically, it had been Dean who had done the manipulating. In March he minimized the problem his testimony would pose to others, apparently hoping to gain White House sponsorship for immunity. "Let's say the President sent me to the grand jury to make a report," he said on the afternoon of March 21, "who could I actually do anything to or cause any problems for? As a practical matter, firsthand knowledge, almost no one." After his first contacts with the prosecutors he kept up his phone calls to Haldeman, his appearance of mutual concern, and his references to "potential" problems on the cover-up, problems he thought possibly could be handled. Only in mid-April, when his bargaining with the prosecutors was under way, did he let it be known that Haldeman and Ehrlichman were in fact his bargaining chips and that he had been positioning himself to get the most from their destruction.

I saw John Dean's testimony on Watergate as an artful blend of truth and untruth, of possible sincere misunderstandings and clearly conscious distortions. In an effort to mitigate his own role, he transplanted his own total knowledge of the cover-up and his own anxiety onto the words and actions of others. In an effort to seem just a subordinate actor, he took the many different levels of understanding, awareness, and concern of those around him and fused them into one.

But as soon as Dean's testimony was over, I once again made the mistake I had been making since the Watergate break-in: I worried about the wrong problem. I went off on a tangent, concentrating all our attention and resources on trying to refute Dean by pointing out his exaggerations, distortions, discrepancies. But even as we geared up to do this, the real issue had already changed. It no longer made any difference that not all of Dean's testimony was accurate. It only mattered if *any* of his testimony was accurate. And Dean's account of the crucial March 21 meeting was more accurate than my own had been. I did not see it then, but in the end it would make less difference that I was not as involved as Dean had alleged than that I was not as uninvolved as I had claimed.

There was another respect in which Dean's testimony caught us unprepared. According to news reports, the Ervin Committee's Democratic members and staff had urged Dean to be sure to build up his opening statement with plenty of "atmospherics" about the White House. He readily obliged, and even more than what he had to say about Watergate, it was from this that we would never recover. This was what gave the political opposition the one thing that they could only have dreamed of: a way of metastasizing Watergate into the other areas of my administration. John Dean dredged up every political machination he could find and offered them as representative of everything we did. He forced the Nixon White House through the prism of his own defense—which was that he was largely the victim of the environment—and produced a portrait devoid of dreams, ideals, serious work, or important goals. He talked about my attempt to have the IRS do checks on our political opponents with no attempt to show how widespread the practice had been among the Democrats in previous years. The fact that we had hired a political investigator was treated as a sinister innovation, when in fact checking up on the political opposition has been part of politics since time out of mind. We paid our investigator with political funds; other administrations had even used the FBI. Dean produced an "enemies list," which even he has since admitted was vastly overplayed by the media. Into all this he folded controversial national security activities—the seventeen wiretaps designed to find the source of foreign policy leaks, the Huston Plan, and the Plumbers—ascribed them to paranoia, and made no effort or attempt to re-create the valid concerns that had produced them.

If the May 22 statement was the American public's first introduction to covert activities undertaken by the government for national security, Dean's testimony was a primer in the dark underside of White House politics. Thanks to the way he did it, everything was perfectly arranged for the Democrats to distance themselves from their own political past and proclaim that my administration had invented original sin.

The Ervin Committee, formally the Senate Select Committee on Presidential Campaign Activities, was a fascinat-

441

ing study in the weaknesses of human nature in general, and in particular of the partisanship and weaknesses of congressional human nature when exposed to massive publicity. The senators and their staffs soon made the heady discovery that whatever they said—or leaked—made news. The result was a steady hemorrhage of leaks usually aimed at undermining the defense of potential witnesses such as Haldeman, Ehrlichman, and Mitchell.

Mike Mansfield publicly chastised the committee. Archibald Cox later compared their tactics to McCarthy's. Senator James Buckley suggested that Ervin interrogate the staff under oath to see who was doing it. Ervin's reply was that that would injure morale. An occasion when a leaker was tracked down and punished exemplified the committee's standard of fairness: Majority Counsel Samuel Dash suspended a staff member who leaked unfavorable comments about Samuel Dash.

The Justice Department prosecutors complained that the committee's leaks and hearings were shattering their cases, and Special Prosecutor Archibald Cox appealed to Ervin not to proceed with open hearings because the publicity would undermine the chance that a prospective defendant could receive a fair trial. Earl Warren had once called it "frontier justice" to haul prospective defendants up before public hearings. But Ervin said that everything had to be done to air the truth. It didn't take long to discover that they had a very special truth in mind.

For example, among the documents the Ervin Committee received from John Dean were two memoranda from Hoover's assistant, William Sullivan. They outlined sensational political abuses of the FBI by earlier Democratic administrations. Ervin's executive assistant announced that the committee would not go into these matters because the allegations were "far, far too personal" and unsubstantiated. "Personal cheap shots," he called them, "rather distasteful."

The original draft of the committee's final report was going to call an aspect of George McGovern's postcampaign fund distribution an "apparent violation of the spirit of the law." When McGovern objected, Ervin had the section removed.

In 1964 Lyndon Johnson's protégé and Senate aide Bobby Baker had been charged with having run a high-finance influence-peddling operation. Many felt that the scandal touched and possibly implicated several Senators and even Johnson, who by then was President. The Democratic majority in Congress voted to keep the Baker case out of public hearings and refused to call any White House aides to testify. Three members of the Ervin Committee—Ervin himself and Senators Daniel Inouye of Hawaii and Herman Talmadge of Georgia—had gone on record seven times to restrict any congressional investigation of the Bobby Baker case. They evidently felt that Watergate deserved a special exception.

Maury Stans was lectured by Ervin for having used dummy committees for campaign funds. Senator Joseph Montoya of New Mexico later claimed that he was "shocked" by the discovery of forgeries on his own campaign finance report, and had no comment when it was reported that $100,000 had been put into dummy committees in Washington after the money had been laundered to prevent disclosure.

The Democrats' chief committee investigator was Carmine Bellino, whose prior political activity for the Kennedys had included tailing a former Republican Congressman during the 1960 campaign. Ervin praised him as a "faithful public servant of exemplary character."

As the first group of witnesses came before the committee, their treatment was in direct response to their willingness to grovel and to implicate others. If they stood up and defended themselves, they were badgered and humiliated. If they exhibited at least a modicum of self-abnegation, they were given first lectures and then commendations. Bernard Levin, the London *Times*'s political commentator, wrote:

> The conduct of the Chairman, Senator Sam Ervin, is so deplorable that the lack of any serious protest against his behavior is in itself a measure of the loss of nerve on the part of so many distinguished Americans, in the press, the academic world and politics itself, who would once, in similar circumstances, have been campaigning vigorously to bring him to heel. . . .
> Worse, however, than Senator Ervin's yokum-hokum is the way in which he has clearly decided that some of those appearing before him under suspicion of various malpractices are heroes, and some villains. . . . The technique, of course,

was exactly the one used by Senator Joseph McCarthy. . . .

What is really wrong with this inquisition is that it appears to be a judicial process but is in fact a political one. . . . Men are having their reputations destroyed in full view of millions; worse, men who may shortly have to face a criminal trial are having their cases literally prejudged, without any of the safeguards of true legal proceedings.

The Democrats on the committee were able to get away with such tactics because they were the majority and because the Republicans were understandably nervous about Watergate. The Republicans on the committee, with the exception of Weicker, worked diligently and seriously to follow up on leads they thought would provide balance. But they had neither the money, the manpower, nor an objective press to help promote and publicize their work.

A fitting epitaph to the fairness and standards employed by the Ervin Committee was provided by Senator Ervin himself when, on March 10, 1974, UPI reported a conversation with him in which he said that an impeachable offense had to be a federal crime and that "no evidence was produced in the Senate Watergate hearings to support impeachment." Another reporter present at the same interview at the same time had written the identical story, so clearly that was what he had said. Before long, Ervin was confronted with the political import of his statement and the adverse effect it might have on the Democratic impeachment move then under way. Finding himself trapped between political necessity and the dictates of principle, he made a quick and ironic choice: despite the documentation refuting him, he apparently chose to contain the damage by denying that he had ever made the statement.

Most Americans are resigned to a modicum of hypocrisy in politics. I am convinced, however, the historians will eventually conclude that even the serious issues raised and abuses revealed by Watergate did not justify such abuses of power as were committed by members of the Ervin Committee. With their prejudicial leaks, their double standards, and their grandstanding behavior, they only confirmed my feeling that this was a partisan attack, a determined effort to turn something minor into something major, and we had to fight back.

There was ample historical precedent for refusing to permit testimony by any White House aides before the Ervin Committee. But I recognized that with the emotional climate now surrounding Watergate, there would be little public tolerance or understanding if I did so. Therefore I waived all executive privilege and permitted members of the White House staff to submit to the Ervin panel's questions. The result was an unprecedented degree of cooperation by the executive branch with a congressional inquiry: 118 hours of public testimony from present and former White House aides and hundreds of hours in informal or private sessions. Even so, the committee members were not satisfied. They still wanted open access to White House files.

Under the Constitution the three branches of government operate like a three-part free-standing scale: each compensates, supplements, and checks the others. But no one branch has the right to dominate, by demanding and receiving the internal working documents of another. The precedent for this point of view goes back to George Washington, who as President refused to surrender executive branch documents to the House of Representatives.

Sam Ervin himself had defended congressional immunity to subpoenas from another branch in 1972, after Democratic Senator Mike Gravel of Alaska read portions of the classified text of the Pentagon Papers into the *Congressional Record*. The question that reached the Supreme Court was whether one of Gravel's aides could legally be compelled to testify about the senator's unauthorized reading of the papers, and Ervin was one of those who argued in a friend-of-the-court brief that one branch should not be allowed to compel testimony about the internal affairs of another branch. The brief insisted: "If an aide must feel that the advice he offers, the knowledge he has, and the assistance he gives to his senator may be called into question by the executive, then he is likely to refrain from acting on those very occasions when the issues are the most controversial and when the senator is most in need of assistance."

Ervin had demonstrated the same approach to the separation of powers in an earlier case involving another of his Democratic friends. During the hearings after Johnson nominated Abe Fortas as Chief Justice, Ervin asked Fortas about a discussion he had had with the President but immediately and genially added, "I will not insist upon your answer because it is a prerogative of communications in the executive branch of the government." He was not to be so genial when given a partisan advantage against a Republican President during Watergate.

On July 7 I sent a letter to Ervin anticipating a formal request for presidential papers. I noted that when historical precedent was examined, our cooperation with the investigation was already extraordinary. There were rumors that they were going to subpoena me personally, so I reminded them that when Harry Truman had been subpoenaed to appear before a committee of Congress in 1953, he had refused.

I told the members of the committee that, like Truman, I would not appear, nor would I provide documents:

> No President could function if the private papers of his office, prepared by his personal staff, were open to public scrutiny. Formulation of sound public policy requires that the President and his personal staff be able to communicate among themselves in complete candor, and that their tentative judgments, their exploration of alternatives, and their frank comments on issues and personalities at home and abroad remain confidential.

Ervin, despite his erstwhile defense of the virtues of separation of powers and the concept of privileged communications, now denounced my "abstruse arguments about separation of powers and executive privilege." On July 12 he sent a letter to the White House saying that he feared our two positions "presented the very grave possibility of a fundamental constitutional confrontation." He requested a meeting to try to avoid such a conflict. It was typical that Ervin's letter to me was leaked to reporters even before it had been delivered to the White House, and that we first learned about it from the reports on the news wires.

THE WHITE HOUSE TAPES REVEALED

I awakened at 5:30 A.M. on July 12 with a stabbing pain in my chest. It had begun before I went to bed; now it was

446

nearly unbearable. It reminded me of the pain I experienced when I had cracked a rib playing football at Whittier. I switched on the light and tried to read, but I was too uncomfortable to be able to concentrate, so I turned the light out again and lay awake until morning.

The White House physicians gave me a brief examination and arrived at different diagnoses: Dr. Tkach thought it was pneumonia; Dr. William Lukash thought it might be simply a digestive disorder. They agreed that I should have a complete battery of tests.

I was lying restlessly in bed about midday when Haig came in and told me that Senator Ervin was on the phone and wanted to speak with me. He was calling about his letter. We talked for sixteen minutes. My voice was subdued because every breath I took caused a sharp pain.

Ervin began by saying that his committee had sent me "a little note."

"I read about your letter," I answered. "Your committee leaks, you know."

He said he did not know how his letter had gotten into the papers and that while they did not want to have a confrontation, they took the view that executive privilege did not cover criminal or political acts. "You want your staff to go through presidential files," I said. "The answer is no. We disagree on that. But I'll think over your letter."

Even this short exchange had fatigued me, but I went on. "What is it you specifically want? I am not going to have anyone going through all my files. We should start, if we have this meeting, by your telling me the areas you think you want."

He said he thought that staff members could work out specifics, but he repeated the totally unacceptable formulation in his letter that had requested presidential papers "relevant to any matters the committee is authorized to investigate." Taken literally, this would mean that his staff would have to go through *all* the papers just to be able to know which ones they wanted to request.

Despite the pain I raised my voice slightly. "Your attitude in the hearings was clear. There's no question who you're out to get," I said.

"We are not out to get anything, Mr. President," he said, "except the truth."

I settled back onto the bed and told him that no one from his staff was going to go through any White House files. I said I was willing to consider a meeting—but just between him and me. "A man-to-man talk might be useful," I said. "I'm cooperating in every way possible, but I have the responsibility to defend the office of the President—just as you thought you had to defend the concept of separation of powers before the Supreme Court. If you have the same objective you had in Gravel's case, we'll get along just fine."

He seemed a bit nonplussed and indicated that he was not optimistic about our being able to work things out. He said he would report to the committee and insisted again that it was not out to get anybody.

I looked up at Haig and Ziegler, who had been in the room during the call. I told them it must have been the fever that had kept me from giving Ervin the cool answers that undoubtedly would have been more effective for our cause. "But," I added, "I said what I believe."

I got up and dressed, and despite the fact that I had a 102-degree temperature, I decided to keep my scheduled appointments for that day. There is a national commotion every time a President is even the slightest bit ill, so I wanted to postpone any indication that I was not feeling well until the last possible moment. I had a half-hour meeting with West German Foreign Minister Walter Scheel, and then Bill Timmons came in to discuss legislative problems. After that I received a report from the members of a commission I had appointed to study the question of fire prevention.

When the schedule was completed, chest X-rays were taken, which confirmed Tkach's diagnosis: I had viral pneumonia. That evening I was driven to Bethesda Naval Hospital.

I was determined to show that even in the hospital I was able to carry out my duties as President. As I received inhalation therapy and underwent tests and X-rays, I continued to take calls and to see Ziegler and Haig. I phoned Kissinger and reviewed the plans for Phase IV of our economic policy with Shultz. The worst thing about the pneumonia was the inability to sleep because the discomfort was so great. During the nights I lay awake counting the minutes. I ended up staying on the phone until late at night, checking on the day's events.

By Sunday, July 15, my temperature had dropped below 100 degrees. For the first time since I entered the hospital I was able to eat a full meal. I had even slept two full hours on Saturday night.

Early Monday morning Haig called to tell me that Haldeman's former aide Alex Butterfield had revealed the existence of the White House taping system to the Ervin Committee staff and that it would become public knowledge later that day.

I was shocked by this news. As impossible as it must seem now, I had believed that the existence of the White House taping system would never be revealed. I thought that at least executive privilege would have been raised by any staff member before verifying its existence.

The impact of the revelation of our taping system was stunning. The headline in the New York *Daily News* was *Nixon Bugged Own Offices*.

Fred Buzhardt sent a letter to Ervin confirming that the system described by Butterfield did exist and pointing out that it was similar to the one that had been employed by the previous administration. Buzhardt's letter provoked swift reactions laced with righteous indignation. *LBJ Aides Disavow System* was the Washington *Post*'s headline. Johnson's former domestic aide, Joseph Califano, said, "I think this is an outrageous smear on a dead President." Arthur Schlesinger, Jr., said that it was "inconceivable" that John Kennedy would have approved such a taping system. Kennedy's former aide, Dave Powers, then curator of the Kennedy Library, denied that there were tapes. But Army Signal Corps technicians who had installed the Johnson taping system gave Fred Buzhardt sworn affidavits about the placement of the machines and microphones, and within a few days the archivist at the Johnson Library in Austin confirmed the existence of the LBJ tapes. Then, the next day, the Kennedy Library admitted that in fact there were 125 tapes and 68 Dictabelt recordings of different meetings and phone conversations.

Haig and I spent several hours in my hospital room

talking about what the revelation of the existence of the tapes would mean. I reflected ironically that just a few months before, on April 10, after I had met with two of the POWs, I had told Haldeman to get rid of all the tapes except those dealing with important national security events. I had made a diary note about it afterward.

Diary

I had meetings with Stockdale and Flynn today. They were just as moving as the meetings I had had earlier with Risner and with Denton. I hope that we have tapes of these conversations.

As a matter of fact, I had a good talk with Haldeman about the tapes—decided that we would go back over the period of time that they have been taken and destroy them except for the national security periods in Cambodia, May 8, and probably December 18, having in mind the fact that otherwise either he or I would be the only ones that could listen to the tapes and decide what could be used—and that would take us just months and months of time.

But this discussion had taken place in the midst of our concerns about Watergate, and three weeks later he was no longer there to do it.

In the hospital I raised the idea of whether we should not destroy the tapes now. Haig said he would have a talk with the lawyers about it. In the meantime we agreed that the taping system itself must be removed.

Over the next three days, while the doctors anxiously tried to keep my meetings to a minimum, I discussed the situation with Haig, Ziegler, Buzhardt, and Garment. Legally the tapes would not actually be evidence until they were subpoenaed. But since we knew that the Ervin Committee or the Special Prosecutor would subpoena them momentarily, it would be a highly controversial move to destroy them. Nonetheless, Buzhardt felt that the tapes were my personal property and he favored destroying them. Garment considered the tapes to be evidence, and while he did not favor releasing them, he made it clear that he would strongly oppose any move to destroy them. Haig made the telling point that, apart from the legal problems it might create, destruction of the tapes would forever seal an impression of guilt in the public mind. When Ted Agnew came to the hospital to visit, he told me I should destroy them.

We contacted Haldeman to find out what he thought I should do. His advice was to claim executive privilege and not surrender an inch of principle to the witch-hunting of Ervin and his committee staff. Haldeman said that the tapes were still our best defense, and he recommended that they not be destroyed.

When I had entered the hospital on July 12, I had been looking forward to fighting our way out of the slump into which Dean's testimony had sent us. But by the time I prepared to leave the hospital on July 20, the revelation of the tapes had changed everything. In the early morning hours of July 19 I had made a note on my bedside pad:

> We must go forward on the business of government for three years. It's the only way we can get by this ordeal. We mustn't let this continuing investigation get to us as the revelation of the existence of the tapes did to Garment and some of the members of the staff. We must be strong and competent. We must go ahead.
> Should have destroyed the tapes after April 30, 1973.

It was a beautiful summer day when I returned to the White House from the hospital. Most of the staff had come out to the Rose Garden to greet me, and as I walked up the steps to the Oval Office I turned around and spoke to them. That brief speech remains my favorite of all the statements I made during this difficult period:

> I feel that we have so little time in the positions that all of us hold and so much to do. With all that we have to do and so little time to do it, at the end of the next three and a half years to look back and think that, but for that day, something went undone that might have been done that would have made a difference in whether we have peace in the world or a better life here at home, that would be the greatest frustration of all.

I turned to the predictable comments the staff would be hearing that, because of my illness and the rough assaults being directed toward me, I should consider either slowing down or resigning. I gave my answer to that idea in one of my father's favorite words: "poppycock." I talked about all the things we could accomplish—prosperity without war, controlling crime, drugs, providing opportunity. Then I said:

> There are these and other great causes that we were elected overwhelmingly to carry forward in November. And what we were elected to do we are going to do, and let others wallow in Watergate, we are going to do our job.

If I had indeed been the knowing Watergate conspirator that I was charged as being, I would have recognized in 1973 that the tapes contained conversations that would be fatally damaging. I would have seen that if I were to survive, they would have to be destroyed.

Many factors bore on my decision not to destroy the tapes. When I listened to them for the first time on June 4, 1973, I recognized that they were a mixed bag as far as I was concerned. There was politically embarrassing talk on them, and they contained many ambiguities, but I recognized that they indisputably disproved Dean's basic charge that I had conspired with him in an obstruction of justice over an eight-month period. I had not listened to the March 21 tape, but Haldeman had, and while I knew it would be difficult to explain in the critical and hostile atmosphere that now existed, he had told me that it could be explained, and I wanted to believe that he was right.

I was also persuaded by Haig's reasoning that destruction of the tapes would create an indelible impression of guilt, and I simply did not believe that the revelation of anything I had actually done would be as bad as that impression. On Saturday, July 21, I made a note outlining this rationale: "If I had discussed illegal action, I would not have taped. If I had discussed illegal action and had taped I would have destroyed the tapes once the investigation began."

Finally I decided that the tapes were my best insurance against the unforeseeable future. I was prepared to believe that others, even people close to me, would turn against me just as Dean had done, and in that case the tapes would give me at least some protection.

Once I had decided not to destroy the tapes, I had to decide whether to release them to the Ervin Committee and the Special Prosecutor or to invoke executive privilege. When President Andrew Jackson had been presented with a congressional request for a White House staff document that had been read at a Cabinet meeting, he had said, "As well might I be required to detail to the Senate the free and private conversations I have held with those officers on any subject relating to their duties and my own." Jackson had thought that this example was a ludicrous extreme but that extreme turned out to be the most moderate position espoused by the Special Prosecutor and the Ervin Committee.

I know that most people think that executive privilege was just a cloak that I drew around me to protect myself from the disclosure of my wrongdoing. But the fact that I wanted to protect myself did not alter the fact that I believed deeply and strongly in the principle and was convinced then—as I am now—that it stands at the very heart of a strong presidency. Even though the application of the principle to this case was flawed by the nature and extent of my personal interest and involvement, I did not want to be the first President in history who acquiesced in a diminution of the principle.

There were other, less abstract reasons for not turning over the tapes. I sensed what Agnew and Buzhardt were sure of: the very existence of the tapes was a tantalizing lure for the political opposition. As far as the Democrats were concerned, fighting the battle to get the tapes could be as politically rewarding as winning it. But if even one tape was yielded, it would only heighten the desire for two more. In his eloquent argument before the court of appeals, our constitutional specialist Charles Alan Wright likened the pressure for the tapes to a "hydraulic force":

> Once there is a hole below the waterline of a ship, no matter how small, the tremendous hydraulic pressure of the sea quickly broadens the gash in the ship and the ship is in danger.
> And it will be that way, too, if the hydraulic pressures of Watergate are thought to permit to tolerate even a very limited infraction of the confidentiality that every President since George Washington has enjoyed.

Shortly after I had heard about Butterfield's disclosure I had written on my bedside notepad: "Tapes—once start, no stopping."

And, finally, I simply was not sure what was on the tapes. If I had been confident that they were without ambiguity and would show me speaking like the romantic ideal of a President pursuing justice undeterred, I suppose that I might have found some way to overcome my inhibitions about releasing them. But they did not—at least the few that I had heard did not—and I could only fear what might be on the others that I had not heard and could not remember. Therefore, I decided to invoke executive privilege to prevent disclosure of the tapes. On Monday, July 23, I sent Senator Ervin a letter informing him that I would not supply any tapes for his committee's investigation.

As soon as Ervin received my letter he convened his committee, which voted unanimously to subpoena five of the taped conversations and a mass of documents relating directly or indirectly to the "activities, participation, responsibilities, or involvement" of some twenty-five individuals in "any alleged criminal acts related to the presidential election of 1972." Cox moved to subpoena nine conversations.

I now believe that from the time of the disclosure of the existence of the tapes and my decision not to destroy them, my presidency had little chance of surviving to the end of its term. Unfortunately my instinct was not so clear or sure at the time, and I did not see that while destroying the tapes might have looked like an admission of guilt, invoking executive privilege to keep them from being made public appeared hardly less so. In the end my refusal damaged the very principle I thought I was protecting. I was the first President to test the principle of executive privilege in the Supreme Court, and by testing it on such weak ground— where my own personal vulnerability would inevitably be perceived as having affected my judgment—I probably ensured the defeat of my cause. Once the public got the impression that I was trying to hide something, the attempts by Ervin and Cox to get the tapes gained increasing public support.

And quite apart from what was on the tapes, the very fact of their existence and the struggle being fought over their possession were about to do what I had been fearing most from the start: they were about to paralyze the presidency.

After hearing Dean's testimony, the Ervin Committee had recessed for a week. When its hearings resumed in July, the media coverage had tapered off considerably, so the witnesses who appeared in rebuttal to Dean did not have nearly so much impact. Only Dean had received complete live television coverage from all three networks on all five days of his testimony. An unnamed television news executive summed up the situation in an article in the Los Angeles *Times* when he said that the networks looked on these hearings as theatre, and as long as they were lively and controversial they would be broadcast. No one was particularly concerned about fairness. As the executive put it, "A man on defense can never match a man on the attack in terms of audience response."

The committee finally began to lose steam. It continued to hear witnesses, but it no longer provided the entertainment television viewers had come to expect; it had simply become overexposed.

Its public death blow was dealt by Pat Buchanan. Appearing as a witness, he responded to the senators with sharp, combative, commonsense answers and documented illustrations of the fact that it was the Democrats who had set the precedents for dirty tricks in American politics. Ervin was visibly shaken and reportedly angry that his staff had exposed him to such embarrassment.

Before long, most of the committee members were looking for a way to close down the hearings. Finally they came up with a face-saving justification: they sanctimoniously announced that they were concerned about prejudicing the rights of defendants.

On August 7, after 37 days of hearings totaling more than 325 hours of network time, the Watergate part of the Ervin Committee's hearings ended. More than 20 percent of that television time had gone to John Dean. When Ervin's gavel banged this section of the investigation to a close, there had been an average of 22 hours of television news shows, specials, and daytime programming on Watergate for every week since the hearings began.

On August 15 I made my second speech to the nation about Watergate. I talked about what I called "the overriding question of what we as a nation can learn from this experience and what we should now do." I said: "The time has come to turn Watergate over to the courts, where the questions of guilt or innocence belong. The time has come for the rest of us to get on with the urgent business of our nation."

I repeated what I called "the simple truth": that I had had no prior knowledge of the Watergate break-in; that I neither took part in nor knew about the subsequent cover-up activities; and that I had neither authorized nor encouraged subordinates to engage in illegal or improper campaign tactics. I said that far from trying to hide the facts, "my effort throughout has been to discover the facts—and to lay those facts before the appropriate law enforcement authorities so that justice could be done and the guilty dealt with."

This speech, with its call to turn Watergate over to the courts, hit a responsive chord. The numbers of telegrams and phone calls to the White House immediately after it was over were the biggest since the days of my Vietnam speeches. People were tired of Watergate.

It was my belief then, and it is still my belief today, that the Democratic majority in Congress used the Watergate scandal as an excuse for indulging in a purposeful policy of ignoring and actually overriding the landslide mandate that my programs and philosophy had received in the 1972 election. Unfortunately, by the way I handled Watergate, I helped them do it.

TRYING TO REGROUP

Three months of Watergate torpor had slowed Congress's work on domestic and foreign affairs to a near halt. My anger at this situation came through in my toast at the state dinner for Prime Minister Tanaka of Japan in July:

It is so easy these days to think in other terms, to think in the minuscule political terms that I think tempt us all from time to time and tempt those who represent the people in both countries—make a small point here, work in the murky field of political partisanship—but what really matters is this: after our short time on this great world stage is completed and we leave, what do we leave?

Do we leave the memory only of the battles we fought, of the opponents we did in, of the viciousness that we created, or do we leave possibly not only the dream but the reality of a new world, a world in which millions of the wonderful young children . . . may grow up in peace and in friendship. . . .

And so, let others spend their time dealing with the murky, small, unimportant, vicious little things. We have spent our time and will spend our time in building a better world.

I was determined not to give up on my election mandate, and in the fall of 1973 I decided to send a second State of the Union message to remind Congress and the American people of the important and unfinished domestic agenda that had gone unattended during the Watergate spring and summer. The September 10 message was launched at a press conference on September 5, during which I reviewed the major categories of national concern: inflation, national defense, and energy.

We had succeeded in holding down spending in 1973 and, despite Watergate, had managed to sustain all my vetoes of budget-busting spending bills. But Congress was now threatening to pass increases that would exceed the budget by at least $6 billion. I therefore called for an effort to keep spending within the budget in order to cut inflation and keep prices down.

In terms of constant dollars, defense spending in 1973 was actually $10 billion less than it had been in 1964 before the Vietnam war began. The draft had been ended and our defense forces were numerically lower than at any time since before the Korean war. Yet the Senate was moving to cut overseas troop strength by nearly 25 percent—without demanding any corresponding cuts by the Soviets. We were winning only narrowly in the congressional appropriations battle for the Trident nuclear submarine and the other important weaponry we needed to give us leverage in SALT.

During the past three years I had sent Congress seven proposals dealing with energy policy and legislation. Congress had not yet acted on any of them. This inaction, I warned, was keeping us at the mercy of the producers of oil in the Mideast, and I asked that immediate attention be paid to this vitally important area of national and international concern. The message described many of the more than fifty bills and programs that I had sent to Congress in 1973 alone and that had been ignored or brushed aside. These included a new federal housing program; proposals for trade reform; proposals for tax reform, particularly in the form of property tax relief for the elderly; environmental bills; education, health, and human affairs bills; and bills relating to crime prevention and control.

On August 22 I announced that I would nominate Henry Kissinger to succeed Bill Rogers as Secretary of State. On September 22 we held the swearing-in ceremony in the East Room, and after Chief Justice Burger had administered the oath, Kissinger talked about our discussion five years earlier during the transition—my insistence that we should not be hampered by preconceptions, or avoid any new departure in the effort to bring peace. He said our objective—achieving a structure of peace— was the same today as then:

> We mean a world which had not just eased tensions but overcome them; a world not based on strength but on justice; a relationship among nations based on cooperation and not equilibrium alone.

Then he added movingly:

> There is no country in the world where it is conceivable that a man of my origin could be standing here next to the President of the United States.

During this period I took stock of the situation within the White House staff. What I saw disturbed me, but I had no solution. Despite my determination that it should not happen, Haig had become bogged down in Watergate; it was like quicksand pulling him back each time he tried to get free to work on foreign and domestic policy problems.

Al Haig, I am sure, would be the first to acknowledge that he ran a very protective White House. It probably would have surprised the press corps to hear the assessments from Cabinet and staff that beneath Haig's far more affable and accessible exterior he was in many ways a more rigid administrator than Bob Haldeman. In fact, Haig purposely set out to structure this kind of White House operation because he felt that during the first term we had made our big mistakes over little things. Watergate was the most obvious case in point: if it had been handled effectively at the outset, it would never have reached this point. Haig was determined not to let this kind of mistake happen again. To prevent it, he drew more and more authority and responsibility to himself.

One problem that Haig had to deal with immediately was that the morale of the White House staff had begun to sink seriously. For many it was a case of sheer physical exhaustion: people who had been used to working ten-hour days were now working twelve and fourteen and seventeen hours a day, trying to handle their own work as well as pitching in on Watergate. But there was also a growing sense that no matter how hard we worked or what we did, we did not gain any ground. Each answer to each charge simply led to another charge requiring another answer— Watergate had become a bottomless pit. We now had a Watergate staff of twelve pitted against the opposition's two hundred. We had no comparable task forces of researchers and investigators to challenge theirs. We needed a well-planned overall strategy, but our lawyers were pulled from case to case with little time to think much beyond the next day's tactics. And I knew that among my lawyers and staff as well there was already a haunting uncertainty about the truth: they recognized that some of my defenses did not hold up to good logic or common sense, and they were naturally reluctant to go out on a limb to expound them.

John Connally soon became disenchanted with his role at the White House. We had planned to match his duties to his talents, but because of Watergate there was never time, and his actual duties as Counsellor to the President remained undefined. While we were in San Clemente in June, Connally told me that he would be leaving before long. He said that he was still supportive but he felt that he had to move on. I tried to talk him into staying, but my heart was not in it; I could not ask a man I liked and respected—and who I hoped would succeed me in the White House in 1976—to tie himself to my troubles.

In a parting press conference Connally told reporters how he felt about their attitudes toward me. "I frankly feel like at this moment if he flew to the moon that you all wouldn't give him credit for courage," he said. "You would say he was fleeing out of fear."

I was also concerned about signs of dissatisfaction in Shultz, Laird, and Harlow. Shultz was discouraged by the downturn in the economy and disillusioned by my handling of Watergate. I considered him one of the ablest members of the Cabinet and asked him to stay on. He did for six months, but finally he said, "I can't, Mr. President. I'm just pooped." I understood. I could not bring myself to urge him to continue to go through the fire that was raging around us. Laird and Harlow felt I was not consulting with them enough on Watergate. There were two reasons that I did not like to discuss the subject with them. First, I felt that it was important for as many people on the staff as possible to stay away from Watergate; second, it was simply a painful subject for me to discuss with anyone. After a while it became easier and easier for me to rely solely on Haig, Ziegler, and the lawyers in dealing with Watergate, even though I knew that this further contributed to the frustration and isolation felt by Laird, Harlow, and others.

On August 29 District Judge John Sirica ruled against us in the Special Prosecutor's suit for nine tapes. No court had ever before in our history compelled a President to produce documents that he had determined not to surrender. Because of the principle of separation of powers, a court can issue an order, but a President has a right—and some scholars would argue, a responsibility—not to obey that order if it infringes on the prerogatives of his independent branch of government. I felt then, and I feel now, that it was fully within my power to refuse to obey Sirica's ruling. In any other case, that is what I would have done. But I recognized the political reality of the Watergate situation, and instead of defying Sirica's order on constitutional principles, I decided to observe the regular procedures of the judicial system and appeal his decision to a higher court.

From the first time that the idea was suggested to me, I had objected to the creation of an independent Watergate Special Prosecutor. For one thing, I thought it was a slap at the ability of the Justice Department to do the job; for another, it was all but inevitable that under the warm glow of press attention and adulation by the Washington establishment, prosecutorial zeal would assume a life of its own.

Unfortunately, in my April 30 speech I had said that I was giving Elliot Richardson "absolute authority to make all decisions bearing upon the prosecution of the Watergate case and related matters." I had, in essence, and as events turned out, put the survival of my administration in his hands. From the time Richardson's confirmation hearings as Attorney General began it was clear that the Senate would hold his nomination hostage until an independent Watergate Special Prosecutor was appointed. Richardson felt compelled to yield to the pressure and began conducting a search for a candidate to fill the position. It took him two weeks and several refusals before he finally selected Professor Archibald Cox of the Harvard Law School.

If Richardson had searched specifically for the man whom I would have least trusted to conduct so politically sensitive an investigation in an unbiased way, he could hardly have done better than choose Archibald Cox. The Washington *Post* described Cox as having "longstanding ties to the Kennedy family." The Boston *Globe* reported that he had actually been recommended to Richardson by Teddy Kennedy. During the 1960 campaign Cox had been in charge of preparing John Kennedy's position papers; he had been a Muskie alternate delegate at the Democratic National Convention in 1972; and he publicly acknowledged that he had voted for McGovern. In a newspaper interview only two weeks before his appointment Cox had caustically criticized John Mitchell as "insensitive" to the importance of civil liberties and mentioned that he had sharp "philosophical and ideological" differences with my administration. When Kissinger learned of the Cox appointment he was shocked. He told me, "Cox will be a disaster. He has been fanatically anti-Nixon all the years I've known him."

Cox was sworn in as Special Prosecutor on May 24. Teddy Kennedy and Mrs. Robert Kennedy were among his guests at the ceremony.

The Special Prosecutor was supposed to supervise the investigation into Watergate and initiate prosecutions if they were justified or required. But shortly after his appointment in May, Cox may have subconsciously revealed his ultimate intention when he told reporters that his great-grandfather had taken part in Andrew Johnson's defense against impeachment. The news reports noted that he smiled as he observed that this family history was "a funny little quirk—or I should say, could become a funny little quirk."

Appointing Archibald Cox was bad enough. But Richardson then compounded the mistake by approving a charter for the Special Prosecution Force that, instead of limiting its responsibility to the area of Watergate, gave it virtual carte blanche to investigate the executive branch. Because of the arm's-length position that we had to observe if the Special Prosecutor was to have any credibility as an independent investigator, we had no role in formulating this charter, which began quite properly by granting him full powers in "investigating and prosecuting offenses against the United States arising out of unauthorized entry into the Democratic National Committee Headquarters at the Watergate." But then it went on to include "all offenses arising out of the 1972 Presidential Election for which the Special Prosecutor deems it necessary and appropriate to assume responsibility, allegations involving the President, members of the White House staff, or Presidential appointees, and any other matters which he consents to have assigned to him by the Attorney General." In addition the charter extended full authority for conducting grand jury proceedings, determining whether to grant immunity, initiating prosecutions, and framing indictments. The Special Prosecution Force was granted virtually unlimited funds, and there was no time limit placed on its activities. It was specifically stated that the Special Prosecutor could be removed only if he were to commit "extraordinary improprieties."

I was shocked and angry when I learned the extent of this charter. Haig talked to Richardson, who insisted that the phrases "allegations involving the President" and "members of the White House staff or Presidential appointees" should be read only in connection with the earlier reference to the 1972 presidential campaign. Of course, it did not work out that way, and Richardson later conceded that he had not foreseen the problems that would arise from giving the Special Prosecutor such unrestricted power.

It did not take long for my worst fears about the Special Prosecution Force to be realized. Of the eleven senior staff members Cox chose, seven had been associated with John, Bobby, or Teddy Kennedy. They included a former Special Assistant to Ramsey Clark, who also served as the head of George McGovern's task force on crime, a former Democratic congressional candidate, and a researcher and speechwriter for Sargent Shriver. The Chicago *Tribune* reported that only one of the top ten staff men was a Republican.

The partisan attitude that permeated the top ranks of the Watergate Special Prosecution Force was exceeded by the fervor of the junior members of its staff, most of whom were brash young lawyers intoxicated with their first real taste of power and with the attention being paid to them by a flattering and fawning press. Reports came back to me of arrogant young men using unsubstantiated charges to threaten and intimidate my personal friends and members of my staff.

Immediately after Cox was appointed, he began his inquiries about White House files. On May 30 he asked about the status of eight files; on June 5 he added six more; on June 11 he wrote asking for the tape of the April 15 conversation with John Dean that I had mentioned to Henry Petersen; the same day he asked for an inventory of twelve files. Then he requested my daily appointment logs covering all my meetings with fifteen different people; then he asked for ITT materials; and then narrative testimony from me. In July there was a leak caused by his staff that he was starting to look into the purchase of my house in San

Clemente to see if any union, corporate, or campaign money had been used. His staff asked for information on government wiretapping and tried to call Secret Service agents to find out the details of their operations. Cox himself acknowledged that this went overboard.

Even though Cox's charter presumably restricted him to the 1972 campaign, he launched an investigation into 1970 campaign funds. He began investigating Secret Service personnel for their handling of demonstrators at rallies even as Richardson pointed out that the Justice Department was already defending some of the men involved in civil actions arising from these incidents. Ranging still further afield, Cox investigated the Plumbers and then launched an investigation of Bebe Rebozo.

By October 12, four months after the Special Prosecutor took over the case that the Justice Department had said was already 90 percent completed, they had brought only one indictment, and that one did not even relate to Watergate. It did not take long to see that they interpreted their power to investigate "all offenses arising out of the 1972 Presidential Election" to mean primarily those alleged to have been committed by the Nixon camp. For example, in 1974 the Special Prosecution Force let the statute of limitations lapse on a campaign fund-raising violation committed by Democratic Finance Chairman Robert Strauss. When a similar situation arose with our Finance Chairman Maury Stans, they asked the court for a waiver of the statute to prevent it from running while proceedings were pending.

No White House in history could have survived the kind of operation Cox was planning. If he were determined to get me, as I was certain that he and his staff were, then given the terms of their charter it would be only a matter of time until they had bored like termites through the whole executive branch. The frustrating thing was that while I saw them as partisan zealots abusing the power I had given them in order to destroy me unfairly, the media presented them and the public largely perceived them as the keepers of the sacred flame of American justice against a wicked President and his corrupt administration. Whenever I tried to state my point of view, I was inevitably discounted as being self-interested and self-serving. I could not imagine any other President allowing a man who derived his authority from the White House to use that power independently to conduct a partisan inquisition at the administration's expense. I certainly did not intend to be the first. Thus, by fall a clash was inevitable, and, thanks to the charter Richardson had given him, Cox was so powerful that the outcome was far from predictable.

AGNEW ACCUSED

Ted Agnew's problems with the U.S. Attorney in Baltimore had remained a peripheral concern of mine ever since April 1973, when Haldeman had first mentioned to me that Agnew was afraid of being embarrassed by the investigations under way there.

In June Elliot Richardson had informed Haig that serious allegations were being made about Agnew; by the middle of July the vague allegations had become a series of specific charges that Agnew while governor of Maryland had taken money in return for granting state contracts. There were also charges that he continued to receive money in return for these past favors while he was Vice President. Agnew was convinced that the young Baltimore prosecutors were out to make a name for themselves at his expense; he pointed out that one of them had worked in Muskie's 1972 campaign—a credential that hardly bespoke detachment.

By the end of July Haig had another report from Richardson. This time it was unequivocal. Haig quoted Richardson as having said that he had never seen such a cut-and-dried case. He said that Agnew was potentially indictable on more than forty counts.

On August 1 Richardson sent Agnew a letter informing him that he was being investigated on allegations of conspiracy, extortion, bribery, and tax fraud. When Haig told me this, I felt that it was time for me to become involved. I arranged to meet with Richardson on Monday, August 6; I asked Buzhardt and Garment to see him before this meeting because I wanted their independent analyses of the case against Agnew. I knew that we were dealing with political dynamite and that I had to be scrupulously careful about the information I was receiving and how it was assessed. After their meeting with Richardson, Buzhardt and Garment sent back gloomy evaluations: they agreed with Richardson that this was one of the most solid cases they had ever seen.

John Mitchell had already sent word to me that Agnew felt that Richardson was out to get him. Agnew remembered that Richardson had opposed his nomination in 1968, and he pointed out that they had disagreed repeatedly on policy matters during meetings of the Domestic Council. Agnew also was convinced that Richardson saw himself as a potential presidential candidate.

Half an hour before my meeting with Richardson on Monday morning, August 6, the White House press office received the first inquiry about rumors that the Vice President was under investigation. We knew that it would be only a matter of time before the story broke.

After a general review of the allegations against Agnew, Richardson told me that the witnesses were believable and in some cases had irrefutable documents. He said there were accusations that the payments had continued through the vice presidential years. Objectively I recognized the weight of Richardson's evidence, but emotionally I was still on Agnew's side. I wanted to believe him. I told Richardson that I expected him to assume full responsibility for seeing to it that Agnew was not railroaded by biased U.S. Attorneys and a predatory press corps.

The next morning, August 7, the *Wall Street Journal* had the scoop: a story attributed to "knowledgeable attorneys" stated that Agnew was under investigation. Haig had told me that Agnew was wavering between fighting and resigning.

That afternoon I met for an hour and a half with Agnew. He walked into my office with the same easy, confident stride he always had and began our conversation by declaring that he was totally innocent of the charges. He said they would not hold up in court, and that if it should ever go that far he would be proved innocent. He repeated to me his feeling that someday the prosecution team in Baltimore would be shown up for what it was.

I told him that I had confidence in his integrity, that I believed him and would stand by him unless clear and final evidence was presented to me that forced me to think otherwise. When he said that he was planning a press conference for the next day, I urged him to consider carefully before he said anything that might haunt him later.

I told him that one man whose fairness I could completely vouch for was Henry Petersen. I said I would arrange with Richardson for Petersen to undertake his own independent investigation of the case and to prepare his own independent recommendation.

By August 8 the newspapers and the networks had begun reporting a series of leaks and attacks on Agnew that became so irresponsible that the New York *Times* and the Washington *Post* ended up criticizing on their editorial pages what was being done on their own news pages.

On August 8 Agnew marched indignantly into the EOB briefing room and denounced the leaks. "I have no intention to be skewered in this fashion," he said. "I have nothing to hide." He denied charges that he received $1,000 a week in kickbacks, calling them "damned lies." He was asked if he had ever had a political slush fund financed by Baltimore County contractors. "Never," he replied. He was asked if he had ever received money for his personal use from any person or company doing business with the state of Maryland or the federal government. "Absolutely not," he said.

Haig and Buzhardt came in to tell me that Agnew's press conference looked like a short-term political triumph. In view of the evidence that was bound to come out, however, they did not see how it could be anything but a long-term disaster. Buzhardt shook his head and said that he could not see how Agnew could have made such blanket denials— "never," "absolutely not"—that simply would not hold up.

I faced an impossible dilemma. I knew the charges against Agnew were serious and completely persuasive to responsible people. But this knowledge was private. The press leaks, and Agnew's impassioned denials, had convinced many people that the charges were a vendetta against him. If I actively defended him, and the charges were later substantiated, I would have succeeded only in further eroding my own already dwindling credibility. If I took a neutral position, Agnew's supporters would think I had let him down. In the end I chose the second course as the sounder approach and decided I would simply have to bear the brunt of the criticism that was to come.

Agnew continued to fight back. On August 21 he had issued a statement charging that some Justice Department officials had decided to indict him in the press regardless of whether the evidence supported their position. Elliot Richardson went on television to deny that the leaks were coming from the Justice Department; later he had to acknowledge that his department was in fact probably responsible for some of the stories.

The concerted press attack against Agnew caused me to reconsider my belief in the dependability of the investigation going on in Baltimore. In a press conference on August 22 I warned that any Justice Department or United States government employee who had leaked information would be dismissed immediately upon discovery.

On September 1 Agnew came in, at his request, in order to bring me up to date on the situation. The strains were beginning to show. He told me bitterly how the prosecutors were pressing him for a wide range of personal financial data going back to 1962. He said that he was considering whether it would not be better for him to seek impeachment by the House than to have a trial in the federal court.

From talking with Agnew I understood the manner in which he had come to think about his actions as governor. State government salaries were meager. He was sure that three-quarters of the governors in other states had done the same kind of thing, namely, accepted campaign contributions from contractors doing business with the state. As he saw it, the whole trumped-up case simply involved campaign contributions that had been used to help meet expenses legitimately incurred by him and his family in their public roles. He argued that the contractors were all well qualified and that there had been no quid pro quo involved. He heatedly denied having received money while Vice President. Once again he complained about the Baltimore prosecutors. He said they were trying to track down everything he had ever bought, and every detail of his personal life.

I was genuinely sympathetic to Agnew, and I shared with him his painful concern about the effect this controversy would have on his family and friends. I said that I could not and would not ever judge his case; but I urged that he, as a lawyer, try to analyze it as objectively as he could. Only then would he be able to make decisions in his own best interests.

I could see that he was no longer as sure as he had been in our first meeting that the charges against him were not provable in court; now he reflected on the fact that no court anywhere near Washington or Maryland could possibly treat him fairly.

On the morning of September 10 Fred Buzhardt and Al Haig brought Agnew a new assessment. Buzhardt, who at my request and with Agnew's consent was keeping me informed of developments in the case, told Agnew that Justice Department officials were convinced that he would be indicted, convicted, and sentenced to a jail term. The gravity of Haig and Buzhardt's report must have had some effect. Within days, Agnew's lawyer, Judah Best, had made the first tentative overtures toward negotiations with the Justice Department.

In the midst of these negotiations I met with Agnew again. He had come a long way since that first session six weeks earlier at which he had protested his complete innocence. Now he asked what I thought he should do and talked poignantly about the problems of going away and starting a new life.

Once again I said that this was a decision only he could make, because only he knew the facts and only he knew those who would be testifying against him. He said that he simply was not going to leave under the terms Richardson was proposing: Richardson wanted to drive him into the ground, he said, and he would fight in court before he would allow that. He would risk jail rather than grovel. After this meeting I had Haig and Buzhardt tell Richardson that he

469

must not force the country into the nightmare of a trial by insisting on unreasonably tough terms.

On Friday, September 21, Buzhardt reported to me that he thought there had been a breakthrough. Richardson and Best had reached agreement on language that would not commit Agnew to a "knowing" acceptance of money for preferential treatment, while still acknowledging that others would allege it. Agnew was going to think about it over the weekend, so Monday would be the day of decision. "I think it is just about over," Buzhardt said.

But Saturday morning brought a new set of leaks. The Washington *Post* carried a front-page story "from two sources" revealing that Agnew's lawyers were bargaining on a plea. Then CBS reported that Henry Petersen had told his associates, "We've got the evidence. We've got it cold."

Buzhardt reported that Agnew was outraged; he was convinced that the leaks had come from the Justice Department and were part of a deliberate strategy to weaken his position in the negotiations. By Sunday he had once again decided to fight.

On Monday morning, September 25, I met with Richardson and Petersen. Petersen went over the principal allegations and gave me his conclusion that it was an "open-and-shut case." He said that Agnew would be found guilty and would have to serve a prison term. Richardson said that he was now ready to send the evidence to the grand jury. I asked Richardson to have the Justice Department prepare an opinion on the question of whether it would be constitutional to indict a Vice President while he was still in office. The Constitution specifically provides that a President can be removed from office only by being impeached and convicted; only then can he be indicted in criminal proceedings and brought to trial for his offenses. Although the Vice President is not specifically mentioned in this clause of the Constitution, I argued that a case could be made that he would be in the same position.

Agnew came in at 10:30 A.M. He told me that he had decided to go to Speaker Carl Albert and request that the House of Representatives undertake a full impeachment inquiry. He still adamantly denied having received any money while Vice President and said that the charges were just part of the effort to sink him. He told me that he would reconsider resigning only if he were granted complete immunity from prosecution. Then, for a moment, his manner changed, and in a sad and gentle voice he asked for my assurance that I would not turn my back on him if he were out of office.

That afternoon Agnew went to Carl Albert's office and presented his formal request for an impeachment proceeding. Though I seriously doubted that it would be granted, I had the congressional relations staff talk with leading House Republicans, urging them to support the request. The next day Albert let it be known that he was rejecting it. The same day, the Justice Department alerted me that its study had concluded that a President could not be indicted while in office, but a Vice President could. I asked that Agnew be informed of this development. That evening Agnew and his family left for California. Haig's impression was that he was going away to think things over, talk with his family, and perhaps prepare them for his resignation.

Agnew's troubles had taken a serious toll. The news stories continued to deluge us and made the Watergate stories seem even worse than they already were. In addition, Agnew's staff had become embittered about our cautious position because they didn't understand the weight of the case against him. Confidence in government—and confidence in me—was already reeling from Watergate and was now being eroded even further. While I still felt enormous personal sympathy for Agnew, over the past days I had grown increasingly disturbed by his prolongation of what seemed an inevitable end and felt he had to resign.

I was at Camp David on Saturday afternoon when Haig called with the latest development. Agnew· had just spoken to a group of Republican women in Los Angeles and told them that during the past several months he had been living in purgatory, finding himself confronted by undefined, unclear, and unattributed accusations. As the audience cheered and waved signs reading "Spiro is my hero," Agnew had proclaimed his innocence, attacked Justice Department officials, and shouted: "I will not resign if indicted! I will not resign if indicted!"

When I received Haig's call, I had just finished talking with Rose Woods, who had come up earlier in the day to start typing the conversation from the tapes subpoenaed by the Special Prosecutor.

I had already begun to anticipate that the court of appeals would rule against us. I wanted to break the paralysis caused by the court battles. Rather than take the case to the Supreme Court I had begun to consider a compromise: submitting written summaries of the tapes subpoenaed by the Special Prosecutor and by the Watergate Committee after national security discussions and other matters irrelevant to Watergate had been deleted.

I had asked Rose to do a quick run-through of the subpoenaed tapes to give us the gist of the conversations without taking the time to prepare complete transcripts. She is such a fast typist that I thought it would take her only a couple of days to finish the whole lot. But she found that the quality of the tapes was so bad and the voices so hard to distinguish that she had to go phrase by phrase, listening to each section several times in order to make out the words. After several hours she had finished only one short passage of the first tape.

I took the earphones and listened myself. At first all I could hear was a complete jumble. I ran the machine back and listened again. Gradually I could make out a few words, but at times the rattling of a cup or the thump of a hand on the desk would obliterate whole passages. The tapes of conversations with John Dean that I had listened to in June had almost all been Oval Office conversations and John Dean's flat, uninflected voice had been picked up reasonably well. It had not occurred to me that the other recordings would not be of the same quality. But in the EOB office the different microphone placements and seating arrangements, the shape of the room, and the height of the arched ceilings apparently created entirely different acoustics. Nor had I considered the problem of understanding a highly modulated voice like Ehrlichman's.

Steve Bull, a White House staff aide, had come to Camp David with Rose to help her locate the subpoenaed conversations on the tapes and cue them on the machine for her. At one point Bull hit upon the ambiguity in the Special Prosecutor's subpoena. The subpoena requested a "Meeting

472

of June 20, 1972, in the President's Executive Office Building ('EOB') Office involving Richard Nixon, John Ehrlichman and H. R. Haldeman from 10:30 A.M. to noon (time approximate)." Bull could not find such a meeting in the logs, which showed only a conversation with Ehrlichman alone, beginning at 10:25 and lasting until 11:20, followed by a separate conversation with Haldeman alone. Bull and Haig talked by phone, and Bull asked about the confusion. Haig talked to Buzhardt and called back to say that, according to Buzhardt, only the Ehrlichman conversation was subpoenaed, not the Haldeman conversation that followed it.

By Sunday night, when we returned to Washington, Rose had worked twenty-nine hours with a Sony tape recorder and a typewriter, and she still had not finished even the first conversation with Ehrlichman.

On Monday morning, October 1, I met with Ziegler, Haig, Laird, and Kissinger and then spent an hour with the President of the commission of the European communities before going to a military promotion ceremony and a bill-signing ceremony. I was in the EOB office when Rose came in visibly agitated.

She said she thought she might have caused a small gap in the Haldeman part of the June 20 tape. For a moment I thought she must have meant the Ehrlichman conversation, because I knew that that was the one she had been working on. When I realized it was the Haldeman conversation I reassured her and told her that since the Haldeman conversation had not been subpoenaed, there was nothing to worry about.

She explained what had happened. At Steve Bull's request the Secret Service had given her a new tape recorder that morning. It was a Uher 5000 machine, a kind that she had never worked with before. Unlike the manually operated Sony she had used at Camp David, the Uher had a foot-pedal control that would help speed up the work considerably by allowing her to type without having continually to shift position back and forth from typewriter to tape recorder. She had been using this new machine only about half an hour when she finally came to what seemed to be the end of the Ehrlichman conversation. She ran the tape ahead

473

to be sure that Ehrlichman had in fact left the room. She had reached a part where she heard Haldeman talking about schedule matters—she heard him say something about Ely, Nevada—when her phone rang and she turned to reach for the phone. When she finished the call, she turned back and started to listen to the tape again. All she could hear was a shrill buzzing sound. She did not know how it had happened. She said she had not heard any words after the reference to Ely. She guessed that she had been on the phone for about four or five minutes.

I called Haig in and told him what had happened, and we checked with Buzhardt to make sure that I was right, that the Haldeman conversation had not been subpoenaed. Buzhardt confirmed this, so the peculiar incident did not seem to present any problem. It had been a busy morning, so Haig and I went for a long drive around Washington in order to talk about the problem that was foremost in my mind: what to do about Agnew. Compared to this, a few minutes missing from a non-subpoenaed tape hardly seemed worth a second thought.

During a press conference on October 3 I again had to walk a verbal tightrope on the Agnew issue. I first came to his defense, urging that he not be tried and convicted in the press. But when the question was asked if there was any truth to Agnew's charge that this had been just a political investigation, I answered that while I had been briefed only on what the witnesses might say, the charges were serious.

After the press conference I left for a weekend in Florida. I asked Buzhardt to come with me. That afternoon he received a call from Judah Best, who said that Agnew was ready to resume discussions about a plea. Best flew to Florida and met with Buzhardt until late into the night. Earlier Best had pointed out to Buzhardt that Agnew was just a few months short of being eligible for retirement with a federal pension. He had wondered if there were not some way to give him a consultancy that would keep him on the government payroll and carry him over the pension deadline. I told Buzhardt that we could not do it at this time. Agnew had also asked if he could keep his Secret Service protection for a while, and he was concerned about what would happen to his staff. I promised that I would see to it that his Secret Service protection was extended, and that we would do our best to find jobs for his staff members.

It was agreed that on Saturday, October 6, Buzhardt would call Richardson to arrange for the talks to begin again.

OCTOBER 1973

On that same Saturday morning we received a cable from Ken Keating, our ambassador in Tel Aviv, reporting that Golda Meir had just told him that Syria and Egypt were in a final countdown for war. Israel was about to be attacked on two fronts: by the Syrians from the north in the Golan Heights, and by the Egyptians from the south in the Sinai Peninsula.

The news of the imminent attack on Israel took us completely by surprise. As recently as the day before, the CIA had reported that war in the Middle East was unlikely, dismissing as annual maneuvers the massive and unusual troop movement that had recently been taking place in Egypt. They had similarly interpreted the dramatic step-up in Syrian military activity as a precautionary move because the Israelis had recently shot down three Syrian jets.

I was disappointed by our own intelligence shortcomings, and I was stunned by the failure of Israeli intelligence. They were among the best in the world, and they, too, had been caught off guard. For the first time since 1948 the Israelis were about to go into a war without having positioned their equipment or having their reserve troops on standby. It was also Yom Kippur—the Day of Atonement—the holiest day in the Jewish calendar, when most Israelis, including many in the armed forces, would be spending the day at home with their families or in synagogue at prayer. It was the one day of the year when Israel was least prepared to defend itself.

It was tragic enough that war was once again going to plague this troubled area. But there was an even more disturbing question mark in the background concerning the role of the Soviet Union. It was hard for me to believe that the Egyptians and Syrians would have moved without the knowledge of the Soviets, if not without their direct encouragement.

In the last few hours before the fighting actually began, Kissinger contacted the Israelis, the Egyptians, and the Soviets to see if war could be prevented. But it was too late. At eight o'clock that morning the Syrians attacked Israel from the north and the Egyptians attacked from the south.

By the end of the first day of fighting, the Egyptians had crossed the Suez Canal and begun a thrust into the Sinai. In the north the Israelis were pushing the Syrians back in the Golan Heights, but they were unable to rout them as they had in earlier conflicts. Israeli losses were heavy. Mrs. Meir, however, was confident that if the Israelis had three or four days in which to mount a counteroffensive, they could turn the military tide on both fronts. We had convened a special meeting of the UN Security Council right after the fighting began, but there was little interest on either side in holding cease-fire discussions. The Soviets objected to our having called the Security Council into session; they clearly thought that the Arabs would win the war on the battlefield if they had enough time to secure their early victories. The French and the British—also Security Council members—were trying to stay at arm's length; they did not share our uniquely close ties with Israel and they knew that Arab oil was at stake in this confrontation.

As far as the American position was concerned, I saw no point in trying to impose a diplomatic cease-fire that neither side wanted or could be expected to observe. It would be better to wait until the war had reached the point at which neither side had a decisive military advantage. Despite the great skepticism of the Israeli hawks, I believed that only a battlefield stalemate would provide the foundation on which fruitful negotiations might begin. Any equilibrium—even if only an equilibrium of mutual exhaustion—would make it easier to reach an enforceable settlement. Therefore, I was convinced that we must not use our influence to bring about a cease-fire that would leave the parties in such imbalance that negotiations for a permanent settlement would never begin. I was also concerned that if the Arabs were actually to start losing this war, the Soviet leaders would feel that they could not stand by and watch their allies suffer another humiliating defeat as they had in 1967.

We had a particularly delicate situation insofar as the

Egyptians were concerned. Beginning in February 1973, with a view toward building better relations, we had had a series of private contacts with them. While we had to keep the interests of the Israelis uppermost during this conflict in which they were the victims of aggression, I hoped that we could support them in such a way that we would not force an irreparable break with the Egyptians, the Syrians, and the other Arab nations. We also had to restrain the Soviets from intervening in any way that would require us to confront them. Underlying all the military complications was the danger that the Arabs would try to bring economic pressure to bear on us by declaring an oil embargo.

The immensely volatile situation created by the unexpected outbreak of this war could not have come at a more complicated domestic juncture. Agnew was beginning the final plea-bargaining negotiations that would lead to his resignation, and I was faced with the need to select his successor. The media were slamming us with daily Watergate charges, and we had just begun reviewing the subpoenaed tapes in preparation for reaching a compromise with the Special Prosecutor in the unfortunate but likely event that the court of appeals ruled against us. And Congress was pushing to assert its authority by passing a far-reaching bill to restrict the President's war powers. All these concerns would be interwoven through the next two weeks. Just as a crisis in one area seemed to be settling down, it would be overtaken by a crisis in another area, until all the crises reached a concerted crescendo as we neared the brink of nuclear war.

By the end of the third day of the Yom Kippur War it was clear that the Israelis had been overconfident about their ability to win a quick victory. The initial battles had gone against them. They had already lost a thousand men—compared with the fewer than 700 lost in the entire 1967 war—and were on the way to losing a third of their tank force. By Tuesday, October 9, the fourth day of the war, we could see that if the Israelis were to continue fighting, we would have to provide them with planes and ammunition to replace their early losses. I had absolutely no doubt or hesitation about what we must do. I met with

Kissinger and told him to let the Israelis know that we would replace all their losses, and asked him to work out the logistics for doing so.

At 6 P.M. Steve Bull stepped in and announced my next appointment. "Mr. President," he said, "the Vice President." Ted Agnew walked in behind him. He had come to inform me officially of what I already knew: he had decided to resign.

We shook hands and sat down in the chairs in front of the fireplace. I spoke first, saying that I knew his decision had been very difficult for him. I knew that he was by nature a man who would almost rather have lost everything fighting, even from his disadvantaged position, than have won the assurance that he would not go to prison at the price of having to compromise with his opponents. I told him how much I had appreciated his hard campaigning in 1968, 1970, and 1972 and the dedicated way he handled all his assignments from me. I asked about his wife and family; I knew how painful it had been for them.

He was particularly embittered by what he considered the hypocrisy of the members of Congress who had formerly served as governors. He repeated his belief that most of the governors in other states had followed practices such as those common in Maryland. He emphasized that he had always awarded contracts on the basis of merit, and he felt that the amounts he had received had been so small that no reasonable critic could claim that they could have influenced him to make a decision that contravened the public interest. He said that he could not see that what he had done was unethical.

He mentioned that after a few months he would like to have some kind of foreign assignment; he thought that he could be particularly effective in a Far Eastern country, perhaps Japan. He said he would appreciate anything that I could do to get some corporation to put him on a retainer as a consultant. I said that if an opportunity arose in which I could help, I would do so. At one point he said that he supposed the IRS would be harassing him the rest of his life. "You know, they were even charting up how much I paid for my neckties," he said bitterly.

Our meeting was over. I shook his hand and told him

that I wished him well. I said that he could always count on me as a friend.

The next day Agnew walked into the federal courtroom in Baltimore and announced that he was pleading nolo contendere to one count of having knowingly failed to report income for tax purposes, and that he was resigning as Vice President.

The judge sentenced him to three years' probation and a $10,000 fine.

Ted Agnew's resignation was a personal tragedy for him and for his family, and a national tragedy as well. I wrote to him on October 10, the day he resigned:

> As Vice President, you have addressed the great issues of our times with courage and candor. Your strong patriotism, and your profound dedication to the welfare of the nation, have been an inspiration to all who have served with you as well as to millions of others throughout the country.
>
> I have been deeply saddened by this whole course of events, and I hope that you and your family will be sustained in the days ahead by a well-justified pride in all that you have contributed to the nation by your years of service as Vice President.

On the morning of October 10 I met with the Republican and Democratic congressional leaders. I said that our objective was to achieve peace without losing the support we had been able to build up in both the Arab and Israeli camps. So far we had succeeded, and neither side felt that we had turned against it. It was clear that none of these men, not even the most ardently pro-Israel among them, was enthusiastic about the prospect of a Mideast war that might involve American participation. Mike Mansfield said, "Mr. President, we want no more Vietnams."

"Is Israel going to lose?" one of the leaders asked apprehensively.

"No," I replied. "We will not let Israel go down the tubes."

Later that morning, as Agnew was entering his plea in a courtroom in Baltimore, the Israeli ambassador came to the White House to deliver a letter from Golda Meir. She wrote:

Early this morning I was told of the decision you made to assure us the immediate flow of U.S. matériel. Your decision will have a great and beneficial influence on our fighting capability. I know that in this hour of dire need to Israel, I could turn to you and count on your deep sympathy and understanding.

We are fighting against heavy odds, but we are fully confident that we shall come out victorious. When we do we will have you in mind.

I had been checking almost hourly with Kissinger to see how our resupply effort was coming. The reports were not good.

"Defense is putting up all kinds of obstacles," he said. Defense Secretary James Schlesinger was apparently concerned about offending the Arabs and therefore did not want to let any Israeli El Al transport planes land at American military bases. Kissinger had finally persuaded him to relent if the planes first stopped in New York and had their tail markings painted over. I agreed that it was important not to offend the Arabs gratuitously, but we now had reports that a massive Soviet airlift of weapons and supplies was under way to Syria and Egypt, and that three Soviet airborne divisions had been put on alert. The Arabs were obviously trying to consolidate their initial military victories. It was unthinkable that Israel should lose the war for lack of weapons while we were spraying paint over Stars of David. "Tell Schlesinger to speed it up," I told Kissinger.

The situation was further complicated when we received intelligence information that our strong ally King Hussein had decided to send a small contingent of Jordanian soldiers to fight with the Syrians. General Brent Scowcroft, who had replaced Haig as Kissinger's deputy, called the Israeli ambassador and expressed our hope that Israel would not widen the war by attacking Jordan.

In the midst of the developing Mideast crisis I had to turn my attention to the selection of the new Vice President.

Several members of Congress came to the White House to talk to me about it. Many of the Democrats were understandably apprehensive at the prospect of the sudden elevation of a strong Republican to a position of such national prominence. Since I would not be able to run again in 1976, my Vice President would enjoy many of the advantages of incumbency if he became the Republican nominee. There was already a drumbeat of demands from the more partisan Democrats that I not appoint anyone who was going to run for President in 1976; they wanted a caretaker Vice President who would simply fill out Agnew's unexpired term.

Mike Mansfield in particular urged that I go the caretaker route. His own choices were Senator John Sherman Cooper of Kentucky and Bill Rogers. He said that Connally, Rockefeller, or Reagan would meet with very strong opposition in Congress. This was, and I am sure was meant to be, a signal that if I nominated one of these dynamic Republican presidential contenders, the Democrats would turn very partisan. I said that the primary criterion had to be the man's qualification for the job, and I deliberately mentioned Jerry Ford as an example of a qualified man. Mansfield lighted his pipe, took some deep puffs, and made no comment.

I asked Republican Party leaders to list their recommendations for Vice President in order of preference and send the lists to Rose Woods. On the afternoon of October 11 I left for Camp David with Rose's compilation of the recommendations and the text of an announcement speech that at my direction had been prepared with four optional endings—for John Connally, for Nelson Rockefeller, for Ronald Reagan, and for Jerry Ford.

Among the approximately 400 top party leaders from all sections of the country and from Congress, the Cabinet, and the White House staff whose recommendations I had solicited, Rockefeller and Reagan were in a virtual tie for first choice; Connally was third; Ford was fourth. Ford, however, was first choice among members of Congress, and they were the ones who would have to approve the man I nominated.

John Connally had been my own first choice. As early as October 6 I had asked Haig to call him and see whether he would take the position if it were offered to him. I had also wanted to know Connally's own assessment of his chances of confirmation. Over the next few days we did some quiet checking, and the reports were all the same: Connally simply could not make it. He would be opposed by an overwhelming number of Democrats who would fear him as the strongest possible Republican candidate in 1976. With all the problems I was having with Watergate, I could not become embroiled in a massive partisan slugging match over the selection of the new Vice President.

I had Haig call Connally again and tell him that, while he still remained my first choice, I was very seriously concerned whether he could survive a confirmation battle. Connally replied that he had been checking through his own sources and had reached the same conclusion.

Looking at the other choices, I concluded that nominating either Rockefeller or Reagan would split the Republican Party down the middle and result in a bitter partisan fight that, while it might not be fatal in terms of confirmation, might leave scars that would not be healed by 1976. This left Jerry Ford.

From the outset of the search for a new Vice President I had established four criteria for the man I would select: qualification to be President; ideological affinity; loyalty; and confirmability. I felt that Jerry Ford was qualified to be President if for any reason I did not complete my term; I knew that his views on both domestic and foreign policy were very close to mine and that he would be a dedicated team player; and there was no question that he would be the easiest to get confirmed.

I returned to the White House early on Friday morning, October 12, and told Haig of my decision. The only other person we informed was Connally. He agreed immediately that Ford was the right choice in the circumstances. I wondered if Connally remembered, as I did, that I had once told him about a conversation I had had with Jerry Ford in 1972, when Ford had told me that in his view Connally was the man for 1976.

Later that morning a somber-faced Haig brought me the news: the court of appeals, in a 5–2 decision, had ruled against us in the tapes case. We now had one week to decide if we wished to appeal the decision to the Supreme Court.

Hugh Scott and Jerry Ford arrived to talk about the congressional schedule for the next few days. I revealed nothing of my decision about the vice presidency. According to some reporters, Ford had been hoping that during this visit he would learn that he was going to be named Vice President, and I was amused by news accounts that he had appeared downcast when he left the White House.

During the afternoon I learned that the plans for resupplying Israel with military equipment had become seriously bottlenecked. Because Israel was a war zone, no insurance company was willing to risk issuing policies for chartered private planes flying there. In order to get around the insurance problem, we raised with the Pentagon the idea of mobilizing a part of the Civil Reserve Air Fleet. The option of flying supplies to the Azores for transshipment to Israel was also considered, and after much discussion we were able to persuade the reluctant Portuguese government to agree to this plan. In the meantime, however, the Soviet airlift was assuming such massive proportions and the Israeli shortages, particularly ammunition, were becoming so serious, that I concluded that any further delay was unacceptable and decided we must use U.S. military aircraft if that was what was necessary to get our supplies through to Israel. I asked Kissinger to convey my decision to the Pentagon and have them prepare a plan. I was shocked when he told me that the Pentagon's proposal was that we send only three C-5A military transport planes to Israel. Their rationale was that sending a small number of planes would cause fewer difficulties with the Egyptians, the Syrians, and also the Soviets. My reaction was that we would take just as much heat for sending three planes as for sending thirty.

I called Schlesinger and told him that I understood his concern and appreciated his caution. I assured him that I was fully aware of the gravity of my decision and that I would accept complete personal responsibility if, as a result, we alienated the Arabs and had our oil supplies cut off. I said if we could not get the private planes, we should use our own military transports. "Whichever way we have to do it, get them in the air, *now*," I told him.

When I was informed that there was disagreement in the Pentagon about which kind of plane should be used for the airlift, I became totally exasperated. I said to Kissinger, "Goddamn it, use every one we have. Tell them to send everything that can fly."

Shortly after seven o'clock on Friday evening, October 12, I had Haig place the call to Jerry Ford at home to tell him that he was my choice for Vice President and to ask if he was prepared to accept. Ford asked if we could call back on another number so that his wife, Betty, could share the call on an extension phone.

After talking with both Jerry and Betty, I went to the Residence to tell Pat the news. "Good," she said. "I guessed it."

At nine that night the announcement was made at a televised ceremony in the East Room. Afterward the family joined me while I ate dinner. I had just finished a small steak when Haig came in to discuss the latest Soviet message, which had been delivered to the White House earlier in the evening.

The message stated that they had heard we were supplying Israel with bombs, air-to-air missiles, planes, and tanks. They said that they had also heard rumors that 150 American Air Force pilots were going to Israel disguised as tourists. No threats were made, but the menacing tone and intention of the message were clear. Of course, there was no mention of the massive Soviet airlift, which was by then supplying an estimated 700 tons of weapons and matériel daily to Syria and Egypt.

This message was premature. Our airlift to Israel had not yet begun at the time he wrote, but the next day, Saturday, October 13, at 3:30 P.M., thirty C-130 transports were on their way to Israel.

By Tuesday we were sending in a thousand tons a day. Over the next few weeks there would be more than 550 American missions, an operation bigger than the Berlin airlift of 1948–49. I also ordered that an additional ten Phantom Jets be delivered to Israel.

In fact, the Israelis had already begun to turn the tide of battle on their own, and with our infusion of new supplies they were able to push all the way to the outskirts of Damascus and were close to encircling the Egyptian forces in the Sinai.

It was not until Saturday morning that I finally had time to go over the decision of the court of appeals, which had ruled against us in the Special Prosecutor's suit for the nine tapes.

In one sense the ruling was a victory, because the court accepted our argument that wholesale access to executive deliberations would cripple the government. The majority opinion said that the ruling should be considered an "unusual and limited" requirement for a President to produce material evidence. But such a victory was relative at best because the majority on the court rejected our contention that only a President could decide whether such material was or was not privileged. Instead they arrogated that power to themselves.

The ruling was a serious blow to me personally, even though I had tried to prepare myself for it, as indicated by notes I had made for discussion with Haig and Ziegler:

We must not kid ourselves; we must face these facts.

After our August 15 statement, Gallup showed us with 38 percent support; since then we've had the August 22 press conference, the September 5 press conference, and a backbreaking schedule of foreign and domestic newsworthy events. We hear from some of our friends in Congress that Congress is in a better mood; that Ervin is going down in public esteem; that the news is not as biased as it was.

Yet both Gallup and Harris show our support going down from 38 in Gallup to 32, and in Harris the number of resignation rising to 31, with 56 opposed.

The question is: are we facing the facts? Aren't we in a losing battle with the media despite the personal efforts I have made over the past month particularly? Are we facing the fact that the public attitudes may have hardened to the point that we can't change them?

The situation was intolerable. Week by week, month by month, we were being worn down, trapped, paralyzed. The Ervin Committee continued its leaks and accusations. It had been four and a half months since Haldeman and Ehrlichman resigned; four months since Cox was named. Nothing had been resolved. The investigations dragged on. Despite the fact that a President can only be impeached, rumors that he wanted to indict me continued. Strong conservatives in Congress and on my staff had long felt that he had to go, both because of the liberal enclave he had established and also because of the parasite he had become, dangerously draining the executive month after month. Firing him seemed the only way to rid the administration of the partisan viper we had planted in our bosom. Whether or not we decided to appeal to the Supreme Court in this particular tapes case, I knew that it would be only a matter of days before Cox would be back for more, and then more after that.

This ruling had come at the worst possible time: we were in the midst of a major world crisis in the Middle East, and in the aftermath of the shattering domestic trauma of the resignation of a Vice President. But any such considerations were extraneous to the timetable imposed on us by the ruling. We had until midnight on Friday either to comply or to file a further appeal.

Appointing a Special Prosecutor had been a major mistake, one that I knew would be difficult and costly to remedy. If I could develop an acceptable compromise on the battle for the tapes, I decided to fire Cox and return the Watergate investigation to the Justice Department, where it had been considered 90 percent complete months earlier and where the investigators would not have the interest Cox and his staff had in self-perpetuation.

When the idea of supplying summaries instead of transcripts of the subpoenaed tapes had first been explored at the end of September, we had begun thinking of finding some outside person who could verify their accuracy. Fred Buzhardt suggested Senator John Stennis of Mississippi. Stennis was a Democrat, the Chairman of the Senate Select Committee on Standards and Conduct, a former judge, and one of the few men in Congress respected by members of both parties for his fairness and integrity. Summaries, we felt, would not compromise the critical question of precedent.

On Sunday, October 14, I saw Stennis for a few minutes after the White House worship service and mentioned the possibility of his verifying the accuracy of some tape summaries. He felt he could handle the job.

The next day, Monday, October 15, Haig called in Elliot Richardson. Cox was officially Richardson's subordinate, and therefore Richardson would be the one who would have to fire him. Richardson, however, was an unpredictable element. He had publicly acknowledged the constitutional foundations of my refusal to hand over tapes when they were first subpoenaed; but he had also promised at his confirmation hearings that he would not fire Cox except for "extraordinary improprieties," and Richardson might feel that if he fired Cox he too would have to resign for breaking his promise to the Senate. After their meeting Haig confirmed that this was indeed how Richardson felt. Besides, I thought, no one could ignore the reality of the situation: Cox had become a Watergate hero.

Richardson's resignation was something we wanted to avoid at all costs. Haig and I decided to approach him with a compromise: we would not insist on firing Cox, but we would go ahead with the Stennis plan. I was still determined that this would be the end of our compromises with Cox. Haig told Richardson this and reported back that Richardson felt that the plan was good and reasonable and that Stennis was perfect for the job. He also said that he had received Richardson's assurance that if Cox refused to accept the Stennis compromise, Richardson would support me in the controversy that was bound to ensue. Haig said that Richardson was confident there would be no problem and that Cox, who had been his mentor at Harvard Law School and with whom he had been friendly ever since, would agree to the compromise.

On Monday Haig and Buzhardt went to see Stennis and confirmed the arrangements. Stennis would verify the line-by-line third-person summaries of the tapes that we produced and attest to the propriety of whatever omissions we made of material that dealt with irrelevant or national security matters. We had also decided to provide the verified summaries to Ervin and Baker for the Watergate Committee.

On October 17 I met in the Oval Office with four Arab Foreign Ministers. Afterward the Saudi Foreign Minister told reporters, "We think the man who could solve the Vietnam war, the man who could have settled the peace all over the world, can easily play a good role in settling and having peace in our area of the Middle East."

At 8:45 P.M. on Thursday, October 18, we received

word of a proposal the Soviets intended to submit to the UN Security Council for a joint Mideast cease-fire resolution. The combination of Israeli successes and our military airlift had proved too much for the Arabs and their Soviet sponsors, who proposed a resolution based on the three principles of a cease-fire in place, immediate withdrawal by the Israelis to the borders described in UN Resolution 242—in other words, to the pre-1967 borders—and the beginning of consultations on a peace agreement.

These terms reflected the familiar Soviet insistence that before any discussions of peace could begin, the Israelis would have to give up the territory they had gained in the 1967 war. This demand was utterly unrealistic, since the Israelis saw this territory not just as their leverage in any negotiations but as essential to their national security in the present environment. Besides, the recent Israeli battlefield successes had given them a decided military advantage, and there was no chance whatever that they would accept willingly the same terms the Arabs would have tried to impose if they had been the victors.

I sent a response that did not commit us to accepting the Soviet proposal but stressed the importance of keeping communications open. I said that our détente would remain incomplete unless peace was achieved in the Middle East and both of us had played a part in it.

In the meantime Haig reported that Richardson had talked with Cox but could not persuade him to compromise. Cox was unwilling to accept Stennis's verification. Richardson told Haig that Cox didn't have the sense of who Stennis was—his integrity—that Washington insiders had. Not only that, Cox wanted specific assurances of total access to all White House documents and tapes in the future. Haig reported that even Richardson thought this was unreasonable. More than ever I wanted Cox fired.

On Thursday and Friday, October 18 and 19, Richardson met twice with Haig, Wright, Garment, and Buzhardt. Haig told me that Richardson had suggested as an alternative to firing Cox, putting what he called "parameters" around him. The Special Prosecutor, as a part of the executive branch, was required to obey the orders of his superiors. The parameters could include an instruction that he was forbidden to sue for any further presidential documents. In the meantime we would bypass Cox with the Stennis compromise by offering the transcripts to the court and to the Ervin Committee.

Haig told me that our lawyers had analyzed Cox's possible reactions to Richardson's proposal and decided that he had three possible choices: he could accept the Stennis compromise; he could reject it and do nothing; or he could reject it and resign. According to Haig, everyone was certain that Cox, if he did not accept the Stennis compromise, would resign in protest against it; this would pose no problem for Richardson.

On October 19, while we were still trying to determine the best way to deal with Cox, a letter arrived from Brezhnev. He said that the situation in the Middle East was becoming more and more dangerous. Since neither the United States nor the Soviet Union wanted to see our relations harmed, he stated that we both should do our utmost to keep events in the Middle East from taking an even more dangerous turn. He suggested that Kissinger come to Moscow for direct talks.

We had reached a critical juncture in the war. The Israelis were now defeating the Arabs on the battlefield, and over the next few days the Soviets would have to decide what they were going to do about it. In the afternoon I sent Congress a request for $2.2 billion in emergency aid for Israel. On October 17 the Organization of Arab Petroleum Exporting Countries had voted to reduce crude oil production. Within a few days after my request for aid to Israel, Abu Dhabi, Libya, Saudi Arabia, Algeria, and Kuwait had imposed total oil embargoes on the United States. Even so, I felt that we could do no less for Israel at such a critical time.

Later that same afternoon, October 19, Haig brought me word of what he called a "tepid" complaint from Richardson about some of the terms of our plan for dealing with Cox. "It's no big problem," Haig said.

At 5:25 P.M., Sam Ervin and Howard Baker arrived at my office. They had been reached in New Orleans and Chicago respectively and brought to Washington aboard Air

Force jets. When I told them about the Stennis compromise, they both seemed pleased and relieved.

Ervin was very respectful during the meeting. Toward the end I told him that I regretted that I had talked to him so bluntly on the telephone in July. He said that he had not realized at the time that I was ill and that no apologies were necessary. After Baker and Ervin had agreed to the Stennis compromise, Haig notified the members of the White House staff, the Cabinet, and Jerry Ford. Everyone was elated by the news.

It was reported to me later that Bryce Harlow, who was helping Haig make the calls to the Cabinet, mistakenly called Elliot Richardson. He quickly apologized, but Richardson gave a petulant reply: "I have never been treated so shabbily." Harlow reported this incident to Haig, who immediately called Richardson and said that he was astonished to hear what he had said to Harlow. Richardson apologized. He told Haig that he was very tired and had had a drink and that things were looking much better to him now.

I announced the Stennis compromise in a statement released at 8:15 that night. I began with a reference to the extremely delicate world situation at that very moment:

> What matters most, in this critical hour, is our ability to act—and to act in a way that enables us to control events, not to be paralyzed and overwhelmed by them. At home, the Watergate issue has taken on overtones of a partisan political contest. Concurrently, there are those in the international community who may be tempted by our Watergate-related difficulties at home to misread America's unity and resolve in meeting the challenges we confront abroad.

Then I described the Stennis compromise and stated that the verified summaries would be sent to Judge Sirica and to the Ervin Committee. Having done this, I announced the instruction to Cox to cease and desist from his Watergate fishing expedition:

> Though I have not wished to intrude upon the independence of the Special Prosecutor, I have felt it necessary to direct him, as an employee of the executive branch, to make

no further attempts by judicial process to obtain tapes, notes, or memoranda of presidential conversations. I believe that with the statement that will be provided to the court, any legitimate need of the Special Prosecutor is fully satisfied and that he can proceed to obtain indictments against those who may have committed any crimes. And I believe that by these actions I have taken today, America will be spared the anguish of further indecision and litigation about tapes.

The initial congressional and public reaction to the Stennis compromise was favorable. Congressional colleagues of both parties expressed confidence in Stennis. David Broder wrote a column describing him as the logical man for the job.

I had immediately agreed to Brezhnev's suggestion that Kissinger go to Moscow for direct talks about the Middle East. At midnight on October 19, just before Kissinger was to leave for Moscow, I phoned him to discuss his trip.

The next morning, Saturday, October 20, I sent a stern letter to Brezhnev. I purposely mitigated the hard language in the text with a handwritten note extending best personal regards from Pat and me to him and Mrs. Brezhnev. Brezhnev, I knew, would understand what this mixture conveyed: if he was willing to get behind a serious peace effort, I would not consider that the Soviet airlift had affected our personal relationship or deflected the course of détente.

Shortly after Kissinger arrived in Moscow, he sent me a letter from Brezhnev, echoing the sentiments of my letter and containing a similar handwritten postscript: "Mrs. Brezhnev is grateful for the regards and in turn joins me in sending our best personal regards to Mrs. Nixon and to you."

Early Saturday afternoon Cox called a press conference. Adopting the air of a modest and even befuddled professor, he said, "I am certainly not out to get the President of the United States. I am even worried, to put it in colloquial terms, that I am getting too big for my britches, that what I see as principle could be vanity.... It is sort of embarrassing to be put in the position to say, well, I don't want the President of the United States to tell me what to do." He said that he was going ahead with his request for the tapes despite the compromise I had offered. He said he questioned whether anyone but Elliot Richardson could give him instructions that he was legally obligated to obey.

I strongly felt that I could not allow Cox to defy openly a presidential directive. I thought of Brezhnev and how it would look to the Soviets if in the midst of our diplomatic showdown with them I were in the position of having to defer to the demands of one of my own employees. Furthermore, I thought that Cox had deliberately exceeded his authority; I felt that he was trying to get me personally, and I wanted him out.

Shortly after two o'clock Haig called Richardson and asked him to fire Cox. Richardson said that he would not, and that he wanted to see me in order to resign. There were rumors that Richardson in conversations with others was now trying to back off from his own role in the formulation of the Stennis compromise and the cease-and-desist directive to Cox.

When Richardson arrived at the White House, Haig appealed to him to withhold his resignation at least until the Mideast crisis had been resolved. The impact of his resignation during this crisis, while Kissinger was meeting with Brezhnev, might have incalculable effects, not just on the Soviets' assessment of our intentions and our strength, but on the morale within our own government. I later asked Len Garment, "If I can't get an order carried out by my Attorney General, how can I get arms to Israel?" But Richardson refused to wait even a few days.

Shortly after 4:30 he was ushered into the Oval Office to tender his resignation. It was an emotional meeting. I talked to him about the gravity of the decision he was making and the ramifications of the things it might precipitate. I told him how serious I thought the next days were going to be with respect to the situation in the Mideast, and I repeated Haig's arguments in a personal appeal to him to delay his resignation in order not to trigger a domestic crisis at such a critical time for us abroad. Again he refused. He thanked me for being such a good friend and for having honored him with so many high appointments.

Richardson's Deputy, William Ruckelshaus, was the next in line to succeed as Attorney General, but he let us know that he too would resign rather than fire Cox. I feared that we were in for a whole chain of such resignations, and I was not sure where it would end. I was, however, prepared to see it through.

The third-ranking official in the Justice Department was the Solicitor General, Robert Bork. The resignations of his two superiors placed Bork in a painfully difficult position. He was no "yes man." But however much he might personally have opposed my decision to fire Cox, he was a constitutional scholar and he felt that I had the constitutional right to do so and that he therefore had the duty to carry out my orders. He said that he would fire Archibald Cox.

At 8:22 P.M. on Saturday, October 20, Ziegler went to the White House briefing room and announced that Cox was being fired, that Richardson and Ruckelshaus had resigned, and that the office of the Watergate Special Prosecutor was being abolished and its functions transferred back to the Justice Department.

The television networks broke into their regular programming with breathless, almost hysterical, bulletins. Later that evening there were special reports on all networks. Commentators and correspondents talked in apocalyptic terms and painted the night's events in terms of an administration coup aimed at suppressing opposition. John Chancellor of NBC began a broadcast thus: "The country tonight is in the midst of what may be the most serious constitutional crisis in its history.... That is a stunning development and nothing even remotely like it has happened in all of our history.... In my career as a correspondent, I never thought I would be announcing these things." Some called it the "Night of the Long Knives" in a tasteless and inflammatory comparison with Hitler's murderous purge of his opposition in 1934. Within twenty-four hours the television and press had labeled the events with the prejudicial shorthand of a "Saturday Night Massacre."

On Monday evening the network news shows ran nineteen different attacks on me by various congressmen; these were balanced by only five defenses, three of them by Bork.

"Has President Nixon gone crazy?" asked columnist Carl Rowan; Ralph Nader said I was "acting like a madman, a tyrant, or both"; "smacks of dictatorship" was Edmund Muskie's judgment. "A reckless act of desperation by a President . . . who has no respect for law and no regard for men of conscience," was Teddy Kennedy's comment. Senator Robert Byrd said that the Cox firing was a "Brown-shirt operation" using "Gestapo tactics." "The wolves are in full cry," countered the New York *Daily News*. The *Star* stated, "The jackboots that some observers seem to hear . . . are largely in their own minds."

By Tuesday, October 23, there were twenty-one resolutions for my impeachment in varying stages of discussion on Capitol Hill. Six newspapers that had formerly been staunch supporters of the administration now called for my resignation. By October 30, in a straight party-line vote, the House Judiciary Committee had voted itself subpoena power; on November 15 the House voted to allocate $1 million to begin the process of impeachment.

Although I had been prepared for a major and adverse reaction to Cox's firing, I was taken by surprise by the ferocious intensity of the reaction that actually occurred. For the first time I recognized the depth of the impact Watergate had been having on America; I suddenly realized how deeply its acid had eaten into the nation's grain. As I learned of the almost hysterical reactions of otherwise sensible and responsible people to this Saturday night's events, I realized how few people were able to see things from my perspective, how badly frayed the nerves of the American public had become. To the extent that I had not been aware of this situation, my actions were the result of serious miscalculation. But to the extent that it was simply intolerable to continue with Cox as Special Prosecutor, I felt I had no other option than to act as I did.

In Moscow on Sunday, October 21, Kissinger and Brezhnev produced the draft of a proposed cease-fire agreement. Brezhnev was to inform Sadat and Asad of its terms, and Kissinger left for Tel Aviv to present it to the Israelis. While he was en route, I sent Mrs. Meir a letter expressing my regret that there had not been more time for consultation and describing the provisions of the proposed agreement:

1. A cease-fire in place.

2. A general call for the implementation of UN Resolution 242 after the cease-fire.

3. Negotiation between the concerned parties aimed at establishing a just and durable peace in the Mideast.

These terms were especially notable because they were the first in which the Soviets had agreed to a resolution that called for direct negotiations between the parties without any conditions or qualifications. It was also the first time that they had accepted a "general call" for adherence to Resolution 242 and not insisted on Israeli withdrawal from the occupied territories as a prerequisite for any further negotiations.

Both the Arabs and the Israelis accepted the terms—without much enthusiasm, to be sure—and on Monday, October 22, the cease-fire went into effect. Within hours, however, the Israelis charged that the Egyptians were violating it and resumed an active offensive and completed their encirclement of the 20,000-man Egyptian Third Army on the east bank of the Suez Canal.

Kissinger, now back in Washington, received a message from the Soviets blaming the Israelis for the breakdown of the cease-fire and informing him that Sadat had suggested that the United States and the Soviet Union agree on measures to ensure the physical disengagement of Egyptian and Israeli forces. Twenty minutes later, at 11 A.M. on October 23, I received an urgent message from Brezhnev over the Washington-Moscow hot line. Although it began, "Esteemed Mr. President," the words were hard and cold. Brezhnev ignored the Egyptian provocations and charged the Israelis with rupturing the cease-fire. He urged that the United States move decisively to stop the violations. He curtly implied that we might even have colluded in Israel's action.

I sent a reply that, according to our information, Egypt was the first party to violate the cease-fire. I added that this was not the time to debate the issue. I said that we had insisted that Israel take immediate steps to cease hostilities, and I urged Brezhnev to do the same on the Egyptian side. I closed by saying that he and I had achieved a historic settlement over the past weekend and should not permit it to be destroyed.

By the time I reached Camp David that afternoon, Brezhnev had sent a message that the Egyptian side was ready for another cease-fire if the Israelis would agree. We sent back a reply urging him to press Syria as well as Egypt to accept the cease-fire. I concluded, "I continue to believe that you and we have done a distinct service to the cause of peace."

That same day, Tuesday, October 23, Charles Alan Wright was scheduled to appear before Judge Sirica and announce my decision on the subpoenaed tapes. The Stennis compromise had fallen apart in the wake of the Cox firing, and shortly before Wright was to leave for the court I met with him, Haig, Garment, and Buzhardt to make the final decision.

I could see that we were going to have to act swiftly or risk an impeachment resolution being raced through the House. This threat argued for yielding the tapes. At the same time, I knew the implications of such compliance, both for the principle of executive privilege and for my personal situation. As a third option I could appeal the decision to the Supreme Court. But that would force an even more binding decision, possibly a negative one, and even greater damage would be done to the presidency and the doctrine of separation of powers.

There were other considerations as well: some congressmen were hinting that Ford's confirmation would be dependent on my surrendering the tapes. Finally, I felt that there was a need to relieve the domestic crisis in order to reduce the temptation the Soviets would feel to take advantage of our internal turmoil by exploiting the international crisis in the Middle East. Everyone at the meeting agreed that I should yield the tapes. It was a wrenching decision for me. I consoled myself that at least these tapes might finally prove that Dean had lied in his testimony against me. That afternoon Wright appeared before the bench and announced, "This President does not defy the law."

On October 24 the second Mideast cease-fire went into effect. But there were alarming new intelligence reports: we received information that seven Soviet airborne divisions, numbering 50,000 men, had been put on alert; and eighty-five Soviet ships, including landing craft and ships carrying troop helicopters, were now in the Mediterranean.

That afternoon Sadat publicly requested that Brezhnev and I send a joint peacekeeping force to the Middle East. The Soviets would obviously back this idea, viewing it as an opportunity to re-establish their military presence in Egypt. Through John Scali, now our ambassador to the UN, we also picked up rumors that the Soviets were plotting for the nonaligned nations to sponsor and support a joint U.S.–U.S.S.R. force whether we liked it or not.

I decided to use our newly opened lines of communication with Egypt to send Sadat a straightforward message:

> I have just learned that a resolution may be introduced into the Security Council this evening urging that outside military forces—including those of the U.S. and U.S.S.R.—be sent to the Middle East to enforce the cease-fire. I must tell you that if such a resolution is introduced into the Security Council, it will be vetoed by the United States for the following reasons:
>
> It would be impossible to assemble sufficient outside military power to represent an effective counterweight to the indigenous forces now engaged in combat in the Middle East.
>
> Should the two great nuclear powers be called upon to provide forces, it would introduce an extremely dangerous potential for direct great-power rivalry in the area.

At nine o'clock that night a new message arrived from Brezhnev. He claimed to have hard information that Israeli armed forces were fighting Egyptian forces on the east bank of the Suez Canal. We knew that this was not true; it had been a relatively quiet day on the battlefront. There was clearly some ulterior motive behind Brezhnev's message, and we would have to wait and see what it was.

An hour later another message from Brezhnev arrived. Kissinger called Dobrynin and read it to him just to be sure there was no mistake, because this message represented perhaps the most serious threat to U.S.–Soviet relations since the Cuban missile crisis eleven years before. Brezhnev repeated his assertion that Israel was fighting despite the Security Council cease-fire. Therefore he urged that the United States and the Soviet Union each immediately dispatch military contingents to the region. He called for an immediate reply and stated that if we did not agree to the joint action he proposed, the Soviets would consider acting unilaterally.

When Haig informed me about this message, I said that he and Kissinger should have a meeting at the White House to formulate plans for a firm reaction to what amounted to a scarcely veiled threat of unilateral Soviet intervention. Words were not making our point—we needed action, even the shock of a military alert.

Late that night I sent Sadat another message, outlining the Soviet proposal and explaining, as I had in my earlier message, why I found intervention unacceptable:

> I asked you to consider the consequences for your country if the two great nuclear countries were thus to confront each other on your soil. I ask you further to consider the impossibility for us for undertaking the diplomatic initiative which was to start with Dr. Kissinger's visit to Cairo on November 7 if the forces of one of the great nuclear powers were to be involved militarily on Egyptian soil.
>
> We are at the beginning of a new period in the Middle East. Let us not destroy it at this moment.

In the meantime Kissinger, Haig, Schlesinger, Scowcroft, Moorer, and Director Colby of the CIA met at eleven o'clock in the White House Situation Room. Their unanimous recommendation was that we should put all American conventional and nuclear forces on military alert. In the early morning hours we flashed the word to American bases, installations, and naval units at home and around the world.

When we were sure the Soviets had picked up the first signs of the alert, I sent a letter to the Soviet Embassy for immediate transmission to Moscow. It was directly to Brezhnev from me, and beneath the diplomatic phraseology it minced no words:

> Mr. General Secretary:
> I have carefully studied your important message of this evening. I agree with you that our understanding to act jointly for peace is of the highest value and that we should implement that understanding in this complex situation.

I must tell you, however, that your proposal for a particular kind of joint action, that of sending Soviet and American military contingents to Egypt, is not appropriate in the present circumstances.

We have no information which would indicate that the cease-fire is now being violated on any significant scale. . . .

In these circumstances, we must view your suggestion of unilateral action as a matter of the gravest concern, involving incalculable consequences.

It is clear that the forces necessary to impose the cease-fire terms on the two sides would be massive and would require closest coordination so as to avoid bloodshed. This is not only clearly infeasible but it is not appropriate to the situation.

I said that I would be prepared to agree that some American and Soviet personnel go to the area, but not as combat forces. Instead, they might be included in an augmented UN force. But even this kind of arrangement would have to follow carefully prescribed lines:

It would be understood that this is an extraordinary and temporary step, solely for the purpose of providing adequate information concerning compliance by both sides with the terms of the cease-fire. If this is what you mean by contingents, we will consider it.

Mr. General Secretary, in the spirit of our agreements this is the time for acting not unilaterally but in harmony and with cool heads. I believe my proposal is consonant with the letter and spirit of our understandings and would ensure a prompt implementation of the cease-fire. . . .

You must know, however, that we could in no event accept unilateral action. . . . As I stated above, such action would produce incalculable consequences which would be in the interest of neither of our countries and which would end all we have striven so hard to achieve.

At 7:15 A.M. on October 25 a message arrived from President Sadat that he understood our position and that he would ask the UN to provide an international peacekeeping force.

I met with Haig and Kissinger at eight, and less than an hour later I briefed the bipartisan leadership on these latest events. The room was hushed as I described the exchanges of the last few hours. When the leaders left, they said that they were fully in support of my actions and my policy, including the military alert.

While we were still waiting for word from Brezhnev that would indicate the Soviet reaction, Kissinger held a press conference. It had been a severe shock to the American people to wake up and find that during the night our armed forces had been placed on worldwide alert, and four of the questions at Kissinger's press conference specifically related to whether the decision to call the alert had been based entirely on the military aspects of the situation. Some even obliquely wondered whether the decision had been totally rational. One reporter commented, "As you know, there has been some line of speculation this morning that the American alert might have been prompted as much perhaps by American domestic requirements as by the real requirements of diplomacy in the Middle East."

Kissinger was taken aback by the hostile and skeptical atmosphere in the room, and he replied icily: "It is a symptom of what is happening to our country that it could even be suggested that the United States would alert its forces for domestic reasons. We do not think it is wise at this moment to go into details of the diplomatic exchanges. . . . Upon the conclusion . . . we will make the record available. . . . And I am absolutely confident that it will be seen that the President had no other choice as a responsible national leader." Later in the press conference he acknowledged that we were undergoing a major domestic crisis, and he added: "It is up to you ladies and gentlemen to determine whether this is the moment to try to create a crisis of confidence in the field of foreign policy as well. . . . But there has to be a minimum of confidence that the senior officials of the American government are not playing with the lives of the American people."

As Kissinger was parrying these questions, a message arrived from Brezhnev. In a few short sentences he announced that the Soviet Union was going to send seventy individual "observers" to the Middle East. This was completely different from the military contingent he had described in his earlier letter. I responded to his message in a similarly low-keyed tone, but strongly expressed my opposition to sending even independent observers:

> I propose that at this time we leave the composition of the UN Observer Force to the discretion of the Secretary-General. . . . We do not believe it necessary to have separate observer forces from individual countries operating in the area.

I evaluated the Soviet behavior during the Mideast crisis not as an example of the failure of détente but as an illustration of its limitations—limitations of which I had always been keenly aware. I told the bipartisan leadership meeting on October 25, "I have never said that the Soviets are 'good guys.' What I have always said is that we should not enter into unnecessary confrontations with them."

The Soviet Union will always act in its own self-interest; and so will the United States. Détente cannot change that. All we can hope from détente is that it will minimize confrontation in marginal areas and provide, at least, alternative possibilities in the major ones.

In 1973 the Soviets, with their presence in the Middle East already reduced, feared that they would lose what little foothold they had left. As our direct approaches to Egypt and the Arab countries had met with increasing success, the Soviets had undoubtedly compensated with increased anti-Israeli bravado. Perhaps this indirectly encouraged the Arab countries, which were fanatically determined to regain the occupied territories from Israel if the Soviets would supply the means. Although Brezhnev heatedly denied it when I talked to him at Summit III in Moscow in June 1974, the Soviets may have gone even further and directly urged the Arabs to attack, lured by the tantalizing prospect that they might actually win a quick victory over the Israelis if they could combine surprise with their vastly superior numbers. The Soviets might also have assumed that the domestic crisis in the United States would deflect or deter us from aiding Israel as much or as fast as we had in the past.

Any such high hopes were dashed by the Israeli counteroffensive made possible by the American airlift. For the second time in six years the Arabs lost most of the Soviet equipment that had been sent them. Moreover, for the first time in an Arab-Israeli conflict the United States conducted itself in a manner that not only preserved but greatly enhanced our relations with the Arabs—even while we were massively resupplying the Israelis. Once they realized that military victory was now beyond their reach for at least the next several years, the Egyptian and Syrian leaders were ready to try the path of negotiation. Thanks to our new policy of carefully cultivated direct relations with the Arab capitals, the Arab leaders had a place other than Moscow to turn.

So obsessive had Watergate become for some reporters and publications that suggestions continued to be made that I had purposely provoked or encouraged the Mideast crisis to distract attention from Watergate and to demonstrate that I was still capable of leadership and action. With this in mind, and thinking about the reporting on the Cox firing, I faced this problem head on at a press conference on October 26. "I have never heard or seen such outrageous, vicious, distorted reporting in twenty-seven years of public life," I said. "And yet I should point out that even in this week, when many thought that the President was shell-shocked, unable to act, the President acted decisively in the interests of peace, in the interests of the country, and I can assure you that whatever shocks gentlemen of the press may have, or others, political people, these shocks will not affect me in my doing my job."

At the end of October there was another hot-line exchange. Brezhnev made a formal complaint about what he called Israeli hostilities; in particular he referred to their handling of food and medical supplies intended for the trapped Egyptian Third Army. He also stated that the recent U.S. alert had surprised him, and he complained that it had not promoted a relaxation of tension.

In my reply I said we would do our part to assist the transport of supplies to the wounded Egyptians in the Third Army. In response to his criticism of the alert I quoted the words he had written threatening to take unilateral action unless we joined his plan to send U.S. and Soviet forces to the Middle East. I stated, "Mr. General Secretary, these are serious words and were taken seriously here in Washington."

I followed up on November 3 with a letter to Brezhnev stating the importance of respecting the principle stated in our agreement on the prevention of nuclear war: that efforts at gaining unilateral advantage at the expense of the other party were inconsistent with the objectives of peaceful relations and the avoidance of confrontations. I repeated the fact that the peace of the world depended on the policies and actions of our two countries—in both a positive and a negative sense.

After almost three weeks Brezhnev replied to this letter. He indicated a willingness to pick up the dialogue of détente where it had left off before the Mideast crisis, and he closed with an unusually personal reference: "We would like, so to say, to wish you in a personal, human way energy and success in overcoming all sorts of complexities, the causes of which are not too easy to understand at a distance."

At the beginning of November Golda Meir came to Washington. We met for an hour in the Oval Office, and she expressed her gratitude for the airlift. "There were days and hours when we needed a friend, and you came right in," she said. "You don't know what your airlift means to us."

"I never believe in little plays when big issues are at stake," I said.

I urged a policy of sensible restraint for Israel. "Sometimes, when you have a situation of attrition, even winners can lose," I reminded her. "The problem that Israel must now consider is whether the policy you are following can succeed. Lacking a settlement, the only policy is constantly being prepared for war. But that really is no policy at all." I said that she could be remembered as the leader who created an Israel that was not burdened with a huge arms budget or with having to fight a war every five years.

Mrs. Meir seemed to understand the essential common sense of what I was saying. She also seemed to appreciate my lack of illusions about the limitations of détente or the nature of the Soviet threat. "When the Europeans talked about détente," she said, "they were bleary-eyed and naïve. But you know exactly what you are doing and who your partners are."

On November 5 Kissinger began the first of many journeys to the Middle East in which he personally guided first Israel and Egypt, and then Israel and Syria, along the unfamiliar and often painful road toward a peaceful settlement of their differences. On November 7, 1973, after six years of tense estrangement, the United States and Egypt resumed diplomatic relations.

After Cox had been fired, I had intended that Henry Petersen and his Justice Department staff would be allowed to complete the Watergate investigation, which they had begun and which was properly their responsibility. But it was evident that Congress was determined to have another Special Prosecutor. It was equally evident that I was in no political position to prevent it.

Robert Bork, as Acting Attorney General, began searching for a new Special Prosecutor. A few days later Haig reported to me that he and Bork had concluded that Leon Jaworski, a successful Houston lawyer, a former president of the American Bar Association, and a prominent Texas Democrat, was the right man for the job. Haig had already tentatively approached Jaworski, who had said he would accept if he could have our agreement that in the event we came to an impasse he could sue me in the courts for evidence. I agreed to this condition, and, as a further guarantee, we announced that there would have to be a supportive consensus of the Majority and Minority Leaders of the House and Senate and the ranking majority and minority members of the House and Senate Judiciary Committees before he could be fired.

Within ten days of the Cox firing and after the high political price I had had to pay for ridding myself of him, I was back in the same trap of having to accept a Watergate Special Prosecutor. But there was one major difference: I had been told that, unlike Cox, Jaworski would be fair and objective. Although as a Democrat he would be under pressure from other Democrats to score partisan points, I was led to believe that he respected the office of the presidency and that therefore he would not mount court challenges just for the plaudits and publicity he would thereby receive. Haig said that Jaworski recognized that the staff assembled by Cox was excessively anti-Nixon and that he was determined not to become their captive. He told Haig that he planned to bring in his own people and would see to it that the staff limited its activity to relevant and proper areas. Haig liked Jaworski and was impressed by him; he told me that Jaworski would be a tough prosecutor but not a partisan who was simply out to get me. On November 1, we announced that Leon Jaworski would be the Special Prosecutor.

I also needed a new Attorney General. The political situation created by Richardson's resignation dictated that in order to get my nominee confirmed, I would have to select someone who would not have to contend with charges of excessive personal loyalty to me. Senator William Saxbe of Ohio had long since established that he was a man without that problem. As my father would have put it, he was as "independent as a hog on ice." His appointment was announced the same day as Jaworski's.

SETBACK AND RALLY

In late September, when we were first preparing for the Stennis compromise, Steve Bull had had some difficulty locating several of the nine subpoenaed conversations. The Secret Service had catalogued the tapes, but their system was informal at best and haphazard at worst. In one case, Bull finally found an apparently missing conversation on a reel that had been erroneously labeled. In the case of a June 20, 1972, phone conversation with John Mitchell, I remembered that I had talked to him from a phone that was in the Family Quarters and therefore not connected to any recording equipment. In another case, that of an April 15, 1973, conversation with John Dean, the tape simply could not be found.

Near the end of October, about a month after Bull's initial search, Fred Buzhardt conducted one of his own. He confirmed that the phone call to Mitchell was from the Residence and had never been recorded. He also confirmed why Bull had not been able to find a tape of the April 15 meeting with Dean.

I usually did not go to the EOB office on Sundays. The Secret Service, who monitored the taping system, had not anticipated that I would have several unusually long conversations there on Saturday and Sunday, April 14 and 15. Thus by the time I sat down with Dick Kleindienst at 1:15 on Sunday afternoon, the reel of tape was near the end. It ran out in midsentence during our conversation, and the afternoon and evening meetings of April 15 with Haldeman, Ehrlichman, Petersen, Kleindienst, and Dean were never recorded.

On October 30 Buzhardt informed Sirica that two of the subpoenaed conversations had never been recorded. We readily agreed to have a panel of experts investigate our explanation for each case. We also offered my written notes of the April 15 meeting with John Dean and the tape of my meeting with him the next day, because a comparison of the April 15 notes and the April 16 tape indicated that we had covered much the same ground in the two sessions.

I was sure that a full explanation of how and why the phone call to Mitchell and the meeting with Dean had failed to be recorded would clear things up completely. I simply did not understand the degree of public anticipation that had developed around these nine subpoenaed tapes; now I can see that it was largely the result of the degree to which my personal credibility had sunk.

The news was met with an outburst of anger and indignation. The next day the media began reporting about two "missing tapes." This was both unfair and misleading: the use of the word *missing* implied that the two tapes had existed in the first place. People felt that I was toying with their patience and insulting their intelligence.

For the first time since the Watergate affair began, the New York *Times* urged editorially that I resign the presidency. *Time,* in its first editorial in fifty years, also said that I should step down. Even old friends, among them the Detroit *News* and ABC's Howard K. Smith, began to express doubts. It was in the wake of the two so-called missing tapes that Senator Edward Brooke of Massachusetts became the first Republican in Congress to urge that I resign.

When Barry Goldwater saw the frenzied turn events

were taking, he went on the air to ask people to "curb their wild stampede, to pause a moment in their tumult and trumpeting" and give thought to the consequences of the hysteria if it continued uncurbed. "In God's name, cool it," he said.

On November 1 I wrote a frustrated note on the top of a briefing paper:

> There were no missing tapes.
> There never were any.
> The conversations in question were not taped.
> Why couldn't we get that across to people?

That same day I left for a weekend in Florida. I looked forward to the chance to get some rest and to try to assess the damage. I had no idea that our problems with the tapes were just beginning.

In April 1973, in a phone conversation with Henry Petersen, I had unthinkingly said that I believed that my April 15 conversation with John Dean had been recorded on tape. Petersen reported my remark to Cox, who later wrote to us requesting this tape for his investigation. In order to avoid revealing the existence of the taping system, I told Buzhardt to write to Cox and tell him that the "tape" I had had in mind was actually the Dictabelt I had made after the meeting. Now it turned out that the April 15 conversation had never been recorded because the tape had run out. But there was worse news still to come. We were about to learn that no Dictabelt could be found either.

I had not actually checked when I told Buzhardt to tell Cox there was a Dictabelt. I had simply assumed that I had made one, since I had been doing so almost daily in that period; my notes of the meeting were clearly marked for dictation. But we could not find a Dictabelt for that conversation.

I had put Buzhardt in an untenable position: first I had had him send a letter to Cox in order to divert him from a tape recording to a Dictabelt; now there was no Dictabelt. Len Garment felt that the public revelation of this latest blunder would throw us into a fatal spin. Beyond that, both he and Buzhardt felt that they were not making any progress or doing any good. We were always in a completely reactive situation, and there seemed to be no prospect for changing that pattern no matter what we did.

On Saturday, November 3, Garment and Buzhardt had come to Florida. Haig brought me a diluted report of his meeting with them, but I sensed what he was saying between the lines: even before we finally confirmed that there was no Dictabelt, they felt they had had it. I could not blame them. They had been hopelessly undermanned, chronically overworked, and regularly undermined by events and now by me. They had both urged, and Haig concurred, that we look for another lawyer, perhaps someone from outside the White House, who would deal with nothing but Watergate.

That weekend in Florida was a new low point for me personally and a turning point for our approach to dealing with Watergate. Even as I realized the depth to which we had plunged, I recognized that there was only one way out. We were under relentless attack by the opposition, and now we were faced with defections by our supporters as well. More than anything else, we had to stop that erosion. "We will take some desperate, strong measure," I told Ziegler, "and this time there is no margin for error."

First, I had to address the increasing number of demands for my resignation. On November 7, at the end of a televised speech on the energy crisis, I turned over the last typed page of the text to the handwritten notes I had made only a few hours earlier. I said:

> Tonight I would like to give my answer to those who have suggested that I resign.
>
> I have no intention whatever of walking away from the job I was elected to do. As long as I am physically able, I am going to continue to work sixteen to eighteen hours a day for the cause of a real peace abroad, and for the cause of prosperity without inflation and without war at home. And in the months ahead I shall do everything that I can to see that any doubts as to the integrity of the man who occupies the highest office in this land—to remove those doubts where they exist.
>
> And I am confident that in those months ahead, the American people will come to realize that I have not violated the trust that they placed in me when they elected me as

President of the United States in the past, and I pledge to you tonight that I shall always do everything that I can to be worthy of that trust in the future.

I decided to begin meeting with different congressional groups until I had personally talked to every Republican in Congress and to all my supporters on the Democratic side. This would not be just a way of presenting my side of the Watergate case and answering whatever questions they had about it; it would also provide an opportunity for beginning to rebuild the badly damaged bridges of communication and shared purposes that had been among the casualties of Watergate. All told, in nine separate two-hour sessions over the next week, I met with 241 Republican and 46 Democratic senators and congressmen. In each meeting I ran over the charges and answered questions, repeating the defense spelled out in my public statements. I explained to Ed Brooke that I would not consider resigning because it would change the American system of government. I remember sitting with Eastland, McClellan, Stennis, and Long, the deans of the Senate, and starting to review the Watergate charges with them. Jim Eastland leaned forward and said, "Mr. President, we don't need to hear any explanations. We don't even want to talk about Watergate. Just tell us what to do to help." Seventy-year-old John Stennis leaned over to Eastland and said, "Quiet, Jim. Let the boy speak."

I told these congressional groups that we would issue white papers on the major charges. I also said that we were contemplating releasing transcripts or summaries of the tapes that had been turned over to the court—something that they had all urged.

Some of the congressmen suggested that I try to put Watergate to rest by making one grandstand play or one dramatic gesture that would answer all the questions and exorcise all the demons. Some suggested that I voluntarily appear before a joint session of Congress and stay until I had answered every question that every member wanted to ask. The suggestion was well intentioned, but I had no confidence whatever that any single gesture would be successful at this late date. Watergate had gone too far for me to be able to dispel it in one speech. As I told one Republican group that urged this as a solution, if I gave a speech

509

and said, "I didn't do it," the Democrats would say, "The son of a bitch is lying"; and the Republicans would say, "Ho hum, he is probably lying but he is our son of a bitch."

I also said that if the charges against me continued in the same partisan way, "I will go down—and I will go down gracefully—but I will not resign." And I tried to tell them I understood what a burden Watergate had been on them: "You have all worked hard, your careers are involved, you are worried about the polls and about whether the money is going to come in for your campaigns. You are wondering why in hell the President can't clear it up and so forth. I'm worried about it too, because these last few months have not been easy."

And I urged some sense of perspective. "I know people say I shouldn't talk about meetings with Brezhnev and Mao, that people aren't interested in that," I said. "But I know that in the history books twenty-five years from now what will really matter is the fact that the President of the United States in the period from 1969 to 1976 changed the world."

In one meeting Jacob Javits leaned over to me reassuringly and said, "Lincoln was called a lot worse things than you, remember that." "I'm catching up," was all I could reply.

The media, ever in search of a simple label for complex events, latched on to one coined by *Newsweek*. An article in the magazine had referred to my stepped-up activities and my televised remarks against impeachment as "Operation Candor." The intent of the label, of course, was to trivialize my effort and to imply that candor was something I thought could be turned on and off like a faucet. A sloppy press corps soon forgot that this label had been its own invention and started using it regularly without putting it in quotation marks or explaining its origin. On December 2 an editorial in the New York *Times* stated authoritatively that: "President Nixon's counteroffensive on Watergate, billed by the White House as 'Operation Candor,' is visibly collapsing."

THE 18-MINUTE GAP

It was during one of the congressional briefing sessions on November 15 that someone asked, "Is there another shoe to drop?"

"As far as I'm concerned," I replied, "as to the guilt of the President, no." But I added, "If the shoes fall, I will be there ready to catch them."

Late that afternoon Haig came into the Oval Office, looking strained and worried. He said that the lawyers had been preparing an index of the tapes that were to be turned over to Sirica. After checking the original subpoena against a supplementary document that had been sent by Cox during the summer, they had now decided that Buzhardt's earlier interpretation, based on the subpoena alone, was wrong. The supplementary document made it clear that the subpoena *did* cover the June 20, 1972, conversation with Haldeman—the tape with the gap.

It was a nightmare. How in hell, I asked, could we have made a mistake about something as fundamental as whether or not a particular conversation was covered by a subpoena? I asked if we could still argue that it wasn't covered by the subpoena. Haig said that he would get Haldeman's notes from June 20, 1972, and try to reconstruct what had been said during the missing segment of our conversation. When the notes finally arrived, they turned out to be a mixed blessing. While they made it clear that we had been talking about Watergate, they indicated that the conversation had been in general terms about the political impact of the incident:

> be sure EOB office is *thoroly* ckd re bugs   at all times—etc.
> what is our counter-attack
>   PR offensive to top this—
>   hit the opposition w/ their activities
>   pt. out libertarians have created public callousness
>   do they justify this less than stealing Pentagon papers, Anderson file etc.?
> we shld be on the attack—for diversion—

There was still more bad news about the gap that day: I learned that it did not run for just the four or five minutes that Rose had estimated as the length of time she had spent on the telephone. Buzhardt informed me that, after playing the tape through, they found that the gap ran 18½ minutes. No one could explain how or why it had happened or account for the shrill buzzing sounds that punctuated the otherwise blank portion.

When we left for a few days in Florida on November 17, Buzhardt stayed in Washington to see if the 18½ minutes of conversation could be electronically recovered. He was also going to see if he could re-create the circumstances that had caused the gap and the peculiar sounds that now appeared on the tape.

On the way back to Washington on Tuesday, November 20, I stopped off in Memphis, Tennessee, to attend a meeting of the Republican Governors Conference. In a private and freewheeling session we covered every major foreign and domestic issue, including Watergate. At one point in the meeting I was asked if there were going to be any more Watergate bombshells. I immediately thought of the tape with the 18½-minute gap—that was certainly in the bombshell category. But we still had not heard from Buzhardt whether the conversation could be recovered, or, failing that, whether we could find some logical explanation of how it had happened. I knew that if I indicated even the remotest possibility of a new bombshell, I would have to say what it was—and I still was not sure of the answer to that myself.

For all these reasons I answered, "If there are, I'm not aware of them."

On the plane on the way back to Washington Haig told me that Buzhardt confirmed that the missing portion of the June 20 conversation was not recoverable. Furthermore, Buzhardt had had no success in his efforts to reproduce the buzzing sound.

The headline in papers all across the country the next morning was my assertion that there would be no more Watergate bombshells. That same morning Buzhardt told Jaworski and Sirica about the 18½-minute gap, and Sirica announced it to the press.

I know that most people think that my inability to explain the 18½-minute gap is the most unbelievable and insulting part of the whole of Watergate. Because of this, I am aware that my treatment of the gap will be looked upon as a touchstone for the candor and credibility of whatever else I write about Watergate. I also know that the only explanations that would readily be accepted are that I erased the tape myself, or that Rose Mary Woods deliberately did so, either on her own initiative or at my direct or indirect request.

But I know I did not do it. And I completely believe Rose when she says that she did not do it. I can only tell the story of the 18½-minute gap—as incomplete and unsatisfactory a story as I know it is—from the vantage point of having watched it bring my reputation and my presidency to new lows of public confidence and esteem.

Haig told me that Garment and Buzhardt were completely panicked by the discovery of the 18½-minute gap. They suspected everyone, including Rose, Steve Bull, and me. Suspicion had now invaded the White House. I even wondered if Buzhardt himself could have accidentally erased the portion beyond the five-minute gap Rose thought she might have caused. Using the simple criterion of access to the tapes, there were many possible suspects. Haig and others joked darkly about "sinister forces" being responsible for the gap, but I think that we all wondered about the various Secret Service agents and technicians who had had free daily access to the tapes, and even about the Secret Service agents who had provided Rose with the new but apparently faulty Uher tape recorder just half an hour before she discovered the gap. We even wondered about Alex Butterfield, who had revealed the existence of the tape system. He had had access to all the tapes; in fact, he had regularly listened to random passages to make sure that the system was working properly. But it would have taken a very dedicated believer in conspiracies to accept that someone would have purposely erased 18½ minutes of this particular tape in order to embarrass me.

After an inconclusive public hearing the matter of the gap was turned over to the grand jury and a panel of court-appointed experts. I believe that the story of these experts represents one of the biggest, and least known, scandals connected with Watergate. The White House is not without blame, because we approved the six "experts" appointed by the court. If we had checked, we would have found that they were experts in the theory of acoustics but not the practicalities of tape recorders.

In a January report the experts concluded that the buzzing sounds had been put on the tape "in the process of erasing and rerecording at least five, and perhaps as many as nine, separate and contiguous segments. Hand operation of the keyboard controls on the recorder was involved in starting and again in stopping the recording of each segment." This conclusion was widely reported; not so widely reported was the fact that it came under immediate attack from other scientists and tape specialists, one of whom called it more a "news release than a solid investigation."

One electronics firm pointed out that the apparently incriminating sounds and magnetic marks attributed by the panel to specific manual erasures could have been made accidentally by a malfunction in the machine that caused the internal power supply to sputter on and off. *Science* magazine reported that other experts agreed with the feasibility of this alternate hypothesis. The only test that the court's experts made of this hypothesis prior to the release of their preliminary report in January was made on a *Sony*, not a Uher 5000. They apparently failed to see this as a lapse in standard scientific testing procedure.

One of the court's experts testified that in testing the machine Rose had used, they "of necessity had to open up the interior . . . and tighten down several screws and quite conceivably, for example, may have tightened a ground connection to a point where it was making more firm contact than previously." When they found a defective part they replaced it—and threw the defective one away! He acknowledged that after they had worked on the machine it no longer produced the buzzing sound they had noticed beforehand.

After this extraordinary admission, Rose's attorney, Charles Rhyne, said, "So in effect you obliterated the evidence which anyone else would need to test your conclusions, did you not?"

"Yes, in large part," was the answer.

Richard Salmon, national manager of Uher of America, Inc., in Inglewood, California, the manufacturer of the machine Rose had used, scathingly criticized the court experts' report. He said that on some of their specially modified machines pressing the "rewind" button in a certain way would cause the machine to erase automatically. Salmon said that by using a display "of great experience and electrical intelligence"—in other words, technical jargon—"they covered up a weak report."

The court paid these six experts $100,000 for their work. It was worthless as a legal document, but it produced more than its money's worth of incriminating headlines.

Rose Woods testified under oath concerning the 18½-minute gap before a court hearing and the grand jury. In the hearing she was subjected to hours of merciless cross-examination on this issue. On July 17, 1974, Leon Jaworski informed Rose's attorney that no case had been developed of any illegal action of any kind by Rose and that no charges would be made against her. He said that his assistant, Richard Ben-Veniste, agreed. Jaworski, however, did not make a public announcement of this fact, and to this day many people are not aware that Rose was exonerated by the Special Prosecutor in regard to the 18½-minute gap.

In late 1973, after the 18½-minute gap had been revealed and it seemed as if nothing worse could happen to us, something worse did.

PROPERTY AND TAXES

From the start of my political career, I had tried to be scrupulously careful in the handling of public money. I grew up in a home where politics was frequently discussed, and where the greatest contempt was reserved for politicians on the take. If anything, I have always gone far beyond most people in government to document and account for public money, whether campaign or government funds. This was why the accusations of financial impropriety made during the fund crisis of 1952 had been particularly searing and embittering.

After the 1968 election I decided to sell all of my stocks and outside holdings. This divestiture was not required by law, but I thought it would be worth going the extra measure to avoid even the appearance of a conflict of interest. I took most of the money from the sale of the stocks and the sale of our New York apartment and put it into the purchase of two houses in Florida and a house in California.

The San Clemente property was a 26-acre tract of land. Personally I could afford to buy only the house itself and the surrounding grounds, about 5.9 acres. In order to keep the adjacent property under my control, I bought the entire tract with the help of a loan from my friend Bob Abplanalp. In December 1970 I sold the 20.1 acres, plus an additional 2.9 acres I had acquired from a neighboring tract, to Rebozo and Abplanalp and retained only the house and the 5.9 acres I had wanted in the first place. In 1973 Rebozo sold his portion to Abplanalp.

In what now seems a bitter irony we decided to keep these transactions private, not because there was anything improper about them, but because I knew how the Washington press corps would play up my acquisition of such a large and expensive property, and the fact that I was doing it with loans from my friends. Once Watergate snowballed and reporters began to tear the skin off every aspect of my life, this innocent secrecy led to suspicions that I could not dispel.

On May 13 Ervin Committee "sources" leaked a story to a California newspaper alleging that up to "$1 million in campaign funds" might have been used to buy my California property. Even when Ervin claimed that he had never heard of such a thing, the newspaper would not retract its story, which was quickly picked up by the national wire services. Early in July a leak caused by the Cox office produced a story indicating that they too were investigating whether union, corporate, or campaign money had been used to buy any of my houses. The stories mushroomed. Other newspapers spread leaked reports that my San Clemente property was underassessed for tax purposes, and papers all across the country carried the story. Subsequently the Orange County Assessment Appeals Board determined that the charge was not true, but it had already left its impression. I sensed that unless we stopped this kind of story immediately, my personal integrity would come under as much of a cloud as my political integrity was now under.

I had nothing to hide concerning my finances and believed that the only defense against these kinds of charges was to put out everything. Therefore we ordered the General Services Administration to begin assembling every document that related to government expenditures at my homes. On May 25 we released a statement recounting the details of the purchase of my property in San Clemente and Key Biscayne. I also paid over $25,000 to have an audit of these transactions prepared, and I released the report to the press on August 27.

Despite these efforts the stories continued to be fabricated and to be printed. For example, the Washington *Star* falsely alleged that C. Arnholt Smith, a wealthy Californian then facing indictment for tax evasion, possibly helped in the purchase of my property. UPI reported that the "Senate Watergate Committee is investigating the possibility that $100,000 given by billionaire Howard Hughes was used to help pay for President Nixon's San Clemente home, a committee source said." ABC reported the equally outrageous charge that I had "a secret private investment portfolio" of $1 million in corporate campaign funds. Jack Anderson later charged I had Swiss bank accounts filled with cash. *Newsweek* even charged that I manipulated family property in such a way that my daughter Tricia may have filed false income tax returns. All these stories and charges were totally false. For at least the third time that I was aware of in my political career, someone in the IRS bureaucracy violated the law and leaked my tax returns to the press. The reporter who wrote the story based on this illegal act won the 1974 Pulitzer Prize for journalism.

At the end of November I announced that I was planning to release my tax returns in their entirety. The IRS, which had twice earlier reviewed and approved my 1971 and 1972 tax returns, informed us that because of all the publicity they were going to reopen their examination. In the meantime, Texas Democratic Congressman Jack Brooks, one of the most partisan men in Congress, used his subcommittee of the House Committee on Government Operations to hold hearings on government expenditures on my houses.

Every modern President has maintained property outside Washington for a change of pace and for the kind of privacy that is impossible in the capital. Johnson regularly visited three locations; Kennedy visited five. I had two of my own—in San Clemente and Key Biscayne—and I also sometimes used Bob Abplanalp's island in the Bahamas. For me as for other Presidents, the government made expenditures on the places I regularly visited in order to ensure my safety when I was working or relaxing there. When I took office, four of my thirty-five predecessors as President had been assassinated and serious attempts had been made on the lives of several others. On the day Robert Kennedy died, Congress passed a new law that established extraordinary security measures to protect all future presidential and vice presidential candidates and incumbents. The legislation called for the full cooperation of government agencies in meeting requests by the Secret Service for protective devices. I was the first President in office after the legislation was passed to receive all the increased protection it provided. At the request of the Secret Service, the General Services Administration, which handles government buildings and supplies, installed intricate warning devices and electronic alarms on the grounds all around my houses; bulletproof glass was put into the windows; special outside lighting was installed. Secret Service command posts and outposts were constructed; landscaping was arranged and rearranged according to Secret Service requirements.

In the end GSA spent $68,000 on my house at San Clemente. The bulk of this amount went for electrical security systems, fire protection, and the replacement of a gas heater with an electric heating system after the Secret Service decided that the less expensive gas system I would have installed was not sufficiently safe. I spent $217,000 of my own money on furnishings and improvements to the San Clemente house.

GSA spent $137,000—all but $7,000 of it on bulletproof glass—on the two adjacent houses I owned in Key Biscayne. We used one as a family residence and the other as an office and work area. At the same time I personally spent $76,000 for remodeling the houses and for improvements on the grounds.

In addition to the money spent on the houses themselves, GSA spent $950,000 on the grounds. This amount covered the installation of security lighting and alarm systems, walls, guard stations, and relandscaping to restore the areas torn up when the protective equipment was installed.

I was no more eager than anyone else would be to pay

for anything that could be legitimately construed as a proper government expense, but a General Accounting Office study concluded that with scattered exceptions, almost all of the $1.1 million spent on my personal properties in California and Florida was spent for protective purposes. In fact, all but $13,400 was specifically requested by the Secret Service. Other items, such as flagpoles and office furniture for my study, were procured under the auspices of the GSA. Flagpoles had routinely been placed at the homes of Presidents and Vice Presidents before me; and the office furniture would all revert to GSA after I left office.

Whenever a President travels there are scores of security and support personnel who have to travel with him to make sure that he is safe and to make sure that his communications facilities are as extensive and secure as they are at the White House or at Camp David. I felt that we also had to take these expenditures into account lest we be accused of trying to hide them. Therefore at my instructions GSA audited every penny the government had spent in San Clemente, Key Biscayne, and Grand Bahama, and on security for my daughters at their homes. More than 20,000 man-hours were devoted to combing 10,000 accounting records and 1,600 files. In the end it cost the government $313,582—50 percent more government money than had been spent on the houses—to answer the congressional and press inquiries. On August 6 we released the totals arrived at by GSA: $1.1 million had been spent on the houses and grounds; $2.5 million had been spent on the office complexes and security measures on government property near the houses; the Defense Department spent $6.1 million for routine presidential communications equipment and support, 60 percent of which would be completely recovered when the equipment was taken away after my presidential term ended; $211,000 more had been spent directly by the Secret Service on equipment connected with their security needs, 90 percent of which would be recovered after I left office.

The next morning, the Washington *Post* and the New York *Times* ran almost identical headlines: *$10 Million Spent on Nixon Homes* wrote the *Post; $10 Million Spent at Nixon Houses* wrote the New York *Times*. Other newspapers and the television news shows adopted the same line.

Not surprisingly, many people felt that this money had been spent on the homes themselves.

Over the next months we tried to correct those stories by pointing out that almost all the money had been spent on security measures. Only 2 percent of that amount had been spent at the houses themselves; almost 90 percent, or $8.9 million, had been spent on administrative and protective support totally divorced from my personal property. But it was a hopeless public relations battle.

Representative Brooks was determined that his house subcommittee hearings would make the most of the story and his plans were only temporarily foiled when two of the subcommittee members, one of them an anti-Nixon Democrat, toured the San Clemente house and pronounced the government expenditures justifiable. The *Wall Street Journal* editorialized, "In short, despite all those headlines, the spending at San Clemente seems to have been a non-story. . . . It might be wise, too, to think about how the press might undo non-stories when they arise."

Before my administration most of the requests for government expenditures at a President's private property had been made orally and informally. The Defense Department had handled the majority of such requests and expenditures for Lyndon Johnson. I was told that Brooks, who had been one of Johnson's most intimate political allies, carefully confirmed the inaccessibility of the full Johnson record before proceeding against me. Even from what little could be reconstructed, however, it was apparent that at least $5 million had been spent on various Texas sites for Johnson, including the LBJ Ranch; the Haywood Ranch and boathouse in Llano County; his suite at Brooke Army Medical Center, San Antonio; and his office at KTBC, the television station Mrs. Johnson owned in Austin. Over $99,000 was spent remodeling and redecorating Johnson's office in Austin; a million dollars was spent carrying out his request for a major redesign of the federal office building there and for construction of a helipad on the roof of the building so that he could fly directly there from the LBJ Ranch. A small house Johnson owned near his ranch was remodeled by GSA according to his detailed instructions, and he then leased it to the Secret Service. Spiro Agnew, incidentally, had provided the Secret Service with two rooms in his house in Maryland without any charge.

Probably the most astonishing testimony to come before Brooks's subcommittee related to expenditures for President Kennedy at Hyannisport; Middleburg, Virginia; Palm Beach; Squaw Island, Massachusetts; and Atoka, Virginia. The records of these expenditures had been kept by a naval aide to Kennedy, and the subcommittee was told that the aide had accidentally dropped them overboard while his ship was either in the Philippines or somewhere near Europe.

In preparing his tally of government expenditures on my houses and properties, Brooks added up every penny paid to every person working, however remotely, in any connection with the presidential office during every trip. Thus he included the salaries of people like cleaners and custodial staff who would have been on the government payroll regardless of my trips. In this way he came up with a total of $17 million. He put it in a report labeled "Confidential," which was promptly leaked. The headline in the New York *Times* was: *U.S. Aid to Nixon Estates Put at $17 Million.* Brooks's subcommittee began its work in the fall of 1973; the final report, however, was not issued until May 1974—just in time for the opening gavel of the House Judiciary Committee's hearings on impeachment. One of the worst distortions to come out of Brooks's investigation was the idea that Bob Abplanalp had benefited from government expenditures at his Grand Bahama home. In fact, when the Secret Service requested the installation of intrusion alarms, fire detection systems, and special generators, Abplanalp paid for them out of his own pocket. He also built a bunkhouse for the Secret Service agents and allowed the government free use of other buildings on the property. All these would have been completely legitimate government expenditures, but Abplanalp paid for them himself, thereby personally saving the government more than $1 million.

I still held the naïve belief that all suspicion and press speculation about my taxes could be dispelled by the facts. Therefore we began to prepare my tax returns for release to the public. I thought that in this way we would firmly and conclusively put to rest the malicious accusations about how I had bought my homes and whether I had paid the taxes I owed.

In a press-conference on November 18 I described my finances over the years. I reminded the reporters of the fact that after fourteen years as congressman, senator, and Vice President, I had a net worth of $47,000 and a 1958 Oldsmobile that needed an overhaul. Such money as I had been able to accumulate was the result of earnings when I was in private life, mainly when I was with the law firm in New York. I concluded:

> I made my mistakes, but in all of my years of public life, I have never profited, never profited from public service—I have earned every cent. And in all of my years of public life, I have never obstructed justice. And I think, too, that I could say that in my years of public life, that I welcome this kind of examination, because people have got to know whether or not their President is a crook. Well, I am not a crook. I have earned everything I have got.

This was not a spur-of-the-moment statement. The attacks on my personal integrity were more disturbing for me and my family than all the other attacks put together. I thought it was essential to put my defense in down-to-earth, understandable language. But it was a mistake. From then on, variations of the line "I am not a crook" were used as an almost constant source of criticism and ridicule.

The first articles on my December 8 release described the extent of the disclosure I had undertaken: "With the release of his income taxes and assorted deeds, mortgages, canceled checks and legal agreements, President Nixon has probably made the fullest disclosure of personal finances in the history of the country." But within only a matter of hours other news reports complained that "most of the issues" were still unresolved. Before long I concluded that the release of the income tax returns had been a mistake. It was the same old story: those who had been demanding that I put out my returns did not really want conclusive proof that the stories about the allegedly illegal purchases of my houses and the supposedly vast secret investment portfolios were false. They seized on the fact that I had large deductions as if it were immoral not to pay more taxes to the government than the law required be paid. They were only looking for ways to keep the stories alive and for any new vulnerability that might turn up.

There were two particular issues raised about my tax returns that were highly complex and on which tax lawyers disagreed. One involved a question about whether I had made a taxable capital gain when I sold some of the San Clemente property to Rebozo and Abplanalp. The accountant who had prepared my taxes insisted that I had not. He found support from some tax professionals and arguments from others. The other controversial question concerned the deduction I had taken for the donation to the National Archives of my prepresidential papers. The idea had come from Lyndon Johnson in 1968 when he told me about the statute providing for the deduction, which, he said, he had been taking for years. He urged that I take advantage of it and recommended that I employ the same expert appraiser he had used to assess the value of his papers. It turned out that a number of public figures had been taking advantage of such deductions long before I found out about them; they included Governor Pat Brown, John Kenneth Galbraith, George Wallace, Hubert Humphrey, Theodore Sorensen, and Arthur Schlesinger, Jr.

Ralph Newman, the appraiser recommended by Johnson, found that in my prepresidential files there were more than a million papers, worth approximately $2 million. In December 1968 I gave a specific portion of these papers to the government and took the allowable tax deduction. Early in 1969 I instructed John Ehrlichman to do what was necessary to make another and larger gift of papers that would spread out the maximum legitimate deductions over the next several years. The papers were delivered to the National Archives on March 27, 1969. A donation of 600,000 documents was appraised at $576,000.

In December 1969 Congress added an amendment to my tax reform act that repealed the provision allowing for any deductions for donations of papers. This amendment was made retroactive to July 25, 1969.

I was confident that the members of my staff and my lawyers, to whom I had delegated the responsibility for preparing my tax returns and executing the documents for the donation of my papers, had taken this change of the law into account and had had everything in order. I was shocked and totally frustrated when, in 1973, I found that this was not the case. A question was raised first by the press and then by the IRS itself about whether the paperwork for my papers donation had actually met the retroactive July deadline.

In the first week of December Bryce Harlow urged that I let the Joint Congressional Committee on Internal Revenue Taxation review the controversial papers gift deduction and the question about the capital gain. He had worked with this committee in the past and found them thorough and objective. Kenneth Gemmill, a prominent tax attorney who helped advise us, shared his views.

On December 8, therefore, I wrote a letter to Wilbur Mills, the chairman of the joint committee, and asked that these two questions be examined. I said that in the event the committee determined that the items had been incorrectly reported, I would pay whatever tax might be due.

On December 13 Mills replied that the joint committee had agreed to consider the case. But he added a new twist. "The committee believes," he wrote, "that the examination should be of all tax items for 1969 through 1972 for the examination to be meaningful." That same day the New York *Times* quoted Mills as saying that he was critical of the deductions I had taken, even if they were legal. "A public official who files a tax return has to be holier-than-thou," Wilbur Mills had said.

I began to fear that I had walked into another trap. My fears were soon borne out. In ordinary times the joint committee may have been, as Harlow had said, objective. But these were not ordinary times. Some of the committee members turned out to be weak and irresponsible; their large staff turned out to be even worse. Philadelphia *Bulletin* columnist Adrian Lee examined the political affiliations of the twenty-five members of the committee's staff and could not find one Republican.

On March 8, 1974, before the committee had reached any findings, Chairman Mills said publicly that he thought I would quit office after their report on my taxes came out.

On March 18 he predicted that I would be out of office by November because of "dismay" over my taxes.

Harlow's reports from the joint committee grew increasingly bleak. The staff had broken a promise by sending its draft report directly to the committee without even giving my lawyers a chance to review its findings or to file their own briefs in support of my case.

In the meantime things on our side were falling disastrously apart. I learned that, without my knowledge, the deed for the gift of the papers had in fact been backdated by one of the lawyers handling it for me. My tax attorneys argued that the deed was not crucial to the gift, and that the important thing was that I had expressed my intent to make the donation and had delivered the papers to the archives three months before the July 25 deadline. Previous court cases supported that view, but the unnerving disclosure of the backdated deed considerably undermined my position with my few supporters on the committee.

The members of the joint committee actually met only twice to consider the question of my taxes: once to accept the assignment in December 1973 and once to receive the thousand-page staff report in April 1974. A majority of the members were not even sufficiently concerned to go over the report or to hear my side of any of the major controversial issues. Senator Carl Curtis of Nebraska decried the staff's work. "No other taxpayer in our country has been treated with the harshness that was given the President of the United States in that report," he said.

In addition to finding against me on the papers donation and the capital gains question, the committee staff report found that I should reimburse the government for the air fare when Pat and the family flew on *Air Force One* with me if they were not performing official functions. No other President had ever been charged for his family in this way; in fact, I was the first President to have reimbursed the government for unofficial flights by members of my family when I was not on board the plane.

The committee staff also disallowed the kind of deduction I had taken for the use of my Florida house as an office, on the ground that I did not have to use my house for this purpose because the government could have built me an office there!

The Republicans on the joint committee expressed shock that the staff had arrogated such power to itself and had then wielded it so arrogantly. Harlow was promised that my supporters would insist that the whole matter be turned over to the IRS, but in the end all of them, with the exception of Carl Curtis, bowed to pressure and did nothing. The political heat was too great.

By this time I had also received a new ruling from the IRS. Although my tax return had been approved in two earlier audits, the IRS now reversed itself and said that I should pay back the deduction I had taken for the gift of the papers, and also pay tax on the San Clemente transaction as a capital gain.

There was an ironic twist involving the gift of the papers. As far as the joint committee and the IRS were concerned, I had not made a legally proper gift. But as far as GSA was concerned I had, and they therefore refused to return my papers to me. In other words, I lost both the deduction and the papers.

My lawyers urged that I go to tax court and fight the ruling. They said that the joint committee and the IRS had clearly bowed to political pressures and that I would win the case in court. But I had already lost the case as far as public opinion was concerned, and at that point that was what mattered to me most. Besides, I had agreed to abide by the joint committee's ruling, and I could hardly go back on that now.

On April 3 I issued a brief statement that I had heard of the joint committee's decision to release a staff analysis of my taxes even before the committee members had had an opportunity to meet and evaluate the staff's findings. I said that I would pay the taxes due because of the disallowance of the deduction for the papers donation and also the taxes on the capital gain.

Over the next several days we received $47,000 from citizens who wanted to help me pay the taxes. Pat and I were deeply touched. Of course, we returned the money. On April 17 Tricia walked into the Lincoln Sitting Room. She said that she and Ed had decided to sell their wedding gifts and give Pat and me the money for the taxes. I assured her we could get a loan to cover the amount. "We don't want to loan the money to you," she said, "we want to give it to you."

In the end, 36 people on the staffs of GSA, GAO, two House committees, the White House staff, and the Secret Service had worked 67 days on the inquiries about Key Biscayne; 33 people had worked for 137 days on San Clemente; the joint committee staff of 23 had put 6 people full-time on my finances, and they worked with 5 full-time IRS people. There had been no fraud on my part, and no impropriety, but the effect of the tax issue was a devastating blow, coming as it did in the crucial months when the Judiciary Committee was beginning to weigh impeachment.

THE ASSAULT BECOMES PERSONAL

Eugene McCarthy once compared the press corps to a flock of blackbirds: one flies off the wire and the others fly off, one flies back and the others return. Something that starts as an idle discussion within the Washington press corps will soon be repeated in wider circles among the Washington establishment, and before long it is being reported, interpreted, and analyzed without a thought to where it originally came from.

As an example of this phenomenon, at some point in the hot, muggy summer of 1973, some of the more influential members of the Washington press corps concluded that I was starting to go off my rocker. They decided that my decision not to answer the Watergate charges until after the Ervin hearings had ended, and my isolation from the press on Watergate, showed that I was peculiarly out of touch with reality. Later that summer, my desire to take private drives without being followed by the press and photographed every moment—something done by President Johnson before me and by President Carter after me—was treated as a sign of mental pathology.

Since they were already thinking along these lines, the press corps had a ready-made explanation when I displayed an outburst of anger at Ron Ziegler in New Orleans. This trip was one of my first public appearances after the Watergate hearings, and we were counting on the large and enthusiastic crowds that had been predicted to help dispel the idea that I was isolated and unpopular because of Watergate. While we were on *Air Force One* we received a Secret Service report that there was a serious threat of an assassination attempt. Personally I would have been willing to take the risk; but I could not endanger the safety of the crowds. Therefore I had to enter the city by an unannounced route.

My temper was already frayed by the time we arrived at the hall where I was scheduled to speak. When I saw Ziegler at the head of a pack of reporters, following right behind me into the VIP waiting room, I took out my frustration by giving him a solid shove and an unmistakable instruction to put the press in the special room that had been provided for them. I apologized immediately afterward to Ziegler, but the incident sent hot flashes through the press corps, and it was portrayed as the desperate flailing of a man at the end of his tether. CBS network news showed the pushing episode *twice* in slow motion.

It was in his influential "Nixon Watch" column in the next issue of *The New Republic* that John Osborne first put into print the talk among reporters that they had detected "something indefinably but unmistakably odd" in my gait and gestures in New Orleans. Some speculated that I was drunk. Osborne, however, said that he believed the assurance of my aides that I did not drink in the daytime, especially not before a speech. His verdict was that it "may just have been the tension taking its toll."

Several weeks later this idea was presumably what accounted for the contention by some reporters and commentators that I had maniacally manufactured the military alert at the time of the Yom Kippur War as a result of the desperate personal and political straits I was in because of Watergate. Considering the combined pressures of the Agnew resignation, the troubled economy, the oil embargo and the fuel shortage, and the Cox firing and its aftermath, many reporters apparently decided that I could only be in a state of mental overload. By early December, the New York *Times* ran a story with the headline *State of Nixon's Health Is a Dimension of Watergate Affair Constantly Being Gauged.* At the daily press briefings reporters began asking questions about whether I was under psychiatric care, if I were using drugs, and if I still prayed or believed in the efficacy of prayer. Theodore White once called reporters' conduct "macabre sadism." There was even a rumor in the press room that I was wearing makeup to disguise a fatal illness. This was a forerunner of the theory that I *planned* to get a serious illness and use that as my excuse for resignation. The final evolution of this bizarre amateur psychiatry was a deduction at the time of my resignation and in the period immediately following it that my problem was a death wish and that I yearned for dramatic extinction.

All these things were conceived, perpetuated, promulgated, and then analyzed by a comparatively small but immensely influential press corps living in the rarefied environment of Watergate-obsessed Washington, feeding on its own inbred ideas.

During this summer and fall of 1973 Pat and I seldom discussed the daily news stories and television broadcasts. She was magnificent in this period of exceptional adversity, just as she had always been before. She felt that in the end we would come out all right and that, above all, we must not allow the attacks to depress us to the point that we would be unable to carry out our duties effectively.

I think of one time in particular when, after an especially difficult day of unrelenting attacks about Watergate, we had to attend the state dinner for Prime Minister Norman Kirk of New Zealand. When the entertainment was over, we saw the Kirks to their car. Just as Pat and I started back through the Grand Foyer on our way upstairs, the Marine Band began playing "The Sound of Music." Following Pat's impulse, we took each other's hands and danced a short fox trot over to the stairs. The press was astonished and the guests delighted. It is a moment I shall always remember.

I believe that the attacks on my financial probity and integrity were the ones that hurt Pat most of all. When she had to join me in signing the statement relating to the preparation of the audit of our taxes, I could sense her tightly controlled anger. She said that she could understand the political attacks that were being made because of Watergate, but she thought that the attacks on our personal and financial integrity were totally unfair. She pointed out how careful she had been in the White House and through all the years we were in government. With a visible shudder she said that this reminded her of the agony and humiliation we had had to endure during the fund crisis in 1952.

At one point a Washington gossip columnist went to extraordinary lengths of innuendo to accuse Pat of unethically keeping jewels given to her as state gifts. In fact, Pat had the jewels listed in a gift register so that there would be no question when they went to the Nixon Library after our administration. Publicly she was charitable about the insults. "It's for the birds," she said laughingly. But privately, she came to me in despair. "What more can they possibly want us to do?" she asked.

Tricia did not make many public appearances during this period, but whenever she was staying with us for a few days she would come to the Lincoln Sitting Room late at night just to be with me while I worked. I knew that deep inside she ached with concern, but she never let Pat or me see it. On a few occasions when we talked about Watergate, she said, "We always have to look down to the end of the road. In the end it will come out all right and that is all that really matters." Ed was a source of steadiness and support for the whole family.

Julie decided that she wanted to go out and fight, and she threw herself into the battle with characteristic verve and intensity. She made as many as six appearances in different parts of the country in one week. David was just starting a new job as a sportswriter with the Philadelphia *Bulletin*, but he joined her when he could. They lived in the front lines of Watergate, and they suffered its brutal assaults every bit as much as I did.

The annual Radio and Television Correspondents' Dinner in Washington is an event at which the political humor of the after-dinner skits and speakers is usually sharp and irreverent. Julie specifically asked to attend the 1973 dinner to prove that we were not ashamed or afraid to appear in public at such events. David decided to go with her and lend his moral support. On the night of the dinner, however, his car ran out of gas as he was driving to meet her. He hitchhiked the rest of the way, but he did not make it in time and Julie had to attend the dinner alone.

Most of the after-dinner humor had to do with Watergate, and the jokes were cutting and brutal. Julie sat with courage through every derisive laugh. After the program she was approached by Ambassador Guillermo Sevilla-Sacasa of Nicaragua, the dean of the Washington diplomatic corps. He whispered to her, "Your father still has one friend." She had steeled herself to the vicious jibes, but this kindness broke her heart. She could no longer hold back the tears, and with all the eyes fixed on her she rushed out of the room.

I did not want Julie to take the brunt of the Watergate questioning, but she could not bear the fact that there did not seem to be anyone else who would speak out for me. Whenever I suggested that she not become so involved, she always replied, "But Daddy, we have to fight."

My immediate family were not the only ones close to me who found themselves under merciless attack from the press. My brothers Don and Ed were called in for questioning. Reporters and investigators also turned on my friends Bob Abplanalp and Bebe Rebozo.

For Bebe Rebozo, 1973 was the beginning of an eighteen-month nightmare of harassment. He was investigated by the IRS, the GAO, and the Miami District Attorney, in addition to being scandalously hounded by the Ervin Committee staff.

Bebe Rebozo is one of the kindest and most generous men I have ever known. He is a man of great character and integrity. Yet anyone who read only the press stories about him, his business dealings, or his friendship with me would have had to conclude that he combined the worst traits of Rasputin and Al Capone.

The main vehicle for the attack was a $100,000 campaign contribution from Howard Hughes. Rebozo had accepted the money on his understanding that it was intended for the 1972 presidential campaign. He kept it in a safe-deposit box in his bank. In 1970, a serious power struggle erupted within the Hughes empire, marked by vicious infighting among several factions. Rebozo remembered the 1962 California gubernatorial campaign and the issue that had been made then of the loan from the Hughes organization to my brother Don. He wanted to make sure that I was not embarrassed again by any connection with Howard Hughes, so he decided not to mention the money to me and simply to hold on to it until after the election, when he thought it could either be used to help pay any deficit the campaign had incurred or for the 1974 congressional election.

In 1973 the IRS was in the midst of conducting an investigation of Hughes's holdings, and Rebozo knew that he would be asked about the $100,000 contribution. He had told me about the money by now, and I said that unless we could obtain the approval of the Hughes organization to put it into the 1974 campaign, we should return it. The money was accordingly returned to Hughes's representative in June 1973. A check of the serial numbers on the bills confirmed that they had all been issued before Rebozo had received the money, thus supporting his claim that he had left the money untouched in the safe-deposit box until he returned it, exactly as he had said.

When the Ervin Committee found out about the Hughes contribution they had a field day with leaks and innuendos, ironically confirming Rebozo's worst fears about the damaging publicity this innocent transaction could create.

There were reports that the Ervin investigation was going to charge that the Hughes money had been put to my personal use and that the money had been a quid pro quo for a Civil Aeronautics Board ruling favorable to Hughes's airline. Other stories reported charges that it was in exchange for an anti-trust favor. UPI said that the Ervin Committee was investigating whether the money had helped to pay for the purchase of my San Clemente home. Some stories referred to the contribution as a "payoff." All these widely reported stories were false.

On October 8 Rebozo was interviewed by the Ervin Committee. UPI ran a report alleging that he had been "hazy" on what happened to the money while it was in his possession. This was outrageously false. The New York *Times* reported charges that the contribution may have been part of an effort to stop a scheduled atomic test, since Hughes feared the effects of nuclear testing in Nevada on his Las Vegas properties. Another article reported that the contribution might have been in exchange for favors on Hughes's tax-exempt medical institute. That story, like the others, was untrue.

The Hughes contribution was not the only weapon used to harass Rebozo. On August 1 ABC had reported that investigators were checking reports that huge sums of illegal campaign contributions had been laundered through gambling casinos in the Bahamas with the aid of his bank, the Key Biscayne Bank; on August 20 ABC reported a story from "committee sources" that the Ervin Committee had subpoenaed the bank's records in connection with contributions run through the Bahamas of possibly $2 million or more. There were no such contributions, and there had been no such "laundering" of them.

On October 22 ABC reported the alleged existence of an illegal "private investment fund" administered on my behalf through the Rebozo bank: "Described by sources close to the investigation as the 'Nixon Checkers Fund of 1973,' the alleged investment portfolio is being probed to determine whether large unreported political contributions may have been diverted to Nixon's personal use." The story said that two corporations might have contributed more than $1 million. The charges were totally false.

In the meantime the Ervin Committee's pursuit of Rebozo was ruthless. It is described in detail in *At That Point in Time,* by the committee's Minority Counsel Fred Thompson. He tells how, in sets of twos and threes, staff investigators went to Miami four separate times to interview Rebozo, each group repeating the questions of the previous group. The committee interviewed his family and his business friends and subpoenaed financial records of everyone with whom he had engaged in business transactions over a period of six years. They also interviewed everyone to whom he had written a check over the last six years.

Rebozo was subjected to fourteen weeks of IRS audits, an investigation by the GAO, an investigation by the Ervin Committee, and an investigation by the Miami District Attorney, and finally the Watergate Special Prosecutor. When in January 1975 Leon Jaworski finally confirmed that there was no evidence for a case against Rebozo, the New York *Times* did not carry the story at all and the Washington *Post* carried only a short report. Not one of the television networks, which had been reporting the false allegations nightly, even mentioned Jaworski's statement.

By the time the Rebozo investigation was finally concluded in October 1975, the Special Prosecutor's office had issued more than 200 subpoenas, questioned 123 people ranging from me to the gardener at my Key Biscayne home, and hauled 28 people before a grand jury. In 1978 internal staff documents from the Special Prosecution Force were made public that showed the lengths to which the investigators were willing to go. A memo by the head of the Rebozo investigation acknowledged that the informant who had prompted their investigation of the secret multimillion-dollar Bahamian bank account supposedly maintained for me by Rebozo turned out to be a "con man with a criminal record" who had made an identical allegation years earlier against Earl Warren. The documents he had shown to back up his story were "determined to be fraudulent." The memo concluded, "Like so many of the Rebozo allegations, it seemed at first to have great potential. Like so many, it lacked critical details. And like so many, it proved utterly baseless."

But this was years later, and in the meantime the Special Prosecutor's office had investigated Rebozo for sixteen months, evidently caring little that they made his life hell.

An estimated $2 million had been spent investigating Bebe Rebozo. In the end all the allegations and innuendos proved false, and he was officially vindicated. In the meantime, of course, he had been unmercifully harassed and defamed. But those who had made the charges, and those who had printed and broadcast them, despite his complete exoneration by the Special Prosecutor's office, did not have the decency to retract them or to apologize for the damage they had done. Bebe Rebozo endured a modern-day Star Chamber of political persecution. His crime was that he was Richard Nixon's friend.

Earlier in 1973 polls had shown that despite a widespread assumption that I was involved in the Watergate cover-up, a majority of the public still believed I was a man of high integrity. The effect of the year's relentless assault was that it began to succeed in doing what the charges of a political cover-up alone could not do: it began to undermine that confidence in my integrity. In the spring of 1974 columnist Nicholas von Hoffman would write:

> But the formal process of legal impeachment has to wait upon a kind of informal social impeachment whereby the man is stripped of the reverence, protections, and deference with which we treat our presidents. He has to be tried, convicted, disgraced and expelled before he is formally accused. . . .
>
> Until a few months ago any American president could have sent the IRS American Express slips and doodles . . . and gotten a pass. . . . Small unflattering tidbits about Nixon and his family are now broadcast and repeated with the special satisfaction of the self-righteous.

Von Hoffman predicted that an inevitable train of events had been set in motion based more on the imperatives of good drama than on questions of impeachable guilt or innocence. He stated that I was going to be impeached "although nobody quite knows why. . . . Nixon's policies such as they were would never get another man impeached. Nevertheless one senses the decision has been made. . . . None of this has to do with whether there are enough votes . . . to do him in now. Before too long there will be."

During my meetings with congressmen in November I had said that I might make the subpoenaed tapes public, in summary form if not in full transcripts. The congressional leadership, particularly Hugh Scott, had strongly urged that I do so. Pat Buchanan was assigned to go over these transcripts and compare them with John Dean's testimony. When I read Buchanan's report of his findings, I was reassured by the thought that anyone reviewing the tapes would agree with my view that Dean had lied when he charged that I had conspired with him for eight months on a Watergate cover-up. I knew that the March 21 tape would cause an uproar. But I was sure that in the end people would recognize that it was what I had done that mattered, not what I said, much less what I had temporarily contemplated.

Haig brought Garment, Harlow, Ziegler, and communications aides Ken Clawson and Dick Moore in on the decision. Each of them first read the tapes, then Buchanan's summaries. Haig tried to soften his report of their opinion for me, but I could tell that they did not share my optimism that if we could weather the many admittedly rough passages, the tapes in their entirety would prove that Dean had lied and I had told the truth. Harlow in particular thought that the tapes would be deadly because the conversations on them were just too realistically political for public consumption.

Buchanan, however, was strongly in favor of releasing the transcripts. I shared his belief that if we could survive the first shock waves, the tapes would end up proving Dean a liar. But I also appreciated Harlow's insight into possible public and congressional reactions, and I felt that in our present parlous situation these considerations would have to be treated as paramount. Therefore, despite the expectations that had been raised by announcing our intention to release the transcripts, I decided not to do so.

On December 2, 1973, William Greider wrote in the Washington *Post*: "What the public has to understand is that if it asks Congress to impeach and try Mr. Nixon, it is really asking for much more than that. Impeachment on these offenses implicitly requires Democrats and Republicans alike . . . to render judgment not just on Mr. Nixon, but on the political past."

"1973 will be a better year," I had dictated in my diary in December 1972. Now, at Camp David on December 23, 1973, I wrote across the top of a page of notes I was making: "Last Christmas here?"

1974

It was difficult to believe that only eight months had passed since Haldeman and Ehrlichman had left, and since the full fury of Watergate had descended on me. It had been a brutal eight months, an endless cycle of blows and rallies followed by further blows. In May I had felt that there was a chance to renew, rebuild, and recover. Now I was reduced to analyzing my situation in the stark terms of the possibilities of simple survival.

It was after the weekend of Cox's dismissal that I first considered what my actions had precipitated. I made notes to myself that I labeled "Analysis":

1. Cox had to go. Richardson would inevitably go with him. Otherwise, if we had waited for Cox making a major mistake which in the public mind would give us what appeared to be good cause for him to go would mean that we had waited until Cox had moved against us.

2. We must learn from the Richardson incident what people we can depend on. Establishment types like Richardson simply won't stand with us when chips are down and they have to choose between their political ambitions and standing by the President who made it possible for them to hold the high positions from which they were now resigning.

3. As far as the tapes were concerned we need to put the final documents in the best possible PR perspective. We must get out the word with regard to no "doctoring" of the tapes.

4. We must compare our situation now with what it was on April 30. Then the action with regard to Haldeman and

Ehrlichman, Gray, Dean, and Kleindienst did not remove the cloud on the President as far as an impression of guilt on his part was concerned. In fact it increased that doubt and rather than satisfying our critics once they had tasted a little blood they liked it so much they wanted far more. Since April 30 we have slipped a great deal. We had 60 percent approval rating in the polls on that date and now we stand at 30 percent at best.

5. Now the question is whether our action on turning over the tapes or the transcripts thereof helps remove the cloud of doubt. Also on the plus side, the Mideast crisis, probably if the polls are anywhere near correct, helped somewhat because it shows the need for RN's leadership in foreign policy.

6. Our opponents will now make an all-out push. The critical question is whether or not the case for impeachment or resignation is strong enough in view of the plus factors I noted in previous paragraph.

At 1:15 A.M. on January 1, 1974, I made this note: "The basic question is: Do I fight all out or do I now begin the long process to prepare for a change, meaning, in effect, resignation?"

Over the past months I had talked about resignation with my family, with a few close friends, and with Haig and Ziegler. But the idea was anathema to me. I believed that my resignation under pressure would change our whole form of government. The change might not be apparent for many years; but once the first President had resigned under fire and thereby established a precedent, the opponents of future Presidents would have a formidable new leverage. It was not hard to visualize a situation in which Congress, confronted with a President it did not like, could paralyze him by blocking him on legislation, foreign affairs, and appointments. Then, when the country was fed up with the resulting stalemate, Congress could claim that it would be better for the country if the President resigned. And Nixon would be cited as the precedent! By forcing Presidents out through resignation, Congress would no longer have to take the responsibility and bear the verdict of history for voting impeachment.

My notes continued:

The *answer—fight*. Fight because if I am forced to resign the press will become a much too dominant force in the nation, not only in this administration but for years to come. Fight because resignation would set a precedent and result in a permanent and very destructive change in our whole constitutional system. Fight because resignation could lead to a collapse of our foreign policy initiatives.

I made another list of notes for myself later that morning, New Year's Day, 1974:

Decision to fight:
1. Resign sets precedent—admits guilt.
2. Lets down friends.
3. Fight now makes possible fight for future as a man of principle.
4. Only substance, not politics, must affect this decision.

Priorities:
1. Press conference and media meetings.
2. Organize our hard core in the House, Senate, among top governors and our friends like Kendall, etc., who were working under Flanigan's direction.
3. Mobilize the Cabinet.
4. Buck up the staff.

Substantive areas:
1. Rodino, Jaworski, et al.
2. Foreign policy initiatives.
3. Run the shop well on the domestic front (energy, et al.).

Style:
1. Confidence.
2. Compassion.
3. Color—the necessity for the interesting.

Be *strong* against unprecedented adversity but avoid intemperate remarks or conduct.

I made still another note on January 5, at 5 A.M.:

Above all else: Dignity, command, faith, head high, no fear, build a new spirit, drive, act like a President, act like a winner. Opponents are savage destroyers, haters. Time to use full power of the President to fight overwhelming forces arrayed against us.

As I assessed the situation, impeachment was not going to be decided on the basis of the law or historical precedent. Impeachment would be an exercise in public persuasion: while I was trying to restore public confidence in my ability to lead, my opposition would be trying to condition the public to the idea that I had to be removed from office.

THE LAST CAMPAIGN

I had thought that 1972 was going to be my last political campaign. But at the beginning of 1974 I recognized that I was about to embark on the campaign of my life.

I was sure that, regardless of the substantive issues involved in the impeachment effort, it was the politics of the situation that would determine the outcome. At each stage the Democrats would be taking the political temperature, trying to determine whether the Republicans would be worse off in the 1974 congressional elections and in the 1976 presidential campaign with a discredited President still in office, or with a new President bearing the political burden of his predecessor's impeachment or resignation. Pressure on the Democratic Congress was intensified by polls that showed that opinion of Congress was at its lowest percentage in the polls' history—even lower than mine!

Many congressional Republicans were now also considering impeachment as a strictly political question in terms of the upcoming off-year elections—in which many of them had an obvious and immediate interest. For them, however, impeachment would clearly be a double-edged sword, because as much as they might want to be rid of me now that it appeared I would be a drag on the party's fortunes in 1974 and 1976, they recognized that many Republicans, particularly the party workers, were outraged by the idea, and that the general public might consider their willingness to see me impeached self-interested and disloyal.

As I increasingly saw it, therefore, the main danger of being impeached would come precisely from the public's being conditioned to the idea that I was going to be impeached. In the end, therefore, it would come down to a race for public support: in other words, a campaign. But this time, instead of campaigning for a political office, I would be campaigning for my political life.

As of December, the opinion polls showed that the people were still undecided. Fifty-four percent were against requiring me to leave office. At the same time, 45 percent would respect me more if I resigned so that the nation could concentrate on other problems than Watergate. The very thing I had been counting on to work in my favor had begun to work against me. In April 1973 I had hoped that the public would get tired of Watergate and apply pressure to Congress and the media to move on to other things. But the congressional and media assault and the controversy over the White House tapes had so embroiled me in Watergate that the public was increasingly seeing me as the roadblock and their desire to move on to other things was affecting their willingness to have me removed. Unless I could do something to stem this tide, it would sweep me out of office.

As I had in every other campaign, I tried to weigh my strengths and weaknesses. As usual, the Democrats had the political edge because they had the numerical majority. Therefore impeachment was *possible* no matter what I did to try to stop it. It was *probable* if the Republicans decided not to help me or not to help me enough.

In fact, my Republican support in Washington had been steadily eroding. By the end of 1973, as the impeachment hearings drew near and as the prospect of the off-year elections threatened to become a personal barometer of public sentiment about me, even the solid middle-ground Republicans, including the party leadership in Congress, had begun to send out signals that unless I could dramatically turn the tide for myself, they would have to begin moving to arm's length. I complained that it was typical Republican minority-party jitters, but in fact it was largely my own fault. Too many who had tried to defend me in the past had been burned, and many no longer felt sufficiently confident or motivated to take further risks for me.

My problems were compounded by the fact that all my activities with my congressional supporters had become uncomfortably self-conscious. No congressman could afford to seem to be too firmly committed to my camp lest he be accused of not considering the case against me on its merits—despite the fact that many on the other side were openly campaigning for impeachment. Normal phone calls and invitations to White House briefings were called into question by the press, and word started to come back that these activities might be made to look like attempts to influence votes and that congressmen would be grateful if I would leave them alone until after the impeachment question had been settled. This effectively barred any real strategy; my primary campaign weapon would have to be doing my job well and continuing to push for recognition of the fact that Watergate mattered so much less than the things I did well. At the same time, increasing irritation and factionalism began to build between the party's liberal and conservative elements. With nerves rubbed raw from all the months of Watergate, and the usual uncertainties of an off-year election campaign, each group tended to view any policy action I took as a concession to the other side in an effort to win votes on impeachment.

Across the country several small but dedicated support groups began to appear. Don Kendall did a superb job trying to rally the business community; Rabbi Baruch Korff of Massachusetts spent his personal savings for an ad that launched a nationwide movement of people who felt that the current assault was not just against me personally but against the presidency as well. Peter Flanigan coordinated the liaison with many of the groups.

The Cabinet had held firm during the rocky passages of the last eight months. Some of them, such as Commerce Secretary Fred Dent and Agriculture Secretary Earl Butz, went out into the country to speak in my behalf. Others stayed in Washington and showed their loyalty simply by doing their jobs despite all the pressures they had to endure. The White House staff was equally superb. I cannot ever adequately thank all those who stood by me. But despite the valor of the staff, everyone was completely exhausted. I do not for a moment concede that we were outclassed, but from the beginning we had been hopelessly outmanned. We reached out for new people. One was James St. Clair, a prominent Boston lawyer who came in to head the legal team. Dean Burch, former Chairman of the Federal Communications Commission, took over the political operation of the White House staff. Ken Cole, the Executive Director of the Domestic Council, became Assistant to the President for Domestic Affairs. These appointments were well received, and they created a certain welcome momentum around the White House. But it would not last long.

Mel Laird soon announced that he was leaving the White

House to begin a new career in the private sector. Jerry Ford had been sworn in as Vice President on December 6, and Laird indicated publicly that he expected Ford would take over many of the domestic policy and congressional liaison functions he had handled. However, Evans and Novak, the Washington *Post* columnists who so regularly reflected Laird's point of view that they were jokingly referred to around Washington as his publicists, wrote that his departure was a signal to Republicans that they were no longer duty-bound to protect the President.

By the end of 1973 my longstanding political opponents began consolidating their efforts to make sure that I would be impeached. The ACLU distributed a fifty-six-page handbook that described ways to hasten and ensure impeachment. The principal ACLU spokesman was candid about their motivation: "There's no civil rights movement. There's no war. There's no social-action movement. I hate to use the word, but it's liberal chic. Impeachment is there." Stewart Mott, McGovern's principal contributor, under the guise of a "public interest" group, published a broadside accusing me of twenty-eight indictable crimes ranging from the war in Vietnam to the Watergate break-in. After Cox was dismissed, Ralph Nader's organization began phoning around the country to promote impeachment. The AFL-CIO announced that impeachment could no longer be avoided and began a nationwide campaign, sending out four million leaflets on "Nineteen Points for Impeachment." An AFL-CIO lobbyist observed in January 1974 that "when the timing is good" they were going to make an "all-out lobbying effort on the Hill" to have me impeached. The serious impact of organized labor's decision to go all out for impeachment was underscored by the fact that nineteen of the twenty-one Democratic members of the House Judiciary Committee had received a total of $189,196 in campaign money from organized labor in the 1972 election. Two of the Republican members had received $2,100. Committee Chairman Peter Rodino had received $30,923.

The question of impeachment would first be debated, and the evidence to justify it would first be investigated, by the

House Judiciary Committee—and one had only to be able to count to know that the House Judiciary Committee was a stacked deck. Twenty-one of its thirty-eight members were Democrats; seventeen were Republicans. Of the twenty-one Democrats, eighteen either came from the party's liberal wing or had reputations as hard-core partisans. Realistic observers of Washington politics conceded at the outset that these eighteen Democrats, despite their pieties about objectivity, were all going to vote for impeachment.

The three remaining Democrats were Southern conservatives: Walter Flowers of Alabama, Ray Thornton of Arkansas, and James Mann of South Carolina. They were the only unpredictable element on the Democratic side, because they had supported me in the past, often going against their party, on matters pertaining to national defense and budget restraint.

The consensus in Washington was that of the seventeen Republicans on the committee, eleven would stand by me. Among the remaining six, some were liberals who had rarely supported me on policy matters, some were facing difficult re-election campaigns, and some had already shown signs of personal disaffection because of Watergate. My only hope of averting a recommendation for impeachment from the committee would be either to hold every Republican and pick up two of the Southern Democrats, or to hold sixteen Republicans and win all three of the Southerners. Either of these outcomes was possible, but extremely remote.

Whatever the opposition from without, there was also an enemy within: the tapes. The biggest danger I saw in the year ahead was that both the Special Prosecutor and the House Judiciary Committee would begin requesting more and more tapes—always with the disclaimer that each request would be the last. But there would never be an end to these requests until all 5,000 hours of tapes had been requested and surrendered. These investigations had taken on a life of their own—I did not understand why more people could not see that. The various investigators were no longer trying to determine the truth of any particular charges against me. They wanted to go through everything, to pursue every lead, no matter how remote, until they found something that would in their view finally justify my removal from office. And for me the continuing nightmare of the tapes was the possibility that, given enough time and enough tapes, they might find what they were looking for.

I wanted to stop it. In the past I had made the grievous mistake of saying I was going to stop it but failing to do so. Then, after paying the political price for refusing, we would cave when the pressure started to build. I regretted not having followed my instincts about this in the past and wanted to begin following them right away. I even talked about destroying the tapes. I argued that the best strategy would be to go to Congress and fling down the gauntlet and declare that enough is enough. I said that I wanted to do it in the State of the Union message on January 30: I would announce that I would provide nothing more to the House Judiciary Committee or the Special Prosecutor.

I was persuaded against it by the argument that using the State of the Union to draw lines and force confrontations would not only heighten the impeachment issue but completely overshadow the important national policy issues in the speech.

So the tapes sat there in the EOB. The ones I had already reviewed were bad enough; now what might be on the others haunted us all. I thought of the peculiar reality for me of Churchill's observation: "The longer one lives, the more one realizes that everything depends upon chance. If anyone will look back over the course of even ten years experience, he will see that tiny incidents, utterly unimportant in themselves, have in fact governed the whole of his fortune and career."

I had no way of remembering everything that was on the tapes, but I was sure that there were many more of the rough political patches that had already brought us to this point. I might survive any number of them, but eventually the accumulated weight would bring me down. Tricia later showed me a note from her diary that reminded me that sometimes people around you understand things better than you understand them yourself:

Something Daddy said makes me feel absolutely hopeless about the outcome. He has since the Butterfield revelation repeatedly stated that the tapes can be taken either way. He has cautioned us that there is nothing damaging on the tapes; he has cautioned us that he might be impeached because of their content. Because he has said the latter, knowing Daddy, the latter is the way he really feels.

So many people had gone out on so many limbs for me already—and I knew better than most of them just how shaky some of those limbs had really been. Now others would have to take that risk if we continued to fight: Haig, Ziegler, the lawyers, the congressmen and senators who would support me during the impeachment hearings, the White House staff. I would have to inspire these people for the battle, even though I knew that in many respects the case was not very inspiring. What enabled me to justify fighting on and asking these people to fight with me and for me was that although the *case* was badly flawed, I convinced myself that the *cause* was noble and important.

As I came to see it, the cause now involved the nature of leadership in American politics. I felt that if I could be hounded from office because of a political scandal like Watergate, the whole American system of government would be undermined and changed. I never for a moment believed that any of the charges against me were legally impeachable— none of them involved "Treason, Bribery, or other high Crimes and Misdemeanors" as enumerated in the Constitution. If I had felt that I was actually guilty of a legally impeachable offense I would not have allowed anyone to extend himself in my defense. I would have resigned immediately. But this impeachment was going to be a political phenomenon; this was confirmed when the House Judiciary Committee could not reach agreement on the constitutional definition of impeachment. In December the New York *Times* reported that two-thirds of the committee's members believed that an impeachable offense did not even have to be a violation of the law. Later, instead of deliberating until a consensus on a definition was reached, it was decided that each member would be allowed to make up his own mind along the way. If there had ever been any doubts before, this decision made it clear that a political rather than a legal standard would govern the impeachment proceedings.

I felt that in terms of the important elements of presidential leadership, I still had much to contribute to America and the world. As crippled as I was and was bound to remain throughout the rest of my term because of Watergate, I was still more experienced than Jerry Ford, who had only just been confirmed as Vice President. And experienced leadership was needed. The North Vietnamese were clearly preparing for a new offensive in Cambodia and South Vietnam, aimed at testing our willingness and ability to enforce the Paris agreement. The Soviets were holding back from concluding a comprehensive SALT agreement and would need a firm U.S. position to encourage them in the right direction. At home, the economy was extremely shaky in the aftermath of its experience with controls, and the impact of the Arab oil embargo was going to make it a long hard winter for whoever was in the White House. The temptation to lash out against the Arabs would have to be kept in check in order to capitalize on the tremendous success of our policy during the Yom Kippur War.

I was aware that the way I had handled Watergate so far and the inherent flaws in my case might endanger the very things I believed required my staying in office. I realized that for many people I had made a mockery of national security and executive privilege by using them, as they saw it, to cover my own guilt. I also realized that many people felt I was irreparably damaging the strength of the presidency by persisting in my determination to be a strong President despite the weakness created by Watergate.

But I did not agree. Rightly or wrongly, I convinced myself that I was being attacked by old opponents for old reasons. I was instinctively geared to fight for my survival. After living and fighting in the political arena for so long, I was not going to give up now and leave the presidency because of something like Watergate. I would fight and do and say whatever I thought was necessary to rally my forces and maintain their confidence for this last campaign.

On January 9, 1974, while I was spending a few days at Sunnylands, the magnificent Palm Springs home of my friend Walter Annenberg, I received a call from John Connally. He is not a man who becomes easily or unnecessarily alarmed, but he sounded agitated as he talked to me. He said that he had just been in Washington and talked to one of his close friends, who was the best source of political intelligence he had ever known. His friend had told him that a group of Republicans, primarily in the House but including one or two senators, some top party leaders among them, had been meeting privately and had concluded that my staying in office would be highly detrimental to all Republicans running in 1974. Some of these people, Connally said, were men who had been my friends in the past. He referred to the group as the "Arizona Mafia." I asked if Goldwater was a part of it, and Connally replied that while Goldwater might be aware of the group's existence and intentions, he was not one of its prime movers. He made it clear that the group was not limited to Arizonans; there were men from the East and the Midwest participating in the discussions. "Some of them are men you think are your very good friends," he said.

The supposed strategy of this alleged group was to delay the vote in the House Judiciary Committee until after the Soviet Summit in June. Then they would have some selected Republican leaders come to the White House and request that I resign in the best interests of the party, particularly because so many of my supporters in the House would lose their seats if I were still in office in November. Connally said that his source had emphasized that Jerry Ford had no knowledge of the group's existence.

Connally repeated that his source for this disturbing intelligence was extremely reliable, and he insisted that I should not brush it off as just another rumor. He urged me to have it checked very carefully. I told him that I would.

When I mentioned this information to Haig he was skeptical, and I agreed that it was the kind of thing that could be expected to turn up in the Washington rumor mills in times like these. Haig checked with Goldwater and reported that Goldwater claimed, and appeared, to be standing firm.

At that time I did not believe there could be an organized Republican conspiracy to force me out of office. However, survival matters most in politics. Washington is ruled by Darwinian forces, and if you are in serious political trouble, you cannot expect generosity or magnanimity for long. Often a consensus develops, sometimes no more than a shared instinct, that the burden of the wounded must be removed in order for the rest to survive.

The State of the Union address was scheduled for January 30 at 9 P.M. Pat and I sat silently in the car on the way from the White House to the Capitol. She knew as well as I did how tense the situation had become. The whole family had discussed whether the members of the House and Senate would receive the speech courteously or whether there might even be an open demonstration of hostility.

As soon as I entered the Chamber door, however, there was a loud, almost raucous burst of applause and cheers. Our small but vocal group of Republican and Democratic loyalists cheered so lustily that their colleagues felt obliged at least to stand, if not to follow suit.

This 1974 State of the Union address was to be the final summing up of my domestic stewardship. I was able to say at the outset: "Tonight, for the first time in twelve years, a President of the United States can report to the Congress on the state of a Union at peace with every nation of the world."

I believe that, had it not been for Watergate, the actual state of the American Union in 1973 would have been acknowledged as proof of the validity of the political philosophy on which I had run in 1972. The events of 1973 almost seemed designed to demonstrate just how inadequate the politics of the left would have been in dealing with the problems we had confronted and in solving them successfully. For example, the Mideast war ironically turned many of the prominent Vietnam doves back into hawks when Israel's safety and survival were at stake. The recurrent inflation showed how recklessly the traditional liberal Democratic dollar politics would have affected the economy. Even Teddy Kennedy and Wilbur Mills tacitly acknowledged this by revising their highly publicized compulsory national health insurance proposal to make it resemble mine. And the realities of the energy crisis forced pragmatic re-evaluations of the fashionable but one-sided environmentalist bias.

The country I had been elected to lead five years earlier had been on the ropes from domestic discord. The cities had been burning and besieged; the college campuses had become battlegrounds; crime was increasing at an alarming rate; drug abuse and drug addiction were increasing; the military draft cast a disruptive shadow over the lives of young Americans; there was no program to deal with the protection of our natural environment; and there were vital areas of social reform and governmental operation that needed attention and consideration.

In the five years of the Nixon administration we could point to some signal successes. The cities were now quiet; the college campuses had once again become seats of learning; the rise in crime had been checked; the drug problem had been massively attacked, abroad as well as at home; the draft had been eliminated; and we had submitted to Congress the nation's first environmental program, as well as major plans for national health care, education reform, revenue-sharing, and government reorganization. In this State of the Union I outlined ten landmark accomplishments that I felt would be possible in 1974: we could break the back of the energy crisis and lay the foundation for meeting our energy needs from our own resources; we could achieve a just and lasting settlement in the Mideast; we could check the rise in prices without causing a recession; we could enact my health care proposals and thereby begin to provide high-quality insurance for every American in a dignified way at an affordable price; we could make states and localities more responsive to local needs; we could make a crucial breakthrough in mass transportation; we could reform federal aid to education in ways that would make it do the most for those who needed it the most; we could begin the task of defining and protecting the right of personal privacy for every American; we could finally and belatedly reform the welfare system; and we could begin establishing an international economic framework in which Americans would share more fully.

As the speech progressed I was surprised and moved by the warm reception it was accorded. By the end I had been interrupted by applause more than thirty times. At one point I came to a line I had not thought particularly exceptional: in discussing the overriding aim of establishing a new structure of peace in the world, I said, "This has been and this will remain my first priority and the chief legacy I hope to leave from the eight years of my presidency." Suddenly the rafters seemed to ring. Almost all the Republicans and even a number of Democrats were on their feet, applauding and cheering. I looked up to my family. They were beaming.

When I had finished the address, I turned over the last page of my text and concluded with an extemporaneous and personal note. The Chamber was completely hushed as I said:

> I would like to add a personal word with regard to an issue that has been of great concern to all Americans over the past

year. I refer, of course, to the investigations of the so-called Watergate affair.

As you know, I have provided to the Special Prosecutor voluntarily a great deal of material. I believe that I have provided all the material that he needs to conclude his investigations and to proceed to prosecute the guilty and to clear the innocent.

I believe the time has come to bring that investigation and the other investigations of this matter to an end. One year of Watergate is enough.

And the time has come, my colleagues, for not only the executive, the President, but the members of Congress, for all of us to join together in devoting our full energies to these great issues that I have discussed tonight which involve the welfare of all of the American people in so many different ways as well as the peace of the world.

I recognize that the House Judiciary Committee has a special responsibility in this area, and I want to indicate on this occasion that I will cooperate with the Judiciary Committee in its investigation. I will cooperate so that it can conclude its investigation, make its decision, and I will cooperate in any way that I consider consistent with my responsibilities to the office of the presidency of the United States.

There is only one limitation. I will follow the precedent that has been followed by and defended by every President from George Washington to Lyndon B. Johnson of never doing anything that weakens the office of the President of the United States or impairs the ability of the Presidents of the future to make the great decisions that are so essential to this nation and the world.

Another point I should like to make very briefly. Like every member of the House and Senate assembled here tonight, I was elected to the office that I hold. And like every member of the House and Senate, when I was elected to that office, I knew that I was elected for the purpose of doing a job and doing it as well as I possibly can. And I want you to know that I have no intention whatever of ever walking away from the job that the people elected me to do for the people of the United States.

Now, needless to say, it would be understatement if I were not to admit that the year 1973 was not a very easy year for me personally or for my family. And as I have already indicated, the year 1974 presents very great and serious problems, as very great and serious opportunities are also presented.

But my colleagues, this I believe: with the help of God, who has blessed this land so richly, with the cooperation of the

Congress, and with the support of the American people, we can and we will make the year 1974 a year of unprecedented progress toward our goal of building a structure of lasting peace in the world and a new prosperity without war in the United States of America.

Back at the White House I found the whole family elated by the reaction to the speech, particularly the ovation that had followed my statement about the eight years of my presidency. Everyone felt that this was a positive sign that there was still a great deal of solid support for me in Congress.

The State of the Union speech seemed to have a generally positive reception. For a while it even seemed to supply the momentum that I had been seeking to break out of the Watergate morass. *New Confident Nixon* was the headline in the New York *Times*.

I decided to take advantage of this situation while it lasted, and I made several trips out into the country. On February 18 I went to Huntsville, Alabama, where more than 20,000 people gathered for an Honor America Day rally. George Wallace was my host, and he could not have been friendlier. On March 15 I went to Chicago for a televised question-and-answer session. The next day I flew to Nashville for the opening of the new Grand Ole Opry House. Three days after that I held a press conference at the convention of the National Association of Broadcasters in Houston. Inspired by the success of these appearances, and buoyed by the obviously sincere enthusiasm of the people I met, I made a note to myself that I would take my case directly to the country right after the Soviet Summit in June.

In the meantime Congress, distracted by impeachment, passed only about half the number of bills it had passed in a similar period the year before.

On December 21, 1973, UN Secretary-General Kurt Waldheim had opened the Geneva Peace Conference on the Middle East. Syria did not attend, but Egypt, Israel, Jordan, the United States, and the U.S.S.R. sent representatives. On December 22 the initial round of talks ended, with instructions to Egypt and Israel to begin immediate discussions on the disengagement of their forces along the Suez Canal.

From January 10 through January 17, 1974, Kissinger began what came to be known as his "shuttle diplomacy."

President Sadat had requested that Kissinger help work out the disagreements between Egypt and Israel relating to the disengagement of their troops. Thanks to the success of our earlier policies, Kissinger had become a common denominator for the two countries: a man both sides felt they could trust, representing an administration both sides thought could and would be evenhanded. The opening of these negotiations with Kissinger as the go-between called for great faith on the part of Golda Meir and for exceptional courage on the part of Anwar Sadat. Kissinger repaid Mrs. Meir's trust and President Sadat's courage with a tireless effort to adjust each side's position until an agreement had been produced that would make a substantial beginning in resolving the differences between Israel and Egypt.

On January 17 the Egyptian-Israeli troop disengagement was finally achieved. It was a tribute to Kissinger's enormous stamina, his incisive intellect, and, not least, his great personal charm. It was an even greater tribute because he had to cope with the burden of a President weakened by political attack at home. .

After I announced the disengagement, I called Mrs. Meir. She sounded as if a weight had been lifted from her. "Your statesmanship has played a key role," I said to her. "It would not have happened except for what you did in October," she replied. "You and Dr. Kissinger deserve great credit for bringing this about," I responded. Before I hung up, she added warmly, "Take care of yourself and get plenty of rest."

I also called President Sadat. "Congratulations on your statesmanship. I'm looking forward to meeting and working together with you for a permanent peace in the Middle East," I said. "Thanks to you and your wise guidance, and the efforts of Dr. Kissinger," he replied.

ENERGY

During the winter of 1973–74 America had an encounter with the future. We passed a milestone of national awareness when we recognized for the first time that the bounty of energy resources we had taken for granted for so long was not as limitless as we had once thought.

This was not something that had happened overnight.

The predicament of the 1970s was the result of shortsighted government policies compounded by decades of wasteful habits.

The United States, with only 6 percent of the world's population, was consuming one-third of the energy used on earth, and the supply of fuel was getting tight.

As early as 1971 I had turned my personal attention to giving an impetus to the production of nuclear energy. I ordered the first American breeder reactor project to begin in the spring of 1971.

By June 4, 1971, our study of the imminent energy problem had evolved into the first Presidential message on energy in our history. In it I urged the continuation of the development of the breeder reactor and committed the administration to the creation of a program for converting coal into clean gaseous fuels and to the acceleration of oil and gas lease sales on the outer continental shelf. I also proposed that all the federal government's energy resource development programs—some fifteen of them —be brought together under one agency. I said, "This message points the way for America—at considerable cost in money, but an investment that is urgent and, therefore, justified—points the way for finding new sources of energy and, at the same time, clean energy that will not pollute the air, will not pollute the environment."

On April 18, 1973, I sent Congress five major new requests involving the energy program. In the twenty-two months since my first message the worsening energy situation had been almost ignored. On our own, the administration had increased funding for experimental research and development by nearly 50 percent, but legislation was needed to forestall the crunch that we saw coming.

I asked Congress to deregulate natural gas and let the price rise with the market so that there would be more money and more incentive in the private sector for additional development. I also requested tax credits for oil exploration, approved extending the deadline on unreasonable environmental regulations, and ended the mandatory quotas on imports. By executive action I tripled the offshore acreage for oil and gas leases. I made requests for further research and development on nuclear and geothermal energy and on shale oil energy resources. I also announced the creation of an Office of Energy Conservation and proposed a new Cabinet-level department dealing exclusively with energy, the Department of Energy and Natural Resources.

In mid-May we began to insist on the voluntary sharing of gasoline resources between the major retailers and independent dealers. On June 29 I named John Love, governor of Colorado, to head the new energy office. I renewed my appeal to Congress, calling for a $10 billion program for energy research over the next five years, to match the anticipated $200 billion that would be spent in the private sector.

I asked that people voluntarily reduce road speeds to fifty miles an hour; this alone would have saved 25 percent of the fuel consumed traveling at seventy miles an hour. I said that the government was going to reduce its energy consumption by 7 percent over the next year and urged that personal consumption voluntarily be cut by 5 percent.

I again appealed to Congress on September 10, when I urged passage of seven bills, including one approving construction of the Alaska pipeline, and others covering deepwater port construction to make bigger fuel imports possible, the deregulation of natural gas, and new legislation on strip mining.

The first distant rumble of a possible Arab oil embargo began in the spring of 1973. By mid-summer King Faisal of Saudi Arabia was warning that unless our policy toward Israel changed, there would be a reduction of the oil sent to us. We stood our ground, and I said in a press conference on September 5: "Both sides need to start negotiating. That is our position. We are not pro-Israel and we are not pro-Arab, and we are not any more pro-Arab because they have oil and Israel hasn't. We are pro-peace and it is the interest of the whole area for us to get those negotiations off dead center."

After the outbreak of the Mideast war on October 6, the Arab position hardened, and by the end of October we were confronted with a full-scale embargo. By November it was clear that we were going to fall as much as 10 percent behind our energy needs, a figure that could rise as high as 17 percent by winter, depending upon weather conditions.

On November 7 I went on television to announce to the American people what I called the "stark fact": we were heading toward the acutest shortage of energy since World War II.

I called for a three-stage conservation effort, involving executive action, state and local action, and congressional action. Heating in federal buildings would be lowered to between 65 and 68 degrees, and I urged the same for private houses. I called for car pooling and asked state and local governments to set speed limits at fifty miles an hour. I asked Congress to pass an emergency energy act that would give me the authority to relax environmental restrictions on a case-by-case basis as I deemed necessary, and would impose special restrictions on the use of energy resources. I asked that the country be returned to daylight-saving time and called for the imposition of a nationwide speed limit of fifty miles an hour on federal highways.

I recalled the dedication that had characterized the Manhattan Project and the unity of spirit that had made the Apollo program a success. It was clear that when the American people decided a particular goal was worth reaching, they could surmount every obstacle to achieve it. Then I announced the beginning of Project Independence, with the goal of attaining energy independence for America by 1980.

Unfortunately only two of the proposals I requested—daylight-saving and a lowered speed limit—made it out of Congress before the Christmas recess. With the important exception of the Alaska pipeline bill, which I signed on November 16, Congress had failed to pass one major energy bill that I had requested.

Although the congressional response was disappointing, the American people rallied through the long winter months of 1973 and 1974. Conservation was working; but the crisis still existed. On November 25 I had to tighten controls still further, banning the sale of gasoline on Sunday, requesting cutbacks in outdoor lighting, and announcing that we were going to have a cutback on gasoline allocations by 15 percent in order to have enough heating oil.

The White House Christmas tree had 80 percent fewer lights that year. And instead of flying to California on *Air Force One* for the holiday season, Pat and I flew on a commercial airliner. We returned on a small Air Force

Jetstar that had to make one refueling stop and got us back to the White House at 3 A.M.

Despite the truly valiant nationwide conservation effort, it was a long winter of energy discontent. Lines at gas stations lengthened. People had to get up in the early hours of cold mornings to get in line for fuel. Even then, a station might not open because its allotted shipment did not arrive. If it did open, it was often only a short time until the supply ran out.

Before long the energy crisis had generated a serious new economic crisis. As early as the spring of 1973 gasoline prices had taken the biggest leap in twenty-two years. The oil-producing countries had the leverage, and they were using it. The National Petroleum Council said that it feared the energy crisis might lead to a recession. The uncertainty began to snowball. A Harris poll showed that 54 percent thought we were heading into a recession. The stock market, which had topped a record high of 1000 at the start of my second term, was now down in the 800s. Every wild rumor gained some nervous credence: gasoline was going to rise to a dollar a gallon; bread would rise to a dollar a loaf. The Wholesale Price Index climbed 18.2 percent in 1973 and the Cost of Living Index registered the biggest rise since 1947. Most of these increases resulted directly from food and fuel prices.

There was no easy place to lay the blame. There was even a lingering disbelief on the part of many Americans that the crisis was real. But every report I received assured me that the crisis had not been contrived by the oil companies. The cause seemed clear: foreign oil imports had risen from $4 a barrel before the crisis to $12 a barrel afterward, and the domestic oil companies were passing on this increase to consumers.

Nor was there a particular school of economics to be made the scapegoat. Walter Heller, economic adviser to several Democratic administrations, said, "The energy crisis caught us with our parameters down. The food crisis caught us too. . . . This was a year of infamy in inflation forecasting. There are many things we just don't know."

As the situation worsened the pressure for radical action—and specifically, for gas rationing—increased. Soon

Senators Mansfield, Proxmire, and Jackson were spearheading a campaign to impose rationing. A number of governors also called for it, and before the winter was over they had been joined by several of my energy experts within the administration.

I strongly opposed this idea. My personal experience at the OPA had convinced me that rationing does not work well even in wartime when patriotism inspires sacrifice. I knew that in peacetime an enormous black market would develop and the entire program would become a fiasco. The huge bureaucracy required to implement rationing would cost millions of dollars, and, like any bureaucracy, it would be determined to perpetuate itself long after it was needed. I was sure that rationing would end up being a cure worse than the illness.

By January 19 I could report real progress: in the month of December national gas consumption was 9 percent below what had been predicted; use of electricity was down 10 percent; the federal government had actually cut back on its energy usage by more than 20 percent; and by executive action I had established a Federal Energy Office in the executive branch and placed Deputy Secretary of the Treasury Bill Simon in charge. Simon moved swiftly to impose a strong hand and was soon dubbed the nation's "energy Czar."

Congress had adjourned for the Christmas holidays without passing any of the legislation I requested, so I met its return in January 1974 with a new appeal for four short-term actions and eleven other priority requests. In my State of the Union address I warned that the energy crisis was now our foremost legislative concern.

From the moment the Arab oil embargo began we had worked unceasingly to end it. Kissinger discussed the problem with both King Faisal and President Sadat. After one of his meetings with Sadat in December, Kissinger sent me a memo describing how he had reminded Sadat of our unique role in bringing peace to the Middle East:

> I told Sadat that without your personal willingness to confront the domestic issue nothing would have been possible. Sadat promised me he would get the oil embargo lifted

during the first half of January and said that he would call for its lifting in a statement which praised your personal role in bringing the parties to the negotiating table and making progress thereafter.

I followed up with a letter to Sadat on December 28:

For my part, I pledge myself to do everything in my power to ensure that my second term as President will be remembered as the period in which the United States developed a new and productive relationship with Egypt and the Arab world. . . .

However, the clearly discriminatory action of the oil producers can totally vitiate the effective contribution the United States is determined to make in the days ahead. Therefore, Mr. President, I must tell you in complete candor that it is essential that the oil embargo and oil production restrictions against the United States be ended at once. It cannot await the outcome of the current talks on disengagement.

A few weeks later, after the Egyptian-Israeli troop disengagement in January, we began urging Sadat even more insistently to help lift the embargo. At the end of the month he wrote to tell me that he had dispatched a special envoy to King Faisal and the other Arab leaders and that they had now agreed to lift the embargo, and a meeting to affirm this decision would be held in February. Unfortunately the meeting turned out to be a stalemate and the embargo continued.

Sadat soon sent me another message through our UN Delegate Shirley Temple Black, who had seen him privately. "I will lift the embargo," he told her. "I will lift it for President Nixon."

By mid-March there were reports that the embargo would be lifted conditionally, depending on the foreign policy behavior of the United States. I addressed these reports in a question-and-answer session in Chicago on March 15:

The United States, as far as the embargo is concerned, is not going to be pressured by our friends in the Mideast or others who might be our opponents to doing something before we are able to do it. And I would only suggest that insofar as any action on the embargo is taken, that if it has any implications of pressure on the United States it would have a countereffect on our efforts to go forward on the peace front, the negotiation front, because it would simply slow down, in my opinion, our very real and earnest efforts to get the disengagement on the Syrian front and also to move towards a permanent settlement.

Finally on March 18, after almost six months, seven of the nine Arab states finally agreed to lift the oil embargo. The decision was not supposed to be conditional on American policy, but it was to be subject to review in June.

The Arab oil embargo caused America's economic output to decline by as much as $15 billion during the first quarter of 1974. But it can be said that the energy crisis of 1974 had at least one positive effect: it made energy consciousness a part of American life.

As the oil embargo was ending, Kissinger resumed his shuttle diplomacy. Now his goal was a Syrian-Israeli troop disengagement. By this time both he and I recognized that we were in a race against time before another incident, inadvertent or otherwise, further froze the Syrian and Israeli positions and perhaps even drew the Egyptians back into the conflict. We were also racing against growing uncertainty in the thinking of some of the Mideastern leaders as the impeachment turmoil steadily threatened to undermine my position. On March 21 I received a report from Henry J. Taylor, a columnist and former ambassador to Switzerland, who had recently seen Sadat. "I am very worried about the President," Sadat had told Taylor. "I need time," he added with concern. "I wonder if I am going to have it. I need six months. You know what I would like to do? I would like to come to Washington and fight for President Nixon."

A WAR OF ATTRITION

On Friday, March 1, John Mitchell, Bob Haldeman, John Ehrlichman, Chuck Colson, Robert Mardian, Gordon Strachan, and Kenneth Parkinson, who had been one of the CRP's lawyers, were indicted on charges of conspiracy and, except for Mardian, on charges of obstruction of justice. All but Parkinson, Colson, and Mardian were also charged with having given false testimony. On March 7 Colson, Ehrlichman, Liddy, and three others were indicted for the break-in at the office of Ellsberg's psychiatrist.

The indictments were not a surprise, but they were still a blow. These men were about to face trials in a city where it would be almost impossible for them to have an impartial jury; a poll taken in Washington showed that 84 percent of the people there already thought they were guilty.

Earlier in the year Haig told me that Jaworski had reassured him that no one currently in the White House was going to be named by the grand jury—including me. Instead, we thought, he was sending grand jury material relating to me to Judge Sirica in a sealed report. On March 18 Sirica directed that this material be sent to the House Judiciary Committee. He also stated that, contrary to recent leaks, the grand jury's report was only a straightforward compilation of evidence and drew no accusatory conclusions.

The political prospects for Republican members of the House and Senate who faced re-election in November 1974 continued to worsen. I believed that the two issues of prosperity in the domestic economy and peace in the world, the same two issues that had swayed off-year elections for as long as I had been in public life, would ultimately tip the balance in this one, too. But many prospective candidates apparently felt that Watergate was going to overshadow everything else and that they would have a better chance to win with Jerry Ford as President.

There were to be five special elections held in the first few months of 1974. Ordinarily these would have attracted only minor interest, but in the superheated climate of the time the media treated them as highly important and significant votes of confidence for me. Of the five, Republican candidates won only one.

On March 19, 1974, Republican Senator James Buckley of New York became the first of my major conservative supporters to call for my resignation. He told reporters that he feared the effects of the "melodrama" of a Senate trial, in which "the Chamber would become a twentieth-century Roman Colosseum, as the performers are thrown to the electronic lions."

I addressed myself to Buckley's point in a press conference that same day:

> While it might be an act of courage to run away from a job that you were elected to do, it also takes courage to stand and fight for what you believe is right, and that is what I intend to do. . . . From the standpoint of statesmanship, for a President of the United States, any President, to resign because of charges made against him which he knew were false and because he had fallen in the polls, I think would not be statesmanship. It might be good politics, but it would be bad statesmanship. And it would mean that our system of government would be changed for all Presidents and all generations in the future.

Four days earlier at a question-and-answer session in Chicago I addressed a similar question by recalling that Senator Fulbright had once demanded Truman's resignation when he was at a low point of his popularity. "Some of the best decisions ever made by Presidents," I said, "were made when they were not too popular."

In March and April I knew that what had been at best only a remote chance to block impeachment in the House Judiciary Committee had now become almost nonexistent. When Chairman Peter Rodino addressed the House of Representatives on February 6—the day of a resolution ratifying the impeachment inquiry—he had said: "We are going to work expeditiously and fairly. . . . Whatever the result, whatever we learn or conclude, let us now proceed with such care and decency and thoroughness and honor that the vast majority of the American people and their children after them will say, 'That was the right course. There was no other way.' "

Among the members of the committee who sat solemnly by when Rodino said this was John Conyers of

Michigan, who had already told the Washington *Star* on March 17, that talk of conscience, evidence, and constitutional factors was "all crap." In the New York *Times Magazine* on April 28 he had described his role on the committee as "making sure Rodino doesn't get *too* damn fair." Another member was Father Robert Drinan of Massachusetts, who had urged impeachment for nearly a year and was frequently seen wearing an "Impeach Nixon" button on his clerical lapel. Robert Kastenmeier of Wisconsin had decorated his office with "Impeach Nixon" bumper strips. Charles Rangel of New York had been quoted by the Associated Press as saying, "There is no doubt in my mind that the President of the United States is a criminal." And Jerome Waldie of California had opened a letter to his constituents by thanking them "for supporting my efforts to impeach President Nixon." These were some of the committee members who, in Rodino's view, were going to proceed with "care and decency and thoroughness and honor" in their investigations into whether the evidence would justify the framing of articles of impeachment against me.

The Democratic majority chose John Doar as their counsel. Renata Adler, who served as one of Doar's aides, has since written in *Atlantic Monthly* that he had advocated my impeachment "months before he became special counsel, long before the inquiry began."

In March, James St. Clair wrote to Doar asking to participate in the hearings and to cross-examine witnesses. The committee finally and reluctantly agreed to allow St. Clair to participate in the closed sessions and to question witnesses, although it would not allow him to cross-examine them. When St. Clair wrote asking if he could see the grand jury material that Sirica had sent to the committee, he was refused.

On March 7 I dictated a memo to Haig in which I said that as far as the impeachment inquiry was concerned, "the law case will be decided by the PR case." That was what I felt we had to get across to St. Clair, Buzhardt, and our supporters in Congress. On March 15 I wrote another note: "St. Clair sees it too much as a trial, not a public relations exercise. We must work on him to get him to understand what we are up against."

My failure to use the State of the Union speech to draw the line firmly once and for all as far as providing more tapes was concerned proved to be the error I had feared it would be. Jaworski on one side, and now the House Judiciary Committee on the other, kept pressuring us for more and more. The Ervin Committee, whose initial request for five taped conversations had been rejected by the court, issued a new series of subpoenas for some 500 tapes and thousands of documents.

We had voluntarily turned over tapes in a civil case brought by Ralph Nader. Nader's lawyer, William Dobrovir, took a copy of one of these tapes and played it, as he was later quoted, "just for fun," at a cocktail party in Georgetown. The Special Prosecutor's office was outraged, but Dobrovir excused himself by saying that it had been an impulsive mistake. He was contradicted by his hostess, who said that he had told her in advance of his plan to bring the tape and play it and that she had told at least one of the guests about it beforehand. Dobrovir had also played the tape for a CBS television news reporter.

In December Jaworski came to us with a plea for access to another group of tapes. Haig told me that Jaworski had assured him that this would be his last request for tapes relating to the break-in and cover-up, and, on this assurance, we yielded. Thus, as of January 8, 1974, every request for tapes or documents that Jaworski had made had been met.

On January 8 and 9 St. Clair received letters asking for more than forty additional tapes—twenty-five of them relating to the break-in and cover-up. Haig was surprised, shocked, and disillusioned by Jaworski's action.

St. Clair wrote Jaworski and reminded him of the specific narrowness of the court ruling requiring us to surrender the nine subpoenaed tapes. Nor could Jaworski maintain that he needed these new tapes in order to obtain Watergate convictions: the year-end report of the Special Prosecution Force stated that enough evidence had been received to consider major indictments, and a prosecutor is not supposed to recommend an indictment unless he feels he already has the evidence needed to get a conviction. Two weeks later Jaworski trapped himself with his own words. In an interview he thought was off the record he revealed that as far as he was concerned, his office already "had the full story of Watergate." St. Clair told Jaworski that I would not give up any more tapes. Jaworski met with St. Clair and seemed to give him yet another assurance that this one additional request would be the last. Haig also met with Jaworski and reported that he was being very expansive and cooperative in evaluating the situation. My notes on Haig's report show these as the major points made by Jaworski:

1. Jaworski had told Haig that the staff he had inherited from Cox had a number of "fanatics" on it and that he was having great difficulty in keeping them under control.
2. Jaworski told Haig that Haldeman was worse off than Ehrlichman. He told him that he was prepared to let Ehrlichman off easy, but that Ehrlichman's attorney had taken too tough a line and, consequently, he had no choice but to proceed against Ehrlichman in the same way that he was proceeding on the charges against Haldeman.
3. Jaworski made what Haig and I considered to be a very interesting comment that "Sirica was really a friend of the President." Sirica, he felt, would not like the attitude of the members of his, Jaworski's, staff who were, in his view, more interested in "getting the President" than in getting the facts.
4. Jaworski disliked Rodino and considered him "publicity mad."
5. Jaworski liked St. Clair.
6. With regard to the additional tapes and documents that Jaworski had just requested, he urged Haig to give him "the softest possible turn-down," and Haig said that we ought to "use Vaseline" in responding to these requests and in handling Jaworski.

On February 13 St. Clair wrote to Jaworski again, saying that he hoped he would have reconsidered the broad scope of his request, and, for the second time, respectfully declining the request for more than forty additional tapes.

Jaworski immediately wrote to Senator Eastland, the Chairman of the Senate Judiciary Committee, acknowledging that he could bring indictments on the evidence he had, but arguing that new tapes "may contain" evidence necessary for future trials. This kind of reasoning could be applied to any and all documents in the presidential files. It was hard to see where, if anywhere, Jaworski would ever draw a line.

The escalating pattern seemed never ending. Because of the original Special Prosecutor's request we had turned over eight conversations; we had also given the prosecutors more than 700 documents. We had voluntarily provided access to seventeen additional tapes since the first court ruling. Now they were back asking for more than forty more.

The House Judiciary Committee would prove no different from the Special Prosecutor in its insatiable demands for tapes and other materials. On March 6 I announced that we would turn over to the committee all the materials we had given to the Special Prosecutor; these comprised some nineteen tapes and more than 700 documents. I also agreed to provide literally boxloads of documents requested by the committee from departments and agencies, ranging from meetings of the Cost of Living Council to high-level sessions on import quotas. I agreed to answer in writing and under oath any question from the committee. I also indicated that I was willing to be interviewed under oath, if that was deemed necessary.

At this time the committee's range of investigations covered scores of policy and political areas—from the secret Cambodian bombing in 1969 to the Cost of Living Council's decisions about the price of hamburger. And the list was still growing.

Before the committee had narrowed down any of its areas of investigation into anything like specific charges against me, and before it had even looked at the 700 documents or listened to the nineteen tapes, a letter was sent demanding over forty more tapes.

I met with House Republican Leader John Rhodes, and he agreed that the committee's request was extremely broad. He confided that some of the committee members had not even known all Doar was doing. But Rhodes was emphatic when he said that, as unjust as it undoubtedly was, no Republican congressman could afford to defend a refusal by the White House to produce any additional evidence the committee requested.

I had to face the fact that we were over a barrel and that my weakened political situation gave the Judiciary

Committee license for an unrestrained fishing expedition. I had no practical choice but to comply with their demands. If I refused, they would vote me in contempt of Congress. I made a note on March 22, 1974, at 2 A.M.: "Lowest day. Contempt equals impeachment."

Since the first of the year impeachment had been like a shifting sea. One day it would be calm, and there would seem to be a chance we could survive. The next day it would turn stormy and survival seemed unlikely. By the end of March almost every day was stormy. In New York, John Mitchell and Maury Stans were on trial in the Vesco case. Some news reports from the trial implied that John Dean had been unrattled in his testimony, whereas Stans and Mitchell had seemed shaken and had not been very effective. Ultimately, both Stans and Mitchell were found innocent, and the jurors told the press that it was Dean they had not believed. But we did not know that in March when the impeachment hearings were gearing up.

The bombshell of my having to pay $400,000 in new taxes because of the disallowance of the deduction for my donation of my papers was still reverberating, and we had just been hit with the leaks that Brooks's subcommittee was charging that $17 million of government funds had been spent on my personal property. The court-appointed tape "experts" had also recently issued one of their series of reports on the 18½-minute gap. In California, John Ehrlichman, on trial for the break-in at Ellsberg's psychiatrist's office, asked and obtained a court subpoena for me to appear at the trial.

We had also received word that John Connally was about to be drawn into a grand jury investigation over illegal contributions alleged to have been made to him from milk producers' organizations. In normal times the Justice Department would not have considered moving against a former Secretary of the Treasury, three-term Governor, and Secretary of the Navy solely on the basis of a highly unreliable informant who succeeded in having the Special Prosecutor's office drop serious charges being brought against him in a totally unrelated matter. But these were not ordinary times. Whenever I met with Connally, he would brush off his own troubles. He was innocent, he said, and there was no way that he could ever be found otherwise. He turned out to be right: in 1975 he was ultimately acquitted on all charges. But in the meantime this was another numbing blow. "Just one time," I said to Ziegler, "will we ever just one time get a break in this long, tortuous year?"

On April 13, for the first time, the Harris poll reported a bare majority, 43 percent to 41 percent, was now in favor of my impeachment.

Haig, Buzhardt, St. Clair, and I decided that because of the political realities of the situation, we had to compromise on the House Judiciary Committee's request for more tapes. We decided to supply the committee with written verbatim transcripts from which only material unrelated to Watergate had been excised. This ultimately became the "Blue Book," a massive, 1,300-page document officially titled *Submission of Recorded Presidential Conversations to the Committee on the Judiciary of the House of Representatives by President Richard Nixon.* Our hope was that this response might, through its sheer bulk, bring home to the public what was being asked of me.

It soon became clear that there were many gray areas in the conversations—material not entirely unrelated to "Watergate," as that term had constantly expanded in meaning—but unrelated to my knowledge and action on the cover-up, which were the issues actually before the committee.

Buzhardt suggested the phrase "Material Unrelated to Presidential Action Deleted," which was typed in the Blue Book transcripts wherever such a deletion was made. In order to verify our decisions in this regard, we offered to invite Rodino and the ranking Republican on the committee, Edward Hutchinson of Michigan, to come to the White House and hear any of the uncut original tapes they chose.

Before we could even complete the Blue Book in response to the House Judiciary Committee's request for 42 tapes, we received a letter requesting 142 more tapes and documents relating to Watergate, the Huston Plan, Daniel Ellsberg, wiretaps, and the visit of Judge Byrne to San Clemente. Not long after this, Peter Rodino warned that the committee might soon be asking for still more tapes and documents dealing with my income taxes, the San Clemente property, campaign dirty tricks, and other matters.

Just before midnight on April 20 I made a note:

> *D Day*
> 1. Any more tapes will destroy the office.
> 2. Leaving the question open will only invite more unreasonable demands.
> 3. Better to fight and lose defending the office than surrender and win a personal victory at disastrous long-range cost to the office of the presidency.

At nine o'clock on the night of April 29 I made a televised address in which I announced that I was yielding the transcripts of the tapes requested by the House Judiciary Committee so that the committee could reach an informed judgment and because the American people were entitled to the facts and the evidence that demonstrated those facts. I said that I hoped that by violating the principle of confidentiality this once I could restore it for the future.

I said that the transcripts I was releasing included all the relevant portions of the subpoenaed conversations, "the rough as well as the smooth, the strategy sessions, the exploration of alternatives, the weighing of human and political costs. . . . These materials—together with those already made available—will tell it all."

Then I continued:

> I realize that these transcripts will provide grist for many sensational stories in the press. Parts will seem to be contradictory with one another and parts will be in conflict with some of the testimony given in the Senate Watergate Committee hearings.
>
> I have been reluctant to release these tapes not just because they will embarrass me and those with whom I have talked—which they will—and not just because they will become the subject of speculation and even ridicule— which they will—and not just because certain parts of them will be seized upon by political and journalistic opponents—which they will.
>
> I have been reluctant because, in these and in all the other conversations in this office, people have spoken their minds freely, never dreaming that specific sentences or even

parts of sentences would be picked out as the subjects of national attention and controversy. . . .

I am confident that the American people will see these transcripts for what they are, fragmentary records from a time more than a year ago that now seems very distant, the records of a President and of a man suddenly being confronted and having to cope with information which, if true, would have the most far-reaching consequences not only for his personal reputation but, more important, for his hopes, his plans, his goals for the people who had elected him as their leader.

In giving you these records—blemishes and all—I am placing my trust in the basic fairness of the American people.

I know in my own heart that through the long, painful, and difficult process revealed in these transcripts I was trying in that period to discover what was right and to do what was right.

It is not possible to describe what it is like to see long-forgotten conversations suddenly reappear as lengthy transcripts. We are conditioned to think of the written word as a form of planned communication, and when the words of an ordinary conversation are put on paper they acquire a rigidity that, despite a literal accuracy in terms of what was said, may completely fail to capture or reflect the nature of the meeting or conversation as it actually took place. An observation can seem like an intention; an offhand comment appears deliberate and premeditated; a passing thought can strike the reader as a prescription for action. Seeing the words there in lifeless type on a page, you realize that there is no way to explain how at one moment in a discussion one person is a devil's advocate and the next moment the roles all shift. Outsiders reading only the words of those conversations about Watergate could know nothing of the torment, the spectrum of concern that lay behind them. More than for the substance, the transcripts would be criticized for the tone of the discussions.

Much of the impact of Watergate throughout the past year had come from the fact that it was breaking new ground in the political awareness of the American people by introducing them to things like government-authorized wiretaps and break-ins, White House taping systems, and the political use of the IRS. As much as many may have suspected beforehand that such things took place, I had to bear the brunt of having revealed the particulars that confirmed those suspicions.

And so it was with the Blue Book transcripts. The American myth that Presidents are always presidential, that they sit in the Oval Office talking in lofty, and quotable phrases, will probably never die—and probably never should, because it reflects an important aspect of the American character.

But the reality of politics and power in the White House is very different. It is a rough game, and the men I have known who have made it there reflect the ability to play rough when necessary and come out on top. There is noble talk in the Oval Office to be sure, high-minded and disinterested. But there are also frustration, worry, anxiety, profanity and, above all, raw pragmatism when it comes to politics and political survival.

With the Blue Book transcripts, as with so many other Watergate revelations, I was in the position of telling the American people things that they did not want to know.

The reaction to the Blue Book was oddly delayed. On May 3, four days after it had been released, I went to a rally in Phoenix. A crowd of 15,000 had gathered inside the auditorium, and when a group of about 150 demonstrators started yelling "Out now," they were shouted into silence. Afterward, at a reception at Barry Goldwater's mountaintop house, both he and John Rhodes came up individually to say how pleased they were with the reception and to assure me that I could continue to count on their support.

By the time I had returned to Camp David from this cross-country swing, however, a surge of negative reaction to the Blue Book had begun to register. Hugh Scott denounced its contents as a "deplorable, shabby, disgusting, and immoral performance by all." The *Wall Street Journal* said editorially that while it could see no good grounds in the transcripts for recommending impeachment, "Still, there is such a thing as moral leadership . . . the 'bully pulpit.' This is what Mr. Nixon has sacrificed for once and all." The Chicago *Tribune* called for my resignation, while other old friends, including the Omaha *World-Herald*, the Kansas City *Times*, the Cleveland *Plain Dealer*, and the Charlotte *Observer*, echoed their sentiments or even endorsed impeachment. They were joined by the Los Angeles *Times*, the Miami *Herald*, and the Providence *Journal*. Jerry Ford felt that he had to make a comment on the transcripts, so he said, "They don't exactly confer sainthood on anyone," and he admitted that he was disappointed by them.

More and more Republicans began to talk about resignation. John Rhodes, his mind apparently changed from just a few days earlier, now said he would accept my decision to resign if I were to make it. He said that my chances of winning in the House had been steadily reduced; at the moment he put the percentage at 51 to 49 against impeachment. John Anderson, the Chairman of the House Republican Conference, suggested that I consider resigning. In the Senate, Marlow Cook of Kentucky and Richard Schweiker of Pennsylvania called for outright resignation, and Milton Young of North Dakota said I should use the Twenty-fifth Amendment to step aside until I had been proved innocent. Barry Goldwater drew attention when he said he was sure I would resign if I were impeached by the House.

I was determined not to panic. I would respect everyone's views and understand the necessity they felt to express them. But I would not quit.

Haig was stunned by the swell of criticism. He said that the combination of the Chicago *Tribune* editorial and Scott's and Rhodes's statements suggested to him a calculated effort to force me out of office. He worried further about news reports of an "informal" conversation Jerry Ford had had with reporters in which he was quoted as having described his concern that my authority had been "crippled" and that Russia might try to take advantage of this situation. Ford was reported to have said that my failing influence could be seen in Teddy Kennedy's successful efforts to secure a congressional cutback on aid to Vietnam, and that he had talked to Kissinger about these concerns but not to me. After this report was published, Ford issued a "clarification," but the damage was done.

Soon the resignation rumors started taking wild turns: there was a report that Ford had asked his staff to go on "red alert," and another that I was going to step down within forty-eight hours and that Kissinger was about to fly back from the Middle East to receive the letter of resignation. There was even a rumor that I had had a stroke.

In an effort to scotch these rumors Haig told reporters that I would consider resignation only if I thought it was in the best interests of the country, and Ziegler released a statement that I had personally approved:

> The city of Washington is full of rumors. All that have been presented to me today are false, and the one that heads the list is the one that says President Nixon intends to resign. His attitude is one of determination that he will not be driven out of office by rumor, speculation, excessive charges, or hypocrisy. He is up for the battle, he intends to fight it and he feels he has a personal and constitutional duty to do so.

The Blue Book proved conclusively that I had not known about the break-in in advance, and that Dean was wrong when he said that he and I had discussed the cover-up over a period of months. On the other hand, it undercut the impression I had left in my public statements that I had reacted like a prosecutor when Dean informed me of the cover-up. But however damaging any or all of it may have been, nothing on the tapes amounted to an impeachable offense.

Unfortunately the main Watergate issue had already shifted, and, as had been the case throughout the past thirteen months, I was in the position of settling a point after everyone had already moved on to another one. The release of the transcripts was good strategy to the extent that it proved conclusively that Dean had not told the truth about everything; and to the extent that it showed that in the areas where he had told the truth, my actions and omissions, while regrettable and possibly indefensible, were not impeachable.

But public opinion is not a court of law, and there would be no trial on this evidence. This was politics, and the effect of the Blue Book was to force Republicans even further into a political corner with me. The transcripts raised the distinctions that responsible congressmen would have to make between what was constitutionally impeachable and what was politically insupportable.

The Blue Book itself would be undermined in early July when the House Judiciary Committee, after suggesting that we had deliberately dropped the most damaging sections from some of the tapes, released its own book of transcripts.

In fact, most of the discrepancies between the committee's version and ours were minor ones that arose because the committee arranged to have its copies of the tapes electronically enhanced, and consequently picked up many words that we had described as "unintelligible." Some of these additional words or sentences helped our case more than hurt it.

But there was one admittedly serious discrepancy that dominated all the others. It was the section of the March 22 tape covering my final discussion with John Mitchell, in which I told him that unlike Eisenhower who cared only that he was "clean," I cared about the men. I told Mitchell that they could go before the Ervin Committee and "stonewall it, let them plead the Fifth Amendment, cover up, or anything else" if they thought they had to. Then I added, "On the other hand, I would prefer . . . that you do it the other way." This section was not in our version of the transcripts.

Transcripts Link Nixon to Cover-up was the Washington *Post* headline when the Judiciary Committee revealed the discrepancy. It was utterly ridiculous to assume that we would have deliberately omitted a damaging section of a tape that we knew the Judiciary Committee already had in its possession. But we took terrible heat for it at the time because we simply did not know what had happened. Only months later, when it no longer mattered, did Fred Buzhardt figure out the answer. Apparently, according to Buzhardt, the committee's copies of the tapes must have been copied from the originals at a higher volume, with the result that the final section of the March 22 tape, which was inaudible on our copy—and evidently also on the Special Prosecutor's copy, which had been made at the same volume level—could be heard on the committee's copy. The bitter irony was that this innocent discrepancy had made us look both sinister and foolish.

On May 5, in the middle of the uproar over the Blue Book, Al Haig met with Leon Jaworski in the Map Room at the White House. Jaworski told Haig that I had been named an unindicted coconspirator by the Watergate grand jury. If this was true, then Jaworski had not been honest with Haig earlier in the year when he had told him that no one in the White House had been named.

We knew Jaworski had doubted whether I could constitutionally be indicted while I was President. But he knew that by naming me an unindicted coconspirator he would have a wild card to produce in the courts when he needed it to get more tapes and to guarantee that he could use the tapes in the Watergate trials. Later Archibald Cox, of all people, would denounce Jaworski's action, calling the technique he used "just a back-handed way of sticking the knife in." By having me charged by the grand jury, a forum that could not judge me, he could prejudice me before the House Judiciary Committee, the forum that could.

Jaworski had a deal to propose: he told Haig that if we would give him eighteen of the sixty-four tapes he had subpoenaed, leaving open the possibility that defendants would request additional ones in the trials, he would drop his suit for the rest and not reveal at this time that the grand jury had named me an unindicted coconspirator. If I would not agree to what he called his "compromise," he was going to announce the grand jury's action in open court in order to strengthen the case against me.

Even after taking so many low blows from so many sources over so many months, I was still surprised that Jaworski would resort to what I felt was a form of blackmail. But the thought of actually ending the courtroom battle over the tapes was like a siren song. Haig felt it too. He said, "We're at the point that we can see the barbed wire at the end of the street. What we have to do is mobilize everything to cut through it." St. Clair, however, was opposed to the so-called compromise; he felt that to cave now would forfeit our position that we would give no more.

Haig urged me at least to listen to the eighteen tapes and not reject the offer out of hand. I returned from Camp David in the evening of May 5, 1974, and went to the EOB office shortly after eight o'clock to begin this task.

I worked until late that night and for several hours the next morning listening to more tapes. I broke just before midday for some appointments and a talk with Scowcroft about the situation in the Middle East. In the afternoon I listened to the tape of my June 23, 1972, conversation with Haldeman—the tape that would emerge publicly three months later as the "smoking gun." I heard Haldeman tell me that Dean and Mitchell had come up with a plan to handle the problem of the investigation's going into areas we didn't want it to go. The plan was to call in Helms and Walters of the CIA and have them restrain the FBI.

I listened further and heard myself asking if Mitchell had known about "this thing to any much of a degree." "I think so. I don't think he knew the details, but I think he knew," Haldeman had answered. His voice did not have a great deal of conviction when he said it, but there he was, a week after the break-in, telling me that he thought Mitchell knew.

I had indicated in all my public statements that the sole motive for calling in the CIA had been national security. But there was no doubt now that we had been talking about political implications that morning. I thought back to my discussion with Haldeman about this very problem in May 1973, when he had insisted that our only motive had been the national security concern that the FBI's investigation might expose CIA operations. I knew he believed it completely then, and so had I. I also knew that no one would ever believe it now. I consoled myself with the thought that there must be other things that were not apparent on these tapes, things that would explain our later belief that we had been thinking about national security. The city was now full of new reports—and provocative new questions—about the CIA's apparent awareness of the break-in before it happened and about its activities during the cover-up. Surely we could not have been so wrong as to have completely rationalized a national security concern where none existed. I thought that perhaps there would be something else, something helpful on another tape.

In the afternoon I talked to Scowcroft, who sent in a report from Kissinger. My letter to Mrs. Meir had apparently had some effect and the Israelis had presented a peace proposal that Kissinger thought had a chance of actually being accepted by the moderate Arab governments.

I wrote across the bottom of the page: "Personal message to K from RN: You are doing a superb job against great odds—regardless of the outcome. But let us hope and work for the best."

The contents of the June 23, 1972, tape were not my primary reason for deciding against Jaworski's "compromise." In another example of miscalculation I did not recognize the tape then as the "smoking gun" it turned out to be. I knew that it would hurt—but so had so many other things, and we had survived them. And perhaps the Court would rule in our favor; in the meantime I did not feel others should listen and have to be answerable for what they heard.

Now I can see that I should have asked Buzhardt to listen to all three June conversations with Haldeman, give me his independent judgment on them, and then have put them out—even though they were in several respects inconsistent with Haldeman's and my public statements of our recollection of the purpose of the meetings. That would have been damaging, but far less so than being forced to make the tapes public after the Supreme Court's decision compelled me to do so.

By this time, however, I had come around to St. Clair's and Buzhardt's view that we should draw the line on producing any further tapes. My instinct was still that we had to put a stop to it.

On Wednesday I notified them both that I had decided not to give up any more tapes. "Perhaps this is Armageddon," I told Ziegler, "but I would rather leave fighting for a principle." That afternoon St. Clair called Jaworski and told him my decision. On May 22 I sent a letter to the House Judiciary Committee informing them that I would not supply any more tapes in response to the constantly escalating requests for them. Now the lines were drawn. April 26 had been a symbolic milestone: if I succeeded in completing my full term as President I would be in the White House for one thousand more days. May 22 was another milestone: with this letter to the House Judiciary Committee, whatever happened, I was about to begin the last leg of the Watergate road.

In January 1973 Washington observers had predicted that I could count on having a margin of between 74 and 125 votes on an impeachment resolution in the House. By March 1974, this margin had been badly worn down by House Judiciary Committee accusations and the attacks on my finances. After the Blue Book was released, Timmons reported a defection of at least twenty-five House members. In mid-May Jerry Ford said that the odds that the committee would vote impeachment were 50–50. The atmosphere spawned more rumors. Now that few people seemed to care about the question of who had ordered the break-in, there was new information that the Democrats themselves had prior knowledge and that the Hughes organization might be involved. And there were stories of strange alliances. In mid-May I received a call from Connally. He had known Jaworski in Texas, and he said he was calling to pass along something Jaworski had told him. The message was: "The President has no friends in the White House."

But then the tide seemed to change, and by June it looked as if things were actually beginning to brighten. Whatever other reasons there might have been, a major one was that the Judiciary Committee's patently unfair tactics had started to backfire.

Rodino had opened the committee's investigation of the evidence with the announcement that the proceedings would be governed by rules of confidentiality. After this announcement the committee had voted itself into closed sessions and then promptly started to leak everything that came into its hands. Every tape was labeled "highly damaging" by the partisans on the committee; my finances were described as even "more explosive." When St. Clair requested that the committee go into open sessions rather than continue its prejudicial game, he was rebuffed.

One of the clearest examples of the committee's conduct was a leak about my diary dictation for the night of March 21, 1973, the day that Dean had described the "cancer" growing close to the presidency. Committee leakers told UPI that I had dictated: "Today is March 21. It wasn't a very eventful day." This leak, which indicated that I was totally blasé about the information Dean had given me—presumably because I was already part of the cover-up—went out over the networks and wires. In fact, what I had dictated was: "As far as the day was concerned it was uneventful, except for the talk with Dean."

The leaks, the posturing, the publicity-mad behavior of the House Judiciary Committee members and staff undermined all their talk about "fairness." At the same time the highly emotional first reaction to the contents and language of the Blue Book transcripts had run its course. On June 5 Timmons reported that Tom Railsback of Illinois, one of the swing Republicans on the committee, was saying that the evidence was simply not overwhelming in the way it would have to be in order to justify impeachment. Robert McClory of Illinois, another Republican, said optimistically that the committee was now evenly divided: eleven votes for impeachment, eleven against, and sixteen on the fence. John Rhodes called me to say that he had found that the attitude in the House and on the Judiciary Committee had grown more positive over the past week. St. Clair said that his experience always told him when things were going bad because there was what he called a "smell of guilt in the courtroom." He said, "There just isn't a smell of guilt in that committee."

There were also reports of new grass roots organizations cropping up across the country to help me. And Haig had finally started to organize the staff into task forces to fight impeachment.

On June 7, 1974, I resumed making detailed diary dictations at the end of each day. I began the first one by summing up the situation as it had appeared at the start of the summer.

Diary

I am not going to try to recap the events of this very difficult time, but will try to put some of the immediate developments in perspective and include some observations with regard to various collateral issues that have arisen.

I have kept in almost daily touch with Timmons in the past couple of weeks, and he believes that we have been gaining slowly but surely among both the Southerners and the Republicans.

Teddy White, interestingly enough, had talked to Rose and then had talked to Ziegler today. He said that two weeks ago he thought that the House would have voted an impeachment and that we would have won in the Senate by a margin of five or six votes. Now he believes that, as he puts it, we have bottomed out and that the House will not vote impeachment if a vote were to occur today.

John Connally strongly held the same opinion. Connally believes, for example, that those who vote for impeachment will find that the next time they come up for election they will be wiped out. Of course, we have been thinking for over a year now that the tide was turning, and then events occur which seem to put us behind the eight ball again.

What will motivate the House members at the present time I think may be their concern that if they impeach, they run the risk of taking the responsibility for whatever goes wrong in foreign and domestic policy after that. They also may be concerned from the Democratic standpoint that if they impeach, they put in office as an incumbent Ford, who would have a united party and an administration behind him against whoever they ran for President. This the Democratic pros must not look to with any relish.

On the plus side, the 18½-minute-gap matter I think is being resolved fairly satisfactorily, although we never know what Jaworski may do.

Bebe is going through another intensive going over with, he said, about a hundred subpoenas to his restaurants, the yacht club, etc. What this poor man has gone through is really unbelievable and it is amazing that he has been able to stand up as well as he has.

I saw Don and Eddie after the luncheon for [Prince] Fahd [of Saudi Arabia]. Both brothers have stood up splendidly under torturous conditions. Don has about forty thousand dollars in legal bills. Eddie has one of twenty thousand for legal fees.

Al Haig told me that the Senate Watergate Committee had a pretty devastating report on Humphrey and also one on Mills. The Republicans have it, but no one of the Republicans, of course, will leak it. The trouble is that the Republicans, like conservatives generally, are responsible and play with Marquis of Queensberry rules, whereas the liberals go just the other way.

The irony of this whole situation is that we are being accused of playing a foul game during the election and so forth, whereas what we have done as compared with previous administrations is hardly worth mentioning, but with the double standard that exists in the media, anything that comes out that hurts the conservatives, and particularly the President, gets enormous play—anything that comes out against one of the Democrats gets a one-day play and then is dropped.

I think one thing that seems to disturb our opponents in the media, in the Congress, and in partisan circles the most is that I have hung on. As I look back over the year, I don't know quite how I have done it. I have had times of considerable discouragement although I have pretty generally been able to cover it so people are unable to see it.

I remember, looking clear back, in May 1973 I think it was, while we were in the swimming pool in Florida, and David was sitting in the Jacuzzi, and he said that he had been thinking about all these things and he felt that all that was necessary was for me to "persevere," as he put it. And that is, of course, about all we've been doing—persevering.

Looking back over the year and just highlighting the events, the mistakes are quite apparent. First, the April 30 speech. Possibly the decision on Haldeman-Ehrlichman was right, although I am not absolutely sure that it was under the circumstances now.

But going on from there, certainly the first major mistake was the appointment of Richardson as Attorney General. Richardson's weakness, which came to light during the Cox firing, should have been apparent. •

Then, of course, came the bombshell of the tapes. This occurred, unfortunately, while I was out at the hospital, and I remember when Haig came in and told me about it and we discussed it. Later Agnew came in and said, maybe you ought to destroy them. Frankly, we thought about it. We should have done it, because none had been subpoenaed at that time. But here Garment, I think primarily, stepped in with the idea that it would be a destruction of evidence or what have you. But all the sorrow and difficulties we have had about the eighteen minutes and the so-called two missing tapes, and, of course, then the tapes themselves and the Supreme Court case would have been avoided had we just bitten the bullet then. But having failed to do so we went on down the line.

The Agnew resignation was necessary although a very serious blow, because while some thought that his stepping aside would take some of the pressure off the effort to get the President, all it did was to open the way to put pressure on the President to resign as well. This is something we have to realize: that any accommodation with opponents in this kind of a fight does not satisfy—it only brings on demands for more.

Of course, the Cox firing probably was the right thing to do even with all the pain and suffering that it caused because, according to Buzhardt and others, Cox was ready to indict the President at that time and that could have been at a time that it could have had a fatal effect with the House, even though our public standing then was probably somewhat higher than it is now.

I think what has irritated me the most has been the handling of my personal finances. We have an excellent case, but we simply couldn't get a proper hearing on it.

On May 20, 1974, the district court hearing Jaworski's suit for the sixty-four new tapes ruled in his favor. I decided to appeal the decision. Jaworski immediately moved to bypass the court of appeals, requesting that the Supreme Court take the case directly. On May 31 the Supreme Court agreed to Jaworski's unusual request. This meant that a final decision could come in as little as a month.

By the end of May Kissinger had spent thirty-two days traveling back and forth between Jerusalem and Damascus in the long and often frustrating attempt to achieve a disengagement between Syrian and Israeli troops. The Egyptian-Israeli disengagement had been easier because Sadat had adopted the attitude that if the major issues could be resolved, the minor ones could be settled at the ongoing Geneva Conference. But the hatred between the Syrians and the Israelis went too deep for them to be able to think this way.

Kissinger was at his finest in these sessions, probing like a surgeon the concerns that separated the two parties, indefatigably seeking the areas of mutual interest that would make an accord possible.

But on May 16 Scowcroft brought Haig a message from Kissinger that he was coming back; he had done the superhuman and it still was not enough. I sent back a firm message of encouragement directing that he give it one more try. I knew he was exhausted, but he was too close to a settlement to let the momentum slacken.

On May 22 I wrote Mrs. Meir to "urge that you and your Cabinet make a supreme effort to seek a compromise which would permit an agreement on the disengagement of forces on the Golan Heights and enable us to move another step away from strife and bloodshed."

On May 29 the prize was won. The impossible had been achieved. Both Israel and Syria accepted the terms, and the disengagement agreement was signed on May 31.

The next step in the American effort had to be an attempt to consolidate the new trust and extend the new dialogue. It was important to move fast while the momentum was still fresh. Plans were therefore activated for a series of major summits in the Mideast. I decided to make personal visits to Egypt, Syria, Saudi Arabia, Jordan, and Israel to help firm up the gains we had made and to lay the groundwork for more progress in the future.

While Kissinger was forging the Syrian-Israeli disengagement, the House Judiciary Committee turned to the topics of wiretaps and the Plumbers. Kissinger had already testified before the Senate Foreign Relations Committee about both subjects, but now the House Judiciary Committee had been given the materials on the case and was treating them with characteristic irresponsibility. The committee began a systematic series of leaks implying that there were discrepancies in Kissinger's statements. Several Foreign Relations Committee members reaffirmed their belief in Kissinger's veracity, but the press would not let up. Early in his first press conference after his shuttle tour de force the questions took an ugly and accusatory turn. He was asked about reports that he had given false testimony to the Foreign Relations Committee and whether he had obtained a lawyer because of the prospect of perjury. His jaw angrily set, Kissinger fired back, "I do not conduct my office as a conspiracy."

This sudden attack on his character and truthfulness, added to the strains of a month of tense shuttling between Israel and Syria, set Kissinger's nerves on edge. He kept his composure during the press conference, but afterward he was shaken and disillusioned. As he analyzed the situation, he was the major symbol of the positive foreign policy accomplishments of the Nixon administration; even while the full-scale attempt to impeach me was under way, he had had the effrontery to show the nation and the world that the United States under my leadership was still able to command respect in the world and achieve significant results despite the drag of Watergate. I agreed with this analysis completely: the voracious forces of the opposition could not allow that to continue.

THE MIDEAST TRIP

Shortly before leaving for the Mideast on June 10, 1974, I dictated two notes about the way the domestic situation had developed.

Diary

As the week ends and as the trip begins, there seems to be a feeling that the momentum is changing somewhat, although we have felt this before and have been disappointed.

One thought that has occurred to me, which I developed at Camp David as I took a walk down the nature trail on a very muddy path, is that from now until approximately the first of August when the Supreme Court will rule, the thing to do is to just treat every day as basically the last one and not to be constantly concerned about what may happen in the future. I have tried to do this over the past year and a half, but it has been very difficult at times because we seem always to be fighting the battle or trying to deal with some new development.

But all in all, looking back over this last fifteen or sixteen months, to me the great tragedy is that it seems to be a year and a half almost that is lost. We have accomplished some good things but I have had to spend an inordinate amount of my time thinking about this problem, and, of course, emotionally it has taken a great deal out of me. We certainly have made our mistakes but perhaps the year has taught us all somewhat more compassion and understanding, although I must say that it has also brought clearly to light the unbelievable battle in which we are engaged and how high the stakes are and how bitter and fanatical the opposition is. We simply have to stick it out.

On June 5 I held a meeting for some of the leaders of the American Jewish community. I was disturbed by what I considered to be their shortsighted outlook.

Diary

I pointed out that hardware alone to Israel was a policy that made sense maybe five years ago but did not make sense today, and that they had to have in mind that each new war would be more and more costly because their neighbors would learn to fight, and there were more of them. And that second, looking into the future, someone would have to hold the ring against the Russians, as we did with the alert in 1973.

I made it very clear there is going to be no blank check in our conversations with the Israelis although, of course, I expressed sympathy for their military needs and, of course, enormous respect for their bravery, etc.

As a matter of fact, whether Israel can survive over a long period of time with a hundred million Arabs around them I think is really questionable. The only long-term hope lies in reaching some kind of settlement now while they can operate from a position of strength, and while we are having such apparent success in weaning the Arabs away from the Soviets and into more responsible paths.

On June 9 we had a lively family dinner. Afterward, while the girls and their husbands went downstairs to watch a movie and Pat went upstairs to finish her packing, I went to the Lincoln Sitting Room and dictated a note describing the problems and opportunities I saw in the historic trip we were to begin the next morning.

Diary

I don't know whether I got across adequately the point that not just this trip when it is concluded, or the two and a half years remaining when it is concluded, will mean that we have secured our goal of a lasting peace. It is going to require tending thereafter by strong Presidents for the balance of this century. And who knows what can happen thereafter.

All I must do is to do everything possible to see that we leave a structure on which future Presidents can build—a structure based on military strength, diplomatic sophistication, intelligence, and, of course, a strong strain of idealism which will lead to progress despite some rough waters through which we will have to pass toward our goal of a permanent peace in that area.

As I complete this day, June 9, I begin this trip recognizing the profound importance it will have for the future as far as the Mideast is concerned, and as far as the American position in the world.

I was fully aware that the success or failure of this trip might make the decisive difference in my being able to continue to exercise presidential leadership abroad and at home despite the merciless onslaught of the Watergate attacks.

Diary

The irony of it all is that, as I told Ziegler, the press—or at least most of the press—will be more obsessed with what happens with the minuscule problems involved in Watergate than they are with the momentous stakes that are involved in what I will be doing and saying in the Mideast.

This is probably a turning point in terms of the whole so-called Watergate issue, but also a turning point insofar as the presidency itself is concerned. I am going to devote myself over this next ten days to doing everything possible to restore some respect for the office as well as for the man.

During the flight to our first stopover, Salzburg, Austria, Haig told me that Kissinger was upset about an editorial in that morning's New York *Times* that accused him of having dissembled in his Senate testimony about the 1969 wiretaps. He said that Kissinger was talking about holding a press conference in Salzburg in order to answer this charge.

"A *Times* editorial isn't a charge, Al," I said. "It's nothing more than a *Times* editorial, and that doesn't mean a goddamn thing. If he holds a press conference, he'll only play into their hands by giving them a Watergate lead for their first story from this trip." I said that if Kissinger felt he had to have a press conference, he should at least not be defensive but approach the question positively on the ground that the wiretaps were legitimate and necessary.

But Kissinger was in no mood to take this advice. He called a press conference and opened it with a long and emotional statement. After going through the details of his testimony on the wiretaps, he introduced an aggrieved personal note. "I have been generally identified, or, it has been alleged that I am supposed to be interested primarily in the balance of power," he said. "I would rather like to think that when the record is written, one may remember that perhaps some lives were saved and that perhaps some mothers can rest more at ease, but I leave that to history. What I will not leave to history is a discussion of my public honor."

The real bombshell came during the question period that followed when, in reply to a question, he said, "I do not believe that it is possible to conduct the foreign policy of the United States under these circumstances when the character and credibility of the Secretary of State is at issue. And if it is not cleared up, I will resign."

I issued a public statement expressing my understanding of Kissinger's desire to defend himself against malicious leaks, adding that all Americans would recognize, as I did, that his honor needed no defense.

All in all, what really concerns me about this attack on Kissinger is the total irresponsibility of the *Times* and Washington *Post* and all of our opponents at a time we are traveling abroad to take him on on this flimsy issue. The mistake that he made, of course, was to hypo his case with the threat to resign, which, among other things, is an empty cannon.

The first reaction to Kissinger's threat to resign was a resounding chorus of support for him. Within a few days, however, even a few of his supporters were calling his Salzburg performance a tantrum, while a small band of critics was claiming that it had been a calculated maneuver to distract attention from the charges against him. But in the end his threat to resign had the effect he desired and put his critics on the defensive. Later, the Senate Foreign Relations Committee reconsidered his testimony and announced that he was still in good standing with them. This, at last, seemed to put the matter to rest.

We stayed overnight in Salzburg in order to get used to the time change.

Diary

I felt good this morning except for the fact that my left leg is having exactly the same symptoms it had when I was in Hawaii and had what was diagnosed as a blood clot. I am having Lukash come over and take a look at it since he was the one who measured it before.

It is much larger than the right leg and it really makes me quite lame. I, of course, will not allow them to do anything which will disrupt the trip at this point.

I was suffering from phlebitis, an inflammation of a vein. After Lukash examined the leg he told me that the danger of phlebitis is that a blood clot might form and break loose into the bloodstream; if it reached the lungs, it could cause a fatal embolism. Fortunately, he seemed to think that the swelling in my leg was in fact the aftermath of the inflammation and that the greatest danger had already passed. He told me to wrap the leg in hot towels at least four times a day and to stay off it as much as possible.

Later I called Haig in and showed him my swollen leg. I told him that I wanted the few people who knew about it to keep it absolutely secret.

We landed in Cairo on June 12 in the hot afternoon sun. President Sadat and his wife were waiting at the airport, and I was immediately impressed by both of them. Sadat is a handsome man, somewhat taller than I had expected from his pictures. In the car he turned to me and said with intense feeling, "This is a great day for Egypt."

As soon as we started on the road to Cairo, I got the first taste of what was perhaps the most tumultuous welcome any American president has ever received anywhere in the world. For mile after mile along both sides of the road people were packed a hundred deep. In Cairo itself the streets and large squares were overflowing. Conservative estimates put the crowd at over a million.

But even more impressive than the sheer number was the obvious sincerity of the crowd's emotion. Sadat seemed to sense what I was thinking, because he leaned over and shouted in my ear so that I could hear him. "This is a real welcome from the heart," he said. "These people are here because they want to be here. You can bring people out, but you can't make them smile." We passed under large arches that had been built across the streets, decorated with huge pictures of Sadat and me, proclaiming us "Great Men Dedicated to Peace and Progress." The noise was overwhelming as a million people yelled "Nik-son, Nik-son, Nik-son!" at the top of their lungs.

When the motorcade finally reached the palace where we would be staying, Sadat suggested that we delay our first meeting for an hour or two. I thought he was simply being polite because of the exertion of standing up and waving for almost an hour under the blazing sun. Only later during the visit did Mrs. Sadat tell me that he took a nap every afternoon. He had suffered two mild heart attacks as recently as 1970 and as a result took extremely cautious care of himself. I later made a diary note: "The thing that I am really concerned about is what would happen if he were to pass from the scene."

In our conversations Sadat showed great subtlety and sophistication. He did not press me privately about U.S.–Israeli ties, although publicly he made a strong appeal for the return of the occupied territories, the rights of the Palestinians, and the status of Jerusalem. Describing his dealings with the Soviets, he said that he had asked them for military help before the October war, and they had not come through. With surprising candor he said, "We just gave up on them."

The crowds got bigger each day we were in Egypt. They jammed the entire route on our three-hour train ride from Cairo to Alexandria as Sadat and I stood waving from an open coach. It was hot and dusty, and the swelling in my leg grew painful from standing so long. But I realized that Sadat felt it was important for as many people as possible to see us together. It was a way of confirming the new Egyptian-American relationship.

One of the pool of reporters aboard the train asked Sadat about the principal contribution the United States could make for continuing peace in the Middle East. In his reply he referred to some of the handmade signs we had seen along the route: "It is to keep the momentum of the whole thing going on, and I must say you have read what my people wrote. They wrote, 'We Trust Nixon.' ... President Nixon never gave a word and didn't fulfill it. He has fulfilled every word he gave. So if this momentum continues, I think we can achieve peace."

I made a diary note about these phenomenal crowds: "I think the estimates that approximately six and a half to seven million people that we saw in Egypt is an honest one. It is in that kind of ball park at any rate. One wonders whether they came out simply because they think we are bringing a bag full of money to deal with their problems. Certainly something of that enters into it. I think more than that was what Sadat told me: that they really feel very strongly a feeling of affection for the Americans. Part of that, of course, is their irritation with the Russians."

Egypt is the key to the Arab world, and thanks to Sadat and the Egyptian people, the trip got off to an excellent start. Our objectives were to provide support to Egypt in pursuing its moderate course and to encourage and strengthen Sadat in his roles as leader of his country and as a constructive and essential influence for any future Middle East negotiations. At the conclusion of the visit, we issued a statement of principles of relations and cooperation between Egypt and the United States that set forth the basis for working together for peace in the Middle East and new plans for economic cooperation. We also agreed to negotiate an agreement under which we would sell non-military nuclear reactors and fuel to Egypt for the production of electrical power.

When we landed in Jidda, Saudi Arabia, the temperature was above 100 degrees. Even so, King Faisal was at the airport waiting to greet us. He looked much older than his admitted sixty-seven—according to our intelligence reports, seventy-two—years.

Faisal saw Zionist and Communist conspiracies everywhere around him. He even put forward what must be the ultimate conspiratorialist notion: that the Zionists were behind the Palestinian terrorists. Despite this obsession, however, and thanks to his intelligence and the experience of many years in power, Faisal was one of the wisest leaders in the entire region.

Saudi Arabia was not directly involved in the Middle East peace negotiations, but Faisal's stature in the Arab world and the substantial financial support he provided to Syria and Egypt gave him a vital role in maintaining the momentum toward peace. I was also able to discuss with him the serious global impact of the high oil prices caused by the recent Arab oil embargo and to encourage his moves to moderate oil prices.

I was as surprised as the reporters who clustered around us when Faisal said at the departure ceremonies, "Anybody who stands against you, Mr. President, in the United States of America or outside the United States of America, or stands against us, your friends in this part of the world, obviously has one aim in mind, namely, that of causing the splintering of the world, the wrong polarization of the world, the bringing about of mischief, which would not be conducive to tranquillity and peace in the world.

591

Therefore, we beseech Almighty God to lend His help to us and to you so that we both can go hand in hand, shoulder to shoulder in pursuance of the noble aims that we both share, namely, those of peace, justice, and prosperity in the world."

My visit to Syria required the most delicate diplomacy of the entire Mideast trip. Syria had been one of the most radically pro-Soviet, anti-Israeli, and anti-American of the Arab nations.

The problems that my visit presented to President Asad were summed up in the story he told me about his eight-year-old son. The boy had watched our airport arrival ceremonies on television, and when Asad returned home that night, he went up to his father and asked, "Wasn't that Nixon the same one you have been telling us for years is an evil man who is completely in control of the Zionists and our enemies? How could you welcome him and shake his hand?" Asad smiled at me and said, "That is the question all my people will ask, and that is why we have to move at a very measured pace as we develop our relations in the future. After all, for years my people have been taught to hate the Americans; and in recent years they have been taught particularly to hate the Nixon who represents the capitalists who have always supported the Israelis. The same Nixon who saved Israel in 1973!"

The agreement to disengage forces in the Golan Heights had been an achievement of substantial proportions, and my visit was an opportunity to encourage, support, and nurture the new Syrian-American relationship that Kissinger had begun. I was convinced that Asad would continue to play the hardest of hard lines in public, but in private he would follow the Arab proverb that he told me during one of our meetings: "When a blind man can see with one eye it is better than not being able to see at all." I was very impressed with President Asad.

Diary

As far as Asad was concerned he exceeded my expectations on the conversations I had had with Henry. He was, as Henry had said, a tough negotiator, but he has a great deal of mystique, tremendous stamina, and a lot of charm. He laughs easily, and I can see he will be a dynamic leader if he can just maintain his judgment. In our last conversation he came down very very hard against any separate peace. But on the other hand, he seemed to be quite reasonable with regard to the various regional approaches we were making. All in all he is a man of real substance, and at his age—forty-four—if he can avoid somebody shooting him or overthrowing him, he will be a leader to be reckoned with in this part of the world.

Pat noted that he had a flat head in the back which she said was probably because he hadn't been turned when he was a baby. What he reminded me of, curiously enough, was that he had a forehead like Pat Buchanan's, and my guess is he has the same kind of brain and drive and single-mindedness that Pat has. The man really has elements of genius, without any question.

In the Syrian capital of Damascus, the oldest continuously inhabited city in the world, American flags were flying for the first time in seven years. Everywhere we went large and friendly crowds turned out to welcome us, despite the fact that our movements and itineraries were given no publicity by the Syrian authorities. I viewed this as a measure of the people's strong desire for friendship with America, for an alternative to the Soviets, and for peace. I noted in my diary, "These people want to be friendly with the U.S. and it runs right down to the rank and file and it goes to the fact that they know the Russians. The Americans, of course, may be in that category soon if we are unable to produce on the peace initiatives that we have begun."

In his toast at the state dinner in my honor President Asad said, "Let us open a new page and begin a new phase in the relations between our two countries." For a President of Syria, this was a dramatic statement. At the conclusion of my visit we announced the resumption of diplomatic relations between our two countries, and I stated our willingness to resume educational and cultural exchanges and to cooperate in Syrian economic growth.

When I said goodbye to Asad at the airport, he kissed

me on both cheeks—the highest compliment that can be paid a visitor and an extraordinarily important gesture for the man who, until a few months earlier, had been the leading anti-American firebrand of the Arab world.

I later reflected on this breakthrough in our relations with Syria.

Diary
All in all, Syria is by far the most difficult country we have in terms of working out some kind of positive continuing relationship. On the other hand, they desperately want to have another string in their bow. They want us in there, probably to play us against the Russians, and that's why on the way back I said that we must explore every possible way to make some moves toward the Syrians in the economic area.

My receptions in Egypt and Syria and my conversations with Sadat and Asad confirmed the tremendous potential of the new role of the United States as a force for peace in the Arab world. If we could provide the lead, these two pragmatic and patriotic men were willing to seek a compromise settlement with Israel as a prerequisite for turning their attention to the development of their own countries. I was also encouraged to see the extent to which the Soviets had alienated their former Arab clients; it was particularly interesting to discover that this was not just the case at the leadership level. As was frequently the case, Manolo, who was traveling with me, was an excellent source of information and insights.

Diary
Manolo gave some interesting sidelights about the trip when we asked him about which country he liked the best. He said that he liked Egypt the best because the Egyptians were so friendly. He said that they all said they were glad to see the Americans come in and the Russians leave. It reminded me of my first conversation with Sadat, where he said that in six months America had gained more in Egyptian popular support than the Russians had been able to gain in twenty years.

594

Manolo said that the Egyptians told him over and over again that the Russians were grim and mean; they lived apart and did not treat the people kindly. He ran into the same thing in Syria, where one of the people working in the kitchen told him that the Americans were smiling and the Russians were always grim. I think one thing we have going for us in this part of the world, and I trust in other parts of the world, is the fact that, with all of our faults, and with the exception of some arrogant Americans, particularly in the foreign service and some business types, most Americans basically like other people. Putting it another way, they want to be liked, and so they go overboard in trying to win other people. The Russians, with their inferiority complex and their single-minded communist determination, are a very different breed. They don't let their good qualities show through except when they are dealing with what they consider to be absolute equals.

I recalled a conversation I had had with Sadat in which I had told him that I thought that the real problem between China and Russia was that, deep down, the Chinese consider themselves superior and more civilized than the Russians. Sadat had smiled and said, "You know, that's exactly the same way we feel: we Egyptians are more civilized than the Russians."

Our reception in Israel, although warm by ordinary standards, was the most restrained of the trip. This was partly because of Israeli domestic problems. Golda Meir had resigned just two months earlier and Yitzhak Rabin had taken over as Prime Minister, heading up a fragile coalition. Given the unpopularity of my Mideast policy in many quarters in Israel, Rabin was understandably unwilling to be more than correct in the treatment he accorded me but he was also bluntly anxious to know how much more aid he could depend on from us.

The primary purpose of my meetings with Rabin and his top Cabinet officials was to make it clear to them that while we would not waver in our total support for Israel's security, we would insist on their playing a sincere and

595

serious part in maintaining the momentum of the peace negotiations that we had begun with Kissinger's shuttle diplomacy and had now confirmed with my trip. In addition to a thorough discussion of the economic and military needs of Israel and a review of further steps that might be taken toward peace, we proposed in a joint statement issued at the conclusion of the visit that we negotiate an agreement on non-military nuclear reactors and fuel supply similar to the one we had concluded with President Sadat.

At the state dinner at the Knesset, the Israeli parliament building, I said that I would exercise the presidential prerogative of breaking precedent: although Golda Meir was no longer Prime Minister, I wanted to propose a special toast to her before the traditional toast to the head of state. I said that of all the world leaders I had met none had greater courage, intelligence, stamina, determination, or dedication to their country than Golda Meir. She was sitting nearby at the head table, and I could see how flustered and flattered she was. I continued, "I thought that I, having worked with her, having become her friend, and she has been my friend, that I might have the honor and the privilege to ask you to join me in a toast to the former Prime Minister. Prime Minister Golda Meir. To Golda."

Typically eloquent even when taken by surprise, she made a brief reply. "As President Nixon says, Presidents can do almost anything, and President Nixon has done many things that nobody would have thought of doing. All I can say, Mr. President, as friends and as an Israeli citizen to a great American President, thank you."

In my formal toast I talked frankly about the task confronting the new Prime Minister and the Knesset:

There are two courses that are open to them. The one is an easy one, an easy one particularly politically, I suppose, and that is the status quo. Don't move, because any movement has risks in it, and therefore resist those initiatives that may be undertaken, that might lead to a negotiation which would perhaps contribute to a permanent, just, and durable peace.

But there is another way. The other, I believe, is the right way. It is the way of statesmanship, not the way of the politician alone. It is a way that does not risk your country's security. That must never be done. But it is a way that recognizes that continuous war in this area is not a solution for Israel's survival and, above all, it is not right that every possible avenue not be explored to avoid it in the interest of the future of those children we saw by the hundreds and thousands on the streets of Jerusalem today.

Our last stop in the Middle East was in Jordan, where I was once again impressed by the charm and intelligence of King Hussein. He and I spent over two hours in a private discussion of his unique role in assisting the settlement of conflicts. He had long been a staunch and loyal friend of the United States, sometimes to his considerable peril, and he affirmed that he would continue to do his part on behalf of restraint and moderation on the long road that lay ahead.

In his toast at the state dinner he gave for us, Hussein generously summed up the meaning of my trip as he saw it: "Mr. President, we join with you in all the hopes and expectations you must have for this memorable 'Journey for Peace' that you are undertaking, and we in the Arab world are grateful that you have made it," he said. "Although you know better than anyone else perhaps that a journey for peace seems to have no ending, your coming to us at this time has been perfectly timed to preserve the momentum that American initiative had begun under your inspired and inspiring leadership."

I concluded my toast that night by saying: "I do not tell you where this journey will end. I cannot tell you when it will end. The important thing is that it has begun."

There was a large crowd waiting on the South Lawn of the White House to welcome Pat and me. Jerry Ford led the official delegation of Cabinet members. He said, "Mr. President, about ten days ago, I was here with many others to wish you Godspeed. Our prayers were with you at that time, and I think it might be appropriate now to quote from that biblical injunction: 'Blessed is the peacemaker.' "

During the next few days, even while preparing for Soviet Summit III, I briefed congressional leaders on the opportunity we had to exert leadership for peace in the Middle East, and I reflected on the Mideast trip in the practical perspective of the domestic reaction to it.

Diary

We must have gotten some lift from the trip, although it seems almost impossible to break through in the polls. Of course, this is not surprising after the terrible banging we are taking. As I pointed out to Ziegler, when he was telling me about the five or six minutes that we were getting on each network while we were away, I said, "Compare that with the eight or ten minutes that they have been hearing on Watergate for over a year!" We can't complain too much about the coverage in the Mideast. It was good. It was very hard to knock the trip. And I think it had an impact. How great and how lasting only time will tell.

The most important thing, of course, is to keep working to make sure the trip bears the fruits of peace—or at least of progress. Sadat constantly emphasized the point that it was unnatural for the Egyptians and the Americans to be enemies, and natural for us to be friends. It was this theme that we heard in Saudi Arabia and also in Syria and Jordan: natural and unnatural, normal and abnormal, etc. This to me is the most significant benefit from the presidential trip as distinguished from all the negotiations. The Arabs really want to be friends of the Americans, and now it's up to us to be their friends and also to prove that friendship with America is worthwhile.

With the congressional leaders I stepped out a little bit ahead of Henry in indicating that we would make Israel strong enough that they would not fear to negotiate, but not so strong that they felt they had no need to negotiate. I would add to that, Israel should also be strong enough so that their neighbors would not be tempted to attack them, and would have an incentive to negotiate.

One thing the Mideast trip did was to put the whole Watergate business into perspective—to make us realize that all the terrible battering we have taken is really pygmy-sized when compared to what we have done and what we can do in the future not only for peace in the world but, indirectly, to effect the well-being of people everywhere. This, I suppose, is what we must always keep front and center regardless of what happens in the future.

On June 13, while I was in Egypt, Fred Buzhardt had suffered a heart attack. Once I was assured that he was going to pull through, I tried to assess the impact his illness would have on our legal situation. This was a particularly busy and important period because we had briefs to file and oral arguments to prepare for the tapes case before the Supreme Court. We also had to prepare for the pretrial hearings in the Watergate cover-up case on defense motions for documents, and to respond to demands for documents from the district court that was hearing the Ellsberg break-in case. There were several other lesser legal battles also being waged. We were trying to assert a claim of executive privilege in a suit brought by Common Cause; and we were getting ready to file an appeal on Sirica's decision to release a section of the September 15, 1972, tape that he himself had earlier judged did not relate to Watergate—one in which I had talked about IRS information on our opponents. And as if these were not enough, the Ervin Committee was still demanding more information, Kissinger was returning to testify on the wiretaps before the Senate Foreign Relations Committee, and the House Judiciary Committee was continuing its rapacious demands for more tapes. Buzhardt's enforced absence would be a serious blow.

There was at least one relatively bright spot: there were reports of behind-the-scenes problems at the House Judiciary Committee. The leaks from both members and staff had become so frequent that Democrats as well as Republicans were expressing their disapproval. An anonymous committee member was quoted in the Washington *Post*, "I think we are a little embarrassed by what we have done."

On June 21, two days after my return from the Mideast, the House Judiciary Committee finished hearing all the evidence on all the charges against me; it ran over 7,000 pages and ultimately filled thirty-eight large printed volumes. The quantity of the evidence was overwhelming, but its quality was weak; most of it had little or no direct bearing on my own actions.

There were also other optimistic signs. Washington columnists noted that John Rhodes, for the first time in weeks, was beginning to emerge as a leader in my behalf. The House pro-impeachment Democrats were now reported to be pushing hard for an early House floor vote because they felt the committee's slow pace had let the momentum slip. The Washington *Post* ran a front-page story that the committee had begun to polarize.

On June 22 I telephoned Louisiana Democrat Joe Waggonner. A veteran of seven terms in the House, Waggonner headed an informal group that sometimes numbered as many as a hundred House Democrats, mainly Southerners, who had often given me support on key issues. He had been a great source of strength to me throughout the whole Watergate period; hardly a week went by that he did not call to reassure me of his continued support. But he was always totally realistic, and he never tried to encourage me falsely. Now he was saying that he had seventy anti-impeachment votes in his group that he thought were pretty solid. The only thing that might change them, he said, would be if for any reason I were held in contempt of the Supreme Court. Other than that he did not think there was any chance for an impeachment. He ended this conversation, as he did every one I ever remember having with him, by saying, "God bless you."

I calculated that if Waggonner had 70 Democratic votes, we would need only 150 Republicans to make a majority against impeachment. That was not an unrealistic goal. On June 22 and 23 I reflected on the tentative new sources of support showing up in Congress, and even in the House Judiciary Committee itself.

Diary
Thank God some of our Republicans on the committee led by [Charles] Wiggins [of California], are standing up. This may be the new factor that could change this situation—change it, that is, with the one caveat—that what happens in the Supreme Court is going to put us to a real test.

I still hope and feel, however, that there would be a fairly good chance this time that the Court, as it looks down to the future of this country and the future of the presidency and for that matter the future of the Court itself, will not want to set such a devastating precedent. But the Court all lives in Washington, are affected by the Washington stories, and the poison they see in the Washington *Post* must really seep in. It's very difficult for people to read it every day and not be affected by it.

In thinking today, after my call with Joe Waggonner, when he said that unless there was contempt of the Supreme Court we would win the impeachment, I realized that we really are looking at about thirty days in which the climactic decision with regard to whether we are able to stay in office or whether we will have to, in effect, refuse to comply with what might be an order of the Court which would violate the constitutional precepts which I have laid forward, will have to be made. What I have to do in these next thirty days is to live every one of them up to the hilt and not be concerned about what happens in between. We just have to be sure that we do everything we can to be worthy of whatever responsibilities we have.

The more I think about this whole impeachment process the more I remember what Ayub Khan said: "Trust is like a thin thread. Once you break it, it is almost impossible to put it together again." This is why as time has gone on, when we add up the Dean week which was just a year ago—and the tape issue—and then Agnew—and then following that up with the two-tapes business—the tax business—and all of the other assaults—the Rebozo thing—the eighteen minutes—it's just miraculous that we are still in the game at all.

We can only thank God for the strength of the family, as I have often said—of some of our close friends, and the iron will of Haig, who I think is the strongest man in the whole group—supported, of course, by Ziegler, Buchanan, and others.

I had a very good talk with Bob Haldeman. He is really a tower of strength. I told him that I knew he must be worried about what was going to happen in September and what he must be going through, and that I felt for him very, very deeply, just as I felt for

601

John Ehrlichman and John Mitchell. He said, well, he just lived day by day and didn't think about the outcome in the end.

When I think, incidentally, of my feeling of depression last night I suppose that something might happen in the future with regard to the Court that would end in eventual impeachment. I thought of all of the others who must be going through much worse—sleepless nights and so forth—people who don't have strong physical or emotional faculties as I have. It's really remarkable that we have so many among our own group who have stood up under a terrible battering, and have taken the worst shots that they could get and have still survived.

I talked to Henry. He seemed to think the mood, as he puts it, had changed. Of course, he has said this before. And, Henry, of course, always puts in the caveat, "unless something big develops."

I also talked to Al Haig. He says he really feels better than he has for a year.

As I analyze things on this rather rainy Sunday, June 23, I must say that we are probably, as Al says, stronger than we were a couple of months ago, and we shall now see what happens as we go to the Soviet Union, come back, and as the tension then focuses as it will almost totally on the whole impeachment process. At least the Mideast trip tended to break the momentum and to focus attention on other subjects. Al feels that the press wants to do that—that they are rather tired of the other subject. I trust he's right, although I think that we will find that many of our opponents will not play that game because they desperately want to get us out.

My family and I tried to make the time we spent together as happy and carefree as possible. I worried about the girls constantly. They were young, and they needed freedom to live their own lives; instead they were having to fight my battles day in and day out. Their constant thoughtfulness was a source of great comfort to me. Julie would often leave her copy of the New English edition of the New Testament on my bedstand, opened to some consoling passage. And Tricia would come to the Lincoln Sitting Room at some of my lowest times and just sit with me while I read or worked, in a quiet tribute of love and support.

I was in the Mideast on Father's Day, but there was a telegram for me from the girls: "Dear Daddy, Happy Father's Day. We are so proud of you and love you very much. Julie and Tricia." My sons-in-law joined to send me a telegram: "Mr. President, A triumphant Father's Day. Our admiration and love. Ed and David."

Because of the demands of Ed's job, he and Tricia stayed in New York and did not make many official appearances. It became a favorite sport of insatiable gossip columnists to fabricate rumors of a "rift" between me and Ed, or even between Tricia and Ed. It finally reached the point that Tricia was forced to issue a statement denying that her marriage was about to break up. In fact, she and Ed seemed to grow stronger and draw closer the more they were forced to endure. In March, without informing me beforehand, they jointly wrote a courageous and eloquent magazine article in my defense.

Julie and David were directly in the blast of the hurricane for the entire final year of my presidency. Living in Washington ensured that they could never escape from the ceaseless media scrutiny or from the stifling atmosphere of the threatened impeachment. Both Julie and David were sturdy young people, but after more than 160 public appearances, many of them searing Watergate sessions, they would have had to be unintelligent and insensitive not to feel the effect. In February 1974 David wrote to me about it:

Julie has undoubtedly mentioned my low spirits this past week. In a nutshell, nothing in my life prepared me for the thunder clap of criminal charges pressed against people I know and respect and essentially on grounds growing out of dedication to your case. . . .

I never accepted that life could be so unfair and it's unquestionably just the beginning. I spent the better part of this week wrestling with my feelings on the situation. I hope I haven't been misunderstood. Last night I discovered an appropriate thought, "There is no despair so absolute as that which comes with the first moment of our first great sorrow when we have not yet known what it is to have suffered and be healed, to have despaired and recovered hope." The quote was from George Eliot, of course. I wondered when it was you experienced your "despair so absolute"—14 years ago, 1 year ago—ours may have been last week? But the point of the passage and of your experience is hope. Under these circumstances hope means determination. We are happy with any part of redeeming the work you have done for America and we aren't alone either, come what may.

It hurt me to see Julie daily grow quieter and more inward. But the only time I recall that she ever let me know of her despair was when we went to Camp David after the release of the Blue Book transcripts. "Everything is so dreary," she said quietly. By the next day she had bounced back, and within a week she and David decided to hold a press conference in response to the storm of criticism of the transcripts and the calls for my resignation that were now coming from friends and enemies alike.

At one point during their press conference a reporter for CBS began talking about the "sins of the fathers" being visited on their children. His implication was that their spontaneous decision to hold the press conference was part of a calculated move to shield me from reporters. Julie's eyes flashed, but the steel in her character helped her restrain emotion as she said:

> I am going to try to control myself in answering the question, because it really does wound me. . . . I am here because Helen Smith had fifty-five calls from the media. . . . Now if the media has a hang-up, an obsession about resignation and feels they must be reassured by members of the family, I feel as a daughter it is my obligation to come out here.
>
> I have seen what my father has gone through, and I am so proud of him that I would never be afraid to come out here and talk to any members of the press about resignation or anything else, even though it goes against my grain because I know he does not want me out here because he does not want anyone to construe that I am trying to answer questions for him. I am not trying to answer questions for him. I am just trying to pray for enough courage to meet his courage.

Pat was, as always, the strongest of all. She worked to keep our spirits high when we were together as a family, while she showed the world that beneath the woman who was loved universally for her warmth, her easy elegance, and her genius for personal understanding, there was a strength of character unmatched, I believe, in the history of American politics.

She was, as Jerry Ford proclaimed her, "First Lady of the World," and on March 11 she made what was to be the last of her trips as my representative abroad. This time she visited Brazil and Venezuela, where she captivated everyone who saw her. Yet on the plane back reporters immediately started pressing her about Watergate, wanting to know just how much pain she had suffered in the last year, just how bad it had been for her. "I really don't wish to speak of it. It's just a personal thing," she said. "Why bring that into the trip?" She repeated what she had said before: that she loved me and knew that I was an honorable, dedicated person.

She worked hard to be an example of dignity under attack. And still they would not let up.

SUMMIT III

In January 1974, the Soviets had agreed to announce the date of Summit III, scheduled to be held in Moscow in the summer. I evaluated this decision either as an act of faith on their part that I was going to prevail over impeachment, or as an indication of their interest in seeing détente continue regardless of who was President.

What was probably the most crucial and hardest fought battle of Summit III took place not in Moscow but in Washington, where the activities of the anti-détente forces reached almost fever pitch just as I was getting ready to leave for the Soviet Union. The liberals were now in full cry with what had become the currently fashionable outrage over Soviet repression of political dissidents and their restriction of Jewish emigration. The conservatives of both parties were still united in their determination either to limit trade with the Soviets or to ban it altogether. The military establishment and its many friends in Congress and the country were up in arms over the prospect that Summit III might actually succeed in producing a breakthrough on limiting offensive nuclear weapons or a limited nuclear test ban.

This convergence of anti-détente forces would have existed regardless of any domestic political problems. But Watergate had badly damaged my ability to defuse, or at least to circumvent, them as effectively as I otherwise might have been able to do.

When Kissinger went to Moscow on March 24 for four days of talks aimed at setting the agenda for Summit III, he reported that Brezhnev seemed to be confronting some of the same problems as we were of military opposition to a permanent agreement to limit offensive nuclear weapons. Thus we knew from the outset that it would be very difficult to produce a major SALT breakthrough at Summit III.

The U.S. military opposition to a new SALT agreement came to a head at the meeting of the National Security Council on the afternoon of June 20 when Secretary of Defense Schlesinger presented the Pentagon's proposal. It amounted to an unyielding hard line against any SALT agreement that did not ensure an overwhelming American advantage. It was a proposal that the Soviets were sure to reject out of hand.

After the arguments on both sides had been stated, I intervened: "I think we should try to use this time to frame a more practical approach to this problem. We have to accept the fact that Secretary Schlesinger's proposal simply has no chance whatever of being accepted by the Soviets, so we should try to work out something consistent with our interests that will."

There was a moment of silence, and then Schlesinger, who was sitting next to me, said, "But, Mr. President, everyone knows how impressed Khrushchev was with your forensic ability in the kitchen debate. I'm sure that if you applied your skills to it you could get them to accept this proposal."

In my diary that night I recorded: "The NSC meeting was a real shocker insofar as the performance of the Chiefs, and particularly of Schlesinger, was concerned. His state-

606

ment that he knew that Khrushchev had been very impressed by my 'forensic ability' and that, with my forensic ability, I could sell the idea that he presented, was really an insult to everybody's intelligence and particularly to mine."

Jerry Ford broke the silence that followed Schlesinger's remark and moved the discussion into the broader area of the defense budget. After this had gone on for a few minutes, I made a statement about the way I viewed the development of détente over the two years remaining to me in the White House.

Diary

Ford is on the kick that we ought to have a huge increase in the defense budget, and that that will give us a bargaining position with the Soviets. He's right in one way, of course, and wrong in another, because we aren't going to be able to bluff them in this particular case.

My great concern, as I said at the meeting, is that whoever might succeed me in this office might not fight these bloody battles that I have had to fight over these past five and a half years—for ABM, for big defense budgets, for the Trident submarine, etc. We could have someone who, despite all the white-hot talk that the United States has to be number one and so forth, would cave in to the peacenik views that the establishment press would undoubtedly be expressing once they got one of their own in office.

That is why it is very important, if we possibly can, to get some constraints on the Soviets at this time. Because later on, if we get into a runaway race, it may be that they will be uninhibited and we will be inhibited. As I tried to point out at the NSC meeting, when the President of the United States makes a decision, it's very different from a decision made by the General Secretary of the Soviet Union. We can be very sure that his decision is one that will and can be carried out. He doesn't have to be too concerned about his public opinion, if at all. When the President of the United States makes a decision, however, he can't ever be absolutely sure that his decision will be carried out. It's certainty versus the uncertainty that weakens, not our actual bargaining position so much, but makes it essential that we take this factor into account in negotiating the terms of any deal that we make with the Soviet. Because if we have an agreement which constrains us both, it means that we will be constraining them in something that they will inevitably do. When we constrain ourselves, it may be that we are constraining ourselves in an area where we wouldn't be doing anything anyway. This, of course, was exactly the situation with regard to the '72 agreement.

It is just as well, however, that we don't fight this battle right now, and if we can just find a way to get the proper language so that we can negotiate it in October and November—and also get the Soviets to agree to some proper numbers, then I think we will have rendered a great service to our national security as well as to some sort of balance in forces generally.

Many of the Defense people don't want any agreement because they want to go ahead willy-nilly with all the defense programs they possibly can and they do not want constraints. The situation has been compounded by the fact that Henry hasn't been able to work on it. He has been so tied down with the Mideast that he hasn't been able to pull this other one together. Maybe it's just as well, however, because this as I said is not the time to fight this battle.

The battle with the military was not the only major problem affecting Summit III. For the first time since the Watergate break-in, Brezhnev expressed concern about my ability to make decisions domestically. He had gone very far out on a limb for détente, and he was understandably concerned that my sudden or unexpected departure from office would leave him in an embarrassing and exposed position within his own hierarchy.

In April 1974 we received a report from Walter Stoessel, now ambassador to Moscow, describing a meeting at which Brezhnev had seemed particularly concerned that our domestic problems could hinder the course of events. "Brezhnev said he respected the President for fighting back, calling this one characteristic of a statesman, and expressed amazement that the United States had reached a point where the President could be bothered about his taxes. He viewed the President's opponents as 'senseless,'" Stoessel reported.

When Gromyko came to see me on April 11, he opened by reassuring me that despite the anti-Soviet stories and articles that appeared in the American press, the Soviets were firmly in support of détente. Then, in an unusually personal moment, Gromyko said that he simply wanted to say to me that he admired my standing up, "despite certain known difficulties," as he put it. "We admire you for it on the human plane," he said.

The rest of our meeting was spent in a wrangle over SALT numbers, a preview of what was to come in Moscow. Thus far, the Soviets were not yielding. Neither were we. When I walked Gromyko to the door of the West Lobby, he said, "We trust you understand that we want you to come and have the meeting and that nothing should interfere with it."

I indicated that I understood. "We will be cursed by future generations if we fail," I said. "We must succeed."

We left Washington on June 25. Our first stop was Brussels, where I attended ceremonies marking the twenty-fifth anniversary of NATO. I thought that it would be especially useful to dramatize the continuing viability of the Atlantic alliance before sitting down with Brezhnev. In my formal statement to the NATO Council, I said that the period of détente was one of great opportunity but also of great danger. We had to face the fact that European politics had changed completely. We had to accept the fact that fear of communism was no longer a practical motivation for NATO; if NATO were to survive, it would need other binding motives to keep it together.

It was just before I left for Brussels that the story of my phlebitis attack during the Mideast trip broke in the American press. The reporters immediately watched my every movement for signs of a limp or pain. In fact, my leg was still swollen and painful, but I was determined not to betray how much.

Diary

It's amazing that my health is as good as it is, and, as I told Ziegler, the main thing about this leg situation is not to let them build it up in a way that they think the President is crippled mentally as well as physically. I feel that at the present time we have it relatively under control but we must make sure that people never get the idea that the President is like Eisenhower in his last year or so, or like Roosevelt, or, for that matter, even like Johnson when everybody felt that Johnson was probably ready to crack up, and was drinking too much and so forth. I think we can avoid this by proper handling.

With our airport reception in Moscow on June 27, Summit III got off to a very auspicious start. Brezhnev himself was there, bounding across the tarmac, to greet me. A fairly large crowd had been allowed to stand behind barriers and wave paper flags. Unlike 1972, there were also crowds along the streets as we drove to the Kremlin.

Shortly after we arrived, Brezhnev invited me to his office for a private talk. He told me about his recent meeting with Teddy Kennedy and Averell Harriman and said that they both supported détente. I told him it was fine for him to meet with leaders of both parties between now and 1976 because we wanted them all to be in support of détente. "Let's get them all a little pregnant," I said.

He said that he had followed the political situation in the United States, and he was convinced that I would be in until 1976.

After the state dinner that night I suggested to Kissinger and Haig that we have a brief meeting in my car, where we could talk without being bugged. Kissinger had seemed depressed all day. As I had guessed, the domestic harassment over the wiretaps still bothered him, as well as his realization after his talks with Gromyko during the afternoon that our negotiating position had been seriously undercut by the anti-détente agitation within the administration.

On the first day of formal sessions we took up the question of a nuclear test ban. The Soviets, as in the past, would not agree to the necessary on-the-ground verification procedures. I was convinced that without such ironclad verification procedures to make sure that they were abiding by the terms, a total test ban was too dangerous to consider. We also had to take into account that such a ban was no longer as meaningful as it would have been when we were the only two nuclear powers, and in those days the Soviets had refused even to consider it. Now neither France nor the P.R.C.—about which the Soviets were especially sensitive—would halt nuclear testing regardless of what we did; nor would Israel or India stop nuclear research.

During Kissinger's preliminary visit to Moscow in March the Soviets had suggested a "threshold" test ban. Under such an arrangement, nuclear weapons could be tested as long as they did not cross a certain threshold of size and force. Since these infractions could be determined by seismic equipment in each country, on-the-ground verification would not be necessary. But at our afternoon session on the first full day of Summit III Brezhnev suddenly suggested that, instead of wrangling about the threshold levels for a limited test ban, we solve the question by agreeing on a comprehensive test ban.

I recorded in my diary, "During this session, Brezhnev was very tough, just like at the dacha in 1972 on Vietnam. He rewrote the script here, and none of us were prepared because it had been their idea in March, which they had explored with Kissinger, to have a threshold test ban."

Since there was no way to forestall this digression if Brezhnev was determined to have it, I decided that the only way to counter was with a vigorously frank and pragmatic approach. If Kosygin and the others expected me to hedge uncomfortably, they would be disappointed by the tone and substance of my reply. "We discussed this issue in very great depth before I came," I replied. "It is true that some in our Senate favor a comprehensive test ban. At the other end of the spectrum, however, there are equal numbers who favor no ban at all, having in mind the problem of verification. We have tried to restrain both sides by setting a low threshold. This is the only way we will get the support of the majority of our Congress. We cannot go to a total test ban," I said.

After a bit of verbal jousting I came back to the subject: "Speaking quite candidly, we have an ironic situation in the United States, as 1976 approaches, with respect to détente.

Those who applaud our efforts toward détente over the past two years now, for reasons that are more partisan than philosophical, would like to see our efforts fail. So, I would not make any enemies if I were intractable here today.

"I do not raise these points to indicate that my position is based simply on these political considerations. I will move in the direction of détente because it is indispensable for the peace of the world, and that is why we want every possible agreement we can make and implement.

"I am in a unique position of being able to bring the American public along in support of détente. I can handle our so-called hawks—but only one step at a time, and I do not want this process to be interrupted. I want it to continue."

I pointed toward the massive gold doors at the entrance to the room. "As we look to those golden doors," I said, "we could say that we all want to reach them. But we will not make it if we try to do it in one step. We will always find, Mr. General Secretary, various factions in the U.S. and in other countries who, for differing reasons, want to see détente fail. And we, on our part, do not want to take a step that we have not prepared the support for. If we did that, we would simply be looking for repudiation."

This bit of plain speaking broke the rhetorical spiral they were building. Brezhnev said he would have to consult with his colleagues and discuss it again later. Then we turned to deciding how early we would have to leave Moscow in order to arrive in the Crimea before nightfall so that I would be able to see the countryside.

I made a diary note of this long and difficult session: "My leg began to swell again after this plenary session. I think I crossed my leg a great deal during it and that seems to start the swelling. It was a pretty tiring exercise, just to hear them go through their usual hard-line statements."

Pat and I flew with Brezhnev from Moscow to the Crimea, where we would continue our discussions at his villa on the outskirts of Yalta on the Black Sea. Since the name Yalta still carried unfavorable connotations, we called this the Oreanda Summit, after the area in which the dacha is situated.

On the way to the Crimea, Brezhnev called his wife from a phone on the plane, and as I noted in my diary, "He is like a child with a new toy when it comes to that sort of thing." I talked to Mrs. Brezhnev and said, "*Ochen priatno,*" a Russian phrase of greeting I had learned, which seemed to please her.

Diary

I told Brezhnev on the plane that the ceremonies at the tomb of the Unknown Soldier in D.C. and in Moscow, where I had laid wreaths, always made me feel the profound importance of the work that we are doing. I said, "That's what our negotiations are all about."

Brezhnev talked about how terrible it was to see thousands of dead people in the war. In winter, he said, it was particularly bad to see them frozen in grotesque shapes. I said, "Like a tragic ballet." Gromyko added, "In the summer when it's hot and the bodies rot it's just as bad."

They have been through some pretty horrible experiences.

The mood lightened during the sixty-four-mile drive from the airport to Oreanda. Brezhnev mentioned my Marine aide, Lieutenant Colonel Jack Brennan. "I like him very much," he said, "he is young and strong and handsome." "The girls all think so, too," I replied, and Brezhnev chuckled for a moment. Then he turned completely serious and looked right at me and said, "Although you and I are older, in history we may do more for our people for peace than any of these younger people."

For most of the hour-and-a-half drive we looked out the windows at the rolling green mountains covered with blue and gold wild flowers. Occasionally we would catch glimpses of the sea in the distance.

Brezhnev clearly loved being in the Crimea, and he enjoyed taking me for walks through the lush greenery surrounding his hillside villa and along the low sea wall. On the first day after we arrived we walked to a small building built partly into the rock, with large picture windows looking out to the sea. He called it a cabana. We went in, took off our coats, and talked privately for over an hour before the others joined us for a plenary session.

Diary

We had a very frank and forthcoming discussion on the subjects he had apparently wanted to talk to me alone about. He looked out to the sea as we sat there and pointed to the hydrofoil. He did some doodling—what it looked like was an arrow with a heart—an arrow through the heart. He first brought up his new idea of a U.S.–Soviet treaty, which others could join, where each country would come to the defense of the other if either country or one of its allies were attacked. This, of course, smacks of condominium in the most blatant sense.

One thing that was particularly interesting about our conversation at the cabana was Brezhnev's complete switch on China. In 1973 he had expressed great concern about it, but now he affected almost complete lack of interest. "Mao is a god," he said, "a very old god. And when he dies there will be a new god." Gromyko, however, took the opposite approach when we talked privately at one of the dinners, warning that the Chinese were a great threat to peace because they had a huge population and would sacrifice anything, including their own cities and their own people, to accomplish their goals.

Diary

Going back to the private session with Brezhnev, I pointed out that if détente unravels in America, the hawks will take over, not the doves, and I urged him to make some sort of a gesture on Jewish emigration if only to pull the rug out from under Jackson and some of the media critics. He proceeded to pull out from his folder the statistics and said he would give them to Dobrynin and Dobrynin would pass them on to Kissinger.

Our conversation ranged freely from the proposed conference on European security to the reduction of nuclear weapons.

614

He pointed out, incidentally, that his predictions with regard to the Mideast proved to be true. He said that under no circumstances, however, did he expect that there would be an Arab attack when he warned me about the explosive situation. That they, as a matter of fact, had done everything that they could to stop it. He was expressive with his gestures at this point—grabbed me by the arm and said, trying to hold them back, but, he said, "We were unable to do so."

When the others joined us at the cabana, the conversation returned to the impasse we had reached over multiple-warhead nuclear missiles, or MIRVs.

"Well, let us examine this question," I said, "because if nothing can be agreed upon, we should know it now." I had concluded that he decided to use this ostensibly casual conversation as the final go-round on SALT at Summit III.

Kissinger stated bluntly that the numbers proposed by the Soviets were impossible for us to accept. If we did, we would have to stop MIRV construction within a year, while the Soviets would be able to continue for four more years.

"This will be represented in the U.S. as our accepting a freeze while permitting the Soviet Union to catch up," Kissinger said. Lest the discussion lose sight of the reality of the situation, he introduced a gentle and subtle threat. "This agreement should be seen not only in terms of the numbers that are established but in terms of what each side could do *without* an agreement," he said. "Without an agreement, for example, we could put MIRVs on 500 more Minuteman missiles."

"In this period?" Gromyko asked, somewhat taken aback.

"Yes, in two years," Kissinger replied firmly. He then introduced our counterproposal on MIRVs. It did not go as far as the Pentagon had urged, but it still provided for a substantially greater number for the U.S. than for the U.S.S.R. "We are restraining our possibilities much more than we are asking for your restraint," Kissinger stated.

The wrangling went on for almost an hour. Suddenly Brezhnev looked across the table at me. In a heavy voice he said, "Mr. President, let me say that if what Dr. Kissinger has outlined is the last word on this subject, there is no basis for an agreement."

He immediately returned to resume the argument with Kissinger, but from that moment I knew that there was no hope for a SALT agreement at Summit III.

Kissinger kept up the fight brilliantly and valiantly. At one point I passed him a note: "Use that 'forensic ability' Schlesinger told us would be sufficient to convince them." But Kissinger could not afford to smile even for a moment. Eventually I sent him another note: "Should be a recess—we appear to be in for endless emphasis on the obvious," and he began steering the discussion to a close. At the first opportunity I broke in and suggested that we keep to the schedule and go on the boat ride that Brezhnev had planned for us.

"I agree. It is time to go out on the water," he said, and immediately led us down to the dock, where we boarded Brezhnev's Soviet Navy yacht for a sail on the Black Sea.

Diary

The boat trip was really done in high style. It was a little rocky and on one occasion some of the plates fell off, but after we all sat down Brezhnev was in good form and the toasts went rather well.

The spirit of Oreanda I described as peace where we reach agreements equally fair to both sides. I also proposed a toast to the diplomats who do the work so that the leaders can rest.

The Brezhnev-Nixon doctrine I described as one that was fair to both nations and one which would leave a legacy of peace for generations to come.

The most interesting session was after lunch, when he joined me in sitting at the back of the boat and we just talked together. He pointed out Yalta and Bear Mountain and all the other points of interest. He became very emotional; he said that he wanted this summit to be one that would be remembered as were the other great events that had taken place, obviously referring, but without saying so, to Yalta.

He put his arm around me and said, "We must do something of vast historical importance. We want every Russian and every American to be friends that talk to each other as you and I are talking to each other here on this boat."

I had many thoughts as the boat went by Yalta and the harbor—in Crimea the war—one of the most useless wars in history and one where both sides lost terribly. About the only thing good that came out of it was the Red Cross.

I made the point, just to try it out on him, that the danger in advanced nations and, of course, the implication included the Soviet Union among them, is the weakening of character. If he thought it through he could have thought of Mao's Red Guards and the Cultural Revolution. Brezhnev agreed and said sociologists and psychiatrists are now studying this question. The point, of course, was that as people got more material goods they became less "hungry," lost their drive, and become almost totally obsessed with self, selfishness, and every kind of abstract idea.

As we later walked back to the dacha after getting off the boat, Gromyko was on my right and I was glad to have a talk with him. He said that his analysis was that I was doing considerably better politically in the United States. He said, "It's really about nothing."

I said that the Crimea had been the cradle of war in the nineteenth century and that we could make it the birthplace of peace in the twentieth century.

On the boat I had said to Brezhnev that our goal must be the reduction of nukes and Brezhnev responded, "We must destroy the evil that we have created." He again came back to the theme that I was always welcome in the Soviet Union, even after '76.

The long boat ride, after the morning walk and the afternoon session, was very tiring. That night I had dinner with Pat alone on the balcony outside our room.

Diary

As we looked out at the sea, there was a three-quarter moon. Pat said that since she was a very little girl, when she looked a the moon, she didn't see a man in the moon or an old lady in the moon—always the

American flag. This, of course, was years before anybody ever thought of a man actually being on the moon or an American flag being there.

She pointed it out to me and, sure enough, I could see an American flag in the moon. Of course, you can see in the moon whatever you want to see.

The next morning Brezhnev and I rode together to the airport. He took advantage of the long ride to importune me again on the Middle East. He said that while Sadat might believe in putting Egypt first, Nasser had appealed to a stronger sentiment of pan-Arabism. I did not repeat for him my analysis of what I considered to be Sadat's brilliant positioning in the flexible middle ground between those extremes.

Diary

I simply said, "Don't let the Mideast become the Balkans for the U.S. and the Soviet Union. Don't let anyplace else, Southeast Asia, the Mideast, or the Caribbean, become a point of difference between us that draws us into conflict, when there are many more important issues that could draw us together." I had used this argument with him in pointing out how Roosevelt, Churchill, and Stalin had gotten along well, particularly emphasizing the Roosevelt-Stalin relationship in fighting the war, because they did not allow differences on what the peace was going to be like to deter them from their main goal of defeating the Nazis.

Of course, historically, my own view is that this was a mistake—that Churchill was right in insisting that there be more discussion at that point and that we should have made some kind of a deal that would have avoided the division of Europe on the basis that it finally came out.

The subject of religion came up, and Brezhnev said, "What the hell difference does it make what God Americans pray to—we recognize all religions. All we care about is whether they are for peace." He again described his policy on Jewish emigration. He said, "As far as I am concerned, I say let all the Jews go and let God go with them."

He spoke of the destruction of civilization from nuclear war and repeated what Khrushchev had said fifteen years earlier: that we must remember that in such a war, the white race would be destroyed and only the yellows and blacks would remain to rule the world.

During this ride I suggested we have a "mini-summit" before the end of the year. Brezhnev enthusiastically agreed. We felt it should not be held in Washington or Moscow but in some place in between; I used the term *halfway house,* and he mentioned Switzerland. I told him it was essential to reach agreement on offensive weapons before the end of the year. Otherwise, I warned, since no agreement had been reached at this summit, Congress would go forward on a greatly increased defense budget. I suggested that Kissinger return to Moscow in September to arrange the agenda, and then Brezhnev and I could meet again in October, November, or December. I said that we must agree in principle on a reduction of military arms, and he nodded his head vigorously.

When we arrived at the airport, Brezhnev went back to Moscow and Pat and I flew to Minsk. I noted in my diary: "On the color side, whereas wild flowers predominated in the Crimea, when we were at Minsk there were purple and yellow flowers—so we had the Whittier colors, purple and gold. Great fields of purple flowers."

The crowds that greeted us everywhere during Summit III seemed genuinely and spontaneously warm. Occasionally someone would shout out "Peace is very important." I noted that in nearly every casual conversation, whether with the people in the street or with the leaders in the Kremlin, the subject invariably turned to one of three topics: the desire for friendship and peace with the United States based on equality; the devastation Russia had suffered in World War II; or pride in Russia's cultural heritage, including the Czarist palaces and buildings. In Minsk the people seemed to reach out to us. Some had tears in their eyes. I felt that such things could not go unnoticed by their leaders. "In the end," I noted in my diary with cautious hope, "the Russian leadership must reflect their people's desires."

On our boat ride, Brezhnev and I had agreed that while Pat and I were in Minsk, Kissinger and Gromyko should make one more attempt at reaching an agreement on limiting offensive nuclear weapons. As soon as I was back in my room in the Kremlin, Kissinger came up to report that he had not been able to make any progress whatever. Gromyko had spent the time nit-picking and was apparently unable or unwilling to negotiate seriously.

In order to be able to talk freely, Kissinger and I went outside and walked up and down in the open courtyard. He was concerned because we would be going home empty-handed on SALT. But the Pentagon's last-minute about-face had made it impossible for us to engage in any flexible negotiating. If we had been able to return with even a controversial SALT agreement, Kissinger was convinced that we would have been able to educate public opinion to accept it. "And," he added, "it's a lot better subject to be debating about than Watergate." Despite this disappointment over SALT, he felt that Summit III had been a success even without a SALT agreement, and he said he did not think that I would be impeached now.

"Well, Henry," I said, as we started back upstairs, "we have to do what is right, regardless of the press analysis or the political consequences. You've done a superb job under enormous pressures against overwhelming odds. You can be proud. Now we shall just have to see where events take us. We have done our best."

It was clear by this time that Summit III was not going to produce any big news as far as new agreements were concerned. Some in the press were already trying out a critical line that attributed this failure to my Watergate troubles, implying that the Soviets were holding out either because they thought I might make greater concessions because I needed a foreign triumph to alleviate my domestic problems or because they thought that I was not going to survive and they might get better terms from my successor.

In normal times Summit III would have been hailed as a successful meeting. It produced the threshold test ban, further restrictions on ABMs, agreements to seek controls on environmental warfare and for cooperation in energy, the opening of additional consulates in both countries, and, most important, the oral agreement I made with Brezhnev for a mini-summit before the end of 1974 for the purpose of reaching agreement on limitations of offensive nuclear weapons.

In my judgment my Watergate problems and the impeachment hearings did not play a major part at Summit III. Our intelligence beforehand—and my distinct impression while in the Soviet Union—was that Brezhnev had decided to go all out for détente and place all his chips on my survival and my ultimate ability to deliver on what I promised. It was the American domestic political fluctuations, most of which had preceded Watergate, that cast the greatest doubt on my reliability: the failure to produce MFN status and the agitation over Soviet Jews and emigration had made it difficult for Brezhnev to defend détente to his own conservatives. Similarly, the military establishments of both countries were bridling against the sudden reality of major and meaningful arms limitation and the real prospect of arms reduction if and as détente progressed. These problems would have existed regardless of Watergate.

Diary

There are some, of course, who will want to put blame on Watergate for our failing to get an agreement on offensive nukes but, on the other hand, I think that it came out about right. We went as far as we could go at this point without raising an issue which could have lost us some of our good conservative supporters, and we did just about what the traffic would bear. As it turned out, it's probably just as well that we were unable to reach any agreement with the Russians on the nuclear front, because to have to take this thing on now would mean that we would have to be opposed to some of our best friends prior to the impeachment vote.

The fact was that neither side was prepared to go any further at Summit III. I think that both Brezhnev and I grasped this situation at the outset, and that is what accounted for his highly personal and warm demeanor. We both understood that if the process of détente could be maintained through a holding-pattern summit, we might be able to make a breakthrough at the next meeting.

Overall, I summarized Summit III as a mixed bag; its success or failure would have to be determined in light of the way events developed before the next meeting at the halfway house.

Diary
There is nit-picking to the effect that it was not as successful as the other two. The main thing is that the process went forward, and this is in itself an achievement. Peace is never going to be achieved once and for all—it must be constantly worked on. That's why these continuing summits between major powers must go forward, even though we don't have great announcements to make after each one.

I am inclined to think that in arranging the next summit, it's the informal meetings which provide the greatest opportunity for progress. I think the formal ones—the plenary sessions—produce the least, because everybody's talking for the record and making a record.

Brezhnev has been much more forthcoming when we meet informally in the car or elsewhere than when we are sitting down in a formal group with others present. The larger the group, the less free the conversation is. This is something that is true in all forms of society, but it is particularly true in the Soviet Union and in the Communist states.

On July 2, the last night of Summit III, we gave a reciprocal dinner at Spaso House, the American ambassador's residence. Brezhnev was the most relaxed I had ever seen him. Even Mrs. Brezhnev, who like most Soviet wives seemed uncomfortable in the limelight of Western visits, opened up and talked freely about her family.

Diary
At dinner Brezhnev spoke very warmly, grabbing me by the arm, first, about the meeting that we would have in between—the so-called halfway summit at halfway house—and second, that after 1976 he wants

to see me. He said he thought he would be in power after that time and, even though because of our Constitution I would not be in, that I would always be welcome in the U.S.S.R.

Brezhnev's granddaughter was very pretty, and he has a very handsome son-in-law as well. Mrs. Brezhnev commented on Tricia, who had visited Russia, saying when she stepped off the plane she looked like a white winter snowflower. At one point, incidentally, he told me about his great-grandchild—a girl—one and a half. Mrs. Brezhnev said that the child had started walking at ten months and I said that taking the first step was always the hardest. He said, yes, that's true. He said in the case of his great-granddaughter now after that first step the only way they could keep from falling down was to almost run. Brezhnev compared this to U.S. and Soviet relations.

He clowned it up a bit by hitting a couple of keys on the piano, which allowed me to say something about playing a duet the next time he came to the United States. It's very difficult, however, to get the Russian elite to respond to any comments that are humorous, particularly when they are in a large group. Individually they will be warm and friendly, but collectively they immediately freeze—they have to watch to see what the others do before they react.

The last morning in Moscow Brezhnev and I held a final meeting alone in his office. I repeated my strong belief that we should try for a SALT accord by the end of the year so that the United States did not go ahead at an increased pace in the development of arms. I also urged what I called "increased communication" between us for taking care of the kind of problems that had arisen in the Middle East.

At the plenary session before we went to St. Vladimir Hall for the final signing ceremony, I said that we must not be discouraged by the fact that we did not settle every issue every time. It was important simply to keep talking.

Diary
The rest of the plenary meeting was really pro forma. They obviously want to put as good a face as

623

possible on the summit as Brezhnev had in his dinner toast the night before when he interestingly enough took some credit for the Soviet Union and détente for the end of the war in Vietnam and holding off in the Mideast. Obviously, in both of these cases this was an overstatement. I think it would be better stated that in both areas the Soviet Union did not play a positive role, but, on the other hand, while they could not take credit for bringing about either of the peace settlements, they could have intervened more strongly than they did and made it impossible for us to accomplish our goal of having any peace settlement at all.

The Soviets ended Summit III with a flourish of ceremony and spectacle. We signed the protocols on the new limitation of ABMs to one site only, the treaty on the limitation of underground nuclear tests, and a joint statement on negotiations to control environmental warfare.

After the signing ceremony we went to St. George Hall, where a buffet that exceeded even the sumptuousness of the one at the end of Summit I had been laid out on two tables running the length of the vast room. While we were talking and toasting each other, I noticed that the small orchestra on the balcony was playing the music that had been played at Tricia's wedding.

To my surprise Brezhnev, Gromyko, Podgorny, and Kosygin all climbed into the car with me for the ride to the airport. Brezhnev sat on the jump seat in front of me. He was extremely quiet on the way out, letting Kosygin and Podgorny do most of the talking. At the airport we performed the traditional farewell ceremonies. Then Brezhnev and I turned and headed toward *Air Force One.*

Diary

As I was walking to the plane, I said that my only regret was that he was not coming with us back to the United States. And he said that, as a matter of fact, he had been thinking the same thing as we drove out to the airport. I really think he had a feeling of loss, and felt sad that the trip was over. He had looked forward to it—had built it up—had hoped that it would achieve a great deal—and now that it was over he was getting somewhat of a letdown.

I think he realizes that it wasn't a "home run," and yet it did make some progress and we talked on several occasions, including the last time at the dinner, of a meeting, perhaps in November, at a neutral place.

I wondered if it would be the last time that I would see Brezhnev. At times he looked very good but at other times he looked very tired. He started very late in the morning—10:30 or eleven o'clock—for every meeting.

My other feeling was one of disappointment on the fact that we couldn't get some sort of agreement on SALT and that the chance of getting it in the future looked pretty hard.

When I got on the plane, I went back through the cabin and said, "Well, we're home again." I recalled on our '53 trip that every time we got on the plane after some very dreary stops we would eat the rather plain food with great relish because it was safe and clean and we would always say, "Well, we're home again." I am sure everybody felt that way when they got on the plane this time.

IMPEACHMENT SUMMER

All the while we were in the Soviet Union, the impeachment effort at home had continued much as before. A few days after my return the House Judiciary Committee began releasing Doar's compilation of evidence on the Watergate break-in and cover-up, thus ensuring that Watergate would dominate the headlines in the weeks before the crucial vote on impeachment. The Ervin Committee also began to leak and then to release accusations from its supposedly secret report.

Despite its headline impact, however, this so-called evidence was generally admitted to be weak. ABC began its evening news with the announcement that there were "no bombshells." "No startling new disclosures," was NBC's verdict. And CBS reported that there were "no shockers, no startling new revelations." Jack Germond of the Washington *Star* summed up by saying, "The smoking pistol has yet to be found in President Nixon's hand."

That the evidence against me fell flat was satisfying; but the situation was still far from reassuring. On July 5 I summarized the situation as I saw it.

Diary

I remember Harlow saying almost a year ago, this issue has no legs to it. He may be right—may have been right, then—but so much has been added on—the personal taxes and all that sort of thing—so many doubts have been raised that one wonders what the situation is now.

I think of myself worrying as I have from time to time—what was going to happen next—and you get that sinking feeling in the bottom of your stomach and sometimes there are nights that are sleepless. I think of people like Kalmbach and Porter and others who are threatened with being sent to prison for fifteen to twenty years and so forth.

Perhaps as years go on attitudes may change, but they have left some deep scars, as I pointed out to both Ziegler and Haig on the plane coming back from Russia. Scars that will remain in the public mind and will not go away. Our only course of action is to keep fighting right through to the last and not to die a thousand deaths in the meantime.

I talked to Bebe too about this situation. Pat had pointed out that Bebe had been almost—she said that he had been really depressed. The whole purpose of course is to discredit, destroy, harass everybody around the President.

Both Pat and Bebe spoke of Rose and that she was really a fighter. I am glad that Pat sensed that from her talk with Rose coming home on the plane because Rose has gone through hell on this whole eighteen-minute business and she certainly has stood up with great character and great courage.

Bebe makes the point when I tell him how regretful I am that he and other decent people have to go through all this hell, he says that my own strength has inspired them all. I am inclined to think that I have not been as strong as I could have been or should have been, but I must say when we have such people like this we can't let them down, and I have got to fight every inch of the way.

In any event, if we can get through the Court and by the impeachment vote we will then have a couple of years to do as many good things for the country as we possibly can. What we have to do is to hold ourselves together through this next very difficult two-month period.

On June 27, 1974, Peter Rodino told a group of reporters that all twenty-one Democrats on the House Judiciary Committee were going to vote for impeachment. With this statement he confirmed what no one had dared say publicly before: the votes were in even before the witnesses had been heard or a defense had been made. Rodino was reprimanded by members of both parties. His first reaction was to try to cover up; he even went before his colleagues in the House and insisted that he had not made the statement. But reporters from the Los Angeles *Times* and ABC who had been there and had heard him confirmed the accuracy of the story.

By this time there was no question in my mind that the House Judiciary Committee was going to vote to impeach me. It was the margin of that vote that would assume a vital importance, because it would have a direct effect on the vote of the full House. The critical votes were still the six swing Republicans and the three Southern Democrats. The way these nine men voted would tell me whether I would be impeached by the House. Timmons had reduced it almost to a science: it was a straightforward example of a multiplier effect. He calculated that each vote we lost in the committee would cost us five votes from our supporters on the floor of the House.

In the first week of July, after we returned from the Soviet Union, Timmons felt we would win at least one of the three Southern Democrats and lose at least two of the six Republicans. If we could hold our losses to these numbers in the committee, then we could be optimistic about beating impeachment in the full House. This analysis found reinforcement from several sides. Godfrey Sperling of the *Christian Science Monitor* wrote that although Watergate was not worn out as an issue, it appeared to be receding from public conversation. Hugh Sidey, *Time*'s White House correspondent, told Henry Kissinger that his editors had decided that I was going to weather the impeachment storm. John Osborne, *The New Republic*'s White House watcher, told Ron Ziegler that he thought the House would not vote to impeach.

There were other hopeful signs of the sort that political pros might be expected to appreciate: RNC Chairman George Bush called the White House to say that he would like to have me appear on a fund-raising telethon; Don Rumsfeld called from Brussels, offering to resign as Ambassador to NATO and return to help work against impeachment among his former colleagues in Congress; and John Rhodes said he was for me unless he was presented with overwhelming evidence he should not be. Haig told me that his talks with the Cabinet members also indicated that the tide had turned. I was encouraged but not overly optimistic as I heard these reports.

Diary

Whatever the case may be, the big battle now is to try and hold the committee as well as we possibly can during the next couple of weeks. Obviously, the Democrats are going to pull out all the stops.

Dean will come again pretty soon and probably slap me around some more, but we don't think there are any other shoes ready to drop, although from the past track record no one can really be sure.

Getting back to Washington always gets you back into really the depths, although Ziegler says that the press is not nearly as hostile. But there is a depressing atmosphere here, and, of course, when you compound this with the family problem it makes it pretty tough. On the other hand, having survived this long I am convinced that we can see it through to the end—however the end comes out.

On July 12 I signed the Congressional Budget and Impoundment Control Act of 1974, a bill that I considered both a personal and a national triumph. After five years of nagging, urging, and pleading, and despite my weakened position because of Watergate, we had finally pushed through legislation that would make Congress face its responsibility for keeping the federal budget at agreed-upon levels.

After the ceremony Jerry Ford came over to me with his big, confident smile. "Don't worry, Mr. President," he said, "you've got this beat. We have a solid fifty-vote margin in the House, and we can build from there." Bryce Harlow, a man who knew Congress as well as any congressman, was also at the ceremony. He added, "Boss, you've got it won."

I wanted to believe these enthusiastic reports, but I knew Washington too well to think that the forces ranged against me would quit or forfeit the battle so easily. Twenty-five years of political instinct told me that despite the superficial appearances, things were not good; in fact, my instinct was stronger than ever that somehow, on some subsurface level, the political tide was flowing fast, and flowing against me.

I tried to pinpoint the reasons for my apprehension. One was the report of the numbers on my side. According to almost every report, there were approximately a hundred members of the House definitely committed to me, about seventy-five openly against me, and the rest were "undecided." I knew from experience that, more often than not, when a congressman tells someone from the White House that he is undecided on a particular question, he is probably against it and is only trying to be polite in declining to state his opposition before the vote is taken.

Another reason was my knowledge of how forceful, organized, and powerful the Democratic congressional leadership was, and how desperate they would become if it looked as though impeachment was actually going to be voted down. Having brought things this far, they would rightly fear the risk of a backlash if the impeachment drive failed and voters began to feel that the agony of Watergate had been prolonged for partisan motives.

Another major unknown was the Supreme Court, which would soon be handing down its ruling on Jaworski's petition for the sixty-four additional tapes. St. Clair was optimistic, but even he conceded that the Court would probably end up voting along political lines, despite the fact that we had the stronger legal case. In the event that the Court ruled flatly against me in the tapes case, I could decide to defy the ruling. But that would almost certainly bring about impeachment and therefore could not realistically be considered. Another choice was to *abide* by the Court's ruling without actually *complying* with it. This would involve some plan to turn over the tapes only in an excerpted form. In fact, I knew that even this approach would not take care of the real problem. I had not heard all the tapes, but I was concerned that in those thousands of hours of conversations there might be material that would be so damaging that I would not want to turn it over. There was already the June 23 tape, which still worried me. As I had noted in my diary on July 21, "Of course, how we handle the 23rd tape is a very difficult call because I don't know how it could be excerpted properly."

The Supreme Court ruling was going to have a tremendous—and almost certainly a detrimental—influence on the course of my impeachment hearings.

Diary

At this time, I must say, I am not particularly optimistic, although I would not be surprised about anything. If only [Burger] and his colleagues can look at the terrible impact if they are coming down in a way that totally destroys executive privilege—the impact that it will have in the future on Presidents. If only they can see that we may come up with a reasonable approach.

In any event, if only we could get over this hurdle without tripping and falling and giving the House some ground for impeachment we can then insist on a vote in the House and then move on to other things.

If they leave any air in the balloon at all, if if we could find a way to comply or abide, this would be the best of all worlds for us because then they could go on with their vote in the House and then we could in the last two years make up for the time that has been lost over the past year and one-half in doing what we were elected to do, the nation's business.

I also felt that the optimists among my supporters had not taken into account the political realities that would come into play when the full House of Representatives was faced with having to vote on an impeachment resolution. In addition to the partisan Democrats who were sure to vote for impeachment regardless of the evidence, an increasing number of Republicans would become concerned that if I were still in office during the November elections, I would be like an albatross around their necks.

If my support in Congress was halfhearted and disorganized, the White House staff was not in much better shape. Haig's eleventh-hour efforts to organize a group that would lead the fight from within the White House was handicapped by the "arm's length" requirement that our congressional supporters had put on their contacts with us. I knew, too, that they were handicapped psychologically by their own uncertainty about the case, by their fear that there might be still another bombshell—and that they might be out on the front line when it hit.

I was also concerned because the economy, which most voters still named as the issue of number-one concern to them, was standing on wobbly postembargo, postfreeze legs. The Dow Jones average had just hit a new four-year low. To the considerable degree that the economy affected national confidence and that national confidence would affect attitudes toward impeachment, this was a cause for the most serious concern. Unfortunately there did not seem to be much that I could do about the problem. I had convened and attended a number of meetings focusing on it, and there was general agreement that the best course was just to wait and ride it out.

Finally, there were the media. I felt that, consciously or subconsciously, they had a vested interest in my impeachment. After all the months of leaks and accusations and innuendo, the media stood to lose if I were vindicated. The defenses never caught up with the charges. For example, after all the damaging press and television coverage of alleged abuses of the IRS, when IRS Commissioner Donald Alexander announced the conclusions of a report that found no one had in fact been harassed as a result of White House intervention—a conclusion later supported by the findings of a joint congressional committee investigation—it was run on page thirty-nine of the New York *Times* and received scant coverage elsewhere. Most of the reporters and commentators were still filtering everything through their own Watergate obsessions. For example, Douglas Kiker of NBC reported that the White House was seeking to create the "impression" of a "busy President, back from an important and exhausting peacemaking mission, trying to do his job" despite harassment from the House Judiciary Committee. Months later, House Judiciary Committee impeachment firebrand Jerome Waldie said he doubted that I would have been forced from office "if the press had not desired it."

These were some of the reasons that my own instincts about the outcome of the impeachment effort were more pessimistic than those of most of my advisers. I often thought of something Tricia had observed several months earlier that seemed to me to be a perfect description of our problem. She had said that trying to explain something like Watergate was just like engaging in trench warfare: despite all the effort and all the blood expended, it was simply impossible to advance.

On July 12 we left Washington to spend two weeks in California. We received word aboard *Air Force One* that John Ehrlichman had been convicted of perjury and of conspiring to violate the civil rights of Daniel Ellsberg's psychiatrist. I was deeply depressed by the tragic irony of this development. Ellsberg, who had leaked top-secret documents, had gone free. Ehrlichman, who was trying to prevent such leaks, had been convicted.

When Pat, Ed, Tricia, and I arrived in San Clemente on the afternoon of July 12, everything seemed to be the same as it had been on every other California trip. We all went for a swim in the pool and then had an early dinner. It was a cool, clear night, and Ed and Tricia decided to take a walk before going to bed. They went through the garden and around the pool out to the golf course. When I bought the house in 1969, some local supporters had formed a group called Friends of the President and had raised money to build and maintain a three-hole golf course on Bob Abplanalp's property, adjacent to mine.

In the diary Tricia kept during this period she recorded the shock she and Ed experienced when they saw the golf course that night:

> Wasted, neglected, ugly, dead. The golf course of "Friends" of the President is no more. The sight is sickening, not because it is a sickening sight, but because of what it signifies. Deserted. Killed. The golf course. The man for whom it was created.
>
> Ed and I came upon it on our first stroll around the grounds, and its quality of finality, of hopelessness, smote us with an almost physical intensity. Ed tried to overcome this feeling with nervous levity. He said, "Looks like someone forgot to water the golf course." Of course we both knew someone had remembered not to water it. We made light of it to Daddy by saying we like to see it wild as it was when we first saw San Clemente. He was not fooled, but politely agreed. He trying to spare us. We trying to spare him. No one was spared.

Despite these dark counterpoints, during the first days of our stay the reports from Washington continued optimistic. I tried to be skeptical and detached, but almost irresistibly I found myself charting out in my diary plans for the future.

Diary

I think what we have to do is to remember that once we get past this election then we have just got to call them as we see them and '75 is the year to do it. '73 would have been the year to do it, as we thoroughly expected to do it when we first began '73, but then with the Watergate thing we lost that whole year and now we are in the election year, but '75 will be our last shot at doing the responsible things that need to be done to get our economy back on the right kind of a track and also to deal philosophically with some of these great issues where this may be the last opportunity for a conservative viewpoint to prevail over the radical leftist viewpoint, which McGovern and his colleagues fought for and lost.

We shall always have to keep in mind Tricia's

philosophy, that we have got to look down to the end of the road to see that we will come out all right, whatever may be and whatever way it is, and then remember that we will look back and see that we shouldn't have been worried about things all along. This is very hard to do, but it is the only thing that can sustain us through these other critical and difficult times. It is the only thing that has sustained us as a matter of fact through the enormous blows that we have been getting from all sides for such a long time.

As I sit here in my upstairs library, I am looking at a really beautiful portrait, hanging over the fireplace. I don't know whether it is a portrait or probably a photograph touched up of my mother when she was twelve years old. She was born in 1885, which would have meant that she would have been ninety years old now. But her face looked somewhat like Julie, I would say, or a combination of Julie and Tricia (very serious, very thoughtful, and very grown-up for a girl of twelve). She was truly a saint, as Helene Drown used to say. Someday I must write a monograph about her, which I think could be a very moving one.

On July 15 there was a violent coup on the strife-torn island of Cyprus. Fighting between the Greek and Turkish Cypriot factions seemed imminent. I suggested to Kissinger that he send Assistant Secretary of State Joe Sisco over to monitor the situation at the scene. I noted in my diary, "The Cyprus thing brought home the fact that with the world in the situation it is, with the peace as fragile as it is in various parts of the world, a shake-up in the American presidency and a change would have a traumatic effect abroad and a traumatic effect at home."

On July 18, James St. Clair was finally, and very reluctantly, given a chance to present a summary of my defense to the House Judiciary Committee. He did a brilliant job, and the overall impact of his appearance was extremely positive. We heard that this impression heightened even further the panic that had set in among the committee Democrats. Soon thereafter the Democrats voted not to allow St. Clair to present a defense of me on television once the public hearings began.

As these all-important hearings approached, Timmons's reports became troubled. He picked up signs that the Democratic leadership was turning on tremendous pressure in preparation for a fight to the finish. Democratic National Chairman Robert Strauss stated publicly that no responsible man could vote other than for impeachment. And we heard that Tip O'Neill was putting pressure on Rodino which Rodino was passing along to Doar to do something to get impeachment back on the track.

On July 18 I tried to evaluate the situation.

Diary

It is a little bit foggy this morning and in a curious way, I think this is the day that I may probably have been preparing for in terms of really shaking up our own thinking to get prepared for the battle of August and perhaps even, if Timmons's more pessimistic views prevail, the battle for the balance of the year in the Senate.

I began to think really about the whole impeachment process and very objectively and coldly. All in all, it appears very possible although not probable, I would have to say that O'Neill's bunch is going to be able certainly to get a majority vote out of the committee and a very damn close vote in the House. This completely leaves out the thing that has been worrying me earlier in the week—the Supreme Court thing.

The problem we have here is trying to hold the line with the Southerners in the House and that means trying to get at least two of them of the committee, and hopefully, for sure, one. We think we have Flowers.

A climactic struggle: that is what we have entered now and I think I have gotten that through to everybody, although I must say that Haig and St. Clair are thinking along these lines themselves.

Haig has agreed that we have got to get the Cabinet out just as soon as St. Clair gets back. In fact, as he said, we have got to push every button and mobilize every asset that we have got. Haig thinks that at a minimum that we should get fourteen votes in the committee. We would hope we could end up with sixteen; of course if we got eighteen that would be a great victory. Sixteen would be manageable (Haig's term), fourteen would be a bit tough, but he thinks still not beyond the point where we could still win on the floor.

Basically, it is like a campaign. We have got to take some risks when everything is on the line.

On July 19 John Doar stood before the members of the House Judiciary Committee and delivered a passionate and, by all accounts, masterful argument calling for my impeachment. The committee had continued its media blitz, releasing mounds of material on different subjects, designed to crescendo toward the public televised hearings to begin on July 24. Everything was moving quickly now, as we approached the time when the hearings would be ended and the vote would be taken.

Diary
I intend to live the next week without dying the death of a thousand cuts. This has been my philosophy throughout my political life. Cowards die a thousand deaths, brave men die only once.

I suppose it could be said that this is our Seventh Crisis in spades. Because the next month will be as hard a month as we will ever go through, but we can only be sustained by two things: one, in the belief that we are right—we are fighting, as all agree, an assault on our entire system of government.

And second, we will be sustained by the fact that at the end it will be over and even if it is over in the terms of an impeachment, we will just have to live with that.

By this time next week we may have both the Court and the committee vote. We can only hope for the best and plan for the worst.

The weekend of July 20 was the last time there was any real hope. On the night of July 21 we all went to a party for some of our old California friends at Roy Ash's house in Bel Air. Tricia's description of the evening in her diary said it all:

> At times it is like being in the eye of the hurricane. It is quite calm, quite still and if your eyes are closed you don't notice the unnatural darkness which surrounds you. You recall moments isolated in time. Yet they exist in the present. You recall a time without "Watergate" or when Watergate simply meant a rather extravagant place to live. An isolated moment. But then your eyes open and the darkness you see is the darkness of the storm.
>
> The sun last shone at the Ash dinner. Their home in Bel Air was a million light-years away from the turmoil. There was a glow of old about the entire evening. The guests, composed of old friends and others that the Ashes felt could be helpful, were in high spirits.
>
> Ever since the Roy Ash party, dating from the day following it, something was lost. Some support. The straw became so brittle and worn that you could almost hear it breaking asunder.

By the beginning of the week of July 22 there had been no new evidence introduced since late June, when it had been generally acknowledged that the evidence was not sufficient to justify impeachment. Nothing factual had changed, but the political ground began to shift. We heard that John Rhodes was going to help us; and that he was not. We were told that Goldwater had said that he was going to ask me to resign; but when Haig called him, Goldwater laughed and said in absolutely no circumstances had he ever said that, nor would he. Perhaps most disturbing, because it was apparently true, we heard that we were in trouble with the three Southern Democrats on the committee: Wilbur Mills was said to be getting to his fellow Arkansan Thornton, while Rodino was reportedly having private sessions with Flowers and O'Neill was rumored to be putting a strong arm on Mann. Most people don't recall it, but long before the new "evidence" of the June 23 tape was produced, the political consensus had already been reached, and the political consensus was to impeach.

"LOWEST POINT IN THE PRESIDENCY"

On the morning of Tuesday, July 23, the day before the House Judiciary Committee's televised hearings were scheduled to begin, Lawrence Hogan, one of the committee's conservative Republicans, called a press conference. In emotional tones he announced that he had decided to vote for my impeachment. Many of his colleagues, and some news commentators, said that Hogan's effort to jump the gun and thereby gain maximum publicity was an effort to shore up his faltering campaign for governor of Maryland. In San Clemente we tried to minimize the damage Hogan caused by concentrating on the many people who criticized him and his motives. But the fact was that he had dealt us a very bad blow. Later that same day, July 23, Timmons called from Washington. He said it was now certain: we had lost all three Southern Democrats on the committee.

I was stunned. I had been prepared to lose one and had steeled myself for losing two. But losing all three meant certain defeat on the House floor. It meant impeachment.

I told Haig bitterly that if this was the result of our hands-off strategy, we could hardly have done worse by outright lobbying. I said that we had to do something to try to get at least one of the Southerners back.

Haig mentioned that one of George Wallace's aides had sent word that I had only to call on Wallace if there was anything he could do to help me. Here was the opportunity to take up Wallace's offer: perhaps the Alabama governor would be willing to call his fellow Alabamian Walter Flowers and remind him that party loyalty need not include supporting the radical surgery of removing a President from office. I agreed that it was worth a try, and Haig said he would arrange the call.

At 3:52 P.M. in my office in San Clemente I picked up the phone. George Wallace was already on the line.

Diary
When I got Wallace on the phone he played it very cozy. He said he couldn't quite hear me at first, and then said that he hadn't expected the call, that nobody had told him about it.

He said he hadn't examined the evidence. That he

prayed for me. That he was sorry that this had to be brought upon me. That he didn't think it was proper for him to call Flowers, that he thought Flowers might resent it and that if he changed his mind he would let me know. I knew when I hung up the phone that he would not change his mind.

The call took only six minutes. When I hung up the phone I turned to Haig and said, "Well, Al, there goes the presidency."

Haig was not ready to give up. He urged that I call Alabama Senator James Allen and ask if he could help with Flowers. I reached Allen in Washington. He was concerned and friendly, but he was too honest to give me any false encouragement. I had to accept the fact that the committee's Southerners were lost.

I called Joe Waggonner, and he said that with the three Southerners gone, he could hope to hold only between thirty and thirty-five of the Waggonner group. This meant that I could not possibly have enough votes on my side when the full House voted. "My guess is," I noted in my diary, "that the Democrats have made a command decision to get me out and Ford in and then tear him up and win in 1976."

That night I sat in my study trying to work on the speech on the economy that I was to give on national television in two days. I tried to organize and outline my thoughts for it, but my mind kept wandering back to the afternoon, and a sense of hopeless loss and despair kept welling up in me.

My options had been reduced to only two: resign or be impeached. I had to decide either to leave the presidency voluntarily, or else confront the hard decision of whether the country could stand six months of having the President on trial in the Senate.

Over the past few weeks I had talked with Haig and Ziegler several times about resigning. Haig argued that resignation would not only look like an admission of guilt, but it would mean a dangerously easy victory for the radicals—not just over me but over the system.

There were also personal factors to consider. My family had already been put through two years of hell, but if I

639

resigned I could expect an onslaught of lawsuits that would cost millions of dollars and take years to fight in the courts. I told Haig that the personal factors must not be the deciding ones. But it was difficult to separate personal considerations from political, party, and national interests.

On the edge of my speech notes I wrote: "12:01 A.M. Lowest point in the presidency, and Supreme Court still to come."

I would not have long to wait.

The next morning I overslept for the first time in several months. I had worked on the speech until 2:30 A.M., and it was after nine o'clock when I picked up the bedside phone. Haig came on the line, and I asked, "How are things going?" In a strained voice he said, "Well, it's pretty rough, Mr. President. I didn't want to wake you until we had the complete text, but the Supreme Court decision came down this morning."

"Unanimous?" I guessed.

"Unanimous. There's no air in it at all," he said.

"None at all?" I asked.

"It's tight as a drum."

This decision in the case of *United States* v. *Nixon* was widely heralded as one of the Court's finest hours. As one television reporter described it, the United States had triumphed. While I understood the reasons for the decision, I thought that the United States had lost. I felt that the presidency itself was a casualty of this ruling.

I asked Haig to come to my study. A few minutes later St. Clair came in, looking very dejected. The problem was not just that we had lost but that we had lost so decisively. We had counted on some air in the Court's ruling, at least some provision for exempting national security materials. We had counted on at least one dissent. For a few minutes we discussed the option of "abiding" by the decision in the Jeffersonian tradition. But after checking with some of our strongest supporters in Washington, we concluded that full compliance was the only option.

I asked St. Clair how long he thought we could take to turn over the sixty-four tapes covered by the decision. He said that with all the problems involved in listening to them and preparing transcripts, we could probably take a month or more.

I thought that we should assess the damage right away. When Haig called Buzhardt to discuss the decision, I took the phone and asked him to listen to the June 23 tape and report back to Haig as soon as possible. This was the tape I had listened to in May on which Haldeman and I discussed having the CIA limit the FBI investigation for political reasons rather than the national security reasons I had given in my public statements. When I first heard it, I knew it would be a problem for us if it ever became public—now I would find out just how much of a problem.

Buzhardt listened to the tape early in the afternoon. When he called back, he told Haig and St. Clair that even though it was legally defensible, politically and practically it was the "smoking gun" we had been fearing. Haig and St. Clair had often remarked that Buzhardt was an alarmist. So Haig called Buzhardt back and asked him to listen to the June 23 tape a second time. After Buzhardt had listened again and made a second report of his impressions, Haig put on a brave front and told me that the tape was apparently "embarrassing" but not completely "unmanageable." "I think we can cope with it," he said.

Diary

> The 23rd tape we have talked over time and time again. Fred has listened to it twice, spoken to St. Clair about it. St. Clair wants to talk to Al about it and listen to it on Monday. When St. Clair and Al came up to see me in the Library to discuss what St. Clair should say about complying with the Supreme Court decision, St. Clair rather airily passed off the 23rd tape by saying—"but just two weeks later you told Gray to go forward with his investigation."

On the night that the Court's ruling was handed down, the House Committee began its televised sessions. The Democrats postured shamefully, pretending that they had not made up their minds. My supporters were eloquent—but they were fighting a lost battle. And now, underneath it all, like slow-fused dynamite waiting to explode, was the June 23 tape.

I was swimming in the ocean at Red Beach near San Clemente on July 27 when the House Judiciary Committee voted on the first article of impeachment. It charged that I had engaged in a "course of conduct" designed to obstruct the investigation of the Watergate case. The vote went exactly the way I had feared: all the Democrats, including the three conservative Southerners, were joined by six of the seventeen Republicans. The article was passed, 27 to 11.

I was getting dressed in the beach trailer when the phone rang and Ziegler gave me the news. That was how I learned that I was the first President in 106 years to be recommended for impeachment: standing in the beach trailer, barefoot, wearing old trousers, a Banlon shirt, and a blue windbreaker emblazoned with the Presidential Seal.

Our family dinner that night was not subdued, but it was more quiet than usual. Afterward, in my study, I made some notes about Pat.

Diary

I remember that Tricia said as we came back from the beach that her mother was really a wonderful woman. And I said, yes. She has been through a lot through the twenty-five years we have been in and out of politics. Both at home and abroad she has always conducted herself with masterful poise and dignity. But, God, how she could have gone through what she does, I simply don't know.

That night and the next I sat up very late trying to grasp the new situation I faced and decide on the best course of action to deal with it.

Diary

And so we will be back on Monday. They will listen to the tapes, and my guess is that they might well come in to me and say, "We just don't think this is manageable." I am referring to St. Clair, Haig, et al.

If we do make that decision, then I have a hard call—that call being as to whether I decide to bite the bullet on resignation or whether I continue to fight it through the House and wait until the House vote and then resign on the basis that I can't put the country through the months that would be involved in an impeachment trial.

Al and Ziegler have been splendid in this period. Ziegler makes the point very strongly that if we ever connote the impression that we have given up, then everybody will run to the hills. Al points out that under no circumstances must we do this for another reason. That if we don't get a third in the House that it would look as if we had run out and so forth.

As a matter of fact, I have had a feeling of calm and strength during this period. This is due in part to the fact that after hearing of the total defection of the Southerners, I realized that we had lost the ball game and faced at least a six-month trial in the Senate.

To a certain extent I think the calmness and strength may have come from somewhere back in my background—perhaps from my father and my mother.

I now recognized in my own mind something that, totally deliberately, I did not convey to my closest associates: the country simply could not afford to have a crippled President for six months.

Diary

We have to try to work out what we can do to live out whatever life I have left as President and thereafter in a decent way.

Looking to the future, I recognize that I would have to face up to the hard fact of how I could take care of our personal expenses in the time ahead. Whether I can sell a book or papers or what have you in order to have the funds that would be needed to maintain an adequate staff in the office and in the house. My present inclination is to sell the property in Florida and take what equity I have there so that I have some cash on hand. As far as the San Clemente house is concerned, I will simply have to make a determination as to whether we want to keep it. It might be that we would be better off to take a reasonably comfortable apartment at some place and live out our lives there.

Needless to say, how we are able to handle our staff like Manolo and Fina—our household staff—and even the minimum staff of Rose and two or three secretaries to work with me on the book, God only knows. But I must not borrow trouble on this at this point. At the present time what I have to do is to recognize that we are in a battle for our lives. It involves the country. The sad thing, as Eddie says, is that the bad guys will have won. He means by that that this would be a very bad thing for the country should I go the resignation route.

Henry came in to see me, very mournful but, bless him, he was thinking only with his heart. A very unusual approach for a man who is so enormously endowed with extraordinary intellectual capacity. He said that his wife had told him that history in four years would look back on the President as a hero. And Al, of course, has made the point that history will show me in the end to have been an outstanding President.

We returned to Washington on Sunday, July 28. Tricia recorded the scene:

> In the hall of the second floor of the White House we said goodbye to Daddy and Mama before Ed and I departed for New York. Daddy came as close to outward emotion as he ever does when he said how much it had meant to him for us to be in California with him. Without further expression, I felt as if these words marked an end of an era. That this was a farewell. A chapter ended forever.

Monday, July 29, was our first full day back in Washington. I was shocked to see the difference that just two weeks had made. Impeachment hysteria had taken over the city. The White House staff was cloaked in gloom. It remained to be seen whether anything could be salvaged of the shattered confidence of the tired men and women in the West Wing and the EOB.

On Tuesday St. Clair returned from a long weekend in Cape Cod, where he had gone to get some rest. Even before the California trip Haig told me that St. Clair had become tired and touchy and that we would have to be careful if we wanted to keep him on the staff. St. Clair listened to the June 23 tape and discussed it with Buzhardt. His breezy optimism disappeared. He not only agreed with Buzhardt that this was the smoking gun, but he said that it so contradicted the arguments he had made before the House Judiciary Committee that he would become party to an obstruction of justice unless it was made public.

As we weighed the damage of the June 23 tape, the House Judiciary Committee passed two more articles of impeachment. Article II, passed on July 29, charged that I had committed an impeachable offense by abusing the powers of the presidency. It contained a number of different charges ranging from an alleged attempt to use the IRS for political purposes to the 1969 national security wiretaps. Article III, passed on July 30, charged that I had committed an impeachable offense by defying the committee's subpoenas for tapes and documents. After voting down two more articles of impeachment—one dealing with the Cambodian bombing and the other with my personal finances—the House Judiciary Committee recessed. The next step would be the vote on each of the three articles of impeachment by the House of Representatives. The opening debate was scheduled for August 19.

On the night of July 30 I could not get to sleep. After tossing and turning for a few hours, I finally put on the light and took a pad of notepaper from the bed table. I wrote the time and date at the top—3:50 A.M., July 31—and I began to outline the choices left to me. There were really only three: I could resign right away; I could stay on until the House had voted on the articles of impeachment and then resign if impeached; or I could fight all the way through the Senate.

For almost three hours I listed the pros and cons: what would be the best for me, for my family, for my friends and supporters? What would be the best for the country?

There were strong arguments against resigning. First and foremost, I was not and never had been a quitter. The idea that I would be running away from the job and ending my career as a weak man was repugnant to me. Resignation would be taken by many, and interpreted by the press, as a blanket admission of guilt. Resignation would set a danger-ous precedent of short-circuiting the constitutional machin-ery that provides for impeachment. I also had to consider that my family and many of my supporters would want me to fight and would be hurt and disillusioned if I gave up before the battle was over.

The arguments in favor of resignation were equally compelling. I knew that after two years of being distracted and divided by Watergate, the nation badly needed a unity of spirit and purpose to face the tough domestic and interna-tional problems that would not wait through the six months of a Senate trial. Besides, I would be crippled politically as soon as the House voted to impeach, and I did not know whether I could subject the country to the ordeal of a weakened presidency during such troubled and important times. From a practical point of view, I also had to face the fact that if I decided to stay and fight, the outcome of the fight was all but settled: I would be defeated and dishon-ored, the first President in history to be impeached and convicted on criminal charges.

Another positive effect of resignation, one I knew to be uppermost in the minds of many Republicans, was that it would free the party from having to defend me. The 1974 elections would not become a referendum on Nixon and Watergate, and their campaigns and their congressional seats would not be held hostage to my political fortunes.

It was almost morning by the time I finished making these notes. My natural instincts welled up and I turned the paper over and wrote on the back: "End career as a fighter."

That was what my instincts and my intuition told me was the right thing to do. As bad as Watergate was, it would be far worse to set the precedent of a presidential resigna-tion—even if the alternative was the removal of a President because of a political scandal. *"End career as a fighter"*—the way it had begun. That was the way I really wanted it.

With Buzhardt and St. Clair now on the side of resigna-tion, Haig's position became pivotal. I would need Haig to rally whatever loyal staff was left and to keep the White House running if I chose not to resign but to face a Senate trial.

On Wednesday, July 31, Haig read the transcripts of the June 23 conversations for the first time.

"Well, what do you think?" I asked when he had finished.

"Mr. President," he said, "I am afraid that I have to agree with Fred and Jim St. Clair. I just don't see how we can survive this one. I know what was really happening there, and I know how you feel about it, but I think that we have to face the facts, and the facts are that the staff won't hold and that public opinion won't hold either, once this tape gets out."

That afternoon Ron Ziegler listened to the tape. I could tell that he too now felt the situation was all but hopeless.

THE DECISION TO RESIGN

On Thursday, August 1, I told Haig that I had decided to resign. If the June 23 tape was not explainable, I could not very well expect the staff to try to explain and defend it.

I said that I planned to take the family to Camp David over the weekend to prepare them and then to resign in a televised speech on Monday night. I would stay in Washington for about two weeks putting things in order, and then fly to San Clemente.

Haig said that we could work out the arrangements however I wanted, but he suggested that I resign even sooner, perhaps the next night, Friday, August 2. Since the June 23 tape was in the group to be handed over to Judge Sirica that morning, Haig thought that I should have resigned and been gone from the scene before the tape surfaced publicly. By that time, he said, so much attention would be focused on the new President that the damaging impact of the tape might be muted.

I decided to think about it, and I asked Haig if in the meantime he would take some notes and then have Ray Price begin work on a resignation speech. I told him that I would acknowledge that I had made mistakes; but I did not want Price to write a groveling mea culpa. I wanted him to say that I no longer had the political support in Congress or in the country that I believed I needed to govern effectively.

I also asked Haig to see Jerry Ford and tell him that I

was thinking of resigning, without indicating when. I said Haig should ask him to be prepared to take over sometime within the next few days. I told him to impress on Ford the need for absolute secrecy. This was a decision I had to make for and by myself—right up to the end. I told him that I would be put in a humiliating position if it got to the point that the Republican National Chairman or a group of senators or congressmen, or a delegation of Cabinet members, began requesting or demanding that I resign. I knew that if that happened, my lifetime instincts of refusing to cave to political pressure might prevail.

I went over to the EOB office early in the afternoon. Now that the decision to resign had been made, I felt that if I could focus strongly enough on carrying it out in all its details, it would be easier to get through the painful decisions and duties of the next few days. I took off my suit coat and put on my favorite old blue sports jacket.

I asked Ron Ziegler to come over. As soon as he came in, I could see that Haig had already talked to him. I confirmed that I was going to resign.

There was a long moment of silence. Ziegler was by instinct a fighter, like me. He said only, "Mr. President, I know you want me to support your decision, so I will."

I told him that I knew Jerry Ford was not experienced in foreign affairs. "But he's a good and decent man, and the country needs that now," I said.

When I told Ziegler about Haig's advice to move quickly and resign the following night, he argued strongly that such a move would be precipitate. He said that there should be at least enough time to prepare properly. I realized that he was right, if for no other reason than that I owed it to my friends and supporters to give them a chance to react to the June 23 tape and get off the hook while I was still in office, rather than leave them behind holding the bag. The least they deserved was the chance to reverse their position if they wanted. So I tentatively decided to wait until Monday night to resign.

After Ziegler had left, I read some of Timmons's congressional reports and listened to the last group of tapes that had to be turned over to Sirica the following week. Around six o'clock I heard that Bebe Rebozo had just arrived from

Miami. I asked Haig if he could arrange a dinner on the *Sequoia,* and an hour later we were sailing up the Potomac under a sultry evening sky.

"You're not going to like this," I said to Rebozo, "but I have decided that I should resign." I will always remember the stricken expression on Rebozo's face when I said this.

"You can't do it," he said. "It's the wrong thing to do. You have got to continue to fight. You just don't know how many people are still for you."

I told him about the June 23 tape and said that once it was released there would certainly be a trial in the Senate, with the likelihood of conviction. He urged that I get Russell Long and other leading senators in to listen to it and not just take the evaluation of a small group of staff.

I said that even if I had a chance in the Senate, the country simply could not afford six months with its President on trial.

As we sailed back toward Washington, I asked Rebozo to help by backing me up with the family. He said he would do everything he could as long as I would promise not to make the decision irrevocable until we made one last try to mount a defense. I agreed. I was touched by his spirit and by his fierce loyalty. But I knew how helpless and hopeless it was.

When we returned to the White House, I went to the Lincoln Sitting Room. It had been a long hard day.

The afternoon of August 2 Haig asked Chuck Wiggins to come in and read the June 23 transcript and give us his preliminary evaluation of its impact.

Haig reported to me that Wiggins said impeachment in the House and conviction in the Senate were now no longer in doubt. He said that when these tapes became known, we would lose all but two or three Republicans on the Judiciary Committee—possibly including himself. He said that unless I planned to withhold the tape from the Court by pleading the Fifth Amendment, I should get ready to resign right away. Like St. Clair, he felt that unless he reported the existence of the tape, he would himself become party to an obstruction of justice. Haig assured him that we would make it public.

That night I began the painful task of telling my family about the June 23 tape and preparing them for the impact it would have on my attempts to remain in office. Tricia's diary recorded the family side of that day:

> Julie called, very down this morning. She informed me that Daddy had had a talk with her that was serious but she hesitated to elaborate over the phone. Immediately I said I was coming right down. She said it was not really necessary. I replied that it was. She agreed.
>
> I pushed the Secret Service button and informed them I would be leaving on the next shuttle for Washington.
>
> Our curious little band departed within ten minutes. While boarding the jet at La Guardia Airport, catcalls, boos, and obscene words were hurled at me by a group of Eastern employees who were lounging around their vehicles. I was caught between two agents, one on the step above me, one on the step below. I attempted to bypass the agent on the step below so that I could verbally take head-on the cowardly group. But the agent was not inclined to cooperate and anyway I thought it more important to make this flight than to protest the treatment.
>
> At the White House, I took the elevator to the second floor, then scurried to the secret stairway at the East Hall and climbed to the third floor. I walked into Julie's room and found her on the telephone. Seeing me, she disengaged herself and I calmly asked her what Daddy had said to her yesterday. "He thinks he must resign." "Why?" "Because he has virtually no support left." "Julie, I can't believe this isn't a nightmare. It cannot be happening."
>
> Julie and I talked some more and I learned that Mama had not been told of Daddy's tentative decision. Mama was in her sitting room at her desk. It is strange how you try to spare those you love from worry. Strange because worry is contagious and is difficult to conceal other than with words. So in the end it is kinder to reveal what the person you are trying to spare already feels. But I was still trying to protect Mama and spare her from grief. Daddy, of course, is always protective of everyone but himself. Mama and I talked briefly and made plans to walk with the dogs later that afternoon.
>
> From her room I entered my own down the hall. I placed a call through the operators to Edward at his office. This is something I refrain from doing, so when he answered he knew

the motive had to be serious. Without going into any details, I said it would be "delightful" if he could come down to Washington that evening for dinner. *Delightful* was a codeword we used to connote trouble. We did not have a codeword for disaster.

After the call I met Bebe in the hall. He looked sick and I asked him how Daddy was. Bebe had just been in the Lincoln Sitting Room with Daddy and he surprisingly (for Bebe is closed-mouthed) told me that Daddy had told him about resigning. Bebe suggested that I should go to Daddy and pretend I knew nothing so that Daddy could tell me himself. This I did.

Daddy was seated in his brown armchair with his feet up on the ottoman. He was fussing with a pipe. He greeted me, "Well, honey, when did you arrive?" And then he began a clear description of the June 23 tape and an analysis of his position. I only interrupted when he began to speak of resigning for the good of the country. I told him for the good of the country he must stay in office.

Then as I was leaving I went over to where he was, put my arms around him, kissed his forehead, and without warning I burst into tears and said brokenly, "You are the most decent person I know."

Emotions for me are usually completely controllable externally. But when Daddy said, "I hope I have not let you down," the tragedy of his ghastly position shattered me.

Mama, Julie, Bebe, David, and I had just been called into the Lincoln Sitting Room by Daddy. Daddy had been talking to us for about twenty minutes when Ed arrived and joined our little band. Just prior to Ed's arrival Daddy picked up the receiver of the nearby phone and asked to speak to Al Haig. Once connected he asked Haig to send over the transcripts of the June 23 tape he had just been describing to us. His tone throughout was almost dispassionate but not quite. In about ten minutes Manolo brought us the papers bearing the bothersome words. Ed arrived and the four of us (Julie, David, Ed, and me) removed ourselves from the room to carefully peruse the transcripts. Julie and David read their copy together. Ed and I read our copy. Ed and I agreed the words could be taken one of two ways depending upon who was judging them.

651

We returned to the Lincoln Sitting Room with its interior deceptively gay-looking from the soft light cast by the fire burning in the fireplace. Each of us in turn expressed his or her opinion. Ed, Julie, and I coming out strongly for not resigning. David was less sure. But all of us were in concert of feeling that we wanted Daddy to do what he felt he should. He spoke of doing the right thing for the country, of how he thought a weak President in the position of being impeached would be a disaster to the country. What would the Soviets not dare to attempt in such a situation? Look what they had already attempted in the last Mideast dispute.

Daddy did not appear overly anguished but rather properly anguished at the events. He was very much in control of his feelings.

Finally there was nothing left to say, and we left Daddy alone in his chair staring into the fire. Undoubtedly more telephone calls would be made and received long after we were gone. We left feeling he still might not resign. In the time we were in that room with Daddy, years had been lived, re-lived.

The future held, he said, either resignation or removal from office by the Senate.

Upstairs Mama, Ed, and I went to the third floor to say good night to Julie and David. We all broke down together, and put our arms around each other in circular, huddle-style fashion. Saying nothing.

I sat alone in the Lincoln Sitting Room that night for several hours, trying to decide the best course of action.

My family's courage moved me deeply. They had been through so much already, and still they wanted to see the struggle through to the end. Pat, who had let the others do most of the talking in our meeting, told me that now, as always before, she was for fighting to the finish.

I decided that instead of resigning on Monday night, I would release the June 23 tape and see the reaction to it. If it was as bad as I expected, then we could resume the countdown toward resignation. If by some miracle the reaction was not so bad and there was any chance that I could actually govern during a six-month trial in the Senate, then we could examine that forlorn option one more time. In a subconscious way I knew that resignation was inevitable. But more than once over the next days I would yield to my

652

desire to fight, and I would bridle as the inexorable end drew near.

I called Haig and told him that Ray Price should stop working on the resignation speech for Monday night and instead begin work on a statement to accompany the release of the June 23 tape.

On Saturday afternoon I decided that we should get out of Washington and go to Camp David. Even up there in the mountains it was hot and humid, so as soon as we could change our clothes we all went for a swim. Then we dressed and sat on the terrace, looking out across the wide valleys. On evenings like this it was easy to see why Franklin Roosevelt had named this place Shangri-la, and I think that each of us had a sense of the mystery and the beauty as well as the history and the tragedy that lay behind our weekend together in this setting.

At every opportunity the young people urged me to fight on. After a swim on Saturday afternoon I was in the sauna when Eddie came in. After sitting for a few minutes in silence, he turned to me in a very controlled but emotional way and said, "You have got to fight 'em, fight 'em, fight 'em."

At dinner on Saturday night we reviewed the situation again, and everyone urged that I at least postpone any decision until after the tape had been released on Monday. I told them I would consider their arguments and delay my decision to resign. For some reason an odd rhyme struck me. I said, "Well, that's settled: we will wait and see. It's fight or flight by Monday night!"

Sunday was a cloudy day, but the clouds did not reach quite to the top of the mountain on which Aspen Lodge is situated. I was awake at dawn, looking out over the great uncharted sea of clouds, pondering the decision yet again.

That afternoon some of the senior staff members and writers came up from Washington. We had decided that a written statement would be better than a speech to discuss the June 23 tape. I wanted the statement to emphasize the fact that as soon as Gray had informed me on July 6, 1972, of his concern about White House intervention, I had told him to press on with the investigation. The lawyers and staff, however, produced a draft that shifted the emphasis of the statement from the contents of the tape to my failure to inform them of its existence.

I handed Haig a page of notes from my yellow pad on which I had formulated the information I wanted the statement to convey. It read: "On July 6 in a telephone conversation FBI Director Gray expressed his concern to me that improper efforts were being made to limit its investigation of the Watergate matter by some White House personnel. I asked him if he had discussed this matter with General Walters. He answered—yes. I asked if Walters agreed with him. He answered—yes. I then told him to press forward with the investigation. This clearly demonstrated that when I was informed that there was no national security objection to a full investigation by the FBI, I did not hesitate to order the investigation to proceed without regard to any political or other considerations. From this time when I was informed that there were no national security interests involved or would be jeopardized by the investigation, the investigation fully proceeded without regard to any political or other considerations."

Haig read the note quickly and said, "It's no use, Mr. President. We've been working all afternoon on this thing, and this is the best we can come up with. I can't make any changes in the statement now. If I do, St. Clair and the other lawyers are going to jump ship, because they claim they weren't told about this beforehand and they based their case before the House Judiciary Committee on a premise that proved to be false."

I did not make an issue of it with Haig. Instead I said, "The hell with it. It really doesn't matter. Let them put out anything they want. My decision has already been made."

THE LAST DAYS

On Monday morning, August 5, the daily press briefing was postponed several times. It was canceled at 1:30, and a statement was promised by three o'clock. Speculation that I was about to resign filled the press lobby. The statement and the lengthy tape transcripts of the June 23 conversations were released at four o'clock. In the rush to produce copies of these transcripts for distribution to the press, some personal references were carelessly and unnecessarily left in.

I had returned to the White House that morning and called the Residence, suggesting that the family have dinner on the *Sequoia*. I did not want them to have to endure the ordeal of watching the evening news broadcasts. I knew what they would be like.

Ed had had to return to New York, so Pat, Julie, David, Tricia, and Rose met me in the Diplomatic Reception Room. As we walked to the cars, about a hundred young staff members, most of them secretaries from the East Wing and West Wing offices, were waiting for us. They stood on the driveway and clapped and cheered. As I shook their hands they said, "Hang in there," "We're still with you," "God bless you, Mr. President."

Out on the river the evening was beautiful. The breeze off the water stirred the sultry air, and we sat on the top deck watching the sunset. When we passed under bridges, reporters and photographers would suddenly surge forward, hanging perilously over the railings, trying to get a closer glimpse or a closer picture.

Everyone valiantly tried to make the evening as happy as possible. They talked about the summer weather and about a movie Julie and David had seen. They talked about the firm way Rose had of fending off impertinent reporters. They talked about everything but what was on everyone's mind.

During dinner I began to reminisce about all sorts of people in so many places who had been good to us over the years. I said that someday, even if it were not for a long time, all the recent experiences we had endured would mean a lot to us because we would see how they had brought us closer together. Everyone agreed that our life in politics had been enriching, the bad as well as the good. There was no talk about resigning that night, but several weeks later I learned that the next morning Pat had begun to organize our clothes, getting them ready for packing.

After dinner the boat turned and began heading back. I had no illusions about what was awaiting us. I knew that while we were sailing on the tranquil river, the city of Washington was being whipped into a frenzy of excitement by the revelation of the June 23 tape. By now everyone would be scrambling for position, and few, if any, would want to be found standing with me.

I asked Rose to call Haig and get a report on the first reactions, and then I went down to my cabin and stretched out on the bed with my left leg elevated as the doctors had ordered.

A few minutes later Rose came down and read me her shorthand notes of her conversation with Haig. "Just tell him that this thing is coming about the way we expected," Haig had told her. Rose continued to read from her notes: "Those in the upper level we expected to be all right are the same—some lower level lost—all ten on first article. The one that Dean Burch talked to regularly"—that would be Goldwater—"is going to keep quiet. Senators Curtis, Cotton, Bennett, Eastland, Stennis, Congressman Waggonner, are very much back of him but concerned about what it will do. He is worried about some others in his group. Rhodes said it was very bad. He didn't say what he was going to do. Talked with three key guys in the Cabinet—no problem with whole Cabinet—all solid."

After Rose left, I turned off the lights and closed my eyes.

I had been planning to hold a Cabinet meeting ever since we returned from San Clemente. Late Monday night I asked Haig to see if he could arrange one for Tuesday morning, August 6.

Although I recognized the inevitability of resignation, no plans had yet been set in motion. Once resignation came, it would be quick and complete; but until then I intended to play the role of President right to the hilt and right to the end. Until my decision had been announced, the government had to remain absolutely stable at home and nations around the world must have no reason to think that America was without a leader. In the meantime I felt that the Cabinet and the White House staff should be reminded that their first responsibility was to their jobs and to the continued functioning of the government.

I knew my Cabinet well, and despite Haig's reports that they were all holding firm I knew that there would be great pressure on them all, and great temptations, to make public demands for my resignation. That was something I had to prevent if I possibly could. I was determined not to appear to have resigned the presidency because of a consensus of staff or Cabinet opinion or because of public pressure from the people around me. For me and no less for the country, I believed that my resignation had to be seen as something that I had decided upon completely on my own.

I was unable to sleep that night, and about two o'clock I walked down to the Lincoln Sitting Room. No fire had been laid, so I stacked some logs together, lighted them with paper, and sat down in my big armchair in front of the blaze. A few minutes later, as I sat lost in thought, the door burst open and two of the night-duty engineers rushed in. When they saw me sitting there, they froze in their tracks. "Mr. President," they said in surprised unison.

Apparently everyone had thought I was in bed, and my amateur fire had set off an alarm. After they recovered from the shock of finding me there, they checked the chimney to make sure that the flue was open.

Just as they left, the younger of the two turned around and said, "Mr. President, I just want you to know that we're praying for you," and quickly closed the door behind him.

I thought about these two men, and about the office workers that afternoon, and about the millions of others like them all across the country who still had faith in me. I knew that by resigning I would let them down.

I went back to bed around three o'clock. We had passed through the first blast of the fire storm, but it was still raging. I knew that it would be following me for the rest of my life.

The Cabinet meeting on Tuesday morning was tense and subdued. During every other crisis of the administration, my entrance had been greeted with applause. Today the Cabinet rose silently as I came into the room and walked around to my chair at the center of the big oblong table.

I opened by saying that we had several major problems to deal with, but I knew that the major subject on their minds was Watergate, and that was what I wanted to talk about first.

I said that I understood how many people were genuinely upset by the June 23 tape. I knew it was a terrible blow to my case because it made clear that there had been discussions about the political advantages of bringing in the

CIA. I thanked the Cabinet members for their statements of support in the past. I knew that many times it had not been easy to stand up for me, and I was grateful when they did. The faces were intent, sober, noncommittal.

I said that I had considered resigning. Resignation would certainly lift a great burden from my shoulders. But I also had to think of the presidency itself. I had to consider whether resigning now because of the tremendous pressures on me to do so would establish a precedent that could start America down the road to a parliamentary type of government in which the executive stays in office only as long as he can win a vote of confidence from the legislative branch. I said that I would not expect any member of the Cabinet to do anything that would be personally embarrassing or politically harmful. My problems were my own responsibility, and I only asked that they try to run their departments especially well over the next weeks and months.

I paused, and Jerry Ford, his voice unnaturally low, said that his situation was particularly difficult. It appeared the vote in the House was going to be unfavorable, and he said that despite his admiration and affection for me, he had decided to remain silent about impeachment from now on. I said that this was the right position, and that no other member of the Cabinet should do anything that might jeopardize his ability to carry on his present responsibilities, or responsibilities he might have in the future, in the event I did leave office.

I repeated that they should not become involved in the impeachment controversy but must instead give their full attention to running their departments. If I became occupied with a Senate trial, I said, I wanted the Cabinet Secretaries to think of themselves as the functioning trustees of the President and the government.

After an uncomfortable pause I said that for the rest of the meeting I wanted to discuss the subjects that the public opinion polls still showed to be the foremost concerns of the American people: inflation and the economy.

There was a brief discussion of the new agricultural appropriations bill, which I said would have to be vetoed because it was an out-and-out giveaway measure, exceeding my budget limitation by $450 million. The discussion then turned to a proposal for an economic summit between

Congress and the executive branch sometime in the near future. Saxbe broke in, saying that perhaps we should wait to see if I would have sufficient leadership to implement any of the economic measures we were discussing. As if spurred on by Saxbe, George Bush indicated that he wanted recognition.

Henry Kissinger's deep, thick voice broke in sharply: "We are not here to give the President excuses. We are here to do the nation's business." There was a moment of embarrassed silence around the table, and then the discussion on the economy resumed until the meeting ended.

After the Cabinet meeting I met with Kissinger in the Oval Office. I told him how much I had appreciated his support and his handling of the foreign policy problems over the last months. Then I told him that I felt I had to resign. He said that, as a friend, he had to agree that it was the best thing. He said that if I decided to fight it through to the Senate I would be picked to death and further dishonored in a trial, and the foreign policy of the nation might not be able to survive such a situation. It was one thing for the President to be under political attack as I had been for the last two years; it was quite another thing, he said, for the President to be in the dock for half a year with his chances for survival in office dubious at best.

I told him that I totally agreed with his appraisal and thanked him for his loyal friendship.

After Kissinger had left, I asked Bill Timmons for a report on the latest congressional defections. It was every bit as bad as I expected it would be. Two days earlier we had estimated that I could almost count on having the thirty-four votes I would need to avoid conviction in the Senate. Today, Timmons said, there were only seven men in the Senate I could count on to be with me if I decided to stay and fight. He said that as the party's former standardbearer, Barry Goldwater had been asked by the Republican congressional leaders to bring me personally their assessment of how hopeless the situation was. I told Haig to make arrangements for Goldwater to see me on Wednesday afternoon. We decided to invite Hugh Scott and John Rhodes to come with him.

Haig said that he had received a phone call from

Haldeman, who was strongly opposed to my resigning. If that was my irrevocable decision, however, Haldeman thought that it would be in my interest to grant him and the other Watergate defendants a full presidential pardon as my last act in office. To make this politically palatable he suggested that these Watergate pardons be combined with amnesty for all Vietnam draft dodgers. The next day I learned that John Ehrlichman had called Rose and Julie with a similar recommendation.

Before we could discuss this any further, Steve Bull came in to say that Rabbi Korff was waiting for his appointment. I had asked Ziegler to tell him that I had decided to resign and that he should not try to change my mind. Rabbi Korff summoned his usual eloquence and said that although he would accept whatever I decided, he felt obligated to say what he thought. "You will be sinning against history if you allow the partisan cabal in Congress and the jackals in the media to force you from office," he said. He spoke with the fire of an Old Testament prophet, but he saw that my mind was made up. He said that if I did resign, I owed it to my supporters to do it with my head high, and not just slip away.

When he left, I buzzed for Rose. I told her that I needed her help in telling the family that I did not want them to go through the agony of watching the television news broadcasts reporting more defections over the June 23 tape. There was no need for them to worry over something we could no longer do anything about. "Tell them that the whole bunch is deserting now and we have no way to lobby them or keep them," I said. I also asked her to tell them that my support was so low I could no longer govern, and that I was going to have to resign.

When Rose left, I took a yellow pad from the desk. At the top I wrote, "Resignation Speech." Working quickly, I filled several pages with notes and outlines.

I asked Haig and Ziegler to come over to the EOB. "Things are moving very fast now," I said, "so I think it should be sooner than later. I have decided on Thursday night. I will do it with no rancor and no loss of dignity. I will do it gracefully." Haig said that it would be an exit as worthy as my opponents were unworthy.

We fell silent. Finally I looked up at them and said,

"Well, I screwed it up good, real good, didn't I?" It was not really a question.

I gave them additional thoughts I wanted included in the first draft of my speech. They both wrote diligently as I dictated. I wanted to say that this had been a difficult time for all of us, and that the situation had now reached a point where it was clear that I did not retain the necessary support to conduct the business of government in a way that would assure that the best interests of the nation were served. I wanted to include a statement that I understood the motivations and considerations of those who were no longer able to stand with me, and that I would be eternally grateful to those who had.

Then the three of us walked from the EOB back to the White House. As we entered the street between the two buildings, reporters rushed out to watch us.

"One thing, Ron, old boy," I said, "we won't have to have any more press conferences, and we won't even have to tell them that either!"

When we reached the end of the Rose Garden, I looked at Haig's face. I suddenly saw how tired he was, how much all the political stress had taken out of this superb military man. "Buck up," I admonished him, and I put my arm around his shoulders.

We parted at the elevator. As I pressed the button, I turned to them and said, "It's settled then. It will be Thursday night."

Since Julie had prepared dinner for David's parents, who were in Washington for a visit, she and David were at their own apartment as I went up to meet the family in the Solarium. Tricia has described the day in her diary:

A day for tears. I could not control their flow. I did not even try.

Mama, Daddy, Rose, and I sat in Mama's room for a bit before dinner. The only emotionally sound one was Daddy.

In my room I began clearing our drawers of five years of memories and became shattered at the significance. I threw clippings, writing, mementos into boxes helter-skelter. Boxes which my tears sealed. I shall not open them again for years.

Rose in tears this afternoon told us (Mama, Julie, me) in

the Solarium that Daddy had irrevocably decided to resign. Now we must all be as stoical as is humanly possible, and show him that this action has our blessing, praise him for it, and show him we love him more than ever. We must not collapse in the face of this ordeal. We must not let him down.

The evening news reports that night were even worse than on Monday. Goldwater was now being quoted as having said privately, "You can only be lied to so often, and it's time to take a stand that we want out." Del Latta, who had been one of my strongest supporters on the House Judiciary Committee, said that when he heard the June 23 tape, he felt he had been run over by a truck.

I sat in the Lincoln Sitting Room thinking about the resignation speech until 2 A.M. When I walked into my bedroom, I found a note from Julie on my pillow. She must have slipped over from her apartment and put it there.

If anything could have changed my mind at this point, this would have done it. But my mind was made up past changing. Not because I was tired and fatigued, and certainly not because I had given up, but because I felt, deep down in my heart and mind, that I had made the decision that was best for the country. I took Julie's note and put it into my briefcase to make sure that it did not get lost in the massive move that was about to take place.

When I got to the Oval Office at ten o'clock on Wednesday morning, August 7, the countdown toward resignation was already proceeding smoothly. That morning Haig had told Jerry Ford to be ready to assume the presidency on very short notice. The first draft of the resignation speech was waiting on my desk. Ray Price had attached a short memo to it saying that the resignation, although sad, was necessary. He said that he hoped I would leave the White House as proud of my accomplishments there as he was proud to have been associated with me and to be my friend. He ended simply, "God bless you; and He will."

I took the speech and started over to the EOB office. As I walked through the West Wing I heard phones ringing in every office. The switchboard was deluged with calls from people who had stood by me through it all. Many had

Agust 6

Dear Daddy —

I love you. Whatever you do I will support. I am very proud of you.

Please wait a week or even ten days before you make this decision. Go through the fire just a little bit longer. You are so strong! I love you.

Julie

Millions support you.

written to me and my family. Some had collected signatures on petitions. Some had sent in money, hoping to contribute to my defense. They were calling to say that I must fight on. That decision, I had to repeat to myself again, was made. Now I did not want to know about these calls.

Staff members seemed to summon up an extra heartiness for their "Good morning, Mr. President!" as I passed by. I went out the West Basement door into the closed street that separates the White House from the Executive Office Building. The crowds waiting outside the iron fence surrounding the White House surged forward when I came into view. Ed Cox had called it a death watch, but I believed that there was more than simple curiosity involved, I felt that these people were drawn by the sense that history was about to happen, and they wanted to be nearby. I could sense the tension of the Secret Service agents, and I moved as quickly as possible up the broad stone stairs and into the office.

I placed a call to Bob Haldeman in California; I felt that I owed it to him to listen to his eleventh-hour plea. A few minutes later he was on the line. The familiar voice sounded energetic and unself-conscious. I told him that I had decided to resign. I said that as much as I was torn by the conflicting principles involved, I thought the country would be better off this way. He urged me to take more time and think it through again, but if I had made up my mind, he would like me to consider issuing a blanket pardon for all the Watergate defendants.

He said the country would be better off if Watergate did not drag on for more months and years with endless subpoenas and lawsuits. With the kind of detachment he used to have when he discussed revenue-sharing, he added that amnesty for Vietnam draft dodgers would deflect criticism of the Watergate pardons.

As he talked, my mind wandered back to the campaign days and the White House days, when his proud and brusque way of dealing with people had aroused fear in some and inspired loyalty in many others. I could not help but feel and share the despair that he must be feeling. I had hoped that after the 1974 election I would be in a position to grant pardons, but I had never foreseen all that would happen. I did not give him an answer.

I called Ziegler for an account of the morning news. He

said that Charles Sandman, hitherto one of my strongest defenders on the Judiciary Committee, had said that the June 23 tape was insurmountable and reckoned that I could command fewer than twelve votes in the whole House. He had said that he thought the Senate must vote to convict.

I had promised Julie that I would see Bruce Herschensohn, one of the most ardent loyalists on the staff. He was emotional as he argued against what he suspected was a course already in motion. His voice shook with conviction when he said that seventy-five years from now, when some young person was confronted with a difficult and seemingly hopeless duty, he should be able to look back and say, "President Nixon didn't give up and neither will I." He argued that the example of a President who faced his attackers and went down defending himself would better serve the American people than any immediate relief that the ending of Watergate would bring them.

I thanked Herschensohn for his frankness and said that he was probably right. The decision was not an easy one, but in a case like this perhaps there were no easy decisions, or even any good decisions, but only decisions that had to be made.

Tricia called and asked if she and Ed could come see me. She described our meeting in her diary:

> We lent our support to whatever Daddy decided to do. Because nothing had been announced publicly, we still wanted to caution him to be sure resignation was the only step to take. We were afraid that in a moment of weakness or discouragement he might make the wrong decision to bring an end to the unbearable harassment. But resignation would not be the end. He would be hounded habitually after leaving office—by trials, lawsuits, etc. We were afraid he would wake up the morning after leaving office feeling he had made a terrible mistake by resigning. Daddy has fought alone many times, almost alone many others. But there comes a point when fighting alone must come to mean fighting against yourself.

A little later Ed and David came in together and argued the case for waiting, even if only for a few days. I told them that I felt that executive authority would be so damaged by a vote of impeachment in the House and a long trial in the Senate that it would be almost impossible to govern.

Ed countered that the most important role for the President was in foreign affairs, and that even crippled by impeachment, I would be a lot stronger and more credible than Ford. He added that from a personal standpoint, my resignation would not accomplish anything. He had worked in the U.S. Attorney's office in New York, and he knew several people on the Special Prosecutor's staff. He said, "I know these people. They are smart and ruthless; they hate you. They will harass you and hound you in civil and criminal actions across this country for the rest of your life if you resign."

After Ed made his point about impeachment not ending my personal troubles, I said to him that this was just like a Greek tragedy: you could not end it in the middle of the second act, or the crowd would throw chairs at the stage. In other words, the tragedy had to be seen through until the end as fate would have it.

David agreed that if I had the personal will to see it through, I should do so. He responded forcefully when I mentioned the argument that I should resign for the good of the party. "You don't owe the party a damn thing," he said. "That was the way Grandad felt, and so should you. Do what you think is best for yourself, and what you think is best for the country." Before they left, they assured me that the family was ready for whatever happened, and would be behind me in whatever I decided to do.

It was after four o'clock. In less than an hour Goldwater, Scott, and Rhodes would arrive. I picked up the draft of the resignation speech again and wrote notes on the bottom of the first page:

> Insert: I have met with leaders of House and Senate, including my strongest supporters in both parties. They have unanimously advised me that because of Watergate matter, I do not and will not have support in Congress for difficult decisions affecting peace abroad and our fight against inflation at home, so essential to lives of every family in America.

Before I realized it, it was five o'clock. I called Steve Bull, who had greeted Goldwater and his colleagues in the West Lobby. "Take the boys into the office," I said, "and make them comfortable until I get over."

They were all seated when I arrived: Barry Goldwater, the former standard-bearer and now the silver-haired patriarch of the party; Hugh Scott, the Senate Republican Leader, and John Rhodes, the House Republican Leader. Over the years I had shared many successes and many failures with these men. Now they were here to inform me of the bleakness of the situation, and to narrow my choices. I pushed back my chair, put my feet up on the desk, and asked them how things looked.

Scott said that they had asked Goldwater to be their spokesman. In a measured voice Goldwater began, "Mr. President, this isn't pleasant, but you want to know the situation, and it isn't good."

I asked how many would vote for me in the Senate. "Half a dozen?" I ventured.

Goldwater's answer was maybe sixteen or perhaps eighteen.

Puffing on his unlighted pipe, Scott guessed fifteen. "It's pretty grim," he said, as one by one he ran through a list of old supporters, many of whom were now against me. Involuntarily I winced at the names of men I had worked to help elect, men who were my friends.

Goldwater said that I might beat Article I and Article III on the House floor, but that even he was leaning toward voting for Article II.

I glanced up at the Presidential Seal set into the ceiling and said, "I don't have many alternatives, do I."

As I looked at their faces, Goldwater and Scott said nothing. Rhodes had not noticed that I had been making a statement rather than asking a question, and he earnestly replied that he did not want to tell the reporters waiting outside that he had discussed any specific alternatives with me.

"Never mind," I said, "there'll be no tears from me. I haven't cried since Eisenhower died. My family has been fine, and I'm going to be all right. I just want to thank you for coming up to tell me."

Scott looked so solemn as they were walking out that I said, "Now that old Harry Truman is gone, I won't have anybody to pal around with." He mustered a bit of a smile.

After the meeting I called Rose and asked her to tell the family that a final check of my dwindling support in Congress had confirmed that I had to resign. I asked her to tell them that Goldwater, Stennis, Scott, and Rhodes were all going to be voting for impeachment. My decision was irrevocable, and I asked her to suggest that we not talk about it anymore when I went over for dinner.

I went back to the Oval Office and asked Kissinger if he could come in. He was contained, quiet, somber. I told him that I had decided to resign the next night. We talked briefly about notifying foreign governments and about sending special messages to the leaders of China, the Soviet Union, and the Middle Eastern countries. Every nation would need reassurance that my departure from the scene would not mean a change in America's foreign policy. They would have little knowledge of Jerry Ford, so I wanted to let them know how strongly he had supported my foreign policy while he was in the House of Representatives and as Vice President, and how they could count on him to continue that policy as President.

For a minute I tried to imagine the different reactions to these cables. What would Chou think in his office in Peking? And how would Chairman Mao take the news, sitting there in the cluttered book-lined study where we had talked just two years ago?

In Moscow it would be the middle of the night when the word arrived. I did not envy the night duty officer who would have to decide whether to wake Brezhnev or wait and give him the news when he got up. Brezhnev had placed so much emphasis on the importance of our personal relationship as the foundation of détente that I suspected his first instinct would be to assess what my resignation would do to his own situation and plan his reaction accordingly.

In Cairo and in Tel Aviv, in Damascus and Amman, the news also would arrive while the cities still slept. Eight weeks ago I had been hailed as a triumphal peacemaker and accorded unprecedented acclaim by their peoples. Now I was resigning the presidency because of a political scandal. How fragile would the peace that we had worked so hard to attain turn out to be?

My mind snapped back to the grim reality of the moment. "Henry," I said, "you know that you must stay here and carry on for Jerry the things that you and I have begun. The whole world will need reassurance that my leaving won't change our policies. You can give them that reassurance, and Jerry will need your help. Just as there is no question but that I must go, there really is no question but that you must stay."

After Kissinger left, I walked alone to the Residence. I had been afraid that this would be the most painful meeting of all. But I had underestimated the character and strength of my family. My wife and daughters remained an indomitable trio. Each one respected the opportunities public life had given her; and when the blows came, each reacted with dignity, courage, and spirit.

Everyone was gathered in the Solarium. Pat was sitting up straight on the edge of the couch. She held her head at the slightly higher angle that is her only visible sign of tension, even to those who know her. As I walked in, she came over and threw her arms around me and kissed me. She said, "We're all very proud of you, Daddy." Tricia was on the couch, with Ed sitting on the arm next to her. Julie sat in one of the bright yellow armchairs, tears standing in her eyes. David stood beside the chair with his hand on her shoulder. Rose, who is as close to us as family, sat on a large ottoman next to my yellow easy chair. I said, "No man who ever lived had a more wonderful family than I have."

I had arranged for Ollie Atkins to take some pictures. Someday, I said, we would be able to talk about this night, and then we would want to remember everything about it. I asked Pat to come down to the Rose Garden for a final photograph, but that was simply expecting too much. Tricia said, "I'll come with you, Daddy."

As we entered the Rose Garden, she took my arm just as she had done three years before when she was married there. Like me, and like my mother, Tricia seldom displays her inner emotions so that people can see them. She smiled

669

at me and looked as young and, if possible, more beautiful than on the day of her wedding.

Finally Ollie said, "I think that's enough, Mr. President." I turned and saw tears in his eyes. I said, "Ollie, keep your chin up!"

We went upstairs, and I asked that the dogs be brought in for the last pictures. No one felt much like posing, so Tricia suggested that we just form a line and link arms as we had done in one of our favorite family photographs taken in front of the Christmas tree in the Blue Room in 1971.

Before Ollie could move into position, Julie broke into tears. I knew that the only way we would get through this night would be to pretend a bravado we did not really feel, so I said that I would have to take over the designing of the photo. I elaborately positioned everyone, and, mercifully, Ollie was quick. After he had snapped some pictures, he turned his head away, but we could all see the tears streaming down his cheeks.

It was too much for Julie. She threw her arms around me sobbing, "I love you, Daddy," she said, and Ollie, through his own tears, captured that moment as well.

I still do not like to look at the pictures from that night. All I can see in them is the tension in the smiles, and the eyes brimming with tears.

No one had much appetite for our last dinner in the White House, so we just asked that trays be brought up to the Solarium. The important thing was that we were together. Because we were there together and so close to each other, it is one of the priceless moments that I will carry with me for the rest of my life. We tried to talk animatedly, even to laugh at the dogs and their comical begging for food. But mostly we ate in silence.

When we had finished, I went to the Lincoln Sitting Room to continue work on the resignation speech. I could even feel a kind of calm starting to settle in now that the family had been told.

•

Ziegler came over to discuss the arrangements for the speech. As we talked about the tremendous swings of fortune we had known over the past two years and about how tragic it was that everything should end so suddenly and so sadly, he recalled a famous quotation from Teddy Roosevelt

I had used often in my campaign speeches. It was the one in which TR had described the "man in the arena,"

> whose face is marred by dust and sweat and blood, who strives valiantly, who errs and comes short again and again because there is not effort without error and shortcoming, but who does actually strive to do the deed, who knows the great enthusiasms, the great devotions, who spends himself in a worthy cause, who at the best knows in the end the triumphs of high achievement and who at worst, if he fails, at least fails while daring greatly.

I decided that I would use this quotation in my resignation speech.

At nine o'clock I picked up the phone to see if Kissinger was still in the office and if he could come over. We talked for an hour about our present relationships with the Chinese and the Soviets, and about our problems in the Middle East, in Europe, and in other parts of the world. We reminisced about the decisions of the past five and a half years. For some reason the agony and the loss of what was about to happen became most acute for me during that conversation. I found myself more emotional than I had been at any time since the decision had been set in motion.

At one point Kissinger blurted out, "If they harass you after you leave office, I am going to resign as Secretary of State, and I am going to tell the world why!"

I told him that the worst thing that could happen to America and to all our initiatives to build a more peaceful world would be for him to resign after I had resigned. There was simply no one else on the horizon who could even shine his shoes, let alone fit into them.

I reminded him how, three years earlier, we had drunk a toast after we received the invitation to go to Peking. I walked down the dark hall to the family kitchen and brought back the same bottle of brandy. Once again we tipped our glasses and solemnly toasted each other. But after a sip we put our glasses down and left them unfinished on the table.

Just as Kissinger was about to leave, I took him from the Lincoln Sitting Room into the Lincoln Bedroom right next to it. In Lincoln's time, long before the West Wing had been built, this had been the President's office. It contains one of the five copies of the Gettysburg Address in Lincoln's own handwriting, as well as the desk he used at his summer White House—the Old Soldiers' Home in the District of Columbia.

I told Kissinger that I realized that, like me, he was not one to wear his religion on his sleeve. I said that we probably had different religious beliefs if we were to examine them in a strictly technical way, but that deep down I knew he had just as strong a belief in a Supreme Being—just as strong a belief in God—as I did. On an impulse I told him how every night, when I had finished working in the Lincoln Sitting Room, I would stop and kneel briefly and, following my mother's Quaker custom, pray silently for a few moments before going to bed. I asked him to pray with me now, and we knelt.

After Kissinger left, I went back to work on the speech. I wrote: "As a private citizen, I shall continue to fight for the great causes to which I have been dedicated throughout my service as congressman, senator, Vice President, and President—peace not just for Americans, but for all nations, prosperity, justice, and opportunity."

A President's power begins slipping away the moment it is known that he is going to leave: I had that in 1952, in 1960, in 1968. On the eve of my resignation I knew that my role was already a symbolic one, and that Gerald Ford's was now the constructive one. My telephone calls and meetings and decisions were now parts of a prescribed ritual aimed at making peace with the past; his calls, his meetings, and his decisions were already the ones that would shape America's future.

Ziegler arrived and described the technical arrangements for the resignation speech and the departure ceremony.

As we walked out of the Lincoln Sitting Room, I asked Manolo to go ahead of us and turn on all the lights. From the outside the second floor of the White House must have looked like the scene of a festive party.

672

Ziegler and I went into each room: the Queen's Bedroom, the Treaty Room, the Yellow Oval Room that Pat had just redecorated and which we had scarcely had a chance to enjoy.

"It's a beautiful house, Ron," I said, as we walked down the long hallway under the glow of the crystal chandeliers.

I asked Manolo to wake me at nine in the morning, and I started toward my room.

"Mr. President," Ziegler called, "it's the right decision."

I nodded. I knew.

"You've had a great presidency, sir," he said as he turned away.

Thursday, August 8, 1974, was the last full day I served as President of the United States. As on other mornings of my presidency, I walked through the colonnade that had been designed by Thomas Jefferson, through the Rose Garden, and into the Oval Office.

I called Haig in and told him that I wanted to veto the agricultural appropriations bill we had discussed in the Cabinet meeting on Tuesday, because I did not want Ford to have to do it on his first day as President. Haig brought the veto statement in, and I signed it. It was the last piece of legislation I acted on as President.

At eleven o'clock Steve Bull came in and said, "Mr. President, the Vice President is here."

I looked up as Jerry Ford came in, somber in his gray suit. His eyes never left me as he approached. He sat down at the side of the desk, and for a moment the room was filled with silence.

Then I said, "Jerry, I know you'll do a good job."

I have never thought much of the notion that the presidency makes a man presidential. What has given the American presidency its vitality is that each man remains distinctive. His abilities become more obvious, and his faults become more glaring. The presidency is not a finishing school. It is a magnifying glass. I thought that Jerry Ford would measure up well under that magnification.

We talked about the problems he would face as soon as

he became President in almost exactly twenty-four hours. I stressed the need to maintain our military strength and to continue the momentum of the peace initiatives in the Middle East. Above all, I said, we must not allow the leaders in Moscow or Peking to seize upon the traumatic events surrounding my resignation as an opportunity to test the United States in Vietnam or anywhere else in the world. We must not let the Communists mistakenly assume that executive authority had been so weakened by Watergate that we would no longer stand up to aggression wherever it occurred.

I said that I was planning to send messages to all the major world leaders that Jerry Ford had been one of the strongest supporters of my policies and that they could count on him to continue those policies with the same firmness and resolve.

Ford asked if I had any particular advice or recommendations for him. I said that as far as I was concerned, the only man who would be absolutely indispensable to him was Henry Kissinger. There was simply no one else who had his wisdom, his tenacity, and his experience in foreign affairs. If he were to leave after I resigned, I said, our foreign policy would soon be in disarray throughout the world. Ford said firmly that he intended to keep Kissinger on for as long as he would be willing to stay.

I also urged him to keep Haig as Chief of Staff, at least during the transition period. Haig, I assured him, was always loyal to the commander he served, and he would be an invaluable source of advice and experience in the days ahead when there would inevitably be a scramble for power within both the Cabinet and the White House staff.

I told Ford that I would always be available to give him advice at any time, but I would never interject myself in any way into his decision-making process. He expressed appreciation for this attitude and said that he would always welcome any of my suggestions, particularly in foreign affairs.

I do not think that Ford knew that he had not been my first choice for Vice President when Agnew resigned, or that he had come in fourth in the informal poll I had taken among Republican leaders. I knew that there were many who did not share my high opinion of Ford's abilities. But I had felt then that Jerry Ford was the right man, and that was why I chose him. I had no reason to regret that decision.

It was noon. It was time for him to go.

"Where will you be sworn in?" I asked as we walked to the door. He said that he had decided not to go to the Capitol because his former colleagues there might turn the occasion into some kind of celebration. I said that I planned to be gone by noon; if he liked, he could be sworn in in the White House, as Truman had been.

I told him about the call I had received from Eisenhower the night before I was inaugurated on January 20, 1969, when he had said that it would be the last time he could call me "Dick." I said, "It's the same with me. From now on, Jerry, you are Mr. President."

Ford's eyes filled with tears—and mine did as well—as we lingered for a moment at the door. I thanked him for his loyal support over the last painful weeks and months. I said that he would have my prayers in the days and years ahead.

After Ford left, I once again walked the familiar route to the EOB office. The West Wing was strangely quiet. Desks that had never been uncluttered were cleared. Only the steady ringing of the phones gave the place a sense of purpose, of life. Everything else seemed frozen.

Fred Buzhardt came in and showed me a letter from Haldeman's attorney, requesting a presidential pardon. Haldeman, ever the efficient Chief of Staff, had included a specially typed page to insert in my resignation speech announcing the pardon and proclaiming a Vietnam amnesty. I told Buzhardt to call the other lawyers after the speech and tell them that I had said no. It was a painful decision not to grant his request, but tying their pardon to the granting of amnesty to Vietnam draft dodgers was unthinkable. And to grant a blanket pardon to all those involved in Watergate would have raised the issue to hysterical political levels. I felt it was vital for the country that my resignation be a healing action, and in the climate then prevailing I was afraid that to couple resignation with a blanket Watergate pardon would vitiate its healing effect.

Haig and Ziegler joined us. Haig had just come from meeting with Jaworski to inform him that I was going to resign. I had told him that I wanted no bargaining with Jaworski. I would not be coaxed out of office by any special deals, or cajoled into resigning in exchange for leniency. I was not leaving from fear, and I would take my chances. "Some of the best writing in history has been done from prison," I said. "Think of Lenin and Gandhi."

Haig said Jaworski believed I had made the right decision, and from their conversation he got the impression that I had nothing further to fear from the Special Prosecutor. I said that, considering the way his office had acted in the past, I had little reason to feel reassured.

Frankly, it galled me that people might think that my decision had been influenced by anything as demeaning as the fear of prosecution, or that the Special Prosecutor and other attackers had forced me out of office. I did not care what else people thought as long as they did not think that I had quit just because things were tough.

I turned to Ziegler and said, "How can you support a quitter? You know, when I was a kid I loved sports. I remember running the mile in track once. By the time we reached the last fifty yards, there were only two of us straggling in for next to last place. Still, I sprinted those last yards just as hard as if I were trying for the first-place ribbon. I have never quit before in my life. Maybe that is what none of you has understood this whole time. You don't quit."

Rose came in to get my final changes for the resignation speech. She was going to type it on the special large-face typewriter we used so that I would not have to wear my glasses on television. She was wearing a pink dress and pink shoes in an attempt, I knew, to defy the darkness of the day.

She said that the family had discussed it, and they wanted to be in the Oval Office when I delivered the speech so that the whole world could see they were with me. I said it was simply out of the question, because I would not be able to get through the speech without breaking up if they were even nearby. She said that they had anticipated my feeling, and so at least wanted to be in the next room when I spoke. I asked her to explain that this was something I would have to do alone, and, as a favor to me, to ask them to stay in the Residence and watch the speech from there.

She said that she also thought I should know that Air Force Colonel Theodore Guy, the head of the POW organization, had called in tears, saying that Rose must not let me resign. I had not given up on them, he had said, and they would not give up on me.

That afternoon I wanted to go from the EOB office back to the White House without any of the usual groups of staff or press or police watching or taking photographs. Ziegler carried out my wishes completely, and we saw no one as he and I made the short walk.

Packing boxes lined the halls of the Family Quarters. I shaved and showered and then picked out the suit and tie that I had worn in Moscow in 1972 when I delivered my speech on television to the Soviet people. It was slate blue, light in texture, and consequently cool under the hot television lights.

I went back to the EOB for a brief meeting with the congressional leaders to inform them officially that I had decided to resign.

I wanted it to be easy for them, and dignified. These men were veterans, and they knew that the coming and going of Presidents, whatever the individual or personal consequences, is not the only thing that matters to the country.

They were right on time, at 7:30 P.M. Carl Albert, the Speaker of the House, was the first to enter.

Before I said a word he blurted out, "I hope you know, Mr. President, that I have nothing to do with this whole resignation business." I said, "I understand, Carl." We talked about coming to Capitol Hill together in the same freshman class in 1947.

I told them all that I had appreciated their support on many issues through the years, and that I was especially grateful for their support during the last Soviet Summit, when I knew that partisan pressures and temptations had been very great. I said that I had always respected them when they had opposed my policies. I was looking directly at Mike Mansfield when I said this, but he did not react at all. He just sat there in a more dour mood than usual, puffing on his pipe. I said, "Mike, I will miss our breakfasts together," and he nodded, but without much responsiveness. Hugh Scott was cordial and more sympathetic than Mansfield. John Rhodes played his usual pleasant but noncommittal role.

Jim Eastland was the only one who seemed really to share my pain. As a Southerner and a conservative, he was always one of the most underestimated men in the Senate. Throughout my career he had been one of my most trusted counselors. In his face was a look of understanding that spoke more than volumes of words.

Finally I rose and put my arm on Carl Albert's shoulder. "I'll miss our breakfasts, too, Carl," I said.

We said goodbye, and they left.

I took a look around the office. My eyes ran over the familiar elephants, the gavels, the framed cartoons and plaques, the books, and the pictures of Pat and Tricia and Julie. I walked out and closed the door behind me. I knew that I would not be back there again.

I walked quickly into the Cabinet Room. Forty-six men were crowded around the table and in the chairs along the walls. Forty-six friends and colleagues in countless causes over three decades. Some of these men had already been in the House for years before I arrived as a freshman from Whittier; some of them had arrived with me in 1947, full of hope and dreams and plans for America. Together over the past five and a half years we had worked together time and again to form the slim but sturdy coalitions that repeatedly beat back the Goliath of liberal Democrats and liberal Republicans in the Senate and the House.

I started to talk about the great moments we had shared together. Without them, I said, it would have been impossible for me to take the initiatives that led to the new relationships with China and Russia, to progress toward peace in the Middle East, and, above all, to the ending of the war in Vietnam on an honorable basis and the return of our POWs.

I said that I wanted to stay and fight, but that a six-month trial in the Senate was too long for the country. I said that a full-time President would be needed now for the tough calls that would be coming up. The presidency is bigger than any man, I said, bigger than any individual

President, and even bigger than their great loyalty. Now it was Jerry Ford they must support with their votes, their affection, and their prayers.

The emotional level in the room was almost unbearable. I could see that many were crying. I looked at my watch. It was approaching 8:30. I had been talking for almost half an hour. When I heard Les Arends, one of my closest and dearest friends, sobbing with grief, I could no longer control my own emotions, and I broke into tears.

"I just hope that I haven't let you down," I said, as I tried to stand up. Everyone was jammed together so tightly that my chair would not move, and Bill Timmons had to pull it back for me. I left the room.

A few minutes later Haig came into the small office next to the Oval Office where I was looking over my speech. He had witnessed the scene in the Cabinet Room, and he was concerned that I might not be able to get through the broadcast. I said, "Al, I'm sorry I cracked up a bit in there, but when I see other people cry, particularly when they are crying for someone else rather than themselves, it just gets to me. I'll be all right now, so there's nothing to worry about."

He said, "Mr. President, the whole group was deeply touched. I know you are going to be able to make a great speech tonight." He left the room, and I sat there by myself.

Two minutes before nine o'clock I went into the Oval Office. I sat in my chair behind the desk while the technicians adjusted the lighting and made their voice check.

At forty-five seconds after nine, the red light on the camera facing my desk went on—it was time to speak to America and the world.

I began by saying how difficult it was for me to leave the battle unfinished, but my lack of congressional support would paralyze the nation's business if I decided to fight on.

In the past few days . . . it has become evident to me that I no longer have a strong enough political base in the Congress to justify continuing that effort. As long as there was such a base, I felt strongly that it was necessary to see the constitutional process through to its conclusion, that to do otherwise would be unfaithful to the spirit of that deliberately difficult process, and a dangerously destabilizing precedent for the future.

But with the disappearance of that base, I now believe that the constitutional purpose has been served, and there is no longer a need for the process to be prolonged.

Then I came to the most difficult sentence I shall ever have to speak. Looking directly into the camera, I said,

Therefore, I shall resign the presidency effective at noon tomorrow.

I continued:

By taking this action, I hope that I will have hastened the start of that process of healing which is so desperately needed in America.

I regret deeply any injuries that may have been done in the course of the events that led to this decision. I would say only that if some of my judgments were wrong—and some were wrong—they were made in what I believed at the time to be in the best interest of the nation.

I talked briefly about America and about the world. I talked about my own attempts in twenty-five years of public life to fight for what I believed in. I recalled that in my first inaugural address I had pledged to consecrate myself and my energies to the cause of peace among nations. I went on:

I have done my very best in all the days since to be true to that pledge. As a result of these efforts, I am confident that the world is a safer place today, not only for the people of America, but for the people of all nations, and that all of our children have a better chance than before of living in peace rather than dying in war.

This, more than anything, is what I hoped to achieve when I sought the presidency. This, more than anything, is what I hope will be my legacy to you, to our country, as I leave the presidency.

Throughout the speech I looked down at the pages of the text, but I did not really read it. That speech was truly in my heart. At the end, I said: "To have served in this office is to have felt a very personal sense of kinship with each and every American. In leaving it, I do so with this prayer: May God's grace be with you in all the days ahead."

The red light blinked off. One by one the blinding television lights were switched off. I looked up and saw the technicians respectfully standing along the wall, pretending that they were not waiting for me to leave so that they could dismantle their equipment. I thanked them and left the Oval Office.

Kissinger was waiting for me in the corridor. He said, "Mr. President, after most of your major speeches in this office we have walked together back to your house. I would be honored to walk with you again tonight."

As we walked past the dark Rose Garden, Kissinger's voice was low and sad. He said that he thought that historically this would rank as one of the great speeches and that history would judge me one of the great Presidents. I turned to him and said, "That depends, Henry, on who writes the history." At the door of the Residence I thanked him and we parted.

I quickly headed for the elevator that would take me to the Family Quarters. The long hall was dark and the police and Secret Service had mercifully been removed or were keeping out of sight. When the doors opened on the second floor, the family was all waiting there to meet me. I walked over to them. Pat put her arms around me. Tricia. Julie. Ed. David. Slowly, instinctively, we embraced in a tender huddle, drawn together by love and faith.

We sat talking for a few minutes about the day and the speech. Suddenly I began to shake violently, and Tricia reached over to hold me. "Daddy!" she exclaimed, "the perspiration is coming clear through your coat!" I told them not to worry. I had perspired heavily during the speech, and I must have caught a chill walking over from the office. In a minute it had passed.

We talked about the initial reactions to the speech, most of which were favorable. Many of the television commentators and newspaper columnists spoke of it as a speech that was aimed at bringing the country together. But this turned out to be the briefest honeymoon of my entire political life; within a few hours came the second thoughts, negative and critical.

Finally I said that we should try to get some sleep because we had a long day ahead of us tomorrow. As we walked out into the hall, we could hear the sound of a crowd chanting outside. A tragicomic scene followed, described in Tricia's diary:

> On Pennsylvania Avenue voices of a crowd chanting were heard. Mama misinterpreted and thought the group was one of supporters when actually it consisted of the same people who throughout Daddy's presidency had hounded his every effort. Now they were singing "Jail to the Chief."
>
> Mama tried to propel Daddy towards the window so that he could see the crowd. Ed and I tried desperately to talk loudly so as to drown them out. We hoped Daddy would not hear their sick message. Even so, I am not sure this last injustice did not escape him.

In fact, I had been able to hear the crowds earlier, before the speech. I did not actually know which side they were on. I assumed they were against me, but I did not really care about the shouters, and they did not bother me.

I asked Manolo to bring some bacon and eggs to me in the Lincoln Sitting Room, and I placed phone calls to friends and supporters and staff members until around 1:30. To each I expressed my appreciation for his support, and I told each that I hoped I had not let him down.

There was a knock at the door and Manolo came in to see if there was anything I wanted before he went to bed. I asked him to turn out all the lights in the Residence. Just as last night had been a time for light, tonight was a time for darkness. A few minutes later I stepped out into the darkened corridor. I was not afraid of knocking into anything in the dark. This house had been my home for almost six years, and I knew every inch of it.

I woke with a start. With the blackout curtains closed I didn't know what time it was. I looked at my watch. It said four o'clock. I had been asleep for only two hours, but I was wide awake.

I put on my robe and decided to make myself something to eat.

To my surprise I found Johnny Johnson, one of the

White House waiters, in the kitchen. I said, "Johnny, what are you doing here so early?"

"It isn't early, Mr. President," he replied. "It's almost six o'clock!"

I looked at my watch again. It had stopped at four.

I told him that instead of having my usual orange juice, wheat germ, and glass of milk, this morning I would like something a little more substantial. I ordered my favorite breakfast of corned beef hash and poached eggs and asked him to bring it down to the Lincoln Sitting Room.

After finishing breakfast I took a yellow pad from my briefcase and began to think of something to say to the administration officials, Cabinet members, and White House staff, who would be coming to the East Room at 9:30 to say goodbye. After what I had been through during the last twenty-four hours, it was difficult to think of anything new to tell them.

There was a knock on the door, and Haig came in. Almost hesitantly, he said, "This is something that will have to be done, Mr. President, and I thought you would rather do it now."

He took a sheet of paper and put it on my desk. I read the single sentence and signed it:

I hereby resign the Office of President of the United States.

It would be delivered in a few hours, at 11:35 A.M. on the 2,027th day of my presidency.

After Haig left, I remembered something I had read in a biography of Theodore Roosevelt, and I asked one of the Residence staff to go over to the EOB office and bring me the books from the edge of my desk. I was sure that the TR book was among them. He came back with Herman Wouk's *The Winds of War*, Allen Drury's *The Throne of Saturn*, and *TR* by Noel Busch. I quickly found what I was looking for and put a marker in the place.

When I called Haig to say a final goodbye, he was in the middle of a staff meeting dealing with the problem of making a smooth transition between administrations. Five minutes later, however, he was standing at the door of the Lincoln Sitting Room.

"The hell with the staff meeting," he said. "I would rather spend these last few minutes with you." I said that words could not express my gratitude for everything he had done for me over the years, and I wished him the very best.

Soon it was time to join the family. David and Julie were waiting in the hall. They were not coming with us but would stay to supervise the shipping of our things to San Clemente. Tricia and Ed came out of their room and stood together, waiting for Pat.

She was wearing a pale pink and white dress, and she tried to smile when she saw us waiting. She was wearing dark glasses to hide the signs of two sleepless nights of preparations and the tears that Julie said had finally come that morning. I knew how much courage she had needed to carry her through the days and night of preparations for this abrupt departure. Now she would not receive any of the praise she deserved. There would be no round of farewell parties by congressional wives, no testimonials, no tributes. She had been a dignified, compassionate First Lady. She had given so much to the nation and so much to the world. Now she would have to share my exile. She deserved so much more.

Manolo came over and said that the residence staff had lined up to say goodbye. I gave a little talk to them, saying that I had been in the great palaces of Europe and Asia and had visited with hundreds of princes and prime ministers in houses of great antiquity and splendor. "But this," I said, "is the best house because this house has a great heart, and that heart comes from those who serve in it."

I said that we had not failed to notice the countless ways and times they had made every guest, whether a king or a retarded child, feel welcome in the President's house. Now they must take the same special care of President Ford and Mrs. Ford. "You're the greatest!" I said, as I shook hands with each of them.

It was time to go downstairs. I asked Ed if he would carry the TR book for me. I had decided to read the passage directly from it, and since there was no time to have it copied on the speech typewriter, for the first time I would have to wear my glasses in public.

Just after 9:30 we went to the elevator. As we rode down, Steve Bull described the arrangement of the East Room and told each member of the family where they were supposed to stand behind me on the platform during my speech. He mentioned that there would be three television cameras. At that news, Pat and Tricia became very upset. It was too much, they said, that after all the agony television had caused us, its prying eye should be allowed to intrude on this last and most intimate moment of all. "That's the way it has to be," I said. "We owe it to our supporters. We owe it to the people."

We stood for a moment steeling ourselves for the ordeal beyond the doors. Pat decided not to wear her dark glasses, and Eddie said that it was proper because this was not a moment to be ashamed of tears. I nodded to Bull, and the doors were opened.

Tricia described our entrance in her diary:

I took three consciously deep breaths to clear the light-headedness that had struck me. One—two—three. I said aloud, "Take three deep breaths." Mama and Julie did so.

As the doors of the hall swung open to the Grand Hall, its beauty was flooded with the startling intensity of the television lights. The warmth they generated surrounded us like a cocoon both pleasant and unpleasant, both comforting and stifling.

The Hall seemed overcrowded with humanity. There seemed to be an electricity in the air produced by the surrounding humanity—an electricity powerful enough to propel our little band forward.

Suddenly I was grabbed from behind. One of the maids (Viola, the laundress, I think) was out of control and sobbing hysterically. I was almost immune from her deep sorrow as I was beyond mere grief itself. I put my arm around her and whispered, "Take care of the new President and his family." Then I extricated myself, conscious of wanting to catch up to the rest of the family who were several steps ahead of me now.

There was a resonance of applause resounding through the House through all who really cared. "Ladies and Gentlemen, the President of the United States of America and Mrs. Nixon. Mr. and Mrs. Edward Cox. Mr. and Mrs. David Eisenhower." Normal. Thunderous applause. Scraping of chairs as people rose to their feet. "Hail to the Chief."

Platform ahead. Step up onto platform. Find name marker. Do not trip over wires. Stand on name marker. Reach for Mama's hand. Hold it. Applause. Daddy is speaking. People are letting tears roll down their cheeks. Must not look. Must not think of it now.

The words themselves were unique for Daddy because they were from the heart. Not formal. I was glad that at the end people at last had a glimpse of the fine person he had always been. At last the "real" Nixon was being revealed as only he could reveal himself. By speaking from the heart people could finally know Daddy. It was not too late.

The emotion in the room was overpowering. For several minutes I could not quiet the applause. After I started to talk, I began to look around. Many of the faces were filled with tears. To this day I can remember seeing Herb Stein, a man I had always respected for his cool and analytical intellectual ability and his dry sense of humor, with tears streaming down his face. I knew that if I continued to look around this way, it would be difficult for me to contain my own emotions. So I turned away from the red eyes of the crowd and looked only at the red eye of the camera, talking to all the nation.

By now I was fighting back a flood tide of emotions. Last night had been the formal speech for history, but now I had a chance to talk personally and intimately to these people who had worked so hard for me and whom I had let down so badly.

This was the nightmare end of a long dream. I had come so far from the little house in Yorba Linda to this great house in Washington. I thought about my parents, and I tried to tell these people about them.

I remember my old man. I think that they would have called him sort of a little man, common man. He didn't consider himself that way. You know what he was? He was a streetcar motorman first, and then he was a farmer, and then he had a lemon ranch. It was the poorest lemon ranch in California, I can assure you. He sold it before they found oil on it.

And then he was a grocer. But he was a great man because he did his job, and every job counts up to the hilt, regardless of what happens.

Nobody will ever write a book, probably, about my mother. Well, I guess all of you would say this about your mother: my mother was a saint. And I think of her, two boys dying of tuberculosis, nursing four others in order that she could take care of my older brother for three years in Arizona, and seeing each of them die, and when they died, it was like one of her own.

Yes, she will have no books written about her. But she was a saint.

I had wanted to find a new way of saying something to the White House staff that would inspire them. I had tried to find a way of urging them, without any platitudes, to look beyond this painful moment. I took the book from Ed, put on my glasses and read the moving tribute Theodore Roosevelt had written when his first wife died:

She was beautiful in face and form and lovelier still in spirit. . . . When she had just become a mother, when her life seemed to be just begun and when the years seemed so bright before her, then by a strange and terrible fate death came to her. And when my heart's dearest died, the light went from my life forever.

Putting down the book, I said that TR had written these words when he was in his twenties. He thought the light had gone out of his life forever. But he went on, and he not only became President, but after that he served his country for many years, always in the arena, always vital. I said that his experience should be an example for everyone to remember.

We think sometimes when things happen that don't go the right way; we think that when you don't pass the bar exam the first time—I happened to, but I was just lucky; I mean, my writing was so poor the bar examiner said, "We have just got to let the guy through." We think that when someone dear to us dies, we think that when we lose an election, we think that when we suffer a defeat, that all is ended. We think, as TR said, that the light had left his life forever.

Not true. It is only a beginning, always. The young must know it; the old must know it. It must always sustain us, because the greatness comes not when things go always good for you, but the greatness comes and you are really tested when you take some knocks, some disappointments, when sadness comes, because only if you have been in the deepest valley can you ever know how magnificent it is to be on the highest mountain. . . .

Always give your best, never get discouraged, never be petty; always remember, others may hate you, but those who hate you don't win unless you hate them, and then you destroy yourself.

Finally it was over. We stepped down from the platform. People were clapping and crying as we went by.

Jerry and Betty Ford were in the Diplomatic Reception Room on the ground floor. As I entered the room, Ford stepped forward to meet me. We shook hands.

"Good luck, Mr. President," I said to him. "As I told you when I named you, I know the country is going to be in good hands with you in the Oval Office."

"Thank you, Mr. President," he replied.

Betty said, "Have a nice trip, Dick."

We walked out under the canopy and started down the long red carpet that led to the steps of *Army One*, the presidential helicopter. Then we were there, quickly shaking hands with Jerry—Pat embracing Betty—kissing Julie—saying goodbye to David. Then I was there alone, Pat, Ed, and Tricia already inside, standing at the top of the steps in the doorway, turning, looking back one last time.

The memory of that scene for me is like a frame of film forever frozen at that moment: the red carpet, the green lawn, the white house, the leaden sky. The starched uniforms and polished shoes of the honor guard. The new President and his First Lady. Julie. David. Rose. So many friends. The crowd, covering the lawn, spilling out onto the balconies, leaning out of the windows. Silent, waving, crying. The elegant curve of the South Portico: balcony above balcony. Someone waving a white handkerchief from the window of the Lincoln Bedroom. The flag on top of the House, hanging limp in the windless, cheerless morning.

I raised my arms in a final salute. I smiled. I waved goodbye. I turned into the helicopter, the door was closed, the red carpet was rolled up. The engines started. The blades began to turn. The noise grew until it almost blotted out thought.

Suddenly, slowly we began to rise. The people on the ground below were waving. Then we turned. The White House was behind us now. We were flying low next to the Washington Monument. Another swing and the Tidal Basin was beneath us and the Jefferson Memorial.

There was no talk. There were no tears left. I leaned my head back against the seat and closed my eyes. I heard Pat saying to no one in particular, "It's so sad. It's so sad."

Another swing, and we were on course for Andrews, where *Air Force One* was waiting for the flight home to California.

Index

691

'The dog *looked* very mean,' said Walt.

'Now you've got the picture,' Garp told him. 'Every night was the same for that dog, and every day he was tied up in an alley beside the café. He was tied to a long chain, which was tied to the front axle of an old army truck, which had been backed into the alley and left there – for good. This truck didn't have any wheels.

'And you know what cinder blocks are,' Garp said. 'The truck was set on blocks so it wouldn't roll an inch on its axles. There was just enough room for the dog to crawl under the truck and lie down out of the rain and the sun. The chain was just long enough so that the dog could walk to the end of the alley and watch the people on the sidewalk and the cars in the street. If you were coming along the sidewalk, you could sometimes see the dog's nose poking out of the alley; that was as far as the chain would reach, and no farther.

'You could hold out your hand to the dog and he would sniff you, but he didn't like to be touched and he never licked your hand the way some dogs do. If you tried to pat him, he would duck his head and slink back into the alley. The way he stared at you made you think it would not be a very good idea to follow him into the alley, or to try very hard to pat him.'

'He would bite you,' Walt said.

'Well, you couldn't be sure,' Garp said. 'He never bit anyone, actually, or I never heard about it if he did.'

'You were there?' Walt said.

'Yes,' Garp said; he knew that the storyteller was always 'there.'

'Walt!' called Helen; it irritated Garp that she eavesdropped on the stories he told the children. 'That is what they mean by "a dog's life,"' Helen called.

But neither Walt nor his father appreciated her interruption. Walt said, 'Go on with the story. What happened to the dog?'

The responsibilities loomed for Garp, every time. What is

the instinct in people that makes them expect something to *happen*? If you begin a story about a person or a dog, something must be going to happen to them. 'Go on!' Walt cried impatiently. Garp, caught up in his art, frequently forgot his audience.

He went on. 'If too many people held out their hands for the dog to sniff, the dog would walk back down the alley and crawl under the truck. You could often see the tip of his black nose poking out from under the truck. He was either under the truck or at the sidewalk end of the alley; he never stopped in between. He had his habits and nothing disturbed them.'

'Nothing?' Walt asked, disappointed – or else worried that nothing was going to happen.

'Well, *almost* nothing,' Garp admitted, and Walt perked up. '*Something* bothered him; there was just one thing. It alone could make the dog furious. It was the only thing that could even make the dog bark. It really drove him crazy.'

'Oh sure, a *cat!*' cried Walt.

'A *terrible* cat,' said Garp in a voice that made Helen stop rereading *The Eternal Husband* and hold her breath. Poor Walt, she thought.

'Why was the cat terrible?' Walt asked.

'Because he teased the dog,' Garp said. Helen was relieved that this was, apparently, all that was 'terrible.'

'Teasing isn't nice,' Walt said, with knowledge; Walt was Duncan's victim in the area of teasing. *Duncan* should be hearing this story, Helen thought. A lesson about teasing is clearly wasted on Walt.

'Teasing is *terrible*,' Garp said. 'But this cat *was* terrible. He was an old cat, off the streets, dirty and mean.'

'What was his name?' Walt asked.

'He didn't have a name,' Garp said. 'Nobody owned him; he was hungry all the time, so he stole food. Nobody could blame him for that. And he had lots of fights with other cats, and nobody could blame him for that either, I suppose. He had only one eye; the other eye had been missing for so long that the hole had closed and the fur had grown over where the eye had been. He didn't have any ears. He must have had to fight all the time.'

'The poor thing!' Helen cried.

'Nobody could blame that cat for the way he was,' Garp said, 'except that he teased the dog. That was wrong; he didn't have to do that. He was hungry, so he had to be sneaky, and nobody took care of him, so he had to fight. But he didn't *have* to tease the dog.'

'Teasing isn't nice,' Walt said again. Very definitely Duncan's story, Helen thought.

'Every day,' said Garp, 'that cat would walk down the sidewalk and stop to wash himself at the end of the alley. The dog would come out from under the truck, running so hard that the chain wriggled behind him like a snake that's just been run over in the road. You ever seen that?'

'Oh sure,' Walt said.

'And when the dog got to the end of his chain, the chain would snap the dog's neck back and the dog would be tugged off his feet and land on the pavement of the alley, sometimes knocking his wind out or hitting his head. The cat would never move. The cat *knew* how long the chain was and he would sit there washing himself with his one eye staring at the dog. The dog went crazy. He barked and snapped and struggled against his chain until the owner of the café, his master, would have to come out and shoo the cat away. Then the dog would crawl back under the truck.

'Sometimes the cat would come right back, and the dog would lie under the truck for as long as he could stand it, which was not very long. He'd lie under there while the cat licked himself all over out on the sidewalk, and pretty soon you could hear the dog begin to whimper and whine, and the cat would just stare down the alley at him and go on washing himself. And pretty soon the dog would start to howl under the truck, and thrash around there as if he were covered with bees, but the cat would just go on washing himself. And finally the dog would lunge out from under the truck and charge up the alley again, snapping his chain behind him – even though he knew what would happen. He knew that the chain would rip him off his feet and choke him, and throw him on the pavement, and that when he got up the cat would still be sitting there, inches away, washing himself. And he'd bark himself hoarse until his master, or someone else, would shoo the cat away.

'That dog *hated* that cat,' Garp said.

'So do I,' Walt said.

'And so did I,' said Garp. Helen felt herself turn against the story – it had such an obvious conclusion. She said nothing.

'Go on,' Walt said. Part of telling a story to a child, Garp knew, is telling (or pretending to tell) a story with an obvious conclusion.

'One day,' said Garp, 'everybody thought the dog had finally lost his mind. For one whole day he ran out from under the truck and all the way up the alley until the chain jerked him off his feet; then he'd do it again. Even when the cat wasn't there, the dog just kept charging up the alley, throwing his weight against the chain and heaving himself to the pavement. It startled some of the people walking on the sidewalk, especially the people who saw the dog coming at them and didn't know that there *was* a chain.

'And that night the dog was so tired that he didn't pace around the café; he slept on the floor as if he were sick. Anyone could have broken into the café that night; I don't think that dog would have woken up. And the next day he did the same thing, although you could tell his neck was sore because he cried out every time the chain snapped him off his feet. And that night he slept in the café as if he were a dead dog who'd been murdered there on the floor.

'His master called a vet,' Garp said, 'and the vet gave the dog some shots – I guess to calm him down. For two days the dog lay on the floor of the café at nighttime and under the truck in the daytime, and even when the cat walked by on the sidewalk, or sat washing himself at the

end of the alley, that dog wouldn't move. That poor dog,'
Garp added.

'He was sad,' Walt said.

'But do you think he was *smart*?' Garp asked.

Walt was puzzled but he said, 'I *think* he was.'

'He was,' Garp said, 'because all the time he'd been running
against the chain, he'd been moving the truck he was tied
to – just a little. Even though that truck had sat there for
years, and it was rusted solid on those cinder blocks and the
buildings could fall down around it before that truck would
budge – *even so*,' Garp said, 'that dog made the truck *move*.
Just a little.

'Do you think the dog moved the truck *enough*?' Garp
asked Walt.

'I think so,' Walt said. Helen thought so, too.

'He needed just a few inches to reach that cat,' Garp
said. Walt nodded. Helen, confident of the gory outcome,
plunged back into *The Eternal Husband*.

'One day,' Garp said, slowly, 'the cat came and sat down
on the sidewalk at the end of the alley and began to lick
his paws. He rubbed his wet paws into his old ear holes
where his ears had been, and he rubbed his paws over his
old grown-together eye hole where his other eye used to be,
and he stared down the alley at the dog under the truck. The
cat was getting bored now that the dog wouldn't come out
anymore. And then the dog came out.'

'I think the truck moved enough,' Walt said.

'The dog ran up the alley faster than ever before, so that
the chain behind him was dancing off the ground, and the
cat never moved although *this* time the dog could reach
him. Except,' said Garp, 'the chain didn't *quite* reach.' Helen
groaned. 'The dog got his mouth over the cat's head but the
chain choked him so badly that he couldn't close his mouth;
the dog gagged and was jerked back – like before – and the
cat, realizing that things had changed, sprang away.'

'God!' Helen cried.

'Oh no,' Walt said.

'Of course, you couldn't fool a cat like that twice,' Garp said. 'The dog had one chance, and he blew it. That cat would never let him get close enough again.'

'What a terrible story!' Helen cried.

Walt, silent, looked as if he agreed.

'But something *else* happened,' Garp said. Walt looked up, alert. Helen, exasperated, held her breath again. 'The cat was so scared he ran into the street – without looking. No matter what happens,' Garp said, 'you don't run into the street without looking, do you, Walt?'

'No,' Walt said.

'Not even if a dog is going to bite you,' Garp said. 'Not *ever*. You *never* run into the street without looking.'

'Oh sure, I know,' Walt said. 'What happened to the cat?'

Garp slapped his hands together so sharply that the boy jumped. 'He was killed like that!' Garp cried. 'Smack! He was dead. Nobody could fix him. He'd have had a better chance if the dog had gotten him.'

'A car hit him?' Walt asked.

'A truck,' Garp said, 'ran right over his head. His brains came out his old ear holes, where his ears used to be.'

'Squashed him?' Walt asked.

'Flat,' said Garp, and he held up his hand, palm level, in front of Walt's serious little face. Jesus, Helen thought, it was Walt's story after all. *Don't run into the street without looking!*

'The end,' said Garp.

'Good night,' Walt said.

'Good night,' Garp said to him. Helen heard them kiss.

'*Why* didn't the dog have a name?' Walt asked.

'I don't know,' Garp said. 'Don't run into the street without looking.'

When Walt fell asleep, Helen and Garp made love. Helen had a sudden insight regarding Garp's story.

'That dog could never move that truck,' she said. 'Not an inch.'

'Right,' Garp said. Helen felt sure he had actually been there.

'So how'd you move it?' she asked him.

'I couldn't move it either,' Garp said. 'It wouldn't budge. So I cut a link out of the dog's chain, at night when he was patrolling the café, and I matched the link at a hardware store. The next night I *added* some links – about six inches.'

'And the cat never ran into the street?' Helen asked.

'No, that was for Walt,' Garp admitted.

'Of course,' Helen said.

'The chain was plenty long enough,' Garp said. 'The cat didn't get away.'

'The dog killed the cat?' Helen asked.

'He bit him in half,' Garp said.

'In a city in Germany?' Helen said.

'No, Austria,' Garp said. 'It was Vienna. I never lived in Germany.'

'But how could the dog have been in the war?' Helen asked. 'He'd have been twenty years old by the time you got there.'

'The dog wasn't in the war,' Garp said. 'He was just a dog. His *owner* had been in the war – the man who owned the café. That's why he knew how to train the dog. He trained him to kill anybody who walked in the café when it was dark outside. When it was light outside, anybody could walk in; when it was dark, even the master couldn't get in.'

'That's nice!' Helen said. 'Suppose there was a fire? There seems to me to be a number of drawbacks to that method.'

'It's a war method, apparently,' Garp said.

'Well,' Helen said, 'it makes a better story than the *dog's* being in the war.'

'You think so, really?' Garp asked her. It seemed to her that he was alert for the first time during their conversation. 'That's interesting,' he said, 'because I just this minute made it up.'

'About the owner's being in the war?' Helen asked.

'Well, more than that,' Garp admitted.

'What part of the story did you make up?' Helen asked him.

'All of it,' he said.

They were in bed together and Helen lay quietly there, knowing that this was one of his trickier moments.

'Well, *almost* all of it,' he added.

Garp never tired of playing this game, though Helen certainly tired of it. He would wait for her to ask: *Which* of it? Which of it is true, which of it is made up? Then he would say to her that it didn't matter; she should just tell him what she didn't *believe*. Then he would change that part. Every part she believed was true; every part she didn't believe needed work. If she believed the whole thing, then the whole thing was true. He was very ruthless as a storyteller, Helen knew. If the truth suited the story, he would reveal it without embarrassment; but if any truth was unsuccessful in a story, he would think nothing of changing it.

'When you're through playing around,' she said, 'I'd just be curious to know what *really* happened.'

'Well, *really*,' said Garp, 'the dog was a beagle.'

'A beagle!'

'Well, actually, a schnauzer. He *was* tied up in the alley all day, but not to an army truck.'

'To a Volkswagen?' Helen guessed.

'To a garbage sled,' Garp said. 'The sled was used to pull the garbage cans out to the sidewalk in the winter, but the schnauzer, of course, was too small and weak to pull it – at any time of the year.'

'And the café owner?' Helen asked. 'He was *not* in the war?'

'*She*,' Garp said. 'She was a widow.'

'Her husband had been killed in the war?' Helen guessed.

'She was a *young* widow,' Garp said. 'Her husband had been killed crossing the street. She was very attached to the dog, which her husband had given her for their first anniversary. But her new landlady would not allow dogs in her apartment, so the widow set the dog loose in the café each night.

'It was a spooky, empty space and the dog was nervous in there; in fact, he crapped all night long. People would stop and peer in the window and laugh at all the messes the dog made. This laughter made the dog more nervous, so he crapped more. In the morning the widow came early – to air out the place and clean up the messes – and she spanked the dog with a newspaper and dragged him cowering out into the alley, where he was tied up to the garbage sled all day.'

'And there was no cat?' Helen asked.

'Oh, there were lots of cats,' Garp said. 'They came into the alley because of the garbage cans for the café. The dog would never touch the garbage, because he was afraid of the widow, and the dog was *terrified* of cats; whenever there was a cat in the alley, raiding the garbage cans, the dog crawled under the garbage sled and hid there until the cat was gone.'

'My God,' said Helen. 'So there was no teasing, either?'

'There is always teasing,' Garp said, solemnly. 'There was a little girl who would come to the end of the alley and call the dog out to the sidewalk, except that the dog's chain wouldn't reach the sidewalk and the dog would yap! and yap! and yap! at the little girl, who stood on the sidewalk and called, "Come on, come on," until someone rolled down a window and yelled at her to leave the poor mutt alone.'

'You were there?' Helen said.

'*We* were there,' Garp said. 'Every day my mother wrote in a room, the only window of which faced that alley. That dog's yapping drove her nuts.'

'So *Jenny* moved the garbage sled,' Helen said, 'and the dog *ate* the little girl, whose parents complained to the police, who had the dog put to sleep. And *you*, of course, were a great comfort to the grieving widow, who was perhaps in her early forties.'

'Her late thirties,' Garp said. 'But that's not how it happened.'

'*What* happened?' Helen asked.

'One night, in the café,' Garp said, 'the dog had a stroke. A number of people claimed to have been responsible for scaring the dog so badly that they caused his stroke. There was a kind of competition in regard to this in the neighborhood. They were always doing things like creeping up to the café and hurling themselves against the windows and doors, shrieking like huge cats – creating a frenzy of bowel movements by the frightened dog.'

'The stroke *killed* the dog, I hope,' Helen said.

'Not quite,' Garp said. 'The stroke paralyzed the dog's hindquarters, so that he could only move his front end and wag his head. The widow, however, clung to the life of this wretched dog as she clung to the memory of her late husband, and she had a carpenter, with whom she was sleeping, build a little cart for the dog's rear end. The cart had wheels on it, so the dog just walked on his front legs and towed his dead hindquarters around on the little cart.'

'My God,' Helen said.

'You wouldn't believe the *noise* of those little wheels,' Garp said.

'Probably not,' said Helen.

'Mother claimed she couldn't hear it,' Garp said, 'but the rolling sound was so pathetic, it was worse than the dog's yapping at the stupid little girl. And the dog couldn't turn a corner very well, without skidding. He'd hop along and then turn, and his rear wheels would slide out beside him, faster than he could keep hopping, and he'd go into a roll. When he was on his side, he couldn't get up again. It seemed I was the only one to see him in this predicament – at least, *I* was always the one who went into the alley and tipped him upright again. As soon as he was back on his wheels, he'd try to bite me,' Garp said, 'but he was easy to outrun.'

'So one day,' Helen said, 'you untied the schnauzer, and he ran into the street without looking. No, excuse me: he *rolled* into the street without looking. And everyone's troubles were over. The widow and the carpenter were married.'

'Not so,' said Garp.

'I want the truth,' Helen said, sleepily. 'What happened to the damn schnauzer?'

'I don't know,' Garp said. 'Mother and I came back to this country, and you know the rest.'

Helen, giving in to sleep, knew that only her silence might get Garp to reveal himself. She knew that this story might be as made up as the other versions, or that the other versions might be largely true – even that *this* one might be largely true. Any combination was possible with Garp.

Helen was already asleep when Garp asked her, 'Which story do you like better?' But lovemaking made Helen sleepy, and she found the sound of Garp's voice, going on and on, enhancing to her drowsiness; it was her most preferred way to fall asleep: after love, with Garp talking.

This frustrated Garp. At bedtime his engines were almost cold. Lovemaking seemed to rev him up and rouse him to moods of marathon talk, eating, all-night reading, general prowling about. In this period he rarely tried to write, though he would sometimes write messages to himself about what he would write later.

But not this night. He instead pulled back the covers and watched Helen sleep; then he covered her again. He went to Walt's room and watched him. Duncan was sleeping at Mrs Ralph's; when Garp shut his eyes he saw a glow on the suburban horizon, which he imagined was the dreaded house of Ralph – in flames.

Garp watched Walt, and this calmed him. Garp relished having such close scrutiny of the child; he lay beside Walt and smelled the boy's fresh breath, remembering when Duncan's breath had turned sour in his sleep in that grown-up's way. It had been an unpleasant sensation for Garp, shortly after Duncan turned six, to smell that Duncan's breath was stale and faintly foul in his sleep. It was as if the process of decay, of slowly dying, was already begun in him. This was Garp's first awareness of the mortality of his son. There appeared with this odor the first discolorations and stains on Duncan's perfect teeth. Perhaps it was just that Duncan was Garp's firstborn child, but Garp worried more about Duncan than he worried about Walt – even though a five-year-old seems more prone (than a ten-year-old) to the usual childhood accidents. And what are *they*? Garp wondered. Being hit by cars? Choking to death on peanuts? Being stolen by strangers? Cancer, for example, was a stranger.

There was so much to worry about, when worrying about children, and Garp worried so much about everything; at times, especially in these throes of insomnia, Garp thought himself to be psychologically unfit for parenthood. Then he worried about *that*, too, and felt all the more anxious for his children. What if their most dangerous enemy turned out to be *him*?

He soon fell asleep beside Walt, but Garp was a fearful dreamer; he was not asleep for long. Soon he was moaning; his armpit hurt. He woke up suddenly, Walt's little fist was snagged in his armpit hair. Walt was moaning, too. Garp untangled himself from the whimpering child, who seemed to Garp to be suffering the same dream Garp had suffered – as if Garp's trembling body had communicated Garp's dream to Walt. But Walt was having his own nightmare.

It would not have occurred to Garp that his instructional story of the war dog, the teasing cat, and the inevitable killer truck could have been terrifying to Walt. But in his dream Walt saw the great abandoned army truck, more the size and shape of a tank, guns and inexplicable tools and evil-looking attachments all over it – the windshield was a slit no bigger than a letter slot. It was all black, of course.

The dog who was tied to the truck was the size of a pony, though leaner and much more cruel. He was loping, in slow motion, toward the end of the alley, his weak-looking chain spiraling behind him. The chain hardly looked strong enough to hold back the dog. At the end of the alley, with his legs all buttery and stumbling over himself, hopelessly clumsy and unable to flee, little Walt bumbled in circles, but he couldn't seem to get himself *going* – to get himself away from that terrible dog. When the chain snapped, the great truck lurched forward as if someone had started it, and the dog was on him. Walt grabbed the dog's fur, sweaty and coarse (his father's armpit), but somehow he lost his grip. The dog was at his throat but Walt was running again, into the street, where trucks like the abandoned army truck rolled heavily past, their massive rear wheels in rows stacked together like giant doughnuts on their sides. And because of the mere gun slits (for windshields) the drivers couldn't see, of course; they couldn't see little Walt.

Then his father kissed him and Walt's dream slipped away, for now. He was somewhere safe again; he could smell his father and feel his father's hands, and he heard his father say, 'It's just a dream, Walt.'

In Garp's dream, he and Duncan had been riding on an airplane. Duncan had to go to the bathroom. Garp pointed down the aisle; there were doors down there, a small kitchen, the pilot's cabin, the lavatory. Duncan wanted to be taken there, to be shown *which* door, but Garp was cross with him.

'You're ten years old, Duncan,' Garp said. 'You can read. Or ask the stewardess.' Duncan crossed his knees and sulked. Garp shoved the child into the aisle. 'Grow up, Duncan,' he said. 'It's one of those doors down there. Go on.'

Moodily, the child walked down the aisle toward the doors. A stewardess smiled at him and rumpled his hair as he passed her, but Duncan, typically, would ask nothing. He got to the end of the aisle and glared back at Garp; Garp waved to him, impatiently. Duncan shrugged his shoulders, helplessly. *Which* door?

Exasperated, Garp stood up. '*Try* one!' he shouted down the aisle to Duncan, and people looked at Duncan standing there. Duncan was embarrassed and opened a door immediately – the one nearest him. He gave a quick, surprised, but uncritical look back to his father before he seemed to be drawn through the door he'd opened. The door slammed itself after Duncan. The stewardess screamed. The plane gave a little dip in altitude, then corrected itself. Everyone looked out the windows; some people fainted, some threw up. Garp ran down the aisle, but the pilot and another official-looking person prevented Garp from opening the door.

'It should always be kept locked, you stupid bitch!' the pilot shouted to the sobbing stewardess.

'I thought it *was* locked!' she wailed.

'Where's it go?' Garp cried. '*God*, where's it go?' He saw that nothing was written on any of the doors.

'I'm sorry, sir,' the pilot said. 'It couldn't be helped.' But Garp shoved past him, he bent a plainclothesman against the back of a seat, he smacked the stewardess out of the aisle. When he opened the door, Garp saw that it went outside – into the rushing sky – and before he could cry aloud for Duncan, Garp was sucked through the open door and into the heavens, where he hurtled after his son.

11

Mrs Ralph

If Garp could have been granted one vast and naïve wish, it would have been that he could make the world *safe*. For children and for grown-ups. The world struck Garp as unnecessarily perilous for both.

After Garp and Helen made love, and Helen fell asleep – after the dreams – Garp got dressed. When he sat on his bed to tie his track shoes, he sat on Helen's leg and woke her up. She reached out her hand to touch him, then felt his running shorts.

'Where are you going?' she asked him.

'To check on Duncan,' he said. Helen stretched up on her elbows, she looked at her watch. It was after one in the morning and she knew Duncan was at Ralph's house.

'*How* are you going to check on Duncan?' she asked Garp.

'I don't know,' Garp said.

Like a gunman hunting his victim, like the child molester the parent dreads, Garp stalks the sleeping spring suburbs, green and dark; the people snore and wish and dream, their lawn mowers at rest; it is too cool for their air conditioners to be running. A few windows are open, a few refrigerators are humming. There is the faint, trapped warble from some televisions tuned in to *The Late Show*, and the blue-gray glow from the picture tubes throbs from a few of the houses. To Garp this glow looks like cancer, insidious and numbing, putting the world to sleep. Maybe television *causes* cancer, Garp thinks; but his real irritation is a *writer's* irritation: he knows that wherever the TV glows, there sits someone who isn't *reading*.

Garp moves lightly along the street; he wants to meet no one. His running shoes are loosely laced, his track shorts flap; he hasn't worn a jock because he hasn't planned to run. Though the spring air is cool, he wears no shirt. In the blackened houses an occasional dog *snorfles* as Garp passes by. Fresh from lovemaking, Garp imagines that his scent is as keen as a cut strawberry. He knows the dogs can smell him.

These are well-policed suburbs and for a moment Garp is apprehensive that he might be caught – in violation of some unwritten dress code, at least guilty of carrying no identification. He hurries, convinced he's coming to Duncan's aid, rescuing his son from the randy Mrs Ralph.

A young woman on an unlighted bicycle almost collides with him, her hair floating behind her, her knees bare and shiny, her breath striking Garp as a startling mixture of a fresh-cut lawn and cigarettes. Garp crouches – she cries out and wobbles her bike around him; she stands up on her pedals and pumps fast away from him, not looking back. Perhaps she thinks he is a would-be exhibitionist – there with his torso and legs bare, ready to drop his shorts. Garp thinks she is coming from some place she shouldn't have been; she is headed for trouble, he imagines. But, thinking of Duncan and Mrs Ralph, Garp has trouble on his mind at this hour.

When Garp first sees Ralph's house, he believes it should be given the Light of the Block award; every window is glaring, the front door is open, the cancerous television is violently loud. Garp suspects Mrs Ralph is having a party, but as he creeps closer – her lawn festooned with dog messes and mangled sports equipment – he feels the house is deserted. The television's lethal rays pulsate through the living room, clogged with piles of shoes and clothes; and crammed against the sagging couch are the casual bodies of Duncan and Ralph, half in their sleeping bags, asleep (of course), but looking as if the television has murdered them. In the sickly TV light their faces look drained of blood.

But where is Mrs Ralph? Out for the evening? Gone to bed with all the lights on and the door open, leaving the boys to be bathed by the television? Garp wonders if she's remembered to shut the oven off. The living room is pockmarked with ashtrays; Garp fears for cigarettes still smoldering. He stays behind the hedges and slinks to the kitchen window, sniffing for gas.

There is a litter of dishes in the sink, a bottle of gin on the kitchen table, the sour smell of slashed limes. The cord to the overhead light, at one time too short, has been substantially lengthened by one sheer leg and hip of a woman's pair of panty hose – severed up the middle, the whereabouts of the other half unclear. The nylon foot, spotted with translucent stains of grease, dangles in the breeze above the gin. There is nothing burning that Garp can smell, unless there's a slow fire under the cat, who lies neatly on top of the stove, artfully spread between burners, its chin resting on the handle of a heavy skillet, its furry belly warmed by the pilot lights. Garp and the cat stare at each other. The cat blinks.

But Garp believes that Mrs Ralph hasn't the necessary concentration to turn herself into a cat. Her home – her *life* – in utter disarray, the woman appears to have abandoned ship, or perhaps passed out upstairs. Is she in bed? Or in the bathtub, drowned? And where is the beast whose dangerous droppings have made a minefield out of the lawn?

Just then there is a thunderous approach down the back staircase of a heavy, falling body that bashes open the stairway entrance door to the kitchen, startling the cat into flight, skidding the greasy iron skillet to the floor. Mrs Ralph sits bare-assed and wincing on the linoleum, a kimono-style robe wide open and roughly tugged above her thick waist, a miraculously unspilled drink in her hand. She looks at the drink, surprised, and sips it; her large, down-pointing breasts shine – they slouch across her freckled chest as she leans back on her elbows and burps. The cat, in a corner of the kitchen, yowls at her, complaining.

'Oh, shut up, Titsy,' Mrs Ralph says to the cat. But when she tries to get up, she groans and lies down flat on her back. Her pubic hair is wet and glistens at Garp; her belly, furrowed with stretch marks, looks as white and parboiled as if Mrs Ralph has been underwater for a long time. 'I'll get you out of here if it's the last thing I do,' Mrs Ralph tells the kitchen ceiling, though Garp assumes she's speaking to the cat. Perhaps she's broken an ankle and is too drunk to feel it, Garp thinks; perhaps she's broken her back.

Garp glides alongside the house to the open front door. He calls inside. 'Anybody home?' he shouts. The cat bolts between his legs and is gone outside. Garp waits. He hears grunts from the kitchen – the strange sounds of flesh slipping.

'Well, as I live and breathe,' says Mrs Ralph, veering into the doorway, her robe of faded flowers more or less drawn together; somewhere, she's ditched her drink.

'I saw all the lights on and thought there might be trouble,' Garp mumbles.

'You're too late,' Mrs Ralph tells him. 'Both boys are dead. I should never have let them play with that bomb.' She probes Garp's unchanging face for any signs of a sense of humor there, but she finds him rather humorless on this subject. 'Okay, you want to see the bodies?' she asks. She pulls him toward her by the elastic waistband of his running shorts. Garp, aware he's not wearing a jock, stumbles quickly after his pants, bumping into Mrs Ralph, who lets him go with a snap and wanders into the living room. Her odor confuses him – like vanilla spilled in the bottom of a deep, damp paper bag.

Mrs Ralph seizes Duncan under his arms and with astonishing strength lifts him in his sleeping bag to the mountainous, lumpy couch; Garp helps her lift Ralph, who's heavier. They arrange the boys, foot to foot on the couch, tucking their sleeping bags around them and setting pillows under their heads. Garp turns off the TV and Mrs Ralph stumbles through the room, killing lights, gathering ashtrays. They are like a married couple, cleaning up after a party. 'Night-y night!' Mrs Ralph whispers to the suddenly dark living room, as Garp trips over a hassock, groping his way toward the kitchen lights. 'You can't go yet,' Mrs Ralph hisses to him. 'You've got to help me get someone *out* of here.' She takes his arm, drops an ashtray; her kimono opens wide. Garp, bending to pick up the ashtray, brushes one of her breasts with his hair. 'I've got this lummox up in my bedroom,' she tells Garp, 'and he won't *go*. I can't make him leave.'

'A lummox?' Garp says.

'He's a real oaf,' says Mrs Ralph, 'a fucking wingding.'

'A wingding?' Garp says.

'Yes, please make him go,' she asks Garp. She pulls out the elastic waistband of his shorts again, and this time she takes an unconcealed look. 'God, you don't *wear* too much, do you?' she asks him. 'Aren't you cold?' She lays her hand flat on his bare stomach. 'No, you're not,' she says, shrugging.

Garp edges away from her. 'Who is he?' Garp asks, fearing he might get involved in evicting Mrs Ralph's former *husband* from the house.

'Come on, I'll show you,' she whispers. She draws him up the back staircase through a narrow channel that passes between the piled laundry and enormous sacks of pet food. No wonder she fell down here, he thinks.

In Mrs Ralph's bedroom Garp looks immediately at the sprawled black Labrador retriever on Mrs Ralph's undulating water bed. The dog rolls listlessly on his side and thumps his tail. Mrs Ralph mates with her dog, Garp thinks, and she can't get him out of her bed. 'Come on, boy,' Garp says. 'Get out of here.' The dog thumps his tail harder and pees a little.

'Not *him*,' Mrs Ralph says, giving Garp a terrific shove; he catches his balance on the bed, which sloshes. The great dog licks his face. Mrs Ralph is pointing to an easy chair at the foot of the bed, but Garp first sees the young man reflected in Mrs Ralph's dressing-table mirror. Sitting naked in the chair, he is combing out the blond end of his thin ponytail, which he holds over his shoulder and sprays with one of Mrs Ralph's aerosol cans. His belly and thighs have the same slick buttered look that Garp saw on the flesh and fur of Mrs Ralph, and his young cock is as lean and arched as the backbone of a whippet.

'Hey, how you doing?' the kid says to Garp.

'Fine, thank you,' Garp says.

'Get rid of him,' says Mrs Ralph.

'I've been trying to get her to just *relax*, you know?' the kid asks Garp. 'I'm trying to get her to just sort of go *with* it, you know?'

'Don't let him talk to you,' Mrs Ralph says. 'He'll bore the shit out of you.'

'Everyone's so tense,' the kid tells Garp; he turns in the chair, leans back, and puts his feet on the water bed; the dog licks his long toes. Mrs Ralph kicks his legs off the bed. 'You see what I mean?' the kid asks Garp.

'She wants you to leave,' Garp says.

'You her husband?' the kid asks.

'That's right,' says Mrs Ralph, 'and he'll pull your scrawny little prick off if you don't get out of here.'

'You better go,' Garp tells him. 'I'll help you find your clothes.'

The kid shuts his eyes, appears to meditate. 'He's really great at that shit,' Mrs Ralph tells Garp. 'All this kid's good for is shutting his damn eyes.'

'Where are your clothes?' Garp asks the boy. Perhaps he's seventeen or eighteen, Garp thinks. Maybe he's old enough for college, or a war. The boy dreams on and Garp gently shakes him by the shoulder.

'Don't touch me, man,' the boy says, eyes still closed. There is something foolishly threatening in his voice that makes Garp draw back and look at Mrs Ralph. She shrugs.

'That's what he said to me, too,' she says. Like her smiles, Garp notices, Mrs Ralph's shrugs are instinctual and sincere. Garp grabs the boy's ponytail and tugs it across his throat and around to the back of his neck; he snaps the boy's head into the cradle of his arm and holds him tightly there. The kid's eyes open.

'Get your clothes, okay?' Garp tells him.

'Don't touch me,' the boy repeats.

'I *am* touching you,' Garp says.

'Okay, okay,' says the boy. Garp lets him get up. The boy is several inches taller than Garp, but easily ten pounds lighter. He looks for his clothes but Mrs Ralph has already found the long purple caftan, absurdly heavy with brocade. The boy climbs into it like armor.

'It was nice balling you,' he tells Mrs Ralph, 'but you should learn to relax more.' Mrs Ralph laughs so harshly that the dog stops wagging his tail.

'You should go back to day one,' she tells the kid, 'and learn everything all over again, from the beginning.' She stretches out on the water bed beside the Labrador, who lolls his head across her stomach. 'Oh, cut it out, Bill!' she tells the dog crossly.

'She's very unrelaxed,' the kid informs Garp.

'You don't know shit about *how* to relax anybody,' Mrs Ralph says.

Garp steers the young man out of the room and down the treacherous back staircase, through the kitchen to the open front door.

'You know, *she* asked me in,' the boy explains. 'It was *her* idea.'

'She asked you to leave, too,' Garp says.

'You know, you're as unrelaxed as she is,' the boy tells him.

'Did the children know what was up?' Garp asks him. 'Were they asleep when you two went upstairs?'

'Don't worry about the kids,' the boy says. 'Kids are beautiful, man. And they know much more than grown-ups think they know. Kids are just perfect people until grown-ups get their hands on them. The kids were just fine. Kids are *always* just fine.'

'You *have* kids?' Garp can't help but mutter; until now Garp has felt great patience toward the young man, but Garp isn't patient on the subject of children. He accepts no other authority there. 'Good-bye,' Garp tells the boy. 'And don't come back.' He shoves him, but lightly, out the open door.

'Don't push me!' the kid shouts, but Garp ducks under the punch and comes up with his arms locked around the kid's waist; to Garp it feels that the kid weighs seventy-five, maybe eighty pounds, though of course he's heavier than that. He bear-hugs the boy and pins his arms behind his back; then he carries him out to the sidewalk. When the kid stops struggling, Garp puts him down.

'You know where to go?' Garp asks him. 'Do you need any directions?' The kid breathes deeply, feels his ribs. 'And don't tell your friends where they can come sniffing around after it,' Garp says. 'Don't even use the phone.'

'I don't even know her name, man,' the kid whines.

'And don't call me "man" again,' says Garp.

'Okay, man,' the kid says. Garp feels a pleasant dryness in his throat, which he recognizes as his readiness to touch someone, but he lets the feeling pass.

'Please walk away from here,' Garp says.

A block away, the boy calls, 'Good-bye, man!' Garp knows how quickly he could run him down; anticipation of such a comedy appeals to him, but it would be disappointing if the boy weren't scared and Garp feels no pressing need to hurt him. Garp waves good-bye. The boy raises his middle finger and walks away, his silly robe dragging – an early Christian lost in the suburbs.

Look out for the lions, kid, Garp thinks, sending a blessing of protection after the boy. In a few years, he knows, Duncan will be that age; Garp can only hope that he'll find it easier to communicate with Duncan.

Back inside, Mrs Ralph is crying. Garp hears her talking

to the dog. 'Oh, Bill,' she sobs. 'I'm sorry I abuse you, Bill. You're so nice.'

'Good-bye!' Garp calls up the stairs. 'Your friend's gone, and I'm going too.'

'Chickenshit!' yells Mrs Ralph. 'How can you leave me like this?' Her wailing grows louder; soon, Garp thinks, the dog will start to bay.

'What can I do?' Garp calls up the stairs.

'You could at least stay and talk to me!' Mrs Ralph shouts. 'You goody-goody chickenshit wingding!'

What's a wingding? Garp wonders, navigating the stairs.

'You probably think this happens to me all the time,' says Mrs Ralph, in utter rumplement upon the water bed. She sits with her legs crossed, her kimono tight around her, Bill's large head in her lap.

Garp, in fact, *does* think so, but he shakes his head.

'I don't get my rocks off by humiliating myself, you know,' Mrs Ralph says. 'For God's sake, sit down.' She pulls Garp to the rocking bed. 'There's not enough water in the damn thing,' Mrs Ralph explains. 'My husband used to fill it all the time, because it leaks.'

'I'm sorry,' Garp says. The marriage-counsel man.

'I hope you never walk out on *your* wife,' Mrs Ralph tells Garp. She takes his hand and holds it in her lap; the dog licks his fingers. 'It's the shittiest thing a man can do,' says Mrs Ralph. 'He just told me he'd been faking his interest in me, "for years"! he said. And *then* he said that almost *any* other woman, young or old, looked better to him than I did. That's not very nice, is it?' Mrs Ralph asks Garp.

'No, it isn't,' Garp agrees.

'Please believe me, I never messed around with anyone until he left me,' Mrs Ralph tells him.

'I believe you,' Garp says.

'It's very hard on a woman's confidence,' Mrs Ralph says. 'Why shouldn't I try to have some fun?'

'You *should*,' Garp says.

'But I'm so *bad* at it!' Mrs Ralph confesses, holding her

hands to her eyes, rocking on the bed. The dog tries to lick her face but Garp pushes him away; the dog thinks Garp is playing with him and lunges across Mrs Ralph's lap. Garp whacks the dog's nose – too hard – and the poor beast whines and slinks away. 'Don't you hurt Bill!' Mrs Ralph shouts.

'I was just trying to help you,' Garp says.

'You don't help *me* by hurting *Bill*,' Mrs Ralph says. 'Jesus, is *every*one bananas?'

Garp slumps back on the water bed, eyes shut tight; the bed rolls like a small sea, and Garp groans. 'I don't know *how* to help you,' he confesses. 'I'm very sorry about your troubles, but there's really nothing I can do, is there? If you want to tell me anything, go ahead,' he says, his eyes still shut tight, 'but nobody can help the way you feel.'

'That's a cheerful thing to say to someone,' Mrs Ralph says. Bill is breathing in Garp's hair. There is a tentative lick at his ear. Garp wonders: Is it Bill or Mrs Ralph? Then he feels her hand grab him under his track shorts, and he thinks, coldly: If I didn't really *want* her to do that, why did I lie down on my back?

'Please don't do that,' he says. She can certainly feel he's not interested, and she lets him go. She lies down beside him, then rolls away, putting her back to him. The bed sloshes violently as Bill tries to wriggle between them, but Mrs Ralph elbows him so hard in his thick rib cage that the dog coughs and abandons the bed for the floor.

'Poor Bill. I'm sorry,' Mrs Ralph says, crying softly. Bill's hard tail thumps the floor. Mrs Ralph, as if to complete her self-humiliation, farts. Her sobbing is steady, like the kind of rain Garp knows can last all day. Garp, the marriage counselor, wonders what could give the woman a little *confidence.*

'Mrs Ralph?' Garp says – then tries to bite back what he's said.

'What?' she says. 'What'd you say?' She struggles up to her elbows and turns her head to glare at him. She heard him, he knows. 'Did you say "Mrs Ralph"?' she asks him. 'Jesus, "Mrs Ralph"!' she cries. 'You don't even know my *name!*'

Garp sits up on the edge of the bed; he feels like joining Bill on the floor. 'I find you very attractive,' he mumbles to Mrs Ralph, but he's facing Bill. 'Really I do.'

'Prove it,' Mrs Ralph says. 'You goddamn liar. Show me.'

'I can't show you,' Garp says, 'but it's not because I don't find you attractive.'

'I don't even give you an erection!' Mrs Ralph shouts. 'Here I am half-naked, and when you're beside me – on my goddamn bed – you don't even have a respectable hard-on.'

'I was trying to conceal it from you,' Garp says.

'You succeeded,' Mrs Ralph says. 'What's my name?'

Garp feels he has never been so aware of one of his terrible weaknesses: how he needs to have people like him, how he wants to be appreciated. With every word, he knows, he is deeper in trouble, and deeper into an obvious lie. Now he knows what a wingding is.

'Your husband must be crazy,' Garp says. 'You look better to *me* than most women.'

'Oh, please stop it,' says Mrs Ralph. 'You must be sick.'

I *must* be, Garp agrees, but he says, 'You should have confidence in your sexuality, believe me. And more important, you should develop confidence in yourself in other ways.'

'There never were any other ways,' Mrs Ralph admits. 'I was never so hot at anything but sex, and now I'm not so hot at sex either.'

'But you're going to school,' Garp says, groping.

'I'm sure I don't know *why*,' Mrs Ralph says. 'Or is that what you mean by developing confidence in other ways?' Garp squints hard, wishes for unconsciousness; when he hears the water bed sound like surf, he senses danger and opens his eyes. Mrs Ralph has undressed, has spread herself out on the bed naked. The little waves are still lapping under her rough-tough body, which confronts Garp like a sturdy rowboat moored on choppy water. 'Show me you've got a hard-on and you can go,' she says. 'Show me your hard-on and I'll believe you like me.'

Garp tries to think of an erection; in order to do this, he shuts his eyes and thinks of someone else.

'You bastard,' says Mrs Ralph, but Garp discovers he is already hard; it was not nearly so difficult as he imagined. Opening his eyes, he's forced to recognize that Mrs Ralph is not without allure. He pulls down his track shorts and shows himself to her. The gesture itself makes him harder; he finds himself liking her damp, curly hair. But Mrs Ralph seems neither disappointed nor impressed with the demonstration; she is resigned to being let down. She shrugs. She rolls over and turns her great round rump to Garp.

'Okay, so you can actually get it up,' she tells him. 'Thank you. You can go home now.'

Garp feels like touching her. Sickened with embarrassment, Garp feels he could come by just looking at her. He blunders out the door, down the wretched staircase. Is the woman's self-abuse all over for *this* night? he wonders. Is Duncan safe?

He contemplates extending his vigil until the comforting light of dawn. Stepping on the fallen skillet and clanging it against the stove, he hears not even a sigh from Mrs Ralph and only a moan from Bill. If the boys were to wake up and need anything, he fears Mrs Ralph wouldn't hear them.

It's 3:30 A.M. in Mrs Ralph's finally quiet house when Garp decides to clean the kitchen, to kill the time until dawn. Familiar with a housewife's tasks, Garp fills the sink and starts to wash the dishes.

When the phone rang, Garp knew it was Helen. It suddenly occurred to him – all the terrible things she could have on her mind.

'Hello,' Garp said.

'Would you tell me what's going on, please?' Helen asked. Garp knew she had been awake a long time. It was four o'clock in the morning.

'Nothing's going on, Helen,' Garp said. 'There was a little trouble here, and I didn't want to leave Duncan.'

'Where is that woman?' Helen asked.

'In bed,' Garp admitted. 'She passed out.'

'From *what*?' Helen asked.

'She'd been drinking,' Garp said. 'There was a young man here, with her, and she wanted me to get him to leave.'

'So then you were alone with her?' Helen asked.

'Not for long,' Garp said. 'She fell asleep.'

'I don't imagine it would take very long,' Helen said, 'with her.'

Garp let there be silence. He had not experienced Helen's jealousy for a while, but he had no trouble remembering its surprising sharpness.

'Nothing's going on, Helen,' Garp said.

'Tell me what you're doing, exactly, at this moment,' Helen said.

'I'm washing the dishes,' Garp told her. He heard her take a long, controlled breath.

'I wonder why you're still there,' Helen said.

'I didn't want to leave Duncan,' Garp told her.

'I think you should bring Duncan home,' Helen said. 'Right now.'

'Helen,' Garp said. 'I've been good.' It sounded defensive, even to Garp; also, he knew he hadn't been quite good enough. 'Nothing has happened,' he added, feeling a little more sure of the truth of that.

'I won't ask you why you're washing her filthy dishes,' Helen said.

'To pass the time,' Garp said.

But in truth he had not examined what he was doing, until now, and it seemed pointless to him – waiting for dawn, as if accidents only happened when it was dark. 'I'm waiting for Duncan to wake up,' he said, but as soon as he spoke he felt there was no sense to that, either.

'Why not just wake him up?' Helen asked.

'I'm good at washing dishes,' Garp said, trying to introduce some levity.

'I know all the things you're good at,' Helen told him, a little too bitterly to pass as a joke.

'You'll make yourself sick, thinking like this,' Garp said. 'Helen, really, please stop it. I haven't done anything wrong.' But Garp had a puritan's niggling memory of the hard-on Mrs Ralph had given him.

'I've already made myself sick,' Helen said, but her voice softened. 'Please come home now,' she told him.

'And leave Duncan?'

'For Christ's sake, wake him up!' she said. 'Or *carry* him.'

'I'll be right home,' Garp told her. 'Please don't worry, don't think what you're thinking. I'll tell you everything that happened. You'll probably love this story.' But he knew he would have trouble telling her *all* this story, and that he would have to think very carefully about the parts to leave out.

'I feel better,' Helen said. 'I'll see you, soon. Please don't wash another dish.' Then she hung up and Garp reviewed the kitchen. He thought that his half hour of work hadn't made enough of a difference for Mrs Ralph to notice that any effort to approach the debris had even been begun.

Garp sought Duncan's clothes among the many, forbidding clots of clothing flung about the living room. He knew Duncan's clothes but he couldn't spot them anywhere; then he remembered that Duncan, like a hamster, stored things in the bottom of his sleeping bag and crawled into the nest with them. Duncan weighed about eighty pounds, plus the bag, plus his junk, but Garp believed he could carry the child home; Duncan could retrieve his bicycle another day. At least, Garp decided, he would not wake Duncan up inside Ralph's house. There might be a scene; Duncan would be fussy about leaving. Mrs Ralph might even wake up.

Then Garp thought of Mrs Ralph. Furious at himself, he knew he wanted one last look; his sudden, recurring erection reminded him that he wanted to see her thick, crude body again. He moved quickly to the back staircase. He could have found her fetid room with his nose.

He looked straight at her crotch, her strangely twisted navel, her rather small nipples (for such big breasts). He should have looked first at her eyes; then he might have realized she was wide-awake and staring back at him.

'Dishes all done?' asked Mrs Ralph. 'Come to say good-bye?'

'I wanted to see if you were all right,' he told her.

'Bullshit,' she said. 'You wanted another look.'

'Yes,' he confessed; he looked away. 'I'm sorry.'

'Don't be,' she said. 'It's made my day.' Garp tried to smile.

'You're too "sorry" all the time,' Mrs Ralph said. 'What a *sorry* man you are. Except to your wife,' Mrs Ralph said. 'You never once said you were sorry to *her*.'

There was a phone beside the water bed. Garp felt he had never so badly misread a person's condition as he had misread Mrs Ralph's. She was suddenly no drunker than Bill; or she had become miraculously undrunk, or she was enjoying that half hour of clarity between stupor and hangover – a half hour Garp had read about, but had always believed was a myth. Another illusion.

'I'm taking Duncan home,' Garp told her. She nodded.

'If I were you,' she said, 'I'd take him home, too.'

Garp fought back another 'I'm sorry,' suppressing it after a short but serious struggle.

'Do me one favor?' said Mrs Ralph. Garp looked at her; she didn't mind. 'Don't tell your wife *everything* about me, okay? Don't make me out to be such a pig. Maybe you could draw a picture of me with a little sympathy.'

'I have pretty good sympathy,' Garp mumbled.

'You have a pretty good *rod* on, too,' said Mrs Ralph, staring at Garp's elevated track shorts. 'You better not bring *that* home.' Garp said nothing. Garp the puritan felt he deserved to take a few punches. 'Your wife really looks after you, doesn't she?' said Mrs Ralph. 'I guess you haven't *always* been a good boy. You know what my husband would have called you?' she asked. 'My husband would have called you "pussy-whipped."'

'Your husband must have been some asshole,' Garp said. It felt good to get a punch in, even a weak punch, but Garp felt foolish that he had mistaken this woman for a slob.

Mrs Ralph got off the bed and stood in front of Garp. Her tits touched his chest. Garp was anxious that his hard-on might poke her. 'You'll be back,' Mrs Ralph said. 'Want to bet on it?' Garp left her without a word.

He wasn't farther than two blocks from Mrs Ralph's house – Duncan crammed down in the sleeping bag, wriggling over Garp's shoulder – when the squad car pulled to the curb and its police-blue light flickered over him where he stood *caught*. A furtive, half-naked kidnapper sneaking away with his bright bundle of stolen goods and stolen looks – and a stolen child.

'What you got there, fella?' a policeman asked him. There were two of them in the squad car, and a third person who was hard to see in the backseat.

'My son,' Garp said. Both policemen got out of the car.

'Where are you going with him?' one of the cops asked Garp. 'Is he all right?' He shined a flashlight in Duncan's face. Duncan was still trying to sleep; he squinted away from the light.

'He was spending the night at a friend's house,' Garp said. 'But it didn't work out. I'm carrying him home.' The policeman shined his light over Garp – in his running costume. Shorts, shoes with racing stripes, no shirt.

'You got identification?' the policeman asked. Garp set Duncan and the sleeping bag, gently, on someone's lawn.

'Of course not,' Garp said. 'If you give me a ride home, I'll show you something.' The policemen looked at each other. They had been called into the neighborhood, hours ago, when a young woman had reported that she was approached by an exhibitionist – at least, by a streaker. Possibly it was a matter of attempted rape. She had escaped him on a bicycle, she said.

'You been out here a long time?' one of the policemen asked Garp.

The third person, in the backseat of the police car, looked out the window at what was going on. When he saw Garp, he said, 'Hey, man, how you doing?' Duncan started to wake up.

'Ralph?' Duncan said.

One policeman knelt beside the boy and pointed the flashlight up at Garp. 'Is this your father?' the cop asked Duncan. The boy was rather wild-eyed; he darted his eyes from his father to the cops to the blue light flashing on the squad car.

The other policeman went over to the person in the backseat of the car. It was the boy in the purple caftan. The police had picked him up while they were cruising the neighborhood for the exhibitionist. The boy hadn't been able to tell them where he lived – because he didn't really live anywhere. 'Do you know that man with the child there?' the policeman asked the boy.

'Yeah, he's a real tough guy,' the kid said.

'It's all right, Duncan,' Garp said. 'Don't be scared. I'm just taking you home.'

'Son?' the policeman asked Duncan. 'Is this your father?'

'You're scaring him,' Garp told the cop.

'I'm not scared,' Duncan said. 'Why are you taking me home?' he asked his father. It seemed that everyone wanted to hear this.

'Ralph's mother was upset,' Garp said; he hoped that would be enough, but the rejected lover in the police car started to laugh. The policeman with the flashlight shone his light on the lover boy and asked Garp if he knew him. Garp thought: There is no end to this in sight.

'My name is Garp,' Garp said, irritably. 'T. S. Garp. I am married. I have two children. One of them – this one, named Duncan, the older – was spending the night with a friend.

I was convinced that this friend's mother was unfit to look after my son. I went to the house and took my son home. Or, I'm still trying to *get* home.

'*That* boy,' Garp said, pointing to the police car, 'was visiting the mother of the friend of my son when I arrived. The mother wanted the boy to leave – *that* boy,' Garp said, again pointing at the kid in the police car, 'and he left.'

'What is this mother's name?' a policeman asked; he was trying to write everything down in a giant pad. After a polite silence, the policeman looked up at Garp.

'Duncan?' Garp asked his son. 'What is Ralph's name?'

'Well, it's being changed,' Duncan said. 'He used to have his father's name, but his mother's trying to get it changed.'

'Yes, but what *is* his father's name?' Garp asked.

'Ralph,' Duncan said. Garp shut his eyes.

'Ralph Ralph?' the policeman with the pad said.

'No, Duncan, please think,' Garp said. 'Ralph's *last* name is what?'

'Well, I think that's the name being changed,' Duncan said.

'Duncan, what is it being changed *from?*' Garp asked.

'You could ask Ralph,' Duncan suggested. Garp wanted to scream.

'Did you say *your* name was Garp?' one of the policemen asked.

'Yes,' Garp admitted.

'And the initials are T. S.?' the policeman asked. Garp knew what would happen next; he felt very tired.

'Yes, T. S.,' he said. 'Just T. S.'

'Hey, Tough Shit!' howled the kid in the car, falling back in the seat, swooning with laughter.

'What does the first initial stand for, Mr Garp?' the policeman asked.

'Nothing,' Garp said.

'Nothing?' the policeman said.

'They're just initials,' Garp said. 'They're all my mother gave me.'

'Your first name is *T*?' the policeman asked.

'People call me Garp,' Garp said.

'What a story, man!' cried the boy in the caftan, but the policeman nearest the squad car rapped on the roof at him.

'You put your dirty feet on that seat again, sonny,' he said, 'and I'll have you licking the crud off.'

'Garp?' said the policeman interviewing Garp. 'I know who you are!' he cried suddenly. Garp felt very anxious. 'You're the one who got that molester in that park!'

'Yes!' said Garp. 'That was me. But it wasn't here, and it was years ago.'

'I remember it as if it were yesterday,' the policeman said.

'What's this?' the other policeman asked.

'You're too young,' the cop told him. 'This is the man named Garp who grabbed that molester in that park – where was it? That *child* molester, that's who it was. And what was it you did?' he asked Garp, curiously. 'I mean, there was something funny, wasn't there?'

'Funny?' said Garp.

'For a *living*,' the policeman said. 'What did you do for a living?'

'I'm a writer,' Garp said.

'Oh, yeah,' the policeman remembered. 'Are you still a writer?'

'Yes,' Garp confessed. He knew, at least, that he wasn't a marriage counselor.

'Well, I'll be,' the policeman said, but something was still bothering him; Garp could tell something was wrong.

'I had a beard then,' Garp offered.

'That's it!' the policeman cried. 'And you've shaved it off?'

'Right,' said Garp.

The policemen had a conference in the red glow of the taillights of the squad car. They decided to give Garp and Duncan a ride home, but they said Garp would still have to show them some information regarding his identity.

'I just don't recognize you – from the pictures – without the beard,' the older policeman said.

'Well, it *was* years ago,' Garp said, sadly, 'and in another town.'

Garp felt uneasy that the young man in the caftan would get to see the house the Garps lived in. Garp imagined the young man would show up one day, asking for something.

'You remember me?' the kid asked Duncan.

'I don't think so,' Duncan said, politely.

'Well, you were almost asleep,' the boy admitted. To Garp he said, 'You're too uptight about children, man. Children make it just fine. This your only child?'

'No, I have another one,' Garp said.

'Man, you ought to have a *dozen* other ones,' the boy said. 'Then maybe you wouldn't get so uptight about just one, you know?' This sounded to Garp like what his mother called the Percy Theory of Children.

'Take your next left,' Garp told the policeman who was driving, 'then a right, and it's on the corner.' The other policeman handed Duncan a lollipop.

'Thank you,' Duncan said.

'What about me?' the kid in the caftan asked. '*I* like lollipops.' The policeman glared; when he turned his back, Duncan gave the kid his lollipop. Duncan was no fan of lollipops, he never had been.

'Thank you,' the boy whispered. 'You see, man?' he said to Garp. 'Kids are just beautiful.'

So is Helen, Garp thought – in the doorway with the light behind her. Her blue, floor-length robe had a high, roll-up collar; Helen had the collar turned up as if she were cold. She also had her glasses on, so that Garp knew she'd been watching for them.

'Man,' whispered the kid in the caftan, elbowing Garp as he got out of the car. 'What's that lovely lady like when she gets her glasses off?'

'Mom! We got arrested,' Duncan called to Helen. The squad car waited at the curb for Garp to get his identification.

'We did *not* get arrested,' Garp said. 'We got a *ride,* Duncan. Everything's *fine,*' he said angrily, to Helen. He ran upstairs to find his wallet among his clothes.

'Is that how you went out?' Helen called after him. 'Dressed like that?'

'The police thought he was kidnapping me,' Duncan said.

'Did they come to the house?' Helen asked him.

'No, Dad was carrying me home,' Duncan said. 'Boy, is Dad weird.'

Garp thundered down the stairs and ran out the door. 'A case of mistaken identity,' Garp muttered to Helen. 'They must have been looking for someone else. For God's sake, don't get upset.'

'I'm *not* upset,' Helen said, sharply.

Garp showed the police his identification.

'Well, I'll be,' the older policeman said. 'It *is* just T. S., isn't it? I suppose it's easier that way.'

'Sometimes it isn't,' Garp said.

As the police car was leaving, the kid called out to Garp, 'You're not a bad guy, man, if you'd just learn to *relax!*'

Garp's impression of Helen's body, lean and tense and shivering in the blue robe, did not relax him. Duncan was wide-awake and jabbering; he was hungry, too. So was Garp. In the predawn kitchen, Helen coolly watched them eat. Duncan told the plot of a long TV movie; Garp suspected that it was actually two movies, and Duncan had fallen asleep before one was over and woken up after the other one had begun. He tried to imagine where and when Mrs Ralph's activities fitted into Duncan's movies.

Helen didn't ask any questions. In part, Garp knew, this was because there was nothing she could say in front of Duncan. But in part, like Garp, she was severely editing what she wanted to say. They were both grateful for Duncan's presence; by the time they got to speak freely to each other, the long wait might make them kinder, and more careful.

At dawn they couldn't wait any longer and they began to talk to each other through Duncan.

'Tell Mommy what the kitchen looked like,' Garp said. 'And tell her about the dog.'

'Bill?'

'Right!' Garp said. 'Tell her about old Bill.'

'What was Ralph's mother wearing while you were there?' Helen asked Duncan. She smiled at Garp. 'I hope she wore more clothes than Daddy.'

'What did you have for supper?' Garp asked Duncan.

'Are the bedrooms upstairs or downstairs?' Helen asked. 'Or both?' Garp tried to give her a look that said: Please don't get started. He could feel her edging the old, worn weapons into easy reach. She had a babysitter or two she could recall for him, and he felt her moving the babysitters into place. If she brought up one of the old, wounding names, Garp had no names ready for retaliation. Helen had no babysitters against her; not yet. In Garp's mind, Harrison Fletcher didn't count.

'How many telephones are there?' Helen asked Duncan. 'Is there a phone in the kitchen and one in the bedroom? Or is the only phone in the bedroom?'

When Duncan finally went to his room, Helen and Garp were left with less than half an hour before Walt would wake up. But Helen had the names of her enemies ready. There is plenty of time to do damage when you know where the war wounds are.

'I love you so much, and I know you so well,' Helen began.

12

It Happens to Helen

Late-night phone calls – those burglar alarms in the heart – would frighten Garp all his life. Who is it that I love? Garp's heart would cry, at the first ring – who's been blasted by a truck, who's drowned in the beer or lies sideswiped by an elephant in the terrible darkness?

Garp feared the receiving of such after-midnight calls, but he once made one – unknowingly – himself. It had been one evening when Jenny was visiting them; his mother had let it slip how Cushie Percy had ruptured in childbirth. Garp had not heard of it, and although he occasionally joked with Helen about his old passion for Cushie – and Helen teased him about her – the news of Cushie *dead* was nearly crippling to Garp. Cushman Percy had been so active – there had been such a hot juiciness about her – it seemed impossible. News of an accident to Alice Fletcher could not have upset him more; he felt more prepared for something happening to her. Sadly, he knew, things *would* always be happening to Quiet Alice.

Garp wandered into the kitchen and without really noticing the time, or remembering when he opened another beer, he discovered that he had dialed the Percys' number; the phone was ringing. Slowly, Garp could imagine the long way back from sleep that Fat Stew had to travel before he could answer the phone.

'God, who are you calling?' Helen asked, coming into the kitchen. 'It's quarter of two!'

Before Garp could hang up, Stewart Percy answered the phone.

'Yes?' Fat Stew asked, worriedly, and Garp could imagine frail and brainless Midge sitting up in bed beside him, as nervous as a cornered hen.

'I'm sorry I woke you,' Garp said. 'I didn't realize it was so late.' Helen shook her head and walked abruptly out of the kitchen. Jenny appeared in the kitchen doorway; on her face was the kind of critical look only a mother can give a son. That is a look with more disappointment in it than the usual anger.

'Who the hell is this?' Stewart Percy said.

'This is Garp, sir,' Garp said, a little boy again, apologizing for his genes.

'Holy shit,' said Fat Stew. 'What do *you* want?'

Jenny had neglected to tell Garp that Cushie Percy had died *months* ago; Garp thought he was offering condolences on a fresh disaster. Thus he faltered.

'I'm sorry, very sorry,' Garp said.

'You said so, you *said* so,' Stewart said.

'I just heard about it,' Garp said, 'and I wanted to tell you and Mrs Percy how truly sorry I was. I may not have demonstrated it, to *you*, sir, but I was really very fond of—'

'You little swine!' said Stewart Percy. 'You mother humper, you Jap ball of shit!' He hung up the phone.

Even Garp was unprepared for this much loathing. But he misunderstood the situation. It would be years before he realized the circumstances of his phone call. Poor Pooh Percy, batty Bainbridge, would one day explain it to Jenny. When Garp called, Cushie had been dead for so long that Stewart did not realize Garp was commiserating with him on *Cushie's* loss. When Garp called, it was the midnight of the dark day when the black beast, Bonkers, had finally expired. Stewart Percy thought that Garp's call was a cruel joke – false condolences for the dog Garp had always hated.

And now, when Garp's phone rang, Garp was conscious

of Helen's grip emerging instinctively from her sleep. When he picked up the phone, Helen had his leg clamped fast between her knees – as if she were holding tight to the life and safety that his body was to her. Garp's mind ran through the odds. Walt was home asleep. And so was Duncan; he was *not* at Ralph's.

Helen thought: It is my father; it's his heart. Sometimes she thought: They've finally found and identified my mother. In a morgue.

And Garp thought: They have murdered Mom. Or they are holding her for ransom – men who will accept nothing less than the public rape of forty virgins before releasing the famous feminist, unharmed. And they'll also demand the lives of my children, and so forth.

It was Roberta Muldoon on the phone, and that only convinced Garp that the victim was Jenny Fields. But the victim was Roberta.

'He's left me,' Roberta said, her huge voice swollen with tears. 'He's thrown me over. *Me!* Can you believe it?'

'Jesus, Roberta,' Garp said.

'Oh, I never knew what *shits* men were until I became a woman,' Roberta said.

'It's Roberta,' Garp whispered to Helen, so that she could relax. 'Her lover's flown the coop.' Helen sighed, released Garp's leg, rolled over.

'You don't even care, do you?' Roberta asked Garp, testily.

'Please, Roberta,' Garp said.

'I'm sorry,' Roberta said. 'But I thought it was too late to call your mother.' Garp found this logic astonishing, since he knew that Jenny stayed up later than he did; but he also liked Roberta, very much, and she had certainly had a hard time.

'He said I wasn't *enough* of a woman, that I confused him, sexually – that *I* was confused sexually!' Roberta cried. 'Oh, God, that *prick*. All he wanted was the novelty of it. He was just showing off for his friends.'

'I'll bet you could have taken him, Roberta,' Garp said. 'Why didn't you beat the shit out of him?'

'You don't understand,' Roberta said. 'I don't *feel* like beating the shit out of anyone, anymore. I'm a *woman!*'

'Don't women ever feel like beating the shit out of someone?' Garp asked. Helen reached over to him and pulled his cock.

'I don't know *what* women feel like,' Roberta wailed. 'I don't know what they're *supposed* to feel like, anyway. I just know what *I* feel like.'

'What's that?' Garp asked, knowing she wanted to tell him.

'I feel like beating the shit out of him *now,*' Roberta confessed, 'but when he was dumping all over me, I just sat there and took it. I even cried. I've been crying all day!' she cried, 'and he even called me up and told me that if I was *still* crying I was faking myself.'

'The hell with him,' Garp said.

'All he wanted was a great big lay,' Roberta said. 'Why are men like that?'

'Well,' Garp said.

'Oh, I know *you're* not,' Roberta said. 'I'm not even attractive to you, probably.'

'Of course you're attractive, Roberta,' Garp said.

'But not to *you,*' Roberta said. 'Don't lie. I'm not sexually attractive, am I?'

'Not really to *me,*' Garp confessed, 'but to lots of *other* men, yes. Of course you are.'

'Well, you're a good friend, that's more important,' Roberta said. 'You're not really sexually attractive to me, either.'

'That's perfectly all right,' Garp said.

'You're too short,' Roberta said. 'I like *longer*-looking people – I mean, sexually. Don't be hurt.'

'I'm not hurt,' Garp said. 'Don't *you* be, either.'

'Of course not,' Roberta said.

'Why not call me in the morning,' Garp suggested. 'You'll feel better.'

'I won't,' Roberta said, sulkily. 'I'll feel *worse*. And I'll feel ashamed that I called you.'

'Why not talk to your doctor?' Garp said. 'The urologist? The fellow who did your operation – he's your friend, isn't he?'

'I think he wants to fuck me,' Roberta said, seriously. 'I think that's all he *ever* wanted to do to me. I think he recommended this whole operation just because he wanted to seduce me, but he wanted to make me a woman first. They're notorious for that – a friend was telling me.'

'A *crazy* friend, Roberta,' Garp said. '*Who's* notorious for that?'

'Urologists,' Roberta said. 'Oh, I don't know – isn't urology a little creepy to you?' It *was*, but Garp didn't want to upset Roberta any further.

'Call Mom,' he heard himself say. '*She'll* cheer you up, she'll think of something.'

'Oh, she *is* wonderful,' Roberta sobbed. 'She always *does* think of something, but I feel I've used her for so much.'

'She loves to help, Roberta,' Garp said, and knew it was, at least, the truth. Jenny Fields was full of sympathy and patience, and Garp only wanted to sleep. 'A good game of squash might help, Roberta,' Garp suggested, weakly. 'Why not come over for a few days and we'll really hit the ball around.' Helen rolled into him, frowned at him, and bit his nipple; Helen liked Roberta, but in the early phase of her sex reassignment Roberta could talk only about herself.

'I just feel so *drained*,' Roberta said. 'No energy, no nothing. I don't even know if I could play.'

'Well, you should *try*, Roberta,' Garp said. 'You should make yourself do something.' Helen, exasperated with him, rolled away from him.

But Helen was affectionate with Garp when he answered these late-night calls; she said they frightened her and she didn't want to be the one to find out what the calls were about. It was strange, therefore, that when Roberta Muldoon called a second time, a few weeks later, *Helen* was the one who answered the phone. It surprised Garp because the phone was on his side of the bed and Helen had to reach over him to pick it up; in fact, this time, she lunged across him and whispered quickly to the phone, 'Yes, what is it?' When she heard it was Roberta, she passed the phone quickly to Garp; it was not as if she'd been trying to let him sleep.

And when Roberta called a third time, Garp felt an absence when he picked up the phone. Something was missing. 'Oh, hello, Roberta,' Garp said. It was Helen's usual grip on his leg: it wasn't there. *Helen* wasn't there, he noticed. He talked reassuringly to Roberta, felt the cold side of his unshared bed, and noted the time was 2 A.M. – Roberta's favorite hour. When Roberta finally hung up, Garp went downstairs to look for Helen, finding her all alone on the living-room couch, sitting up with a glass of wine and a manuscript in her lap.

'Couldn't sleep,' she said, but there was a look on her face – it was a look Garp couldn't immediately place. Although he thought he recognized that look, he also thought he had never seen that look on Helen.

'Reading papers?' he asked; she nodded, but there was only one manuscript in front of her. Garp picked it up.

'It's just student work,' she said, reaching for it.

The student's name was Michael Milton. Garp read a paragraph of the paper. 'It sounds like a story,' Garp said. 'I didn't know you assigned *fiction* writing to your students.'

'I don't,' Helen said, 'but they sometimes show me what they do, anyway.'

Garp read another paragraph. He thought that the writer's style was self-conscious and forced, but there were no errors on the page; it was, at least, competent writing.

'He's one of my graduate students,' Helen said. 'He's very bright, but . . .' She shrugged, but her gesture had the sudden mock casualness of an embarrassed child.

'But what?' Garp said. He laughed – that Helen could look so girlish at this late hour.

But Helen took her glasses off and showed him that *other*

look again, that look he had first seen and couldn't place. Anxiously, she said, 'Oh, I don't know. *Young,* maybe. He's just young, you know. Very bright, but young.'

Garp flipped a page, read half of another paragraph, gave the manuscript back to her. He shrugged. 'It's all shit to me,' he said.

'No, it's not shit,' Helen said, seriously. Oh, Helen the judicious teacher, Garp thought, and announced he was going back to bed. 'I'll be up in a little while,' Helen told him.

Then Garp saw himself in the mirror in the upstairs bathroom. That was where he finally identified that look he'd seen, strangely out of place, on Helen's face. It was a look Garp recognized because he'd seen it before – on his own face, from time to time, but never on Helen's. The look Garp recognized was *guilty,* and it puzzled him. He lay awake a long time but Helen did not come up to bed. In the morning Garp was surprised that although he'd only glanced at the graduate student's manuscript, the name of Michael Milton was the first thing to come to his mind. He looked cautiously at Helen, now lying awake beside him.

'Michael Milton,' Garp said quietly, not to her, but loud enough for her to hear. He watched her unresponding face. Either she was daydreaming, and far away, or she simply had not heard him. Or, he thought, the name of Michael Milton was already on her mind, so that when Garp uttered it, it was the name that she was *already* saying – to herself – and she had not noticed that Garp had spoken it.

Michael Milton, a third-year graduate student in comparative literature, had been a French major at Yale, where he graduated with indifferent distinction; he had earlier graduated from the Steering School, though he tended to play down his prep school years. Once he knew that *you* knew he had gone to Yale, he tended to play that down, too, but he never played down his Junior Year Abroad – in France. To listen to Michael Milton, you would not guess that he'd spent only a year in Europe because he managed to give you the impression that he'd lived in France all his young life. He was twenty-five.

Though he'd lived so briefly in Europe, it appeared that he'd bought all the clothes for his lifetime there: the tweed jackets had wide lapels and flared cuffs, and both the jackets and the slacks were cut to flatter the hips and the waist; they were the kind of clothes that even the Americans of Garp's days at Steering referred to as 'Continental.' The collars of Michael Milton's shirts, which he wore open at the throat (always with *two* unbuttoned buttons), were floppy and wide with a kind of Renaissance flair: a manner betraying both carelessness and intense perfection.

He was as different from Garp as an ostrich is different from a seal. The body of Michael Milton was an elegant body, when dressed; unclothed, he resembled no animal so much as he resembled a heron. He was thin and tallish, with a slouch his tailored tweed jackets concealed. He had a body like coat hangers – the perfect body to hang clothes on. Stripped, he had barely a body at all.

He was Garp's opposite in almost every way, except that Michael Milton had in common with Garp a tremendous self-confidence; he shared with Garp the virtue, or the vice, of arrogance. Like Garp, he was aggressive in the way only someone who believes totally in himself can be aggressive. It had been these qualities, long ago, that had first attracted Helen to Garp.

Now here were the qualities, newly attired; they manifested themselves in a much different form, yet Helen recognized them. She was not usually attracted to rather dandified young men who dressed and spoke as if they had grown world-weary and wisely sad in Europe, when, in fact, they had spent most of their short lives in the backseats of cars in Connecticut. But, in her girlhood, Helen had not *usually* been attracted to wrestlers, either. Helen liked confident men, provided that their confidence was not absurdly misplaced.

What attracted Michael Milton to Helen was what attracted many men and few women to her. She was, in her thirties, an alluring woman not simply because she was beautiful but because she was perfect-looking. It is an important distinction to note that she looked not only as if she had taken good care of herself, but that she had good reason to have done so. This frightening but fetching look, in Helen's case, was not misleading. She was a very successful woman. She looked to be in such total possession of her life that only the most confident men could continue to look at her if she looked back at them. Even in bus stations, she was a woman who was stared at only until she looked back.

In the corridors surrounding the English Department, Helen was not used to being stared at at all; everyone looked when they could, but the looks were furtive. She was, therefore, unprepared for the long, frank look that young Michael Milton gave her one day. He simply stopped in the hall and watched her walking toward him. It was actually Helen who turned her eyes away from his; he turned and watched her walk away from him, down the hall. He said to someone beside him, loud enough for Helen to hear: 'Does she teach here or *go* here? What's she *do* here, anyway?' Michael Milton asked.

In the second semester of that year, Helen taught a course in Narrative Point of View; it was a seminar for graduate students, and for a few advanced undergraduates. Helen was interested in the development and sophistication of narrative technique, with special attention to point of view, in the modern novel. In the first class she noticed the older-looking student with the thin, pale mustache and the nice shirt with the two buttons unbuttoned; she turned her eyes away from him and distributed a questionnaire. It asked, among other questions, why the students thought they were interested in this particular course. In answer to that question, a student named Michael Milton wrote: 'Because, from the first time I saw you, I wanted to be your lover.'

After that class, alone in her office, Helen read that answer to her questionnaire. She thought she knew which one of the people in the class Michael Milton was; if she'd known it was someone else, some boy she hadn't even noticed, she would have shown the questionnaire to Garp. Garp might have said, 'Show me the fucker!' Or: 'Let's introduce him to Roberta Muldoon.' And they would both have laughed, and Garp would have teased her about leading her students on. Because the intentions of the boy, whoever he was, would have been aired between them, there would have been no possibility of actual connection; Helen knew that. When she didn't show the questionnaire to Garp, she felt already guilty – but she thought that if Michael Milton was who she thought he was, she would like to see this go a little further. At that moment, in her office, Helen honestly did not foresee it going *more* than a little further. What would have been the harm of a little?

If Harrison Fletcher had still been her colleague, she would have shown *him* the questionnaire. Regardless – whoever Michael Milton was, even if he *was* that disturbing-looking boy – she would have brought up the matter with Harrison. Harrison and Helen, in the past, had some secrets of this kind, which they kept from Garp and Alice; they were permanent but innocent secrets. Helen knew that sharing Michael Milton's interest in her with Harrison would have been another way to avoid any actual connection.

But she did not mention Michael Milton to Garp, and Harrison, of course, had left to seek his tenure elsewhere. The handwriting on the questionnaire was black, eighteenth-century calligraphy, the kind that can only be carved with a special pen; Michael Milton's written message looked more permanent than print, and Helen read it over and over again. She noted the other answers to the questionnaire: date of birth, years in school, previous courses in the Department of English or in comparative literature. She checked his transcript; his grades were good. She called two colleagues who'd had Michael Milton in courses last semester; she derived from them both that Michael Milton was a good student, aggressive and proud to the point of being vain. She gathered from both her colleagues, though they did not actually say so, that Michael Milton was both gifted and unlikable. She thought of the deliberately unbuttoned buttons on his shirt (she was *sure*, now, that it was he) and she imagined buttoning them up. She thought of that wispy mustache, a thin trace upon his lip. Garp would later comment on Michael Milton's mustache, saying that it was an insult to the world of hair and to the world of lips; Garp thought that it was so much the merest imitation of a mustache that Michael Milton would do his face a favor to shave it off.

But Helen liked the strange little mustache on the lip of Michael Milton.

'You just don't like *any* mustaches,' Helen said to Garp.

'I don't like *that* mustache,' he said. 'I've got nothing against mustaches, in general,' Garp insisted, though in truth Helen was right: Garp hated all mustaches, ever since his encounter with the Mustache Kid. The Mustache Kid had spoiled mustaches for Garp, forever.

Helen also liked the length of Michael Milton's sideburns, curly and blondish; Garp's sideburns were cropped level to his dark eyes, almost at the tops of his ears – although his hair was thick and shaggy, and always just long enough to cover the ear that Bonkers ate.

Helen also noticed that her husband's eccentricities were beginning to bother her. Perhaps she just noticed them more, now that he was so fitfully involved in his writing slump; when he was writing, perhaps he had less time to devote to his eccentricities? Whatever the reason, she found them irksome. His driveway trick, for example, infuriated her; it was even contradictory. For someone who fussed and worried so much about the safety of the children – about reckless drivers, about leaking gas, and so forth – Garp had a way of entering their driveway and garage, after dark, that terrified Helen.

The driveway turned sharply uphill off a long downhill

road. When Garp knew the children were in bed, asleep, he would cut the engine *and* the lights and coast *up* the black driveway; he would gather enough momentum from leaving the downhill road to roll over the lip at the top of the driveway and down into their dark garage. He said he did it so that the engine and the headlights would not wake up the children. But he had to start the car to turn it around to drive the babysitter home, anyway; Helen said his trick was simply for a thrill – it was puerile and dangerous. He was always running over toys left in the blackened driveway, and crashing into bicycles not moved far enough to the rear of the garage.

Once a babysitter had complained to Helen that she hated coasting *down* the driveway with the engine and the headlights out (*another* trick: he would pop the clutch and snap on the lights just before they reached the road).

Am *I* the one who's restless? Helen wondered. She had not thought of herself as restless until she thought of *Garp's* restlessness. And for how long had she really been irritated by Garp's routines and habits? She didn't know. She only knew that she *noticed* she was irritated by them almost from the moment she read Michael Milton's questionnaire.

Helen was driving to her office, wondering what she would say to the rude and conceited boy, when the gear knob of the Volvo's stick shift came off in her hand – the exposed shaft scratched her wrist. She swore as she pulled the car over and examined the damage to herself and to the gearshift.

The knob had been falling off for weeks, the screw threads were stripped, and Garp had several times attempted to make the knob stay on the stick-shift shaft with tape. Helen had complained about this half-assed method of repair, but Garp never claimed to be handy and the care of the car was one of Helen's domestic responsibilities.

This division of labor, though largely agreed upon, was sometimes confusing. Although Garp was the homemaker among them, Helen did the ironing ('because,' Garp said, 'it's *you* who cares about pressed clothes'), and Helen got the car serviced ('because,' Garp said, 'you're the one who drives it every day; you know best when something has to be fixed'). Helen accepted the ironing, but she felt that Garp should deal with the car. She did not like accepting a ride in the service truck from the garage to her office – sitting in the greasy cab with some young mechanic who paid less than adequate attention to his driving. The garage where the car was fixed was a friendly enough place to Helen, but she resented having to be there at all; and the comedy of *who* would drive her to work after she dropped off the car had finally worn thin. 'Who's free to take Mrs Garp to the university?' the boss mechanic would cry into the dank and oily darkness of the vehicle pits. And three or four boys, eager but begrimed, would drop their wrenches and their needle-nosed pliers, would lug and heave themselves out of the pits, would bolt forward and volunteer to share – for a brief, heady moment – that tight cab aclank with auto parts, which would take the slender Professor Garp to work.

Garp pointed out to Helen that when *he* took the car, the volunteers were slow to appear; he frequently waited in the garage for an hour, finally coaxing some laggard to drive him home. His morning's work thus shot, he decided the Volvo was Helen's chore.

They had both procrastinated about the gearshift knob. 'If you just call to order a new one,' Helen told him, 'I'll drive there and let them screw it on while I wait. But I *don't* want to leave the car for a day while they fart around trying to fix *this* one.' She had tossed the knob to him, but he'd carried it out to the car and had taped it, precariously, back on the shaft.

Somehow, she thought, it always fell off when *she* was driving; but, of course, she drove the car more than he did.

'Damn,' she said, and drove to her office with the bare, ugly gearshift uncovered. It hurt her hand every time she had to shift the car, and her scratched wrist bled a little on the fresh skirt of her suit. She parked the car and carried the gear knob with her, across the parking lot, toward her office building. She contemplated throwing it down a storm sewer, but it had little numbers printed on it; in her office she could call the garage and tell them what the little numbers were. *Then* she could throw it away, wherever she liked; or, she thought, I can *mail* it to Garp.

It was in this mood, beset with trivia, that Helen encountered the smug young man slouched in the hall by her office door with the top two buttons of his nice shirt unbuttoned. The shoulders of his tweed jacket were, she noticed, slightly padded; his hair was a bit too lank, and too long, and one end of his mustache – as thin as a knife – drooped too far down at the corner of his mouth. She was not sure if she wanted to love this young man or *groom* him.

'You're up early,' she told him, handing him the gearshift knob so that she could unlock her office door.

'Have you hurt yourself?' he asked. 'You're bleeding.' Helen would think later that it was as if he had a nose for blood, because the slight scratch on her wrist had almost stopped bleeding.

'Are you going to be a doctor?' she asked him, letting him inside her office.

'I *was* going to be,' he said.

'What stopped you?' she asked, still not looking at him, but moving about her desk, straightening what was straight already; and adjusting the venetian blind, which had been left exactly as she wanted it. She took her glasses off, so that when she looked at him he was soft and fuzzy.

'Organic chemistry stopped me,' he said. 'I dropped the course. And besides, I wanted to live in France.'

'Oh, you've lived in France?' Helen asked him, knowing that's what she was supposed to ask him, knowing it was one of the things he thought was special about himself, and he didn't hesitate to slip it in. He had even slipped it in the questionnaire. He was *very* shallow, she saw right away; she hoped he was the slightest bit intelligent, but she felt curiously relieved by his shallowness – as if this made him less dangerous to her, and left her a little freer.

They talked about France, which was fun for Helen, because she talked about France as well as Michael Milton talked about it, and she had never been to Europe. She also told him that she thought he had a poor reason for taking her course.

'A poor reason?' he pressed her, smiling.

'First of all,' Helen said, 'it's a totally unrealistic expectation to have for the course.'

'Oh, you already *have* a lover?' Michael Milton asked her, still smiling.

Somehow he was so frivolous that he didn't insult her; she didn't snap at him that it was enough to have a husband, that it was none of his business, or that she was out of his league. She said, instead, that for what he wanted he should at least have registered for independent study. He said he'd be glad to switch courses. She said she never took on any new independent study students in the second semester.

She knew she had not entirely discouraged him, but she had not been exactly encouraging, either. Michael Milton talked to her, seriously, for an hour – about the subject of her course in narration. He discussed Virginia Woolf's *The Waves* and *Jacob's Room* very impressively, though he was not so good on *To the Lighthouse* and Helen knew he only pretended to have read *Mrs Dalloway*. When he left, she was forced to agree with her two colleagues who'd evaluated Michael Milton previously: he was glib, he was smug, he was facile, and all that was unlikable; but he had a certain brittle smartness, however shiny and thin it was – and it was *also*, somehow, unlikable. What her colleagues had overlooked was his audacious smile and his way of wearing clothes as if he were defiantly undressed. But Helen's colleagues were men; they could not have been expected to define the precise audacity of Michael Milton's smile the way Helen could define it. Helen recognized it as a smile that said to her: I already know you, and I know everything you like. It was an infuriating smile, but it tempted her; she wanted to wipe it off his face. One way of wiping it off, Helen knew, would be to show Michael Milton that he *didn't* know her – or what she really liked – at all.

She also knew that not too many ways of showing him were open to her.

When she first shifted the Volvo, driving home, the point of the uncovered stick-shift shaft dug sharply into the heel of her hand. She knew exactly where Michael Milton had left the gear knob – on the window ledge above the wastebasket, where the janitor would find it and probably throw it away. It looked as if it *ought* to be thrown away, but Helen remembered that she had not phoned in the little numbers to the car garage. That would mean that she, or Garp, would have to call the car garage and try to order a new knob *without* the goddamn numbers – giving the year and model of the car, and so forth, and inevitably ending up with a knob that wasn't right.

But Helen decided she was not going back to her office, and she had enough on her mind already without trying to remember to call the janitor and tell him not to throw away the knob. Besides, it might already be too late.

And anyway, Helen thought, it's not just *my* fault. It's Garp's fault, too. Or, she thought, it's really nobody's fault. It's just one of those things.

But she did not *quite* feel guiltless; not yet. When Michael Milton gave her his papers to read – his old papers, from his other courses – she accepted them and read them, because at least this was an allowable, still-innocent subject for them to discuss: his work. When he grew bolder, and more attached to her, and he showed her even his *creative* work, his short stories and pathetic poems about France, Helen still felt that their long conversations were guided by the critical, constructive relationship between a student and a teacher.

It was all right to have lunch together; they had his *work* to talk about. Perhaps both of them knew that the work was not so special. For Michael Milton, *any* topic of conversation that justified his being with Helen was all right. For Helen, she was still anxious about the obvious conclusion – when he simply ran out of work; when they had consumed all the papers he'd had time to write; when they'd mentioned every book they had in common. Then Helen knew they would need a new subject. She also knew that this was only *her* problem – that Michael Milton already knew what the inevitable subject between them was. She knew he was smugly and irritatingly waiting for her to make up her mind; she occasionally wondered if he would be bold enough to raise his original answer to her questionnaire again, but she didn't think so. Perhaps both of them knew that he wouldn't have to – that the next move was hers. He would show her how grown-up he was by being patient. Helen wanted, above all, to surprise him.

But among these feelings that were new to her, there was one she disliked; she was most unused to feeling guilty – for Helen Holm always felt right about everything she did, and she needed to feel guiltless about this, too. She felt close to achieving this guilt-free state of mind, but she did not quite have it; not yet.

It would be Garp who provided her with the necessary feeling. Perhaps he sensed he had competition; Garp got started as a writer out of a sense of competition, and he finally broke out of his writing slump with a similar, competitive surge.

Helen, he knew, was *reading* someone else. It did not occur to Garp that she might be contemplating more than literature, but he saw with a typical writer's jealousy that someone else's *words* were keeping her up at night. Garp had first courted Helen with 'The Pension Grillparzer.' Some instinct told him to court her again.

If that had been an acceptable motive to get a young writer *started*, it was a dubious motive for his writing now – especially after he'd been stopped for so long. He might

have been in a necessary phase, rethinking everything,
letting the well refill, preparing a book for the future with a
proper period of silence. Somehow the new story he wrote
for Helen reflected the forced and unnatural circumstances
of its conception. The story was written less out of any real
reaction to the viscera of life than it was written to relieve
the anxieties of the writer.

It was possibly a necessary exercise for a writer who
had not written in too long, but Helen did not care for
the urgency with which Garp shoved the story at her. 'I
finally finished something,' he said. It was after dinner; the
children were asleep; Helen wanted to go to bed with him
– she wanted long and reassuring lovemaking, because she
had come to the end of what Michael Milton had written;
there was nothing more for her to read, or for them to
talk about. She knew she should not show the slightest
disappointment in the manuscript Garp gave her, but her
tiredness overwhelmed her and she stared at it, crouching
between dirty dishes.

'I'll do the dishes alone,' Garp offered, clearing the way
to his story for her. Her heart sank; she had read too much.
Sex, or at least romance, was the subject she had at last come
to; Garp had better provide it or Michael Milton would.

'I want to be loved,' Helen told Garp; he was gathering up
the dishes like a waiter who was confident of a large tip. He
laughed at her.

'Read the story, Helen,' he said. '*Then* we'll get laid.'

She resented *his* priorities. There could be no comparison
between Garp's *writing* and the student work of Michael
Milton; though gifted among students, Michael Milton,
Helen knew, would only be a *student* of writing all his life.
The issue was not writing. The issue is *me*, Helen thought;
I want someone paying attention to me. Garp's manner of
courtship was suddenly offensive to her. The *subject* being
courted was somehow Garp's writing. That is *not* the subject
between us, Helen thought. Because of Michael Milton,
Helen was way ahead of Garp at considering the spoken

and unspoken subjects between people. 'If people only told each other what was on their minds,' wrote Jenny Fields – a naïve but forgivable lapse; both Garp and Jenny knew how difficult it was for people to do that.

Garp cautiously washed the dishes, waiting for Helen to read his story. Instinctively – the trained teacher – Helen took out her red pencil and began. That is *not* how she should read my story, Garp thought; I'm not one of her students. But he went on quietly washing the dishes. He saw there was no stopping her.

VIGILANCE
by T. S. Garp

Running my five miles a day, I frequently encounter some smart-mouthed motorist who will pull alongside me and ask (from the safety of the driver's seat), 'What are you in training for?'

Deep and regular breathing is the secret; I am rarely out of breath; I never pant or gasp when I respond. 'I am staying in shape to chase cars,' I say.

At this point the responses of the motorists vary; there are degrees of stupidity as there are degrees of everything else. Of course, they never realize that I don't mean them – I'm not staying in shape to chase *their* cars; not out on the open road, at least. I let them go out there, though I sometimes believe that I *could* catch them. And I do not run on the open road, as some motorists believe, to attract attention.

In my neighborhood there is no place to run. One must leave the suburbs to be even a middle-distance runner. Where I live there are four-way stop signs at every intersection; the blocks are short, and those right-angle corners are hard on the balls of the feet. Also, the sidewalks are threatened by dogs, festooned with the playthings of children, intermittently splashed with lawn sprinklers. And just when there's some running room, there's an elderly person taking up the whole sidewalk, precarious on crutches or armed with quacking canes. With good conscience one does not yell 'Track!' to such a person. Even passing the aged at a safe distance, but with my usual speed, seems to alarm them; and it's not my intention to cause heart attacks.

So it's the open road for training, but it's the suburbs I'm in training *for*. In my condition I am more than a match for a car caught speeding in my neighborhood. Provided they make an even halfhearted halt at the stop signs, they cannot hit over fifty before they have to brake for the next intersection. I always catch up to them. I can travel across lawns, over porches, through swing sets and the children's wading pools; I can burst through hedges, or hurdle them. And since my engine is quiet – and steady, and always in tune – I can *hear* if other cars are coming; I don't have to stop at the stop signs.

In the end I run them down, I wave them over; they always stop. Although I am clearly in impressive car-chasing condition, that is not what intimidates the speeders. No, they are almost always intimidated by my *parenthood*, because they are almost always young. Yes, my parenthood is what sobers them, almost every time. I begin simply. 'Did you see my children back there?' I ask them, loudly and anxiously. Veteran speeders, upon being asked such a question, are immediately frightened that they have *run over* my children. They are instantly defensive.

'I have two young children,' I tell them. The drama is deliberate in my voice – which, with this sentence, I allow to tremble a little. It is as if I am holding back tears, or unspeakable rage, or both. Perhaps they think I am hunting a kidnapper, or that I suspect them of being child molesters.

'What happened?' they invariably ask.

'You *didn't* see my children, did you?' I repeat. 'A little boy pulling a little girl in a red wagon?' This is, of course, a fiction. I have two boys, and they're not so little; they have no wagon. They may have been watching television at the time, or riding their bikes in the park – where it's safe, where there are no cars.

'No,' the bewildered speeder says. 'I saw children, *some* children. But I don't think I saw *those* children. *Why?*'

'Because you almost killed them,' I say.

'But I didn't *see* them!' the speeder protests.

'You were driving too fast to see them!' I say. This is sprung on them as if it were proof of their guilt; I always pronounce this sentence as if it were hard evidence. And they're never sure. I've rehearsed this part so well. The sweat from my hard sprint, by now, drips off my mustache and the point of my chin, streaking the driver's-side door. They know only a father who genuinely fears for his children would run so hard, would stare like such a maniac, would wear such a cruel mustache.

'I'm sorry,' they usually say.

'This is a neighborhood *full* of children,' I always tell them. 'You have other places you can drive fast, don't you? *Please*, for the children's sake, don't speed here anymore.' My voice, now, is never nasty; it is always beseeching. But they see that a restrained fanatic resides behind my honest, watering eyes.

Usually it's just a young kid. Those kids have a need to dribble a little oil; they want to race the frantic pace of the music on their radios. And I don't expect to change their ways. I only hope they'll do it somewhere else. I concede that the open road is theirs; when I train there, I keep my place. I run in the stuff of the soft shoulder, in the hot sand and gravel, in the beer-bottle glass – among the mangled cats, the maimed birds, the mashed condoms. But in my neighborhood, the car is not king; not yet.

Usually they learn.

After my five-mile run I do fifty-five push-ups, then five hundred-yard dashes, followed by fifty-five situps, followed by fifty-five neck bridges. It's not that I care so much for the number five; it's simply that strenuous and mindless exertion is easier if one doesn't have to keep track of too many different numbers. After my shower (about five o'clock), through the late afternoon, and in the course of the evening, I allow myself *five* beers.

I do not chase cars at night. Children should not be playing outside at night – in my neighborhood, or in any other neighborhood. At night, I believe, the car is king of the whole modern world. Even the suburbs.

At night, in fact, I rarely leave my house, or allow the

members of my family to venture out. But once I went to investigate an obvious accident – the darkness suddenly streaked with headlights pointing straight up and exploding; the silence pierced with a metal screaming and the shriek of ground glass. Only half a block away, in the dark and perfect middle of my street, a Land Rover lay upside-down and bleeding its oil and gas in a puddle so deep and still I could see the moon in it. The only sound: the *ping* of heat in the hot pipes and the dead engine. The Land Rover looked like a tank tumbled by a land mine. Great juts and tears in the pavement revealed that the auto had rolled over and over before coming to rest here.

The driver's-side door could be opened only slightly, but enough to miraculously turn on the door light. There in the lit cab, still behind the steering wheel – still upside-down and still alive – was a fat man. He looked unharmed. The top of his head rested gingerly on the ceiling of the cab, which of course was now the floor, but the man seemed only dimly sensitive to this change in his perspective. He looked puzzled, chiefly, by the presence of a large brown bowling ball that sat alongside his head, like another head; he was, in fact, cheek to cheek with this bowling ball, which he perhaps felt touching him as he might have felt the presence of a lover's severed head – formerly resting on his shoulder.

'Is that you, Roger?' the man asked. I couldn't tell whether he was addressing me or the bowling ball.

'It is not Roger,' I said, answering for us both.

'That Roger is a moron,' the man explained. 'We crossed our balls.'

That the fat man was referring to a bizarre sexual experience seemed unlikely. I assumed that the fat man referred to bowling.

'This is *Roger's* ball,' he explained, indicating the brown globe against his cheek. 'I should have known it wasn't my ball because it wouldn't fit in my bag. My ball will fit in *anyone's* bag, but Roger's ball is really strange. I was trying to fit it in my bag when the Land Rover went off the bridge.'

Although I knew there was no bridge in my entire neighborhood, I tried to visualize the occurrence. But I was distracted by the gurgle of spilling gasoline, like beer down a thirsty man's throat.

'You should get out,' I told the upside-down bowler.

'I'll wait for Roger,' he replied. 'Roger will be right along.'

And sure enough, along came another Land Rover, as if they were a separated twosome from a column of an army on the move. Roger's Land Rover came along with its headlights out and did not stop in time; it plowed into the fat bowler's Land Rover and together, like coupled boxcars, they jarred each other another tough ten yards down the street.

It appeared that Roger *was* a moron, but I merely asked him the expected question: 'Is that you, Roger?'

'Yup,' said the man, whose throbbing Land Rover was dark and creaking; little fragments of its windshield and head-lights and grille dropped to the street like noisy confetti.

'That could *only* be Roger!' groaned the fat bowler, still upside-down – and still alive – in his lit cab. I saw that his nose bled slightly; it appeared that the bowling ball had bashed him.

'You moron, Roger!' he called out. 'You've got my *ball!*'

'Well, someone's got *my* ball, then,' Roger replied.

'*I've* got your ball, you moron,' the fat bowler declared.

'Well, that's not the answer to everything,' Roger said. 'You've got *my* Land Rover.' Roger lit a cigarette in the blackened cab; he did not appear interested in climbing out of the wreck.

'You should set up flares,' I suggested to him, 'and that fat man should get out of your Land Rover. There's gasoline everywhere. I don't think you should smoke.' But Roger only continued smoking and ignoring me in the cavelike silence of the second Land Rover, and the fat bowler again cried out – as if he were having a dream that was starting over, at the beginning – 'Is that *you*, Roger?'

I went back to my house and called the police. In the daytime, in my neighborhood, I would never have tolerated such mayhem, but people who go bowling in each other's Land Rovers are not the usual suburban speeders, and I decided they were legitimately lost.

'Hello, Police?' I said.

I have learned what you can and what you can't expect of the police. I know that they do not really support the notion of citizen arrest; when I have reported speeders to them, the results have been disappointing. They don't seem interested in learning the details. I am told there are people whom the police are interested in apprehending, but I believe the police are basically sympathetic to speeders; and they do not appreciate citizens who make arrests for them.

I reported the whereabouts of the bowlers' accident, and when the police asked, as they always ask, who was calling, I told them, 'Roger.'

That, I knew – knowing the police – would be interesting. The police are always more interested in bothering the person who reports the crime than they are interested in bothering the criminals. And sure enough, when they arrived, they went straight after Roger. I could see them all arguing under the streetlamps, but I could catch only snatches of their conversation.

'He's Roger,' the fat bowler kept saying. 'He's Roger through and through.'

'I'm not the Roger who called you fuckers,' Roger told the police.

'That's true,' the fat bowler declared. 'This Roger wouldn't call the police for anything.'

And after a while they began to call out into our dark suburb for another Roger. 'Is there another Roger here?' one policeman called.

'Roger!' screamed the fat bowler, but my dark house and the dark houses of my neighbors were appropriately silent. In daylight, I knew, they would all be gone. Only their oil slicks and their broken glass would remain.

Relieved – and, as always, pleased with the destruction of automotive vehicles – I watched until almost dawn, when the hulking, coupled Land Rovers were finally separated and towed away. They were like two exhausted rhinos caught fornicating in the suburbs. Roger and the fat bowler stood arguing, and swinging their bowling balls, until the streetlamps in our block were extinguished; then, as if on signal, the bowlers shook hands and departed in different directions – on foot, and as if they knew where they were going.

The police came interrogating in the morning, still concerned with the possibility of another Roger. But they learned nothing from me – just as they learn nothing, apparently, whenever I report a speeder to them. 'Well, if it happens again,' they tell me, 'be sure to let us know.'

Fortunately, I have rarely needed the police; I am usually effective with first offenders. Only once have I had to stop the *same* driver – and him, only twice. He was an arrogant young man in a blood-red plumber's truck. Lurid-yellow lettering advertised on the cab that the plumber handled Roto-Rootering needs and all plumbing services:

O. FECTEAU, OWNER & HEAD PLUMBER

With two-time offenders I come more quickly to the point.

'I'm calling the cops,' I told the young man. 'And I'm calling your boss, old O. Fecteau; I should have called him the last time.'

'I'm my own boss,' the young man said. 'It's *my* plumbing business. Fuck off.'

And I realized I was facing O. Fecteau himself – a runty but successful youth, unimpressed with standard authority.

'There are children in this neighborhood,' I said. 'Two of them are mine.'

'Yeah, you already told me,' the plumber said; he revved his engine as if he were clearing his throat. There was a hint of menace in his expression, like the trace of pubic beard he was growing on his young chin. I rested my hands on the door – one on the handle, one on the rolled-down window.

'Please don't speed here,' I said.

'Yeah, I'll try,' said O. Fecteau. I might have let it go at that, but the plumber lit a cigarette and smiled at me. I thought I saw on his punk's face *the leer of the world*.

'If I catch you driving like that again,' I said, 'I'll stick your Roto-Rooter up your ass.'

We stared at each other, O. Fecteau and I. Then the plumber gunned his engine and popped his clutch; I had to leap back to the curb. In the gutter I saw a little metal dump truck, a child's toy; the front wheels were missing. I snatched it up and ran after O. Fecteau. Five blocks later I was close enough to throw the dump truck, which struck the plumber's cab; it made a good noise but it bounced off harmlessly. Even so, O. Fecteau slammed on his brakes; about five long pipes were flipped out of the pickup part of the truck, and one of those metal drawers sprang open, disgorging a screwdriver and several spools of heavy wire. The plumber jumped down from his cab, banging the door after himself; he had a Stillson wrench in his hand. You could tell he was sensitive about collecting dents on his blood-red truck. I grabbed one of the fallen pipes. It was about five feet long and I quickly smashed the truck's left taillight with it. For some time now, things have just been coming naturally to me in fives. For example, the circumference, in inches, of my chest (expanded): fifty-five.

'Your taillight's broken,' I pointed out to the plumber. 'You shouldn't be driving around that way.'

'I'm going to call the cops on *you*, you crazy bastard!' said O. Fecteau.

'This is a citizen arrest,' I said. 'You broke the speed limit, you're endangering the lives of my children. We'll go see the cops together.' And I poked the long pipe under the truck's rear license plate and folded the plate like a letter.

'You touch my truck again,' the plumber said, 'and you're in trouble.' But the pipe felt as light in my hands as a badminton racket; I swung it easily and shattered the other taillight.

'You're already in trouble,' I pointed out to O. Fecteau. 'You ever drive in this neighborhood again, you better stay in first gear and use your flasher.' First, I knew (swinging the pipe), he would need to *repair* his flasher.

There was an elderly woman, just then, who came out of her house to observe the commotion. She recognized me immediately. I catch up to a lot of people at her corner. 'Oh, good for you!' she called. I smiled to her and she tottered toward me, stopping and peering into her well-groomed lawn where the toy dump truck arrested her attention. She seized it, with obvious distaste, and carried it over to me. I put the toy and the pieces of broken glass and plastic from the taillights and the flasher into the back of the pickup. It is a clean neighborhood; I despise litter. On the open road, in training, I see nothing but litter. I put the other pipes in back, too, and with the long pipe I still held (like a warrior's javelin) I nudged the screwdriver and the spools of wire that had fallen by the curb. O. Fecteau gathered them up and returned them to the metal drawer. He is probably a better plumber than a driver, I thought; the Stillson wrench looked very comfortable in his hand.

'You should be ashamed of yourself,' the old woman told O. Fecteau. The plumber glared at her.

'He's one of the worst ones,' I told her.

'Imagine that,' the old lady said. 'And you're a big boy,' she told the plumber. 'You should know better.'

O. Fecteau edged back to the cab, looking as if he would hurl his wrench at me, then leap into his truck and back over the old biddy.

'Drive carefully,' I told him. When he was safely in the cab, I slid the long pipe into the pickup. Then I took the old woman's arm and helped her along the sidewalk.

When the truck tore away from the curb, with that stink of scorched rubber and a noise as raw as bones leaving their sockets, I felt the old lady tremble through the frail point of her elbow; something of her fear passed into me, and I realized how risky it was to make anyone as angry as I had made O. Fecteau. I could hear him, maybe five blocks away, driving furiously fast, and I prayed for all the dogs and cats and children who might be near the street. Surely, I thought, modern life is about five times as difficult as life used to be.

I should stop this crusade against speeders, I thought. I go too far with them, but they make me so angry – with their carelessness, their dangerous, sloppy way of life, which I view as so directly threatening to my own life and the lives of my children. I have always hated cars, and hated people who drove them stupidly. I feel such anger toward people who take such risks with other people's lives. Let them race their cars – but in the desert! We would not allow an outdoor rifle range in the suburbs! Let them jump out of airplanes, if they want – but over the ocean! *Not* where my children live.

'What would this neighborhood be like without you?' the old woman wondered aloud. I can never remember her name. Without me, I thought, this neighborhood would probably be *peaceful*. Perhaps deadlier, but peaceful. 'They all drive so fast,' the old lady said. 'If it weren't for you, I sometimes think they'd be having their smashups right in my living room.' But I felt embarrassed that I shared such anxiety with eighty-year-olds – that my fears are more like their nervous, senile worries than they are the normal anxieties of people my own *young* middle age.

What an incredibly dull life I have! I thought, aiming the old woman toward her front door, steering her over the cracks in the sidewalk.

Then the plumber came back. I thought the old woman was going to die in my arms. The plumber drove over the curb and hurtled past us, over the old woman's lawn, flattening a whiplike young tree and nearly rolling over when he wheeled the truck into a U-turn that uprooted a sizable hedge and tore divots from the ground the size of five-pound steaks. Then down to the sidewalk the truck fled – an explosion of tools flying free of the pickup as the rear wheels jounced over the curb. O. Fecteau was off up the street, once more terrorizing my neighborhood; I saw the violent plumber jump the curb again at the corner of Dodge and Furlong – where he grazed the back of a parked car, springing open the car's trunk on impact and leaving it flapping.

Helping the shaken old lady inside, I called the police – and my wife, to tell her to keep the children indoors. The plumber was berserk. This is how I help the neighborhood, I thought: I drive mad men madder.

The old woman sat in a paisley chair in her cluttered living room, as carefully as a plant. When O. Fecteau returned – this time driving within inches of the living room bay window, and through the gravel beds for the baby trees, his horn blaring – the old woman never moved. I stood at the door, awaiting the ultimate assault, but I thought it wiser not to show myself. I knew that if O. Fecteau saw me, he would attempt to drive *in* the house.

By the time the police arrived, the plumber had rolled his truck in an attempt to avoid a station wagon at the intersection of Cold Hill and North Lane. He had broken his collarbone and was sitting upright in the cab, though the truck lay on its side; he wasn't able to climb out the door above his head, or he hadn't tried. O. Fecteau appeared calm; he was listening to his radio.

Since that time, I have tried to provoke the offending drivers less; if I sense them taking offense at my stopping them and presuming to criticize their vile habits, I simply tell them I am informing the police and quickly leave.

That O. Fecteau turned out to have a long history of violent overreactions to social situations did not allow me to forgive myself. 'Look, it's all the better you got that plumber off the road,' my wife told me – and she usually criticizes my meddlesomeness in the behavior of others. But I could only think that I had driven a workingman off his rocker, and that *during* his outburst, *if* O. Fecteau had killed a child, whose fault would it have been? Partly mine, I think.

In modern times, in my opinion, either everything is a moral question or there are no more moral questions. Nowadays, there are no compromises or there are only compromises. Never influenced, I keep my vigil. There is no letting up.

Don't say anything, Helen told herself. Go kiss him and rub against him; get him upstairs as fast as you can, and talk about the damn story later. *Much* later, she warned herself. But she knew he wouldn't let her.

The dishes were done and he sat across the table from her.

She tried her nicest smile and told him, 'I want to go to bed with you.'

'You don't like it?' he asked.

'Let's talk in bed,' she said.

'Goddamn it, Helen,' he said. 'It's the first thing I've finished in a long time. I want to know what you think of it.'

She bit her lip and took her glasses off; she had not made a single mark with her red pencil. 'I love you,' she said.

'Yes, yes,' he said, impatiently. 'I love you, too, but we can *fuck* anytime. What about the *story*?' And she finally relaxed; she felt he had released her, somehow. I *tried*, she thought; she felt hugely relieved.

'Fuck the story,' she said. 'No, I *don't* like it. And I don't want to talk about it, either. You don't care to regard what *I* want, obviously. You're like a little boy at the dinner table – you serve yourself first.'

'You don't like it?' Garp said.

'Oh, it's not *bad*,' she said, 'it's just not much of anything. It's a trifle, it's a little ditty. If you're warming up to something, I'd like to see what it is – when you get to it. But this is nothing, you must know that. It's a toss-off, isn't it? You can do tricks like this with your left hand, can't you?'

'It's *funny*, isn't it?' Garp asked.

'Oh, it's *funny*,' she said, 'but it's funny like *jokes* are funny. It's all one-liners. I mean, what *is* it? A self-parody? You're not old enough, and you haven't written enough, to start mocking yourself. It's self-serving, it's self-justifying; and it's not about anything except yourself, really. It's cute.'

'Son of a bitch,' said Garp. '*Cute?*'

'You're always talking about people who write well but don't have anything to say,' Helen said. 'Well, what do you call this? It's no "Grillparzer," certainly; it isn't worth a fifth of what "Grillparzer" is worth. It isn't worth a *tenth* of that story,' Helen said.

'"The Pension Grillparzer" is the first big thing I wrote,' Garp said. 'This is completely different; it's another kind of fiction altogether.'

'Yes, one is about something and one is about nothing,'

Helen said. 'One is about people and one is about only *you*. One has mystery *and* precision, and one has only wit.' When Helen's critical faculties were engaged, they were difficult to disengage.

'It's not fair to compare them,' Garp said. 'I know this is *smaller*.'

'Then let's not talk anymore about it,' Helen said.

Garp sulked for a minute.

'You didn't like *Second Wind of the Cuckold*, either,' he said, 'and I don't suppose you'll like the next one any better.'

'*What* next one?' Helen asked him. 'Are you writing another novel?'

He sulked some more. She *hated* him, making her do this to him, but she wanted him and she knew she loved him, too.

'Please,' she said. 'Let's go to bed.'

But now he saw *his* chance for a little cruelty – and/or a little truth – and his eyes shone at her brightly.

'Let's not say another word,' she begged him. 'Let's go to bed.'

'You think "The Pension Grillparzer" is the best thing I've written, don't you?' he asked her. He knew already what she thought of the second novel, and he knew that, despite Helen's fondness for *Procrastination*, a first novel is a first novel. Yes, she *did* think 'Grillparzer' was his best.

'So far, yes,' she said, softly. 'You're a *lovely* writer, you *know* I think so.'

'I guess I just haven't lived up to my potential,' Garp said, nastily.

'You will,' she said; the sympathy and her love for him were draining from her voice.

They stared at each other; Helen looked away. He started upstairs. 'Are you coming to bed?' he asked. His back was to her; his intentions were hidden from her – his feelings for her, too: either hidden from her or buried in his infernal *work*.

'Not right now,' she said.

He waited on the stairs. 'Got something to *read?*' he asked.

'No, I'm through reading for a while,' she said.

Garp went upstairs. When she came up to him, he was already asleep, which made her despair. If he'd had her on his mind at all, how *could* he have fallen asleep? But, actually, he'd had so much on his mind, he'd been confused; he had fallen asleep because he was bewildered. If he'd been able to focus his feelings on any *one* thing, he'd still have been awake when she came upstairs. They might have saved a lot of things, then.

As it was, she sat beside him on the bed and watched his face with more fondness than she thought she could stand. She saw he had a hard-on, as severe as if he *had* been waiting up for her, and she took him into her mouth and sucked him softly until he came.

He woke up, surprised, and he was very guilty-looking – when he appeared to realize where he was, and with whom. Helen, however, was not in the least guilty-looking; she looked only sad. Garp would think, later, that it was as if Helen had *known* he had been dreaming of Mrs Ralph.

When he came back from the bathroom, she was asleep. She had quickly drifted off. Guiltless at last, Helen felt freed to have her dreams. Garp lay awake beside her, watching the astonishing innocence upon her face – until the children woke her.

13

Walt Catches Cold

When Walt caught colds, Garp slept badly. It was as if he were trying to breathe for the boy, and for himself. Garp would get up in the night to kiss and nuzzle the child; anyone seeing Garp would have thought that he could make Walt's cold go away by catching it himself.

'Oh, God,' Helen said. 'It's just a cold. Duncan had colds all winter when he was five.' Nearing eleven, Duncan seemed to have outgrown colds; but Walt, at five, was fully in the throes of cold after cold – or it was one long cold that went away and came back. By the March mud season, Walt's resistance struck Garp as altogether gone; the child hacked himself and Garp awake each night with a wet, wrenching cough. Garp sometimes fell asleep listening to Walt's chest, and he would wake up, frightened, when he could no longer hear the thump of the boy's heart; but the child had merely pushed his father's heavy head off his chest so that he could roll over and sleep more comfortably.

Both the doctor and Helen told Garp, 'It's just a cough.'

But the imperfection in Walt's nightly breathing scared Garp right out of his sleep. He was usually awake, therefore, when Roberta called; the late-night anguish of the large and powerful Ms Muldoon was no longer frightening to Garp – he had come to expect it – but Garp's own fretful sleeplessness made Helen short-tempered.

'If you were back at work, on a book, you'd be too tired to lie awake half the night,' she said. It was his imagination that was keeping him up, Helen told him; one sign that he hadn't been writing enough, Garp knew, was when he had too much imagination left over for other things. For example, the onslaught of dreams: Garp now dreamed *only* of horrors happening to his children.

In a dream, there was one horror that took place while Garp was reading a pornographic magazine. He was just looking at the same picture, over and over again; the picture was very pornographic. The wrestlers on the university team, with whom Garp occasionally worked out, had a peculiar vocabulary for such pictures. This vocabulary, Garp noted, had not changed since his days at Steering, when the wrestlers on Garp's team spoke of such pictures in the same fashion. What had changed was the increased availability of the pictures, but the names were the same.

The picture Garp looked at in the dream was considered among the highest in the rankings of pornographic pictures. Among pictures of naked women, there were names for how much you could see. If you could see the pubic hair, but not the sex parts, that was called a bush shot – or just a bush. If you could see the sex parts, which were sometimes partially hidden by the hair, that was a beaver; a beaver was better than just a bush; a beaver was the whole thing: the hair and the parts. If the parts were *open*, that was called a *split* beaver. And if the whole thing *glistened*, that was the best of all, in the world of pornography: that was a wet, split beaver. The wetness implied that the woman was not only naked and exposed and open, but she was also *ready*.

In his dream, Garp was looking at what the wrestlers called a wet, split beaver when he heard children crying. He did not know whose children they were, but Helen and his mother, Jenny Fields, were with them; they all came down the stairs and filed past him, where he struggled to hide from them what he'd been looking at. They had been upstairs and something terrible had awakened them; they were on their way farther downstairs – going to the basement as if the basement were a bomb shelter. And with that thought, Garp heard the dull *crump* of bombing – he noted the crumbling plaster, he saw the flickering lights – and he grasped the terror of what was approaching them. The children, two by two, marched whimpering after Helen and Jenny, who led them to the bomb shelter as soberly as nurses. If they looked at Garp at all, they regarded him with vague sadness and with scorn, as if he had let them all down and was powerless to help them now.

Perhaps he had been looking at the wet, split beaver instead of watching for enemy planes? This, true to the nature of dreams, was forever unclear: precisely *why* he felt so guilty, and *why* they looked at him as if they'd been so abused.

At the end of the line of children were Walt and Duncan, holding hands; the so-called buddy system, as it is employed at summer camps, appeared in Garp's dream to be the natural reaction to a disaster among children. Little Walt was crying, the way Garp had heard him cry when he was caught in the grip of a nightmare, unable to wake up. 'I'm having a bad dream,' he sniveled. He looked at his father and almost shouted to him, 'I'm having a bad dream!'

But in Garp's dream, Garp could not wake the child from *this* one. Duncan looked stoically over his shoulder at his father, a silent and bravely doomed expression on his beautiful young face. Duncan was appearing very grown-up lately. Duncan's look was a secret between Duncan and Garp: that they both knew it was *not* a dream, and that Walt could not be helped.

'Wake me up!' Walt cried, but the long file of children was disappearing into the bomb shelter. Twisting in Duncan's grip (Walt came to about the height of Duncan's elbow), Walt looked back at his father. 'I'm having a *dream!*' Walt screamed, as if to convince himself. Garp could do nothing; he said nothing; he made no attempt to follow them – down these last stairs. And the dropping plaster coated everything white. The bombs kept falling.

'You're having a dream!' Garp screamed after little Walt.

'It's just a bad dream!' he cried, though he knew he was lying.

Then Helen would kick him and he'd wake up.

Perhaps Helen feared that Garp's run-amuck imagination would turn away from Walt and turn on her. Because if Garp had given half the worry to Helen that he seemed compelled to give to Walt, Garp might have realized that something was going on.

Helen thought she was in control of what was going on; she at least had controlled how it began (opening her office door, as usual, to the slouching Michael Milton, and bidding him enter her room). Once inside, she closed the door behind him and kissed him quickly on the mouth, holding his slim neck so that he couldn't even escape for breath, and grinding her knee between his legs; he kicked over the wastebasket and dropped his notebook.

'There's nothing more to discuss,' Helen said, taking a breath. She raced her tongue across his upper lip; Helen was trying to decide if she liked his mustache. She decided she liked it; or, at least, she liked it for now. 'We'll go to your apartment. Nowhere else,' she told him.

'It's across the river,' he said.

'I know where it is,' she said. 'Is it clean?'

'Of course,' he said. 'And it's got a great view of the river.'

'I don't care about the view,' Helen said. 'I want it clean.'

'It's pretty clean,' he said. 'I can clean it better.'

'We can only use your car,' she said.

'I don't have a car,' he said.

'I know you don't,' Helen said. 'You'll have to get one.'

He was smiling now; he'd been surprised, but now he was feeling sure of himself again. 'Well, I don't have to get one *now*, do I?' he asked, nuzzling his mustache against her neck; he touched her breasts. Helen unattached herself from his embrace.

'Get one whenever you want,' she said. 'We'll never use mine, and I won't be seen walking with you all over town, or riding on the buses. If *anyone* knows about this, it's over.

Do you understand?' She sat down at her desk, and he did not feel invited to walk around her desk to touch her; he sat in the chair her students usually sat in.

'Sure, I understand,' he said.

'I love my husband and will never hurt him,' Helen told him. Michael Milton knew better than to smile.

'I'll get a car, right away,' he said.

'And clean your apartment, or *have* it cleaned,' she said.

'Absolutely,' he said. Now he dared to smile, a little. 'What kind of car do you want me to get?' he asked her.

'I don't care about that,' she told him. 'Just get one that runs; get one that isn't in the garage all the time. And don't get one with bucket seats. Get one with a long seat in front.' He looked more surprised and puzzled than ever, so she explained to him: 'I want to be able to lie down, comfortably, across the front seat,' she said. 'I'll put my head in your lap so that no one will see me sitting up beside you. Do you understand?'

'Don't worry,' he said, smiling again.

'It's a small town,' Helen said. 'No one must know.'

'It's not *that* small a town,' Michael Milton said, confidently.

'Every town is a small town,' Helen said, 'and this one is smaller than you think. Do you want me to tell you?'

'Tell me what?' he asked her.

'You're sleeping with Margie Tallworth,' Helen said. 'She's in my Comp. Lit. 205; she's a junior,' Helen said. 'And you see another *very* young undergraduate – she's in Dirkson's English 150; I think she's a *freshman*, but I don't know if you've slept with her. Not for lack of trying, if you haven't,' Helen added. 'To my knowledge you've not touched any of your fellow graduate students; not yet,' Helen said. 'But there's surely someone I've missed, or there *has* been.'

Michael Milton was both sheepish and proud at the same time, and the usual command he held over his expressions escaped him so completely that Helen didn't like the expression she saw on his face and she looked away.

'*That's* how small this town, and every town, is,' Helen said. 'If you have me,' she told him, 'you can't have any of those others. I know what young girls notice, and I know how much they're inclined to *say*.'

'Yes,' Michael Milton said; he appeared ready to take notes.

Helen suddenly thought of something, and she looked momentarily startled. 'You *do* have a driver's license?' she asked.

'Oh yes!' Michael Milton said. They both laughed, and Helen relaxed again; but when he came around her desk to kiss her, she shook her head and waved him back.

'And you won't ever touch me here,' she said. 'There will be nothing intimate in this office. I don't lock my door. I don't even like to have it shut. Please open it, now,' she asked him, and he did as he was told.

He got a car, a huge Buick Roadmaster, the *old* kind of station wagon – with real wooden slats on the side. It was a 1951 Buick Dynaflow, heavy and shiny with pre-Korea chrome and real oak. It weighed 5,550 pounds, or almost three tons. It held seven quarts of oil and nineteen gallons of gasoline. Its original price was $2,850 but Michael Milton picked it up for less than six hundred dollars.

'It's a straight-eight cylinder, three-twenty cubic, power steering, with a single-throat Carter carb,' the salesman told Michael. 'It's not too badly rusted.'

In fact, it was the dull, inconspicuous color of clotted blood, more than six feet wide and seventeen feet long. The front seat was so long and deep that Helen could lie across it, almost without having to bend her knees – or without having to put her head in Michael Milton's lap, though she did this anyway.

She did not put her head in his lap because she *had* to; she liked her view of the dashboard, and being close to the old smell of the maroon leather of the big, slick seat. She put her head in his lap because she liked feeling Michael's leg stiffen and relax, his thigh shifting just slightly between the brake and the accelerator. It was a quiet lap to put your head in because the car had no clutch; the driver needed to move just one leg, and just occasionally. Michael Milton thoughtfully carried his loose change in his left front pocket, so there were only the soft wales of his corduroy slacks, which made a faint impression on the skin of Helen's cheek – and sometimes his rising erection would touch her ear, or reach up into the hair on the back of her neck.

Sometimes she imagined taking him into her mouth while they drove across town in the big car with the gaping chrome grille like the mouth of a feeding fish – *Buick Eight* in script across the teeth. But that, Helen knew, would not be safe.

The first indication that the whole thing might not be safe was when Margie Tallworth dropped Helen's Comp. Lit. 205, without so much as a note of explanation concerning what she might not have liked about the course. Helen feared it was not the course that Margie hadn't liked, and she called the young Miss Tallworth into her office to ask her for an explanation.

Margie Tallworth, a junior, knew enough about school to know that no explanation was required; up to a certain point in any semester, a student was free to drop any course without the instructor's permission. 'Do I have to have a reason?' the girl asked Helen, sullenly.

'No, you don't,' Helen said. 'But if you *had* a reason, I just wanted to hear it.'

'I don't have to have a reason,' Margie Tallworth said. She held Helen's gaze longer than most students could hold it; then she got up to leave. She was pretty and small and rather well dressed for a student, Helen thought. If there was any consistency to Michael Milton's former girlfriend and his present taste, it appeared only that he liked women to wear nice clothes.

'Well, I'm sorry it didn't work out,' Helen said, truthfully, as Margie was leaving; she was still fishing for what the girl might actually *know*.

She knew, Helen thought, and quickly accused Michael.

'You've blown it already,' she told him coldly, because she *could* speak coldly to him – over the phone. 'Just *how* did you drop Margie Tallworth?'

'Very gently,' Michael Milton said, smugly. 'But a drop is a drop, no matter how different the ways of doing it are.' Helen did not appreciate it when he attempted to instruct her – except sexually; she indulged the boy that, and he seemed to need to be dominant there. That was different for her, and she didn't really mind. He was sometimes rough, but not ever dangerous, she thought; and if she firmly resisted something, he stopped. Once she had had to tell him, 'No! I don't like that, I won't do that.' But she had added, 'Please,' because she wasn't *that* sure of him. He had stopped; he had been forceful with her, but in another way – in a way that was all right with her. It was exciting that she couldn't trust him completely. But not trusting him to be *silent* was another matter; if she knew he had talked about her, that would be that.

'I didn't tell her anything,' Michael insisted. 'I said, "Margie, it's all over," or something like that. I didn't even tell her there was another woman, and I *certainly* said nothing about you.'

'But she's probably heard you talk about me, before,' Helen said. 'Before this started, I mean.'

'She never liked your course, anyway,' Michael said. 'We *did* talk about that once.'

'She never liked the course?' Helen said. This truly surprised her.

'Well, she's not very bright,' Michael said, impatiently.

'She'd better not know,' Helen said. 'I mean it: you better find out.'

But he found out nothing. Margie Tallworth refused to speak to him. He tried to tell her, on the phone, that it was all because an old girlfriend had come back to him – she had arrived from out of town; she'd had no place to stay; one thing had led to another. But Margie Tallworth had hung up on him before he could polish the story.

Helen smoked a little more. She watched Garp anxiously for a few days – and once she felt actual guilt, when she made love to Garp; she felt guilty that she had made love to him not because she wanted to but because she wanted to reassure him, *if* he had been thinking that anything was wrong.

He hadn't been thinking, not much. Or: he *had* thought, but only once, about the bruises on the small, tight backs of Helen's thighs; though he was strong, Garp was a very gentle man with his children and his wife. He also knew what fingermark bruises looked like because he was a wrestler. It was a day or so later that he noticed the same small fingermark bruises on the backs of Duncan's arms – just where Garp held him when Garp wrestled with the boy – and Garp concluded that he gripped the people he loved harder than he meant to. He concluded that the fingermarks on Helen were also his.

He was too vain a man to be easily jealous. And the name he had woken with – on his lips, one morning – had eluded him. There were no more papers by Michael Milton around the house, keeping Helen up at night. In fact, she was going to bed earlier and earlier; she needed her rest.

As for Helen, she developed a fondness for the bare, sharp shaft of the Volvo's stick shift; its bite at the end of the day, driving home from her office, felt good against the heel of her hand, and she often pressed against it until she felt it was only a hair away from the pressure necessary to break her skin. She could bring tears to her eyes, this way, and it made her feel clean again, when she arrived home – when the boys would wave and shout at her, from the window where the TV was; and when Garp would announce what dinner he had prepared for them all, when Helen walked into the kitchen.

Margie Tallworth's possible knowledge had frightened Helen, because although Helen had said to Michael – and to herself – that it would be over the instant anyone knew,

Helen now knew that it would be more difficult to end than she had first imagined. She hugged Garp in his kitchen and hoped for Margie Tallworth's ignorance.

Margie Tallworth *was* ignorant, but she was not ignorant of Michael Milton's relationship with Helen. She was ignorant of many things but she knew about that. She was ignorant in that she thought her own shallow infatuation with Michael Milton had 'surpassed,' as she would say, 'the sexual'; whereas, she assumed, Helen was merely amusing herself with Michael. In truth, Margie Tallworth had absolutely *wallowed* in, as she would say, 'the sexual'; it is difficult, in fact, to know what *else* her relationship with Michael Milton had been about. But she was not altogether wrong in assuming that this was what Helen's relationship with Michael Milton was also about. Margie Tallworth was ignorant in that she assumed too much, too much of the time; but in this case she had assumed correctly.

Back when Michael Milton and Helen were actually talking about Michael's 'work,' Margie assumed – even then – that they were fucking. Margie Tallworth did not believe there was another kind of relationship that one could have with Michael Milton. In this one way, she was not ignorant. She may have known the kind of relationship Helen had with Michael before Helen knew it herself.

And through the one-way glass of the fourth-floor ladies' room, in the English and Literature Building, it was possible for Margie Tallworth to look through the tinted windshield of the three-ton Buick, gliding like the coffin of a king out of the parking lot. Margie could see Mrs Garp's slender legs stretched along the long front seat. It was a peculiar way to ride in a car with other than the best of friends.

Margie knew their habits better than she understood her own; she took long walks, to try to forget Michael Milton, and to familiarize herself with the whereabouts of Helen's house. She was soon familiar with the habits of Helen's husband, too, because Garp's habits were much more constant than *any*one's: he padded back and forth, from room to room, in the mornings; perhaps he was out of a job. That fitted Margie Tallworth's assumptions of the likely cuckold: a man who was out of work. At midday he burst out the door in track clothes and ran away; miles later, he returned and read his mail, which nearly always came when he was gone. Then he padded back and forth in the house again; he undressed, in pieces, on the way to the shower, and he was slow to dress when he was out of the shower. One thing did not fit her image of the cuckold: Garp had a good body. And why did he spend so much time in the kitchen? Margie Tallworth wondered if perhaps he was an unemployed cook.

Then his children came home and they broke Margie Tallworth's soft little heart. He looked quite nice when he played with his children, which also fitted Margie's assumptions of what a cuckold was like: someone who had witless good fun with his children while his wife was out getting *planked*. 'Planked' was also a word that the wrestlers Garp knew used, and they had used it back at those blood-and-blue days at Steering, too. Someone was always bragging about planking a wet, split beaver.

So one day, when Garp burst out the door in his track clothes, Margie Tallworth waited only as long as it took him to run away; then she went up on the Garps' porch with a perfumed note, which she intended to drop in his mail. She had thought very carefully that he would have time to read the note and (hopefully) recover himself before his children came home. This was how she assumed such news was absorbed: suddenly! Then there was a reasonable period of recovery and one got ready to face the children. Here was another case of something Margie Tallworth was ignorant of.

The note itself had given her trouble because she was not good with words. And it was perfumed not by intention but simply because every piece of paper Margie Tallworth owned was perfumed; if she had thought about it, she would have realized perfume was inappropriate to this note, but that was another of the things she was ignorant of. Even her schoolwork was perfumed; when Helen had read Margie Tallworth's first essay for Comp. Lit. 205, she had cringed at its *scent*.

What Margie's note to Garp said was:

Your Wife Is 'Involved with' Michael Milton

Margie Tallworth would grow up to be the sort of person who said that someone 'passed away' instead of died. Thus she sought delicacy with the words that Helen was 'involved with' Michael Milton. And she had this sweetly smelling note in her hand, and she was poised on the Garps' porch with it, when it began to rain.

Nothing made Garp turn back from a run faster than rain. He hated getting his running shoes wet. He would run in the cold, and run in the snow, but when it rained, Garp ran home, swearing, and cooked for an hour in a foul-weather mood. Then he put on a poncho and caught the bus to the gym in time for wrestling practice. On the way, he picked up Walt from day care and took Walt to the gym with him; he called home when he got to the gym to see if Duncan was back from school. Sometimes he gave Duncan instructions, if the meal was still cooking, but usually he just cautioned Duncan about riding his bike and he quizzed him about emergency phone numbers: did Duncan know what to dial in case of fire, explosion, armed robbery, mayhem in the streets?

Then he wrestled, and after practice he popped Walt into the shower with himself; by the time he called home again, Helen was there to come pick them up.

Therefore, Garp did not like rain; although he enjoyed wrestling, rain complicated his simple plans. And Margie Tallworth was unprepared to see him suddenly panting and angry behind her on the porch.

'Aaahhh!' she cried; she clutched her scented note as

tightly as if it were the main artery of an animal whose blood flow she wished she could *stop*.

'Hello,' said Garp. She looked like a babysitter to him. He had trained himself off babysitters some time ago. He smiled at her with frank curiosity – that is all.

'Aaa,' said Margie Tallworth; she couldn't speak. Garp looked at the crushed message in her hand; she shut her eyes and held the note out to him, as if she were putting her hand into a fire.

If at first Garp had thought she was one of Helen's students, wanting something, now he thought something else. He saw that she couldn't speak, and he saw the extreme self-consciousness of her handing him the note. Garp's experience with speechless women who handed out notes self-consciously was limited to Ellen Jamesians, and he suppressed a momentary flame of anger – that another creepy Ellen Jamesian was introducing herself to him. Or had she come to bait him about something – the reclusive son of the exciting Jenny Fields?

Hi! I'm Margie. I'm an Ellen Jamesian,

her stupid note would say.

Do You Know What an Ellen Jamesian Is?

The next thing you know, Garp thought, they'll be organized like the religious morons who bring those righteous pamphlets about Jesus to one's very door. It sickened him, for example, that the Ellen Jamesians were now reaching girls as young as this one; she was too young to know, he thought, whether she wanted a tongue in her life or not. He shook his head and waved the note away.

'Yes, yes, I know, I know,' Garp said. 'So what?'

Poor Margie Tallworth was unprepared for this. She had come like an avenging angel – her terrible duty, and what a burden it was to her! – to bring the bad news that somehow must be made known. But he *knew* already! And he didn't even care.

She clutched her note in both her hands, so tightly to her pretty, trembling breasts that more of the perfume was *expressed* from it – or from *her* – and a wave of her young-girl smell passed over Garp, who stood glaring at her.

'I said, "So what?"' Garp said. 'Do you actually expect me to have respect for someone who cuts her own tongue off?'

Margie forced a word out. 'What?' she said; she was frightened now. *Now* she guessed why the poor man padded around his house all day, out of work: he was insane.

Garp had distinctly heard the word; it was not a gagged 'Aaahhh' or even a little 'Aaa' – it was not the word of an amputated tongue. It was a whole word.

'What?' he said.

'What?' she said, again.

He stared at the note she held against herself.

'You can *talk*?' he said.

'Of course,' she croaked.

'What's *that*?' he asked, and pointed to her note. But now she was afraid of him – an insane cuckold. God knows what he might do. Murder the children, or murder her; he looked strong enough to murder Michael Milton with one arm. And every man looked evil when he was questioning you. She backed away from him, off the porch.

'Wait!' Garp cried. 'Is that a note for *me*? What *is* that? Is it something for Helen? Who are you?'

Margie Tallworth shook her head. 'It's a mistake,' she whispered, and when she turned to flee, she collided with the wet mailman, spilling his bag and knocking herself back into Garp. Garp had a vision of Duna, the senile bear, bowling a mailman down a Viennese staircase – outlawed forever. But all that happened to Margie Tallworth was that she fell to the floor of the porch; her stockings tore and she skinned one knee.

The mailman, who assumed he'd arrived at an awkward moment, fumbled for Garp's mail among his strewn letters, but Garp was now only interested in what message the crying girl had for him. 'What *is* it?' he asked her, gently; he tried to help her to her feet, but she wanted to sit where she was. She kept sobbing.

'I'm sorry,' Margie Tallworth said. She had lost her nerve; she had spent a minute too long around Garp, and now that she thought she rather *liked* him, it was hard for her to imagine giving him this news.

'Your knee's not too bad,' Garp said, 'but let me get something to clean you up.' He went inside for antiseptic for her cut, and bandages, but she took this opportunity to limp away. She could not face him with this news, but she could not withhold it from him, either. She left her note for him. The mailman watched her hobble down the side street toward the corner where the buses stopped; he wondered briefly what the Garps were up to. They seemed to get more mail than other families, too.

It was all those letters Garp wrote, which poor John Wolf, his editor, struggled to answer. And there were copies of books to review; Garp gave them to Helen, who at least read them. There were Helen's magazines; it seemed to Garp there were a great many. There were Garp's two magazines, his only subscriptions: *Gourmet* and *Amateur Wrestling News*. There were, of course, bills. And a letter rather frequently from Jenny; it was all she wrote these days. And a letter now and then, short and sweet, from Ernie Holm.

Sometimes Harry Fletcher wrote them both, and Alice still wrote with exquisite fluency, about nothing at all, to Garp.

And now among the usual was a note, reeking of perfume and wet with tears. Garp put down the bottle of antiseptic and the bandages; he did not bother to look for the girl. He held the crumpled note and thought he knew, more or less, what it would be about.

He wondered why he hadn't thought of it before, because there were so many things that pointed to it; now that he thought of it, he supposed he *had* thought of it before, only

not quite this consciously. The slow unwrapping of the note
– so it wouldn't tear – made sounds as crisp as autumn,
though all around Garp it was a cold March, the hurt
ground thawing to mud. The little note snapped like bones
as he opened it. With the escaping perfume, Garp imagined
he could still hear the girl's sharp little yelp: 'What?'

He knew 'what'; what he *didn't* know was 'with whom'
– that name, which had kicked around in his mind, one
morning, but then was gone. The note, of course, would
provide him with the name: Michael Milton. It sounded
to Garp like a special kind of new ice cream at that shop
he took the boys to. There was Strawberry Swirl, Chock-full
of Chocolate, Mocha Madness, and Michael Milton. It was
a *disgusting* name – a flavor Garp could taste – and Garp
tramped to the storm sewer and wadded the vile-smelling
note into pieces and stuffed them through the grate. Then
he went inside the house and read the name in a phone
book, over and over again.

It seemed to him now that Helen had been 'involved
with' someone for a long time; it seemed that he had known
it for some time, too. But the *name!* Michael Milton! Garp
had classified him – to Helen – at a party where Garp had
been introduced to him. Garp had told Helen that Michael
Milton was a 'wimp'; they had discussed his mustache.
Michael Milton! Garp read the name so many times, he was
still peering into the phone book when Duncan got home
from school and assumed that his father was once more
searching a directory for his make-believe people.

'Didn't you get Walt yet?' Duncan asked.

Garp had forgotten. And Walt has a cold, too, Garp
thought. The boy shouldn't have to wait for me, with a
cold.

'Let's go get him together,' Garp said to Duncan. To
Duncan's surprise, Garp threw the phone book into the
trash barrel. Then they walked to the bus stop.

Garp was still in his track clothes, and it was still raining; Duncan found this odd, too, but he didn't say anything

about it. He said, 'I got two goals today.' For some reason, all they played at Duncan's school was soccer – fall, winter, and spring, they played only soccer. It was a small school, but there was another reason for all the soccer; Garp forgot what it was. He had never liked the reason, anyway. 'Two goals,' Duncan repeated.

'That's great,' Garp said.

'One was a header,' Duncan said.

'With your head?' Garp said. 'That's wonderful!'

'Ralph gave me a perfect pass,' Duncan said.

'That's *still* wonderful,' Garp said. 'And good for Ralph.' He put his arm around Duncan, but he knew Duncan would be embarrassed if he tried to kiss him; it is Walt who lets me kiss him, Garp thought. Then he thought of kissing Helen and almost stepped in front of the bus.

'Dad!' Duncan said. And in the bus he asked his father, 'Are you okay?'

'Sure,' Garp said.

'I thought you'd be up at the wrestling room,' Duncan said. 'It *is* raining.'

From Walt's day care you could look across the river and Garp tried to place the exact location, there, of Michael Milton's address, which he had memorized from the phone book.

'Where were you?' Walt complained. He coughed; his nose dripped; he felt hot. He expected to go wrestling whenever it rained.

'Why don't we *all* go to the wrestling room, as long as we're downtown?' Duncan said. He was increasingly logical, but Garp said no, he didn't want to wrestle today. 'Why not?' Duncan wanted to know.

'Because he's got his running stuff on, dummy,' Walt said.

'Oh, shut up, Walt,' Duncan said. They more or less fought on the bus, until Garp told them they couldn't. Walt was sick, Garp reasoned, and fighting was bad for his cold.

'I'm not sick,' Walt said.

'Yes, you are,' Garp said.

'Yes, you are,' Duncan teased.

'Shut up, Duncan,' Garp said.

'Boy, you're in a great mood,' Duncan said, and Garp wanted to kiss him; Garp wished to assure Duncan that he wasn't really in a bad mood, but kissing embarrassed Duncan, so Garp kissed Walt instead.

'Dad!' Walt complained. 'You're all wet and sweaty.'

'Because he's got his running stuff on, dummy,' Duncan said.

'He called me a dummy,' Walt told Garp.

'I heard him,' Garp said.

'I'm not a dummy,' Walt said.

'Yes, you are,' Duncan said.

'Shut up, both of you,' Garp said.

'Dad's in a great mood, isn't he, Walt?' Duncan asked his brother.

'Sure is,' Walt said, and they decided to tease their father, instead of fight among themselves, until the bus deposited them – a few blocks from the house in the increasing rain. They were a soggy threesome when they were still a block from home, and a car that had been going too fast slowed suddenly beside them; the window was rolled down, after a struggle, and in the steamy interior Garp saw the frazzled, glistening face of Mrs Ralph. She grinned at them.

'You seen Ralph?' she asked Duncan.

'Nope,' Duncan said.

'The moron doesn't know enough to come out of the rain,' she said. 'I guess *you* don't, either,' she said sweetly, to Garp; she was still grinning and Garp tried to smile back at her, but he couldn't think of anything to say. He must have had poor control of his expression, he suspected, because Mrs Ralph wouldn't usually pass up the opportunity to go on teasing him in the rain. Yet, instead, she looked suddenly shocked by Garp's ghastly smile; she rolled her window back up.

'See ya,' she called, and drove off. Slowly.

'See ya,' Garp mumbled after her; he admired the woman

but he was thinking that maybe even *this* horror would eventually come to pass: that he *would* see Mrs Ralph.

In the house he gave Walt a hot bath, slipping into the tub with him – an excuse, which he often took, to wrestle with that little body. Duncan was too big for Garp to fit in the tub with him anymore.

'What's for supper?' Duncan called upstairs.

Garp realized he had forgotten supper.

'I forgot supper,' Garp called.

'You *forgot?*' Walt asked him, but Garp dunked Walt in the tub, and tickled him, and Walt fought back and forgot about the issue.

'You forgot *supper?*' Duncan hollered from downstairs.

Garp decided he was not going to get out of the tub. He kept adding more hot water; the steam was good for Walt's lungs, he believed. He would try to keep the child in the tub with him as long as Walt was content to play.

They were still in the bath together when Helen got home.

'Dad forgot supper,' Duncan told her immediately.

'He forgot supper?' Helen said.

'He forgot all about it,' Duncan said.

'Where *is* he?' Helen asked.

'He's taking a bath with Walt,' Duncan said. 'They've been taking a bath for *hours.*'

'Heavens,' said Helen. 'Maybe they've drowned.'

'Wouldn't you love *that?*' Garp hollered from his bath, upstairs. Duncan laughed.

'He's in a great mood,' Duncan told his mother.

'I can see that he is,' Helen said. She put her hand softly on Duncan's shoulder, being careful not to let him know that she was actually leaning on him for support. She felt suddenly unsure of her balance. Poised at the bottom of the stairs, she called up to Garp, 'Had a bad day?'

But Garp slipped underwater; it was a gesture of control, because he felt such hatred for her and he didn't want Walt to see it or hear it.

There was no answer and Helen tightened her grip on Duncan's shoulder. Please, *not in front of the children,* she thought. It was a new situation for her – that she should find herself in the defensive position in a matter of some contention with Garp – and she felt frightened.

'Shall I come up?' she called.

There was still no answer; Garp could hold his breath a long time.

Walt shouted back downstairs to her, 'Dad's underwater!'

'Dad is so *weird,*' Duncan said.

Garp came up for air just as Walt yelled again, 'He's holding his breath!'

I hope so, Helen thought. She didn't know what to do, she couldn't move.

In a minute or so, Garp whispered to Walt, 'Tell her I'm *still* underwater, Walt. Okay?'

Walt appeared to think this was a fiendishly clever trick and he yelled downstairs to Helen, 'Dad's *still* underwater!'

'Wow,' Duncan said. 'We should time him. It must be a record.'

But now Helen felt panicked. Duncan moved out from under her hand – he was starting up the stairs to see this breath-holding feat – and Helen felt that her legs were lead.

'He's *still* underwater!' Walt shrieked, though Garp was drying Walt with a towel and had already started to drain the tub; they stood naked on the bathmat by the big mirror together. When Duncan came into the bathroom, Garp silenced him by putting a finger to his lips.

'Now, say it *together,*' Garp whispered. 'On the count of three, "He's still under!" One, two, three.'

'He's *still* under!' Duncan and Walt howled together, and Helen felt her own lungs burst. She felt a scream escape her but no sound emerged, and she ran up the stairs thinking that only her husband could have conceived of such a plot to pay her back: *drowning* himself in front of their children and leaving her to explain to them why he did it.

She ran crying into the bathroom, so surprising Duncan and Walt that she had to recover almost immediately – in order not to frighten them. Garp was naked at the mirror, slowly drying between his toes and watching her in a way she remembered that Ernie Holm had taught his wrestlers how to *look* for openings.

'You're too late,' he told her. 'I already died. But it's touching, and a little surprising, to see that you *care.*'

'We'll talk about this later?' she asked him, hopefully – and smiling, as if it had been a good joke.

'We fooled you!' Walt said, poking Helen on that sharp bone above her hip.

'Boy, if we'd pulled that on *you,*' Duncan said to his father, 'you'd have really been pissed at us.'

'The children haven't eaten,' Helen said.

'Nobody's eaten,' Garp said. 'Unless you have.'

'I can wait,' she told him.

'So can I,' Garp told her.

'I'll get the kids something,' Helen offered, pushing Walt out of the bathroom. 'There must be eggs, and cereal.'

'For *supper?*' Duncan said. 'That sounds like a *great* supper,' he said.

'I just forgot, Duncan,' Garp said.

'I want toast,' Walt said.

'You can have toast, too,' Helen said.

'Are you sure you can handle this?' Garp asked Helen.

She just smiled at him.

'God, even *I* can handle *toast,*' Duncan said. 'I think even *Walt* can fix cereal.'

'The eggs are tricky,' Helen said; she tried to laugh.

Garp went on drying between his toes. When the kids were out of the bathroom, Helen poked her head back in. 'I'm sorry, and I love you,' Helen said, but he wouldn't look up from his deliberate procedure with the towel. 'I never wanted to hurt you,' she went on. 'How did you find out? I have *never* once stopped thinking of you. Was it that girl?'

Helen whispered, but Garp gave all his attention to his toes.

When she had set out food for the children (as if they were *pets!* she would think to herself, later), she went back upstairs to him. He was still in front of the mirror, sitting naked on the edge of the tub.

'He means nothing; he never took anything away from you,' she told him. 'It's all over now, really it is.'

'Since when?' he asked her.

'As of now,' she said to Garp. 'I just have to tell him.'

'*Don't* tell him,' Garp said. 'Let him guess.'

'I can't do that,' Helen said.

'There's shell in my egg!' Walt hollered from down-stairs.

'My toast is burnt!' Duncan said. They were plotting together to distract their parents from each other – whether they knew it or not. Children, Garp thought, have some instinct for separating their parents when their parents ought to be separated.

'Just eat it!' Helen called to them. 'It's not so bad.'

She tried to touch Garp but he slipped past her, out of the bathroom; he started to dress.

'Eat up and I'll take you to a movie!' he called to the kids.

'What are you doing that for?' Helen asked him.

'I'm not staying here with you,' he said. 'We're going out. You call that wimpish asshole and say good-bye.'

'He'll want to see me,' Helen said, dully – the reality of having it over, now that Garp knew about it, was working on her like Novocain. If she had been sensitive to how much she'd hurt Garp, at first, now her feelings for him were dead-ening slightly and she was feeling for herself again.

'Tell him to eat his heart out,' Garp said. 'You won't see him. No last fucks for the road, Helen. Just tell him good-bye. On the phone.'

'Nobody said anything about "last fucks,"' Helen said.

'Use the phone,' Garp said. 'I'll take the kids out. We'll see a movie. Please have it over with before we come back. You *won't* see him again.'

'I won't, I promise,' Helen said. 'But I *should* see him, just once – to tell him.'

'I suppose you feel you've handled this very decently,' Garp said.

Helen, to a point, *did* feel so; she didn't say anything. She felt she had never lost sight of Garp and the children during this indulgence; she felt justified in handling it *her* way, now.

'We should talk about this later,' she said to him. 'Some perspective will be possible, later.'

He would have struck her if the children hadn't burst into the room.

'One, two, three,' Duncan chanted to Walt.

'The cereal is stale!' Duncan and Walt hollered together.

'Please, boys,' Helen said. 'Your father and I are having a little fight. Go downstairs.'

They stared at her.

'Please,' Garp said to them. He turned away from them so they wouldn't see him crying, but Duncan probably knew, and surely Helen knew. Walt probably didn't catch it.

'A fight?' Walt said.

'Come on,' Duncan said to him; he took Walt's hand. Duncan pulled Walt out of the bedroom. 'Come *on*, Walt,' Duncan said, 'or we won't get to see the movie.'

'Yeah, the movie!' Walt cried.

To his horror, Garp recognized the attitude of their leaving – Duncan leading Walt away, and down the stairs; the smaller boy turning and looking back. Walt waved, but Duncan pulled him on. Down and gone, into the bomb shelter. Garp hid his face in his clothes and cried.

When Helen touched him, he said, 'Don't touch me,' and went on crying. Helen shut the bedroom door.

'Oh, *don't*,' she pleaded. 'He isn't worth this; he wasn't *any*thing. I just *enjoyed* him,' she tried to explain, but Garp shook his head violently and threw his pants at her. He was still only half dressed – an attitude that was perhaps, Helen realized, the most compromising for men: when they were not one thing and also not another. A woman half dressed seemed to have some power, but a man was simply not as handsome as when he was naked, and not as secure as when he was clothed. 'Please get dressed,' she whispered to him, and handed him back his pants. He took them, he pulled them on; and went on crying.

'I'll do just what you want,' she said.

'You won't see him again?' he said to her.

'No, not once,' she said. 'Not ever again.'

'Walt has a cold,' Garp said. 'He shouldn't even be going out, but it's not too bad for him at a movie. And we won't be late,' he added to her. 'Go see if he's dressed warmly enough.' She did.

He opened her top drawer, where her lingerie was, and pulled the drawer from the dresser; he pushed his face into the wonderful silkiness and scent of her clothes – like a bear holding a great trough of food in his forepaws, and then losing himself in it. When Helen came back into the room and caught him at this, it was almost as if she'd caught him masturbating. Embarrassed, he brought the drawer down across his knee and cracked it; her underwear flew about. He raised the cracked drawer over his head and smacked it down against the edge of the dresser, snapping what felt like the spine of an animal about the size of the drawer. Helen ran from the room and he finished dressing.

He saw Duncan's fairly well finished supper on Duncan's plate; he saw Walt's uneaten supper on Walt's plate, and on various parts of the table and floor. 'If you don't eat, Walt,' Garp said, 'you'll grow up to be a *wimp.*'

'I'm not going to grow up,' Walt said.

That gave Garp such a shiver that he turned on Walt and startled the child. 'Don't *ever* say that,' Garp said.

'I don't *want* to grow up,' Walt said.

'Oh, I see,' Garp said, softening. 'You mean, you *like* being a kid?'

'Yup,' Walt said.

'Walt is *so* weird,' Duncan said.

'I am *not!*' Walt cried.

'You are so,' Duncan said.

'Go get in the car,' Garp said. 'And stop fighting.'

'*You* were fighting,' Duncan said, cautiously; no one reacted and Duncan tugged Walt out of the kitchen. 'Come on,' he said.

'Yeah, the *movie!*' Walt said. They went out.

Garp said to Helen, 'He's not to come here, under any circumstances. If you let him in this house, he won't get out alive. And you're not to go out,' he said. 'Under any circumstances. Please,' he added, and he had to turn away from her.

'Oh, darling,' Helen said.

'He's such an *asshole!*' Garp moaned.

'It could never be anyone like *you*, don't you see?' Helen said. 'It could *only* be someone who wasn't at all like you.'

He thought of the babysitters and Alice Fletcher, and his inexplicable attraction to Mrs Ralph, and of course he knew what she meant; he walked out the kitchen door. It was raining outside, and already dark; perhaps the rain would freeze. The mud in the driveway was wet but firm. He turned the car around; then, by habit, he edged the car to the top of the driveway and cut the engine and the lights. Down the Volvo rolled, but he knew the driveway's dark curve by heart. The kids were thrilled by the sound of the gravel and the slick mud in the growing blackness, and when he popped the clutch at the bottom of the driveway, and flicked on the lights, both Walt and Duncan cheered.

'What movie are we going to see?' Duncan asked.

'Anything you want,' Garp said. They drove downtown to have a look at the posters.

It was cold and damp in the car and Walt coughed; the windshield kept fogging over, which made it hard to see what was playing at the movie houses. Walt and Duncan continued to fight about who got to stand in the gap between the bucket seats; for some reason, this had always been the prime spot in the backseat for them, and they had always fought over who got to stand or kneel there – crowding each other and bumping Garp's elbow when he used the stick shift.

'Get out of there, both of you,' Garp said.

'It's the only place you can see,' Duncan said.

'*I'm* the only one who has to see,' Garp said. 'And this defroster is such *junk*,' he added, 'that *no* one can see out the windshield anyway.'

'Why don't you write the Volvo people?' Duncan suggested.

Garp tried to imagine a letter to Sweden about the inadequacies of the defrost system, but he couldn't sustain the idea for very long. On the floor, in back, Duncan kneeled on Walt's foot and pushed him out of the gap between the bucket seats; now Walt cried *and* coughed.

'I was here first,' Duncan said.

Garp downshifted, hard, and the uncovered tip of the stick-shift shaft bit into his hand.

'You see this, Duncan?' Garp asked, angrily. 'You see this gearshift? It's like a *spear*. You want to fall on that if I have to stop hard?'

'Why don't you get it fixed?' Duncan asked.

'Get *out* of the goddamn gap between the seats, Duncan!' Garp said.

'The stick shift has been like that for months,' Duncan said.

'For *weeks*, maybe,' Garp said.

'If it's dangerous, you should get it fixed,' Duncan said.

'That's your mother's job,' Garp said.

'She says it's *your* job, Dad,' Walt said.

'How's your cough, Walt?' Garp asked.

Walt coughed. The wet rattle in his small chest seemed oversized for the child.

'Jesus,' Duncan said.

'That's great, Walt,' Garp said.

'It's not *my* fault,' Walt complained.

'Of course it isn't,' Garp said.

'Yes, it is,' Duncan said. 'Walt spends half his life in *puddles.*'

'I do not!' Walt said.

'Look for a movie that looks interesting, Duncan,' Garp said.

'I can't see unless I kneel between the seats,' Duncan said.

They drove around. The movie houses were all on the same block but they had to drive past them a few times to decide upon *which* movie, and then they had to drive by them a few more times before they found a place to park.

The children chose to see the only film that had a line waiting to see it, extending out from under the cinema marquee along the sidewalk, streaked now with a freezing rain. Garp put his own jacket over Walt's head, so that very quickly Walt resembled some ill-clothed street beggar – a damp dwarf seeking sympathy in bad weather. He promptly stepped in a puddle and soaked his feet; Garp then picked him up and listened to his chest. It was almost as if Garp thought the water in Walt's wet shoes dripped immediately into his little lungs.

'You're so *weird*, Dad,' Duncan said.

Walt saw a strange car and pointed it out. The car moved quickly down the soaked street; splashing through the garish puddles, it threw the reflected neon upon itself – a big dark car, the color of clotted blood; it had wooden slats on its sides, and the blond wood glowed in the streetlights. The slats looked like the ribs of the long, lit skeleton of a great fish gliding through moonlight. 'Look at that car!' Walt cried.

'Wow, it's a *hearse*,' Duncan said.

'No, Duncan,' Garp said. 'It's an old Buick. Before your time.'

The Buick that Duncan mistook for a hearse was on its

way to Garp's house, although Helen had done all she could to discourage Michael Milton from coming.

'I *can't* see you,' Helen told him when she called. 'It's as simple as that. It's over, just the way I said it would be if he ever found out. I won't hurt him any more than I already have.'

'What about me?' Michael Milton said.

'I'm sorry,' Helen told him. 'But you *knew*. We both knew.'

'I want to *see* you,' he said. 'Maybe tomorrow?'

But she told him that Garp had taken the kids to a movie for the sole purpose that she finish it tonight.

'I'm coming over,' he told her.

'Not here, no,' she said.

'We'll go for a drive,' he told her.

'I can't go out, either,' she said.

'I'm coming,' Michael Milton said, and he hung up.

Helen checked the time. It would be all right, she supposed, if she could get him to leave quickly. Movies were at least an hour and a half long. She decided she wouldn't let him in the house – not under any circumstances. She watched for the headlights to come up the driveway, and when the Buick stopped – just in front of the garage, like a big ship docking at a dark pier – she ran out of the house and pushed herself against the driver's-side door before Michael Milton could open it.

The rain was turning to a semisoft slush at her feet, and the icy drops were hardening as they fell – they had some sting as they struck her bare neck, when she bent over to speak to him through the rolled-down window.

He immediately kissed her. She tried to lightly peck his cheek but he turned her face and forced his tongue into her mouth. All over again she saw the corny bedroom of his apartment: the poster-sized print above his bed – Paul Klee's *Sinbad the Sailor*. She supposed this was how he saw himself: a colorful adventurer, but sensitive to the beauty of Europe.

Helen pulled back from him and felt the cold rain soak her blouse.

'We can't just *stop*,' he said, miserably. Helen couldn't tell if it was the rain through the open window or tears that streaked his face. To her surprise, he had shaved his mustache off, and his upper lip looked slightly like the puckered, undeveloped lip of a child – like Walt's little lip, which looked lovely on Walt, Helen thought; but it wasn't her idea of the lip for a lover.

'What did you do to your mustache?' she asked him.

'I thought you didn't like it,' he said. 'I did it for you.'

'But I *liked* it,' she said, and shivered in the freezing rain.

'Please, get in with me,' he said.

She shook her head; her blouse clung to her cold skin and her long corduroy skirt felt as heavy as chain mail; her tall boots slipped in the stiffening slush.

'I won't take you anywhere,' he promised. 'We'll just sit here, in the car. We can't just *stop*,' he repeated.

'We knew we'd have to,' Helen said. 'We knew it was just for a little while.'

Michael Milton let his head sink against the glinting ring of the horn; but there was no sound, the big Buick was shut off. The rain began to stick to the windows – the car was slowly being encased in ice.

'Please get *in*,' Michael Milton moaned. 'I'm not leaving here,' he added, sharply. 'I'm not afraid of him. I don't have to do what he says.'

'It's what *I* say, too,' Helen said. 'You have to go.'

'I'm not going,' Michael Milton said. 'I know about your husband. I know everything about him.'

They had never talked about Garp; Helen had forbidden it. She didn't know what Michael Milton meant.

'He's a minor writer,' Michael said, boldly. Helen looked surprised; to her knowledge, Michael Milton had never read Garp. He'd told her once that he never read living writers; he claimed to value the perspective he said one could gain only when a writer had been dead for a while. It is fortunate that

Garp didn't know *this* about him – it would certainly have added to Garp's contempt for the young man. It added somewhat to Helen's disappointment with poor Michael, now.

'My husband is a very good writer,' she said softly, and a shiver made her twitch so hard that her folded arms sprang open and she had to fold them closed at her breasts again.

'He's not a *major* writer,' Michael declared. 'Higgins said so. You certainly must be aware of how your husband is regarded in the department.'

Higgins, Helen was aware, was a singularly eccentric and troublesome colleague, who managed at the same time to be dull and cloddish to the point of sleep. Helen hardly felt Higgins was representative of the department – except that like many of her more insecure colleagues, Higgins habitually gossiped to the graduate students about his fellow department members; in this desperate way, perhaps, Higgins felt he gained the students' trust.

'I was not aware that Garp *was* regarded by the department, one way or another,' Helen said coolly. 'Most of them don't read anything very contemporary.'

'Those who do say he's minor,' Michael Milton said.

This competitive and pathetic stand did not warm Helen's heart to the boy and she turned to go back inside the house.

'I won't go!' Michael Milton screamed. 'I'll *confront* him about us! Right now. He can't tell us what to do.'

'*I'm* telling you, Michael,' Helen said.

He slumped against the horn and began to cry. She went over and touched his shoulder through the window.

'I'll sit with you a minute,' Helen told him. 'But you *must* promise me that you'll leave. I won't have him or my children see this.'

He promised.

'Give me the keys,' Helen said. His look of baleful hurt – that she didn't trust him not to drive off with her – touched Helen all over again. She put the keys in the deep flap pocket of her long skirt and walked around to the passenger side and let herself in. He rolled up his window, and they sat, not touching, the windows fogging around them, the car creaking under a coat of ice.

Then he completely broke down and told her that she had meant more to him than all of France – and she knew what France had meant to him, of course. She held him, then, and wildly feared how much *time* had passed, or was passing there in the frozen car. Even if it was not a long movie, they must still have a good half hour, or forty-five minutes; yet Michael Milton was nowhere near ready to leave. She kissed him, strongly, hoping this would help, but he only began to fondle her wet, cold breasts. She felt all over as frozen to him as she had felt outside in the hardening sleet. But she let him touch her.

'Dear Michael,' she said, thinking all the while.

'How can we stop?' was all he said.

But Helen had already stopped; she was only thinking about how to stop *him*. She shoved him up straight in the driver's position and stretched across the long seat, pulling her skirt back down to cover her knees, and putting her head in his lap.

'Please *remember*,' she said. 'Please try. This was the nicest part for me – just letting you drive me in the car, when I knew where we were going. Can't you be happy – can't you just remember that, and let it go?'

He sat rigid behind the steering wheel, both hands struggling to stay gripped to the wheel, both thighs tensed under her head, his erection pressing against her ear.

'Please try to just let it go at that, Michael,' she said softly. And they stayed this way a moment, imagining that the old Buick was carrying them to Michael's apartment again. But Michael Milton could not sustain himself on imagination. He let one hand stray to the back of Helen's neck, which he gripped very tightly; his other hand opened his fly.

'Michael!' she said, sharply.

'You said you always wanted to,' he reminded her.

'It's *over*, Michael.'

'Not yet, it isn't,' he said. His penis grazed her forehead, bent her eyelashes, and she recognized that this was the old Michael – the Michael of the apartment, the Michael who occasionally liked to treat her with some *force*. She did not appreciate it now. But if I resist, she thought, there will be a scene. She had only to imagine *Garp* as a part of the scene to convince herself that she should avoid *any* scene, at any cost.

'Don't be a bastard, don't be a prick, Michael,' she said. 'Don't spoil it.'

'You always said you wanted to,' he said. 'But it wasn't safe, you said. Well, now it's safe. The car isn't even moving. There can't be any accidents now,' he said.

Oddly, she realized, he had suddenly made it easier for her. She did not feel concerned anymore with letting him down gently; she felt grateful to him that he had helped her to sort her priorities so forcefully. Her priorities, she felt enormously relieved to know, were Garp and her children. Walt shouldn't be out in this weather, she thought, shivering. And Garp was more *major* to her, she knew, than all her minor colleagues and graduate students together.

Michael Milton had allowed her to see himself with what struck Helen as a necessary vulgarity. *Suck him off*, she thought bluntly, putting him into her mouth, and *then* he'll leave. She thought bitterly that men, once they had ejaculated, were rather quick to abandon their demands. And from her brief experience in Michael Milton's apartment, Helen knew that this would not take long.

Time was also a factor in her decision; there was at least twenty minutes remaining in even the shortest movie they could have gone to see. She set her mind to it as she might have done if it were the last task remaining to a messy business, which might have ended better but could also have turned out worse; she felt slightly proud that she had at least proved to herself that her family *was* her first priority. Even Garp might appreciate this, she thought; but one day, not right away.

She was so determined that she hardly noticed Michael Milton's grip loosen on her neck; he returned both hands to the steering wheel, as if he were actually piloting this experience. Let him think what he wants to think, she thought. She was thinking of her family, and she did not notice that the sleet was now nearly as hard as hail; it rattled off the big Buick like the tapping of countless hammers, driving little nails. And she did not sense the old car groaning and snapping under its thickening tomb of ice.

And she did not hear the telephone, ringing in her warm house. There was too much weather, and other interference, between her house and where she lay.

It was a stupid movie. Typical of the children's taste in films, Garp thought; typical of the taste in a university town. Typical of the entire country. Typical of the *world!* Garp raged, in his heart, and paid more attention to Walt's labored breathing – the thick rivulets of snot from his tiny nose.

'Be careful you don't choke on that popcorn,' he whispered to Walt.

'I won't choke,' Walt said, never taking his eyes from the giant screen.

'Well, you can't *breathe* very well,' Garp complained, 'so just don't put too much in your mouth. You might inhale it. You can't breathe through your nose, at all – that's perfectly clear.' And he wiped the child's nose again. 'Blow,' he whispered. Walt blew.

'Isn't this great?' Duncan whispered. Garp felt how hot Walt's snot was; the child must have a temperature of nearly 102°! he thought. Garp rolled his eyes at Duncan.

'Oh, just great, Duncan,' Garp said. Duncan had meant the movie.

'You should relax, Dad,' Duncan suggested, shaking his head. Oh, I *should*, Garp knew; but he couldn't. He thought of Walt, and what a perfect little ass he had, and strong little legs, and how sweet his sweat smelled when he'd been running and his hair was damp behind his ears. A body that perfect should not be sick, he thought. I should have let *Helen* go out on this miserable night; I should have made her call that twerp from her office – and tell him to put it in his ear, Garp thought. Or in a light socket. And turn on the juice!

I should have called that candy-ass myself, Garp thought. I should have visited him in the middle of the night. When Garp walked up the aisle to see if they had a phone in the lobby, he heard Walt still coughing.

If she hasn't already gotten in touch with him, Garp thought, I'll tell her *not* to keep trying; I'll tell her it's *my* turn. He was at that point in his feelings toward Helen where he felt betrayed but at the same time honestly loved and important to her; he had not had time enough to ponder *how* betrayed he felt – or how much, truly, she had been trying to keep him in her mind. It was a delicate point, between hating her and loving her terribly – also, he was not without sympathy for whatever she'd wanted; after all, he knew, the shoe on the other foot had also been worn (and was certainly thinner). It even seemed unfair, to Garp, that Helen, who had always meant so well, had been caught like this; she was a good woman and she certainly deserved better luck. But when Helen did not answer the phone, this point of delicacy in Garp's feelings toward her quite suddenly escaped him. He felt only rage, and only betrayal.

Bitch! he thought. The phone rang and rang.

She went out, to meet him. Or they're even doing it in our house! he thought – he could hear them saying, 'One last time.' That puny fink with his pretentious short stories about fragile relationships, which *almost* developed in badly lit European restaurants. (Perhaps someone wore the wrong glove and the moment was lost forever; there was one where a woman decides *not* to, because the man's shirt was too tight at his throat.)

How could Helen have read that crap! And how *could* she have touched that foppish body?

'But the movie isn't half over,' Duncan protested. 'There's going to be a duel.'

'I want to see the duel,' Walt said. 'What's a duel?'

'We're leaving,' Garp told them.

'No!' Duncan hissed.

'Walt's sick,' Garp mumbled. 'He shouldn't be here.'

'I'm not sick,' Walt said.

'He's not *that* sick,' Duncan said.

'Get out of those seats,' Garp told them; he had to grab the front of Duncan's shirt, which made Walt get up and stumble into the aisle first. Duncan, grumbling, scuffed after him.

'What's a *duel*?' Walt asked Duncan.

'It's real neat,' Duncan said. 'Now you won't ever see it.'

'Cut it out, Duncan,' Garp said. 'Don't be mean.'

'*You're* the one who's mean,' Duncan said.

'Yeah, Dad,' said Walt.

The Volvo was shrouded in ice, the windshield solid with it; there were various scrapers and broken snow brushes and junk of that sort, somewhere in the trunk, Garp supposed. But by March the winter driving had worn out much of this equipment, or the children had played with it and lost it. Garp wasn't going to take the time to clean the windshield, anyway.

'How can you see?' Duncan asked.

'I live here,' Garp said. 'I don't have to see.'

But, in fact, he had to roll down the driver's-side window and stick his face out into the raining sleet, as hard as hail; he drove toward home that way.

'It's *cold*,' Walt shivered. 'Shut the window!'

'I need it open to see,' Garp said.

'I thought you didn't have to see,' Duncan said.

'I'm too cold!' Walt cried. Dramatically, he coughed.

But all of this, as Garp saw it, was Helen's fault. She was to blame – for however Walt suffered his cold, or for its growing worse: it was *her* fault. And for Duncan's disappointment in his father, for that unforgivable way in the theater that Garp had grabbed the boy and stood him up out of his seat: *she* was to blame. The bitch with her runt lover!

But at the moment his eyes were teary in the cold wind and the sleet, and he thought to himself how he loved Helen and would *never* be unfaithful to her again – never hurt her like this, he would promise her that.

At the same moment Helen felt her conscience clear. Her love for Garp was very fine. And she sensed that Michael Milton was about to be released; he was exhibiting the familiar signs. The angle that he bent at the waist and the peculiar way he pointed his hips; the straining of that muscle, used for little else, on the inside of his thigh. It's almost over, Helen thought. Her nose touched the cold brass of his belt buckle and the back of her head bumped the bottom of the steering wheel, which Michael Milton gripped as if he expected the three-ton Buick to suddenly leave the ground.

Garp hit the bottom of his driveway at about forty miles per hour. He came off the downhill road in third gear and accelerated just as he exited; he glimpsed how the driveway was glazed with frozen slush, and he worried momentarily that the Volvo might slip on the short uphill curve. He held the car in gear until he felt what grip he had of the road; it was good enough, and he popped the sharp stick shift into neutral – a second before he killed the engine and flicked out the headlights.

They coasted up, into the black rain. It was like that moment when you feel an airplane lift off the runway; the children both cried out in excitement. Garp could feel the children at his elbow, crowding each other for the one favored position in the gap between the bucket seats.

'How can you see *now?*' Duncan asked.

'He doesn't have to see,' Walt said. There was a high thrill in Walt's voice, which suggested to Garp that Walt wished to reassure himself.

'I know this by heart,' Garp assured them.

'It's like being underwater!' cried Duncan; he held his breath.

'It's like a dream!' said Walt; he reached for his brother's hand.

14

The World According to Marcus Aurelius

That was how Jenny Fields became a kind of nurse again; after all her years in her white uniform, nursing the women's movement, Jenny was appropriately dressed for her role. It was at Jenny's suggestion that the Garp family moved into the Fields estate at Dog's Head Harbor. There were many rooms for Jenny to take care of them in, and there was the healing sound of the sea, rushing in and out, rinsing everything clean.

All his life, Duncan Garp would associate the sound of the sea with his convalescence. His grandmother would remove the bandage; there was a kind of tidal irrigation of the hole where Duncan's right eye had been. His father and mother could not stand the sight of that empty hole, but Jenny was an old hand at staring down wounds until they went away. It was with his grandmother, Jenny Fields, that Duncan would see his first glass eye. 'See?' Jenny said. 'It's big and brown; it's not quite as pretty as your left one, but you just make sure the girls see your left one first.' It was not a very feminist thing to say, she supposed, but Jenny always said that she was, first and foremost, a nurse.

Duncan's eye was gouged out when he was flung forward between the bucket seats; the uncovered tip of the stick-shift shaft was the first thing to break his fall. Garp's right arm, reaching into the gap between the seats, was too late; Duncan passed under it, putting out his right eye and breaking three fingers of his right hand, which was jammed into the seat-belt release mechanism.

By no one's estimate could the Volvo have been moving faster than twenty-five – at the most, thirty-five – miles per hour, but the collision was astonishing. The three-ton Buick did not yield quite an inch to Garp's coasting car. Inside the Volvo the children were like eggs out of the egg box – loose inside the shopping bag – at the moment of impact. Even inside the Buick, the jolt had surprising ferocity.

Helen's head was flung forward, narrowly missing the steering column, which caught her at the back of her neck. Many wrestlers' children have hardy necks, because Helen's did not break – though she wore a brace for almost six weeks, and her back would bother her the rest of her life. Her right collarbone was broken, perhaps by the rising slam of Michael Milton's knee, and her nose was gashed across the bridge – requiring nine stitches – by what must have been Michael Milton's belt buckle. Helen's mouth was snapped shut with such force that she broke two teeth and required two neat stitches in her tongue.

At first she thought she had bitten her tongue off, because she could feel it swimming in her mouth, which was full of blood; but her head ached so severely that she didn't dare open her mouth, until she had to breathe, and she couldn't move her right arm. She spat what she thought was her tongue into the palm of her left hand. It wasn't her tongue, of course. It was what amounted to three quarters of Michael Milton's penis.

The warm wash of blood over her face felt, to Helen, like gasoline; she began to scream – not for her own safety, but for Garp's and the children's. She knew what had hit the Buick. She struggled to get out of Michael Milton's lap because she had to see what had happened to her family. She dropped what she thought was her tongue on the floor of the Buick and with her good left arm she *punched* Michael Milton, whose lap pinned her against the steering column. It was only then that she heard other screams above her own. Michael Milton was screaming, of course, but Helen heard beyond him – to the Volvo. That was *Duncan* who was screaming, she was sure, and Helen fought her left arm across Michael Milton's bleeding lap to the door handle. When the door opened, she pushed Michael out of the Buick; she felt incredibly strong. Michael never once corrected his bent-double, sitting-up position; he lay on his side in the freezing slush as if he were still in the driver's seat, though he bellowed and bled like a steer.

When the door light came on in the huge Buick, Garp could dimly see the gore in the Volvo – Duncan's streaming face, split with his gaping wail. Garp began to bellow, too, but his bellow issued forth no louder than a whimper; his own, odd sound scared him so much that he tried to talk softly to Duncan. It was then that Garp realized he couldn't talk.

When Garp had flung out his arm to break Duncan's fall, he had turned almost sideways in the driver's seat and his face had struck the steering wheel hard enough to break his jaw and mangle his tongue (twelve stitches). In the long weeks of Garp's recovery, at Dog's Head Harbor, it is fortunate for Jenny that she'd had much experience with Ellen Jamesians, because Garp's mouth was wired shut and his messages to his mother were written ones. He sometimes wrote pages and pages, on the typewriter, which Jenny would then read aloud to Duncan – because, although Duncan could read, he was instructed not to strain his remaining eye more than was necessary. In time, the eye would compensate for the other eye's loss, but Garp had much to say that was immediate – and no way to say it. When he sensed that his mother was editing his remarks – to Duncan, and to Helen (to whom he also wrote pages and pages) – Garp would grunt his protest through his wires, holding his sore tongue very still. And Jenny Fields, like the good nurse she was, would wisely move him to a private room.

'This is the Dog's Head Harbor Hospital,' Helen said to Jenny once. Although Helen could talk, she said little; she did not have pages and pages to say. She spent most of her convalescence in Duncan's room, reading to the boy, because Helen was a much better reader than Jenny, and there were only two stitches in Helen's tongue. In this period of recovery, Jenny Fields could deal with Garp better than Helen could deal with him.

Helen and Duncan often sat side by side in Duncan's room. Duncan had a fine, one-eyed view of the sea, which he watched all day as if he were a camera. Getting used to having one eye is something like getting used to the world through a camera; there are similarities in depth of field, and in the problems of focus. When Duncan seemed ready to discover this, Helen bought him a camera – a single-lens reflex camera; for Duncan, that kind made the most sense.

It was in this period of time, Duncan Garp would recall, that the thought of being an artist, a painter and a photographer, first occurred to him; he was almost eleven. Although he had been athletic, his one eye would make him (like his father) forever leery of sports involving balls. Even running, he said, he was bothered by the lack of peripheral vision; Duncan claimed it made him clumsy. It was eventually added to Garp's sadness that Duncan did not care for wrestling, either. Duncan spoke in terms of the camera, and he told his father that one of his problems with depth of field included not knowing how far away the mat was. 'When I wrestle,' he told Garp, 'I feel like I'm going downstairs in the dark; I don't know when I get to the bottom until I *feel* it.' Garp concluded, of course, that the accident had made Duncan insecure about sports, but Helen pointed out to him that Duncan had always had a certain timidity, a reserve – even though he was good at games, and clearly well coordinated, he'd always had a tendency not to participate. Not as energetically, certainly, as Walt – who was intrepid, who flung his body into every new circumstance with faith and grace and with temerity. Walt, Helen said, was the real athlete between them. After a while, Garp supposed she was right.

'Helen *is* often right, you know,' Jenny told Garp one night at Dog's Head Harbor. The context of this remark could have been anything, but it was sometime soon after the accident, because Duncan had his own room, and Helen had her own room, and Garp had *his* own room, and so forth.

Helen is often right, his mother had told him, but Garp looked angry and wrote Jenny a note.

Not this *time, Mom,*

said the note, meaning – perhaps – Michael Milton. Meaning: the whole thing.

It was not expressly because of Michael Milton that Helen resigned. The availability of Jenny's big hospital on the ocean, as both Garp and Helen would come to think of it, was a way to leave the unwanted familiarity of their house, and of that driveway.

And in the faculty code of ethics, 'moral turpitude' is listed as one ground for revoking tenure – though this never came to debate; sleeping with students was not generally treated too harshly. It might be a hidden reason why a faculty member wasn't given tenure; it would rarely be a reason for revoking someone's tenure. Helen may have supposed that biting off three quarters of a student's penis was fairly high on the scale of conceivable abuse to students. Sleeping with them simply happened, though it was not encouraged; there were many worse ways of evaluating students and categorizing them for life. But amputation of their genitalia was certainly severe, even for bad students, and Helen must have felt inclined to punish herself. So she denied herself the pleasure of continuing at the task she had prepared for, so well, and she removed herself from the arousement that books and their discussion had always meant to her. In her later life, Helen would spare herself considerable unhappiness by refusing to feel guilty; in her later life, the whole business with Michael Milton would more often make

her angry than it would make her sad – because she was
strong enough to believe that she was a good woman, which
she was, who'd been made to suffer disproportionately for
a trivial indiscretion.

But at least for a time, Helen would heal herself and her
family. Never having had a mother, and having had little
chance to use Jenny Fields in that way, Helen submitted to
this period of hospitalization at Dog's Head Harbor. She
calmed herself by nursing Duncan, and she hoped that
Jenny could nurse Garp.

This aura of the hospital was not new to Garp, whose
earliest experiences – with fear, with dreams, with sex –
had all occurred in the infirmary atmosphere of the old
Steering School. He adapted. It helped him that he had to
write out what he wanted to say, because this made him
careful; it made him reconsider many of the things he might
have *thought* he wanted to say. When he saw them written
down – these raw thoughts – he realized that he couldn't
or shouldn't say them; when he went to revise them, he
knew better and threw them away. There was one for Helen,
which read:

Three quarters is not enough.

He threw it away.

Then he wrote one for Helen that he *did* give to her.

I don't blame you.

Later, he wrote another one.

I don't blame me, either,

the note said.

Only in this way can we be whole again,

Garp wrote to his mother.

And Jenny Fields padded whitely through the salt-damp house, room to room with her nursing ways and Garp's notes. It was all the writing he could manage.

Of course, the house at Dog's Head Harbor was used to recoveries. Jenny's wounded women had gotten hold of themselves there; these sea-smelling rooms had histories of sadnesses outlived. Among them, the sadness of Roberta Muldoon, who had lived there with Jenny through the most difficult periods of her sex reassignment. In fact, Roberta had failed at living alone – and at living with a number of men – and she was back living at Dog's Head Harbor with Jenny again when the Garps moved in.

As the spring warmed up, and the hole that had been Duncan's right eye slowly healed and was less vulnerable to sticking bits of sand, Roberta took Duncan to the beach. It was on the beach that Duncan discovered his depth-of-field problem as it was related to a thrown ball, because Roberta Muldoon tried playing catch with Duncan and very soon hit him in the face with the football. They gave up the ball, and Roberta contented Duncan with diagraming, in the sand, all the plays she once ran at the tight end position for the Philadelphia Eagles; she focused on the part of the Eagles offense that concerned her, when she was Robert Muldoon, No. 90 and she relived for Duncan her occasional touchdown passes, her dropped balls, her offside penalties, her most vicious hits. 'It was against the Cowboys,' she told Duncan. 'We were playing in Dallas, when that snake in the grass – Eight Ball, everyone called him – came up on my blind side . . .' And Roberta would regard the quiet child, who had a blind side for life, and she would deftly change the subject.

To Garp, Roberta's subject was the ticklish detail of sex reassignment, because Garp seemed interested and Roberta knew that Garp probably liked hearing about a problem so thoroughly removed from his own.

'I always knew I should have been a girl,' she told Garp.

'I dreamed about having love made to me, by a man, but in the dreams I was always a woman; I was *never* a man having love made to me by another man.' There was more than a hint of distaste in Roberta's references to homosexuals, and Garp thought it strange that people in the process of making a decision that will plant them firmly in a minority, forever, are possibly less tolerant of other minorities than we might imagine. There was even a bitchiness about Roberta, when she complained of the other troubled women who came to get well at Dog's Head Harbor with Jenny Fields. 'That damn lesbian crowd,' Roberta said to Garp. 'They're trying to make your mother into something she isn't.'

'I sometimes think that's what Mom is *for*,' Garp teased Roberta. 'She makes people happy by letting them think she is something she isn't.'

'Well, they tried to confuse me,' Roberta said. 'When I was preparing myself for the operation, they kept trying to talk me out of it. "Be gay," they said. "If you want men, have them as you are. If you become a woman, you'll just be taken advantage of," they told me. They were all cowards,' Roberta concluded, though Garp knew, sadly, that Roberta *had* been taken advantage of, over and over again.

Roberta's vehemence was not unique; Garp pondered how these other women in his mother's house, and in her care, had *all* been victims of intolerance – yet most of them he'd met seemed especially intolerant of each other. It was a kind of infighting that made no sense to Garp and he marveled at his mother sorting them all out, keeping them happy and out of each other's hair. *Robert* Muldoon, Garp knew, had spent several months in drag before his actual operation. He'd go off in the morning dressed as Robert Muldoon; he went out shopping for women's clothes, and almost no one knew that he paid for his sex change with the banquet fees he collected for the speeches he gave to boys' clubs and men's clubs. In the evenings, at Dog's Head Harbor, Robert Muldoon would model his new clothes for Jenny and the critical women who shared her house.

When the estrogen hormones began to enlarge his breasts and shift the former tight end's shape around, Robert gave up the banquet circuit and marched forth from the Dog's Head Harbor house in mannish women's suits and rather conservative wigs; he tried *being* Roberta long before he had the surgery. Clinically, now, Roberta had the same genitalia and urological equipment as most other women.

'But of course I can't conceive,' she told Garp. 'I don't ovulate and I don't menstruate.' Neither do millions of other women, Jenny Fields had reassured her. 'When I came home from the hospital,' Roberta said to Garp, 'do you know what *else* your mother told me?'

Garp shook his head; 'home' to Roberta, Garp knew, was Dog's Head Harbor.

'She told me I was less sexually ambiguous than most people she knew,' Roberta said. 'I really needed that,' she said, 'because I had to use this horrible dilator all the time so that my vagina wouldn't close; I felt like a *machine*.'

Good old mom,

Garp scribbled.

'There's such sympathy for people, in what you *write*,' Roberta told him, suddenly. 'But I don't see that much sympathy in you, in your real life,' she said. It was the same thing Jenny had always accused him of.

But now, he felt, he had more. With his jaw wired shut, with his wife with her arm in a sling all day – and Duncan with only half his pretty face intact – Garp felt more generous toward the other wretches who wandered into Dog's Head Harbor.

It was a summer town. Out of season, the bleached shingled house with its porches and garrets was the only occupied mansion along the gray-green dunes and the white beach at the end of Ocean Lane. An occasional dog sniffed through the bone-colored driftwood, and retired people, living some miles inland, in their former summer houses, occasionally strolled the shore, scrutinizing the shells. In summer there were lots of dogs and children and mothers' helpers all over the beach, and always a bright boat or two in the harbor. But when the Garps moved in with Jenny, the shoreline seemed abandoned. The beach, littered with the debris washed in with the high tides of winter, was deserted. The Atlantic Ocean, through April and through May, was the livid color of a bruise – was the color of the bridge of Helen's nose.

Visitors to the town, in the off-season, were quickly spotted as lost women in search of the famous nurse, Jenny Fields. In summer, these women often spent a whole day in Dog's Head Harbor trying to find someone who knew where Jenny lived. But the permanent residents of Dog's Head Harbor all knew: 'The last house at the end of Ocean Lane,' they told the damaged girls and women who asked for directions. 'It's as big as a hotel, honey. You can't miss it.'

Sometimes these searchers would trudge out to the beach first and view the house for a long time before they got up the nerve to come see if Jenny was home; sometimes Garp would see them, single or in twos and threes, squatting on the windy dunes and watching the house as if they were trying to read the degree of sympathy therein. If there were more than one, they conferred on the beach; one of them was elected to knock on the door while the others huddled on the dunes, like dogs told to stay! until they're called.

Helen bought Duncan a telescope, and from his room with a sea view Duncan spied on the trepid visitors and often announced their presence hours before the knock on the door. 'Someone for Grandma,' he'd say. Focusing, always focusing. 'She's about twenty-four. Or maybe fourteen. She has a blue knapsack. She has an orange with her but I don't think she's going to eat it. Someone's with her but I can't see her face. She's lying down; no, she's being sick. No, she's wearing a kind of mask. Maybe she's the other one's mother – no, her sister. Or just a friend.

'Now she's eating the orange. It doesn't look very good,' Duncan would report. And Roberta would look, too; and sometimes Helen. It was often Garp who answered the door.

'Yes, she's my mother,' he'd say, 'but she's out shopping right now. Please come in, if you want to wait for her.' And he would smile, though all the time he would be scrutinizing the person as carefully as the retired people along the beach looked at their seashells. And before his jaw healed, and his mauled tongue grew back together, Garp would answer the door with a ready supply of notes. Many of the visitors were not in the least surprised by being handed notes, because this was the only way they communicated, too.

Hello, my name is Beth. I'm an Ellen Jamesian.

And Garp would give her his:

Hello, my name is Garp. I have a broken jaw.

And he'd smile at them, and hand them a second note, depending on the occasion. One said:

There's a nice fire in the wood stove in the kitchen; turn left.

And there was one that said:

Don't be upset. My mother will be back very soon. There are other women here. Would you like to see them?

It was in this period that Garp took to wearing a sport jacket again, not out of nostalgia for his days at Steering, or in Vienna – and certainly not out of any necessity to be well dressed at Dog's Head Harbor, where Roberta seemed the only woman who was concerned with what she wore – but only because of his need for pockets; he carried so many notes.

He tried running on the beach but he had to give it up; it jarred his jaw and jangled his tongue against his teeth. But he walked for miles along the sand. He was returning from a walk the day the police car brought the young man to Jenny's house; arm in arm, the policemen helped him up the big front porch.

'Mr Garp?' one of the policemen asked.

Garp dressed in running gear for his walks; he didn't have any notes on him, but he nodded, yes, he was Mr Garp.

'You know this kid?' the policeman asked.

'Of course he does,' the young man said. 'You cops don't ever believe anybody. You don't know how to *relax*.'

It was the kid in the purple caftan, the boy Garp had escorted from the boudoir of Mrs Ralph – what seemed to Garp like years ago. Garp considered not recognizing him, but he nodded.

'The kid's got no money,' the policeman explained. 'He doesn't live around here, and he's got no job. He's not in school anywhere and when we called his folks, they said they didn't even know where he *was* – and they didn't sound very interested to find out. But he says he's staying with you – and you'll speak up for him.'

Garp, of course, couldn't speak. He pointed to his wire mesh and imitated the act of writing a note on his palm.

'When'd you get the braces?' the kid asked. 'Most people have them when they're younger. They're the craziest-looking braces I ever saw.'

Garp wrote out a note on the back of a traffic violation form that the policeman handed him.

Yes, I'll take responsibility for him. But I can't speak up for him because I have a broken jaw.

The kid read the note over the policeman's shoulder.

'Wow,' he said, grinning. 'What happened to the *other* guy?'

He lost three quarters of his prick, Garp thought, but he

did not write this on a traffic violation form, or on anything else. Ever.

The boy turned out to have read Garp's novels while he was in jail.

'If I'd known you were the author of those books,' the kid said, 'I would never have been so disrespectful.' His name was Randy and he had become an ardent Garp fan. Garp was convinced that the mainstream of his fans consisted of waifs, lonely children, retarded grown-ups, cranks, and only occasional members of the citizenry who were not afflicted with perverted taste. But Randy had come to Garp as if Garp were now the only guru Randy obeyed. In the spirit of his mother's home at Dog's Head Harbor, Garp couldn't very well turn the boy away.

Roberta Muldoon took on the task of briefing Randy on the accident to Garp and his family.

'Who's the great big lovely chick?' Randy asked Garp in an awed whisper.

Don't you recognize her?

Garp wrote.

She was a tight end for the Philadelphia Eagles.

But even Garp's sourness could not dim Randy's likable enthusiasm; not right away. The boy entertained Duncan for hours.

God knows how,

Garp complained to Helen.

He probably tells Duncan about all his drug experiences.

'The boy's not on anything,' Helen assured Garp. 'Your mother asked him.'

Then he relates to Duncan the exciting history of his criminal record,

Garp wrote.

'Randy wants to be a writer,' Helen said.

Everyone wants to be a writer!

Garp wrote. But it wasn't true. *He* didn't want to be a writer – not anymore. When he tried to write, only the deadliest subject rose up to greet him. He knew he had to forget it – not fondle it with his memory and exaggerate its awfulness with his art. That was madness, but whenever he thought of writing, his only subject greeted him with its leers, its fresh visceral puddles, and its stink of death. And so he did not write; he didn't even try.

At last Randy went away. Though Duncan was sorry to see him go, Garp felt relieved; he did not show anybody else the note Randy left for him.

I'll never be as good as you – at anything. Even if that's true, you could be a little more generous about how you rub that in.

So I'm not kind, Garp thought. What else is new? He threw Randy's note away.

When the wires came off and the rawness left his tongue, Garp ran again. As the weather warmed up, Helen swam. She was told it was good for restoring her muscle tone and strengthening her collarbone, though this still hurt her – especially the breaststroke. She swam for what seemed to be miles, to Garp: straight out to sea, and then along the shoreline. She said she went out so far because the water was calmer there; closer to shore, the waves interfered with her. But Garp worried. He and Duncan sometimes used the telescope to watch her. What am I going to do if something happens? Garp wondered. He was a poor swimmer.

'Mom's a good swimmer,' Duncan assured him. Duncan was also becoming a good swimmer.

'She goes out too far,' Garp said.

By the time the summer people arrived, the Garp family took its exercise in slightly less ostentatious ways; they played on the beach or in the sea only in the early morning. In the crowded moments of the summer days, and in the early evenings, they watched the world from the shaded porches of Jenny Fields' home; they withdrew to the big cool house.

Garp got a little better. He began to write – gingerly, at first: long plot outlines, and speculations about his characters. He avoided the main characters; at least he thought they were the main characters – a husband, a wife, a child. He concentrated instead on a detective, an outsider to the family. Garp knew what terror would lurk at the heart of his book, and perhaps for that reason he approached it through a character as distant from his personal anxiety as the police inspector is distant from the crime. What business do I have writing about a police inspector? he thought, and so he made the inspector into someone even Garp could understand. Then Garp stood close to the stink itself. The bandages came off Duncan's eye hole and the boy wore a black patch, almost handsome against his summer tan. Garp took a deep breath and began a novel.

It was in the late summer of Garp's convalescence that *The World According to Bensenhaver* was begun. About that time, Michael Milton was released from a hospital, walking with a postsurgical stoop and a woebegone face. Due to an infection, the result of improper drainage – and aggravated by a common urological problem – he had to have the remaining quarter of his penis removed in an operation. Garp never knew this; and at this point, it might not even have cheered him up.

Helen knew Garp was writing again.

'I won't read it,' she told him. 'Not one word of it. I know you have to write it, but I never want to see it. I don't mean to hurt you, but you have to understand. *I* have to forget it; if *you* have to write about it, God help you. People bury these things in different ways.'

'It's not about "it," exactly,' he told her. 'I do not write autobiographical fiction.'

'I know that, too,' she said. 'But I won't read it just the same.'

'Of course, I understand,' he said.

Writing, he always knew, was a lonely business. It was hard for a lonely thing to feel that much lonelier. Jenny, he knew, would read it; she was tough as nails. Jenny watched them all get well; she watched new patients come and go.

One was a hideous young girl named Laurel, who made the mistake of sounding off about Duncan one morning at breakfast. 'Could I sleep in another part of the house?' she asked Jenny. 'There's this creepy kid – with the telescope, the camera, and the eye patch? He's like a fucking pirate, spying on me. Even little boys like to paw you over with their eyes – even with *one* eye.'

Garp had fallen while running in the predawn light on the beach; he had hurt his jaw again, and was – again – wired shut. He had no old notes handy for what he wanted to say to this girl, but he scribbled very hastily on his napkin.

Fuck you,

he scribbled, and threw the napkin at the surprised girl.

'Look,' the girl said to Jenny, 'this is just the kind of routine I had to get away from. Some *man* bullying me all the time, some ding-dong threatening me with his big-prick violence. Who needs it? I mean, especially *here* – who needs it? Did I come here for more of the same?'

Fuck you to death,

said Garp's next note, but Jenny ushered the girl outside and told her the history of Duncan's eye patch, and his telescope, and his camera, and the girl tried very hard to avoid Garp during the last part of her stay.

Her stay was just a few days, and then someone was there to get her: a sporty car with New York plates and a man who *looked* like a ding-dong – and someone who had, actually, threatened poor Laurel with 'big-prick violence,' all the time.

'Hey, you dildos!' he called to Garp and Roberta, who were sitting on the large porch swing, like old-fashioned lovers. 'Is this the whorehouse where you're keeping Laurel?'

'We're not exactly "keeping" her,' Roberta said.

'Shut up, you big dyke,' said the New York man; he came up on the porch. He'd left the motor running to his sports car, and its idle charged and calmed itself – charged and calmed itself, and charged again. The man wore cowboy boots and green suede bell-bottom pants. He was tall and chesty, though not quite as tall and chesty as Roberta Muldoon.

'I'm not a dyke,' Roberta said.

'Well, you're no vestal virgin either,' the man said. 'Where the fuck is Laurel?' He wore an orange T-shirt with bright green letters between his nipples.

SHAPE UP!

the letters read.

Garp searched his pockets for a pencil to scribble a note, but all he came up with was old notes: all the old standbys, which did not seem to apply to this rude person.

'Is Laurel expecting you?' Roberta Muldoon asked the man, and Garp knew that Roberta was having a sex-identity problem again; she was goading the moron in hopes that she could then feel justified in beating the shit out of him. But the man, to Garp, looked as if he might make a fair match for Roberta. All that estrogen had changed more than Roberta's shape, Garp thought – it had unmuscled the former Robert Muldoon, to a degree that Roberta seemed prone to forget.

'Look, sweethearts,' the man said, to both Garp and Roberta. 'If Laurel doesn't get her ass out here, I'm going to clean house. What kind of fag joint is this, anyway? Everyone's heard of it. I didn't have any trouble finding out where she went. Every screwy bitch in New York knows about this cunt hangout.'

Roberta smiled. She was beginning to rock back and forth on the big porch swing in a way that was making Garp feel sick to his stomach. Garp clawed through his pockets at a frantic rate, scanning note after worthless note.

'Look, you clowns,' the man said. 'I *know* what sort of douche bags hang out here. It's a big lesbian scene, right?' He prodded the edge of the big porch swing with his cowboy boot and set the swing to moving oddly. 'And what are *you?*' he asked Garp. 'You the *man* of the house? Or the court eunuch?'

Garp handed the man a note.

There's a nice fire in the wood stove in the kitchen; turn left.

But it was August; that was the wrong note.

'What's this shit?' the man said. And Garp handed him another note, the first one to fly out of his pocket.

Don't be upset. My mother will be back very soon. There are other women here. Would you like to see them?

'*Fuck* your mother!' the man said. He started toward the big screen door. 'Laurel!' he screamed. 'You in there? You bitch!'

But it was Jenny Fields who met him in the doorway.

'Hello,' she said.

'I know who *you* are,' the man said. 'I recognize the dumb uniform. My Laurel's not your type, sweetie; she *likes* to fuck.'

'Perhaps not with you,' said Jenny Fields.

Whatever abuse the man in the SHAPE UP! T-shirt was then

prepared to deliver to Jenny Fields went unsaid. Roberta Muldoon threw a cross-body block on the surprised man, hitting him from behind and a little to one side of the backs of his knees. It was a flagrant clip, worthy of a fifteen-yard penalty in Roberta's days as a Philadelphia Eagle. The man hit the gray boards of the porch deck with such force that the hanging flowerpots were set swinging. He tried but could not get up. He appeared to have suffered a knee injury common to the sport of football – the very reason, in fact, why clipping was a fifteen-yard penalty. The man was not plucky enough to hurl further abuse, at anyone, from his back; he lay with a calm, moonlike expression upon his face, which whitened slightly in his pain.

'That was too *hard*, Roberta,' Jenny said.

'I'll get Laurel,' Roberta said, sheepishly, and she went inside. In Roberta's heart of hearts, Garp and Jenny knew, she was more feminine than anyone; but in her body of bodies, she was a highly trained rock.

Garp had found another note and he dropped it on the New York man's chest, right where it said SHAPE UP! It was a note Garp had many duplicates of.

Hello, my name is Garp. I have a broken jaw.

'My name is Harold,' the man said. 'Too bad about your jaw.'

Garp found a pencil and wrote another note.

Too bad about your knee, Harold.

Laurel was fetched.

'Oh, baby,' she said. 'You *found* me!'

'I don't think I can drive the fucking car,' Harold said. Out on Ocean Lane the man's sport car still chugged like an animal interested in eating sand.

'*I* can drive, baby,' Laurel said. 'You just never *let* me.'

'Now I'll let you,' Harold groaned. 'Believe me.'

'Oh, baby,' Laurel said.

Roberta and Garp carried the man to the car. 'I think I really need Laurel,' the man confided to them. 'Fucking bucket seats,' the man complained, when they had gingerly squeezed him in. Harold was large for his car. It was the first time in what seemed like years, to Garp, that Garp had been this near to an automobile. Roberta put her hand on Garp's shoulder, but Garp turned away.

'I guess Harold needs me,' Laurel told Jenny Fields, and gave a little shrug.

'But why does *she* need *him?*' said Jenny Fields, to no one in particular, as the little car drove away. Garp had wandered off. Roberta, punishing herself for her momentarily lapsed femininity, went to find Duncan and mother him.

Helen was talking on the phone to the Fletchers, Harrison and Alice, who wanted to come visit. That might help us, Helen thought. She was right, and it must have boosted Helen's confidence in herself – to be right about something again.

The Fletchers stayed a week. There was at last a child for Duncan to play with, even if it was not his age and not his sex; it was, at least, a child who knew about his eye, and Duncan lost most of his self-consciousness about the eye patch. When the Fletchers left, he was more willing to go to the beach by himself, even at those times of the day when he might encounter other children – who might ask him or, of course, tease him.

Harrison provided Helen with a confidant, as he had been for her before; she was able to tell Harrison things about Michael Milton that were simply too raw to tell Garp, and yet she needed to say them. She needed to talk about her anxieties for her marriage, now; and how she was dealing with the accident so differently from Garp. Harrison suggested another child. Get pregnant, he advised. Helen confided that she was no longer taking the pills, but she did not tell Harrison that Garp had not slept with her – not since it had happened. She didn't really need to tell Harrison that; Harrison noted the separate rooms.

Alice encouraged Garp to stop the silly notes. He could talk if he tried, if he wasn't so vain about how he sounded. If *she* could talk, certainly he could spit the words out, Alice reasoned – teeth wired together, delicate tongue, and all; he could at least try.

'Alish,' Garp said.

'Yeth,' said Alice. 'That'th my name. What'th yours?'

'Arp,' Garp managed to say.

Jenny Fields, passing whitely to another room, shuddered like a ghost and moved on.

'I *mish* him,' Garp confessed to Alice.

'You mith him, yeth, of *courth* you do,' said Alice, and she held him while he cried.

It was quite some time after the Fletchers left when Helen came to Garp's room in the night. She was not surprised to find him lying awake, because he was listening to what she'd heard, too. It was why she couldn't sleep.

Someone, one of Jenny's late arrivals – a new guest – was taking a bath. First the Garps had heard the tub being drawn, then they'd heard the plunking in the water – now the splashing and soapy sounds. There was even a little light singing, or the person was humming.

They remembered, of course, the years Walt had washed himself within their hearing, how they would listen for any telltale slipping sounds, or for the most frightening sound of all – which was no sound. And then they'd call, 'Walt?' And Walt would say, 'What?' And they would say, 'Okay, just checking!' To make sure that he hadn't slipped under and drowned.

Walt liked to lie with his ears underwater, listening to his fingers climbing the walls of the tub, and often he wouldn't hear Garp or Helen calling him. He'd look up, surprised, to see their anxious faces suddenly above him, peering over the rim of the tub. 'I'm all right,' he'd say, sitting up.

'Just *answer*, for God's sake, Walt,' Garp would tell him. 'When we call you, just answer us.'

'I didn't hear you,' Walt said.

'Then keep your head out of the water,' Helen said.

'But how can I wash my hair?' Walt asked.

'That's a lousy way to wash your hair, Walt,' Garp said. 'Call me. *I'll* wash your hair.'

'Okay,' said Walt. And when they left him alone, he'd put his head underwater again and listen to the world that way.

Helen and Garp lay beside each other on Garp's narrow bed in one of the guest rooms in one of the garrets at Dog's Head Harbor. The house had so many bathrooms – they couldn't even be sure which bathroom they were listening to, but they listened.

'It's a woman, I think,' Helen said.

'Here?' Garp said. 'Of *course* it's a woman.'

'I thought at first it was a child,' Helen said.

'I know,' Garp said.

'The humming, I guess,' Helen said. 'You know how he used to talk to himself?'

'I know,' Garp said.

They held each other in the bed that was always a little damp, so close to the ocean and with so many windows open all day, and the screen doors swinging and banging.

'I want another child,' said Helen.

'Okay,' Garp said.

'As soon as possible,' Helen said.

'Right away,' said Garp. 'Of course.'

'If it's a girl,' Helen said, 'we'll name her Jenny, because of your mother.'

'Good,' said Garp.

'I don't know, if it's a boy,' said Helen.

'Not Walt,' Garp said.

'Okay,' Helen said.

'Not *ever* another Walt,' said Garp. 'Although I know some people do that.'

'I wouldn't want to,' Helen said.

'Some other name, if it's a boy,' Garp said.

'I hope it's a girl,' said Helen.

'I won't care,' Garp said.

'Of course. Neither will I, really,' said Helen.

'I'm so sorry,' Garp said; he hugged her.

'No, *I'm* so sorry,' she said.

'No, *I'm* so sorry,' said Garp.

'*I* am,' Helen said.

'*I* am,' he said.

They made love so carefully. Helen imagined that she was Roberta Muldoon, fresh out of surgery, trying out a brand-new vagina. Garp tried not to imagine anything.

Whenever Garp began imagining, he only saw the bloody Volvo. There were Duncan's screams, and outside he could hear Helen calling; and someone else. He twisted himself from behind the steering wheel and kneeled on the driver's seat; he held Duncan's face in his hands, but the blood would not stop and Garp couldn't see everything that was wrong.

'It's okay,' he whispered to Duncan. 'Hush, you're going to be all right.' But because of his tongue, there were no words – only a soft spray.

Duncan kept screaming, and so did Helen, and someone else kept groaning – the way a dog dreams in its sleep. But what did Garp hear that frightened him so? What *else*?

'It's all right, Duncan, believe me,' he whispered, incomprehensibly. 'You're going to be all right.' He wiped the blood from the boy's throat with his hand; nothing at the boy's throat was cut, he could see. He wiped the blood from the boy's temples, and saw that they were not bashed in. He kicked open the driver's-side door, to be sure; the door light went on and he could see that one of Duncan's eyes was darting. The eye was looking for help, but Garp could see that the eye could see. He wiped more blood with his hand, but he could not find Duncan's other eye. 'It's okay,' he whispered to Duncan, but Duncan screamed even louder.

Over his father's shoulder, Duncan had seen his mother

at the Volvo's open door. Blood streamed from her gashed nose and her sliced tongue, and she held her right arm as if it had broken off somewhere near her shoulder. But it was the *fright* in her face that frightened Duncan. Garp turned and saw her. Something else frightened him.

It was not Helen's screaming, it was not Duncan's screaming. And Garp knew that Michael Milton, who was grunting, could grunt himself to death – for all Garp cared. It was something else. It was not a sound. It was *no* sound. It was the absence of sound.

'Where's Walt?' Helen said, trying to see into the Volvo. She stopped screaming.

'Walt!' cried Garp. He held his breath. Duncan stopped crying.

They heard nothing. And Garp knew Walt had a cold you could hear from the next room – even two rooms away, you could hear that wet rattle in the child's chest.

'Walt!' they screamed.

Both Helen and Garp would whisper to each other, later, that at that moment they imagined Walt with his ears underwater, listening intently to his fingers at play in the bathtub.

'I can still see him,' Helen whispered, later.

'All the time,' Garp said. 'I know.'

'I just shut my eyes,' said Helen.

'Right,' Garp said. 'I know.'

But Duncan said it best. Duncan said that sometimes it was as if his missing right eye was not entirely gone. 'It's like I can still see out of it, sometimes,' Duncan said. 'But it's like memory, it's not real – what I see.'

'Maybe it's become the eye you see your dreams with,' Garp told him.

'Sort of,' Duncan said. 'But it seems so real.'

'It's your *imaginary* eye,' Garp said. 'That can be very real.'

'It's the eye I can still see Walt with,' Duncan said. 'You know?'

'I know,' Garp said.

* * *

Many wrestlers' children have hardy necks, but not all the children of wrestlers have necks that are hardy enough.

For Duncan and Helen, now, Garp seemed to have an endless reservoir of gentleness; for a year, he spoke softly to them; for a year, he was never impatient with them. They must have grown impatient with his delicacy. Jenny Fields noticed that the three of them needed a year to nurse each other.

In that year, Jenny wondered, what did they do with the *other* feelings human beings have? Helen hid them; Helen was very strong. Duncan saw them only with his missing eye. And Garp? He was strong, but not that strong. He wrote a novel called *The World According to Bensenhaver*, into which all his *other* feelings flew.

When Garp's editor, John Wolf, read the first chapter of *The World According to Bensenhaver*, he wrote to Jenny Fields. 'What in hell is going on out there?' Wolf wrote to Jenny. 'It is as if Garp's grief has made his heart perverse.'

But T. S. Garp felt guided by an impulse as old as Marcus Aurelius, who had the wisdom and the urgency to note that 'in the life of a man, his time is but a moment . . . his sense a dim rushlight.'

15

The World According to Bensenhaver

Hope Standish was at home with her son, Nicky, when Oren Rath walked into the kitchen. She was drying the dishes and she saw immediately the long, thin-bladed fisherman's knife with the slick cutting edge and the special, saw-toothed edge that they call a disgorger-scaler. Nicky was not yet three; he still ate in a high chair, and he was eating his breakfast when Oren Rath stepped up behind him and nudged the ripper teeth of his fisherman's knife against the child's throat.

'Set them dishes aside,' he told Hope. Mrs Standish did as she was told. Nicky gurgled at the stranger; the knife was just a tickle under his chin.

'What do you want?' Hope asked. 'I'll give you anything you want.'

'You sure will,' said Oren Rath. 'What's your name?'

'Hope.'

'Mine's Oren.'

'That's a nice name,' Hope told him.

Nicky couldn't turn in the high chair to see the stranger who was tickling his throat. He had wet cereal on his fingers, and when he reached for Oren Rath's hand, Rath stepped up beside the high chair and touched the fine, slicing edge of his fisherman's blade to the fleshy pouch of the boy's cheek. He made a quick cut there, as if he were briefly outlining the child's cheekbone. Then he stepped back to observe Nicky's surprised face, his simple cry; a thread-thin line of blood appeared, like the stitching for a pocket, on the boy's cheek. It was as if the child had suddenly developed a gill.

'I mean business,' said Oren Rath. Hope started toward Nicky but Rath waved her back. 'He don't need you. He just don't care for his cereal. He wants a cookie.' Nicky bawled.

'He'll choke on it, when he's crying,' Hope said.

'You want to argue with me?' said Oren Rath. 'You want to talk about choking? I'll cut his pecker off and stuff it down his throat – if you want to talk about choking.'

Hope gave Nicky a zwieback and he stopped crying.

'You see?' said Oren Rath. He picked up the high chair with Nicky in it and hugged it to his chest. 'We're going to the bedroom now,' he said; he nodded to Hope. 'You first.'

They went down the hall together. The Standish family lived in a ranch house then; with a new baby, they had agreed that ranch houses were safer in the case of a fire. Hope went into the bedroom and Oren Rath put down the high chair with Nicky in it, just outside the bedroom door. Nicky had almost stopped bleeding; there was just a little blood on his cheek; Oren Rath wiped this off with his hand, then wiped his hand on his pants. Then he stepped into the bedroom after Hope. When he closed the door, Nicky started to cry.

'Please,' Hope said. 'He really might choke, and he knows how to get out of that high chair – or it might tip over. He doesn't like to be alone.'

Oren Rath went to the night table and slashed through the phone cord with his fisherman's knife as easily as a man halving a very ripe pear. 'You don't want to argue with me,' he said.

Hope sat down on the bed. Nicky was crying, but not hysterically; it sounded as if he might stop. Hope started crying, too.

'Just take off your clothes,' Oren said. He helped her undress. He was tall and reddish-blond, his hair as lank and as close to his head as high grass beaten down by a flood. He smelled like silage and Hope remembered the turquoise pickup she'd noticed in the driveway, just before he appeared in her kitchen. 'You've even got a rug in the bedroom,' he said to her. He was thin but muscular; his hands were large and clumsy, like the feet of a puppy who's going to be a big dog. His body seemed almost hair-less, but he was so pale, so very blond, that his hair was hard to see against his skin.

'Do you know my husband?' Hope asked him.

'I know when he's home and when he ain't,' Rath said. 'Listen,' he said suddenly; Hope held her breath. 'You hear? Your kid don't even mind it.' Nicky was murmuring vowel sounds outside the bedroom door, talking wetly to his zwieback. Hope began crying harder. When Oren Rath touched her, awkward and fast, she thought she was so dry that she wouldn't even get big enough for his horrible finger.

'Please wait,' she said.

'No arguing with me.'

'No, I mean I can help you,' she said. She wanted him in and out of her as fast as possible; she was thinking of Nicky in the high chair in the hall. 'I can make it nicer, I mean,' she said, unconvincingly; she did not know how to say what she was say-ing. Oren Rath grabbed one of her breasts in such a way that Hope knew he had never touched a breast before; his hand was so cold, she flinched. In his awkwardness, he butted her in the mouth with the top of his head.

'No arguing,' he grunted.

'Hope!' someone called. They both heard it and froze. Oren Rath gaped at the cut phone cord.

'Hope?'

It was Margot, a neighbor and a friend. Oren Rath touched the cool, flat blade of his knife to Hope's nipple.

'She's going to walk right in here,' Hope whispered. 'She's a good friend.'

'My God, Nicky,' they could hear Margot say, 'I see you're eat-ing all over the house. Is your mother getting dressed?'

'I'll have to fuck you both and kill everybody,' whispered Oren Rath.

Hope scissored his waist with her good legs and hugged him, knife and all, to her breasts. 'Margot!' she screamed. 'Grab Nicky and run! *Please!*' she shrieked. 'There's a crazy man who's going to kill us all! Take Nicky, take Nicky!'

Oren Rath lay stiffly against her as if it were the first time he'd ever been hugged. He did not struggle, he did not use his knife. They both lay rigid and listened to Margot dragging Nicky down the hall and out the kitchen door. One leg of the high chair was snapped off against the refrigerator, but Margot didn't stop to remove Nicky from the chair until she was half a block down the street and kicking open her own door.

'Don't kill me,' Hope whispered. 'Just go, quickly, and you'll get away. She's calling the police, right now.'

'Get dressed,' said Oren Rath. 'I ain't had you yet, and I'm going to.' Where he'd butted her with the oval crown of his head, he had split her lip against her teeth and made her bleed. 'I mean business,' he repeated, but uncertainly. He was as rough-boned and graceless as a young steer. He made her put her dress on without any underwear, he shoved her barefoot down the hall, carrying his boots under his arm. Hope didn't realize until she was beside him in the pickup that he had put on one of her husband's flannel shirts.

'Margot has probably written down the license number of this truck,' she told him. She turned the rearview mirror so that she could see herself; she dabbed at her split lip with the broad, floppy collar of her dress. Oren Rath stiff-armed her in the ear, rapping the far side of her head off the passenger door of the cab.

'I need that mirror to see,' he said. 'Don't mess around or I'll really hurt you.' He'd taken her bra with him and he used it to tie her wrists to the thick, rusty hinges of the glove-compartment door, which gaped open at her.

He drove as if he were in no special hurry to get out of town. He did not seem impatient when he got stuck at the long traffic light near the university. He watched all the pedestrians crossing the street; he shook his head and clucked his tongue when he saw how some of the students were dressed. Hope could see her husband's office window from where she sat in the truck's cab, but she didn't know if he would be in his office or actually, at that moment, teaching a class.

In fact, he was in his office – four floors up. Dorsey Standish looked out his window and saw the lights change; the traffic was allowed to flow, the hordes of marching students were temporarily restrained at the gates to the crosswalks. Dorsey Standish liked watching traffic. There are many foreign and flashy cars in a university town, but here these cars were contrasted with the vehicles of the natives: farmers' trucks, slat-sided conveyors of pigs and cattle, strange harvesting machinery, everything muddy from the farms and county roads. Standish knew nothing about farms, but he was fascinated by the animals and the machines – especially the dangerous, baffling vehicles. There went one, now, with a chute – for what? – and a latticework of cables that pulled or suspended something heavy. Standish liked to try to visualize how everything worked.

Below him a lurid turquoise pickup moved ahead with the traffic; its fenders were pockmarked, its grille bashed in and black with mashed flies and – Standish imagined – the heads of imbedded birds. In the cab beside the driver Dorsey Standish thought he saw a pretty woman – something about her hair and profile reminded him of Hope, and a flash of the woman's dress struck him as a color his wife liked to wear. But he was four floors up; the truck was past him, and the cab's rear window was so thickly caked with mud that he couldn't glimpse more of her. Besides, it was time for his nine-thirty class. Dorsey Standish decided it was unlikely that a woman riding in such an ugly truck would be at all pretty.

'I bet your husband is screwing his students all the time,' said Oren Rath. His big hand, with the knife, lay in Hope's lap.

'No, I don't think so,' Hope said.

'Shit, you don't know *nothing*,' he said. 'I'm going to fuck you so good you won't ever want it to stop.'

'I don't care what you do,' Hope told him. 'You can't hurt my baby now.'

'I can do things to *you*,' said Oren Rath. 'Lots of things.'

'Yes. You mean business,' Hope said, mockingly.

They were driving into the farm country. Rath didn't say anything for a while. Then he said, 'I'm not as crazy as you think.'

'I don't think you're crazy at all,' Hope lied. 'I think you're just a dumb, horny kid who's never been laid.'

Oren Rath must have felt at this moment that his advantage of terror was slipping away from him, fast. Hope was seeking *any* advantage she might find, but she didn't know if Oren Rath was sane enough to be humiliated.

They turned off the county road, up a long dirt driveway toward a farmhouse whose windows were blurred with plastic insulation; the scruffy lawn was strewn with tractor parts and other metal trash. The mailbox said: R, R, W, E & O RATH.

These Raths were not related to the famous sausage Raths, but it appeared that they were pig farmers. Hope saw a series of outbuildings, gray and slanted with rusted roofs. On the ramp by the brown barn a full-grown sow lay on her side, breathing with difficulty; beside the pig were two men who looked to Hope like mutants of the same mutation that had produced Oren Rath.

'I want the black truck, now,' Oren said to them. 'People are out looking for this one.' He used his knife matter-of-factly to slice through the bra that bound Hope's wrists to the glove compartment.

'Shit,' one of the men said.

The other man shrugged; he had a red blotch on his face – a kind of birthmark, which was the color and nubbled surface of a raspberry. In fact, that is what his family called him: Raspberry Rath. Fortunately, Hope didn't know this.

They had not looked at Oren or at Hope. The hard-breathing sow shattered the barnyard calm with a rippling fart. 'Shit, there she goes again,' the man without the birthmark said; except for his eyes, *his* face was more or less normal. His name was Weldon.

Raspberry Rath read the label on a brown bottle he held out toward the pig like a drink: '"May produce excessive gas and flatulence," it says.'

'Don't say anything about producing a pig like *this*,' Weldon said.

'I need the black truck,' Oren said.

'Well, the key's in it, Oren,' said Weldon Rath. 'If you think you can manage by yourself.'

Oren Rath shoved Hope toward the black pickup. Raspberry was holding the bottle of pig medicine and staring at Hope when she said to him, 'He's kidnapping me. He's going to rape me. The police are already looking for him.'

Raspberry kept staring at Hope, but Weldon turned to Oren. 'I hope you ain't doing nothing too stupid,' he said.

'I ain't,' Oren said. The two men now turned their total attention to the pig.

'I'd wait another hour and then give her another squirt,' Raspberry said. 'Ain't we seen enough of the vet this week?' He scratched the mud-smeared neck of the sow with the toe of his boot; the sow farted.

Oren led Hope behind the barn where the corn spilled out of the silo. Some piglets, barely bigger than kittens, were playing in it. They scattered when Oren started the black pickup. Hope started to cry.

'Are you going to let me go?' she asked Oren.

'I ain't had you yet,' he said.

Hope's bare feet were cold and black with the spring muck. 'My feet hurt,' she said. 'Where are we going?'

She'd seen an old blanket in the back of the pickup, matted and flecked with straw. *That's* where she imagined she was going: into the cornfields, then spread on the spongy spring ground – and when it was over and her throat was slit, and she'd been disemboweled with the fisherman's knife, he'd wrap her up in the blanket that was lumped stiffly on the floor of the pickup as if it covered some stillborn livestock.

'I got to find a good place to *have* you,' said Oren Rath. 'I would of kept you at home, but I'd of had to share you.'

Hope Standish was trying to figure out the foreign machinery of Oren Rath. He did not *work* like the human beings she was accustomed to.

'What you're doing is wrong,' she said.

'No, it isn't,' he said. 'It *ain't*.'

'You're going to rape me,' Hope said. 'That's wrong.'

'I just want to *have* you,' he said. He hadn't bothered to tie her to the glove compartment this time. There was nowhere she could go. They were driving only on those mile-long plots of county roads, driving slowly west in little squares, the way a knight advances on a chessboard: one square ahead, two sideways, one sideways, two ahead. It seemed purposeless to Hope, but then she wondered if he didn't know the roads so very well that he knew how to cover a considerable distance without ever passing through a town. They saw only the signposts for towns, and although they couldn't have moved more than thirty miles from the university, she didn't recognize any of the names: Coldwater, Hills, Fields, Plainview. Maybe they *aren't* towns, she thought, but only crude labels for the natives who lived here – identifying the land for them, as if they didn't know the simple words for the things they saw every day.

'You don't have any right to do this to me,' Hope said.

'Shit,' he said. He pumped his brakes hard, throwing her forward against the truck's solid dashboard. Her forehead bounced off the windshield, the back of her hand was mashed against her nose. She felt something like a small muscle or a very light bone give way in her chest. Then he tromped on the accelerator and tossed her back into the seat. 'I hate arguing,' he said.

Her nose bled; she sat with her head forward, in her hands, and the blood dripped on her thighs. She sniffed a little; the blood dripped over her lip and filmed her teeth. She tipped her head back so that she could taste it. For some reason, it calmed her – it helped her to think. She knew there was a rapidly blueing knot on her forehead, swelling under her smooth skin. When she ran her hand up to her face and touched the lump, Oren Rath looked at her and laughed. She spit at him – a thin phlegm laced pink with blood. It caught his cheek and ran down to the collar of her husband's flannel shirt. His hand, as flat and broad as the sole of a boot, reached for her hair. She grabbed his forearm with both her hands, she jerked his wrist to her mouth and bit into the soft part where the hairs don't always grow and the blue tubes carry the blood.

She meant to kill him in this impossible way but she barely

had time to break the skin. His arm was so strong that he snapped her body upright and across his lap. He pushed the back of her neck against the steering wheel – the horn blew through her head – and he broke her nose with the heel of his left hand. Then he returned that hand to the wheel. He cradled her head with his right hand, holding her face against his stomach; when he felt that she wasn't struggling, he let her head rest on his thigh. His hand lightly cupped her ear, as if to hold the sound of the horn inside her. She kept her eyes shut against the pain in her nose.

He made several left turns, more right turns. Each turn, she knew, meant they had driven one mile. His hand now cupped the back of her neck. She could hear again, and she felt his fingers working their way into her hair. The front of her face felt numb.

'I don't want to kill you,' he said.

'*Don't*, then,' Hope said.

'*Got* to,' Oren Rath told her. 'After we do it, I'll *have* to.'

This affected her like the taste of her own blood. She knew he didn't care for arguing. She saw that she had lost a step: her rape. He was going to do it to her. She had to consider that it was done. What mattered now was *living*; she knew that meant outliving him. She knew that meant getting him caught, or getting him killed, or killing him.

Against her cheek, she felt the change in his pocket; his blue jeans were soft and sticky with farm dust and machine grease. His belt buckle dug into her forehead; her lips touched the oily leather of his belt. The fisherman's knife was kept in a sheath, she knew. But where was the sheath? She couldn't see it; she didn't dare to hunt for it with her hands. Suddenly, against her eye, she felt his penis stiffening. She felt then – for really the first time – almost paralyzed, panicked beyond helping herself, no longer able to sort out the priorities. Once again, it was Oren Rath who helped her.

'Look at it this way,' he said. 'Your kid got away. I was going to kill the kid, too, you know.'

The logic of Oren Rath's peculiar version of sanity made

everything sharpen for Hope; she heard the other cars. There were not many, but every few minutes or so there was a car passing. She wished she could see, but she knew they were not as isolated as they had been. *Now*, she thought, before he gets to where we're going – if he even knows where we're going. She thought he did. At least, before he gets off this road – before I'm somewhere, again, where there aren't any people.

Oren Rath shifted in his seat. His erection was making him uncomfortable. Hope's warm face in his lap, his hand in her hair, was reaching him. *Now*, Hope thought. She moved her cheek against his thigh, just slightly; he did not stop her. She moved her face in his lap as if she were making herself more comfortable, against a pillow – against his *prick*, she knew. She moved until the bulge under his rank pants rose untouched by her face. But she could reach it with her breath; it stuck up out of his lap near her mouth, and she began to breathe on it. It hurt too much to breathe out of her nose. She drew her lips into an O-shaped kiss, she focused her breathing, and, very softly, she blew.

Oh, Nicky, she thought. And Dorsey, her husband. She would see them again, she hoped. To Oren Rath she gave her warm, careful breath. On him she focused her one, cold thought: I'm going to *get* you, you son of a bitch.

It was apparent that the sexual experience of Oren Rath had not previously involved such subtleties as Hope's directed breathing. He tried to move her head in his lap so that he would once again have contact with her hot face, but at the same time he didn't want to disturb her soft breath. What she was doing made him want *more* contact, but it was excruciating to imagine losing the teasing contact he now had. He began to squirm. Hope didn't hurry. It was his movement that finally brought the bulge of sour jeans to touch her lips. She closed them there, but didn't move her mouth. Oren Rath felt only a hot wind passing through the crude weave of his clothes; he groaned. A car approached, then passed him; he corrected the truck. He was aware he was beginning to wander across the center of the road.

'What are you doing?' he asked Hope. She, very lightly,

applied her teeth to his swollen clothes. He brought his knee up, pumped the brake, jarred her head, hurt her nose. He forced his hand between her face and his lap. She thought he was going to really hurt her but he was struggling with his zipper. 'I've seen pictures of this,' he told her.

'Let me,' she said. She had to sit up just a little to get his fly open. She wanted to get a look at where they were; they were still out in the country, of course, but there were painted lines on the road. She took him out of his pants and into her mouth without looking at him.

'Shit,' he said. She thought she would gag; she was afraid she would be sick. Then she got him into the back of her cheek where she thought she could take a lot of time. He was sitting so stiffly still, but trembling, that she knew he was already far beyond even his imaginary experiences. That steadied Hope; it gave her confidence, and a sense of time. She went ahead with it very slowly, listening for other cars. She could tell he had slowed down. At the first sign she had that he was leaving this road, she would have to change her plans. Could I bite the damn thing off? she wondered. But she thought that she probably couldn't – at least, not quickly enough.

Then two trucks went by them, closely following each other; in the distance she thought she heard another car's horn. She started working faster – he raised his lap higher. She thought their truck had speeded up. A car passed them – awfully close, she thought. Its horn blared at them. 'Fuck you!' Oren Rath yelled after it; he was beginning to jounce up and down in the seat, hurting Hope's nose. Hope now had to be careful not to hurt him; she wanted to hurt him very much. Just make him lose his head, she encouraged herself.

Suddenly there was the sound of gravel spraying the underside of the truck. She closed her mouth fast around him. But they were neither crashing nor turning off the road; he was pulling abruptly to the roadside and stopping. The truck stalled out. He put both his hands on either side of her face; his thighs hardened and slapped against her jaw. I'm going to choke on it, she thought, but he was lifting her face up, out of his lap. 'No!

No!' he cried. A truck, flinging tiny stones, tore by them and cut into his words. 'I don't have the *thing* on,' he said to her. 'If you have any germs, they'll swim right up me.'

Hope sat on her knees, her lips hot and sore, her nose throbbing. He was going to put on a rubber, but when he tore it from its little tinfoil package, he stared at it as if it wasn't at all what he expected to see – as if he thought they were bright green! As if he didn't know how to put it on. 'Take your dress off,' he said; he was embarrassed that she was looking at him. She could see the cornfields on either side of the road, and the back side of a billboard a few yards away from them. But there were no houses, no signs, no intersecting roads. No cars and trucks were coming. She thought her heart would simply stop.

Oren Rath tore himself out of her husband's shirt; he threw it out his window; Hope saw it flap in the road. He scraped his boots off on the brake pedal, whacking his narrow blond knees on the steering wheel. 'Shove over!' he said. She was wedged against the passenger-side door. She knew – even if she could get out the door – that she couldn't outrun him. She didn't have any shoes – and his feet appeared to have a dog's rough pads.

He was having trouble with his pants; he clutched the rolled-up rubber in his teeth. Then he was naked – he'd flung his pants somewhere – and he shoved the rubber down over himself as if his penis were no more sensitive than a turtle's leathery tail. She was trying to unbutton her dress and her tears were coming back, though she was fighting them, when he suddenly caught her dress and began to yank it over her head; it caught on her arms. He jerked her elbows painfully behind her back.

He was too long to fit in the cab. One door had to be open. She reached for the handle over her head but he bit her in the neck. 'No!' he hollered. He thrashed his feet around – she saw his shin was bleeding; he'd cut it on the rim of the horn – and his hard heels struck the door handle on the driver's side. With both feet, he launched the door open. She saw the gray smear of the road over his shoulder – his long ankles stuck out into the traffic lane, but there was no traffic now. Her head hurt; she was jammed against the door. She had to wriggle herself back down the seat, farther under him, and her movement made him yell something unintelligible. She felt his rubbered prick slipping over her stomach. Then his whole body braced and he bit into her shoulder fiercely. He'd come!

'Shit!' he cried. 'I *done* it already!'

'No,' she said, hugging him. 'No, you can do *more*.' She knew that if he thought he was through with her, he would kill her.

'Much more,' she said in his ear, which smelled like dust. She had to wet her fingers to wet herself. God, I'll never get him inside me, she thought, but when she found him with her hand, she knew that the rubber was the lubricated kind.

'Oh,' he said. He lay still on top of her; he seemed surprised by where she'd put him, as if he didn't really know what was where. 'Oh,' he repeated.

Oh, what now? Hope wondered. She held her breath. A car, a flash of red, whined past their open door – the horn blast and some muffled, derisive hoots fading away from them. Of course, she thought: we look like two farmers fucking off the side of the road; it's probably done all the time. No one will stop, she thought, unless it's the police. She imagined a bread-faced trooper appearing over Rath's lurching shoulder, writing out a ticket. 'Not on the road, buddy,' he'd be saying. And when she screamed at him, 'Rape! He's *raping* me,' the trooper would wink at Oren Rath.

The bewildered Rath seemed to be feeling rather cautiously for something inside her. If he's just come, Hope thought, how much time do I have before he comes again? But he seemed more like a goat than a human to her, and the babylike gurgle in his throat, hot against her ear, seemed close to the last sound she imagined she'd hear.

She looked at everything she could see. The keys dangling from the ignition were too far to reach; and what could she do with a set of keys? Her back hurt and she pushed her hand against the dashboard to try to shift his weight on her; this excited him and made him grunt against her. 'Don't move,' he said; she tried to do what he said. 'Oh,' he said, approvingly. 'That's real good.

I'll kill you quick. You won't even know it. You just do like that, and I'll kill you good.'

Her hand grazed a metal button, smooth and round; her fingers touched it and she did not even have to turn her face away from him and look at it to know what it was. It opened the glove compartment and she pushed it. The spring-release door was a sudden weight in her hand. She said a long and loud 'Aaahhh!' to conceal the sound of the things in the glove compartment that rattled around. Her hand touched cloth, her fingers felt grit. There was a spool of wire, something sharp, but too small – things like screws and nails, a bolt, perhaps a hinge to something else. There was nothing she could use. Reaching around in there was hurting her arm; she let her hand trail to the floor of the cab. When another truck passed them – catcalls and bloops from the air horn, and no sign of even slowing down for a better look – she started to cry.

'I *got* to kill you,' Rath moaned.

'Have you done this before?' she asked him.

'Sure,' he said, and he thrust into her – stupidly, as if his brute lunges could impress her.

'And did you kill them, too?' Hope asked. Her hand, aimless now, toyed with something – some material – on the floor of the cab.

'They were animals,' Rath admitted. 'But I had to kill them, too.' Hope sickened, her fingers clutched the thing on the floor – an old jacket or something.

'Pigs?' she asked him.

'Pigs!' he cried. 'Shit, *no*body fucks pigs,' he told her. Hope thought that probably *some*body did. 'They was sheep,' Rath said. 'And one calf.' But this was hopeless, she knew. She felt him shrinking inside her; she was distracting him. She choked a sob that felt like it would split her head if it ever escaped her.

'Please *try* to be kind to me,' Hope said.

'Don't talk any,' he said. 'Move like you did.'

She moved, but apparently not the right way. 'No!' he shouted. His fingers dug into her spine. She tried moving another way.

'Yup,' he said. He moved, now, determined and purposeful –
mechanical and dumb.

Oh, God, Hope thought. Oh, Nicky. And Dorsey. Then she
felt what she held in her hands: his pants. And her fingers, suddenly as wise as a Braille reader's, located the zipper and moved
on; her fingers passed over the change in the pocket, they slipped
around the wide belt.

'Yup, yup, yup,' said Oren Rath.

Sheep, Hope thought to herself; and one calf. 'Oh, *please* concentrate!' she cried aloud to herself.

'Don't talk!' said Oren Rath.

But now her hand held it: the long, hard, leather sheath. That
is the little hook, her fingers told her, and that is the little metal
clasp. And that – oh, yes! – is the head of the thing, the bony
handle of the fisherman's knife he had used to cut her son.

Nicky's cut was not serious. In fact, everyone was trying to figure
out how he got it. Nicky was not talking yet. He enjoyed looking in the mirror at the thin, half-moon slit that was already
closed.

'Must have been something very sharp,' the doctor told the
police. Margot, the neighbor, had thought she'd better call a
doctor, too; she'd found blood on the child's bib. The police had
found more blood in the bedroom; a single drop on the cream-
white bedspread. They were puzzled about it; there was no other
sign of violence, and Margot had seen Mrs Standish leave. She
had looked all right. The blood was from Hope's split lip – from
the time Oren Rath had butted her – but there was no way any
of them could know that. Margot thought there might have
been sex, but she wasn't suggesting it. Dorsey Standish was too
shocked to think. The police did not think there had been time
for sex. The doctor knew no blow had been connected with
Nicky's cut – probably not even a fall. 'A razor?' he suggested.
'Or a very sharp knife.'

The police inspector, a solidly round and florid man, a year
away from his retirement, found the cut phone cord in the
bedroom. 'A knife,' he said. 'A sharp knife with some *weight* to

it.' His name was Arden Bensenhaver, and he had once been a police superintendent in Toledo, but his methods had been judged as unorthodox.

He pointed at Nicky's cheek. 'It's a flick wound,' he said. He demonstrated the proper wrist action. 'But you don't see many flick knives around here,' Bensenhaver told them. 'It's a flick-type of wound, but it's probably some kind of hunting or fishing knife.'

Margot had described Oren Rath as a farm kid in a farm truck, except that the truck's color revealed the unnatural influence of the town and the university upon the farmers: turquoise. Dorsey Standish did not even associate this with the turquoise truck he had seen, or the woman in the cab whom he'd thought had resembled Hope. He still didn't understand anything.

'Did they leave a note?' he asked. Arden Bensenhaver stared at him. The doctor looked down at the floor. 'You know, about a *ransom?*' Standish said. He was a literal man struggling for a literal hold. Someone, he thought, had said 'kidnap'; wasn't there ransom in the case of kidnap?

'There's no note, Mr Standish,' Bensenhaver told him. 'It doesn't look like that kind of thing.'

'They were in the bedroom when I found Nicky outside the door,' Margot said. 'But she was all right when she left, Dorsey. I saw her.'

They hadn't told Standish about Hope's panties, discarded on the bedroom floor; they'd been unable to find the matching bra. Margot had told Arden Bensenhaver that Mrs Standish was a woman who usually wore a bra. She had left barefoot; they knew that, too. And Margot had recognized Dorsey's shirt on the farm kid. She'd got only a partial reading of the license plate; it was an in-state, commercial plate, and the first two numbers placed it within the county, but she hadn't gotten them all. The rear plate had been spattered with mud, the front plate was missing.

'We'll find them,' Arden Bensenhaver said. 'There's not much in the way of turquoise trucks around here. The county sheriff's boys will probably know it.'

'Nicky, what happened?' Dorsey Standish asked the boy. He

sat him on his lap. 'What happened to Mommy?' The child pointed out the window. 'So he was going to *rape* her?' Dorsey Standish asked them all.

Margot said, 'Dorsey, let's wait until we know.'

'Wait?' Standish said.

'You got to excuse me asking you,' said Arden Bensenhaver, 'but your wife wasn't seeing anybody, was she? You know.'

Standish was mute at the question, but it seemed as if he were importantly considering it. 'No, she wasn't,' Margot told Bensenhaver. 'Absolutely not.'

'I got to ask Mr Standish,' Bensenhaver said.

'God,' Margot said.

'No, I don't think she was,' Standish told the inspector.

'Of course she wasn't, Dorsey,' Margot said. 'Let's go take Nicky for a walk,' she said to him. She was a busy, businesslike woman whom Hope liked very much. She was in and out of the house five times a day; she was always in the process of finishing something. Twice a year she had her phone disconnected, and connected again; it was like trying to stop smoking is for some people. Margot had children of her own but they were older – they were in school all day – and she often watched Nicky so that Hope could do something by herself. Dorsey Standish took Margot for granted; although he knew she was a kind and generous person, those were not qualities that especially arrested his attention. Margot, he realized now, wasn't especially attractive, either. She was not *sexually* attractive, he thought, and a bitter feeling rose up in Standish: he thought that no one would ever try to rape Margot – whereas Hope was a beautiful woman, anyone could see. Anyone would want her.

Dorsey Standish was all wrong about that; he didn't know the first thing about rape – that the victim hardly ever matters. At one time or another, people have tried to force sex on almost anyone imaginable. Very small children, very old people, even dead people; also animals.

Inspector Arden Bensenhaver, who knew a good deal about rape, announced that he had to get on with his job.

*   *   *

Bensenhaver felt better with lots of open space around him. His first employment had been the nighttime beat in a squad car, cruising old Route 2 between Sandusky and Toledo. In the summers it was a road speckled with beer joints and little homemade signs promising BOWLING! POOL! SMOKED FISH! and LIVE BAIT! And Arden Bensenhaver would drive slowly over Sandusky Bay and along Lake Erie to Toledo, waiting for the drunken carfuls of teenagers and fishermen to play chicken with him on that unlit, two-lane road. Later, when he was the police superintendent of Toledo, Bensenhaver would be driven, in the daytime, over that harmless stretch of road. The bait shops and beer palaces and fast-food services looked so exposed in the daylight. It was like watching a once-feared bully strip down for a fight; you saw the thick neck, the dense chest, the wristless arms – and then, when the last shirt was off, you saw the sad, helpless paunch.

Arden Bensenhaver hated the night. Bensenhaver's big plea with the city government of Toledo had been for better lighting on Saturday nights. Toledo was a workingman's city, and Bensenhaver believed that if the city could afford to light itself, brightly, on Saturday night, half the gashings and maimings – the general bodily abusings – would stop. But Toledo had thought the idea was dim. Toledo was as unimpressed with Arden Bensenhaver's ideas as it was questioning of his methods.

Now Bensenhaver relaxed in all this open country. He had a perspective on the dangerous world that he always wanted to have: he was circling the flat, open land in a helicopter – above it all, the detached overseer observing his contained, well-lit kingdom. The county deputy said to him, 'There's only one truck around here that's *turquoise*. It's those damn Raths.'

'Raths?' Bensenhaver asked.

'There's a whole family of them,' the deputy said. 'I hate going out there.'

'Why?' Bensenhaver asked; below him, he watched the shadow of the helicopter cross a creek, cross a road, move alongside a field of corn and a field of soybeans.

'They're all weird,' the deputy said. Bensenhaver looked at

him – a young man, puffy-faced and small-eyed, but pleasant; his long hair hung in a hunk under his tight hat, almost touching his shoulders. Bensenhaver thought of all the football players who wore their hair spilling out under their helmets. They could *braid* it, some of them, he thought. Now even lawmen looked like this. He was glad he was retiring soon; he couldn't understand why so many people *wanted* to look the way they did.

'"Weird"?' said Bensenhaver. Their language was all the same, too, he thought. They used just four or five words for almost everything.

'Well, I got a complaint about the younger one just last week,' the deputy said. Bensenhaver noted this casual use of 'I' – as in 'I got a complaint' – when in fact Bensenhaver knew that the sheriff, or his office, would have received the complaint, and that the sheriff probably thought it was simple enough to send this young deputy out on it. But why did they give me such a young one for *this*? Bensenhaver wondered.

'The youngest brother's name is Oren,' the deputy said. 'They all have weird names, too.'

'What was the complaint?' Bensenhaver asked; his eyes followed a long dirt driveway to what appeared to be a random dropping of barns and outbuildings, one of which he knew was the main farmhouse, where the *people* lived. But Arden Bensenhaver couldn't tell which one that might be. To him, all the buildings looked vaguely unfit for animals.

'Well,' the deputy said, 'this kid Oren was screwing around with someone's dog.'

'"Screwing around"?' Bensenhaver asked patiently. That could mean anything, he thought.

'Well,' the deputy said, 'the people whose dog it was thought that Oren was trying to *fuck* it.'

'*Was* he?' Bensenhaver asked.

'Probably,' the deputy said, 'but I couldn't tell anything. When I got there, Oren wasn't around – and the dog *looked* all right. I mean, how could I tell if the dog had been fucked?'

'Should've *asked* it!' said the copter pilot – a kid, Bensenhaver

realized, even younger than the deputy. Even the deputy looked
at him with contempt.

'One of these half-wits the National Guard gives us,' the
deputy whispered to Bensenhaver, but Bensenhaver had spotted
the turquoise truck. It was parked out in the open, alongside a
low shed. No attempt had been made to conceal it.

In a long pen a tide of pigs surged this way and that, driven
crazy by the hovering helicopter. Two lean men in overalls
squatted over a pig that lay sprawled at the foot of a ramp to
a barn. They looked up at the helicopter, shielding their faces
from the stinging dirt.

'Not so close. Put it down over on the lawn,' Bensenhaver
told the pilot. 'You're scaring the animals.'

'I don't see Oren, or the old man,' the deputy said. 'There's
more of them than those two.'

'You ask those two where Oren is,' Bensenhaver said. 'I want
to look at that truck.'

The men obviously knew the deputy; they hardly watched
him approach. But they watched Bensenhaver, in his dull
dun-colored suit and tie, crossing the barnyard toward the
turquoise pickup. Arden Bensenhaver didn't look at them, but
he could see them just the same. They are *morons*, he thought.
Bensenhaver had seen all kinds of bad men in Toledo – vicious
men, unjustifiably angry men, dangerous men, cowardly and
ballsy thieves, men who murdered for money, and men who
murdered for sex. But Bensenhaver had not seen quite such
benign corruption as he thought he saw on the faces of Weldon
and Raspberry Rath. It gave him a chill. He thought he'd better
find Mrs Standish, quickly.

He didn't know what he was looking for when he opened
the door of the turquoise pickup, but Arden Bensenhaver
knew how to look for unknowns. He saw it immediately – it
was easy: the slashed bra, a piece of it still tied to the hinge of
the glove-compartment door; the other two pieces were on the
floor. There was no blood; the bra was a soft, natural beige; very
classy, Arden Bensenhaver thought. He had no style himself,
but he'd seen dead people of all kinds, and he could recognize

something of a person's style in the clothes. He put the pieces of the silky bra into one hand; then he put both hands into the floppy, stretched pockets of his suit jacket and started across the yard toward the deputy, who was talking to the Rath brothers.

'They haven't seen the kid all day,' the deputy told Bensenhaver. 'They say Oren sometimes stays away overnight.'

'Ask them who's the last one who drove that truck,' Bensenhaver said to the deputy; he wouldn't look at the Raths; he treated them as if they couldn't possibly understand him, directly.

'I already asked them that,' the deputy said. 'They say they don't remember.'

'Ask them when's the last time a pretty young woman rode in that truck,' Bensenhaver said, but the deputy didn't have time; Weldon Rath laughed. Bensenhaver felt grateful that the one with the blotch on his face, like a wine spill, had kept quiet.

'Shit,' Weldon said. 'There's no "pretty young woman" around here, no pretty young woman ever sat her ass in that truck.'

'Tell him,' said Bensenhaver to the deputy, 'that he is a liar.'

'You're a liar, Weldon,' the deputy said.

Raspberry Rath said to the deputy, 'Shit, who is he, coming in here, telling us what to do?'

Arden Bensenhaver took the three pieces of the bra from his pocket. He looked at the sow lying beside the men; she had one frightened eye, which appeared to be looking at all of them at once, and it was hard to tell where her other eye was looking.

'Is that a boy pig or a girl pig?' asked Bensenhaver.

The Raths laughed. 'Anyone can see it's a sow,' Raspberry said.

'Do you ever cut the balls off the boy pigs?' Bensenhaver asked. 'Do you do that yourselves or do you have others do it for you?'

'We castrate them ourselves,' said Weldon. He looked a little like a boar himself, with wild tufts of hair sprouting upward, out of his ears. 'We know all about castrating. There's nothing to it.'

'Well,' said Bensenhaver, holding up the bra for them and the deputy to see. 'Well, that's exactly what the new law provides for – in the case of these sexual crimes.' Neither the deputy nor the Raths spoke. 'Any sexual crime,' Bensenhaver said, 'is now punishable by castration. If you fuck anybody you shouldn't,' said Bensenhaver, 'or if you assist in the act of getting a person fucked – by not helping us to stop it – then we can castrate you.'

Weldon Rath looked at his brother, Raspberry, who looked a little puzzled. But Weldon leered at Bensenhaver and said, 'You do it yourselves or do you have others do it for you?' He nudged his brother. Raspberry tried to grin, pulling his birth-mark askew.

But Bensenhaver was deadpan, turning the bra over and over in his hands. 'Of course we don't do it,' he said. 'There's all new equipment for it now. The National Guard does it. That's why we got the National Guard helicopter. We just fly you right out to the National Guard hospital and fly you right back home again. There's nothing to it,' he said. 'As you know.'

'We have a big family,' Raspberry Rath said. 'There's a lot of us brothers. We don't know from one day to the next who's riding around in what truck.'

'There's another truck?' Bensenhaver asked the deputy. 'You didn't tell me there was another truck.'

'Yeah, it's black. I forgot,' the deputy said. 'They have a black one, too.' The Raths nodded.

'Where is it?' Bensenhaver asked. He was contained but tense.

The brothers looked at each other. Weldon said, 'I haven't seen it in a while.'

'Might be that Oren has it,' said Raspberry.

'Might be our father who's got it,' Weldon said.

'We don't have time for this shit,' Bensenhaver told the deputy, sharply. 'We'll find out what they weigh – then see if the pilot can carry them.' The deputy, thought Bensenhaver, is almost as much of a moron as the brothers. 'Go on!' Bensenhaver said to the deputy. Then, with impatience, he turned to Weldon Rath. 'Name?' he asked.

'Weldon,' Weldon said.

'Weight?' Bensenhaver asked.

'Weight?' said Weldon.

'What do you weigh?' Bensenhaver asked him. 'If we're going to lug you off in the copter, we got to know what you weigh.'

'One-eighty-something,' Weldon said.

'You?' Bensenhaver asked the younger one.

'One-ninety-something,' he said. 'My name's Raspberry.' Bensenhaver shut his eyes.

'That's three-seventy-something,' Bensenhaver told the deputy. 'Go ask the pilot if we can carry that.'

'You're not taking us anywhere, now, are you?' Weldon asked.

'We'll just take you to the National Guard hospital,' Bensenhaver said. 'Then if we find the woman, and she's all right, we'll take you home.'

'But if she ain't all right, we get a lawyer, right?' Raspberry asked Bensenhaver. 'One of those people in the courts, right?'

'If who *ain't* all right?' Bensenhaver asked him.

'Well, this woman you're looking for,' Raspberry said.

'Well, if she's not all right,' Bensenhaver said, 'then we already got you in the hospital and we can castrate you and send you back home the same day. You boys know more about what's involved than I do,' he admitted. 'I've never seen it done, but it doesn't take long, does it? And it doesn't bleed much, does it?'

'But there's courts, and a lawyer!' Raspberry said.

'Of course there is,' Weldon said. 'Shut up.'

'No, no more courts for this kind of thing – not with the new law,' Bensenhaver said. 'Sex crimes are special, and with the new machines, it's just so easy to castrate someone that it makes the most sense.'

'Yeah!' the deputy hollered from the helicopter. 'The weight's okay. We can take them.'

'Shit!' Raspberry said.

'Shut up,' said Weldon.

'They're not cutting *my* balls off!' Raspberry yelled at him. 'I didn't even get to *have* her!' Weldon hit Raspberry so hard in the stomach that the younger man pitched over sideways and landed on the prostrate pig. It squealed, its short legs spasmed, it *evacuated* suddenly, and horribly, but otherwise it didn't move. Raspberry lay gasping beside the sow's stenchful waste, and Arden Bensenhaver tried to knee Weldon Rath in the balls. Weldon was too quick, though; he caught Bensenhaver's leg at the knee and tossed the old man over backwards, over Raspberry and the poor pig.

'Goddamnit,' Bensenhaver said.

The deputy drew his gun and fired one shot in the air. Weldon dropped to his knees, holding his ears. 'You all right, Inspector?' the deputy asked.

'Yes, of course I am,' Bensenhaver said. He sat beside the pig and Raspberry. He realized, without the smallest touch of shame, that he felt toward them more or less equally. 'Raspberry,' he said (the name itself made Bensenhaver close his eyes), 'if you want to keep your balls on, you tell us where the woman is.' The man's birthmark flashed at Bensenhaver like a neon sign.

'You keep still, Raspberry,' Weldon said.

And Bensenhaver told the deputy, 'If he opens his mouth again, *shoot* his balls off, right here. Save us the trip.' Then he hoped to God that the deputy was not so stupid that he would actually do it.

'Oren's got her,' Raspberry told Bensenhaver. 'He took the black truck.'

'Where'd he take her?' Bensenhaver asked.

'Don't know,' Raspberry said. 'He took her for a ride.'

'Was she all right when she left here?' Bensenhaver asked.

'Well, she was all right, I guess,' Raspberry said. 'I mean, I don't think Oren had hurt her yet. I don't think he'd even *had* her yet.'

'Why not?' Bensenhaver asked.

'Well, if he'd already had her,' Raspberry said, 'why would he want to keep her?' Bensenhaver again shut his eyes. He got to his feet.

'Find out how long ago,' he told the deputy. 'Then fuck up

that turquoise truck so they can't drive it. Then get your ass back to the copter.'

'And leave them here?' the deputy asked.

'Sure,' Bensenhaver said. 'There'll be plenty of time to cut their balls off, later.'

Arden Bensenhaver had the pilot send a message that the abductor's name was Oren Rath, and that he was driving a black, not a turquoise, pickup. This message meshed interestingly with another one: a state trooper had received a report that a man all alone in a black pickup had been driving dangerously, wandering in and out of his rightful driving lane, 'looking like he was drunk, or stoned, or something else.' The trooper had not followed this up because, at the time, he'd thought he was supposed to be more concerned about a *turquoise* pickup. Arden Bensenhaver, of course, couldn't know that the man in the black pickup hadn't really been alone – that, in fact, Hope Standish had been lying with her head in his lap. The news simply gave Bensenhaver another of his chills: if Rath was alone, he had already done something to the woman. Bensenhaver yelled to the deputy to hurry over to the copter – that they were looking for a black pickup that had last been seen on the bypass that intersects the system of county roads near the town called Sweet Wells.

'Know it?' Bensenhaver asked.

'Oh, yeah,' the deputy said.

They were in the air again, below them the pigs once more in a panic. The poor, medicated pig that had been fallen on was lying as still as when they'd come. But the Rath brothers were fighting – it appeared, quite savagely – and the higher and farther from them that the helicopter moved, the more the world returned to a level of sanity of which Arden Bensenhaver approved. Until the tiny fighting figures, below and to the east, were no more than miniatures to him, and he was so far from their blood and fear that when the deputy said he thought that Raspberry could whip Weldon, if Raspberry just didn't allow himself to get scared, Bensenhaver laughed his Toledo deadpan laugh.

'They're *animals*,' he said to the deputy, who, despite whatever young man's cruelty and cynicism were in him, seemed a little shocked. 'If they both killed each other,' Bensenhaver said, 'think of the food they would have eaten in their lifetimes that other human beings could now eat.' The deputy realized that Bensenhaver's lie about the new law – about the instant castration for sexual crimes – was more than a farfetched story: for Bensenhaver, although he knew it was clearly *not* the law, it was what he thought the law *should* be. It was one of Arden Bensenhaver's Toledo methods.

'That poor woman,' Bensenhaver said; he wrung the pieces of her bra in his thick-veined hands. 'How old is this *Oren?*' he asked the deputy.

'Sixteen, maybe seventeen,' the deputy said. 'Just a kid.' The deputy was at least twenty-four himself.

'If he's old enough to get a hard-on,' Arden Bensenhaver said, 'he's old enough to have it cut off.'

But *what* should I cut? Oh, *where* can I cut him? wondered Hope – the long, thin fisherman's knife now snug in her hand. Her pulse thrummed in her palm, but to Hope it felt as if the knife had a heartbeat of its own. She brought her hand very slowly up to her hip, up over the edge of the thrashed seat to where she could glimpse the blade. Should I use the saw-toothed edge or the one that looks so sharp? she thought. How do you kill a man with one of these? Alongside the sweating, swiveling ass of Oren Rath that knife in her hand was a cool and distant miracle. Do I slash him or stick him? She wished she knew. Both his hot hands were under her buttocks, lifting her, jerking up. His chin dug into the hollow near her collarbone like a heavy stone. Then she felt him slip one of his hands out from under her, and his fingers, reaching for the floor, grazed her hand that held the knife.

'Move!' he grunted. 'Now move.' She tried to arch her back but couldn't; she tried to twist her hips, but she couldn't. She felt him groping for his own peculiar rhythm, trying to find the last pace that would make him come. His hand – under her now

– spread over the small of her back; his other hand clawed the floor.

Then she knew: he was looking for the knife. And when his fingers found the empty sheath, she would be in trouble.

'Aaahhh!' he cried.

Quick! she thought. Between the ribs? Into his side – and slide the knife up – or straight down as hard as she could between the shoulder blades, reaching all the way through his back to a lung, until she felt the point of the thing poking her own crushed breast? She waved her arm in the air above his hunching back. She saw the oily blade glint – and *his* hand, suddenly rising, flung his empty pants back toward the steering wheel.

He was trying to push himself up off her, but his lower half was locked into his long-sought rhythm; his hips shuddered in little spasms he couldn't seem to control, while his chest rose up, off her chest, and his hands shoved hard against her shoulders. His thumbs crawled toward her throat. 'My knife?' he asked. His head whipped back and forth; he looked behind him, he looked above him. His thumbs pried her chin up; she was trying to hide her Adam's apple.

Then she scissored his pale ass. He could not stop pumping down there, though his brain must have known there was suddenly another priority. 'My knife?' he said. And she reached over his shoulder and (faster than she herself could see it happen) she slid the slim-edged side of the blade across his throat. For a second, she saw no wound. She only knew that he was choking her. Then one of his hands left her throat and went to find his own. He hid from her the gash she'd expected to see. But at last she saw the dark blood springing between his tight fingers. He brought his hand away – he was searching for *her* hand, the one that held the knife – and from his slashed throat a great bubble burst over her. She heard a sound like someone sucking the bottom of a drink with a clogged straw. She could breathe again. Where were his hands? she wondered. They seemed, at once, to loll beside her on the seat and to be darting like panicked birds behind his back.

She stabbed the long blade into him, just above his waist,

thinking that perhaps a kidney was there, because the blade went in so easily, and out again. Oren Rath laid his cheek against her cheek like a child. He'd have screamed then, of course, but her first slash had cut cleanly through his windpipe and his vocal cords.

Hope now tried the knife higher up, but encountered a rib, or something difficult; she had to probe and, unsatisfied, withdrew the knife after only a few inches. He was flopping on her now, as if he wanted to get off her. His body was sending distress signals to itself, but the signals were not getting all the way through. He heaved himself against the back of the seat, but his head wouldn't stay up and his penis, still moving, attached him still to Hope. She took advantage of this opportunity to insert the knife again. It slipped into his belly at the side and moved straightaway to within an inch of his navel before engaging some major obstruction there – and his body slumped back on top of her, trapping her wrist. But this was easy; she twisted her hand and the slippery knife came free. Something to do with his bowels relaxed. Hope was overwhelmed with his wetness and with his smell. She let the knife drop to the floor.

Oren Rath was emptying, by quartfuls – by gallons. He felt actually lighter on top of her. Their bodies were so slick that she slipped out from under him easily. She shoved him over on his back and crouched beside him on the truck's puddled floor. Hope's hair was gravid with blood – his throat had fountained over her. When she blinked, her eyelashes stuck to her cheeks. One of his hands twitched and she slapped it. 'Stop,' she said. His knee rose, then flopped down. 'Stop it, stop now,' Hope said. She meant his heart, his life.

She would not look at his face. Against the dark slime coating his body, the white, translucent condom hugged his shrunken cock like a congealed fluid quite foreign to the human matter of blood and bowel. Hope recalled a zoo, and a gob of camel spit upon her crimson sweater.

His balls contracted. That made her angry. 'Stop,' she hissed. The balls were small and rounded and tight; then they fell slack. '*Please* stop,' she whispered. 'Please die.' There was a tiny sigh, as if someone had let out a breath too small to bother taking back. But Hope squatted for some time beside him, feeling her heart pound and confusing her pulse with his own. He had died fairly quickly, she realized later.

Out the open door of the pickup, Oren Rath's clean white feet, his drained toes, pointed upward in the sunlight. Inside the sun-baked cab, the blood was coagulating. Everything clotted. Hope Standish felt the tiny hairs on her arms stiffen and tug her skin as her skin dried. Everything that was slick was turning sticky.

I should get dressed, Hope thought. But something seemed wrong with the weather.

Out the truck windows Hope saw the sunlight flicker, like a lamp whose light is shone through the blades of a fast fan. And the gravel at the roadside was lifted up in little swirls, and dry shards and stubble from last year's corn were whisked along the flat, bare ground as if a great wind was blowing – but not from the usual directions: *this* wind appeared to be blowing straight down. And the noise! It was like being in the afterblow of a speeding truck, but there was still no traffic on the road.

It's a tornado! Hope thought. She hated the Midwest with its strange weather; she was an Easterner who could understand a hurricane. But tornadoes! She'd never seen one, but the weather forecasts were always full of 'tornado watches.' What does one *watch* for? she'd always wondered. For *this*, she guessed – this whirling din all around her. These clods of earth flying. The sun turned brown.

She was so angry, she struck the cool, viscid thigh of Oren Rath. After she had lived through *this*, now there was a fucking tornado, too! The noise resembled a train passing over the pelted truck. Hope imagined the funnel descending, other trucks and cars already caught up in it. Somehow, she could hear, their engines were still running. Sand flew in the open door, stuck to her glazed body; she groped for her dress – discovered the empty armholes where the sleeves had been; it would have to do.

But she would have to step outside the truck to put it on. There was no room to maneuver beside Rath and his gore, now dappled with roadside sand. And out there, she had no doubt, her dress would be torn from her hands and she would be sucked up naked into the sky. 'I am not sorry,' she whispered. 'I am *not* sorry!' she screamed, and again she struck at the body of Rath.

Then a voice, a terrible voice – loud as the loudest loudspeaker – shook her in the cab. 'IF YOU'RE IN THERE, COME OUT! PUT YOUR HANDS OVER YOUR HEAD. COME OUT. CLIMB INTO THE BACK OF THE PICKUP AND LIE THE FUCK DOWN!'

I am actually dead, thought Hope. I'm *already* in the sky and it's the voice of God. She was not religious and it seemed fitting, to Hope: if there were a God, God *would* have a bullying, loudspeaker voice.

'COME OUT NOW,' God said. 'DO IT NOW.'

Oh, why not? she thought. You big fucker. What can you do to me next? Rape was an outrage even God couldn't understand.

In the helicopter, shuddering above the black truck, Arden Bensenhaver barked into the megaphone. He was sure that Mrs Standish was dead. He could not tell the sex of the feet he saw protruding from the open door of the cab, but the feet hadn't moved during the helicopter's descent, and they seemed so naked and drained of any color in the sunlight that Bensenhaver was sure that they were *dead* feet. That Oren Rath could be the one who was dead had not crossed the deputy's or Bensenhaver's mind.

But they couldn't understand why Rath would have abandoned the truck, after performing his foul acts, and so Bensenhaver had told the pilot to hold the helicopter just above the pickup. 'If he's still in there with her,' Bensenhaver told the deputy, 'maybe we can scare the bastard to death.'

When Hope Standish brushed between those stiff feet and huddled alongside the cab, trying to shield her eyes from the flying sand, Arden Bensenhaver felt his finger go limp against the trigger of the megaphone. Hope tried to wrap her face in her flapping dress but it snapped around her like a torn sail; she felt her way along the truck toward the tailgate, cringing against the stinging gravel that clung to the places on her body where the blood hadn't quite dried.

'It's the *woman*,' the deputy said.

'Back off!' Bensenhaver told the pilot.

'Jesus, what happened to her?' the deputy asked, frightened. Bensenhaver roughly handed him the megaphone.

'Move *away*,' he said to the pilot. 'Set this thing down across the road.'

Hope felt the wind shift, and the clamor in the tornado's funnel seemed to pass over her. She kneeled at the side of the road. Her wild dress quieted in her hands. She held it to her mouth because the dust was choking her.

A car came along, but Hope was unaware of it. The driver passed in the proper lane – the black pickup off the road to his right, the helicopter settling down off the road to his left. The bloody, praying woman, naked and caked with grit, took no notice of him driving past her. The driver had a vision of an angel on a trip back from hell. The driver's reaction was *so* delayed that he was a hundred yards beyond everything he'd seen before he surprisingly attempted a U-turn in the road. Without slowing down. His front wheels caught the soft shoulder and slithered him across the road ditch and into the soft spring earth of a plowed bean field, where his car sank up to his bumpers and he could not open his door. He rolled down his window and peered across the mire to the road – like a man who'd been sitting peacefully on a dock when the dock broke free from the shore, and he was drifting out to sea.

'Help!' he cried. The vision of the woman had so terrified him that he feared there might be more like her around, or that whoever had made her look that way might be in search of another victim.

'Jesus Christ,' said Arden Bensenhaver to the pilot, 'you'll have to go see if that fool is all right. Why do they let everyone drive a car?' Bensenhaver and the deputy dropped out of the helicopter and into the same lush muck that had trapped the driver. 'Goddamnit,' Bensenhaver said.

'Mother,' said the deputy.

Across the road, Hope Standish looked up at them for the first time. Two swearing men were wallowing toward her out of a muddy field. The blades of the helicopter were slowing down. There was also a man peeping witlessly out the window of his car, but that seemed far away. Hope stepped into her dress. One armhole, where a sleeve had been, was torn open and Hope had to pin a flap of material to her side with her elbow, or else leave her breast exposed. It was then that she noticed how sore her shoulders and her neck were.

Arden Bensenhaver, out of breath and soaked with mud from his knees down, was in front of her suddenly. The mud made his trousers hug his legs so that, to Hope, he looked like an old man wearing knickers. 'Mrs Standish?' he asked. She turned her back to him and hid her face, nodding. 'So much blood,' he said, helplessly. 'I'm sorry we took so long. Are you hurt?'

She turned and stared at him. He saw the swelling around both eyes and her broken nose – and the blue bulge on her forehead. 'It's mostly *his* blood,' she said. 'But I was raped. He did it,' she told Bensenhaver.

Bensenhaver had his handkerchief out; he seemed about to dab at her face with it, as he might wipe the mouth of a child, but then he despaired at what a job it would be to clean her up and he put his handkerchief away. 'I'm sorry,' he said. 'I'm so sorry. We got here as fast as we could. We saw your baby and he's fine,' Bensenhaver said.

'I had to put him in my mouth,' Hope said to him. Bensenhaver shut his eyes. 'And then he fucked me and fucked me,' she said. 'He was going to kill me, later – he told me he would. I *had* to kill him. And I'm not sorry.'

'Of *course* you're not,' Bensenhaver said. 'And you *shouldn't* be, Mrs Standish. I'm sure you did the very best thing.' She nodded her head to him, then stared down at her feet. She put one hand out toward Bensenhaver's shoulder and he let her lean against him, though she was slightly taller than Bensenhaver and in order to rest her head against him, she had to scrunch down.

Bensenhaver was aware of the deputy then; he had been to the cab to look at Oren Rath and had vomited all over the truck's front fender and in full view of the pilot who was walking the shocked driver of the stuck car across the road. The deputy, with his face the bloodless color of Oren Rath's sunlit feet, was imploring Bensenhaver to come *see*. But Bensenhaver wanted Mrs Standish to feel every possible reassurance.

'So you killed him after he raped you, when he was relaxed, not paying attention?' he asked her.

'No, *during*,' she whispered against his neck. The awful reek of her almost got to Bensenhaver, but he kept his face very close to her, where he could hear her.

'You mean, *while* he was raping you, Mrs Standish?'

'Yes,' she whispered. 'He was still inside me when I got his knife. It was in his pants, on the floor, and he was going to use it on me when he was finished, so I *had* to,' she said.

'Of course you did,' Bensenhaver said. 'It doesn't matter.' He meant that she should have killed him anyway – even if he hadn't been planning to kill her. To Arden Bensenhaver there was no crime as serious as rape – not even murder, except perhaps the murder of a child. But he knew less about that; he had no children of his own.

He had been married seven months when his pregnant wife had been raped in a Laundromat while he waited outside for her in the car. Three kids had done it. They had opened one of the big spring-doored dryers and sat her ass on the open door, pushed her head into the warm dryer where she could only scream into the hot, muffling sheets and pillowcases and hear her own voice boom and bounce around the great metal drum. Her arms were in the dryer with her head, so she was helpless. Her feet couldn't even reach the floor. The spring door made her jounce up and down under all three of them, although she probably tried not to move. The boys had no idea, of course, that they were raping the police superintendent's wife. And all the bright lighting possible for downtown Toledo on a Saturday night would not have saved her.

They were an early-morning couple, the Bensenhavers. They

were young still, and they took their laundry to the Laundromat together, Monday morning before breakfast; they read the newspapers during the wash cycle. Then they put their laundry in the dryer and went home and had breakfast. Mrs Bensenhaver picked it up on her way downtown to the police station with Bensenhaver. He would wait in the car while she went inside to get it; sometimes, someone would have taken it out of the dryer while they were having breakfast and Mrs Bensenhaver would have to run it for another few minutes. Bensenhaver then waited. But they liked the early morning because there was rarely anyone else in the Laundromat.

Only when Bensenhaver saw the three kids leaving did he start to worry about how long his wife had been collecting the dry laundry. But it does not take very long to rape someone, even three times. Bensenhaver went into the Laundromat where he saw his wife's legs sticking out of the dryer; her shoes had fallen off. Those were not the first dead feet Bensenhaver had seen, but they were very important feet to him.

She had suffocated in her own clean wash – or she had vomited, and choked – but they had not meant to kill her. That part had been an accident, and at the trial a great deal had been made of the unplanned nature of Mrs Bensenhaver's death. Their attorney had said that the boys had planned 'to just rape her – not kill her, too.' And the phrase '*just* rape' – as in 'She was *just raped*, lucky thing, a wonder she wasn't killed!' – appalled Arden Bensenhaver.

'It's *good* that you killed him,' Bensenhaver whispered to Hope Standish. 'We couldn't have done nearly enough to him,' he confided to her. 'Nothing like he deserved. Good for you,' he whispered. 'Good for you.'

Hope had expected another sort of police experience, a more critical investigation – at least, a more suspicious cop, and certainly a man very different from Arden Bensenhaver. She was so grateful, for one thing, that Bensenhaver was an *old* man, clearly in his sixties – like an uncle to her, or even more sexually remote: a grandfather. She said she felt better, that she was all right; when she straightened up and stood away from him, she saw she had smeared his shirt collar and his cheek with blood, but Bensenhaver hadn't noticed or didn't care.

'Okay, show me,' Bensenhaver said to the deputy, but again he smiled gently at Hope. The deputy led him to the open cab.

'Oh, my God,' the driver of the stuck car was saying. 'Dear Jesus, look at this, and what's *that*? Christ, look, I think that's his *liver*. Isn't that what a liver looks like?' The pilot gawked in mute wonder and Bensenhaver caught both men by their coat shoulders and steered them roughly away. They started toward the rear of the truck, where Hope was composing herself, but Bensenhaver hissed at them, 'Stay away from Mrs Standish. Stay *away* from the truck. Go radio our position,' he told the pilot. 'They'll need an ambulance or something here. We'll take Mrs Standish with us.'

'They'll need a plastic bag for *him*,' said the deputy, pointing to Oren Rath. 'He's all over the place.'

'I can see with my own eyes,' said Arden Bensenhaver. He looked inside the cab and whistled admiringly.

The deputy started to ask, 'Was he doing it when . . .'

'That's right,' said Bensenhaver. He put his hand into a horrible mess by the accelerator pedal, but he didn't seem to mind. He was reaching for the knife on the floor of the passenger's side. He picked it up in his handkerchief; he looked it over carefully, wrapped it in the handkerchief, and put it in his pocket.

'Look,' the deputy whispered, conspiratorially. 'Did you ever hear of a *rapist* wearing a rubber?'

'It's not common,' Bensenhaver said. 'But it's not unknown.'

'It's weird to me,' said the deputy. He looked amazed as Bensenhaver pinched the prophylactic tight, just below its bulge; Bensenhaver snapped the rubber off and held it, without spilling a drop, up to the light. The sack was as large as a tennis ball. It hadn't leaked. It was full of blood.

Bensenhaver looked satisfied; he tied a knot in the condom, the way you'd knot a balloon, and he flung it so far into the bean field that it was out of sight.

'I don't want someone suggesting that it might *not* have been a rape,' Bensenhaver said softly to the deputy. 'Got it?'

He didn't wait for the deputy to answer; Bensenhaver went to the back of the truck to be with Mrs Standish.

'How old was he – that boy?' Hope asked Bensenhaver.

'Old enough,' Bensenhaver told her. 'About twenty-five or twenty-six,' he added. He did not want anything to diminish her survival – particularly, in her own eyes. He waved to the pilot, who was to help Mrs Standish aboard. Then he went to clear things with the deputy. 'You stay here with the body and the bad driver,' he told him.

'I'm not a bad driver,' the driver whined. 'Christ, if *you'd* seen that lady there – in the road . . .'

'And keep anyone away from the truck,' Bensenhaver said. On the road was the shirt belonging to Mrs Standish's husband; Bensenhaver picked it up and trotted to the helicopter in his funny, overweight way of running. The two men watched Bensenhaver climb aboard the helicopter and rise away from them. The weak spring sun seemed to leave with the copter and they were suddenly cold and didn't know where to go. Not in the truck, certainly, and sitting in the driver's car meant crossing that field of muck. They went to the pickup, lowered the tailgate, and sat on it.

'Will he call a tow truck for my car?' the driver asked.

'He'll probably forget,' the deputy said. He was thinking about Bensenhaver; he admired him, but he feared him, and he also thought that Bensenhaver was not to be totally trusted. There were questions of orthodoxy, if that's what it was, which the deputy had never considered. Mainly, the deputy just had too many things to think about at one time.

The driver paced back and forth in the pickup, which irritated the deputy because it jounced him on the tailgate. The driver avoided the foul, bunched blanket crammed in the corner next to the cab; he cleared a see-through spot on the dusted and caked rear window so that he could, occasionally, squint inside the cab at the rigid and disemboweled body of Oren Rath. All the blood was dry now, and through the mottled rear window the body looked to the driver to be similar, in color and in gloss, to an eggplant. He went and sat down on the tailgate beside the deputy, who got up, walked back in the truck, and peered in the window at the gashed corpse.

'You know what?' the driver said. 'Even though she was all messed up, you could tell what a really good-looking woman she was.'

'Yes, you could,' the deputy agreed. The driver now paced around in the back of the truck with him, so the deputy went to the tailgate and sat down.

'Don't get sore,' the driver said.

'I'm not sore,' the deputy said.

'I don't mean that I can sympathize with anyone who'd want to *rape* her, you know,' the driver said.

'I know what you don't mean,' said the deputy.

The deputy knew he was over his head in these matters, but the simplemindedness of the driver forced the deputy to adopt what he imagined was Bensenhaver's attitude of contempt for *him*.

'You see a lot of this, huh?' the driver asked. 'You know: rape and murder.'

'Enough,' the deputy said with self-conscious solemnity. He had never seen a rape or murder before, and he realized that even now he had not actually seen it through his own eyes as much as he'd been treated to the experience through the eyes of Arden Bensenhaver. He had seen rape and murder according to Bensenhaver, he thought. The deputy felt very confused; he sought some point of view all his own.

'Well,' said the driver, peering in the rear window again, 'I seen some stuff in the service, but nothing like this.'

The deputy couldn't respond.

'This is like war, I guess,' the driver said. 'This is like a bad hospital.'

The deputy wondered if he should let the fool look at Rath's body, if it mattered or not, and to whom? Certainly it couldn't matter to Rath. But to his unreal family? To the deputy? – *he* didn't know. And would Bensenhaver object?

'Hey, don't mind my asking you a personal question,' the driver said. 'Don't get sore, okay?'

'Okay,' said the deputy.

'Well,' the driver said. 'What happened to the rubber?'

'*What* rubber?' asked the deputy; he might have had some questions concerning Bensenhaver's sanity, but the deputy had no doubt that, in this case, Bensenhaver had been right. In the world according to Bensenhaver, no trivial detail should make less of rape's outrage.

Hope Standish, at that moment, felt safe at last in Bensenhaver's world. She floated and dipped over the farmlands beside him, trying not to be sick. She was beginning to notice things about her body again – she could smell herself and feel every sore spot. She felt such disgust, but here was this cheerful policeman who sat there admiring her – his heart touched by her violent success.

'Are you married, Mr Bensenhaver?' she asked him.

'Yes, Mrs Standish,' he said. 'I am.'

'You've been awfully nice,' Hope told him, 'but I think I'm going to be sick now.'

'Oh, sure,' said Bensenhaver; he grabbed a waxy paper bag at his feet. It was the pilot's lunch bag; there were some uneaten french-fried potatoes at the bottom and the grease had turned the waxed paper translucent. Bensenhaver could see his own hand, through the french fries and through the bottom of the bag. 'Here,' he said. 'You go right ahead.'

She was already retching; she took the bag from him and turned her head away. The bag did not feel big enough to contain what vileness she was sure she held inside her. She felt Bensenhaver's hard, heavy hand on her back. With his other hand, he held a strand of her matted hair out of her way. 'That's right,' he encouraged her, 'keep it coming, get it all out and you'll feel much better.'

Hope recalled that whenever Nicky was being sick, she told him the same thing. She marveled how Bensenhaver could even turn her vomiting into a victory, but she *did* feel much better – the rhythmic heaving was as soothing to her as his calm, dry hands, holding her head and patting her back. When the bag ripped and spilled, Bensenhaver said, 'Good riddance, Mrs Standish! You don't need the bag. This is a National Guard helicopter. We'll let the National Guard clean it up! After all – what's the National Guard *for*?'

The pilot flew on, grimly, his expression never changing.

'What a day it's been for you, Mrs Standish!' Bensenhaver went on. 'Your husband is going to be so proud of you.' But Bensenhaver was thinking that he'd better make sure; he'd better have a talk with the man. It was Arden Bensenhaver's experience that husbands and other people did not always take a rape in the right way.

16

The First Assassin

'What do you mean, "This is Chapter One"?' Garp's editor, John Wolf, wrote him. 'How can there be any more of *this*? There is entirely too much as it stands! How can you possibly go on?'

'It goes on,' Garp wrote back. 'You'll see.'

'I don't *want* to see,' John Wolf told Garp on the phone. 'Please drop it. At least put it aside. Why don't you take a trip? It would be good for you – and for Helen, I'm sure. And Duncan can travel now, can't he?'

But Garp not only insisted that *The World According to Bensenhaver* was going to be a novel; he insisted that John Wolf try to sell the first chapter to a magazine. Garp had never had an agent; John Wolf was the first man to deal with Garp's writing, and he managed everything for him, just as he managed everything for Jenny Fields.

'*Sell* it?' John Wolf said.

'Yes, sell it,' Garp said. 'Advance publicity for the novel.'

This had happened with Garp's first two books; excerpts had been sold to magazines. But John Wolf tried to tell Garp that *this* chapter was (1) unpublishable and (2) the worst possible publicity – should anyone be fool enough to publish it. He said that Garp had a 'small but serious' reputation as a writer, that his first two novels had been decently reviewed – had won him respected supporters and a 'small but serious' audience. Garp said he *hated* the reputation of 'small but serious,' though he could see that this appealed to John Wolf.

'I would rather be rich and wholly outside *caring* about what the idiots call "serious,"' he told John Wolf. But who is ever outside caring about that?

Garp actually felt that he could buy a sort of isolation from the real and terrible world. He imagined a kind of fort where he and Duncan and Helen (and a new baby) could live unmolested, even untouched by what he called 'the rest of life.'

'What *are* you talking about?' John Wolf asked him.

Helen asked him, too. And so did Jenny. But Jenny Fields *liked* the first chapter of *The World According to Bensenhaver*. She thought it had all its priorities in order – that it knew whom to heroize in such a situation, that it expressed the necessary outrage, that it made properly grotesque the vileness of *lust*. Actually, Jenny's fondness for the first chapter was more troubling to Garp than John Wolf's criticism. Garp suspected his mother's literary judgment above all things.

'My God, look at *her* book,' he kept saying to Helen, but Helen, as she promised, would not allow herself to be drawn in; she would not read Garp's new novel, not one word of it.

'Why does he suddenly want to be *rich?*' John Wolf asked Helen. 'What's all this about?'

'I don't know,' Helen said. 'I think he believes it will protect him, and all of us.'

'From *what?*' John Wolf said. 'From *whom?*'

'You'll have to wait until you read the whole book,' Garp said to his editor. 'Every business is a shitty business. I am trying to treat this book like business, and I want you to treat it that way, too. I don't care if you *like* it; I want you to *sell* it.'

'I am not a vulgar publisher,' John Wolf said. 'And you are not a vulgar writer, either. I'm sorry I have to remind you.' John Wolf's feelings were hurt, and he was angry at Garp for presuming to talk about a business that John Wolf understood far better than Garp. But he knew Garp had been through a bad time, he knew Garp was a good writer who would write more and (he thought) better books, and he wanted to continue publishing him.

'Every business is a shitty business,' Garp repeated. 'If you think the book is vulgar, then you should have *no* trouble selling it.'

'That's not the only way it works,' Wolf said, sadly. 'No one knows what makes books sell.'

'I've heard that before,' Garp said.

'You have no call to speak to me like this,' John Wolf said. 'I'm your friend.' Garp knew that was true, so he hung up the telephone and answered no mail and finished *The World According to Bensenhaver* two weeks before Helen delivered, with only Jenny's help, their third child – a daughter, who spared Helen and Garp the problem of having to agree upon a boy's name that in no way resembled the name of Walt. The daughter was named Jenny Garp, which was the name Jenny Fields would have had if she had gone about the business of having Garp in a more conventional way.

Jenny was delighted to have someone at least partially named after her. 'But there's going to be some confusion,' she warned, 'with two of us around.'

'I've always called you "Mom,"' Garp reminded her. He did not remind his mother that a fashion designer had already named a dress after her. It was popular in New York for about a year: a white nurse's uniform with a bright red heart sewn over the left breast. A JENNY FIELDS ORIGINAL, the heart said.

When Jenny Garp was born, Helen said nothing. Helen was grateful; she felt for the first time since the accident that she was delivered from the insanity of grief that had crushed her with the loss of Walt.

The World According to Bensenhaver, which was Garp's deliverance from the same insanity, resided in New York, where John Wolf read it over and over again. He had arranged to have the first chapter published in a porno magazine of such loathsome crudity that he felt sure even Garp would be convinced of the book's doom. The magazine was called *Crotch Shots*, and it was full of exactly that – those wet, split beavers of Garp's childhood, between the pages of his story of violent rape and obvious revenge. At first Garp accused John Wolf of deliberately placing the chapter there, of not even trying the better magazines. But Wolf assured Garp that he had tried them all; that this was the bottom line of the list – this was exactly how Garp's story was interpreted. Lurid, sensational violence and sex of no redeeming value whatsoever.

'That's not what it's about,' Garp said. 'You'll see.'

But Garp often wondered about the first chapter of *The World According to Bensenhaver*, which had been published in *Crotch Shots*. If it had been read at all. If anyone who bought those magazines ever looked at the words.

'Perhaps they read some of the stories after they masturbate to the pictures,' Garp wrote to John Wolf. He wondered if that was a good mood to be read in: after masturbation, the reader was at least relaxed, possibly lonely ('a good state in which to read,' Garp told John Wolf). But maybe the reader felt guilty, too; and humiliated, and overwhelmingly responsible (that was *not* such a good condition in which to read, Garp thought). In fact, he knew, it was not a good condition in which to *write*.

The World According to Bensenhaver is about the impossible desire of the husband, Dorsey Standish, to protect his wife and child from the brutal world; thus Arden Bensenhaver (who is forced to retire from the police, for repeated unorthodoxy in his methods of arrest) is hired to live like an armed uncle in the house with the Standish family – he becomes the lovable family bodyguard, whom Hope must finally reject. Though the worst of the real world has been visited upon Hope, it is her husband who *fears* the world most. After Hope insists that Bensenhaver not live with them, Standish continues to support the old policeman as a kind of hovering angel. Bensenhaver is paid to tail the child, Nicky, but Bensenhaver is an aloof and curious kind of watchdog, subject to fits of his own awful memories; he gradually seems more of a menace to the Standishes than he seems a protector. He is described as 'a lurker at the last edge of light – a retired enforcer, barely alive on the rim of darkness.'

Hope counters her husband's anxiety by insisting they have a second child. The child is born, but Standish seems destined to create one monster of paranoia after another; now more relaxed about possible assaults upon his wife and children, he begins to suspect that Hope is having an affair. Slowly, he realizes that this would wound him more than if she were raped (again). Thus he doubts his love for her, and doubts himself; guiltily, he begs Bensenhaver to spy on Hope and determine if she is faithful. But Arden Bensenhaver will no longer do Dorsey's worry work for him. The old policeman argues that he was hired to protect Standish's family from the outside world – not to restrict the free choices of the family to live as it wants. Without Bensenhaver's support, Dorsey Standish panics. One night he leaves the house (and the children) unprotected while he goes out to spy on his wife. While Dorsey is gone, the younger child chokes to death on a piece of Nicky's chewing gum.

Guilt abounds. In Garp's work, guilt always abounds. With Hope, too – because she *was* seeing someone (although who could blame her). Bensenhaver, morbid with responsibility, has a stroke. Partially paralyzed, he moves back in with the Standishes; Dorsey feels responsible for him. Hope insists they have *another* child, but the events have made Standish determinedly sterile. He agrees that Hope should encourage her lover – but merely to 'impregnate' herself, as he puts it. (Ironically, this was the *only* part of the book that Jenny Fields called 'far-fetched.')

Once again, Dorsey Standish seeks 'a control situation – more like a laboratory experiment at life than life itself,' Garp wrote. Hope cannot adjust to such a clinical arrangement; emotionally, either she has a lover or she doesn't. Insisting that the lovers meet for the sole purpose of 'impregnating' Hope, Dorsey tries to control the whereabouts, the number and length of their meetings. Suspecting that Hope is meeting her lover clandestinely, as well as according to plan, Standish alerts the senile Bensenhaver to the existence of a prowler, a potential kidnapper and rapist, whose presence in the neighborhood has already been detected.

Still not satisfied, Dorsey Standish takes to sudden, un-announced visits at his own house (at times when he's least expected home); he never catches Hope at anything, but Bensenhaver, armed and deadly with senility, catches Dorsey. A cunning invalid, Arden Bensenhaver is surpris-ingly mobile and silent in his wheelchair; he is also still unorthodox in his methods of arrest. In fact, Bensenhaver shoots Dorsey Standish with a twelve-gauge shotgun from a distance of less than six feet. Dorsey had been hiding in the upstairs cedar closet, stumbling among his wife's shoes, waiting for her to make a phone call from the bedroom, which – from the closet – he could overhear. He deserves to be shot, of course.

The wound is fatal. Arden Bensenhaver, thoroughly mad, is taken away. Hope is pregnant with her lover's child. When the child is born, Nicky – now twelve – feels unburdened by the relaxing tension in the family. The terrible anxiety of Dorsey Standish, which has been so crippling to all their lives, is at last lifted from them. Hope and her children live on, even cheerfully dealing with the wild rantings of old Bensenhaver, too tough to die, who goes on and on with his versions of the nightmarish world from his wheelchair in an old-age home for the criminally insane. He is seen, finally, as belonging where he is. Hope and her children visit him often, not merely out of kindness – for they are kind – but also to remind themselves of their own precious sanity. Hope's endurance, and the survival of her two children, make the old man's ravings tolerable, finally even comic to her.

That peculiar old-age home for the criminally insane, by the way, bears an astonishing resemblance to Jenny Fields' hospital for wounded women at Dog's Head Harbor.

It is not so much that 'the world according to Bensenhaver' is *wrong,* or even misperceived, as it is out of proportion to the world's need for sensual pleasure, and the world's need and capacity for warmth. Dorsey Standish 'is not true to the world,' either; he is too vulnerable to how *delicately* he loves his wife and children; he is seen, together with Bensenhaver, as 'not well suited for life on this planet.' Where immunity counts.

Hope – and, the reader hopes, her children – may have better chances. Somehow implicit in the novel is the sense that women are better equipped than men at enduring fear and brutality, and at containing the anxiousness of feeling how vulnerable we are to the people we love. Hope is seen as a strong survivor of a weak man's world.

John Wolf sat in New York, hoping that the visceral reality of Garp's language, and the intensity of Garp's characters, somehow rescued the book from sheer soap opera. But, Wolf thought, one might as well call the thing *Anxiousness of Life;* it would make a fantastic series for daytime television, he thought – if suitably edited for invalids, senior citizens, and preschool children. John Wolf concluded that *The World According to Bensenhaver,* despite the 'visceral reality of Garp's language,' and so forth, was an X-rated soap opera.

Much later, of course, even Garp would agree; it was his worst work. 'But the fucking world never gave me credit for the first two,' he wrote to John Wolf. 'Thus I was owed.' That, Garp felt, was the way it worked most of the time.

John Wolf was more basically concerned: that is, he wondered if he could justify the book's publication. With books he did not absolutely take to, John Wolf had a system that rarely failed him. At his publishing house, he was envied for his record of being right about those books destined to be popular. When he said a book was going to be popular – distinct from being good or likable or not – he was almost always right. There were many books that were popular without his saying so, of course, but no book he'd ever claimed *would* be popular was ever *un*popular.

Nobody knew how he did it.

He did it first for Jenny Fields – and for certain, surprising books, every year or two, he had been doing it ever since.

There was a woman who worked in the publishing house who once told John Wolf that she never read a book that didn't make her want to close it and go to sleep. She was a challenge to John Wolf, who loved books, and he spent many years giving this woman good books and bad books to read; the books were alike in that they put this woman to sleep. She just didn't like to read, she told John Wolf; but he would not give up on her. No one else in the publishing house ever asked this woman to read anything at all; in fact, they never asked this woman's opinion of *any*thing. The woman moved through the books lying all around the publishing house as if these books were ashtrays and she was a nonsmoker. She was a cleaning woman. Every day she emptied the wastebaskets; she cleaned everyone's office when they went home at night. She vacuumed the rugs in the corridors every Monday, she dusted the display cases every Tuesday, and the secretaries' desks on Wednesdays; she scrubbed the bathrooms on Thursdays and sprayed air freshener on everything on Fridays – so that, she told John Wolf, the entire publishing house had the whole weekend to gather up a good smell for the next week. John Wolf had watched her for years and he'd never seen her so much as glance at a book.

When he asked her about books and she told him how unlikable they were to her, he kept using her to test books he wasn't sure of – and the books he thought he was *very* sure of, too. She was consistent in her dislike of books and John Wolf had almost given up on her when he gave her the manuscript of *A Sexual Suspect*, the autobiography of Jenny Fields.

The cleaning woman read it overnight and asked John Wolf if she could have a copy of her very own to read – over and over again – when the book was published.

After that, John Wolf sought her opinion scrupulously. She did not disappoint him. She did not like most things, but when she liked something, it meant to John Wolf that nearly everybody else was at least sure to be able to read it.

It was almost by rote that John Wolf gave the cleaning woman *The World According to Bensenhaver*. Then he went home for the weekend and thought about it; he tried to call her and tell her not even to try to read it. He remembered the first chapter and he didn't want to offend the woman, who was somebody's grandmother, and (of course) some-body's mother, too – and, after all, she never knew she was *paid* to read all the stuff John Wolf gave her to read. That she had a rather whopping salary for a cleaning lady was known only to John Wolf. The woman thought *all* good cleaning ladies were well paid, and *should* be.

Her name was Jillsy Sloper, and John Wolf marveled to note that there was not one Sloper with even the first initial of J. in the New York phone directory. Apparently Jillsy didn't like phone calls any more than she liked books. John Wolf made a note to apologize to Jillsy the first thing Monday morning. He spent the rest of a miserable weekend trying to phrase to himself exactly how he would tell T. S. Garp that he believed it was in his own best interests, and certainly in the best interests of the publishing house, NOT to publish *The World According to Bensenhaver*.

It was a hard weekend for him, because John Wolf liked Garp and he believed in Garp, and he also knew that Garp had no friends who could advise him against embarrassing himself – which is one of the valuable things friends are for. There was only Alice Fletcher, who so loved Garp that she would love, indiscriminately, everything he uttered – or else she would be silent. And there was Roberta Muldoon,

whose literary judgment, John Wolf suspected, was even
more newfound and awkward (if existent at all) than her
adopted sex. And Helen wouldn't read it. And Jenny Fields,
John Wolf knew, was not biased toward her son in the
way a mother is usually biased; she had demonstrated
the dubious taste to *dislike* some of the better things her son
had written. The problem with Jenny, John Wolf knew, was
one of subject matter. A book *about* an important subject
was, to Jenny Fields, an important book. And Jenny Fields
thought that Garp's new book was all about the stupid male
anxieties that women are asked to suffer and endure. How a
book was written never mattered to Jenny.

That was one thread that interested John Wolf in
publishing the book. If Jenny Fields liked *The World According
to Bensenhaver*, it was at least a potentially controversial
book. But John Wolf, like Garp, knew that Jenny's status
as a political figure was due largely to a general, hazy
misunderstanding of Jenny.

Wolf thought and thought about it, all weekend, and he
completely forgot to apologize to Jillsy Sloper the first thing
Monday morning. Suddenly there was Jillsy, red-eyed and
twitching like a squirrel, the ratted manuscript pages of *The
World According to Bensenhaver* held fast in her rough brown
hands.

'Lawd,' Jillsy said. She rolled her eyes; she shook the
manuscript in her hands.

'Oh, Jillsy,' John Wolf said. 'I'm sorry.'

'Lawd!' Jillsy crowed. 'I never had a worse weekend. I got
no sleep, I got *no* food, I got *no* trips to the cemetery to see
my family and my friends.'

The pattern of Jillsy Sloper's weekend seemed strange to
John Wolf but he said nothing; he just listened to her, as he
had listened to her for more than a dozen years.

'This man's *crazy*,' Jillsy said. 'Nobody sane ever wrote a
book like this.'

'I shouldn't have given it to you, Jillsy,' John Wolf said. 'I
should have remembered that first chapter.'

'*First* chapter ain't so bad,' Jillsy said. 'That first chapter ain't *nothin'*. It's that nine*teenth* chapter that got me,' Jillsy said. 'Lawd, Lawd!' she crowed.

'You read nineteen chapters?' John Wolf asked.

'You didn't give me no more than nineteen chapters,' Jillsy said. 'Jesus Lawd, is there *another* chapter? Do it keep goin' *on?*'

'No, no,' John Wolf said. 'That's the end of it. That's all there is.'

'I should hope so,' Jillsy said. 'Ain't nothin' left to go on *with*. Got that crazy old cop where he belongs – at long last – and that crazy husband with his head blowed off. That's the *only* proper state for that husband's head, if you ask me: blowed off.'

'You *read* it?' John Wolf said.

'Lawd!' Jillsy screamed. 'You'd think it was *him* who got raped, the way he went on and on. If you ask me,' Jillsy said, 'that's just like men: rape you half to death one minute and the next minute go crazy fussin' over who you're *givin'* it to – of your own free will! It's not *their* damn business, either way, is it?' Jillsy asked.

'I'm not sure,' said John Wolf, who sat bewildered at his desk. 'You didn't like the book.'

'*Like* it?' Jillsy cawed. 'There's nothin' to like about it,' she said.

'But you *read* it,' John Wolf said. 'Why'd you read it?'

'Lawd,' Jillsy said, as if she were sorry for John Wolf – that he was so hopelessly stupid. 'I sometimes wonder if you know the first thing about all these books you're makin',' she said; she shook her head. 'I sometimes wonder why *you're* the one who's makin' the books and *I'm* the one who's cleanin' the bathrooms. Except I'd rather clean the bathrooms than read most of them,' Jillsy said. 'Lawd, Lawd.'

'If you hated it, why'd you read it, Jillsy?' John Wolf asked her.

'Same reason I read anythin' for,' Jillsy said. 'To find out what *happens*.'

John Wolf stared at her.

'Most books you *know* nothin's gonna happen,' Jillsy said. 'Lawd, *you* know that. Other books,' she said, 'you know just *what's* gonna happen, so you don't have to read them, either. But *this* book,' Jillsy said, 'this book's so *sick* you *know* somethin's gonna happen, but you can't imagine *what*. You got to be sick yourself to imagine what happens in *this* book,' Jillsy said.

'So you read it to find out?' John Wolf said.

'There surely ain't no other reason to read a book, is there?' Jillsy Sloper said. She put the manuscript heavily (for it was large) on John Wolf's desk and hitched up the long extension cord (for the vacuum cleaner) which Jillsy wore on Mondays like a belt around her broad middle. 'When it's a book,' she said, pointing to the manuscript, 'I'd be happy if I could have a copy of my own. If it's okay,' she added.

'You want a copy?' John Wolf asked.

'If it's no trouble,' Jillsy said.

'Now that you know what happens,' John Wolf said, 'what would you want to read it *again* for?'

'Well,' Jillsy said. She looked confused; John Wolf had never seen Jillsy Sloper look confused before – only sleepy. 'Well, I might *lend* it,' she said. 'There might be someone I know who needs to be reminded what men in this world is like,' she said.

'Would you ever read it again yourself?' John Wolf asked.

'Well,' Jillsy said. 'Not *all* of it, I imagine. At least not all at once, or not right away.' Again, she looked confused. 'Well,' she said, sheepishly, 'I guess I mean there's *parts* of it I wouldn't mind readin' again.'

'Why?' John Wolf asked.

'Lawd,' Jillsy said, tiredly, as if she were finally impatient with him. 'It feels so *true*,' she crooned, making the word *true* cry like a loon over a lake at night.

'It feels so true,' John Wolf repeated.

'Lawd, don't you *know* it is?' Jillsy asked him. 'If you don't know when a book's *true*,' Jillsy sang to him, 'we really *ought* to trade jobs.' She laughed now, the stout three-pronged plug for the vacuum-cleaner cord clutched like a gun in her fist. 'I do wonder, Mr Wolf,' she said, sweetly, 'if you'd know when a bathroom was *clean*.' She went over and peered in his wastebasket. 'Or when a wastebasket was empty,' she said. 'A book feels true when it feels true,' she said to him, impatiently. 'A book's true when you can say, "Yeah! That's just how damn people *behave* all the time." *Then* you know it's true,' Jillsy said.

Leaning over the wastebasket, she seized the one scrap of paper lying alone on the bottom of the basket; she stuffed it into her cleaning apron. It was the crumpled-up first page of the letter John Wolf had tried to compose to Garp.

Months later, when *The World According to Bensenhaver* was going to the printers, Garp complained to John Wolf that there was no one to dedicate the book to. He would not have it *in memory of* Walt, because Garp hated that kind of thing: 'that cheap capitalizing,' as he called it, 'on one's autobiographical accidents – to try to hook the reader into thinking you're a more serious *writer* than you are.' And he would not dedicate a book to his mother, because he hated, as he called it, 'the free ride everyone else gets on the name of Jenny Fields.' Helen, of course, was out of the question, and Garp felt, with some shame, that he couldn't dedicate a book to Duncan if it was a book he would not allow Duncan to read. The child wasn't old enough. He felt some distaste, as a father, for writing something he would forbid his own children to read.

The Fletchers, he knew, would be uncomfortable with a book dedicated to them, as a couple; and to dedicate a book to Alice, alone, might be insulting to Harry.

'Not to *me*,' John Wolf said. 'Not this one.'

'I wasn't thinking of you,' Garp lied.

'How about Roberta Muldoon?' John Wolf said.

'The book has absolutely nothing to *do* with Roberta,' Garp said. Though Garp knew that Roberta, at least, wouldn't object to the dedication. How funny to write a book really no one would like to have dedicated to them!

'Maybe I'll dedicate it to the Ellen Jamesians,' Garp said, bitterly.

'Don't make trouble for yourself,' John Wolf said. 'That's just plain stupid.'

Garp sulked.

For Mrs Ralph?

he thought. But he still didn't know her real name. There was Helen's father – his good old wrestling coach, Ernie Holm – but Ernie wouldn't understand the gesture; it would hardly be a book Ernie would like. Garp hoped, in fact, that Ernie wouldn't read it. How funny to write a book you hope someone doesn't read!

To Fat Stew

he thought.

For Michael Milton
In Memory of Bonkers

He bogged down. He could think of no one.

'I know someone,' John Wolf said. 'I could ask her if she'd mind.'

'Very funny,' Garp said.

But John Wolf was thinking of Jillsy Sloper, the person, he knew, who was responsible for getting this book of Garp's published at all.

'She's a very special woman who *loved* the book,' John Wolf told Garp. 'She said it was so "true."'

Garp was interested in the idea.

'I gave her the manuscript for one weekend,' John Wolf said, 'and she couldn't put it down.'

'Why'd you give her the manuscript?' Garp asked.

'She just seemed *right* for it,' John Wolf said. A good editor will not share all his secrets with anyone.

'Well, okay,' Garp said. 'It seems *naked*, having no one. Tell her I'd appreciate it. She's a *close* friend of yours?' Garp asked. Garp's editor winked at him and Garp nodded.

'What's it all mean, anyway?' Jillsy Sloper asked John Wolf, suspiciously. 'What's it mean, he wants to "dedicate" that terrible book to me?'

'It means that your response was valuable to him,' John Wolf said. 'He thinks the book was written almost with you in mind.'

'Lawd,' Jillsy said. 'With me in mind? What's *that* mean?'

'I told him how you responded to his book,' John Wolf said, 'and he thinks you're the perfect audience, I guess.'

'The perfect audience?' Jillsy said. 'Lawd, he *is* crazy, isn't he?'

'He's got no one else to dedicate it to,' John Wolf admitted.

'Kind of like needin' a witness for a weddin'?' Jillsy Sloper asked.

'Kind of,' John Wolf guessed.

'It don't mean I *approve* of the book?' Jillsy asked.

'Lord, no,' John Wolf said.

'Lawd, no, huh?' Jillsy said.

'No one's going to blame you for anything in the book, if that's what you mean,' John Wolf said.

'Well,' said Jillsy.

John Wolf showed Jillsy where the dedication would be; he showed her other dedications in other books. They all looked nice to Jillsy Sloper and she nodded her head, gradually pleased by the idea.

'One thing,' she said. 'I won't have to *meet* him, or anythin', will I?'

'Lord, no,' said John Wolf, so Jillsy agreed.

There remained only one more stroke of genius to launch *The World According to Bensenhaver* into that uncanny half-light where occasional 'serious' books glow, for a time, as also 'popular' books. John Wolf was a smart and cynical man. He knew about all the shitty autobiographical associations that make those rabid readers of gossip warm to an occasional fiction.

Years later, Helen would remark that the success of *The World According to Bensenhaver* lay entirely in the book jacket. John Wolf was in the habit of letting Garp write his own jacket flaps, but Garp's description of his own book was so ponderous and glum that John Wolf took matters into his own hands; he went straight to the dubious heart of the matter.

'*The World According to Bensenhaver*,' the book jacket flap said, 'is about a man who is so fearful of bad things happening to his loved ones that he creates an atmosphere of such tension that bad things are almost certain to occur. And they do.

'T. S. Garp,' the jacket flap went on, 'is the only child of the noted feminist Jenny Fields.' John Wolf shivered slightly when he saw this in print, because although he had written it, and although he knew very well *why* he had written it, he also knew that it was information Garp *never* wanted mentioned in connection with his own work. 'T. S. Garp is also a father,' the jacket flap said. And John Wolf shook his head in shame to see the garbage he had written there. 'He is a father who has recently suffered the tragic loss of a five-year-old son. Out of the anguish that a father endures in the aftermath of an accident, this tortured novel emerges . . .' And so forth.

It was, in Garp's opinion, the cheapest reason to read of all. Garp always said that the question he most hated to be asked, about his work, was how much of it was 'true' – how much of it was based on 'personal experience.' *True* – not in the good way that Jillsy Sloper used it, but true as in 'real life.' Usually, with great patience and restraint, Garp would say that the autobiographical basis – if there even was one – was the least interesting level on which to read a novel. He would

always say that the art of fiction was the act of *imagining*
truly – was, like any art, a process of selection. Memories
and personal histories – 'all the recollected traumas of
our unmemorable lives' – were suspicious models for fiction,
Garp would say. 'Fiction has to be better made than life,'
Garp wrote. And he consistently detested what he called
'the phony mileage of personal hardship' – writers whose
books were 'important' because something important had
happened in their lives. He wrote that the *worst* reason for
anything being part of a novel was that it really happened.
'*Everything* has really happened, sometime!' he fumed. 'The
only reason for something to happen in a novel is that it's
the perfect thing to have happen at that time.'

'Tell me *any*thing that's ever happened to you,' Garp told
an interviewer once, 'and I can improve upon the story; I
can make the details better than they were.' The interviewer,
a divorced woman with four young children, one of whom
was dying of cancer, had her face firmly fixed in disbelief.
Garp saw her determined unhappiness, and its terrible
importance to her, and he said to her, gently, 'If it's sad –
even if it's *very* sad – I can make up a story that's sadder.' But
he saw in her face that she would never believe him; she
wasn't even writing it down. It wouldn't even be a part of
her interview.

And John Wolf knew this: one of the first things most
readers *want* to know is everything they can about a writer's
life. John Wolf wrote Garp: 'For most people, with limited
imaginations, the idea of improving on reality is pure bunk.'
On the book jacket flap of *The World According to Bensenhaver*,
John Wolf created a bogus sense of Garp's importance
('the only child of the noted feminist Jenny Fields') and
a sentimental sympathy for Garp's personal experience
('the tragic loss of a five-year-old son'). That both pieces of
information were essentially irrelevant to the *art* of Garp's
novel did not deeply concern John Wolf. Garp had made
John Wolf sore with all his talk about preferring riches to
seriousness.

'It's not your best book,' John Wolf wrote Garp, when he sent the galleys for Garp to proofread. 'One day you'll know that, too. But it *is* going to be your biggest book; just wait and see. You can't imagine, yet, how you're going to hate many of the reasons for your success, so I advise you to leave the country for a few months. I advise you to read only the reviews *I* send to you. And when it blows over – because everything blows over – you can come back home and pick up your considerable surprise at the bank. And you can hope that *Bensenhaver*'s popularity is big enough to make people go back and read the first two novels – for which you *deserve* to be better known.

'Tell Helen I am *sorry,* Garp, but I think you must know: I have always had your own interests at heart. If you want to *sell* this book, we'll sell it. "Every business is a shitty business," Garp. I am quoting *you.*'

Garp was very puzzled by the letter; John Wolf, of course, had not shown him the jacket flaps.

'Why are you *sorry?*' Garp wrote back. 'Don't weep; just sell it.'

'Every business is a shitty business,' Wolf repeated.

'I know, I *know,*' Garp said.

'Take my advice,' Wolf said.

'I *like* reading the reviews,' Garp protested.

'Not these, you won't,' John Wolf said. 'Take a trip. Please.' Then John Wolf sent the jacket flap copy to Jenny Fields. He asked her for her confidence, and her help in getting Garp to leave the country.

'Leave the country,' Jenny said to her son. 'It's the best thing you can do for yourself and your family.' Helen was actually keen on the idea; she'd never been abroad. Duncan had read his father's first story, 'The Pension Grillparzer,' and he wanted to go to Vienna.

'Vienna's not *really* like that,' Garp told Duncan, but it touched Garp very much that the boy liked the old story. Garp liked it, too. In fact, he was beginning to wish that he liked everything else he had written half as much.

'With a new baby, why go to Europe?' Garp complained. 'I don't know. It's complicated. The passports – and the baby will need lots of shots, or something.'

'You need some shots yourself,' said Jenny Fields. 'The baby will be perfectly safe.'

'Don't you want to see Vienna again?' Helen asked Garp.

'Ah, just imagine, the scene of your old crimes!' John Wolf said heartily.

'Old crimes?' Garp mumbled. 'I don't know.'

'Please, Dad,' Duncan said. Garp was a sucker to what Duncan wanted; he agreed.

Helen cheered up and even took a glance at the galleys of *The World According to Bensenhaver,* though it was a quick, nervous glance, and she had no intention of doing any real reading therein. The first thing she saw was the dedication.

For Jillsy Sloper

'Who in God's name is Jillsy Sloper?' she asked Garp.

'I don't know, really,' Garp said; Helen frowned at him. 'No, *really,*' he said. 'It's some girlfriend of John's; he said she loved the book – couldn't put it down. Wolf took it as a kind of omen, I guess; it was *his* suggestion, anyway,' Garp said. 'And I thought it was nice.'

'Hm,' said Helen; she put the galleys aside.

They both imagined John Wolf's girlfriend in silence. John Wolf had been divorced before they met him; though the Garps had gotten to meet some of Wolf's grown-up children, they had never met his first and only wife. There had been a conservative number of girlfriends, all smart and sleekly attractive women – all younger than John Wolf. Some working girls, in the publishing business, but mostly young women with divorces of their own, and money – always money, or always the *look* of money. Garp remembered most of them by how nicely they smelled, and how their lipstick tasted – and the high-gloss, touchable quality of their clothes.

Neither Garp nor Helen could ever have imagined Jillsy Sloper, the offspring of a white person and a quadroon – which made Jillsy an octoroon, or one-eighth Negro. Her skin was a sallow brown, like a lightly stained pine board. Her hair was straight and short and waxy-black, beginning to gray at her bangs, which were coarsely chopped above her shining, wrinkled forehead. She was short, with long arms, and her ring finger was missing from her left hand. By the deep scar on her right cheek, one could imagine that the ring finger had been cut off in the same battle, by the same weapon – perhaps during a bad marriage, for she had certainly had a bad marriage. Which she never spoke of.

She was about forty-five and looked sixty. She had the trunk of a Labrador retriever about to have puppies, and she shuffled whenever and wherever she walked because her feet killed her. In a few years she would so long ignore the lump she could feel in her own breast, which no one else ever felt, that she would die needlessly of cancer.

She had an unlisted phone number (as John Wolf discovered) only because her former husband threatened to kill her every few months, and she tired of hearing from him; the reason she had a phone at all was that her children needed a place to call collect so that they could ask her to send them money.

But Helen and Garp, when they imagined Jillsy Sloper, did not for a moment see anyone approximating this sad, hardworking octoroon.

'John Wolf seems to be doing everything for this book except writing it,' Helen said.

'I wish he *had* written it,' Garp suddenly said. Garp had reread the book, and he felt full of doubt. In 'The Pension Grillparzer,' Garp thought, there was a certainty concerning how the world behaved. In The World According to Bensenhaver, Garp had felt less certain – an indication he was getting older, of course; but artists, he knew, should also get *better*.

*   *   *

With baby Jenny and one-eyed Duncan, Garp and Helen left for Europe out of a cool New England August; most transatlantic travelers were headed the other way.

'Why not wait until after Thanksgiving?' Ernie Holm asked them. But *The World According to Bensenhaver* would be published in October. John Wolf had received various responses to the uncorrected proofs he circulated through the summer; they had all been enthusiastic responses – enthusiastically praising the book, or enthusiastically condemning it.

He'd had difficulty keeping Garp from seeing the advance copies of the actual book – the book jacket, for example. But Garp's own enthusiasm for the book was so sporadic, and generally low, that John Wolf had been able to stall him.

Garp was now excited about the trip, and he was talking about other books he was going to write. ('A good sign,' John Wolf told Helen.)

Jenny and Roberta drove the Garps to Boston, where they took a plane to New York. 'Don't worry about the airplane,' Jenny said. 'It won't fall.'

'Jesus, Mom,' Garp said. 'What do you know about airplanes? They fall all the time.'

'Keep your arms in constant motion, like wings,' Roberta told Duncan.

'Don't scare him, Roberta,' Helen said.

'I'm not scared,' Duncan said.

'If your father keeps *talking*, you can't fall,' Jenny said.

'If he keeps talking,' Helen said, 'we'll never *land*.' They could see that Garp was all wound up.

'I'll *fart* all the way, if you don't leave me alone,' Garp said, 'and we'll go in a great explosion.'

'You better write often,' Jenny said.

Remembering dear old Tinch, and his last trip to Europe, Garp told his mother, 'This time I'm just going to ab-ab-ab*sorb* a lot, Mom. I'm not going to write a w-w-word.' They both laughed at this, and Jenny Fields even cried a little, although only Garp noticed; he kissed his mother good-bye.

Roberta, whose sex reassignment had made her a dynamite kisser, kissed everyone several times.

'Jesus, Roberta,' Garp said.

'I'll look after the old girl while you're gone,' Roberta said, her giant arm dwarfing Jenny, who looked so small and suddenly very gray beside her.

'I don't need any looking after,' Jenny Fields said.

'It's Mom who looks after everyone else,' Garp said.

Helen hugged Jenny, because she knew how true that was. From the airplane, Garp and Duncan could see Jenny and Roberta waving from the observation deck. There had been some seat changes because Duncan had wanted a window seat on the left-hand side of the plane. 'The right-hand side is just as nice,' a stewardess said.

'Not if you don't have a right eye,' Duncan told her, pleasantly, and Garp admired how the boy was feeling so bold about himself.

Helen and the baby sat across the aisle from them. 'Can you see Grandma?' Helen asked Duncan.

'Yes,' Duncan said.

Although the observation deck was suddenly overrun with people wanting to see the takeoff, Jenny Fields – as always – stood out in her white uniform, even though she was short. 'Why does Nana look so tall?' Duncan asked Garp, and it was true: Jenny Fields towered head and shoulders above the crowd. Garp realized that Roberta was lifting his mother up as if his mother were a child. 'Oh, *Roberta's* got her!' Duncan cried. Garp looked at his mother hefted up in the air to wave good-bye to him, safe in the arms of the old tight end; Jenny's shy, confident smile touched him, and he waved out the window to her, although Garp knew that Jenny couldn't see inside the plane. For the first time, his mother looked old to him; he looked away – across the aisle, at Helen with their new child.

'Here we go,' Helen said. Helen and Garp held hands across the aisle when the plane lifted off, because, Garp knew, Helen was terrified of flying.

In New York, John Wolf put them up in his apartment; he gave Garp and Helen and baby Jenny his own bedroom and graciously offered to share the guest room with Duncan.

The grown-ups had a late dinner and too much cognac. Garp told John Wolf about the next three novels he was going to write.

'The first one is called *My Father's Illusions*,' Garp said. 'It's about an idealistic father who has many children. He keeps establishing little utopias for his kids to grow up in, and after his kids grow up he becomes a founder of small colleges. But all of them go broke – the colleges and the kids. The father keeps trying to give a speech at the U.N., but they keep throwing him out; it's the same speech – he keeps revising and revising it. Then he tries to run a free hospital; it's a disaster. Then he tries to institute a nationwide free-transportation system. Meanwhile, his wife divorces him and his children keep growing older, and turning out unhappy, or fucked-up – or just perfectly normal, you know. The only thing the children have in common are these dreadful memories of the utopias their father tried to have them grow up in. Finally, the father becomes the governor of Vermont.'

'Vermont?' John Wolf asked.

'Yes, Vermont,' Garp said. 'He becomes governor of Vermont, but he really thinks of himself as a king. More utopias, you see.'

'*The King of Vermont!*' John Wolf said. 'That's a better title.'

'No, no,' Garp said. 'That's another book. No relation. The second book, after *My Father's Illusions*, will be called *The Death of Vermont*.'

'Same cast of characters?' Helen asked.

'No, no,' Garp said. 'Another story. It's about the death of Vermont.'

'Well, I like something that is what it says it is,' John Wolf said.

'One year spring doesn't come,' Garp said.

'Spring never does come to Vermont, anyway,' Helen said.

'No, no,' Garp said, frowning. 'This year summer doesn't come, either. Winter never stops. It warms up one day and all the buds appear. Maybe in May. One day in May there are buds on the trees, the next day there are leaves, and the next day the leaves have all turned. It's fall already. The leaves fall off the trees.'

'A short foliage season,' Helen said.

'Very funny,' Garp said. 'But that's what happens. It's winter again; it will be winter forever.'

'The people die?' John Wolf asked.

'I'm not sure about the people,' Garp said. 'Some leave Vermont, of course.'

'Not a bad idea,' Helen said.

'Some stay, some die. Maybe they all die,' Garp said.

'What's it mean?' John Wolf asked.

'I'll know when I get there,' Garp said. Helen laughed.

'And there's a *third* novel, after that?' John Wolf asked.

'It's called *The Plot against the Giant*,' Garp said.

'That's a poem by Wallace Stevens,' Helen said.

'Yes, of course,' Garp said, and he recited the poem for them.

THE PLOT AGAINST THE GIANT

First Girl

When this yokel comes maundering,
Whetting his hacker,
I shall run before him,
Diffusing the civilest odors
Out of geraniums and unsmelled flowers.
It will check him.

Second Girl

I shall run before him,
Arching cloths besprinkled with colors

As small as fish-eggs.
The threads
Will abash him.

      Third Girl
Oh, la . . . le pauvre!
I shall run before him,
With a curious puffing.
He will bend his ear then.
I shall whisper
Heavenly labials in a world of gutturals.
It will undo him.

'What a nice poem,' Helen said.
'The novel is in three parts,' Garp said.
'Girl One, Girl Two, Girl Three?' John Wolf asked.
'And *is* the giant undone?' Helen asked.
'Is he ever,' Garp said.
'Is he a *real* giant, in the novel?' John Wolf asked.
'I don't know, yet,' Garp said.
'Is he *you?*' Helen asked.
'I hope not,' Garp said.
'I hope not, too,' said Helen.
'Write that one first,' John Wolf said.
'No, write it last,' Helen said.
'*The Death of Vermont* seems the logical one to write last,'
John Wolf said.
'No, I see *The Plot against the Giant* as last,' Garp said.
'Wait and write it after I'm dead,' Helen said.
Everyone laughed.
'But there are only three,' John Wolf said. 'What then?
What happens after the three?'
'I die,' Garp said. 'That will make six novels altogether,
and that's enough.'
Everyone laughed again.
'And do you also know *how* you die?' John Wolf asked
him.

'Let's stop this,' Helen said. And to Garp she said, 'If you say, "In an airplane," I will not forgive you.' Behind the lightly drunk humor in her voice, John Wolf detected a seriousness; it made him stretch his legs.

'You two better go to bed,' he said. 'And get rested for your trip.'

'Don't you want to know how I die?' Garp asked them.

They didn't say anything.

'I kill myself,' Garp said, pleasantly. 'In order to become fully established, that seems almost necessary. I mean it, *really*,' Garp said. 'In the present fashion, you'll agree this is one way of recognizing a writer's seriousness? Since the *art* of the writing doesn't always make the writer's seriousness apparent, it's sometimes necessary to reveal the depth of one's personal anguish by other means. Killing yourself seems to mean that you were serious after all. It's *true*,' Garp said, but his sarcasm was unpleasant and Helen sighed; John Wolf stretched again. 'And thereafter,' Garp said, 'much seriousness is suddenly revealed in the work – where it had escaped notice before.'

Garp had often remarked, irritably, that this would be his final duty as a father and provider – and he was fond of citing examples of the middling writers who were now adored and read with great avidity *because* of their suicides. Of those writer-suicides whom he, too – in some cases – truly admired, Garp only hoped that, at the moment the act was accomplished, at least some of them had known about this lucky aspect of their unhappy decision. He knew perfectly well that people who really killed themselves did not romanticize suicide in the least; *they* did not respect the 'seriousness' that the act supposedly lent to their work – a nauseating habit in the book world, Garp thought. Among readers *and* reviewers.

Garp also knew *he* was no suicide; he knew it somewhat less surely after the accident to Walt, but he knew it. He was as distant from suicide as he was from rape; he could not imagine actually doing it. But he liked to imagine the suicidal writer grinning at his successful mischief, while once more he read and revised the last message he would leave – a note aching with despair, and appropriately humorless. Garp liked to imagine that moment, bitterly: when the suicide note was perfect, the writer took the gun, the poison, the plunge – laughing hideously, and full of the knowledge that he had at last got the better of the readers and reviewers. One note he imagined was: 'I have been misunderstood by you idiots for the last time.'

'What a sick idea,' Helen said.

'The perfect writer's death,' said Garp.

'It's late,' John Wolf said. 'Remember your flight.'

In the guest room, where John Wolf wanted to fall asleep, he found Duncan Garp still wide-awake.

'Excited by the trip, Duncan?' Wolf asked the boy.

'My father's been to Europe before,' Duncan said. 'But *I* haven't.'

'I know,' John Wolf said.

'Is my father going to make a lot of money?' Duncan asked.

'I hope so,' John Wolf said.

'We don't really need it, because my grandmother has so much,' Duncan said.

'But it's nice to have your own,' John Wolf said.

'Why?' Duncan asked.

'Well, it's nice to be famous,' John Wolf said.

'Do you think my father's going to be famous?' Duncan asked.

'I *think* so,' John Wolf said.

'My grandmother's already famous,' Duncan said.

'I know,' John Wolf said.

'I don't think she likes it,' Duncan said.

'Why?' John Wolf asked.

'Too many strangers around,' Duncan said. 'That's what Nana says; I've heard her. "Too many strangers in the house."'

'Well, your dad probably won't be famous in quite the

same *way* that your grandmother is,' John Wolf said.

'How many different ways are there to be famous?' Duncan asked.

John Wolf expelled a long, restrained breath. Then he began to tell Duncan Garp about the differences between very popular books and just successful ones. He talked about political books, and controversial books, and works of fiction. He told Duncan the finer points of book publishing; in fact, he gave Duncan the benefit of more of his personal opinions about publishing than he had ever given Garp. Garp wasn't really interested. Duncan wasn't, either. Duncan would not remember *one* of the finer points; he fell asleep rather quickly after John Wolf started explaining.

It was simply John Wolf's tone of voice that Duncan loved. The long story, the slow explanation. It was the voice of Roberta Muldoon – of Jenny Fields, of his mother, of Garp – telling him stories at night in the house at Dog's Head Harbor, putting him to sleep so soundly that he wouldn't have any nightmares. Duncan had gotten used to that tone of voice, and he had been unable to fall asleep in New York without it.

In the morning, Garp and Helen were amused by John Wolf's closet. There was a pretty nightgown belonging, no doubt, to one of John Wolf's recent, sleek women – someone who had *not* been asked to spend last night. There were about thirty dark suits, all with pinstripes, all quite elegant, and all failing to fit Garp by about three extra inches in the pant legs. Garp wore one he liked to breakfast, with the pants rolled up.

'Jesus, you have a lot of suits,' he said to John Wolf.

'Take one,' John Wolf said. 'Take two or three. Take the one you're wearing.'

'It's too long,' Garp said, holding up a foot.

'Have it shortened,' John Wolf said.

'You don't have *any* suits,' Helen told Garp.

Garp decided he liked the suit so well that he wanted to wear it to the airport, with the pant legs pinned up.

'Jesus,' Helen said.

'I'm slightly embarrassed to be seen with you,' John Wolf confessed, but he drove them to the airport. He was making absolutely certain that the Garps got out of the country.

'Oh, your book,' he said to Garp, in the car. 'I keep forgetting to get you a copy.'

'I noticed,' Garp said.

'I'll send you one,' John Wolf said.

'I never even saw what went on the jacket,' Garp said.

'A photograph of you, on the back,' John Wolf said. 'It's an old one – it's one you've seen, I'm sure.'

'What's on the front?' Garp said.

'Well, the title,' John Wolf said.

'Oh, really?' Garp said. 'I thought maybe you decided to leave the title off.'

'Just the title,' John Wolf said, 'over a kind of photograph.'

'"A kind of photograph,"' Garp said. '*What* kind of photograph?'

'Maybe I have one in my briefcase,' Wolf said. 'I'll look, at the airport.'

Wolf was being careful; he had already let it slip that he thought *The World According to Bensenhaver* was an 'X-rated soap opera.' Garp hadn't seemed bothered. 'Mind you, it's awfully well *written*,' Wolf had said, 'but it's still, somehow, soap opera; it's too *much*, somehow.' Garp had sighed. '*Life*,' Garp had said, 'is too much, somehow. *Life* is an X-rated soap opera, John,' Garp had said.

In John Wolf's briefcase was a snip-out of the front cover of *The World According to Bensenhaver*, missing the back-jacket photograph of Garp and, of course, the jacket flaps. John Wolf planned to hand this snip-out to Garp just moments before they said good-bye. This snip-out of the front cover was sealed in an envelope; the envelope was sealed in another envelope. John Wolf felt pretty certain that Garp would not be able to undo the thing and look at it until he was safely seated in the plane.

When Garp got to Europe, John Wolf would send him the rest of the book jacket for *The World According to Bensenhaver.* Wolf felt certain that it would not make Garp quite angry enough to fly home.

'This is bigger than the other plane,' Duncan said, at the window on the left-hand side, a little in front of the wing.

'It has to be bigger because it's going all the way across the ocean,' Garp said.

'Please don't mention that again,' Helen said. Across the aisle from Duncan and Garp, a stewardess was fashioning an intriguing sling for baby Jenny, who hung on the back of the seat in front of Helen like someone else's baby or a papoose.

'John Wolf said you were going to be rich and famous,' Duncan told his father.

'Hm,' Garp said. He was involved in the tedious process of opening the envelopes John Wolf had given him; he was having a hell of a time with them.

'Are you?' Duncan asked.

'I *hope* so,' Garp said. At last he looked at the cover of *The World According to Bensenhaver.* He could not tell if it was the sudden, apparent weightlessness of the great airplane, leaving the ground, that gave him such a chill – or if it was the photograph.

Blown up in black and white, with grains as fat as flakes of snow, was a picture of an ambulance unloading at a hospital. The glum futility on the gray faces of the attendants expressed the fact that there was no need to hurry. The body under the sheet was small and completely covered. The photograph had the quick, fearful quality of the entrance marked EMERGENCY at any hospital. It *was* any hospital, and any ambulance – and any small body arriving too late.

A kind of wet finish glazed the photograph, which – with its grainy aspect, and the fact that this accident appeared to have happened on a rainy night – made it a picture out of *any* cheap newspaper; it was any catastrophe. It was *any* small death, anywhere, anytime. But of course it only reminded Garp of the gray despairing on all their faces when they were struck by the sight of Walt lying broken.

The cover of *The World According to Bensenhaver,* an X-rated soap opera, shouted a grim warning: this was a disaster story. The cover called for your cheap but immediate attention; it got it. The cover promised you a sudden, sickening sadness; Garp knew that the book would deliver it.

If he could have read the jacket-flap description of his novel and his life, at that time, he might very well have taken the next plane back to New York as soon as he landed in Europe. But he would have time to resign himself to this kind of advertising – just as John Wolf had planned. By the time Garp read the jacket flaps, he'd already have absorbed that horrible front-cover photograph.

Helen would never absorb it, and she never forgave John Wolf for it, either. Nor would she ever forgive him for the back-cover photograph of Garp. It was a picture, taken several years before the accident, of Garp with Duncan and Walt. Helen had taken the picture, and Garp had sent it to John Wolf instead of a Christmas card. Garp was on a dock in Maine. He was wearing nothing but a bathing suit and he looked in terrific physical shape. He was. Duncan stood behind him, his lean arm rested on his father's shoulder; Duncan also wore a bathing suit, he was very tan, with a white sailor's cap cocked jauntily on his head. He grinned into the camera, staring it down with his beautiful eyes.

Walt sat on Garp's lap. Walt was so fresh out of the water that he was as slick as a seal puppy; Garp was trying to wrap him warmly in a towel, and Walt was squirming. Wildly happy, his clownish, round face beamed at the camera – at his mother taking the picture.

When Garp looked at that picture, he could feel Walt's cold, wet body growing warm and dry against him.

Beneath the photograph, the caption cashed in on one of the least noble instincts of human beings.

T. S. GARP WITH HIS CHILDREN
(BEFORE THE ACCIDENT)

The implication was that if you read the book, you would find out *what* accident. Of course, you wouldn't. *The World According to Bensenhaver* would tell you nothing about that accident, really – although it is fair to say that accidents play an enormous part in the novel. The only thing you would really learn about the accident referred to under the photograph was contained in the garbage that John Wolf wrote on the jacket flap. But, even so, that photograph – of a father with his doomed children – had a way of *hook*ing you.

People bought the book by the sad son of Jenny Fields in droves.

On the airplane to Europe, Garp had only the picture of the ambulance to use his imagination on. Even at that altitude, he could imagine people buying the book in droves. He sat feeling disgusted at the people he imagined buying the book; he also felt disgusted that he had written the kind of book that could attract people in droves.

'Droves' of anything, but especially of people, were not comforting to T. S. Garp. He sat in the airplane wishing for more isolation and privacy – for himself and for his family – than he would ever know again.

'What will we do with all the money?' Duncan asked him suddenly.

'All the money?' Garp said.

'When you're rich and famous,' Duncan said. 'What will we do?'

'We'll have lots of fun,' Garp told him, but his handsome son's one eye pierced him with doubt.

'We'll be flying at an altitude of thirty-five thousand feet,' the pilot said.

'Wow,' said Duncan. And Garp reached for his wife's hand across the aisle. A fat man was making his unsure way down the aisle to the lavatory; Garp and Helen could only look at each other and convey a kind of hand-in-hand contact with their eyes.

In his mind's eye, Garp saw his mother, Jenny Fields, all in white, held up in the sky by the towering Roberta Muldoon. He did not know what it meant, but his vision of Jenny Fields raised above a crowd chilled him in the same way that the ambulance on the cover of *The World According to Bensenhaver* had chilled him. He began talking to Duncan, about anything at all.

Duncan began talking about Walt and the undertow – a famous family story. For as far back as Duncan could remember, the Garps had gone every summer to Dog's Head Harbor, New Hampshire, where the miles of beach in front of Jenny Fields' estate were ravaged by a fearful undertow. When Walt was old enough to venture near the water, Duncan said to him – as Helen and Garp had, for years, said to Duncan – 'Watch out for the undertow.' Walt retreated, respectfully. And for three summers Walt was warned about the undertow. Duncan recalled all the phrases.

'The undertow is bad today.'

'The undertow is strong today.'

'The undertow is *wicked* today.' *Wicked* was a big word in New Hampshire – not just for the undertow.

And for years Walt watched out for it. From the first, when he asked what *it* could do to you, he had only been told that it could pull you out to sea. It could suck you under and drown you and drag you away.

It was Walt's fourth summer at Dog's Head Harbor, Duncan remembered, when Garp and Helen and Duncan observed Walt watching the sea. He stood ankle-deep in the foam from the surf and peered into the waves, without taking a step, for the longest time. The family went down to the water's edge to have a word with him.

'What are you doing, Walt?' Helen asked.

'What are you looking for, dummy?' Duncan asked him.

'I'm trying to see the Under Toad,' Walt said.

'The what?' said Garp.

'The Under Toad,' Walt said. 'I'm trying to *see* it. How *big* is it?'

And Garp and Helen and Duncan held their breath; they realized that all these years Walt had been dreading a giant *toad*, lurking offshore, waiting to suck him under and drag him out to sea. The terrible Under Toad.

Garp tried to imagine it with him. Would it ever surface? Did it ever float? Or was it always down under, slimy and bloated and ever-watchful for ankles its coated tongue could snare? The vile Under Toad.

Between Helen and Garp, the Under Toad became their code phrase for anxiety. Long after the monster was clarified for Walt ('Under*tow*, dummy, not Under Toad!' Duncan had howled), Garp and Helen evoked the beast as a way of referring to their own sense of danger. When the traffic was heavy, when the road was icy – when depression had moved in overnight – they said to each other, 'The Under Toad is strong today.'

'Remember,' Duncan asked on the plane, 'how Walt asked if it was green or brown?'

Both Garp and Duncan laughed. But it was neither green nor brown, Garp thought. It was me. It was Helen. It was the color of bad weather. It was the size of an automobile.

In Vienna, Garp felt, the Under Toad was strong. Helen did not seem to feel it, and Duncan, like an eleven-year-old, passed from one feeling to the next. The return to the city, for Garp, was like returning to the Steering School. The streets, the buildings, even the paintings in the museums, were like his old teachers, grown older; he barely recognized them, and they did not know him at all. Helen and Duncan saw everything. Garp was content to walk with baby Jenny; he strolled her through the long, warm fall in a carriage as baroque as the city itself – he smiled and nodded to all the tongue-clucking elderly who peered into the carriage and approved of his new baby. The Viennese appeared well fed and comfortable with luxuries that looked new to Garp;

the city was years away from the Russian occupation, the memory of the war, the reminders of ruins. If Vienna had been dying, or already dead, in his time there with his mother, Garp felt that something new but common had grown in the old city's place.

At the same time, Garp liked showing Duncan and Helen around. He enjoyed his personal history tour, mixed with the guidebook history of Vienna. 'And this is where Hitler stood when he first addressed the city. And this is where I used to shop on Saturday mornings.

'This is the fourth district, a Russian zone of occupation; the famous Karlskirche is here, and the Lower and Upper Belvedere. And between the Prinz-Eugen-Strasse, on your left, and the Argentinierstrasse is the little street where Mom and I . . .'

They rented some rooms in a nice pension in the fourth district. They discussed enrolling Duncan in an English-speaking school, but it was a long drive, or a long Strassenbahn ride every morning, and they didn't really plan on staying even half the year. Vaguely, they imagined Christmas at Dog's Head Harbor with Jenny and Roberta and Ernie Holm.

John Wolf finally sent the book, complete book jacket and all, and Garp's sense of the Under Toad grew unbearably for a few days, then kicked deeper, beneath the surface. It appeared to be gone. Garp managed a restrained letter to his editor; he expressed his sense of personal hurt, his understanding that this had been done with the best intentions, businesswise. But . . . and so forth. How angry could he really be – at Wolf? Garp had provided the package; Wolf had only promoted it.

Garp heard from his mother that the first reviews were 'not nice,' but Jenny – on John Wolf's advice – did not enclose any reviews with her letter. John Wolf clipped the first rave from among the important New York reviews: 'The women's movement has at last exhibited a significant influence on a significant male writer,' wrote the reviewer, who was an associate professor of women's studies somewhere. She went on to say that *The World According to Bensenhaver* was 'the first in-depth study, by a man, of the peculiarly *male* neurotic pressure many women are made to suffer.' And so forth.

'Christ,' Garp said, 'it sounds as if I wrote a *thesis*. It's a fucking *novel*, it's a *story*, and I made it up!'

'Well, it sounds as if she *liked* it,' Helen said.

'It's not *it* she liked,' Garp said. 'She liked something else.'

But the review helped to establish the rumor that *The World According to Bensenhaver* was 'a feminist novel.'

'Like me,' Jenny Fields wrote her son, 'it appears you are going to be the beneficiary of one of the many popular misunderstandings of our time.'

Other reviews called the book 'paranoid, crazed, and crammed with gratuitous violence and sex.' Garp was not shown most of those reviews, but they probably didn't hurt the sales, either.

One reviewer admitted that Garp was a serious writer whose 'tendencies toward baroque exaggeration have run amuck.' John Wolf couldn't resist sending Garp that review – probably because John Wolf agreed with it.

Jenny wrote that she was becoming 'involved with' New Hampshire politics.

'The New Hampshire gubernatorial race is taking all our time,' Roberta Muldoon wrote.

'How could anyone give all her time to a New Hampshire governor?' Garp wrote back.

There was, apparently, some feminist issue at stake, and some generally illiberal nonsense and crimes the incumbent governor was actually proud of. The administration boasted that a raped fourteen-year-old had been denied an abortion, thus stemming the tide of nationwide degeneracy. The governor truly *was* a crowing, reactionary moron. Among other things, he appeared to believe that poor people should not be helped by the state or federal government, largely because the condition of the poor seemed to the governor of New Hampshire to be a deserved punishment – the just and moral judgment of a Superior Being. The incumbent governor was obnoxious and clever; for example, the sense of *fear* that he successfully evoked: that New Hampshire was in danger of being victimized by *teams* of New York divorcees.

The divorced women from New York allegedly were moving into New Hampshire in droves. Their intentions were to turn New Hampshire women into lesbians, or at the very least to encourage them to be unfaithful to their New Hampshire husbands; their intentions also included the seduction of New Hampshire husbands, and New Hampshire high school boys. The New York divorcees apparently represented widespread promiscuity, socialism, alimony, and something ominously referred to, in the New Hampshire press, as 'Group Female Living.'

One of the centers for this alleged Group Female Living was Dog's Head Harbor, of course, 'the den of the radical feminist Jenny Fields.'

There had also been a widespread increase, the governor said, of venereal disease – 'a known problem among these Liberationists.' He was a terrific liar. The candidate running for governor against this well-liked fool was, apparently, a woman. Jenny and Roberta and (Jenny wrote) 'teams of New York divorcees' were running her campaign.

Somehow, in the sole New Hampshire newspaper of statewide distribution, Garp's 'degenerate' novel was referred to as 'the new feminist Bible.'

'A violent hymn to the moral depravity and sexual danger of our time,' wrote one West Coast reviewer.

'A pained protest against the violence and sexual combat of our groping age,' said another newspaper, somewhere else.

Whether it was liked or disliked, the novel was largely looked upon as *news*. One way for novels to be successful is for the fiction to resemble somebody's version of the news.

That is what happened to *The World According to Bensenhaver*; like the stupid governor of New Hampshire, Garp's book became news.

'New Hampshire is a backwoods state with base politics,' Garp wrote his mother. 'For God's sake, don't get involved.'

'That's what you always say,' Jenny wrote. 'When you come home, you're going to be famous. Then let me see *you* try not to get involved.'

'Just watch me,' Garp wrote her. 'Nothing could be easier.'

His involvement with the transatlantic mail had momentarily distracted Garp from his sense of the awesome and lethal Under Toad, but now Helen told him that she detected the presence of the beast, too.

'Let's go home,' she said. 'We've had a nice time.'

They got a telegram from John Wolf. 'Stay where you are,' it said. 'People are buying your book in droves.'

Roberta sent Garp a T-shirt.

NEW YORK DIVORCEES ARE GOOD
FOR NEW HAMPSHIRE

the T-shirt said.

'My God,' Garp said to Helen. 'If we're going home, let's at least wait until after this mindless election.'

Thus he missed, thankfully, the 'dissenting feminist opinion' of *The World According to Bensenhaver,* published in a giddy, popular magazine. The novel, the reviewer said, 'steadfastly upholds the sexist notion that women are chiefly an assemblage of orifices and the acceptable prey of predatory males . . . T. S. Garp continues the infuriating male mythology: the good man is the bodyguard of his family, the good woman never willingly lets another man enter her literal or figurative door.'

Even Jenny Fields was cajoled into 'reviewing' her son's novel, and it is fortunate that Garp never saw this, either. Jenny said that although it was her son's best novel – because it was his most serious subject – it was a novel 'marred by repeated male obsessions, which could become tedious to women readers.' However, Jenny said, her son was a good writer who was still young and would only get better. 'His heart,' she added, 'is in the right place.'

If Garp had read that, he might have stayed in Vienna a lot longer. But they made their plans to leave. As usual, anxiousness quickened the Garps' plans. One night Duncan was not home from the park before dark and Garp, running out to look for him, called back to Helen that this was the final sign; they would leave as soon as possible. City life, in general, made Garp too fearful for Duncan.

Garp ran along the Prinz-Eugen-Strasse toward the Russian War Memorial at the Schwarzenbergplatz. There was a pastry shop near there, and Duncan liked pastry, although Garp had repeatedly warned the child that it would ruin his supper. 'Duncan!' he ran calling, and his voice against the stolid stone buildings bounced back to him like the froggy belching of the Under Toad, the foul and warty beast whose sticky nearness he felt like breath.

But Duncan was munching happily on a Grillparzertorte in the pastry shop.

'It gets dark earlier and earlier,' he complained. 'I'm not *that* late.'

Garp had to admit it. They walked home together. The Under Toad disappeared up a small, dark street – or else it's not interested in Duncan, Garp thought. He imagined he felt the tug of the tide at his own ankles, but it was a passing feeling.

The telephone, that old cry of alarm – a warrior stabbed on guard duty, screaming his shock – startled the pension where they lived and brought the trembling landlady like a ghost to their rooms.

'Bitte, bitte,' she came pleading. She conveyed, with little shakes of excitement, that the call was from the United States.

It was about two in the morning, the heat was off, and

Garp shivered after the old woman, down the corridor of the pension. 'The hall rug was thin,' he recalled, 'the color of a shadow.' He had written that, years ago. And he looked for the rest of his cast: the Hungarian singer, the man who could only walk on his hands, the doomed bear, and all the members of the sad circus of death he had imagined.

But they were gone; only the old woman's lean, erect body guided him – her erectness unnaturally formal, as if she were overcorrecting a stoop. There were no photographs of speed-skating teams on the walls, there was no unicycle parked by the door to the W.C. Down a staircase and into a room with a harsh overhead light, like a hasty operating room set up in a city under siege, Garp felt he followed the Angel of Death – midwife to the Under Toad whose swampy smell he sniffed at the mouthpiece of the phone.

'Yes?' he whispered.

And for a moment was relieved to hear Roberta Muldoon – another sexual rejection; perhaps that was all. Or perhaps an update on the New Hampshire gubernatorial race. Garp looked up at the old, inquiring face of the landlady and realized that she had not taken the time to put in her teeth; her cheeks were sucked into her mouth, the loose flesh drooped below her jawline – her whole face was as slack as a skeleton's. The room reeked of toad.

'I didn't want you to see it on the news,' Roberta was saying. 'If it would be on TV over there – I couldn't know for sure. Or even the newspapers. I just didn't want you to find out that way.'

'Who won?' Garp asked, lightly, though he knew that this call had little to do with the new or old governor of New Hampshire.

'She's been *shot* – your mother,' Roberta said. 'They've killed her, Garp. A bastard shot her with a deer rifle.'

'Who?' Garp whispered.

'A *man!*' Roberta wailed. It was the worst word she could use: a man. 'A man who hated women,' Roberta said. 'He was a hunter,' Roberta sobbed. 'It was hunting season, or it was almost hunting season, and no one thought there was anything wrong about a man with a rifle. He shot her.'

'Dead?' Garp said.

'I caught her before she fell,' Roberta cried. 'She never struck the ground, Garp. She never said a word. She never knew what happened, Garp. I'm sure.'

'Did they get the man?' Garp asked.

'Someone shot him, or he shot himself,' Roberta said.

'Dead?' Garp asked.

'Yes, the bastard,' Roberta said. 'He's dead, too.'

'Are you alone, Roberta?' Garp asked her.

'No,' Roberta wept. 'There are a lot of us here. We're at *your* place.' And Garp could imagine them all, the wailing women at Dog's Head Harbor – their leader murdered.

'She wanted her body to go to a med school,' Garp said. 'Roberta?'

'I hear you,' Roberta said. 'That's just so awful.'

'That's what she wanted,' Garp said.

'I know,' Roberta said. 'You've got to come home.'

'Right away,' Garp said.

'We don't know what to *do*,' Roberta said.

'What *is* there to do?' Garp asked. 'There's nothing to do.'

'There should be *something*,' Roberta said, 'but she said she never wanted a funeral.'

'Certainly not,' Garp said. 'She wanted her body to go to a med school. You get that accomplished, Roberta: that's what Mom would have wanted.'

'But there ought to be *some*thing,' Roberta protested. 'Maybe not a *religious* service, but something.'

'Don't you get involved in anything until I get there,' Garp told her.

'There's a lot of talk,' Roberta said. 'People want a rally, or something.'

'I'm her only family, Roberta,' Garp said. 'You tell them that.'

'She meant a lot to a *lot* of us, you know,' Roberta said, sharply.

Yes, and it got her killed! Garp thought, but he said nothing.

'I tried to look after her!' Roberta cried. 'I told her not to go in that parking lot!'

'Nobody's to blame, Roberta,' Garp said, softly.

'*You* think somebody's to blame, Garp,' Roberta said. 'You always do.'

'Please, Roberta,' Garp said. 'You're my best friend.'

'*I'll* tell you who's to blame,' Roberta said. 'It's *men*, Garp. It's your filthy murderous sex! If you can't *fuck* us the way you want to, you kill us in a hundred ways!'

'Not *me*, Roberta, please,' Garp said.

'Yes, you too,' Roberta whispered. 'No man is a woman's friend.'

'I'm *your* friend, Roberta,' Garp said, and Roberta cried for a while – a sound as acceptable to Garp as rain falling on a deep lake.

'I'm so sorry,' Roberta whispered. 'If I'd seen the man with the gun – just a second sooner – I could have blocked the shot. I *would* have, you know.'

'I know you would have, Roberta,' Garp said; he wondered if *he* would have. He felt love for his mother, of course; and now an aching loss. But did he ever feel such *devotion* to Jenny Fields as the followers among her own sex?

He apologized to the landlady for the lateness of the phone call. When he told her that his mother was dead, the old woman crossed herself – her sunken cheeks and her empty gums were mute but clear indications of the family deaths she had herself outlived.

Helen cried for the longest time; she would not let Jenny's namesake, little Jenny Garp, out of her arms. Duncan and Garp searched the newspapers, but the news would be a day getting to Austria – except for the marvel of television.

Garp watched his mother's murder on his landlady's TV.

There was some election nonsense at a shopping plaza in New Hampshire. The landscape had a vaguely seacoast appearance, and Garp recognized the place as being a few miles from Dog's Head Harbor.

The incumbent governor was in favor of all the same, swinish, stupid things. The woman running against him seemed educated and idealistic and kind; she also seemed to barely restrain her anger at the same, swinish, stupid things the governor represented.

The parking lot at the shopping plaza was circled by pickup trucks. The pickups were full of men in hunting coats and caps; apparently they represented local New Hampshire interests – as opposed to the interest in New Hampshire taken by the New York divorcees.

The nice woman running against the governor was also a kind of New York divorcee. That she had lived fifteen years in New Hampshire, and her children had gone to school there, was a fact more or less ignored by the incumbent governor, and by his supporters who circled the parking lot in their pickup trucks.

There were lots of signs; there was a steady jeering.

There was also a high school football team, in uniform – their cleats clacking on the cement of the parking lot. One of the woman candidate's children was on the team and he had assembled the football players in the parking lot in hopes of demonstrating to New Hampshire that it was perfectly manly to vote for his mother.

The hunters in their pickup trucks were of the opinion that to vote for this woman was to vote for faggotry – and lesbianism, and socialism, and alimony, and New York. And so forth. Garp had the feeling, watching the telecast, that those things were not tolerated in New Hampshire.

Garp and Helen and Duncan, and baby Jenny, sat in the Viennese pension about to watch the murder of Jenny Fields. Their bewildered old landlady served them coffee and little cakes; only Duncan ate anything.

Then Jenny Fields had her turn to speak to the assembled people in the parking lot. She spoke from the back of a pickup truck; Roberta Muldoon lifted her up to the tailgate and adjusted the microphone for her. Garp's mother looked very small in the pickup truck, especially beside Roberta, but Jenny's uniform was so white that she stood out, bright and clear.

'I am Jenny Fields,' she said – to some cheers and some whistles and some hoots. There was a blaring of horns from the pickup trucks circling the parking lot. The police were telling the pickup trucks to move on; they moved on, and came back, and moved on again. 'Most of you know who I am,' Jenny Fields said. There were more hoots, more cheers, more blowing of horns – and a single sharp gunshot as conclusive as a wave breaking on the beach.

No one saw where it came from. Roberta Muldoon held Garp's mother under her arms. Jenny's white uniform seemed struck by a small dark splash. Then Roberta dropped down from the tailgate with Jenny in her arms and knifed through the breaking crowd like an old tight end carrying the ball for a hard first down. The crowd parted; Jenny's white uniform was almost concealed in Roberta's arms. There was a police car moving to intercept Roberta; when they neared each other, Roberta held out the body of Jenny Fields toward the squad car. For a moment Garp saw his mother's unmoving white uniform lifted above the crowd and into the arms of a policeman, who helped her and Roberta into the car.

The car, as they say, sped away. The camera was distracted by an apparent shoot-out taking place among the circling pickup trucks and several more police cars. Later, there was the still body of a man in a hunting coat lying in a dark puddle of what looked like oil. Later still, there was a close-up of what the newsmen would only identify as 'a deer rifle.'

It was pointed out that the deer season had not officially opened.

Except for the fact that there had been no nudity in the telecast, the event was an X-rated soap opera from start to finish.

Garp thanked the landlady for allowing them to watch

the news. Within two hours they were in Frankfurt, where they changed planes for New York. The Under Toad was not on the plane with them – not even for Helen, who was so afraid of planes. For a while, they knew, the Under Toad was elsewhere.

All Garp could think, somewhere over the Atlantic Ocean, was that his mother had delivered some adequate 'last words.' Jenny Fields had ended her life saying, 'Most of you know who I am.' On the airplane, Garp tried out the line.

'Most of you know who I am,' he whispered. Duncan was asleep, but Helen overheard him; she reached across the aisle and held Garp's hand.

Thousands of feet above sea level, T. S. Garp cried in the airplane that was bringing him home to be famous in his violent country.

The First Feminist Funeral,
and Other Funerals

'Ever since Walt died,' wrote T. S. Garp, 'my life has felt like an epilogue.'

When Jenny Fields died, Garp must have felt his bewilderment increase – that sense of time passing with a plan. But what was the plan?

Garp sat in John Wolf's New York office, trying to comprehend the plethora of plans surrounding his mother's death.

'I didn't authorize a funeral,' Garp said. 'How can there be a funeral? Where is the body, Roberta?'

Roberta Muldoon said patiently that the body was where Jenny wanted her body to go. It was not her body that mattered, Roberta said. There was simply going to be a kind of memorial service; it was better not to think of it as a 'funeral.'

The newspapers had said it was to be the first feminist funeral in New York.

The police had said that violence was expected.

'The first feminist funeral?' Garp said.

'She meant so much to so many women,' Roberta said. 'Don't be angry. You didn't *own* her, you know.'

John Wolf rolled his eyes.

Duncan Garp looked out the window of John Wolf's office, forty floors above Manhattan. It probably felt to

Duncan a little like being on the plane he had just got off.

Helen was making a phone call in another office. She was trying to reach her father in the good old town of Steering; she wanted Ernie to meet their plane out of New York when it landed in Boston.

'All right,' Garp said, slowly; he held the baby, little Jenny Garp, on his knee. 'All right. You know I don't approve of this, Roberta, but I'll go.'

'You'll *go*?' John Wolf said.

'No!' Roberta said. 'I mean, you don't *have* to,' she said.

'I know,' Garp said. 'But you're right. She probably would have liked such a thing, so I'll go. What's going to happen at it?'

'There's going to be a lot of speeches,' Roberta said. 'You don't want to go.'

'And they're going to read from her book,' John Wolf said. 'We've donated some copies.'

'But *you* don't want to go, Garp,' Roberta said, nervously. 'Please don't go.'

'I want to go,' Garp said. 'I promise you I won't hiss or boo – no matter what the assholes say about her. I have something of hers I might read myself, if anyone's interested,' he said. 'Did you ever see that thing she wrote about being called a feminist?' Roberta and John Wolf looked at each other; they looked stricken and gray. 'She said, "I hate being called one, because it's a label I didn't choose to describe my feelings about men or the way I write."'

'I don't want to argue with you, Garp,' Roberta said. 'Not now. You know perfectly well she said other things, too. She *was* a feminist, whether she liked the label or not. She was simply one for pointing out all the injustices to women; she was simply for allowing women to live their own lives and make their own choices.'

'Oh?' said Garp. 'And did she believe that *everything* that happened to women happened to them *because* they were women?'

'You have to be stupid to believe that, Garp,' Roberta said. 'You make us all sound like Ellen Jamesians.'

'Please stop it, both of you,' John Wolf said.

Jenny Garp squawked briefly and slapped Garp's knee; he looked at her, surprised – as if he'd forgotten she was a live thing there in his lap.

'What is it?' he asked her. But the baby was quiet again, watching some pattern in the landscape of John Wolf's office that was invisible to the rest of them.

'What time is this wingding?' Garp asked Roberta.

'Five o'clock in the afternoon,' Roberta said.

'I believe it was chosen,' John Wolf said, 'so that half the secretaries in New York could walk off their jobs an hour early.'

'Not all the working women in New York are secretaries,' Roberta said.

'The secretaries,' said John Wolf, 'are the only ones who'll be *missed* between four and five.'

'Oh boy,' Garp said.

Helen came in and announced that she could not reach her father on the phone.

'He's at wrestling practice,' Garp said.

'The wrestling season hasn't begun yet,' Helen said. Garp looked at the calendar on his watch, which was several hours out of sync with the United States; he had last set it in Vienna. But Garp knew that wrestling at Steering did not officially begin until after Thanksgiving. Helen was right.

'When I called his office at the gym, they said he was at home,' Helen told Garp. 'And when I called home, there was no answer.'

'We'll rent a car at the airport,' Garp said. 'And anyway, we can't leave until tonight. I have to go to this damn funeral.'

'No, you *don't* have to,' Roberta insisted.

'In fact,' Helen said, 'you *can't.*'

Roberta and John Wolf again looked stricken and gray; Garp simply looked uninformed.

'What do you mean, I *can't?*' he asked.

'It's a feminist funeral,' Helen said. 'Did you *read* the paper, or did you stop at the headlines?'

Garp looked accusingly at Roberta Muldoon, but she looked at Duncan looking out the window. Duncan had his telescope out, spying on Manhattan.

'You can't go, Garp,' Roberta admitted. 'It's true. I didn't tell you because I thought it would really piss you off. I didn't think you'd *want* to go, anyway.'

'I'm not *allowed?*' Garp said.

'It's a funeral for *women,*' Roberta said. '*Women* loved her, women will mourn her. That's how we wanted it.'

Garp glared at Roberta Muldoon. '*I* loved her,' he said. 'I'm her only child. Do you mean I can't go to this wingding because I'm a *man?*'

'I wish you wouldn't call it a wingding,' Roberta said.

'What's a wingding?' Duncan asked.

Jenny Garp squawked again, but Garp didn't listen to her. Helen took her from him.

'Do you mean no men are allowed at my mother's funeral?' Garp asked Roberta.

'It's not exactly a funeral, as I told you,' Roberta said. 'It's more like a rally – it's a kind of reverent demonstration.'

'I'm going, Roberta,' Garp said. 'I don't care what you *call* it.'

'Oh boy,' Helen said. She walked out of the office with baby Jenny. 'I'm going to try to get my father again,' she said.

'I see a man with one arm,' Duncan said.

'Please don't go, Garp,' Roberta said softly.

'She's right,' John Wolf said. 'I wanted to go, too. I was her editor, after all. But let them have it their way, Garp. I think Jenny would have liked the idea.'

'I don't care what she would have liked,' Garp said.

'That's probably true,' Roberta said. 'That's another reason you shouldn't be there.'

'You don't know, Garp, how some of the women's

movement people have reacted to your *book,*' John Wolf advised him.

Roberta Muldoon rolled her eyes. The accusation that Garp was cashing in on his mother's reputation, and the women's movement, had been made before. Roberta had seen the advertisement for *The World According to Bensenhaver,* which John Wolf had instantly authorized upon Jenny's assassination. Garp's book appeared to cash in on that tragedy, too – the ad conveyed a sick sense of a poor author who's lost a son 'and now a mother, too.'

It is fortunate Garp never saw that ad; even John Wolf regretted it.

The World According to Bensenhaver sold and sold and sold. For years it would be controversial; it would be taught in colleges. Fortunately, Garp's other books would be taught in colleges, sporadically, too. One course taught Jenny's autobiography together with Garp's three novels and Stewart Percy's *A History of Everett Steering's Academy.* The purpose of that course, apparently, was to figure out everything about Garp's *life* by hunting through the books for those things that appeared to be *true.*

It is fortunate Garp never knew anything about that course, either.

'I see a man with one leg,' announced Duncan Garp, searching the streets and windows of Manhattan for all the crippled and misarranged – a task that could take years.

'Please stop it, Duncan,' Garp said to him.

'If you really want to go, Garp,' Roberta Muldoon whispered to him, 'you'll have to go in drag.'

'If it's all that tough for a man to get in,' Garp snapped at Roberta, 'you better hope they don't have a chromosome check at the door.' He felt instantly sorry he'd said that; he saw Roberta wince as if he'd slapped her and he took both her big hands in his and held them until he felt her squeeze him back. 'Sorry,' he whispered. 'If I've got to go in drag, it's a good thing you're here to help me dress up. I mean, you're an old hand at that, right?'

'Right,' Roberta said.

'This is ridiculous,' John Wolf said.

'If some of those women recognize you,' Roberta told Garp, 'they'll tear you limb from limb. At the very least, they won't let you in the door.'

Helen came back in the office with Jenny Garp squawking on her hip.

'I've called Dean Bodger,' she told Garp. 'I asked him to try to reach Daddy. It's just not like him, to be nowhere.'

Garp shook his head.

'We should just go to the airport now,' Helen told him. 'Rent a car in Boston, drive to Steering. Let the children rest,' she said. 'Then if you want to run back to New York on some crusade, you can do it.'

'*You* go,' Garp said. 'I'll take a plane and rent my own car later.'

'That's silly,' Helen said.

'And needlessly expensive,' Roberta said.

'I have a lot of money now,' Garp said; his wry smile to John Wolf was not returned.

John Wolf volunteered to take Helen and the kids to the airport.

'One man with one arm, one man with one leg, two people who limped,' said Duncan, 'and someone without any nose.'

'You should wait awhile and get a look at your father,' Roberta Muldoon said.

Garp thought of himself: a grieving ex-wrestler, in drag for his mother's memorial service. He kissed Helen and the children, and even John Wolf. 'Don't worry about your dad,' Garp told Helen.

'And don't worry about Garp,' Roberta told Helen. 'I'm going to disguise him so that everyone will leave him alone.'

'I wish *you'd* try to leave everyone alone,' Helen told Garp.

There was suddenly another woman in John Wolf's

crowded office; no one had noticed her, but she had been trying to get John Wolf's attention. When she spoke, she spoke out in a single, clear moment of silence and everyone looked at her.

'Mr Wolf?' the woman said. She was old and brown-black-gray, and her feet appeared to be killing her; she wore an electrical extension cord, wrapped twice around her thick waist.

'Yes, Jillsy?' John Wolf said, and Garp stared at the woman. It was Jillsy Sloper, of course; John Wolf should have known that writers remember names.

'I was wonderin',' Jillsy said, 'if I could get off early this afternoon – if you'd say a word for me, because I want to go to that funeral.' She spoke with her chin down, a stiff mutter of bitten words – as few as possible. She did not like to open her mouth around strangers; also, she recognized Garp and she didn't want to be introduced to him – not ever.

'Yes, of course you can,' John Wolf said, quickly. He didn't want to introduce Jillsy Sloper to Garp any more than *she* wanted it.

'Just a minute,' Garp said. Jillsy Sloper and John Wolf froze. 'Are you Jillsy Sloper?' Garp asked her.

'No!' John Wolf blurted. Garp glared at him.

'How do you do?' Jillsy said to Garp; she would not look at him.

'How do *you* do?' Garp said. He could see at a glance that this sorrowful woman had *not*, as John Wolf said, 'loved' his book.

'I'm sorry about your mom,' Jillsy said.

'Thank you very much,' Garp said, but he could see – they *all* could see! – that Jillsy Sloper was seething about something.

'She was worth two or three of *you*!' Jillsy suddenly cried to Garp. There were tears in her muddy-yellow eyes. 'She was worth four or five of your terrible books!' she crooned. 'Lawd,' she muttered, leaving them all in John Wolf's office. 'Lawd, Lawd!'

Another person with a limp, thought Duncan Garp, but he could see that his father did not want to hear about his body count.

At the first feminist funeral held in the city of New York, the mourners appeared unsure how to behave. This was perhaps the result of the gathering's being not in a church but in one of those enigmatic buildings of the city university system – an auditorium, old with the echo of speeches no one had listened to. The giant space was slightly seedy with the sense of past cheering – for rock bands, and for the occasional, well-known poet. But the space was also serious with the certain knowledge that large lectures had taken place there; it was a room in which hundreds of people had taken notes.

The name of the space was School of Nursing Hall – thus it was oddly appropriate as a place of tribute to Jenny Fields. It was hard to tell the difference between the mourners wearing their Jenny Fields Originals, with the little red hearts stitched over the breast, and the real nurses, forever white and unfashionable, who had other reasons to be in the environs of the nursing school but had paused to peek in on the ceremonies – either curious or genuinely sympathetic, or both.

There were many white uniforms among the enormous, milling, softly mumbling audience, and Garp immediately cursed Roberta. 'I *told* you I could have dressed as a nurse,' Garp hissed. 'I could have been a little less conspicuous.'

'I thought you'd be conspicuous as a nurse,' Roberta said. 'I didn't know there'd be so many.'

'It's going to be a fucking national trend,' Garp muttered. 'Just wait and see,' he said, but he said no more; he huddled small and garish beside Roberta, feeling that everyone was looking at him and somehow sensing his maleness – or at least, as Roberta had warned him, his hostility.

They sat dead-center in the massive auditorium, only three rows back from the stage and the speakers' platform; a sea of women had moved in and sat behind them – rows and

rows of them – and farther back, at the wide-open rear of
the hall (where there were no seats), the women who were
less interested in seating themselves for the entire ritual, but
who'd wanted to come pay their respects, filed slowly in one
door and slowly out another. It was as if the larger, seated
audience were the open casket of Jenny Fields that the slow-
walking women had come to observe.

Garp, of course, felt that *he* was an open casket, and all
the women were observing him – his pallor, his hue, his
preposterous disguise.

Roberta had done this to him, perhaps to get even with
him for his bullying her into letting him come at all – or for
his cruel crack concerning her chromosomes. Roberta had
dressed Garp in a cheap turquoise jumpsuit, the color of
Oren Rath's pickup truck. The jumpsuit had a gold zipper
that ran from Garp's crotch to Garp's throat. Garp did not
adequately fill the hips of the suit, but his breasts – or,
rather, the falsies Roberta had fashioned for him – strained
against the snap-flap pockets and twisted the vulnerable
zipper askew.

'What a set you have!' Roberta had told him.

'You animal, Roberta,' Garp had hissed to her.

The shoulder straps of the huge, hideous bra dug into his
shoulders. But whenever Garp felt that a woman was staring
at him, perhaps doubting his sex, he would simply turn
himself sideways to her and show off. Thus eliminating any
possible doubt, or so he hoped.

He was less sure of the wig. A tousled whore's head of
honey-blond hair, under which his own scalp itched.

A pretty green silk scarf was at his throat.

His dark face was powdered a sickly gray, but this concealed, Roberta said, his stubble of beard. His rather thin
lips were cherry-colored, but he kept licking them and had
smeared the lipstick at one corner of his mouth.

'You look like you've just been kissed,' Roberta reassured
him.

Though Garp was cold, Roberta had not allowed him to

wear his ski parka – it made his shoulders look too thick. And on Garp's feet was a towering pair of knee-high boots – a kind of cherry vinyl that matched, Roberta said, his lipstick. Garp had seen himself reflected in a storefront window and he'd told Roberta that he thought he looked like a teenage prostitute.

'An *aging* teenage prostitute,' Roberta had corrected him.

'A faggot parachutist,' Garp had said.

'No, you look like a woman, Garp,' Roberta had assured him. 'Not a woman with especially good taste, but a woman.'

So Garp sat squirming in School of Nursing Hall. He twisted the itchy rope braids of his ridiculous purse, a scraggily hemp thing with an oriental design, barely big enough to hold his wallet. In her large, bursting shoulder bag, Roberta Muldoon had hidden Garp's real clothes – his other identity.

'This is Manda Horton-Jones,' Roberta whispered, indicating a thin, hawk-nosed woman speaking nasally and with her rodential head pointed down; she read a stiff, prepared speech.

Garp didn't know who Manda Horton-Jones was; he shrugged, enduring her. The speeches had ranged from strident, political calls for unity to disturbed, painful, personal reminiscences of Jenny Fields. The audience did not know whether to applaud or to pray – whether to voice approval or to nod grimly. The atmosphere was both one of mourning and one of urgent togetherness – with a strong sense of marching forth. Thinking about it, Garp supposed this was natural and fitting, both to his mother and to his dim perception of what the women's movement *was*.

'This is Sally Devlin,' Roberta whispered. The woman now climbing to the speakers' platform looked pleasant and wise and vaguely familiar. Garp felt immediately the need to defend himself from her. He didn't mean it, but solely to goad Roberta, Garp whispered, 'She has nice legs.'

'Nicer than yours,' Roberta said, pinching his thigh

painfully between her strong thumb and her long, pass-catching index finger – one of the fingers, Garp supposed, that had been broken so many times during Roberta's fling as a Philadelphia Eagle.

Sally Devlin looked down on them with her soft, sad eyes as if she were silently scolding a classroom of children who were not paying attention – not even sitting still.

'That senseless murder does not really merit all this,' she said, quietly. 'But Jenny Fields simply helped so many *individuals*, she simply was so patient and generous with women who were having a bad time. Anyone who's ever been helped by someone else should feel terrible about what's happened to her.'

Garp felt truly terrible, at that moment; he heard a combined sigh and sob of hundreds of women. Beside him, Roberta's broad shoulders shook against him. He felt a hand, perhaps of the woman sitting directly behind him, grip his own shoulder, cramped in the terrible turquoise jumpsuit. He wondered if he was about to be slapped for his offensive, inappropriate attire, but the hand just held on to his shoulder. Perhaps the woman needed support. At this moment, Garp knew, they all felt like sisters, didn't they?

He looked up to see what Sally Devlin was saying, but his own eyes were teary and he could not see Ms Devlin clearly. He could *hear* her, though: she was sobbing. Great heartfelt and heaving cries! She was trying to get back to her speech but her eyes couldn't find her place on the page; the page rattled against the microphone. Some very powerful-looking woman, whom Garp thought he had seen before – one of those bodyguard types he had often seen with his mother – tried to help Sally Devlin off the platform, but Ms Devlin didn't want to leave.

'I wasn't going to do this,' she said, still crying – meaning her sobs, her loss of control. 'I had more to say,' she protested, but she could not get hold of her voice. 'Damn it,' she said, with a dignity that moved Garp.

The big tough-looking woman found herself alone at

the microphone. The audience waited quietly. Garp felt a tremble, or maybe a tug, from the hand on his shoulder. Looking at Roberta's large hands, folded in her lap, Garp knew that the hand on his shoulder must be very small.

The big tough-looking woman wanted to say something, and the audience waited. But they would wait forever to hear a word from her. Roberta knew her. Roberta stood up beside Garp and began to applaud the big, hard-looking woman's silence – her exasperating quiet in front of the microphone. Other people joined Roberta's applause – even Garp, though he had no idea why he was clapping.

'She's an Ellen Jamesian,' Roberta whispered to him. 'She *can't* say anything.' Yet the woman melted the audience with her pained, sorry face. She opened her mouth as if she were singing, but no sound came out. Garp imagined he could see the severed stump of her tongue. He remembered how his mother supported them – these crazies; Jenny was wonderful to every single one of them who came to her. But Jenny had finally admitted her disapproval of what they had done – perhaps only to Garp. 'They're making victims of themselves,' Jenny had said, 'and yet that's the same thing they're angry at men for doing to them. Why don't they just take a vow of silence, or never speak in a man's presence?' Jenny said. 'It's not logical: to maim yourself to make a point.'

But Garp, now touched by the mad woman in front of him, felt the whole history of the world's self-mutilation – though violent and illogical, it expressed, perhaps like nothing else, a terrible hurt. 'I am really *hurt*,' said the woman's huge face, dissolving before him in his own swimmy tears.

Then the little hand on his shoulder hurt *him*; he remembered himself – a man at a ritual for women – and he turned around to see the rather tired-looking young woman behind him. Her face was familiar, but he didn't recognize her.

'I know you,' the young woman whispered to him. She did not sound *happy* that she knew him, either.

Roberta had warned him not to open his mouth to anyone, not even to *try* to speak. He was prepared for handling that problem. He shook his head. He took a pad of paper out of the flap pocket, which was crushed against his mammoth, false bosom, and he snatched a pencil out of his absurd purse. The sharp, clawlike fingers of the woman bit into his shoulder, as if she were keeping him from running away.

Hi! I'm an Ellen Jamesian,

Garp scribbled on the pad; he tore the slip off and handed it to the young woman. She didn't take it.

'Like hell you are,' she said. 'You're T. S. Garp.'

The word *Garp* bounced like the burp of an unknown animal into the silence of the suffering auditorium, still conducted by the quiet Ellen Jamesian onstage. Roberta Muldoon turned around and looked panic-stricken; she had never seen this particular young woman in her life.

'I don't know who your big playmate is,' the young woman told Garp, 'but you're T. S. Garp. I don't know where you got that dumb wig or those big tits, but I'd know you anywhere. You haven't changed a bit since you were fucking my sister – fucking her to *death*,' the young woman said. And Garp knew who his enemy was: the last and youngest of the Percy Family Horde. Bainbridge! Little Pooh Percy, who was wearing diapers as a preteen, and, for all Garp knew, might be wearing them still.

Garp looked at her; Garp had bigger tits than she did. Pooh was asexually attired, her haircut was similar to a popular and unisexual style, her features were neither delicate nor coarse. Pooh wore a U.S. Army shirt with sergeant stripes and a campaign button for the woman who'd hoped to be the new governor of the State of New Hampshire. With a shock, Garp realized that the woman running for governor was Sally Devlin. He wondered if she'd won!

'Hello, Pooh,' Garp said, and saw her wince – a *hated* nickname, obviously, and one she was never called anymore. 'Bainbridge,' Garp muttered, but it was too late to make friends. It was *years* too late. It was too late from the night Garp had bitten off Bonkers' ear, had violated Cushie in the Steering School infirmary, had not ever really loved her – had not come to her wedding, and not to her funeral.

Whatever grudge against Garp this was, or whatever loathing for men in general, Pooh Percy had *her* enemy at her mercy – at last.

Roberta's big warm hand was at the small of Garp's back and her heavy voice urged him, 'Get out of here, move fast, don't say a word.'

'There's a *man* here!' Bainbridge Percy shouted to the grieving silence of School of Nursing Hall. That even brought a small sound – perhaps a grunt – from the troubled Ellen Jamesian onstage. 'There's a man here!' Pooh screamed. 'And he's T. S. Garp. *Garp* is here!' she cried.

Roberta tried to lead him to the aisle. A tight end is chiefly a good blocker, secondarily a pass-receiver, but even the former Robert Muldoon could not quite move all these women.

'Please,' Roberta said. 'Excuse us, please. She was his *mother* – you must know that. Her only child.'

My only *mother!* Garp thought, plowing against Roberta's back; he felt Pooh Percy's needlelike claws rake his face. She snatched his wig off; he snatched it back and clutched it to his big bosom, as if it mattered to him.

'He fucked my sister to *death!*' Pooh Percy wailed. How *this* perception of Garp had convinced her, Garp would never know – but convinced of it Pooh clearly was. She climbed over the seat he had abandoned and moved in behind him and Roberta – who finally broke through, into the aisle.

'She was my mother,' Garp said to a woman he was passing, a woman who looked like a potential mother herself. She was pregnant. In the woman's scornful face Garp saw reason and kindness; he also saw restraint and contempt.

'Let him pass,' the pregnant woman murmured, but without much feeling.

Others seemed more sympathetic. Someone cried out that he had a right to be there – but there were other things shouted, rather lacking sympathy of any kind.

Farther up the aisle he felt his falsies punched; he put his hand out for Roberta and realized Roberta had (as they say in football) been taken out of the play. She was down. Several young women wearing navy pea coats appeared to be sitting on her. It occurred to Garp that they might think Roberta was *also* a man in drag; their discovery that Roberta was real could be painful.

'Take off, Garp!' Roberta cried.

'Yes, *run*, you little fucker!' one woman in a pea coat hissed.

He ran.

He was almost up to the milling women at the rear of the hall when someone's blow landed where it was aimed. He had not been hit in the balls since a wrestling practice at Steering – so many years ago, he realized he had forgotten the total incapacity that resulted. He covered himself and lay curled on one hip. They kept trying to rip his wig out of his hands. And his tiny purse. He held on as if this were some mugging. He felt a few shoes, a few slaps, and then the minty breath of an elderly woman breathing in his face.

'Try to get up,' she said, gently. He saw she was a nurse. A real nurse. There was no fashionable heart sewn above her breast; there was just the little brass-and-blue nameplate – she was R.N. So-and-So.

'My name is Dotty,' the nurse told him; she was at least sixty.

'Hello,' Garp said. 'Thank you, Dotty.'

She took his arm and led him at a fast pace through the remaining mob. No one appeared to want to hurt him when he was with her. They let him go.

'Do you have money for a cab?' the nurse named Dotty asked him when they were outside School of Nursing Hall.

'Yes, I think so,' Garp said. He checked his horrid purse; his wallet was safely there. And his wig – tousled still further – was under his arm. Roberta had Garp's real clothes and Garp looked in vain for any sign of Roberta emerging from the first feminist funeral.

'Put that wig on,' Dotty advised him, 'or you'll be mistaken for one of those transvestites.' He struggled to put it on; she helped him. 'People are really rough on transvestites,' Dotty added. She took several bobby pins from her own gray head of hair and fastened Garp's wig more decently in place.

The scratch on his cheek, she told him, would stop bleeding very soon.

On the steps of School of Nursing Hall, a tall black woman who looked like an even match for Roberta shook her fist at Garp but said not a word. Perhaps she was another Ellen Jamesian. A few other women were gathering there and Garp feared they might be thinking over the advisability of an open attack. Oddly at the fringe of their group, but seeming to have no connection with them, was a wraith-like girl, or barely grown-up child; she was a dirty blond-headed girl with piercing eyes the color of coffee-stained saucers – like a drug-user's eyes, or someone long involved in hard tears. Garp felt frozen by her stare, and frightened of her – as if she were *really* crazy, a kind of teenage hit man for the women's movement, with a gun in her oversized purse. He clutched his own ratty bag, recalling that his wallet was at least full of credit cards; he had enough cash for a cab to the airport and the credit cards could get him a flight to Boston and the bosom, so to speak, of his remaining family. He wished he could relieve himself of his ostentatious tits, but there they were, as if he'd been born with them – and born, too, in this alternately tight and baggy jumpsuit. It was all he had and it would have to do. From the din escaping from School of Nursing Hall, Garp knew that Roberta was deep in the throes of debate – if not combat. Someone who had fainted, or had been mauled, was carried out; more police went in.

'Your mother was a first-rate nurse and a woman who made every woman proud,' the nurse named Dotty told him. 'I'll bet she was a good mother, too.'

'She sure was,' Garp said.

The nurse got him a cab; the last he saw of her, she was walking away from the curb, back toward School of Nursing Hall. The other women who'd seemed so threatening, on the steps outside the building, appeared to be not interested in molesting her. More police were arriving; Garp looked for the strange saucer-eyed girl, but she was not among the other women.

He asked the cabby who the new governor of New Hampshire was. Garp tried to conceal the depth of his voice, but the cabby, familiar with the eccentricities of his job, seemed unsurprised at both Garp's voice and Garp's appearance.

'I was out of the country,' Garp said.

'You didn't miss nothin', sweetie,' the cabby told him. 'That broad broke down.'

'Sally Devlin?' said Garp.

'She cracked up, right on the TV,' the cabby said. 'She was so flipped out over the assassination, she couldn't control herself. She was givin' this speech but she couldn't get through it, you know?

'She looked like a real idiot to me,' the cabby said. 'She couldn't be no governor if she couldn't control herself no better than that.'

And Garp saw the pattern of the woman's loss emerging. Perhaps the foul incumbent governor had remarked that Ms Devlin's inability to control her emotions was 'just like a woman.' Disgraced by her demonstration of her feelings for Jenny Fields, Sally Devlin was judged not competent enough for whatever dubious work being a governor entailed.

Garp felt ashamed. He felt ashamed of other people.

'In my opinion,' the cabby said, 'it took something like that shooting to show the people that the woman couldn't handle the job, you know?'

'Shut up and drive,' Garp said.

'Look, honey,' the cabby said. 'I don't have to put up with no *abuse.*'

'You're an asshole and a moron,' Garp told him, 'and if you don't drive me to the airport with your mouth shut, I'll tell a cop you tried to paw me all over.'

The cabby floored the accelerator and drove for a while in furious silence, hoping the speed and recklessness of his driving would scare his passenger.

'If you don't slow down,' Garp said, 'I'll tell a cop you tried to rape me.'

'Fucking weirdo,' the cabby said, but he slowed down and drove to the airport without another word. Garp put the money for the tip on the taxi's hood and one of the coins rolled into the crack between the hood and fender. 'Fucking *women,*' the cabby said.

'Fucking *men,*' said Garp, feeling – with mixed feelings – that he had done his duty to ensure that the sex war went on.

At the airport they questioned Garp's American Express card and asked for further identification. Inevitably, they asked him about the initials T. S. The airline ticket-maker was clearly not in touch with the literary world – not to know who T. S. Garp was.

He told the ticket-maker that T. was for Tillie, S. was for Sarah.

'Tillie Sarah Garp?' the ticket-maker said. She was a young woman, and she clearly disapproved of Garp's oddly fetching but whorish appearance. 'Nothing to check, and no carry-on luggage?' Garp was asked.

'No, nothing,' he said.

'You have a coat?' the stewardess asked him, also giving him a condescending appraisal.

'No coat,' Garp said. The stewardess gave a start at the deepness of his voice. 'No bags and nothing to hang up,' he said, smiling. He felt that all he had was *breasts* – these terrific knockers Roberta had made for him – and he walked slouched and stoop-shouldered to try to hold them back. There was no holding them back, though.

As soon as he chose a seat, some man chose to sit beside him. Garp looked out the window. Passengers were still hurrying to his plane. Among them, he saw a wraithlike, dirty blond-haired girl. She had no coat and no carry-on luggage, either. Just that oversized purse – big enough for a bomb. Thickly, Garp sensed the Under Toad – a wriggle at his hip. He looked toward the aisle, so that he would notice where the girl chose to sit, but he looked into the leering face of the man who'd taken the aisle seat beside him.

'Perhaps, when we're in the air,' the man said, knowingly, 'I could buy you a little drink?' His small, close-together eyes were riveted on the twisted zipper of Garp's straining turquoise jumpsuit.

Garp felt a peculiar kind of unfairness overwhelm him. He had not asked to have such an anatomy. He wished he could have spent a quiet time, just talking, with that wise and pleasant-looking woman, Sally Devlin, the failed gubernatorial candidate from New Hampshire. He would have told her that she was too good for the rotten job.

'That's some *suit* you got,' said Garp's leering seat partner.

'Go stick it in your ear,' Garp said. He was, after all, the son of a woman who'd slashed a masher at a movie in Boston – years ago, long ago.

The man struggled to get up, but he couldn't; his seat belt would not release him. He looked helplessly at Garp. Garp leaned over the man's trapped lap; Garp gagged on his own dose of perfume, which he remembered Roberta slathering over him. He got the seat-belt clasp to operate properly and released the man with a sharp snap. Then Garp growled a menacing whisper in the man's very red ear. 'When we're in the air, cutie,' he whispered to the frightened fellow, 'go blow yourself in the bathroom.'

But when the man deserted Garp's company, the aisle seat was vacant, inviting someone else. Garp glared challengingly at the empty seat, daring the next man on the make to sit there. The person who approached Garp shook his momentary confidence. She was very thin, her girlish hands bony and clutching her oversized purse. She didn't ask first; she just sat down. The Under Toad is a very young girl today, Garp thought. When she reached into her purse, Garp caught her wrist and pulled her hand out of the bag and into her lap. She was not strong, and in her hand there was no gun; there was not even a knife. Garp saw only a pad of paper and a pencil with the eraser bitten down to a nub.

'I'm sorry,' he whispered. If she was not an assassin, he guessed he knew who or what she was. 'Why is my life so full of people with impaired speech?' he wrote once. 'Or is it only because I'm a writer that I notice all the damaged voices around me?'

The nonviolent waif on the airplane beside him wrote hastily and handed him a note.

'Yes, yes,' he said, wearily. 'You're an Ellen Jamesian.' But the girl bit her lip and fiercely shook her head. She pushed the note into his hand.

My name is Ellen James,

the note informed Garp.

I am not an Ellen Jamesian.

'You're *the* Ellen James?' he asked her, though it was unnecessary and he knew it – just looking at her, he should have known. She was the right age; not so long ago she would have been that eleven-year-old child, raped and untongued. The dirty-saucer eyes were, up close, not dirty; they were simply bloodshot, perhaps insomniac. Her lower lip was ragged; it looked like the pencil eraser – bitten down.

She scribbled more.

I came from Illinois. My parents were killed in an auto accident, recently. I came East to meet your mother. I wrote her a letter and she

actually answered *me! She wrote me a wonderful reply. She invited me
to come stay with her. She also told me to read all your books.*

Garp turned these tiny pages of notepaper; he kept
nodding; he kept smiling.

But your mother was killed!

From the big purse Ellen James pulled a brown bandanna
into which she blew her nose.

*I went to stay with a women's group in New York. But I already
knew too many Ellen Jamesians. They're all I know; I get hundreds
of Christmas cards,*

she wrote. She paused for Garp to read that line.
'Yes, yes, I'm sure you do,' he encouraged her.

*I went to the funeral, of course. I went because I knew you'd be there. I
knew you'd come,*

she wrote; she stopped, now, to smile at him. Then she hid
her face in her dirty brown bandanna.
'You wanted to see *me?*' Garp said.
She nodded, fiercely. She pulled from the big bag her
mangled copy of *The World According to Bensenhaver.*

The best rape story I have ever read,

wrote Ellen James. Garp winced.

Do you know how many times I have read this book?

she wrote. He looked at her teary, admiring eyes. He shook
his head, as mutely as an Ellen Jamesian. She touched his
face; she had a childlike inability with her hands. She held
up her fingers for him to count. All of one little hand and

most of the other. She had read his awful book eight times.

'Eight times,' Garp murmured.

She nodded, and smiled at him. Now she settled back in the plane seat, as if her life were accomplished, now that she was sitting beside him, en route to Boston – if not with the woman she had admired all the way from Illinois, at least with the woman's only son, who would have to suffice.

'Have you been to college?' Garp asked her.

Ellen James held up one dirty finger; she made an unhappy face.

'One year?' Garp translated. 'But you didn't like it. It didn't work out?'

She nodded eagerly.

'And what do you want to be?' he asked her, barely keeping himself from adding: *When you grow up.*

She pointed to him and blushed. She actually touched his gross breasts.

'A writer?' Garp guessed. She relaxed and smiled; he understood her so easily, her face seemed to say. Garp felt his throat constricting. She struck him as one of those doomed children he had read about: the ones who have no antibodies – they have no natural immunities to disease. If they don't live their lives in plastic bags, they die of their first common cold. Here was Ellen James of Illinois, out of her sack.

'*Both* your parents were killed?' Garp asked. She nodded, and bit again her chewed lip. 'And you have no other family?' he asked her. She shook her head.

He knew what his mother would have done. He knew Helen wouldn't mind; and of course Roberta would always be of help. And all those women who'd been wounded and were now healed, in their fashion.

'Well, you have a family *now*,' Garp told Ellen James; he held her hand and winced to hear himself make such an offer. He heard the echo of his mother's voice, her old soap-opera role: The Adventures of Good Nurse.

Ellen James shut her eyes as if she had fainted for joy.

When the stewardess asked her to fasten her seat belt, Ellen James didn't hear; Garp fastened her belt for her. All the short flight to Boston the girl wrote her heart out.

I hate the Ellen Jamesians,

she wrote.

I would never do this to myself.

She opened her mouth and pointed to the wide absence in there. Garp cringed.

I want to talk; I want to say everything,

wrote Ellen James. Garp noticed that the gnarled thumb and index finger of her writing hand were easily twice the size of the unused instruments on her other hand; she had a writing muscle such as he'd never seen. No writer's cramp for Ellen James, he thought.

The words come and come,

she wrote. She waited for his approval, line by line. He would nod; she would go on. She wrote him her whole life. Her high school English teacher, the only one who mattered. Her mother's eczema. The Ford Mustang that her father drove too fast.

I have read everything,

she wrote. Garp told her that Helen was a big reader, too; he thought she would like Helen. The girl looked very hopeful.

Who was your favorite writer when you were a boy?

'Joseph Conrad,' Garp said. She sighed her approval.

Jane Austen was mine.

'That's fine,' Garp said to her.

At Logan Airport she was almost asleep on her feet; Garp steered her up the aisles and leaned her on the counters while he filled out the necessary forms for the rental car.

'T. S.?' the rental-car person asked. One of Garp's falsies was slipping sideways and the rental-car person appeared anxious that this entire turquoise body might self-destruct.

In the car north, on the dark road to Steering, Ellen James slept like a kitten curled in the backseat. In the rearview mirror Garp noted that her knee was skinned, and that the girl sucked her thumb while she slept.

It had been a proper funeral for Jenny Fields, after all; some essential message had passed from mother to son. Here he was, playing nurse to someone. More essentially, Garp finally understood what his mother's talent had been; she had right instincts – *Jenny Fields always did what was right.* One day, Garp hoped, he would see the connection between this lesson and his own writing, but that was a personal goal – like others, it would take a little time. Importantly, it was in the car north to Steering, with the real Ellen James asleep and in his care, that T. S. Garp decided he would try to *be* more like his mother, Jenny Fields.

A thought, it occurred to him, that would have pleased his mother greatly if it had only come to him when she was alive.

'Death, it seems,' Garp wrote, 'does not like to wait until we are prepared for it. Death is indulgent and enjoys, when it can, a flair for the dramatic.'

Thus Garp, with his defenses down and his sense of the Under Toad fled from him – at least, since his arrival in Boston – walked into the house of Ernie Holm, his father-in-law, carrying the sleeping Ellen James in his arms. She might have been nineteen, but she was easier to carry than Duncan.

Garp was not prepared for the grizzled face of Dean Bodger, alone in Ernie's dim living room, watching TV. The old dean, who would soon retire, seemed to accept that Garp was dressed as a whore, but he stared with horror at the sleeping Ellen James.

'Is she . . .'

'She's asleep,' Garp said. 'Where's everyone?' And with the voicing of his question, Garp heard the cold hop of the Under Toad thudding across the cold floors of the silent house.

'I tried to reach you,' Dean Bodger told him. 'It's Ernie.'

'His heart,' Garp guessed.

'Yes,' Bodger said. 'They gave Helen something to help her sleep. She's upstairs. And I thought I'd stay until you got here – you know: so that if the children woke up and needed anything, they wouldn't disturb her. I'm sorry, Garp. These things sometimes come all at once, or they seem to.'

Garp knew how Bodger had liked his mother, too. He put the sleeping Ellen James on the living-room couch and turned off the sickly TV, which was turning the girl's face bluish.

'In his sleep?' Garp asked Bodger, pulling off his wig. 'Did you find Ernie here?'

Now the poor dean looked nervous. 'He was on the bed upstairs,' Bodger said. 'I called up the stairs, but I knew I'd have to go up and find him. I fixed him up a little before I called anyone.'

'Fixed him up?' Garp said. He unzipped the terrible turquoise jump suit and ripped off his breasts. The old dean perhaps thought this was a common traveling disguise of the now-famous writer.

'Please don't ever tell Helen,' Bodger said.

'Tell her what?' Garp asked.

Bodger brought out the magazine – out from under his bulging vest. It was the issue of *Crotch Shots* where the first chapter of *The World According to Bensenhaver* had been published. The magazine looked very worn and used.

'Ernie had been looking at it, you know,' Bodger said. 'When his heart stopped.'

Garp took the magazine from Bodger and imagined the death scene. Ernie Holm had been masturbating to the split-beaver pictures when his heart quit. There was a joke during Garp's days at Steering that this was the preferred way to 'go'. So Ernie had gone that way, and the kindly Bodger had pulled up the coach's pants and hidden the magazine from the coach's daughter.

'I had to tell the medical examiner, you know,' Bodger said.

A nasty metaphor from his mother's past came up to Garp in a wave, like nausea, but he did not express it to the old dean. Lust lays another good man low! Ernie's lonely life depressed Garp.

'And your mom,' sighed Bodger, shaking his head under the cold porch light that glowed into the black Steering campus. 'Your mom was someone special,' the old man mused. 'She was a real fighter,' the scrappy Bodger said, with pride. 'I still have copies of the notes she wrote to Stewart Percy.'

'You were always nice to her,' Garp reminded him.

'She was worth a hundred Stewart Percys, you know, Garp,' Bodger said.

'She sure was,' Garp said.

'You know *he's* gone, too?' Bodger said.

'Fat Stew?' said Garp.

'Yesterday,' Bodger said. 'After a long illness – you know what that usually means, don't you?'

'No,' Garp said. He hadn't ever thought about it.

'Cancer, usually,' Bodger said, gravely. 'He had it for a long time.'

'Well, I'm sorry,' Garp said. He was thinking of Pooh, and of course of Cushie. And his old challenger, Bonkers, whose ear in his dreams he could still taste.

'There's going to be some confusion about the Steering chapel,' Bodger explained. 'Helen can tell you, she understands. Stewart has a service in the morning; Ernie has his later in the day. And, of course, you know the bit about Jenny?'

'What bit?' Garp asked.

'The memorial?'

'God, no,' Garp said. 'A memorial *here?*'

'There are girls here now, you know,' Bodger said. 'I should say *women,*' he added, shaking his head. 'I don't know; they're awfully young. They're girls to me.'

'Students?' Garp said.

'Yes, students,' Bodger said. 'The girl students voted to name the infirmary after her.'

'The infirmary?' Garp said.

'Well, it's never had a name, you know,' Bodger said. 'Most of our buildings have names.'

'The Jenny Fields Infirmary,' Garp said, numbly.

'Sort of nice, isn't it?' Bodger asked; he wasn't too sure if Garp would think so, but Garp didn't care.

In the long night, baby Jenny woke up once; by the time Garp had moved himself away from Helen's warm and deeply sleeping body, he saw that Ellen James had already found the crying baby and was warming a bottle. Odd cooing and grunting sounds, appropriate to babies, came softly out of the tongueless mouth of Ellen James. She had worked in a day-care center in Illinois, she had written Garp on the plane. She knew all about babies, and could even make noises like them.

Garp smiled at her and went back to bed.

In the morning he told Helen about Ellen James and they talked about Ernie.

'It was good that he went in his sleep,' Helen said. 'When I think of your mother.'

'Yes, yes,' Garp told her.

Duncan was introduced to Ellen James. One-eyed and

no-tongued, thought Garp, my family will pull together.

When Roberta called to describe her arrest, Duncan – who was the least-tired talking human in the house – explained to her about Ernie's heart attack.

Helen found the turquoise jumpsuit and the huge, loaded bra in the kitchen wastebasket; it seemed to cheer her up. The cherry-colored vinyl boots actually fit her better than they had fit Garp, but she threw them out, anyway. Ellen James wanted the green scarf, and Helen took the girl shopping for some more clothes. Duncan asked for and received the wig, which – to Garp's irritation – he wore most of the morning.

Dean Bodger called, to ask to be of use.

A man who was the new director of Physical Facilities for the Steering School stopped at the house to talk confidentially with Garp. The Physical Facilities director explained that Ernie had lived in a school house, and as soon as it was convenient for Helen, Ernie's things should be moved out. Garp had understood that the original Steering family house, Midge Steering Percy's house, had been given back to the school some years ago – a gift of Midge and Fat Stew, for which a ceremony had been arranged. Garp told the Physical Facilities director that he hoped Helen had as much time to move out as Midge would be given.

'Oh, we'll *sell* that albatross,' the man confided to Garp. 'It's a lemon, you know.'

The Steering family house, in Garp's memory, was no lemon.

'All that history,' Garp said. 'I should think you'd want it – and it was a gift, after all.'

'The plumbing's terrible,' the man said. He implied that, in their advancing senility, Midge and Fat Stew had let the place fall into a wretched state. 'It may be a lovely old house, and all that,' the young man said, 'but the school has to look ahead. We've got enough *history* around here. We can't sink our housing funds into history. We need more buildings that the school can *use*. No matter what you do with that old mansion, it's just another family house.'

When Garp told Helen that the Steering Percy house was going to be sold, Helen broke down. Of course she was really crying for her father, and for everything, but the thought that the Steering School did not even *want* the grandest house of their childhood years depressed both Garp and Helen.

Then Garp had to check with the organist at the Steering chapel so that the same music would not be played for Ernie that, in the morning, would be played for Fat Stew. This mattered to Helen; she was upset, so Garp didn't question the seeming meaninglessness, to him, of his errand.

The Steering chapel was a squat Tudor attempt at a building; the church was so wreathed in ivy that it appeared to have thrust itself up out of the ground and was struggling to break through the matted vines. The pant legs of John Wolf's dark, pin-striped suit dragged under Garp's heels as he peered into the musty chapel – he had never delivered the suit to a proper tailor, but had attempted to take up the pants himself. The first wave of gray organ music drifted over Garp like smoke. He thought he had come early enough, but to his dread he saw that Fat Stew's funeral had already begun. The audience was old and hardly recognizable – those ancients of the Steering School community who would attend *anyone's* death, as if, in double sympathy, they were anticipating their own. *This* death, Garp thought, was chiefly attended because Midge was a Steering; Stewart Percy had made few friends. The pews were pockmarked with widows; their little black hats with veils were like dark cobwebs that had fallen on the heads of these old women.

'I'm glad you're here, Jack,' a man in black said to Garp. Garp had slipped almost unnoticed into a back pew; he was going to wait out the ordeal and then speak to the organist. 'We're short some muscle for the casket,' the man said, and Garp recognized him – he was the hearse driver from the funeral home.

'I'm not a pallbearer,' Garp whispered.

'You've *got* to be,' the driver said, 'or we'll never get him out of here. He's a *big* one.'

The hearse driver smelled of cigars, but Garp had only to glance about the sun-dappled pews of the Steering chapel to see that the man was right. White hair and baldness winked at him from the occasional male heads; there must have been thirteen or fourteen canes hooked on the pews. There were two wheelchairs.

Garp let the driver take his arm.

'They said there'd be more *men*,' the driver complained, 'but nobody healthy showed up.'

Garp was led to the pew up front, across from the family pew. To his horror an old man lay stretched out in the pew Garp was supposed to sit in and Garp was waved, instead, into the Percy pew, where he found himself seated next to Midge. Garp briefly wondered if the old man stretched out in the pew was another body waiting his turn.

'That's Uncle Harris Stanfull,' Midge whispered to Garp, nodding her head to the sleeper, who looked like a dead man across the aisle.

'Uncle *Horace Salter*, Mother,' said the man on Midge's other side. Garp recognized Stewie Two, red-faced with corpulence – the eldest Percy child and sole surviving son. He had something to do with aluminum in Pittsburgh. Stewie Two hadn't seen Garp since Garp was five; he showed no signs of knowing who Garp was. Neither did Midge indicate that she knew *any*body, anymore. Wizened and white, with brown blotches on her face the size and complexity of unshelled peanuts, Midge had a jitter in her head that made her bob in her pew like a chicken trying to make up its mind what to peck.

At a glance Garp saw that the pallbearing would be handled by Stewie Two, the hearse driver, and himself. He doubted that they could manage it. How awful to be this unloved! he thought, looking at the gray ship that was Stewart Percy's casket – fortunately closed.

'I'm sorry, young man,' Midge whispered to Garp; her gloved hand rested as lightly on his arm as one of the Percy family parakeets. 'I don't recall your *name*,' she said, gracious into senility.

'Uh,' Garp said. And somewhere between the names 'Smith' and 'Jones,' Garp stumbled on a word that escaped him. 'Smoans,' he said, surprising both Midge and himself. Stewie Two did not appear to notice.

'Mr Smoans?' Midge said.

'Yes, Smoans,' Garp said. 'Smoans, Class of '61. I had Mr Percy in history.' My Part of the Pacific.

'Oh, yes, Mr Smoans! How thoughtful of you to come,' Midge said.

'I was sorry to hear of it,' Mr Smoans said.

'Yes, we *all* were,' Midge said, looking cautiously around the half-empty chapel. A convulsion of some kind made her whole face shake, and the loose skin on her cheeks made a soft slapping noise.

'Mother,' Stewie Two cautioned her.

'Yes, yes, Stewart,' she said. To Mr Smoans, she said, 'It's a pity, not all of our children could be here.'

Garp, of course, knew that Dopey's strained heart had already quit him, that William was lost in a war, that Cushie was a victim of making babies. Garp guessed he knew, vaguely, where poor Pooh was. To his relief, Bainbridge Percy was *not* in the family pew.

It was there in the pew of remaining Percys that Garp remembered another day.

'Where do we go after we die?' Cushie Percy once asked her mother. Fat Stew belched and left the kitchen. All the Percy children were there: William, whom a war was waiting for; Dopey, whose heart was gathering fat; Cushie, who could not reproduce, whose vital tubes would tangle; Stewie Two, who turned into aluminum. And only God knows what happened to Pooh. Little Garp was there, too – in the sumptuous country kitchen of the vast, grand Steering family house.

'Well, after death,' Midge Steering Percy told the children – little Garp, too – 'we all go to a big *house*, sort of like this one.'

'But *bigger*,' Stewie Two said, seriously.

'I hope so,' said William, worriedly.

Dopey didn't get what was meant. Pooh was not old enough to talk. Cushie said she didn't believe it – only God knows where *she* went.

Garp thought of the vast, grand Steering family house – now for sale. He realized that he wanted to buy it.

'Mr Smoans?' Midge nudged him.

'Uh,' Garp said.

'The coffin, Jack,' whispered the hearse driver. Stewie Two, bulging beside him, looked seriously toward the enormous casket that now housed the debris of his father.

'We need four,' the driver said. 'At least four.'

'No, I can take one side myself,' Garp said.

'Mr Smoans looks very strong,' Midge said. 'Not very *large*, but strong.'

'Mother,' Stewie Two said.

'Yes, yes, Stewart,' she said.

'We need four. That's all there is to it,' the driver said.

Garp didn't believe it. *He* could lift it.

'You two on the other side,' he said, 'and up she goes.'

A frail mutter reached Garp from the mourners at Fat Stew's funeral, aghast at the apparently unmovable casket. But Garp believed in himself. It was just death in there; of course it would be heavy – the weight of his mother, Jenny Fields, the weight of Ernie Holm, and of little Walt (who was the heaviest of all). God knows what they all weighed together, but Garp planted himself on one side of Fat Stew's gray gunboat of a coffin. He was ready.

It was Dean Bodger who volunteered to be the necessary fourth.

'I never thought *you'd* be here,' Bodger whispered to Garp.

'Do you know Mr Smoans?' Midge asked the dean.

'Smoans, '61,' Garp said.

'Oh yes, *Smoans*, of course,' Bodger said. And the catcher of pigeons, the bandy-legged sheriff of the Steering School, lifted his share of the coffin with Garp and the others. Thus they launched Fat Stew into another life. Or into another house, hopefully bigger.

Bodger and Garp trailed behind the stragglers limping and tottering to the cars that would transport them to the Steering cemetery. When the aged audience was no more around them, Bodger took Garp to Buster's Snack and Grill, where they sat over coffee. Bodger apparently accepted that it was Garp's habit to disguise his sex in the evening and change his name during the day.

'Ah, Smoans,' Bodger said. 'Perhaps now your life will settle down and you'll be happy and prosperous.'

'At least prosperous,' Garp said.

Garp had completely forgotten to ask the organist not to repeat Fat Stew's music for Ernie Holm. Garp hadn't noticed the music, anyway; he wouldn't recognize it if it were repeated. And Helen hadn't been there; she wouldn't know the difference. Neither, Garp knew, would Ernie.

'Why don't you stay with us awhile?' Bodger asked Garp; with his strong, pudgy hand, sweeping the bleary windows in Buster's Snack and Grill, the dean indicated the campus of the Steering School. 'We're not a *bad* place, really,' he said.

'You're the only place I know,' Garp said, neutrally.

Garp knew that his mother had chosen Steering once, at least for a place to bring up children. And Jenny Fields, Garp knew, had right instincts. He drank his coffee and shook Dean Bodger's hand affectionately. Garp had one more funeral to get through. Then, with Helen, he would consider the future.

18

Habits of the Under Toad

Although she received a most cordial invitation from the Department of English, Helen was not sure about teaching at the Steering School.

'I thought you wanted to teach again,' Garp said, but Helen would wait awhile before accepting a job at the school where girls were not admitted when she was a girl.

'Perhaps, when Jenny's old enough to go,' Helen said. 'Meanwhile, I'm happy to read, just read.' As a writer, Garp was both envious and mistrustful of people who read as much as Helen.

And they were both developing a fearfulness that worried them; here they were, thinking so cautiously about their lives, as if they were truly old people. Of course Garp had always had this obsession about protecting his children; now, at last, he saw that Jenny Fields' old notion of wanting to continue living with her son was not so abnormal after all.

The Garps would stay at Steering. They had all the money they would ever need; Helen didn't *have* to do anything, if she didn't want to. But Garp needed something to do.

'You're going to write,' Helen said, tiredly.

'Not for a while,' Garp said. 'Maybe never again. At least not for a while.'

This really did strike Helen as a sign of rather premature senility, but she had come to share his anxiousness – his desire to keep what he had, including sanity – and she knew that he shared with her the vulnerability of conjugal love.

She did not say anything to him when he went to the Steering Athletic Department and offered himself as Ernie Holm's replacement. 'You don't have to pay me,' he told them. 'Money doesn't matter to me; I just want to be the wrestling coach.' Of course they had to admit he would do a decent job. What had been a strong program would begin to slump without a replacement for Ernie.

'You don't want any money?' the chairman of the Athletic Department asked him.

'I don't *need* any money,' Garp told him. 'What I need is something to *do* – something that's *not* writing.' Except for Helen, no one knew that there were only two things in this world that T. S. Garp ever learned to do: he could write and he could wrestle.

Helen was perhaps the only one who knew why he couldn't (at the moment) write. Her theory would later be expressed by the critic A. J. Harms, who claimed that Garp's work was progressively weakened by its closer and closer parallels to his personal history. 'As he became more autobiographical, his writing grew narrower; also, he became less comfortable about doing it. It was as if he knew that not only was the work more *personally* painful to him – this memory dredging – but the work was slimmer and less imaginative in every way,' Harms wrote. Garp had lost the freedom of *imagining* life truly, which he had so early promised himself, and us all, with the brilliance of 'The Pension Grillparzer.' According to Harms, Garp could now be truthful only by *remembering*, and that method – as distinct from imagining – was not only psychologically harmful to him but far less fruitful.

But the hindsight of Harms is easy; Helen knew this was Garp's problem the day he accepted the job as wrestling coach at the Steering School. He would be nowhere near as good as Ernie, they both knew, but he would run a respectable program and Garp's wrestlers would always win more than they would lose.

'Try fairy tales,' Helen suggested; she thought of his writing more often than *he* did. 'Try making something up, the whole thing – completely made up.' She never said, 'Like "The Pension Grillparzer"'; she never mentioned it, although she knew that he now agreed with her: it was the best he had done. Sadly, it had been the first.

Whenever Garp would try to write, he would see only the dull, undeveloped facts of his personal life: that gray parking lot in New Hampshire, the stillness of Walt's small body, the hunters' glossy coats and their red caps – and the sexless, self-righteous fanaticism of Pooh Percy. Those images went nowhere. He spent a great deal of time fussing with his new house.

Midge Steering Percy never knew who bought her family's mansion, and her gift to the Steering School. If Stewie Two ever found it out, he was at least smart enough never to tell his mother, whose memory of Garp was clouded by her fresher memory of the nice Mr Smoans. Midge Steering Percy died in a nursing home in Pittsburgh; because of what Stewie Two had to do with aluminum, he had moved his mother into a nursing home not far from where all that metal was made.

God knows what happened to Pooh.

Helen and Garp fixed up the old Steering mansion, as it was called by many in the school community. The name Percy faded fast; in most memories, now, Midge was always referred to as Midge *Steering*. Garp's new home was the classiest place on or near the Steering campus, and when the Steering students gave guided tours of the campus to parents, and to prospective Steering students, they rarely said, 'And this is where T. S. Garp, the writer, lives. It was the original Steering family house, circa 1781.' The students were more playful than that; what they usually said was, 'And this is where our wrestling coach lives.' And the parents would look at one another politely, and the prospective student would ask, 'Is wrestling a *big* sport at Steering?'

Very soon, Garp thought, Duncan would be a Steering

student; it was an unembarrassed pleasure that Garp looked forward to. He missed Duncan's presence in the wrestling room, but he was happy that the boy had found his place: the swimming pool – where either his nature or his eyesight, or both, felt completely comfortable. Duncan sometimes visited the wrestling room, swaddled in towels and shivering from the pool; he sat on the soft mats under one of the blow heaters, getting warm.

'How you doing?' Garp would ask him. 'You're not wet, are you? Don't drip on the mat, okay?'

'No, I won't,' Duncan would say. 'I'm just fine.'

More frequently, Helen visited the wrestling room. She was reading everything again, and she would come to the wrestling room to read – 'like reading in a sauna,' she often said – occasionally looking up from what she was reading when there was an unusually loud slam or a cry of pain. The only thing that had ever been hard for Helen, about reading in a wrestling room, was that her glasses kept fogging up.

'Are we already middle-aged?' Helen asked Garp one night in their beautiful house, from the front parlor of which, on a clear night, they could see the window squares of light in the Jenny Fields Infirmary; and look over the green-black lawn to the solitary night-light above the door of the infirmary annex – far away – where Garp had lived as a child.

'Jesus,' Garp said. 'Middle-aged? We are already *retired* – that's what we are. We skipped middle age altogether and moved directly into the world of the *elderly.*'

'Does that depress you?' Helen asked him, cautiously.

'Not yet,' Garp said. 'When it starts to depress me, I'll do something else. Or I'll do *some*thing, anyway. I figure, Helen, that we got a head start on everyone else. We can afford to take a long time-out.'

Helen grew tired of Garp's wrestling terminology, but she had grown up with it, after all; it was water off a duck, for Helen Holm. And although Garp wasn't writing, he seemed, to Helen, to be happy. Helen read in the evenings, and Garp watched TV.

*   *   *

Garp's work had developed a curious reputation, not altogether unlike what he would have wanted for himself, and even stranger than John Wolf had imagined. Although it embarrassed Garp and John Wolf to see how politically *The World According to Bensenhaver* was both admired and despised, the book's reputation had caused readers, even if for the wrong reasons, to return to Garp's earlier work. Garp politely refused invitations to speak at colleges, where he was wanted to represent one side or another of so-called women's issues; also, to speak on his relationship to his mother and her work, and the 'sex roles' he ascribed to various characters in his books. 'The destruction of art by sociology and psychoanalysis,' he called it. But there were an almost equal number of invitations for him simply to read from his own fiction; an occasional one or two of these – especially if it was somewhere Helen wanted to go – he accepted.

Garp was happy with Helen. He wasn't unfaithful to her, anymore; that thought seldom occurred to him. It was perhaps his contact with Ellen James that finally cured him of ever looking at young girls in that way. As for other women – Helen's age, and older – Garp exercised a willpower that was not especially difficult for him. Enough of his life had been influenced by lust.

Ellen James, who was eleven when she was raped and untongued, was nineteen when she moved in with the Garps. She was immediately an older sister to Duncan, and a fellow member of the maimed society to which Duncan shyly belonged. They were so close. She helped Duncan with his homework, because Ellen James was very good at reading and writing. Duncan interested Ellen in swimming, and in photography. Garp built them a darkroom in the Steering mansion, and they spent hours in the dark, developing and developing – Duncan's ceaseless babble, concerning lens openings and light, and the wordless *oooh*'s and *aaah*'s of Ellen James.

Helen bought them a movie camera, and Ellen and Duncan wrote a screenplay together and acted in their own movie – the story of a blind prince whose vision is partially restored by kissing a young cleaning woman. Only one of the prince's eyes is restored to sight because the cleaning woman allows the prince only to kiss her on the cheek. She is embarrassed to let anyone kiss her on the lips because she has lost her tongue. Despite their handicaps, and their compromises, the young couple marries. The involved story is told through pantomime and subtitles, which Ellen wrote. The best thing about the film, Duncan would say later, is that it's only seven minutes long.

Ellen James was also a great help to Helen with baby Jenny. Ellen and Duncan were expert babysitters with the girl, whom Garp took to the wrestling room on Sunday afternoons; there, he claimed, she would learn to walk and run and fall without hurting herself, although Helen claimed that the mat would give the child the misconception that the world underfoot felt like a barely firm sponge.

'But that is what the world *does* feel like,' Garp said.

Since he had stopped writing, the only ongoing friction in Garp's life concerned his relationship with his best friend, Roberta Muldoon. But Roberta was not the *source* of the friction. When Jenny Fields was dead and gone, Garp discovered that her estate was tremendous, and that Jenny, as if to plague her son, had designated *him* to be the executor of her last wishes for her fabulous loot and the mansion for wounded women at Dog's Head Harbor.

'Why *me?*' Garp had howled. 'Why not *you?*' Garp yelled at Roberta. But Roberta Muldoon was rather hurt that it *hadn't* been her.

'I can't imagine. Why you, indeed?' Roberta admitted. 'Of all people.'

'Mom was out to get me,' Garp decided.

'Or she was out to make you *think*,' Roberta suggested. 'What a good mother she was!'

'Oh boy,' Garp said.

For weeks he puzzled over the single sentence that stated Jenny's intentions for the spending of her money and the use of her enormous seacoast house.

I want to leave a place where worthy women can go to collect themselves *and just be themselves, by themselves.*

'Oh boy,' Garp said.

'A kind of foundation?' Roberta guessed.

'The Fields Foundation,' Garp suggested.

'That's terrific!' Roberta said. 'Yes, *grants* for women – and a place to go.'

'To go do *what*?' Garp said. 'And grants *for* what?'

'To go get well, if they have to, or to go be by themselves, if that's what they need,' Roberta said. 'And to write, if that's what they do – or paint.'

'Or a home for unwed mothers?' Garp said. 'A *grant* for "getting well"? Oh boy.'

'Be serious,' Roberta said. 'This is important. Don't you see? She wanted *you* to understand the need, she wanted you to have to deal with the problems.'

'And who decides if a woman is "worthy"?' Garp asked. 'Oh boy, Mom!' he cried out. 'I could wring your neck for this shit!'

'*You* decide,' Roberta said. '*That's* what will make you think.'

'How about *you*?' Garp asked. 'This is your kind of thing, Roberta.'

Roberta was clearly torn. She shared with Jenny Fields the desire to educate Garp and other men concerning the legitimacy and complexity of women's needs. She also thought Garp would be rather terrible at this, and she knew she would do it very well.

'We'll do it together,' Roberta said. 'That is, you're in charge, but I'll advise you. I'll tell you when I think you're making a mistake.'

'Roberta,' Garp said, 'you're *always* telling me I'm making a mistake.'

Roberta, at her most flirtatious, kissed him on the lips and clubbed him on the shoulder – in both cases, so hard that he winced.

'Jesus,' Garp said.

'The Fields Foundation!' Roberta cried. 'It's going to be wonderful.'

Thus was *friction* kept in the life of T. S. Garp, who without friction of some kind would probably have lost his senses and his grip upon the world. It was friction that kept Garp alive, when he wasn't writing; Roberta Muldoon and the Fields Foundation would provide him with friction, at the very least.

Roberta became the in-residence administrator of the Fields Foundation at Dog's Head Harbor; the house became, all at once, a writers' colony, a recovery center, and a birth-advisory clinic – and the few well-lit garret rooms provided light and solitude for painters. Once women knew that there *was* a Fields Foundation, there were many women who wondered who was eligible for aid. Garp wondered, too. All applicants wrote Roberta, who assembled a small staff of women who alternately liked and disliked Garp – but always argued with him. Together, twice a month, Roberta and her Board of Trustees would assemble in Garp's grouchy presence and choose among the applicants.

In good weather they sat in the balmy side-porch room of the Dog's Head Harbor estate, although Garp increasingly refused to go there. 'All the weirdos-in-residence,' Garp told Roberta. 'They remind me of other times.' So then they met at Steering, in the Steering family mansion, the wrestling coach's home, where Garp felt slightly more comfortable in the company of these fierce women.

He would have felt *more* comfortable, no doubt, to have met them all in the wrestling room. Though even there, Garp knew perfectly well, the former Robert Muldoon would have made Garp struggle for his every point.

*　　　*　　　*

Applicant No. 1,048 was named Charlie Pulaski.

'I thought they had to be *women*,' Garp said. 'I thought there was at least *one* firm criterion.'

'Charlie Pulaski *is* a woman,' Roberta told Garp. 'She's just always been called Charlie.'

'I should say that was enough to disqualify her,' someone said. It was Marcia Fox – a lean, spare poet with whom Garp frequently crossed swords, although he admired her poems. He could never be that economical.

'What does Charlie Pulaski *want*?' Garp asked, by rote. Some of the applicants only wanted money; some of them wanted to live at Dog's Head Harbor for a while. Some of them wanted lots of money *and* a room at Dog's Head Harbor, forever.

'She just wants money,' Roberta said.

'To change her name?' asked Marcia Fox.

'She wants to quit her job and write a book,' Roberta said.

'Oh boy,' said Garp.

'Advise her to keep her job,' said Marcia Fox; she was one of those writers who resented other writers, and would-be writers.

'Marcia even resents *dead* writers,' Garp told Roberta.

But Marcia and Garp both read a manuscript submitted by Ms Charlie Pulaski, and they agreed that she should hold on to whatever job she could get.

Applicant No. 1,073, an associate professor of microbiology, wanted time off from her job to write a book, too.

'A novel?' Garp asked.

'Studies in molecular virology,' said Dr Joan Axe; she was on leave from the Duke University Medical Center to do some research of her own. When Garp asked her what it was, she had told him, mysteriously, that she was interested in 'the unseen diseases of the bloodstream.'

*　　　*　　　*

Applicant No. 1,081 had an uninsured husband who was killed in a plane crash. She had three children under the age of five and she needed fifteen more semester hours to complete her M.A. degree, in French. She wanted to go back to school, get the degree, and find a decent job; she wanted money for this – and rooms enough for her children, and for a babysitter, at Dog's Head Harbor.

The Board of Trustees unanimously decided to award the woman sufficient money to complete her degree and to pay a live-in babysitter; but the children, the babysitter, *and* the woman would all have to live wherever the woman chose to complete her degree. Dog's Head Harbor was *not* for children and babysitters. There were women there who would go crazy upon the sight or sound of a single child. There were women there whose lives had been made miserable by babysitters.

That was an easy one to decide.

No. 1,088 caused some problems. She was the divorced wife of the man who had killed Jenny Fields. She had three children, one of whom was in a reform school for preteens, and her child-support payments had stopped when her husband, Jenny Fields' assassin, was shot by a barrage from the New Hampshire State Police and some other hunters with guns who had been cruising the parking lot.

The deceased, Kenny Truckenmiller, had been divorced less than a year. He'd told friends that the child support was breaking his ass; he said that women's lib had screwed up his wife so much that she divorced him. The lawyer who got the job done, in favor of Mrs Truckenmiller, was a New York divorcee. Kenny Truckenmiller had beaten his wife at least twice weekly for almost thirteen years, and he had physically and mentally abused each of his three children on several occasions. But Mrs Truckenmiller had not known enough about herself, or what rights she might possibly have, until she read *A Sexual Suspect*, the autobiography of Jenny Fields. That started her thinking that perhaps the suffering of her weekly beatings, and the abuse of her children, was actually Kenny Truckenmiller's fault; for thirteen years she had thought it was *her* problem, and her 'lot in life.'

Kenny Truckenmiller had blamed the women's movement for the self-education of his wife. Mrs Truckenmiller had always been self-employed, a 'hairstylist' in the town of North Mountain, New Hampshire. She went right on being a hairstylist when Kenny was forced, by the court, to move out of her house. But now that Kenny was no longer driving a truck for the town, Mrs Truckenmiller found the support of her family difficult by hairstyling alone. She wrote in her nearly illegible application that she had been forced to compromise herself 'to make ends meet,' and that she did not care to repeat the act of compromising herself in the future.

Mrs Truckenmiller, who never once referred to herself as having a first name, realized that the loathing for her husband was so great as to prejudice the board against her. She would understand, she wrote, if they chose to ignore her.

John Wolf, who was (against his will) an honorary member of the board – and valued for his shrewd financial head – said immediately that nothing could be better or wider publicity for the Fields Foundation than awarding 'this unfortunate relation of Jenny's killer' what she asked for. It would be instant news; it would show the nonpolitical nature of the foundation's intentions; it would pay for itself, John Wolf decided, in that it would surely gain the foundation untold sums in gift donations.

'We're already doing pretty well on gift donations,' Garp hedged.

'Suppose she's just a whore?' Roberta suggested of the unfortunate Mrs Truckenmiller; they all stared at her. Roberta had an advantage among them: of being able to think like a woman *and* like a Philadelphia Eagle. 'Just think a minute,' Roberta said. 'Suppose she's just a floozy, someone who *compromises herself* all the time, and always has – and thinks nothing of it. Then, suddenly, we're a *joke*; then we've been had.'

'So we need a character reference,' said Marcia Fox.

'Someone's got to see the woman, talk with her,' Garp suggested. 'Find out if she's honorable, if she's really *trying* to live independently.'

They all stared at him.

'Well,' Roberta said, '*I'm* not about to discover whether she's a whore or not.'

'Oh no,' Garp said. 'Not *me*.'

'Where's North Mountain, New Hampshire?' asked Marcia Fox.

'Not *me*,' John Wolf said. 'I'm out of New York too much of the time as it is.'

'Oh boy,' Garp said. 'Suppose she recognizes me? People *do*, you know.'

'I doubt *she* will,' said Hilma Bloch, a psychiatric social worker whom Garp detested. 'Those people most motivated to read autobiographies, such as your mother's, are rarely attracted to fiction – or only tangentially. That is, if she read *The World According to Bensenhaver* she would have done so only because of who you are. And that would not have been sufficient reason to cause her to finish the book; in all probability – and given the fact that she's a hairstylist, after all – she would have bogged down and *not* read it. And not remembered your picture on the cover, either – only your face, and only vaguely (you *were* a face in the news, of course, but really only around the time of Jenny's murder). Surely, at that time, Jenny's face was the face to recall. A woman like this watches a lot of television; she's not a book-world person. I strongly doubt that a woman like this would even have a picture of you in her mind.'

John Wolf rolled his eyes away from Hilma Bloch. Even Roberta rolled her eyes.

'Thank you, Hilma,' said Garp, quietly. It was decided that Garp would visit Mrs Truckenmiller 'to determine something more concrete about her character.'

'At least find out her first name,' said Marcia Fox.

'I'll bet it's Charlie,' Roberta said.

They passed on to the reports: who was living, presently, at Dog's Head Harbor; whose tenancy was expiring; who was about to move in. And what were the problems there, if any?

There were two painters – one in the south garret, one in the north. The south-garret painter coveted the north-garret painter's *light,* and for two weeks they didn't get along; not a word to each other at breakfast, and accusations concerning lost mail. And so forth. Then, it appeared, they became lovers. Now only the north-garret painter was painting at all – studies of the south-garret painter, who modeled all day in the good light. Her nakedness, about the upstairs of the house, bothered at least one of the writers, an outspoken anti-lesbian playwright from Cleveland who had trouble sleeping, she said, because of the sound of the waves. It was probably the lovemaking of the painters that bothered her; she was described as 'overextended,' anyway, but her complaints ceased once the other writer-in-residence suggested that all the Dog's Head Harbor guests read aloud the parts of the dramatist's play in progress. This was done, successfully for all, and the upper floors of the house were now happy.

The 'other writer,' a good short-story writer whom Garp had enthusiastically recommended a year ago, was about to move out, however; her term of residency was expiring. Who would go in her room?

The woman whose mother-in-law had just won custody of her children, following the suicide of her husband?

'I *told* you not to accept her,' Garp said.

The two Ellen Jamesians who just, one day, showed up?

'Now wait a minute,' Garp said. 'What's this? Ellen Jamesians? Showing up? That's not allowed.'

'Jenny always took them in,' Roberta said.

'This is *now*, Roberta,' Garp said.

The other members of the board were more or less

in agreement with him; Ellen Jamesians were not much admired – they never had been, and their radicalism (now) seemed growingly obsolete and pathetic.

'It's almost a tradition, though,' Roberta said. She described two 'old' Ellen Jamesians, who'd been back from a bad time in California. Years ago they had stayed at Dog's Head Harbor; returning there, Roberta argued, was a kind of sentimental recovery for them.

'Jesus, Roberta,' Garp said. 'Get rid of them.'

'They were people your mother always took care of,' Roberta said.

'At least they'll be *quiet*,' said Marcia Fox, whose economy of tongue Garp *did* admire. But only Garp laughed.

'I think you should get them to leave, Roberta,' Dr Joan Axe said.

'They really resent the entire *society*,' Hilma Bloch said. 'That could be infectious. On the other hand, they are almost the essence of the *spirit* of the place.'

John Wolf rolled his eyes.

'There is the doctor researching cancer-related abortions,' Joan Axe said. 'What about her?'

'Yes, put *her* on the second floor,' Garp said. 'I've *met* her. She'll scare the shit out of anyone who tries to come upstairs.' Roberta frowned.

The downstairs of the Dog's Head Harbor mansion was the largest part, containing two kitchens and four complete baths; as many as twelve could sleep, very privately, downstairs, and there were still the various conference rooms, as Roberta now called them – they were parlors and giant dens in the days of Jenny Fields. And a vast dining room where food, mail, and whoever wanted company collected all during the day and night.

It was the most social floor of Dog's Head Harbor, usually not suited for the writers and painters. It was the best floor for the potential suicides, Garp had told the board, 'because they'll be forced to drown themselves in the ocean rather than jump out the windows.'

But Roberta ran the place in a strong, motherly, tight-end fashion; she could talk almost anyone out of anything, and if she couldn't, she could overpower anybody. She had been much more successful at making the local police her allies than Jenny ever had been. Occasional unhappies were picked up by the police, far down the beach, or wailing on the boardwalks of the village; they were always gently returned to Roberta. The Dog's Head Harbor Police were all football fans, full of respect for the savage line play and the vicious downfield blocking of the former Robert Muldoon.

'I would like to make a motion that *no* Ellen Jamesian be eligible for aid and comfort from the Fields Foundation,' Garp said.

'Second,' said Marcia Fox.

'This is open to discussion,' Roberta told them all. 'I don't see the necessity of having such a rule. We are not in the business of supporting what we largely would agree is a stupid form of political expression, but that doesn't mean that one of these women without a tongue couldn't be genuinely in need of help – I'd say, in fact, they have already demonstrated a definite need to locate themselves, and we can expect to go on hearing from them. They are truly needful people.'

'They are insane,' Garp said.

'This is too general,' said Hilma Bloch.

'There *are* productive women,' Marcia Fox said, 'who have *not* given up their voices – in fact, they are fighting to *use* their voices – and I am not in favor of rewarding stupidity and self-imposed silence.'

'There are virtues in silence,' Roberta argued.

'Jesus, Roberta,' Garp said. And then he saw a light in this dark subject. For some reason, the Ellen Jamesians made him angrier than his image, even, of the Kenny Trucken-millers of this world; and although he saw that the Ellen Jamesians were fading from fashion, they could not fade fast enough to suit Garp. He wanted them gone; he wanted them more than gone – he wanted them disgraced. Helen had already told him that his hatred of them was inappropriate to what they were.

'It's just madness, and simpleminded – what they've done,' Helen said. 'Why can't you ignore them, and leave them alone?'

But Garp said, 'Let's ask Ellen James. That's fair, isn't it? Let's ask Ellen James for *her* opinion of the Ellen Jamesians. Jesus, I'd like to *publish* her opinion of them. Do you know how they've made *her* feel?'

'This is too personal a matter,' Hilma Bloch said. They had all met Ellen; they all knew that Ellen James *hated* being tongueless and hated the Ellen Jamesians.

'Let's back off this, for now,' John Wolf said. 'I move we table the motion.'

'Damn,' Garp said.

'All right, Garp,' Roberta said. 'Let's vote it, right now.' They all knew they would vote it down. That would get rid of it.

'I withdraw the motion,' Garp said, nastily. 'Long live the Ellen Jamesians.'

But *he* did not withdraw.

It was madness that had killed Jenny Fields, his mother. It was extremism. It was self-righteous, fanatical, and monstrous self-pity. Kenny Truckenmiller was only a special kind of moron: a true believer who was also a thug. He was a man who pitied himself so blindly that he could make absolute enemies out of people who contributed only the ideas to his undoing.

And how was an Ellen Jamesian any different? Was not her gesture as desperate, and as empty of an understanding of human complexity?

'Come *on*,' John Wolf said. 'They haven't *murdered* anyone.'

'Not yet,' Garp said. 'They have the equipment. They are capable of making mindless decisions, and they believe they are so *right*.'

'There's more to killing someone than that,' Roberta said. They let Garp seethe. What else could they do? It was not one of Garp's better points: tolerance of the intolerant. Crazy people made him crazy. It was as if he personally resented them giving in to madness – in part, because he so frequently labored to behave sanely. When some people gave up the labor of sanity, or failed at it, Garp suspected them of not trying hard enough.

'Tolerance of the intolerant is a difficult task that the times asks of us,' Helen said. Although Garp knew Helen was intelligent, and often more far-seeing than he was, he was rather blind about the Ellen Jamesians.

They, of course, were rather blind about him.

The most radical criticism of Garp – concerning his relationship to his mother *and* his own works – had come from various Ellen Jamesians. Baited by them, he baited them back. It was hard to see why it should have started, or *if* it should have, but Garp had become a case of controversy among feminists largely through the goading of Ellen Jamesians – and Garp goading them in return. For the very *same* reasons, Garp was liked by many feminists and disliked by as many.

As for the Ellen Jamesians, they were no more complicated in their feelings for Garp than they were complicated in their symbology: their tongues hacked off for the hacked-off tongue of Ellen James.

Ironically, it would be Ellen James who escalated this longtime cold war.

She was in the habit, constantly, of showing Garp her writing – her many stories, her remembrances of her parents, of Illinois; her poems; her painful analogies to speechlessness; her appreciations of the visual arts, and swimming. She wrote wisely and craftily and with penetrating energy.

'She's the real thing,' Garp kept telling Helen. 'She's got the ability, but she's also got the passion. And I believe she'll have the stamina.'

The aforementioned 'stamina' was a word Helen let slide away, because she feared for Garp that he had given up his.

He certainly had the ability, and the passion; but she felt he'd also taken a narrow path – he'd been misdirected – and only stamina would let him grow back in all the other ways.

It saddened her. For the time being, Helen kept thinking, she would content herself with whatever Garp got passionate about – the wrestling, even the Ellen Jamesians. Because, Helen believed, energy begets energy – and sooner or later, she thought, he would write again.

So Helen did not interfere too vehemently when Garp got excited about the essay Ellen James showed him. The essay was: 'Why I'm Not an Ellen Jamesian,' by Ellen James. It was powerful and touching and it moved Garp to tears. It recounted her rape, her difficulty with it, her parents' difficulty with it; it made what the Ellen Jamesians did seem like a shallow, wholly political imitation of a very private trauma. Ellen James said that the Ellen Jamesians had only prolonged her anguish; they had made her into a very public casualty. Of course, Garp was susceptible to being moved by public casualties.

And of course, to be fair, the better of the Ellen Jamesians had *meant* to publicize the general dread that so brutally menaced women and girls. For many of the Ellen Jamesians, the imitation of the horrible untonguing had not been 'wholly political.' It had been a most personal identification. In some cases, of course, Ellen Jamesians were women who had also been raped; what they meant was that they *felt* as if their tongues were gone. In a world of men, they felt as if they had been shut up forever.

That the organization was full of crazies, no one would deny. Not even some Ellen Jamesians would have denied that. It was generally true that they were an inflammatory political group of feminist extremists who often detracted from the extreme seriousness of other women, and other feminists, around them. But Ellen James' attack on them was as inconsiderate of the occasional individuals among the Ellen Jamesians as the action of the group had been inconsiderate of Ellen James – not really thinking how an eleven-year-old girl would have preferred to get over her horror more privately.

Everyone in America knew how Ellen James had lost her tongue, except the younger generation, just now growing up, who often confused Ellen with the Ellen Jamesians; this was a most painful confusion for Ellen, because it meant that she was suspected of having done it to herself.

'It was a necessary rage for her to have,' Helen said to Garp, about Ellen's essay. 'I'm sure she needed to write it, and it's done her a world of good to say all this. I've told her that.'

'*I've* told her she should publish it,' Garp said.

'No,' Helen said. 'I really don't think so. What good does it do?'

'What *good?*' Garp asked. 'Well, it's the *truth*. And it will be good for Ellen.'

'And for *you?*' Helen asked, knowing that he wanted a kind of public humiliation of the Ellen Jamesians.

'Okay,' he said, 'okay, okay. But she's *right*, goddamnit. Those nuts ought to hear it from the original source.'

'But why?' said Helen. 'For whose good?'

'Good, good,' Garp muttered, though in his heart he must have known that Helen was right. He told Ellen she should file her essay. Ellen wouldn't communicate with either Garp or Helen for a week.

It was not until John Wolf called Garp that either Garp or Helen realized Ellen had sent the essay to John Wolf.

'What am I supposed to do with it?' he asked.

'God, send it back,' Helen said.

'No, damn it,' Garp said. 'Ask *Ellen* what she wants you to do with it.'

'Old Pontius Pilate, washing his hands,' Helen said to Garp.

'What do *you* want to do with it?' Garp asked John Wolf.

'*Me?*' John Wolf said. 'It means nothing to me. But I'm sure it's publishable. I mean, it's very well written.'

'That's not why it's publishable,' Garp said, 'and you know it.'

'Well, no,' John Wolf said. 'But it's also *nice* that it's well said.'

Ellen told John Wolf she wanted it published. Helen tried to talk her out of it. Garp refused to get involved.

'You *are* involved,' Helen told him, 'and by saying nothing,' you know you'll get what you want: that painful attack published. That's what you want.'

So Garp spoke to Ellen James. He tried to be enthusiastic in his reasoning to her – why she shouldn't publicly say all those things. These women were sick, sad, confused, tortured, abused by others, and now self-abused – but what point was there in criticizing them? Everyone would forget them in another five years. They'll hand out their notes and people will say, 'What's an Ellen Jamesian? You mean you can't talk? You got no tongue?'

Ellen looked sullen and determined.

I won't forget them!

she wrote Garp.

Not in 5 years, not in 50 years will I ever forget them; I will remember them the way I remember my tongue.

Garp admired how the girl liked to use the good old semicolon. He said softly, 'I think it's better not to publish this, Ellen.'

Will you be angry with me if I do?

she asked.

He admitted he would not be angry.

And Helen?

'Helen will only be angry with *me*,' Garp said.

'You make people too angry,' Helen told him, in bed. 'You get them all wound up. You *inflame*. You should lay off. You should do your own work, Garp. Just your own work. You used to say politics were stupid, and they meant nothing to you. You were right. They *are* stupid, they *do* mean nothing. You're doing this because it's *easier* than sitting down and making something up, from scratch. And you know it. You're building bookshelves all over the house, and finishing floors, and fucking around in the *garden*, for Christ's sake.

'Did I marry a handyman? Did I ever expect you to be a crusader?

'You should be writing the books and letting other people make the shelves. And you know I'm right, Garp.'

'You're right,' he said.

He tried to remember what had enabled him to imagine that first sentence of 'The Pension Grillparzer.'

'My father worked for the Austrian Tourist Bureau.'

Where had it come from? He tried to think of sentences like it. What he got was a sentence like this: 'The boy was five years old; he had a cough that seemed deeper than his small, bony chest.' What he got was memory, and that made muck. He had no pure imagination anymore.

In the wrestling room, he worked out three straight days with the heavyweight. To punish himself?

'More fucking around in the garden, so to speak,' said Helen.

Then he announced he had a mission, a trip to make for the Fields Foundation. To North Mountain, New Hampshire. To determine if a Fields Foundation Fellowship would be wasted on a woman named Truckenmiller.

'More fucking around in the garden,' Helen said. 'More bookshelves. More politics. More crusades. That's the kind of thing people do who *can't* write.'

But he was gone; he was out of the house when John Wolf called to say that a very well read and much seen magazine

was going to publish 'Why I'm Not an Ellen Jamesian,' by
Ellen James.

John Wolf's voice over the phone had the cold, unseen,
quick flick of the tongue of old You-Know-Who – the Under
Toad, that's who, Helen thought. But she didn't know why;
not yet.

She told Ellen James the news. Helen forgave Ellen,
immediately, and even allowed herself to be excited with
her. They took a drive to the shore with Duncan and little
Jenny. They bought lobsters – Ellen's favorite – and enough
scallops for Garp, who was not crazy about lobster.

Champagne!

Ellen wrote in the car.

Does champagne go with lobster and scallops?

'Of course,' Helen said. 'It *can*.' They bought champagne.
They stopped at Dog's Head Harbor and invited Roberta to
dinner.

'When will Dad be back?' Duncan asked.

'I don't know where North Mountain, New Hampshire,
is,' Helen said, 'but he *said* he'd be back in time to eat with
us.'

That's what he told me, too,

said Ellen James.

NANETTE'S BEAUTY SALON in North Mountain, New Hampshire, was really the kitchen of Mrs Kenny Truckenmiller,
whose first name was Harriet.

'Are you Nanette?' Garp asked her timidly, from the
outside steps, frosted with salt and crunchy with melting
slush.

'There ain't no Nanette,' she told him. 'I'm Harriet

Truckenmiller.' Behind her, in the dark kitchen, a large dog strained and snarled; Mrs Truckenmiller kept the dog from getting to Garp by thrusting her long hip back against the lunging beast. Her pale, scarred ankle wedged open the kitchen door. Her slippers were blue; in her long robe, her figure was lost, but Garp could see she was tall – and that she had been taking a bath.

'Uh, do you do *men's* hair?' he asked her.

'No,' she said.

'But *would* you?' Garp asked her. 'I don't trust barbers.'

Harriet Truckenmiller looked suspiciously at Garp's black knit ski hat, which was pulled down over his ears and concealed all his hair but the thick tufts that touched his shoulders from the back of his short neck.

'I can't see your hair,' she said. He took the stocking hat off, his hair wild with static electricity and tangled in the cold wind.

'I don't want just a haircut,' Garp said, neutrally, eyeing the woman's sad, drawn face and the soft wrinkles beside her gray eyes. Her own hair, a washed-out blond, was in curlers.

'You don't have no appointment,' Harriet Truckenmiller said.

The woman was no whore, he could plainly see. She was tired and frightened of him.

'What exactly do you want done to your hair, anyway?' she asked him.

'Just a trim,' Garp mumbled, 'but I like a slight curl in it.'

'A curl?' said Harriet Truckenmiller, trying to imagine this from Garp's crown of very straight hair. 'Like a permanent, you mean?' she asked.

'Well,' he said, running his hand sheepishly through the snarls. 'Whatever you can do with it, you know?'

Harriet Truckenmiller shrugged. 'I have to get dressed,' she said. The dog, devious and strong, thrust most of his stout body between her legs and jammed his broad, grimacing face into the opening between the storm and the main door. Garp tensed for the attack, but Harriet Truckenmiller brought her big knee up sharply and staggered the animal with a blow to its muzzle. She twisted her hand into the loose skin of its neck; the dog moaned and melted into the kitchen behind her.

The frozen yard, Garp saw, was a mosaic of the dog's huge turds captured in ice. There were also three cars in the yard; Garp doubted if any of them ran. There was a woodpile, but no one had stacked it. There was a TV antenna, which at one time might have been on the roof; now it leaned against the beige aluminum siding of the house, its wires running like a spiderweb out a cracked window.

Mrs Truckenmiller stepped back and opened the door for Garp. In the kitchen he felt his eyes dry from the heat of the wood stove; the room smelled of baking cookies and hair rinse – in fact, the kitchen seemed divided between the functions of a kitchen and the paraphernalia of Harriet's business. A pink sink with a shampoo hose; cans of stewed tomatoes; a three-way mirror framed with stage lights; a wooden rack with spices and meat tenderizer; the rows of ointments, lotions, and goo. And a steel stool over which a hair dryer hung suspended from a steel rod – like an original invention of an electric chair.

The dog was gone, and so was Harriet Truckenmiller; she had slipped away to dress herself, and her surly companion appeared to have gone with her. Garp combed his hair; he looked in the mirror as if he were trying to remember himself. He was about to be altered and rendered unrecognizable to all, he imagined.

Then the door to the outside opened and a big man in a hunting coat with a hunter's red cap walked in; he had an enormous armload of wood, which he carried to the wood box by the stove. The dog, who all along had been crouched under the sink – inches away from Garp's trembling knees – moved quickly to intercept the man. The dog slunk quietly, not even growling; the man was known here.

'Go lie down, you damn fool,' he said, and the dog did as it was told.

'Is that you, Dickie?' called Harriet Truckenmiller, from somewhere in another part of the house.

'Who else was you expectin'?' he shouted; then he turned and saw Garp in front of the mirror.

'Hello,' Garp said. The big man called Dickie stared. He was perhaps fifty; his huge red face looked scraped by ice, and Garp recognized immediately, from his familiarity with Duncan's expressions, that the man had a glass eye.

''Lo,' Dickie said.

'I got a customer!' Harriet called.

'I see you do,' said Dickie. Garp nervously touched his hair, as if he could suggest to Dickie how important his hair was to him – to have come all the way to North Mountain, New Hampshire, and NANETTE'S BEAUTY SALON, for what must have appeared to Dickie to be the simple need of a haircut.

'He wants a *curl*!' called Harriet. Dickie kept his red cap on, though Garp could plainly see that the man was bald.

'I don't know what you *really* want, fella,' Dickie whispered to Garp, 'but a curl is all you get. You hear?'

'I don't trust barbers,' Garp said.

'I don't trust *you*,' Dickie said.

'Dickie, he hasn't done anything,' Harriet Truckenmiller said. She was dressed in rather tight turquoise slacks, which reminded Garp of his discarded jumpsuit, and a print blouse full of flowers that never grow in New Hampshire. Her hair was tied back with a scarf of unmatching plants, and she had done her face, but not overdone it; she looked 'nice,' like somebody's mother who bothered to keep herself up. She was, Garp guessed, a few years younger than Dickie, but just a few.

'He don't want no *curl*, Harriet,' Dickie said. 'What's he want to have his hair played with for, huh?'

'He don't trust barbers,' Harriet Truckenmiller said. For

a brief moment Garp wondered if Dickie were a barber; he didn't think so.

'I really don't mean any disrespect,' Garp said. He had seen all he needed to see; he wanted to go tell the Fields Foundation to give Harriet Truckenmiller all the money she needed. 'If this makes anyone uncomfortable,' Garp said, 'I'll just forget it.' He reached for his parka, which he'd put on an empty chair, but the big dog had the parka pinned down on the floor.

'Please, you can stay,' Mrs Truckenmiller said. 'Dickie's just lookin' after me.' Dickie looked ashamed of himself; he stood with one mighty boot on top of the other.

'I brung you some dry wood,' he said to Harriet. 'I guess I shoulda *knocked*.' He pouted by the stove.

'*Don't*, Dickie,' Harriet said to him, and she kissed him fondly on his big pink cheek.

He left the kitchen with one last glare for Garp.

'Hope you get a good haircut,' Dickie said.

'Thank you,' said Garp. When he spoke, the dog shook his parka.

'Here, stop that,' Harriet told the dog; she put Garp's parka back on the chair. 'You can go if you want to,' Harriet said, 'but Dickie won't bother you. He's just lookin' after me.'

'Your husband?' Garp asked, though he doubted it.

'My husband was Kenny Truckenmiller,' Harriet said. 'Everybody knows that, and no matter who you are, you know who *he* was.'

'Yes,' Garp said.

'Dickie's my brother. He just worries about me,' Harriet said. 'Some guys have been messin' around, since Kenny's gone.' She sat at the bright counter of mirrors, beside Garp, and leaned her long, veiny hands on her turquoise thighs. She sighed. She did not look at Garp when she spoke. 'I don't know what you heard, and I don't care,' she said. 'I do *hair – just* hair. If you really want somethin' done to your hair, I'll do it. But that's all I do,' Harriet said. 'No matter what anybody told you, I don't mess around. Just hair.'

'Just hair,' Garp said. 'I just want my hair done, that's all.'

'That's good,' she said, still not looking at him.

There were little photographs stuck under the molding and framed against the mirrors. One was a wedding picture of young Harriet Truckenmiller and her grinning husband, Kenny. They were awkwardly maiming a cake.

Another photograph was of a pregnant Harriet Truckenmiller holding a young baby; there was another child, maybe Walt's age, leaning his cheek against her hip. Harriet looked tired but not daunted. And there was a photograph of Dickie; he was standing next to Kenny Truckenmiller, and they were both standing next to a gutted deer, hung upside-down from the branch of a tree. The tree was in the front yard of NANETTE'S BEAUTY SALON. Garp recognized that photograph quickly; he had seen it in a national magazine after Jenny's assassination. The photograph apparently demonstrated to the simpleminded that Kenny Truckenmiller was a born-and-raised killer: besides shooting Jenny Fields, he had at one time shot a deer.

'Why *Nanette?*' Garp asked Harriet later, when he dared look only at her patient fingers and not at her unhappy face – and not at his hair.

'I thought it sounded sort of French,' Harriet said, but she knew he was from somewhere in the outside world – outside North Mountain, New Hampshire – and she laughed at herself.

'Well, it *does*,' Garp said, laughing with her. 'Sort of,' he added, and they both laughed in a friendly way.

When he was ready to go, she wiped the slobber of the dog off his parka with a sponge. 'Aren't you even going to look at it?' she asked him. She meant the hairdo; he took a breath and confronted himself in the three-way mirror. His hair, he thought, was beautiful! It was his same old hair, the same color, even the same length, but it seemed to fit his head for the first time in his life. His hair clung to his skull, yet it was still light and fluffy; a slight wave in it made his broken nose and his squat neck appear less severe. Garp seemed to himself to fit his own face in a way he had never thought possible. This was the first beauty salon he had ever been to, of course. In fact, Jenny had cut his hair until he married Helen, and Helen had cut his hair after that; he had never even been to a barber.

'It's lovely,' he said; his missing ear remained artfully hidden.

'Oh, go on,' Harriet said, giving him a pleasant little shove – but, he would tell the Fields Foundation, *not* a suggestive shove; not at all. He wanted to tell her then that he was Jenny Fields' son, but he knew that his motive for doing so would have been wholly selfish – to have been personally responsible for moving someone.

'It is unfair to take advantage of anyone's emotional vul-nerability,' wrote the polemical Jenny Fields. Thus Garp's new creed: capitalize not on the emotions of others. 'Thank you and good-bye,' he said to Mrs Truckenmiller.

Outside, Dickie wielded a splitting ax in the woodpile. He did it very well. He stopped splitting when Garp appeared. 'Good-bye,' Garp called to him, but Dickie walked over to Garp – with the ax.

'Let's get a look at the hairdo,' Dickie said.

Garp stood still while Dickie examined him.

'You were a friend of Kenny Truckenmiller's?' Garp asked.

'Yup,' Dickie said. 'I was his *only* friend. I introduced him to Harriet,' Dickie said. Garp nodded. Dickie eyed the new hairdo.

'It's tragic,' Garp said; he meant everything that had happened.

'It ain't bad,' Dickie said; he meant Garp's hair.

'Jenny Fields was my mother,' Garp said, because he wanted someone to know, and he felt certain he was taking no emotional advantage of Dickie.

'You didn't tell *her* that, did you?' Dickie said, pointing toward the house, and Harriet, with his long ax.

'No, no,' Garp said.

'That's good,' Dickie said. 'She don't want to hear nothin' like that.'

'I didn't think so,' Garp said, and Dickie nodded approvingly. 'Your sister is a very nice woman,' Garp added.

'She *is*, she is,' Dickie said, nodding fiercely.

'Well, so long,' Garp said. But Dickie touched him lightly with the handle of the ax.

'I was one of them who shot him,' Dickie said. 'You know that?'

'You shot Kenny?' Garp said.

'I was *one* of them who did,' Dickie said. 'Kenny was crazy. Somebody had to shoot him.'

'I'm very sorry,' Garp said. Dickie shrugged.

'I liked the guy,' Dickie said. 'But he got crazy at Harriet, and he got crazy at your mother. He wouldn't ever have got well, you know,' Dickie said. 'He just got sick about women. He got sick for good. You could tell he wasn't ever going to get over it.'

'A terrible thing,' said Garp.

'So long,' Dickie said; he turned back to his woodpile. Garp turned toward his car, across the frozen turds that dotted the yard. 'Your hair looks good!' Dickie called to him. The remark seemed sincere. Dickie was splitting logs again when Garp waved to him from the driver's seat of his car. In the window of NANETTE'S BEAUTY SALON Harriet Truckenmiller waved to Garp: it was not a wave meant to encourage him, or anything, he was quite sure. He drove back through the village of North Mountain – he drank a cup of coffee in the one diner, he got gas at the one gas station. Everyone looked at his pretty hair. In every mirror, *Garp* looked at his pretty hair! Then he drove home, arriving in time for the celebration: Ellen's first publication.

If it made him as uneasy as the news had made Helen, he did not admit it. He sat through the lobster, the scallops, and the champagne, waiting for Helen or Duncan to comment on his hair. It was only when he was doing the dishes that Ellen James handed him a soggy note.

You had your hair done?

He nodded, irritably.

'I don't like it,' Helen told him, in bed.

'I think it's terrific,' Garp said.

'It's not like you,' Helen said; she was doing her best to muss it up. 'It looks like the hair on a corpse,' she said in the darkness.

'A corpse!' Garp said. 'Jesus.'

'A body prepared by an undertaker,' said Helen, almost frantically running her hands through his hair. 'Every little hair in place,' she said. 'It's too perfect. You don't look alive!' she said. Then she cried and cried and Garp held her and whispered to her – trying to find out what the matter was.

Garp did not share her sense of the Under Toad – not this time – and he talked and talked to her, and made love to her. Finally, she fell asleep.

The essay by Ellen James, 'Why I'm Not an Ellen Jamesian,' appeared to engender no immediate fuss. It takes a while for most Letters to the Editor to be printed.

There were the expectable personal letters to Ellen James: condolences from idiots, propositions from sick men – the ugly, antifeminist tyrants and baiters of women who, as Garp had warned Ellen, would see themselves as being on *her* side.

'People will always make sides,' Garp said, '– of everything.'

There was not a written word from a single Ellen Jamesian.

Garp's first Steering wrestling team produced an 8-2 season as it approached its final dual meet with its archrival, the bad boys from Bath. Of course, the team's strength rested on some very well coached wrestlers whom Ernie Holm had brought along for the last two or three years, but Garp had kept everyone sharp. He was trying to estimate the wins and losses, weight class by weight class, in the upcoming match with Bath – sitting at the kitchen table in the vast house now in memory of Steering's first family – when Ellen James burst upon him, in tears, with the new issue of the magazine that had published her a month ago.

Garp felt he should have warned Ellen about magazines, too. They had, of course, published a long, epistolary essay written by a score of Ellen Jamesians, in response to Ellen's bold announcement that she felt used by them and she disliked them. It was just the kind of controversy magazines love. Ellen felt especially betrayed by the magazine's editor, who had obviously revealed to the Jamesians that Ellen James now lived with the notorious T. S. Garp.

Thus the Ellen Jamesians had *that* to get their teeth into: Ellen James, poor child, had been brainwashed into her antifeminist stance by the male villain, Garp. The betrayer of his mother! The smirking capitalizer on women's-movement politics! In the various letters, Garp's relationship with Ellen James was referred to as 'seductive,' 'slimy,' and 'underhanded.'

I'm sorry!

Ellen wrote.

'It's okay, it's okay. Nothing's your fault,' Garp assured her.

I'm not an antifeminist!

'Of course you're not,' Garp told her.

They make everything so black and white.

'Of course they do,' said Garp.

That's why I hate them. They force you to be like them – or else you're their enemy.

'Yes, yes,' Garp said.

I wish I could talk.

And then she dissolved, crying on Garp's shoulder, her wordless, angry blubber rousing Helen from the far-off reading room of the great house, driving Duncan from the darkroom, and waking baby Jenny from her nap.

So, foolishly, Garp decided to take them on, these grown-up crazies, these devout fanatics who – even when their chosen symbol rejected them – insisted they knew more about Ellen James than Ellen James knew about herself.

'Ellen James is *not* a symbol,' Garp wrote. 'She is a rape victim who was raped and dismembered before she was old enough to make up her own mind about sex and men.' Thus he began; he went on and on. And, of course, they published it – liking any fuel to any fire. It was also the first published piece of *anything* by T. S. Garp since the famous novel, *The World According to Bensenhaver.*

Actually, it was the second. In a little magazine, shortly after Jenny's death, Garp published his first and only poem. It was a strange poem; it was about condoms.

Garp felt his life was marred by condoms – man's device to spare himself and others the consequences of his lust. Our lifetime, Garp felt, was stalked by condoms – condoms in the parking lots in the early mornings, condoms discovered by children in the playing sand of the beaches, condoms used for messages (one to his mother, on the doorknob of their tiny wing apartment in the infirmary annex). Condoms unflushed down the dormitory toilets of the Steering School. Condoms lying slick and cocky in public urinals. Once a condom delivered with the Sunday paper. Once a condom in the mailbox at the end of the driveway. And once a condom on the stick-shift shaft of the old Volvo; someone had used the car overnight, but not for driving.

Condoms found Garp the way ants found sugar. He traveled miles, he changed continents, and there – in the bidet of the otherwise spotless but unfamiliar hotel room . . . there – in the backseat of the taxi, like the removed eye of a large fish . . . there – eyeing him, from the bottom of his shoe, where he picked it up, somewhere. From *every*where condoms came to him and vilely surprised him.

Condoms and Garp went way back. They were somehow joined at the beginning. How often he recalled his first condom shock, the condoms in the cannon's mouth!

It was a fair poem, but almost no one read it because it was gross. Many more people read his essay on Ellen James vs the Ellen Jamesians. That was news; that was a contemporary event. Sadly, Garp knew, that is more interesting than art.

Helen begged him not to be baited, not to get involved. Even Ellen James told him that it was *her* fight; she did not ask for his support.

'More fucking around in the garden,' Helen warned. 'More bookshelves.'

But he wrote angrily and well; he said more firmly what Ellen James had meant. He spoke with eloquence for those serious women who suffered, by association, 'the radical self-damage' of the Ellen Jamesians – 'the kind of shit that gives feminism a bad name.' He could not resist putting them down, and though he did it well, Helen rightly asked, 'For *whom*? Who is serious who doesn't already *know* the Ellen Jamesians are crazy? No, Garp, you've done this for *them* – not for Ellen, either. You've done it for the fucking Ellen Jamesians! You've done it to *get* to them. And why? Jesus, in another year no one would have remembered them – or why they did what they did. They were a *fashion*, a stupid fashion, but you couldn't just let them pass by. *Why?*'

But he was sullen about it, with the predictable attitude of someone who has been *right* – at all costs. And, therefore, wonders if he was wrong. It was a feeling that isolated him from everyone – even from Ellen. She was ready to be quits with it, she was sorry she had started it.

'But *they* started it,' Garp insisted.

Not really. The first man who raped someone, and tried to hurt her so she couldn't tell – he started it,

said Ellen James.

'Okay,' Garp said. 'Okay, okay.' The girl's sad truth hurt him. Hadn't he only wanted to defend her?

The Steering wrestling team whipped Bath Academy in the season's final dual meet and finished 9-2, with a second-place team trophy in the New England tournament and one individual champion, a 167-pounder whom Garp had personally done the most work with. But the season was over; Garp, the retired writer, once more had too much time on his hands.

He saw a lot of Roberta. They played endless games of squash; between them, they broke four rackets in three months and the little finger on Garp's left hand. Garp had an unmindful backswing that accounted for nine stitches across the bridge of Roberta's nose; Roberta hadn't had any stitches since her Eagle days and she complained about them bitterly. On a cross-court charge, Roberta's long knee gave Garp a groin injury that had him hobbling for a week.

'Honestly, you two,' Helen told them. 'Why don't you just go off and have a torrid affair. It would be *safer.*'

But they were the best of friends, and if ever such urges occurred – for either Garp or Roberta – they were quickly made into a joke. Also, Roberta's love life was at last coolly organized; like a born woman, she valued her privacy. And she enjoyed the directorship of the Fields Foundation at Dog's Head Harbor. Roberta reserved her sexual self for not infrequent but never excessive flings upon the city of New York, where she kept a calm number of lovers on edge for her sudden visits and trysts. 'It's the only way I can manage it,' she told Garp.

'It's a good enough way, Roberta,' Garp said. 'Not everyone is so fortunate – to have this separation of power.'

And so they played more squash, and when the weather

warmed, they ran on the curvy roads that stretched from Steering to the sea. On one road, Dog's Head Harbor was a flat six miles from Steering; they often ran from one mansion to the other. When Roberta did her business in New York, Garp ran alone.

He was alone, nearing the halfway point to Dog's Head Harbor – where he would turn around and run back to Steering – when the dirty-white Saab passed him, appeared to slow down, then sped ahead of him and out of sight. That was the only thing strange about it. Garp ran on the left-hand side of the road so that he could see the cars approaching closest to him; the Saab had passed him on the right, in its proper lane – nothing funny about it.

Garp was thinking about a reading he had promised to give at Dog's Head Harbor. Roberta had talked him into reading to the assembled Fields Foundation fellows and their invited guests; he was, after all, the chief trustee – and Roberta frequently organized small concerts and poetry readings, and so forth – but Garp was leery of it. He disliked readings – and especially now, to women; his put-down of the Ellen Jamesians had left so many women feeling raw. Most serious women, of course, agreed with him, but most of them were also intelligent enough to recognize a kind of personal vindictiveness in his criticisms of the Ellen Jamesians, which was stronger than logic. They sensed a kind of killer instinct in him – basically male and basically intolerant. He was, as Helen said, too intolerant of the intolerant. Most women surely thought Garp had written the truth about the Ellen Jamesians, but was it necessary to have been so rough? In his own wrestling terminology, perhaps Garp was guilty of unnecessary roughness. It was his roughness many women suspected, and when he read now, even to mixed audiences – at colleges, mainly, where roughness seemed presently unfashionable – he was aware of a silent dislike. He was a man who had publicly lost his temper; he had demonstrated that he could be cruel.

And Roberta had advised him not to read a sex scene; not that the Fields Foundation fellows were essentially hostile, but they *were* wary, Roberta said. 'You have lots of other scenes to read,' Roberta said, 'besides sex.' Neither of them mentioned the possibility that he might have anything *new* to read. And it was mainly for this reason – that he had nothing new to read – that Garp had grown increasingly unhappy about giving readings, anywhere.

Garp topped the slight hill by a farm for black Angus cattle – the only hill between Steering and the sea – and passed the two-mile mark on his run. He saw the blue-black noses of the beasts pointed at him, like double-barreled guns over a low stone wall. Garp always spoke to the cattle; he mooed at them.

The dirty-white Saab was now approaching him, and Garp moved into the dust of the soft shoulder. One of the black Angus mooed back at Garp; two shied away from the stone wall. Garp had his eyes on them. The Saab was not going very fast – did not appear reckless. There seemed no reason to keep an eye on it.

It was only his memory that saved him. Writers have very selective memories, and fortunately, for Garp, he had chosen to remember how the dirty-white Saab had slowed – when it first passed him, going the other way – and how the driver's head appeared to be lining him up in the rearview mirror.

Garp looked away from the Angus and saw the silent Saab, engine cut, coasting straight at him in the soft shoulder, a trail of dust spuming behind its quiet white shape and over the intent, hunched head of the driver. The driver, aiming the Saab at Garp, was the closest visual image Garp would ever have of what a ball turret gunner who was at work *looked* like.

Garp took two bounds to the stone wall and vaulted it, not seeing the single line of electric fencing above the wall. He felt the tingle in his thigh as he grazed the wire, but he cleared the fence, and the wall, and landed in the wet green stubble of the field, chewed and pockmarked by the herd of Angus.

He lay hugging the wet ground, he heard the croak of the vile-tasting Under Toad in his dry throat – he heard the explosion of hooves as the Angus thundered away from him. He heard the rock-and-metal meeting of the dirty-white Saab with the stone wall. Two boulders, the size of his head, bounced lazily beside him. One wild-eyed Angus bull stood his ground, but the Saab's horn was stuck; perhaps the steady blare kept the bull from charging.

Garp knew he was alive; the blood in his mouth was only because he had bitten his lip. He moved along the wall to the point of impact, where the bashed Saab was imbedded. Its driver had lost more than her tongue.

She was in her forties. The Saab's engine had driven her knees up around the mangled steering column. She had no rings on her hands, which were short-fingered and reddened by the rough winter, or winters, she had known. The Saab's door post on the driver's side, or else the windshield's frame, had struck her face and dented one temple and one cheek. This left her face a little lopsided. Her brown, blood-matted hair was ruffled by the warm summer wind, which blew through the hole where the windshield had been.

Garp knew she was dead because he looked in her eyes. He knew she was an Ellen Jamesian because he looked in her mouth. He also looked in her purse. There was only the predictable notepad and pencil. There were lots of used and new notes, too. One of them said:

Hi! My name is . . .

and so forth. Another one said:

You asked for this.

Garp imagined that this was the note she had intended to stick under the bloody waistband of his running shorts when she left him dead and mangled by the side of the road.

Another note was almost lyrical; it was the one the newspapers would love to use, and reuse.

I have never been raped, and I have never wanted to be. I have never been with a man, and I have never wanted to be, either. My whole life's meaning has been to share the suffering of Ellen James.

Oh boy, Garp thought, but he left that note to be discovered with her other things. He was not the sort of writer, or the sort of man, who concealed important messages – even if the messages were insane.

He had aggravated his old groin injury by vaulting the stone wall and the electric fence, but he was able to jog back toward town until a yogurt truck picked him up; Garp and the yogurt driver went to tell the police together.

By the time the yogurt driver passed the scene of the accident, on his way to discover Garp, the black Angus had escaped through the rent in the stone wall and were milling around the dirty-white Saab like large, beastly mourners surrounding this fragile angel killed in a foreign car.

Maybe *that* was the Under Toad I felt, Helen thought, lying awake beside the soundly sleeping Garp. She hugged his warm body; she nestled in the smell of her own rich sex all over him. Maybe that dead Ellen Jamesian was the Under Toad, and now she's gone, thought Helen; she squeezed Garp so hard that he woke up.

'What is it?' he asked. But, wordless as Ellen James, Helen hugged his hips; her teeth chattered against his chest and he hugged her until she stopped shivering.

A 'spokesperson' for the Ellen Jamesians remarked that this was an isolated act of violence, not sanctioned by the society of Ellen Jamesians but obviously provoked by the 'typically male, aggressive, rapist personality of T. S. Garp.' They were not taking responsibility for this 'isolated act,' the Jamesians declared, but they were not surprised or especially sorry about it, either.

Roberta told Garp that, under the circumstances, if he didn't feel like reading to a group of women, she would understand. But Garp read to the assembled Fields Foundation fellows and their assorted guests at Dog's Head Harbor – a crowd of less than one hundred people, cozily comfortable in the sun room of Jenny's estate. He read them 'The Pension Grillparzer,' which he introduced by saying, 'This is the first and best thing I ever wrote, and I don't even know how I thought it up. I think it is about death, which I didn't even know very much about when I wrote it. I know more about death now, and I'm not writing a word. There are eleven major characters in this story and seven of them die; one of them goes mad; one of them runs away with another woman. I'm not going to give away what happens to the other two characters, but you can see that the odds for surviving this story aren't great.'

Then he read to them. Some of them laughed; four of them cried; there were lots of sneezes and coughs, perhaps because of the ocean dampness; nobody left and everyone applauded. An older woman in the back, by the piano, slept soundly through the entire story, but even she applauded at the end; she woke up to the applause and joined in it, happily.

The event seemed to charge Garp. Duncan had attended the reading – it was his favorite among his father's works (actually, one of the few things his father had written that Duncan had been allowed to read). Duncan was a talented young artist and he had more than fifty drawings of the characters and situations in his father's story, which he revealed to Garp after Garp drove them both home. Some of the drawings were fresh and unpretentious; all of them were thrilling to Garp. The old bear's withered flanks engulfing the absurd unicycle; the grandmother's matchstick ankles appearing frail and exposed under the W.C. door. The evil mischief in the dream man's excited eyes! The floozy beauty

of Herr Theobald's sister ('. . . as if her life and her com-
panions had never been exotic to *her* – as if they had
always been staging a ludicrous and doomed effort at
reclassification'). And the brave optimism of the man who
could only walk on his hands.

'How long have you been doing this?' Garp asked Duncan;
he could have wept, he felt so proud.

It charged him, very much. He proposed to John Wolf a
special edition, a *book* of 'The Pension Grillparzer,' illustrated
by Duncan. 'The story's good enough to be a book all by
itself,' Garp wrote John Wolf. 'And I'm certainly well known
enough for it to sell. Except for a little magazine, and an
anthology or two, it's really never been published before.
Besides, the drawings are lovely! And the story really holds
up.

'I hate it when a writer starts cashing in on a reputation –
publishing all the shit in his drawers, and republishing all
the *old* shit that deserved to be missed. But this isn't a case
of that, John; you know it isn't.'

John Wolf knew. He thought Duncan's drawings *were*
fresh and unpretentious, but also not really very good; the
boy was not yet thirteen – no matter how talented he was.
But John Wolf also knew a good idea for publishing when
he saw it. To be sure, of course, he gave the book the Secret
Jillsy Sloper Test; Garp's story, and especially Duncan's
drawings, passed Jillsy's scrutiny with the highest praise. Her
only reservations concerned Garp's using too many words
she didn't know.

A father and son book, John Wolf thought, would be nice
for Christmas. And the sad gentleness of the story, its full
pity and its mild violence, would perhaps ease the tension
of Garp's war with the Ellen Jamesians.

The groin healed, and Garp ran the road from Steering to
the sea all summer, nodding his recognition to the brooding
Angus every day; they now had the safety of that fortunate
stone wall in common, and Garp felt forever identified with
these large, lucky animals. Happily grazed, and happily

bred. And slaughtered, one day, quickly. Garp did not think of their slaughter. Or his own. He watched out for cars, but not nervously.

'An isolated act,' he told Helen and Roberta and Ellen James. They nodded, but Roberta ran with him whenever she could. Helen thought she would feel more at ease when the weather got cold again and Garp ran on the indoor track in the Miles Seabrook Field House. Or when he started wrestling again, and rarely went out at all. Those warm mats and that padded room were a safety symbol to Helen Holm, who had grown up in such an incubator.

Garp, too, looked forward to another wrestling season. And to the father and son publication of *The Pension Grillparzer* – a tale by T. S. Garp, illustrated by Duncan Garp. At last, a Garp book for children *and* for grown-ups! It was also, of course, like starting over. Going back to the beginning and getting a fresh start. What a world of illusions blossoms with the idea of 'starting over.'

Suddenly, Garp started writing again.

He started by writing a letter to the magazine that had published his attack on the Ellen Jamesians. In the letter he apologized for the vehemence and self-righteousness of his remarks. 'Although I believe Ellen James was used by these women, who had little concern for the real-life Ellen James, I can see that the *need* to use Ellen James in some way was genuine and great. I feel, of course, at least partially responsible for the death of that very needful and violent woman who felt provoked enough to try to kill me. I am sorry.'

Of course, apologies are rarely acceptable to true believers – or to anyone who believes in *pure* good, or in pure evil. The Ellen Jamesians who responded, in print, all said that Garp was obviously afraid for his own life; they said he obviously feared an endless line of hit men (or 'hit persons') whom the Ellen Jamesians would send after him until they got him. They said that along with being a male swine, and a bully of women, T. S. Garp was clearly 'a yellow chickenshit coward with no balls.'

If Garp saw these responses, he appeared not to care; it is likely that he never read them. He wrote to apologize, mainly, because of his *writing;* it was an act meant to clear his desk, not his conscience; he meant to rid his mind of the garden-tending, bookshelf-making trivia that had occupied his time while he was waiting to write seriously again. He thought he would make peace with the Ellen Jamesians and then forget them, although Helen could *not* forget them. Ellen James certainly could not forget them, either, and even Roberta was alert and edgy whenever she was out with Garp.

About a mile beyond the bull farm, one fine day when they were running toward the sea, Roberta felt suddenly convinced that the approaching Volkswagen housed another would-be assassin; she threw a magnificent cross-body block on Garp and belted him off the soft shoulder and down a twelve-foot embankment into a muddy ditch. Garp sprained an ankle and sat howling at Roberta from the stream bed. Roberta seized a rock, with which she threatened the Volkswagen, which was full of frightened teenagers returning from a beach party; Roberta talked them into making room for Garp, whom they drove to the Jenny Fields Infirmary.

'You are a *menace!*' Garp told Roberta, but Helen was especially happy for Roberta's presence – her tight end's instinct for blind-side hits and cheap shots.

Garp's sprained ankle kept him off the road for two weeks and stepped up his writing. He was working on what he called his 'father book,' or 'the book of fathers'; it was the first of the three projects he had jauntily described to John Wolf the night before he left for Europe – this one was the novel to be called *My Father's Illusions*. Because he was inventing a father, Garp felt more in touch with the spirit of pure imagination that he felt had kindled 'The Pension Grillparzer.' A long way from which he had been falsely led. He had been too impressed by what he now called the 'mere accidents and casualties of daily life, and the understandable trauma resulting therefrom.' He felt cocky again, as if he could make up anything.

'My father wanted us all to have a better life,' Garp began, 'but better than *what* – he was not so sure. I do not think that he knew what life was; only that he wanted it *better*.'

As he did in 'The Pension Grillparzer,' he *made up* a family; he gave himself brothers and sisters and aunts – both an eccentric and an evil uncle – and he felt he was a novelist again. A plot, to his delight, thickened.

In the evenings Garp read aloud to Ellen James and Helen; sometimes Duncan stayed up and listened, and sometimes Roberta stayed for supper, and he would read to her, too. He became suddenly generous in all matters concerning the Fields Foundation. In fact, the other board members were exasperated with him: Garp wanted to give *every* applicant something. 'She sounds sincere,' he kept saying. 'Look, she's had a hard life,' he told them. 'Isn't there enough money?'

'Not if we spend it this way,' Marcia Fox said.

'If we don't discriminate between these applicants more than you suggest,' said Hilma Bloch, 'we are lost.'

'Lost?' Garp said. 'How could *we* get lost?' Overnight, it seemed to them all (except Roberta), Garp had become the weakest sort of liberal: he would evaluate no one. But he was full of imagining the whole, sad histories of his fictional family; thus full of sympathy, he was a soft touch in the real world.

The anniversary of Jenny's murder, and of the sudden funerals for Ernie Holm and Stewart Percy, passed quickly for Garp in the midst of his renewed creative energy. Then the wrestling season was again upon him; Helen had never seen him so taken up, so completely focused and relentless. He became again the determined young Garp who had made her fall in love, and she felt so drawn to him that she often cried when she was alone – without knowing why. She was alone too much; now that Garp was busy again, Helen realized she had kept herself inactive too long. She agreed to let the Steering School employ her, so that she could teach and use her mind for her own ideas again.

She also taught Ellen James to drive a car and Ellen drove twice a week to the state university, where she took a creative writing course. 'This family isn't big enough for two writers, Ellen,' Garp teased her. How they all cherished the good mood he was in! And now that Helen was working again, she was much less anxious.

In the world according to Garp, an evening could be hilarious and the next morning could be murderous.

Later, they would often remark (Roberta, too) how good it was that Garp got to see the first edition of *The Pension Grillparzer* – illustrated by Duncan Garp, and out in time for Christmas – before he saw the Under Toad.

19

Life After Garp

He loved epilogues, as he showed us in 'The Pension Grillparzer.'

'An epilogue,' Garp wrote, 'is more than a body count. An epilogue, in the disguise of wrapping up the past, is really a way of warning us about the future.'

That February day, Helen heard him telling jokes to Ellen James and Duncan at breakfast; he certainly sounded as if he felt good about the future. Helen gave little Jenny Garp a bath, and powdered her and oiled her scalp and clipped her tiny fingernails and zipped her into a yellow playsuit that Walt once wore. Helen could smell the coffee Garp had made, and she could hear Garp hurrying Duncan off to school.

'Not *that* hat, Duncan, for Christ's sake,' Garp said. 'That hat couldn't keep a bird warm. It's twelve below.'

'It's twelve *above*, Dad,' Duncan said.

'That's academic,' Garp said. 'It's very cold, that's what it is.'

Ellen James must have come in through the garage door then, and written out a note, because Helen heard Garp say that he'd help her in a minute; obviously, Ellen couldn't start the car.

Then it was quiet in the great house for a while; as if from far away, Helen heard only the squeak of boots in the snow and the slow cranking of the car's cold engine. 'Have a good day!' she heard Garp call to Duncan, who must have been walking down the long driveway – off to school.

'Yup!' Duncan called. 'You, too!'

The car started; Ellen James would be driving off to the university. 'Drive carefully!' Garp called after her.

Helen had her coffee alone. Occasionally, the in-articulateness with which baby Jenny talked to herself reminded Helen of the Ellen Jamesians – or of Ellen, when she was upset – but not this morning. The baby was playing quietly with some plastic things. Helen could hear Garp's typewriter – that was all.

He wrote for three hours. The typewriter would burst for three or four pages, then be silent for such a long time that Helen imagined Garp had stopped breathing; then, when she had forgotten about it and was lost in her reading, or in some task with Jenny, the typewriter would burst out again.

At eleven-thirty in the morning Helen heard him call Roberta Muldoon. Garp wanted a squash game before wrestling practice, if Roberta could get away from her 'girls,' as Garp called the Fields Foundation fellows.

'How are the girls today, Roberta?' Garp said.

But Roberta couldn't play. Helen heard the disappointment in Garp's voice.

Later, poor Roberta would repeat and repeat how she *should* have played; if only she had played, she went on saying, maybe she would have spotted it coming – maybe she would have been around, alert and edgy, recognizing the spoor of the real world, the paw prints Garp had always overlooked or ignored. But Roberta Muldoon could not play squash.

Garp wrote for another half hour. Helen knew he was writing a letter; somehow she could tell the difference in the sound of the typing. He wrote to John Wolf about *My Father's Illusions*; he was pleased with how the book was coming along. He complained that Roberta took her job too seriously and was letting herself get out of shape; *no* administrative job was worth as much time as Roberta gave to the Fields Foundation. Garp said that the low sales figures on *The Pension Grillparzer* were about what he expected; the main thing was that it was 'a lovely book' – he liked looking at it, and giving it to people, and its rebirth had been a rebirth for him. He said he expected a better wrestling season than last year, although he had lost his starting heavyweight to a knee operation and his one New England champion had graduated. He said that living with someone who read as much as Helen was both irritating and inspiring; he wanted to give her something to read that would make her close her other books.

At noon he came and kissed Helen, and fondled her breasts, and kissed baby Jenny, over and over again, while he dressed her in a snowsuit that had also been worn by Walt – and before Walt, even Duncan had gotten some wear out of it. Garp drove Jenny to the day-care center as soon as Ellen James came back with the car. Then Garp showed up at Buster's Snack and Grill for his customary cup of tea with honey, his one tangerine, and his one banana. That was all the lunch he ran or wrestled on; he explained why to a new teacher in the English Department – a young man fresh out of graduate school who adored Garp's work. His name was Donald Whitcomb, and his nervous stutter reminded Garp, affectionately, of the departed Mr Tinch and the race in his pulse he still felt for Alice Fletcher.

This particular day, Garp was eager to talk about writing to anyone, and young Whitcomb was eager to listen. Don Whitcomb would remember that Garp told him what the act of starting a novel felt like. 'It's like trying to make the dead come alive,' he said. 'No, no, that's not right – it's more like trying to keep everyone alive, forever. Even the ones who must die in the end. They're the most important to keep alive.' Finally, Garp said it in a way that seemed to please him. 'A novelist is a doctor who sees only terminal cases,' Garp said. Young Whitcomb was so awed that he wrote this down.

It would be Whitcomb's biography, years later, that the would-be biographers of Garp would all envy and despise. Whitcomb reflected that this Bloom Period in Garp's writing (as Whitcomb called it) was really due to Garp's sense of mortality. The attempt on Garp's life by the Ellen Jamesian in the dirty-white Saab, Whitcomb claimed, had given Garp the urgency necessary to make him write again. Helen would endorse that thesis.

It was not a bad idea, although Garp would surely have laughed at it. He really had forgotten the Ellen Jamesians, and he was not on the lookout for more of them. But unconsciously, perhaps, he might have been feeling that urgency young Whitcomb expressed.

In Buster's Snack and Grill, Garp held Whitcomb enthralled until it was time for wrestling practice. On his way out (leaving Whitcomb to pay, the young man later recalled, good-naturedly), Garp ran into Dean Bodger, who had just spent three days hospitalized with some heart complaint.

'They found nothing wrong,' Bodger complained.

'But did they find your heart?' Garp asked him.

The dean, young Whitcomb, and Garp all laughed. Bodger said he'd brought only *The Pension Grillparzer* with him to the hospital, and since it was so short a book, he'd been able to read it completely three times. It was a gloomy story to read in a hospital, Bodger said, though he was glad to report that he had not yet had the grandmother's dream; thus he knew he would live awhile longer. Bodger said he had loved the story.

Whitcomb would remember that Garp then grew embarrassed, though he was obviously pleased by Bodger's praise. Whitcomb and Bodger waved good-bye to him. Garp forgot his skier's knit hat, but Bodger told Whitcomb he would bring it to Garp – at the gym. Dean Bodger said to Whitcomb that he liked dropping in on Garp in the wrestling room, occasionally. 'He is so in his element there,' Bodger said.

Donald Whitcomb was no wrestling fan but he talked

enthusiastically about Garp's writing. The young and the old man agreed: Garp was a man with remarkable energy.

Whitcomb recalled that he returned to his small apartment in one of the dormitories and tried to write down everything that had impressed him about Garp; he had to stop, unfinished, in time for supper. When Whitcomb went to the dining hall, he was one of the few people at the Steering School who'd heard nothing about what had happened. It was Dean Bodger – his eyes red-rimmed, his face suddenly years older – who stopped young Whitcomb going into the dining hall. The dean, who had left his gloves at the gym, clutched Garp's ski hat in his cold hands. When Whitcomb saw that the dean still had Garp's hat, he knew – even before looking in Bodger's eyes – that something was wrong.

Garp missed his hat as soon as he trotted out on the snowy footpath that led from Buster's Snack and Grill to the Sea-brook Gymnasium and Field House. But rather than go back for it, he stepped up his usual pace and ran to the gym. His head was cold when he got there, in less than three minutes; his toes were cold, too, and he warmed his feet in the steamy trainer's room before putting on his wrestling shoes.

He talked briefly with his 145-pounder in the trainer's room. The boy was getting his little finger taped to his ring finger so that he would give some support to what the trainer said was only a sprain. Garp asked if there'd been an X-ray; there had been, and it was negative. Garp tapped his 145-pounder on the shoulder, asked him what he weighed in at, frowned at the answer – which was probably a lie, and still about five pounds too heavy – and went to suit up.

He stopped again in the trainer's room before going to practice. 'Just to put some Vaseline on one ear,' the trainer recalled. Garp had a cauliflower ear in progress, and the Vaseline made his ear slippery; he thought this protected it. Garp did not like wrestling in a headgear; those ear guards had not been part of the required uniform when he'd been a wrestler, and he saw no reason to wear one now.

He jogged a mile around the indoor track with his 152-pounder before opening the wrestling room. Garp challenged the boy to a sprint in the last lap, but the 152-pounder had more left than Garp and beat him by six feet at the end. Garp then 'played' with the 152-pounder – in lieu of warming up – in the wrestling room. He took the kid down easily, about five or six times, then rode him around the mat for about five minutes – or until the boy showed signs of tiring. Then Garp allowed the boy to reverse him; Garp let the 152-pounder try to pin him while he defended himself on the bottom. But there was a muscle in Garp's back that was tight, that would not stretch enough to suit him, so Garp told the 152-pounder to go play with someone else. Garp sat by himself against the padded wall, sweating happily and watching the room fill up with his team.

He let them warm up on their own – he hated organized calisthenics – before demonstrating the first of the drills he wanted them to practice. 'Get a partner, get a partner,' he said, by rote. And he added, 'Eric? Get a *harder* partner, Eric, or you'll work with me.'

Eric, his 133-pounder, had a habit of coasting through workouts with the second-string 115-pounder, who was Eric's roommate and best friend.

When Helen came in the wrestling room, the temperature was up to 85° or so, and climbing. The coupled boys upon the mat were already breathing hard. Garp was intently watching a time clock. 'One minute left!' Garp yelled. When Helen walked by him, he had a whistle in his mouth – so she did not kiss him.

She would remember that whistle, and not kissing him, for as long as she would live – which would be a long time.

Helen went to her usual corner of the wrestling room, where she could not easily be fallen on. She opened her book. Her glasses fogged up; she wiped them off. She had her glasses on when the nurse entered the wrestling room, at the farthest end of the room from Helen. But Helen never looked up from her book unless there was a loud body slam upon the mat or an unusually loud cry of pain. The nurse closed the wrestling-room door behind her and moved quickly past the grappling bodies toward Garp, with his time clock in his hands and his whistle in his mouth. Garp took the whistle out and hollered, 'Fifteen seconds!' That was all the time *he* had left, too. Garp put the whistle back in his mouth and got ready to blow.

When he saw the nurse, he mistook her for the kindly nurse named Dotty who had helped him escape from the first feminist funeral. Garp was simply judging her by her hair, which was iron-gray and in a braid, coiled like a rope around her head – it was a wig, of course. The nurse smiled at him. There was probably no one Garp felt as comfortable with as a nurse; he smiled back at her, then glanced at the time clock: ten seconds.

When Garp looked up at the nurse again, he saw the gun. He had just been thinking about his mother, Jenny Fields, and how she must have looked when she walked into the wrestling room, not quite twenty years ago. Jenny was younger than this nurse, he was thinking. If Helen had looked up and seen this nurse, Helen might have been fooled again into thinking that her missing mother had finally decided to come out of hiding.

When Garp saw the gun, he also noticed that it wasn't a real nurse's uniform; it was a Jenny Fields Original with the characteristic red heart sewn over the breast. It was then that Garp saw the nurse's breasts – they were small but they were too firm and youthfully erect for a woman with iron-gray hair; and her hips were too slim, her legs too girlish. When Garp looked again at her face, he saw the family resemblance: the square jawline that Midge Steering had given to all her children, the sloping forehead that had been the contribution of Fat Stew. The combination gave all the Percys' heads the shape of violent navy vessels.

The first shot forced the whistle out of Garp's mouth with a sharp *tweet!* and caused the time clock to fly from his hands. He sat down. The mat was warm. The bullet had traveled through his stomach and had lodged in his spine. There were fewer than five seconds remaining on the time clock when Bainbridge Percy fired a second time; the bullet struck Garp's chest and drove him, still in a sitting position, back against the padded wall. The stunned wrestlers, who were only boys, seemed incapable of motion. It was Helen who tackled Pooh Percy to the mat and kept her from firing a third shot.

Helen's screams aroused the wrestlers. One of them, the second-string heavyweight, pinned Pooh Percy belly down to the mat and ripped her hand with the gun in it out from under her; his pumping elbow split Helen's lip, but Helen hardly felt it. The starting 145-pounder, with his little finger taped to his ring finger, wrenched the gun out of Pooh's hand by breaking her thumb.

At the moment her bone *clicked*, Pooh Percy screamed; even Garp saw what had become of her – the surgery must have been recent. In Pooh Percy's open, yelling mouth, anyone near her could see the black gathering of stitches, like ants clustered on the stump of what had been her tongue. The second-string heavyweight was so frightened of Pooh that he squeezed her too hard and cracked one of her ribs; Bainbridge Percy's recent madness – to become an Ellen Jamesian – was certainly painful to her.

'Igs!' she screamed. 'Ucking igs!' An 'ucking ig' was a 'fucking pig,' but you had to be an Ellen Jamesian to understand Pooh Percy now.

The starting 145-pounder held the gun at arm's length, pointed down to the mat and into an empty corner of the wrestling room. 'Ig!' Pooh gagged at him, but the trembling boy stared at his coach.

Helen held Garp steady; he was starting to slide against the wall. He could not talk, he knew; he could not feel, he could not touch. He had only a keen sense of smell, his brief eyesight, and his vivid memory.

Garp was glad, for once, that Duncan wasn't interested in wrestling. By virtue of his preference for swimming,

Duncan had missed seeing this; Garp knew that Duncan would either just be getting out of school or already at the swimming pool.

Garp was sorry for Helen – that she was here – but he was happy to have her scent nearest him. He savored it, among those other intimate odors in the Steering wrestling room. If he could have talked, he would have told Helen not to be frightened of the Under Toad anymore. It surprised him to realize that the Under Toad was no stranger, was not even mysterious; the Under Toad was very familiar – as if he had always known it, as if he had grown up with it. It was yielding, like the warm wrestling mats; it smelled like the sweat of clean boys – and like Helen, the first and last woman Garp loved. The Under Toad, Garp knew now, could even look like a nurse: a person who is familiar with death and trained to make practical responses to pain.

When Dean Bodger opened the wrestling-room door with Garp's ski hat in his hands, Garp had no illusions that the dean had arrived, once again, to organize the rescue party – to catch the body falling from the infirmary annex, four floors above where the world was safe. The world was not safe. Dean Bodger, Garp knew, would do his best to be of service; Garp smiled gratefully to him, and to Helen – and to his wrestlers; some of them were weeping now. Garp looked fondly at his sobbing second-string heavyweight who lay crushing Pooh Percy to the mat; Garp knew what a difficult season the poor, fat boy was about to experience.

Garp looked at Helen; all he could move was his eyes. Helen, he saw, was trying to smile back at him. With his eyes, Garp tried to reassure her: don't worry – so what if there is no life after death? There is life after Garp, believe me. Even if there is only death after death (after death), be grateful for small favors – sometimes there is birth after sex, for example. And, if you are very fortunate, sometimes there is sex after birth! Oh yeth, as Alice Fletcher would have said. And if you have life, said Garp's eyes, there is hope you'll have energy. And never forget, there is memory, Helen, his eyes told her.

'In the world according to Garp,' young Donald Whitcomb would write, 'we are obliged to remember everything.'

Garp died before they could move him from the wrestling room. He was thirty-three, the same age as Helen. Ellen James was just starting her twenties. Duncan was thirteen. Little Jenny Garp was going on three. Walt would have been eight.

The news of Garp's death promoted the immediate printing of a third and fourth edition of the father and son book, *The Pension Grillparzer*. Over a long weekend, John Wolf drank too much and contemplated leaving publishing; it sometimes nauseated him to see how a violent death was so good for business. But it comforted Wolf to realize how Garp would have taken the news. Even Garp could not have imagined that his own death would be *better* than a suicide at establishing *his* literary seriousness and his fame. Not bad for someone who, at thirty-three, had written one good short story and perhaps one and a half good novels out of three. Garp's rare manner of dying was, in fact, so perfect that John Wolf had to smile when he imagined how pleased Garp would have been with it. It was a death, Wolf thought, which in its random, stupid, and unnecessary qualities – comic and ugly and bizarre – underlined everything Garp had ever written about how the world works. It was a death scene, John Wolf told Jillsy Sloper, that only Garp could have written.

Helen would remark bitterly, but only once, that Garp's death was really a kind of suicide, after all. 'In the sense that his whole *life* was a suicide,' she said, mysteriously. She would later explain that all she meant was, 'He made people too angry.'

He had made Pooh Percy too angry; at least that was clear.

He made others pay him tribute, small and strange. The

Steering School cemetery got the honor of his gravestone, if not his body; like his mother's, Garp's body went to medicine. The Steering School also chose to honor him by naming after him its one remaining building that was not named after anybody else. It was old Dean Bodger's idea. If there was a Jenny Fields Infirmary, the good dean argued, then there should be a Garp Infirmary Annex.

In later years the functions of these buildings would alter slightly, although they would remain, in name, the Fields Infirmary and the Garp Annex. The Fields Infirmary would one day become the old wing of the new Steering Health Clinic and Laboratories; the Garp Annex would become a building used chiefly for storage – a kind of warehouse for medical, kitchen, and classroom supplies; it could also be used for epidemics. Of course, there weren't many epidemics anymore. Garp probably would have liked the idea: to have a storage building named after him. He wrote once that a novel was 'only a place for storage – of all the meaningful things that a novelist isn't able to use in his life.'

He would have liked the idea of an epilogue, too – so here it is: an epilogue 'warning us about the future,' as T. S. Garp might have imagined it.

ALICE AND HARRISON FLETCHER would remain married, through thick and through thin – in part, their marriage lasted because of Alice's difficulty with finishing anything. Their only child, a daughter, would play the cello – that large and cumbersome and silken-voiced instrument – in a manner so graceful that the pure, deep sound of it aggravated Alice's speech defect for hours after each performance. Harrison, who would get and hold his tenure after a while, would outgrow his habits with his prettier students about the time his talented daughter began to assert herself as a serious musician.

Alice, who would never complete her second novel, or her third or fourth, would never have a second child, either. She remained smoothly fluent on the page, and agonizing in the flesh. Alice never again took to 'other men' to the degree that she had taken to Garp; even in her memory, he was a passion that was strong enough to keep her from ever becoming close to Helen. And Harry's old fondness for Helen seemed to fade with each of his fast-fading affairs, until the Fletchers rarely kept track of the surviving Garps at all.

Once Duncan Garp met the Fletcher daughter in New York, after her maiden cello solo in that dangerous city; Duncan took her to dinner.

'Does he look like his mother?' Harrison asked the girl.

'I don't remember her very well,' the daughter said.

'Did he make a *path* at you?' Alice asked.

'I don't *think* so,' said her daughter, whose first-chosen and best-loved partner would always be that big-hipped cello.

The Fletchers, both Harry and Alice, would die in their ripe middle age, when their airplane – to Martinique – crashed during the Christmas holidays. One of Harrison's students had driven them to the airport.

'If you live in New England,' Alice confided to the student, 'you owe yourthelf a holiday in the *thun*. Right, Harrithon?'

Helen had always thought that Alice was 'a little loony.'

HELEN HOLM, who most of her life would be known as Helen Garp, would live a long, long time. A slim, dark woman with an arresting face and precise language, she would have her lovers but never remarry. Each lover suffered the presence of Garp – not only in Helen's relentless memory, but in the articles of fact that Helen surrounded herself with in the Steering mansion, which she rarely left: for example, Garp's books, and all of Duncan's photographs of him, and even Garp's wrestling trophies.

Helen maintained that she could never forgive Garp for dying so young and leaving her to live so much of her life alone – he had also spoiled her, she claimed, for ever considering seriously the possibility of living with another man.

Helen would become one of the most respected teachers the Steering School ever had, though she would never lose her sense of sarcasm about the place. She had some friends there, though they were few: old Dean Bodger, until he died, and the young scholar, Donald Whitcomb, who would become as enchanted with Helen as he was enchanted with the work of Garp. There was also a woman, a sculptor, who was an artist-in-residence – someone Roberta had introduced Helen to.

John Wolf was a lifelong friend whom Helen forgave in small pieces, but never completely, for his success at making Garp a success. Helen and Roberta remained close, too – Helen occasionally joining Roberta for Roberta's famous flings upon the city of New York. The two of them, growing older and more eccentric, were guilty of lording it over the Fields Foundation for years. In fact, the wit of their running commentary on the outside world became almost a tourist attraction at Dog's Head Harbor; from time to time, when Helen was lonely or bored at Steering – when her children were grown up and pursuing their own lives, elsewhere – she went to stay with Roberta at Jenny Fields' old estate. It was always lively there. When Roberta died, Helen appeared to age twenty years.

Very late in her life – and only after she had complained to Duncan that she had survived all her favorite contemporaries – Helen Holm was stricken suddenly with an illness that affects the body's mucous membranes. She would die in her sleep.

She had successfully outlived many cutthroat biographers who were waiting for her to die so that they could swoop in on the remains of Garp. She had protected his letters, the unfinished manuscript of *My Father's Illusions*, most of his journals and jottings. She told all the would-be biographers, exactly as *he* would have, 'Read the work. Forget the life.'

She herself wrote several articles, which were respected in her field. One was called 'The Adventurer's Instinct in Narration.' It was a comparative study of the narrative technique of Joseph Conrad and Virginia Woolf.

Helen always considered herself as a widow left with *three* children – Duncan, baby Jenny, and Ellen James, who all survived Helen and wept copiously at her death. They had been too young and too astonished to weep as much for Garp.

DEAN BODGER, who wept almost as much as Helen at Garp's death, remained as loyal as a pit bull, and as tenacious. Long after his retirement, he still stormed the Steering campus by night, unable to sleep, fitfully capturing lurkers and lovers who slunk along the footpaths and hugged each other to the spongy ground – under the soft bushes, alongside the beautiful old buildings, and so forth.

Bodger remained active at Steering for as long as it took Duncan Garp to graduate. 'I saw your father through, boy,' the dean told Duncan. 'I'll see you through, too. And if they let me, I'll stay to see your sister through.' But they finally forced his retirement; they cited to themselves, among other problems, his habit of talking to himself during chapel, and his bizarre arrests, at midnight, of the boys and girls caught out after hours. They also mentioned the dean's recurring fantasy: that it had been the young Garp he caught in his arms – one night, years ago – and not a pigeon. Bodger refused to move from the campus, even when he was retired, and despite – or, perhaps, because of – his obstinacy, he became Steering's most honored emeritus. They would drag him out for all the school's ceremonies; they would totter him up to the stage, introduce him to people who didn't know who he was, and then they would lead him away. Perhaps because they could display him on these dignified occasions, they tolerated his odd behavior; long through his seventies, for example, Bodger would be convinced – sometimes for weeks at a time – that he was *still* the dean.

'You *are* the dean, really,' Helen liked to tease him.

'Of course I am!' Bodger roared.

They saw each other often, and as Bodger grew deafer, and deafer, he was more frequently seen on the arm of that nice Ellen James, who had her ways of talking to people who couldn't hear.

Dean Bodger remained loyal even to the Steering wrestling team, whose glory years soon faded from the memories of most. The wrestlers were never again to have a coach the equal of Ernie Holm, or even the equal of Garp. They became a losing team, yet Bodger always supported them, hollering through the last bout to the poor Steering boy flopping on his back, about to be pinned.

It was at a wrestling match that Bodger died. In the unlimited class – an unusually close match – the Steering heavyweight lay floundering with his equally exhausted and out-of-shape opponent; like beached baby whales, they groveled for the upper hand and the winning points as the clock ran down. 'Fifteen seconds!' the announcer boomed. The big boys struggled. Bodger rose to his feet, stamping and urging. 'Gott!' he squawked, his German emerging at the end.

When the bout ended and the stands emptied, there was the retired dean – dead in his seat. It took much comforting from Helen for the sensitive young Whitcomb to gain control of his grief at Bodger's loss.

DONALD WHITCOMB would never sleep with Helen, despite rumors among the envious would-be biographers who longed to get their hands on Garp's property and Garp's widow. Whitcomb would be a monkish recluse all his life, which he spent in virtual hiding at the Steering School. It was his happy fortune to have discovered Garp there, moments before Garp's death, and his happy fortune, too, to find himself befriended and looked after by Helen. She trusted him to adore her husband perhaps even more uncritically than she did.

Poor Whitcomb would always be referred to as 'the young Whitcomb,' even though he would not always be young. His face would never grow a beard, his cheeks would be forever pink – under his brown, his gray, his finally frost-white hair. His voice would remain a stuttering, eager yodel; his hands would wring themselves forever. But it would be Whitcomb whom Helen would trust with the family and literary record.

He would be Garp's biographer. Helen would read all but the last chapter, which Whitcomb waited for years to write; it was the chapter eulogizing her. Whitcomb was *the* Garp scholar, the final Garp authority. He had the proper meekness for a biographer, Duncan always joked. He was a good biographer from the Garp family's point of view; Whitcomb believed everything that Helen told him – he believed every note that Garp left – or every note that Helen *told* him Garp left.

'Life,' Garp wrote, 'is sadly *not* structured like a good old-fashioned novel. Instead, an ending occurs when those who are meant to peter out have petered out. All that's left is memory. But even a nihilist has a memory.'

Whitcomb even loved Garp at his most whimsical and at his most pretentious.

Among Garp's things, Helen found this note.

'No matter what my fucking last words were, please say they were these: "I have always known that the pursuit of excellence is a lethal habit."'

Donald Whitcomb, who loved Garp uncritically – in the manner of dogs and children – said that those indeed were Garp's last words.

'If Whitcomb said so, then they were,' Duncan always said.

Jenny Garp and Ellen James – they agreed about this, too.

It was a family matter – keeping Garp from the biographers,

wrote Ellen James.

'And why not?' asked Jenny Garp. 'What does he owe the

public? He always said he was only grateful for other artists, and to the people who *loved* him.'

So who else deserves to have a piece of him, now?

wrote Ellen James.

Donald Whitcomb was even faithful to Helen's last wish. Although Helen was old, her final illness was sudden, and it had to be Whitcomb who defended her deathbed request. Helen did not want to be buried in the Steering School cemetery, alongside Garp and Jenny, her father and Fat Stew – and all the others. She said that the *town* cemetery would do her just fine. She did not want to be left to medicine, either; since she was so old, she was sure there was little left of her body that anyone could possibly use. She wanted to be cremated, she told Whitcomb, and her ashes were to remain the property of Duncan and Jenny Garp and Ellen James. After burying some of her ashes, they could do anything they chose with what ashes remained, but they could *not* scatter them anywhere on the property of the Steering School. She would be damned, Helen told Whitcomb, if the Steering School, which did not admit women students when she had been of age, would get to have any part of her now.

The gravestone in the town cemetery, she told Whitcomb, should say simply that she was Helen Holm, daughter of the wrestling coach Ernie Holm, and that she had not been allowed to attend the Steering School because she was a girl; furthermore, she was the loving wife of the novelist T. S. Garp, whose gravestone could be seen in the Steering School cemetery, because he was a boy.

Whitcomb was faithful to this request, which amused Duncan especially.

'How Dad would have loved *this!*' Duncan kept saying. 'Boy, I can just hear him.'

How Jenny Fields would have applauded Helen's decision was a point made most often by Jenny Garp and Ellen James.

*   *   *

ELLEN JAMES would grow up to be a writer. She was 'the real thing,' as Garp had guessed. Her two mentors – Garp and the ghost of his mother, Jenny Fields – would somehow prove overbearing for Ellen, who because of them both would not ever write much nonfiction or fiction. She became a very good poet – though, of course, she was not much on the reading circuit.

Her wonderful first book of poems, *Speeches Delivered to Plants and Animals,* would have made Garp and Jenny Fields very proud of her; it did make Helen very proud of her – they were good friends, and they were also like mother and daughter.

Ellen James would outlive the Ellen Jamesians, of course. Garp's murder drove them deeper underground, and their occasional surfacing over the years would be largely disguised, even embarrassed.

Hi! I'm mute,

their notes finally said. Or:

I've had an accident – can't talk. But I write good, as you can see.

'You aren't one of those Ellen Somebodies, are you?' they were occasionally asked.

A what?

they learned to reply. And the more honest among them would write:

No. Not now.

Now they were just women who couldn't speak. Un-ostentatiously, most of them worked hard to discover what they *could* do. Most of them turned, constructively, to helping those who also couldn't do something. They were good at helping disadvantaged people, and also good at helping people who felt too sorry for themselves. More and more their labels left them, and one by one these speechless women appeared under names more of their own making.

Some of them even won Fields Foundation fellowships for the things they did.

Some of them, of course, went on trying to be Ellen Jamesians in a world that soon forgot what an Ellen Jamesian was. Some people thought that the Ellen Jamesians were a criminal gang who flourished, briefly, near mid-century. Others, ironically, confused them with the very people that the Ellen Jamesians had originally been protesting: rapists. One Ellen Jamesian wrote Ellen James that she stopped being an Ellen Jamesian when she asked a little girl if she knew what an Ellen Jamesian was.

'Someone who rapes little boys?' the little girl replied.

There was also a bad but very popular novel that followed Garp's murder by about two months. It took three weeks to write and five weeks to publish. It was called *Confessions of an Ellen Jamesian* and it did much to drive the Ellen Jamesians even wackier or simply away. The novel was written by a man, of course. His previous novel had been called *Confessions of a Porn King,* and the one before that had been called *Confessions of a Child Slave Trader.* And so forth. He was a sly, evil man who became something different about every six months.

One of his cruelly forced jokes, in *Confessions of an Ellen Jamesian,* was that he conceived of his narrator-heroine as a lesbian who doesn't realize until *after* she's cut off her tongue that she has made herself undesirable as a *lover,* too.

The popularity of this vulgar trash was enough to embarrass some Ellen Jamesians to death. There were, actually, suicides. 'There are *always* suicides,' Garp wrote, 'among people who are unable to say what they mean.'

But, in the end, Ellen James sought them out and be-friended them. It was, she thought, what Jenny Fields would have done. Ellen took to giving poetry readings with Roberta Muldoon, who had a huge, booming voice. Roberta would read Ellen's poems while Ellen sat beside her, looking as if she were wishing very hard that she could say her own poems. This brought out of hiding a lot of Ellen Jamesians who had been wishing *they* could talk, too. A few of them became Ellen's friends.

Ellen James would never marry. She may have known an occasional man, but more because he was a fellow poet than because he was a man. She was a good poet and an ardent feminist who believed in living like Jenny Fields and believed in writing with the energy and the personal vision of T. S. Garp. In other words, she was stubborn enough to have personal opinions, and she was also kind to other people. Ellen would maintain a lifelong flirtation with Duncan Garp – her younger brother, really.

The death of Ellen James would cause Duncan much sorrowing. Ellen, at an advanced age, became a long-distance swimmer – about the time she succeeded Roberta as the director of the Fields Foundation. Ellen worked up to swimming several times across the wide neck of Dog's Head Harbor. Her last and best poems used swimming and 'the ocean's pull' as metaphors. But Ellen James remained a girl from the Midwest who never thoroughly understood the undertow; one cold fall day, when she was too tired, it got her.

'When I swim,' she wrote to Duncan, 'I am reminded of the strenuousness, but also the gracefulness, of arguing with your father. I can also feel the sea's eagerness to get *at* me – to get at my dry middle, my landlocked little heart. My landlocked little ass, your father would say, I'm sure. But we tease each other, the sea and I. I suppose *you* would say, you raunchy fellow, that this is my substitute for sex.'

FLORENCE COCHRAN BOWLSBY, who was best known to Garp as Mrs Ralph, would live a life of larkish turmoil, with no substitute for sex in sight – or, apparently, in need. She actually completed a Ph.D. in comparative literature and was eventually tenured by a large and confused English Department whose members were only unified by their terror of her. She had, at various times, seduced and scorned nine of the thirteen senior members – who were alternately admitted to and then ridiculed from her bed. She would be referred to by her students as 'a dynamite teacher,' so that she at least demonstrated to other people, if not to herself, some confidence in an area other than sex.

She would hardly be referred to at all by her cringing lovers, whose tails between their legs were all remindful to Mrs Ralph of the manner in which Garp had once left her house.

In sympathy, at the news of Garp's shocking death, Mrs Ralph was among the very first to write to Helen. 'His was a seduction,' Mrs Ralph wrote, 'whose non-occurrence I have always regretted but respected.'

Helen came to rather like the woman, with whom she occasionally corresponded.

Roberta Muldoon also had occasion to correspond with Mrs Ralph, whose application for a Fields Foundation fellowship was rejected. Roberta was quite surprised by the note sent the Fields Foundation by Mrs Ralph.

Up yours,

the note said. Mrs Ralph did not appreciate rejection.

Her own child, Ralph, would die before her; Ralph became quite a good newspaperman and, like William Percy, was killed in a war.

BAINBRIDGE PERCY, who was best known to Garp as Pooh, would live a long, long time. The last of a train of psychiatrists would claim to have rehabilitated her, but Pooh Percy may simply have emerged from analysis – and a number of institutions – too thoroughly *bored* with rehabilitation to be violent anymore.

However it was achieved, Pooh was, after a great while, peaceably reintroduced to social intercourse; she reentered public life, a functioning if not speaking member of society, more or less safe and (finally) useful. It was in her fifties that she became interested in children; she worked especially well and patiently with the retarded. In this capacity, she would frequently meet other Ellen Jamesians, who in their various ways were also rehabilitated – or, at least, vastly changed.

For almost twenty years Pooh would not mention her dead sister, Cushie, but her fondness for children eventually confused her. She got herself pregnant when she was fifty-four (no one could imagine how) and she was returned to institutional observation, convinced, as she was, that she would die in childbirth. When this didn't occur, Pooh became a devoted mother; she also continued her work with the retarded. Pooh Percy's own child, for whom her mother's violent history would be a severe shock in her later life, was fortunately *not* retarded; in fact, she would have reminded Garp of Cushie.

Pooh Percy, some said, became a positive example for those who would forever put an end to capital punishment: her rehabilitation was so impressive. Only not to Helen, and to Duncan Garp, who would wish to their graves that Pooh Percy had died at that moment when she last cried 'Ig!' in the Steering wrestling room.

One day Pooh *would* die, of course; she would succumb to a stroke in Florida, where she was visiting her daughter. It was a small consolation to Helen that Helen would outlive her.

The faithful Whitcomb would choose to describe Pooh Percy as Garp had once described her, following his escape from the first feminist funeral. 'An androgynous twerp,' Garp said to Dean Bodger, 'with a face like a ferret and a mind completely sodden by spending nearly fifteen years in diapers.'

*　　　*　　　*

That official biography of Garp, which Donald Whitcomb titled *Lunacy and Sorrow: The Life and Art of T. S. Garp*, would be published by the associates of JOHN WOLF, who would not live to see the good book in print. John Wolf had contributed much effort to the book's careful making, and he had worked in the capacity of an editor to Whitcomb – over most of the manuscript – before his untimely demise.

John Wolf died of lung cancer in New York at a relatively young age. He had been a careful, conscientious, attentive, even elegant man – most of his life – but his deep restlessness and unrelieved pessimism could only be numbed and disguised by smoking three packs of unfiltered cigarettes per day from the time he was eighteen. Like many busy men who maintain an otherwise calm and managed air about themselves, John Wolf smoked himself to death.

His service to Garp, and to Garp's books, is inestimable. Although he may from time to time have held himself responsible for the fame which, in the end, provoked Garp's own violent killing, Wolf was far too sophisticated a man to dwell on such a narrow view. Assassination, in Wolf's opinion, was 'an increasingly popular amateur sport of the times'; and 'political true believers,' as he called nearly everybody, were always the sworn enemy of the artist – who insisted, however arrogantly, on the superiority of a *personal* vision. Besides, Wolf knew, it was not only that Pooh Percy had become an Ellen Jamesian, and had responded to Garp's baiting; hers was a grievance as old as childhood, possibly aggravated by politics but basically as deep as her long need for diapers. Pooh had gotten it into her head that Garp's and Cushie's love for fucking each other had finally been lethal to Cushie. At least, it is true, it was lethal to Garp.

A professional in a world that too often worshiped the contemporaneity it had created, John Wolf insisted to his end that his proudest publication was the father and son edition of *The Pension Grillparzer*. He was proud of the early Garp novels, of course, and came to speak of *The World According to Bensenhaver* as 'inevitable – when you consider the violence Garp was exposed to.' But it was 'Grillparzer' that elevated Wolf – it and the unfinished manuscript of *My Father's Illusions*, which John Wolf looked upon, lovingly and sadly, as 'Garp's road back to his right way to write.' For years Wolf edited the messy first draft of the unfinished novel; for years he consulted with Helen, and with Donald Whitcomb, about its merits and its faults.

'Only after I'm dead,' Helen insisted. 'Garp would let nothing go if he didn't think it was finished.' Wolf agreed, but he died before Helen. Whitcomb and Duncan would be left to publish *My Father's Illusions* – considerably posthumously.

It was Duncan who spent the most time with John Wolf during Wolf's torturous dying of lung cancer. Wolf lay in a private hospital in New York, sometimes smoking a cigarette through a plastic tube inserted in his throat.

'What would your father say to this?' Wolf asked Duncan. 'Wouldn't it suit one of *his* death scenes? Isn't it properly grotesque? Did he ever tell you about the prostitute who died in Vienna, in the Rudolfinerhaus? What was her name?'

'Charlotte,' Duncan said. He was close to John Wolf. Wolf had even come to like the early drawings Duncan had done for *The Pension Grillparzer*. And Duncan had moved to New York; he told Wolf that his first sense of knowing he wanted to be a painter, as well as a photographer, was his view of Manhattan from John Wolf's office – the day of the first feminist funeral in New York.

In a letter John Wolf dictated to Duncan from his death-bed, Wolf left word for his associates that Duncan Garp was to be allowed to come look at Manhattan from his office for as long as the publishing company occupied the building.

For many years after John Wolf died, Duncan took advantage of the offer. A new editor moved into Wolf's office, but the name of Garp made all the editors in that publishing house scurry.

For years secretaries would come in and say, 'Excuse me, it's that young *Garp*. To look out the window again.'

Duncan and John Wolf spent the many hours it took John Wolf to die discussing how good a writer Garp was.

'He would have been very, very special,' John Wolf told Duncan.

'*Would* have been, maybe,' Duncan said. 'But what else could you say to me?'

'No, no, I'm not lying; there's no need,' Wolf said. 'He had the vision, and he always had the language. But mainly vision; he was always personal. He just got sidetracked for a while, but he was back on the beam with that new book. He was back to the good impulses again. "The Pension Grillparzer" is his most charming, but it's not his most original; he was still too young; there are other writers who could have written that story. *Procrastination* is an original idea, and a brilliant first novel – but it's a first novel. *Second Wind of the Cuckold* is very funny, and his best title; it's also very original, but it's a novel of manners – and rather narrow. Of course, *The World According to Bensenhaver* is his most original, even if it *is* an X-rated soap opera – which it is. But it's so harsh; it's raw food – good food, but *very* raw. I mean, who wants it? Who needs to suffer such abuse?

'Your father was a difficult fellow; he never gave an inch – but that's the point: he was always following his nose; wherever it took him, it was always *his* nose. And he was ambitious. He started out daring to write about the *world* – when he was just a *kid*, for Christ's sake, he still took it on. Then, for a while – like a lot of writers – he could only write about himself; but he also wrote about the world – it just didn't come through as cleanly. He was starting to get bored with writing about his life and he was beginning to write about the whole world again; he was just starting. And Jesus, Duncan, you must remember he was a *young* man! He was thirty-three.'

'And he had energy,' Duncan said.

'Oh, he would have written a lot, there's no question,' John Wolf said. But he began to cough and had to stop talking.

'But he could never just relax,' Duncan said. 'So what

was the point? Wouldn't he have just burned himself out, anyway?'

Shaking his head – but delicately, not to loosen the tube in his throat – John Wolf went on coughing. 'Not him!' Wolf gasped.

'He could have just gone on and on?' Duncan asked. 'You think so?'

The coughing Wolf nodded. He would die coughing.

Roberta and Helen would attend his funeral, of course. The rumor-mongers would be hissing, because it was often speculated in the small town of New York that John Wolf had looked after more than Garp's *literary* estate. Knowing Helen, it seems unlikely that she would ever have had such a relationship with John Wolf. Whenever Helen heard how she was linked with someone, Helen would just laugh. Roberta Muldoon was more vehement.

'With John Wolf?' Roberta said. 'Helen and Wolf? You've got to be kidding.'

Roberta's confidence was well founded. On occasion, when she flung herself upon the city of New York, Roberta Muldoon had enjoyed a tryst or two with John Wolf.

'And to think I used to watch you play!' John Wolf told Roberta once.

'You can *still* watch me play,' Roberta said.

'I mean football,' John Wolf said.

'There are better things than football,' said Roberta.

'But you do so many things well,' John Wolf told her.

'Ha!'

'But you *do*, Roberta.'

'All men are liars,' said Roberta Muldoon, who *knew* this was true because she had once been a man.

ROBERTA MULDOON, formerly Robert Muldoon, No. 90 of the Philadelphia Eagles, would outlive John Wolf – and most of her lovers. She would not outlive Helen, but Roberta lived long enough to grow at last comfortable with her sex reassignment. Approaching fifty, she would remark to Helen that she suffered the vanity of a middle-aged man *and* the anxieties of a middle-aged woman, 'but,' Roberta added, 'this perspective is not without advantages. Now I always know what men are going to say before they say it.'

'But *I* know, too, Roberta,' Helen said. Roberta laughed her frightening boomer of a laugh; she had a habit of bear-hugging her friends, which made Helen nervous. Roberta had once broken a pair of Helen's glasses.

Roberta had successfully dwarfed her enormous eccentricity by becoming responsible – chiefly to the Fields Foundation, which she ran so vigorously that Ellen James had given her a nickname.

Captain Energy.

'Ha!' Roberta said. 'Garp was Captain Energy.'

Roberta was also greatly admired in the small community of Dog's Head Harbor, for Jenny Fields' estate had never been so respectable, in the old days, and Roberta was a far more outgoing participant in the affairs of the town than Jenny had ever been. She spent ten years as the chairperson of the local school board – although, of course, she could never have a child of her own. She organized, coached, and pitched on the Rockingham County Women's Softball Team – for twelve years, the best team in the state of New Hampshire. Once upon a time, the same, stupid, swinish governor of New Hampshire suggested that Roberta be given a chromosome test before she be allowed to play in the title game; Roberta suggested that the governor should meet her, just before the start of the game – on the pitcher's mound – 'and see if he can fight like a man.' Nothing came of it, and – politics being what they are – the governor threw out the first ball. Roberta pitched a shutout, chromosomes and all.

And it is to the credit of the athletic director of the Steering School that Roberta was offered the position of offensive line coach for the Steering football team. But the former tight end politely refused the job. 'All those young boys,' Roberta said sweetly. 'I'd get in terrible trouble.'

Her favorite young boy, all her life, was Duncan Garp, whom she mothered and sistered and smothered with her perfume and her affection. Duncan loved her; he was one of the few male guests ever allowed at Dog's Head Harbor, although Roberta was angry with him and stopped inviting him for a period of almost two years – following Duncan's seduction of a young poet.

'His father's son,' Helen said. 'He's charming.'

'The boy is *too* charming,' Roberta told Helen. 'And that poet was not stable. She was also far too old for him.'

'You sound jealous, Roberta,' Helen said.

'It was a violation of *trust*,' Roberta said loudly. Helen agreed that it was. Duncan apologized. Even the poet apologized.

'*I* seduced *him*,' she told Roberta.

'No you didn't,' Roberta said. 'You *couldn't*.'

All was forgiven one spring in New York when Roberta surprised Duncan with a dinner invitation. 'I'm bringing this smashing girl, just for you – a friend,' Roberta told him, 'so wash the paint off your hands, and wash your hair and look nice. I've told her you're nice, and I know you *can* be. I think you'll like her.'

Thus having set Duncan up with a date, who was a woman of *her* choice, Roberta felt somehow better. Over a long period it came out that Roberta had *hated* the poet whom Duncan had slept with, and that was the worst of the problem.

When Duncan crashed his motorcycle within a mile of a Vermont hospital, Roberta was the first to get there; she had been skiing farther north; Helen had called her, and Roberta beat Helen to the hospital.

'Riding a motorcycle in the snow!' Roberta roared. 'What would your father say?' Duncan could barely whisper. Every limb appeared in traction; there was a complication involving a kidney, and unknown to both Duncan and

Roberta – at the time – one of his arms would have to come off.

Helen and Roberta and Duncan's sister, Jenny Garp, waited for three days until Duncan was out of danger. Ellen James was too shaken to come wait with them. Roberta railed the whole time.

'What should he *be* on a motorcycle for – with only one eye? What kind of peripheral vision is *that?*' Roberta asked. 'One side is always blind.'

That had been what had happened, exactly. A drunk had run a stoplight and Duncan had seen the car too late; when he'd tried to outmaneuver the car, the snow had locked him in place and held him, an almost motionless target, for the drunken driver.

Everything had been broken.

'He is too much like his father,' Helen mourned. But, Captain Energy knew, in some ways Duncan was *not* like his father. Duncan lacked *direction*, in Roberta's opinion.

When Duncan was out of danger, Roberta broke down in front of him.

'If you get killed before I die, you little son of a bitch,' she cried, 'it will *kill* me! *And* your mother, probably – and Ellen, possibly – but you can be sure about me. It will absolutely *kill* me, Duncan, you little bastard!' Roberta wept and wept, and Duncan wept, too, because he knew it was true: Roberta loved him and was terribly vulnerable, in that way, to whatever happened to him.

Jenny Garp, who was only a freshman at college, dropped out of school so that she could stay in Vermont with Duncan while Duncan got well. Jenny had graduated from the Steering School with the highest honors; she would have no trouble returning to college when Duncan recovered. She volunteered her help to the hospital as a nurse's aide, and she was a great source of optimism for Duncan, who had a long and painful convalescence ahead of him. Duncan, of course, had some experience with convalescence.

Helen came from Steering to see him every weekend;

Roberta went to New York to look after the deplorable state of Duncan's live-in studio. Duncan was afraid that all his paintings and photographs, and his stereo, would be stolen.

When Roberta first went to Duncan's studio-apartment, she found a lank, willowy girl living there, wearing Duncan's clothes, all splattered with paint; the girl was not doing such a hot job with the dishes.

'Move out, honey,' Roberta said, letting herself in with Duncan's key. 'Duncan's back in the bosom of his family.'

'Who are you?' the girl asked Roberta. 'His mother?'

'His *wife*, sweetheart,' Roberta said. 'I've always gone for younger men.'

'His *wife*?' the girl said, gawking at Roberta. 'I didn't know he was *married*.'

'His kids are coming up in the elevator,' Roberta told the girl, 'so you better use the stairs. His kids are practically as big as me.'

'His *kids*?' the girl said; she fled.

Roberta had the studio cleaned and invited a young woman she knew to move in and watch after the place; the woman had just undergone a sexual transformation and she needed to match her new identity with a new place to live. 'It will be perfect for you,' Roberta told the new woman. 'A luscious young man owns it, but he'll be away for months. You can take care of his things, and have dreams about him, and I'll let you know when you have to move out.'

In Vermont, Roberta told Duncan, 'I hope you clean up your life. Stop the motorcycles and the mess – and stop the girls who don't know the first thing about you. My God: sleeping with strangers. You're not your father yet; you haven't gotten down to *work*. If you were really *being* an artist, Duncan, you wouldn't have *time* for all the other shit. All the self-destruction shit, particularly.'

Captain Energy was the only one who could talk to Duncan that way – now that Garp was gone. Helen could not criticize him. Helen was too happy just to have Duncan alive, and Jenny was ten years younger than Duncan; all she could do was look up to him, and love him, and be there while he took so long to heal. Ellen James, who loved Duncan fiercely and possessively, became so exasperated with him that she would throw her notepad and her pencil in the air; and then, of course, she had nothing to say.

'A one-eyed, one-armed painter,' Duncan complained. 'Oh boy.'

'Be happy you've still got one head and one heart,' Roberta told him. 'Do you know many painters who hold the brush in *both* hands? You need two eyes to drive a motorcycle, dummy, but only one to paint.'

Jenny Garp, who loved her brother as if he were her brother *and* her father – because she had been too young to know her father, really – wrote Duncan a poem while he recuperated in the hospital. It was the first and only poem young Jenny Garp ever wrote; she did *not* have the artistic inclination of her father and her brother. And only God knows what inclination Walt might have had.

> Here lies the firstborn, lean and long,
> with one arm handy and one arm gone,
> with one eye lit and one gone out,
> with family memories, clout by clout.
> This mother's son must keep intact
> the remains of the house that Garp built.

It was a lousy poem, of course, but Duncan loved it.

'I'll keep myself intact,' he promised Jenny.

The young transsexual, whom Roberta had placed in Duncan's studio-apartment, sent Duncan get-well postcards from New York.

The plants are doing okay, but the big yellow painting by the fireplace was warping – I don't think it was stretched properly – so I took it down and leaned it with the others in the pantry, where it's colder. I *love* the blue painting, and the drawings – *all*

the drawings! And the one Roberta tells me is a self-portrait, of
you – I love that especially.

'Oh boy,' Duncan groaned.

Jenny read him all of Joseph Conrad, who had been
Garp's favorite writer when Garp was a boy.

It was good for Helen that she had her teaching duties to
distract her from worrying about Duncan.

'That boy will straighten out,' Roberta assured her.

'He's a young *man*, Roberta,' Helen said. 'He's not a *boy*
anymore – although he certainly acts like one.'

'They're all boys to me,' Roberta said. 'Garp was a boy. *I*
was a boy, before I became a girl. Duncan will always be a
boy, to me.'

'Oh boy,' Helen said.

'You ought to take up some sport,' Roberta told Helen. 'To
relax you.'

'Please, Roberta,' Helen said.

'Try *running*,' Roberta said.

'*You* run, I'll read,' Helen said.

Roberta ran all the time. In her late fifties she was
becoming forgetful of using her estrogen, which must be
used for the whole of a transsexual's life to maintain a female
body shape. The lapses in her estrogen, and her stepped-
up running, made Roberta's large body change shape, and
change back again, before Helen's eyes.

'I sometimes don't know what's *happening* to you, Roberta,'
Helen told her.

'It's sort of exciting,' Roberta said. 'I never know what I'm
going to feel like; I never know what I'm going to *look* like,
either.'

Roberta ran in three marathon races after she was fifty, but
she developed problems with bursting blood vessels and
was advised, by her doctor, to run shorter distances. Twenty-
six miles was too much for a former tight end in her fifties
– 'old Number Ninety,' Duncan occasionally teased her.
Roberta was a few years older than Garp and Helen, and had

always looked it. She went back to running the old six-mile route she and Garp used to take, between Steering and the sea, and Helen never knew when Roberta might suddenly arrive at the Steering house, sweaty and gasping and wanting to use the shower. Roberta kept a large robe and several changes of clothes at Helen's house for these occasions, when Helen would look up from her book and see Roberta Muldoon in her running costume – her stopwatch held like her heart in her big pass-catching hands.

Roberta died that spring Duncan was hospitalized in Vermont. She had been doing wind sprints on the beach at Dog's Head Harbor, but she'd stopped running and had come up on the porch, complaining of 'popping sounds' in the back of her head – or possibly in her temples; she couldn't exactly locate them, she said. She sat on the porch hammock and looked at the ocean and let Ellen James go get her a glass of ice tea. Ellen sent a note out to Roberta with one of the Fields Foundation fellows.

Lemon?

'No, just sugar!' Roberta called.

When Ellen brought the ice tea, Roberta downed the whole glass in a few gulps.

'That's perfect, Ellen,' Roberta said. Ellen went to fix Roberta another glass. 'Perfect,' Roberta repeated. 'Give me another one just like that one!' Roberta called. 'I want a *whole life* just like that one!'

When Ellen came back with the ice tea, Roberta Muldoon was dead in the hammock. Something had popped, something had burst.

If Roberta's death struck Helen and made her feel low, Helen had Duncan to worry about – for once, a grateful distraction. Ellen James, whom Roberta had supported so much, was spared an overdose of grief by her sudden responsibilities – she was busy taking over Roberta's job at the Fields Foundation; she had big shoes to fill, as they say. In fact, size 12. Young Jenny Garp had never been as close to Roberta as Duncan had been; it was Duncan, still in traction, who took it the hardest. Jenny stayed with him and gave him one pep talk after another, but Duncan could remember Roberta and all the times she had bailed out the Garps before – Duncan especially.

He cried and cried. He cried so much, they had to change a cast on his chest.

His transsexual tenant sent him a telegram from New York.

I'LL GET OUT NOW. NOW THAT R. IS GONE. IF YOU DON'T FEEL
COMFORTABLE ABOUT MY BEING HERE. I'LL GO. I WONDER. COULD
I HAVE THAT PICTURE OF HER. THE ONE OF R. AND YOU. I ASSUME
THAT'S YOU. WITH THE FOOTBALL. YOU'RE IN THE JERSEY WITH THE
90 THAT'S TOO BIG FOR YOU.

Duncan had never answered her cards, her reports on the welfare of his plants and the exact location of his paintings. It was in the spirit of old No. 90 that he answered her now, whoever she was – this poor confused boy-girl whom Roberta, Duncan knew, would have been kind to.

Please stay as long as you want to [*he wrote to her*]. But I like that photograph, too. When I get back on my feet, I'll make a copy just for you.

Roberta had told him to pull his life together and Duncan regretted he would not be able to *show* her that he could. He felt a responsibility now, and wondered at his father, *being* a writer when he was so young – having children, having *Duncan*, when he was so young. Duncan made lots of resolutions in the hospital in Vermont; he would keep most of them, too.

He wrote Ellen James, who was still too upset at his accident to come see him all plastered and full of pins.

Time we both got to work, though I have some catching up to
do – to catch up to you. With 90 gone, we're a smaller family.
Let's work at not losing anybody else.

He would have written to his mother that he intended to
make her proud of him, but he would have felt silly saying it
and he knew how tough his mother was – how little *she* ever
needed pep talks. It was to young Jenny that Duncan turned
his new enthusiasm.

'Goddamnit, we've got to have energy,' Duncan told his
sister, who had plenty of energy. 'That's what you missed –
by not knowing the old man. Energy! You've got to get it on
your own.'

'*I've* got energy,' Jenny said. 'Jesus, what do you think I've
been *doing* – just taking care of *you*?'

It was a Sunday afternoon; Duncan and Jenny always
watched the pro football on Duncan's hospital TV. It was
a further good omen, Duncan thought, that the Vermont
station carried the game, that Sunday, from Philadelphia.
The Eagles were about to get creamed by the Cowboys. The
game, however, didn't matter; it was the before-the-game
ceremony that Duncan appreciated. The flag was at half-
mast for the former tight end Robert Muldoon. The score-
board flashed 90! 90! 90! Duncan noted how the times had
changed; for example, there were feminist funerals everywhere now; he had just read about a big one in Nebraska.
And in Philadelphia the sports announcer managed to say,
without snickering, that the flag flew at half-mast for *Roberta*
Muldoon.

'*She* was a fine athlete,' the announcer mumbled. 'A great
pair of hands.'

'An extraordinary person,' agreed the co-announcer.

The first man spoke again. 'Yeah,' he said, 'she didda
lot for . . .' and he struggled, while Duncan waited to hear
for *whom* – for freaks, for weirdos, for sexual disasters, for
his father and his mother and himself and Ellen James.
'She didda lot for people wid *complicated* lives,' the sports

announcer said, surprising himself *and* Duncan Garp – but with dignity.

The band played. The Dallas Cowboys kicked off to the Philadelphia Eagles; it would be the first of many kickoffs that the Eagles would receive. And Duncan Garp could imagine his father, appreciating the announcer's struggle to be tactful and kind. Duncan actually imagined Garp whooping it up with Roberta; somehow, Duncan felt that Roberta would be there – privy to her own eulogy. She and Garp would be hilarious at the awkwardness of the news.

Garp would mimic the announcer: 'She didda lot for refashioning da vagina!'

'Ha!' Roberta would roar.

'Oh boy!' Garp would holler. 'Oh boy.'

When Garp had been killed, Duncan remembered, Roberta Muldoon had threatened to have her sexual reversal *reversed*. 'I'd rather be a lousy *man* again,' she wailed, 'than think there are women in this world who are actually *gloating* over this filthy murder by that filthy *cunt!*'

Stop it! Stop it! Don't ever say that word!

scribbled Ellen James.

There are only those of us who loved him, and those of us who didn't know him – men and women,

wrote Ellen James.

Then Roberta Muldoon had picked them all up, one by one; she gave to them – formally, seriously, and generously – her famous bear hug.

When Roberta died, some *talking* person among the Fields Foundation fellows at Dog's Head Harbor called Helen on the phone. Helen, gathering herself – once again – would be the one to call Duncan in Vermont. Helen would advise young Jenny how to break the news to Duncan. Jenny Garp had inherited a fine bedside manner from her famous grandmother, Jenny Fields.

'Bad news, Duncan,' young Jenny whispered, kissing her brother on the lips. 'Old Number Ninety has dropped the ball.'

DUNCAN GARP, who survived both the accident that cost him an eye and the accident that cost him an arm, became a good and serious painter; he was something of a pioneer in the artistically suspect field of color photography, which he developed with his painter's eye for color and his father's habit of an insistent, *personal* vision. He did not make nonsense images, you can be sure, and he brought to his painting an eerie, sensual, almost narrative realism; it was easy, knowing who he was, to say that this was more of a *writer's* craft than it was a craft that belonged in a picture – and to criticize him, as he was criticized, for being too 'literal.'

'Whatever *that* means,' Duncan always said. 'What do they expect of a one-eyed, one-armed artist – and the son of Garp? No flaws?'

He had his father's sense of humor, after all, and Helen was very proud of him.

He must have made a hundred paintings in a series called *Family Album* – the period of his work he was best known for. They were paintings modeled from the photographs he had taken as a child, after his eye accident. They were of Roberta, and his grandmother, Jenny Fields; his mother swimming at Dog's Head Harbor; his father running, with his healed jaw, along the beach. There was one series of a dozen small paintings of a dirty-white Saab; the series was called *The Colors of the World*, because, Duncan said, all the colors of the world are visible in the twelve versions of the dirty-white Saab.

There were baby pictures of Jenny Garp, too; and in the large, group portraits – largely imagined, not from any photograph – the critics said that the blank face, or the repeated figure (very small) with its back to the camera, was always Walt.

Duncan did not want children of his own. 'Too vulnerable,' he told his mother. 'I couldn't stand watching them grow up.' What he meant was, he couldn't stand watching them *not* grow up.

Since he felt that way, Duncan was fortunate not to have children be an issue in his life – they weren't even a worry. He came home from his four months of hospitalization in Vermont and found an extremely lonely transsexual living in his New York studio-apartment. She had made the place look as if a real artist already lived there, and by a curious process – it was almost a kind of osmosis of his things – she already seemed to know a great deal about him. She was in love with him, too – just from pictures. Another gift to Duncan's life from Roberta Muldoon! And there were some who said – Jenny Garp, for example – that she was even beautiful.

They were married, because if ever there was a boy with no discrimination in his heart about transsexuals, that boy was Duncan Garp.

'It's a marriage made in Heaven,' Jenny Garp told her mother. She meant Roberta, of course; Roberta was in Heaven. But Helen was a natural at worrying about Duncan; since Garp had died, she'd had to take over much of the worrying. And since Roberta had died, Helen felt she'd had to take over *all* the worrying.

'I don't know, I don't know,' Helen said. Duncan's marriage made her anxious. 'That damn Roberta,' Helen said. 'She always got her way!'

But this way there's no chance of unwanted pregnancy,

wrote Ellen James.

'Oh, stop it!' Helen said. 'I sort of *wanted* grandchildren, you know. One or two, anyway.'

'*I'll* give them to you,' Jenny promised.

'Oh boy,' Helen said. 'If I'm still alive, kid.'

Sadly, she wouldn't be, although she would get to see Jenny pregnant and be able to *imagine* she was a grandmother.

'Imagining something is better than remembering something,' Garp wrote.

And Helen certainly had to be happy with how Duncan's life straightened out, as Roberta had promised.

After Helen's death, Duncan worked very hard with the meek Mr Whitcomb; they made a respectable presentation out of Garp's unfinished novel, *My Father's Illusions*. Like the father and son edition of *The Pension Grillparzer*, Duncan illustrated what there was of *My Father's Illusions* – a portrait of a father who plots ambitiously and impossibly for a world where his children will be safe and happy. The illustrations Duncan contributed were largely portraits of Garp.

Sometime after the book's publication, Duncan was visited by an old, old man whose name Duncan could not remember. The man claimed to be at work on 'a critical biography' of Garp, but Duncan found his questions irritating. The man asked over and over again about the events leading up to the terrible accident where Walt was killed. Duncan wouldn't tell him anything (Duncan didn't *know* anything), and the man went away empty-handed – biographically speaking. The man was Michael Milton, of course. It had appeared to Duncan that the man was missing something, though Duncan couldn't have known that Michael Milton was missing his penis.

The book he supposedly was writing was never seen, and no one knows what happened to him.

If the world of the reviewer seemed content, after the publication of *My Father's Illusions*, to call Garp merely an 'eccentric writer,' a 'good but not a great writer,' Duncan didn't mind. In Duncan's own words, Garp was 'original' and 'the real thing.' Garp had been the type, after all, to compel blind loyalty.

'*One-eyed* loyalty,' Duncan called it.

He had a long-standing code with his sister, Jenny,

and with Ellen James; the three of them were as thick as thieves.

'Here's to Captain Energy!' they would say, when they were drinking together.

'There's no sex like transsex!' they would shout, when they were drunk, which occasionally embarrassed Duncan's wife – although she certainly agreed.

'How's the energy?' they would write and phone and telegraph each other, when they wanted to know what was up. And when they had plenty of energy, they would describe each other as 'full of Garp.'

Although Duncan would live a long, long time, he would die unnecessarily and, ironically, *because* of his good sense of humor. He would die laughing at one of his own jokes, which was surely a Garp-family thing to do. It was at a kind of coming-out party for a new transsexual, a friend of his wife's. Duncan aspirated an olive and choked to death in just a few seconds of violent laughter. That is a horrible and stupid way to die, but everyone who knew him said that Duncan would not have objected – either to that form of death, or to the life he'd had. Duncan Garp always said that his father suffered the death of Walt more than anyone in the family suffered anything else. And among the chosen forms of death, death finally was the same. 'Between men and women,' as Jenny Fields once said, 'only death is shared equally.'

Jenny Garp, who in the field of death had much more specific training than her famous grandmother, would not have agreed. Young Jenny knew that, between men and women, not even death gets shared equally. Men get to die more, too.

JENNY GARP would outlive them all. If she had been at the party where her brother choked to death, she probably could have saved him. At least she would have known exactly what to do. She was a doctor. She always said it was her time in the Vermont hospital, looking after Duncan, that had made up her mind to turn to medicine – not her famous grand-mother's history of nursing, because Jenny Garp knew that only secondhand.

Young Jenny was a brilliant student; like her mother, she absorbed everything – and everything she learned she could redeliver. Like Jenny Fields, she got her feeling for people as a roamer of hospitals – inching what kindness was possible, and recognizing what wasn't.

While she was an intern, she married another young doctor. Jenny Garp would not give up her name, how-ever; she stayed a Garp, and, in a frightful war with her husband, she saw that her three children would all be Garps, too. She would divorce, eventually – and remarry, but in no hurry. That second time would suit her. He was a painter, much older than herself, and if any of her family had been alive to nag her, they would have no doubt warned her that she was imagining something of Duncan in the man.

'So what?' she would have said. Like her mother, she had her own mind; like Jenny Fields, she kept her own name.

And her father? In what way was Jenny Garp even slightly like him – whom she never really knew? She was only a baby, after all, when he died.

Well, she *was* eccentric. She made a point of going into every bookstore and asking for her father's books. If the store was out of stock, she would order. She had a writer's sense of immortality: if you're in print and on the shelves, you're alive. Jenny Garp left fake names and addresses all over America; the books she ordered would be sold to *some-one*, she reasoned. T. S. Garp would not go out of print – at least not in his daughter's lifetime.

She was also avid in her support of the famous feminist, her grandmother, Jenny Fields; but like her father, Jenny Garp did not put much stock in the *writing* of Jenny Fields. She did not bother bookstores about keeping *A Sexual Suspect* on the shelves.

Most of all, she resembled her father in the *kind* of doctor she became. Jenny Garp would turn her medical mind to research. She would not have a private practice. She would go to hospitals only when *she* was sick. Instead, Jenny spent a number of years working closely with the Connecticut Tumor Registry; she would eventually direct a branch of the National Cancer Institute. Like a good writer, who must love and worry each detail, Jenny Garp would spend hours noticing the habits of a single human cell. Like a good writer, she was ambitious; she hoped she would get to the bottom of cancer. In a sense, she would. She would die of it.

Like other doctors, Jenny Garp took that sacred oath of Hippocrates, the so-called father of medicine, wherein she agreed to devote herself to something like the life Garp once described to young Whitcomb – although Garp was concerned with a *writer's* ambitions ('. . . trying to keep everyone alive, forever. Even the ones who must die in the end. They're the most important to keep alive'). Thus, cancer research did not depress Jenny Garp, who liked to describe herself as her father had described a novelist.

'A doctor who sees only terminal cases.'

In the world according to her father, Jenny Garp knew, we must have energy. Her famous grandmother, Jenny Fields, once thought of us as Externals, Vital Organs, Absentees, and Goners. But in the world according to Garp, we are all terminal cases.

THE END

AFTERWORD:
TWENTY YEARS AGO
BY JOHN IRVING

On the twentieth anniversary of the publication of *The World According to Garp*, John Irving described the experience of writing *Garp*, its reception, and its meaning. Here are his thoughts.

My eldest son, Colin, who is now thirty-three, was twelve when he first read *The World According to Garp* – in manuscript, and with me anxiously awaiting his reaction. (I still believe there are scenes in the book that are unsuitable for twelve-year-olds.) Although *Garp* was my fourth novel, it was the first one Colin could read, and I remember feeling both proud and nervous at the prospect of being judged by one of my children; that the book was dedicated to Colin, and to his younger brother Brendan, made the moment even more tense and exciting.

Surely everyone knows the two most common questions that are asked of any novelist. What is your book about? And is it autobiographical? These questions and their answers have never been of compelling interest to me – if it's a good novel, both the questions and the answers are irrelevant – but while my twelve-year-old son was reading *The World According to Garp*, I anticipated that these were the very questions he would ask me, and I thought very hard about how I might answer him.

Now, twenty years later – and having written nine novels – it occurs to me that I have never thought as hard about my answers to those 'irrelevant' questions as I did when Colin was reading *Garp*. What I mean, of course, is that it's perfectly understandable and completely permissible for a twelve-year-old to ask those questions, whereas (in my opinion) an adult has no business asking them. An adult who reads a novel should know what the book is 'about'; an adult should also know that whether a novel is autobiographical or not is beside the point – unless the alleged adult is hopelessly inexperienced or totally innocent of the ways of fiction.

Anyway, while Colin was off in his room reading the manuscript of *Garp*, I found myself agonizing over what the novel was 'about.' To my horror, and full of self-loathing, I jumped to the conclusion that the book was about the temptations of lust – lust leads just about everyone to a miserable end. There is even a chapter called 'More Lust,' as if there weren't enough already. I was positively ashamed of how much lust was in the book, not to mention how punitive a novel I thought it was; indeed, every character in the story who indulges his or her lust is severely punished. And, among the culprits and the victims, physical mutilations abound: characters lose eyes and arms and tongues – even penises!

It had seemed at one time, when I was beginning the novel, that the polarization of the sexes was a dominant theme; the story was about men and women growing farther and farther apart. Just look at the plot: a remarkable, albeit outspoken, woman (Garp's mother, Jenny Fields) is killed by a lunatic male who hates women; and Garp himself is assassinated by a lunatic female who hates men.

'In this dirty-minded world,' Jenny thinks, 'you are either somebody's wife or somebody's whore – or fast on your way to becoming one or the other. If you don't fit either category, then everyone tries to make you think there is something wrong with you.' But there is nothing wrong with Garp's mother. In her autobiography, Jenny writes: 'I wanted a job and I wanted to live alone. That made me a sexual suspect. Then I wanted a baby, but I didn't want to have to share my body or my life to have one. That made me a sexual suspect, too.' And being what she calls 'a sexual suspect' also makes Jenny a target of antifeminist hatred – just as Garp, her son, becomes a target of radical feminists.

But the principal point about Garp's mother is stated in the first chapter: 'Jenny Fields discovered that you got more respect from shocking other people than you got from trying to live your own life with a little privacy.' Today, twenty years later, Jenny's discovery seems more true – not to mention more defensible – than it seemed to me in 1978. And I don't always agree with Jenny. 'Between men and women,' she says, 'only death is shared equally.' Late in the novel, in the last chapter, I disagree with her as follows: '. . . between men and women, not even death gets shared equally. Men get to die more, too.'

There was a time when Jenny threatened to take over the novel, when I wasn't at all sure if Garp or his mother was the main character; something of my indecision remains. I once wanted to begin the book with Chapter 11 (the 'Mrs Ralph' chapter), but that would have necessitated a flashback of 278 pages. I next tried beginning the novel with Chapter 9, the chapter called 'The Eternal Husband.' My first sentence was: 'In the Yellow Pages of Garp's phone directory, Marriage was listed near Lumber.' I used to think the novel was about marriage, specifically the perils of marriage – more specifically, the threat of lust to marriage. 'Garp had never realized,' I wrote, 'that there were more marriage counselors than lumberyards.' (Is it any wonder I was anxious that a twelve-year-old was reading this book?)

And, at another time, *The World According to Garp* began with Chapter 3 ('What He Wanted to Be When He Grew Up') – for isn't the novel also about that? Garp wants to be a writer; it is a novel about a novelist, although almost no reader of the book remembers it as such. Yet Garp's origins as an author are crucial to the story – 'the beginning of a writer's long-sought trance, wherein the world falls under one embracing tone of voice.' And from the beginning, there was an epilogue. I knew everything that happened before I began – I always do. 'An epilogue,' Garp writes, 'is more than a body count. An epilogue, in the disguise of wrapping up the past, is really a way of warning us about the future.'

But to begin the novel as I once tried, with Chapter 3, was too historical, too emotionally remote. 'In 1781 the widow and children of Everett Steering founded Steering Academy, as it was first called, because Everett Steering had announced to his family, while carving his last Christmas goose, that his only disappointment with *his* town was that he had not provided his boys with an academy capable of preparing them for a higher education. He did not mention his girls.' There again is the sexual-polarization theme – as early as 1781!

Meanwhile, in the privacy of his room, Colin was reading on and on. *The World According to Garp* would never have satisfied a twelve-year-old if it had been only a novel about a novelist, although much of what mattered to me about the book was exactly that. I shall always see Garp prowling in his neighborhood at night, taking a dim view of his neighbors' television sets. 'There is the faint, trapped warble from some televisions tuned in to *The Late Show*, and the blue-gray glow from the picture tubes throbs from a few of the houses. To Garp this glow looks like cancer, insidious and numbing, putting the world to sleep. Maybe television *causes* cancer, Garp thinks; but his real irritation is a *writer's* irritation: he knows that wherever the TV glows, there sits someone who isn't *reading.*'

And what of the Under Toad? Colin was familiar with its source. It was his brother Brendan who misunderstood him one summer at the beach on Long Island. 'Watch out for the undertow, Brendan,' Colin warned him – at the time, Brendan was six. (Colin was ten.) Brendan had never heard

of an undertow; he thought Colin said Under Toad. Somewhere, under the water, lurked a dangerous toad.

'What can it do to you?' Brendan asked his brother.

'Pull you under, suck you out to sea,' Colin said.

That did it for Brendan at the beach – he wouldn't go
near the ocean. It was weeks later when I saw him standing at some distance from the water's edge, staring into the
waves.

'What are you doing?' I asked him.

'I'm looking for the Under Toad,' Brendan said. 'How big
is it? What color is it? How fast can it swim?'

The World According to Garp wouldn't exist without the
Under Toad. Brendan got me started.

To my surprise, Colin didn't ask me what the book was
'about' – he told me. 'It's about the fear of death, I think,'
Colin began. 'Maybe more accurately, the fear of the death
of children – or of anyone you love.'

I remembered then that, among my other attempts to
begin the novel, I had long ago begun with what would
become the last sentence ('. . . in the world according to
Garp, we are all terminal cases'), and I recalled how that
sentence had moved through the book; I kept pushing it
ahead. It was once the first sentence of the second chapter;
later it was the last sentence of the tenth chapter, and so
on, until it became the end of the novel – the only possible
ending. Not surprisingly, Garp describes a novelist as 'a
doctor who sees only terminal cases.'

Yet Colin, my twelve-year-old, surprised me by telling
me what my book was about. The 'Mrs Ralph' chapter, my
first false beginning, begins as follows: 'If Garp could have
been granted one vast and naïve wish, it would have been
that he could make the world *safe*. For children and for
grown-ups. The world struck Garp as unnecessarily perilous for both.' At age twelve, Colin had zeroed in on that.
Garp lives in 'a safe suburb of a small, safe city,' but neither
he nor his children are safe. The Under Toad will get him
in the end – as it gets his mother, as it gets his younger son.

'Just be careful!' Garp is always telling his children, as I am still telling mine.

It is a novel about being careful, and about that not being enough.

The real beginning to the book, the one I finally chose, describes Jenny's habit of carrying a scalpel in her purse. Jenny is a nurse, and an unmarried woman who wants nothing to do with men; she carries the scalpel for self-defense. And so *The World According to Garp* begins with an act of violence – Jenny cuts a soldier, a stranger who thrusts his hand under her dress (her nurse's uniform). 'Garp's mother, Jenny Fields, was arrested in Boston in 1942 for wounding a man in a movie theater.' Finally, it was just that simple; I began at the beginning of the main story, before Jenny is pregnant with Garp – at the moment she decides she wants to have a baby without having a husband.

Interestingly, Colin never asked me if the novel was autobiographical. But a year after the publication of *The World According to Garp*, I visited the Northfield Mount Hermon School – a private secondary school in Massachusetts. I had been invited to give a reading to the students, and I'd accepted the invitation because Colin had recently been admitted to the school – he would be a student there in the coming academic year – and I thought it would be an opportunity for Colin to see something of the place and meet a few of the young men and women who would soon be his fellow students. Therefore Colin came with me to the reading, after which there were some questions from the audience. (It had been announced to the audience that Colin would be attending Northfield Mount Hermon in the fall – he'd already been introduced to the crowd.) Unexpectedly, a very pretty young woman asked Colin a question – she didn't ask me.

'Is Garp your dad – is your father Garp?' the girl asked.

Poor Colin! He must have been embarrassed, but you would not have known it from his unflappable composure; he was a little younger than the assembled students, but he suddenly struck me as much older and more wary than most of them. Furthermore, he was an expert on *The World According to Garp*.

'No, my dad isn't Garp,' Colin replied, 'but my father's fears are Garp's fears – they are any father's fears.' (Colin was fourteen, going on thirty-three.)

So that's what *The World According to Garp* is about – a father's fears. As such, the novel is and isn't 'autobiographical.' Just ask Colin, or Brendan, or – in a few years, when he's old enough to read it – my youngest son, Everett. (As of this writing, Everett is six.)

I may have written this novel twenty years ago, but I go back there almost every day – back to those fears. Even the smallest detail of *The World According to Garp* is an expression of fear; even the curious pockmark on the face of the Viennese prostitute – it is also an expression of that most terrible fear. 'The silvery gouge on her forehead was nearly as big as her mouth; her pockmark looked to Garp like a small, open grave.' A child's grave . . .

When Garp was published, people who'd lost children wrote to me. 'I lost one, too,' they told me. I confessed to them that I hadn't lost any children. I'm just a father with a good imagination. In my imagination, I lose my children every day.

LAST NIGHT IN TWISTED RIVER

John Irving

'A premier storyteller, master of the tragicomic and among the first rank of contemporary novelists'
Los Angeles Times

'We don't always have a choice how we get to know one another. Sometimes, people fall into our lives cleanly – as if out of the sky, or as if there were a direct flight from Heaven to Earth – the same sudden way we lose people, who once seemed they would always be part of our lives.'

In 1954, in the cookhouse of a logging and sawmill settlement in northern New Hampshire, an anxious twelve-year-old boy fatally mistakes the local constable's girlfriend for a bear. Both the twelve-year-old and his father become fugitives – to Boston, to southern Vermont, to Toronto – pursued over the years by the implacable constable. Their lone protector is a fiercely libertarian logger, once a river driver, who befriends them and distantly watches over them like a vast, idiosyncratic guardian…

'Irving's instincts are so basically sound, his talent for story-telling so bright and strong that he gets down to the truth of his time'
The New York Times Book Review

'Irving is among the few novelists who can write a novel about grief and fill it with ribald humour soaked in irony'
USA Today

'His instinctive mark is the moral choice stripped bare, and his aim is impressive. What's more, there's hardly a writer alive who can match his control of the omniscient point of view'
Washington Post Book World

9780552776578

A PRAYER FOR OWEN MEANY

John Irving

'A work of genius'

Independent

'If you care about something you have to protect it. If you're lucky enough to find a way of life you love, you have to find the courage to live it.'

Eleven-year-old Owen Meany, playing in a Little League baseball game in Gravesend, New Hampshire, hits a foul ball and kills his best friend's mother. Owen doesn't believe in accidents; he believes he is God's instrument. What happens to Owen after that 1953 foul ball is both extraordinary and terrifying.

'Originality has distinguished all Mr Irving's books, but in *A Prayer For Owen Meany* it achieves a new pitch and a new profundity … Irrepressible'

Independent

'Marvellously funny … What better entertainment is there than a serious book which makes you laugh?'

Spectator

9780552993692

THE CIDER HOUSE RULES

John Irving

'Difficult to define, impossible not to admire'
Daily Telegraph

'The reason Homer Wells kept his name was that he came back to St Cloud's so many times, after so many failed foster homes, that the orphanage was forced to acknowledge Homer's intention to make St Cloud's his home.'

Homer Wells' odyssey begins among the apple orchards of rural Maine. As the oldest unadopted child at St Cloud's orphanage, he strikes up a profound and unusual friendship with Wilbur Larch, the orphanage's founder – a man of rare compassion and an addiction to ether. What he learns from Wilbur takes him from his early apprenticeship in the orphanage surgery, to an adult life running a cider-making factory and a strange relationship with the wife of his closest friend.

'Wry, laconic, he sketches his characters with an economy that springs from a feeling for words and mastery over his craft. This superbly original book is one to be read and remembered'
The Times

'Funnier than *Garp* ... it's an irresistibly readable yarn spun by a master's voice'
Time Out

'Like the rest of Irving's fiction, it is often disconcerting, but always exciting and provoking'
Observer

9780552992046

A WIDOW FOR ONE YEAR

John Irving

'Irving's storytelling has never been better'
New York Times

'One night when she was four and sleeping in the bottom bunk of her bunk bed, Ruth Cole awoke to the sound of lovemaking – it was coming from her parents' bedroom.'

This is the story of Ruth Cole. It is told in three parts: on Long Island, in the summer of 1958, when she is only four; in 1990, when she is an unmarried woman whose personal life is not nearly as successful as her literary career; and in the autumn of 1995, when Ruth Cole is a forty-one-year-old widow and mother. She's also about to fall in love for the first time.

'Wickedly knowing, mischievously post-modern and magical realist along the lines of Gunter Grass, Gabriel Garcia Marquez and Robertson Davies'
Time Out

'Gripping, full of horror and humour'
Literary Review

'A compelling chronicle of love and loss ... His most intricate and fully imagined novel'
San Francisco Chronicle

9780552997966

A SON OF THE CIRCUS

John Irving

'Compulsively readable'
Guardian

*'The doctor was fated to go back to Bombay; he would keep return-
ing again and again – if not forever, at least for as long as there
were dwarves in the circus.'*

Born a Parsi in Bombay, sent to university and medical school
in Vienna, Dr Farrokh Daruwalla is a Canadian citizen – a
fifty-nine-year-old orthopaedic surgeon, living in Toronto.
Once, twenty years ago, Dr Daruwalla was the examining
physician of two murder victims in Goa. Now, two decades
later, the doctor will be reacquainted with the murderer.

'[Irving] is at the peak of his powers … he plunges the
reader into one sensual or grotesque scene after another
with cheerful vigour and a madcap tenderness for life …
entertainment on a grand scale'
The Economist

'More plot twists than the Ramayana and a cast of characters
that includes dwarves, prostitutes, movie stars, transvestites
and at least one serial killer'
Daily Telegraph

'Irving has given us that treat of treats, a wide-ranging fiction
of massive design and length that encapsulates our world
with intelligence and sugars the pill with wit'
Mail on Sunday

9780552996051